PIMLICO

123

ROBERT LOUIS STEVENSON

Frank McLynn was educated at Wadham College, Oxford, and the University of London. He was Alistair Horne Research Fellow at St Antony's College, Oxford, in 1987-88, and now works as a full-time writer. He is the author of biographies of H. M. Stanley and Richard Burton, as well as several books relating to the Jacobite movement, including *Charles Edward Stuart*, which was shortlisted for the 1989 McVitie's Prize for Scottish Writer of the Year, and *The Jacobite Army in England*, which won the 1985 Cheltenham Prize for Literature. His most recent books are *Hearts of Darkness: The European Exploration of Africa* (also available in Pimlico) and *Fitzroy Maclean*.

ROBERT LOUIS STEVENSON

A Biography

FRANK McLYNN

PIMLICO

PIMLICO

20 Vauxhall Bridge Road, London SW1V 2SA

London Melbourne Sydney Auckland Johannesburg
and agencies throughout the world

First published by Hutchinson 1993
Pimlico edition 1994

Printed and bound in Great Britain

ISBN 0-7126-5893-9

Contents

Illustrations
(between pages 184-185 and pages 376-377)

Photographic Acknowledgements

British Library 19; Edinburgh City Museums – Lady Stair's House: 1-10, 12-18, 20-29, 31, 33, 34, 36; Mansell Collection: 11, 30, 32, 35.

Introduction

This book has been written in the firm conviction that Robert Louis Stevenson is Scotland's greatest writer of English prose. It is usual to regard Sir Walter Scott as the man to whom this title is due, and it is true that, *in terms of achievement*, Scott takes the palm. Achievement and natural giftedness are, however, very different qualities: one may take the example of the two great Soviet composers Shostakovich and Prokofiev, of whom the former's achievement was more impressive but the latter's intrinsic genius was greater. So it seems to me to be with Scott and Stevenson, and this truth has often been obscured by those who talk of Scott as Stevenson's literary 'father'. I am wholeheartedly behind Gerard Manley Hopkins, who told Robert Bridges: 'I think that Robert Lewis (sic) Stevenson shows more genius in a page than Scott in a volume.'[1] With Scott history and politics were always primary, storytelling secondary; with Stevenson it was the reverse, and perhaps this is why *Kidnapped, Catriona* and *The Master of Ballantrae*, despite their seemingly antiquarian Jacobite point of departure, still live today, while *Waverley* and *Redgauntlet*, for all their merits, have the musty smell of the historical museum. Scott has a ponderousness that sometimes touches depths of tragic profundity, but Stevenson is a shrewder judge of human nature, has a better sense of irony and humour and, above all, is a deeper psychologist and a more modern figure in his appreciation of the multiple ambiguities of the universe. Moreover, if one's taste runs to economy rather than prolixity, Stevenson will always win over Scott. Nothing in Scott is so tersely effective in the true Scottish idiom as Alan Breck's description of James More in *Catriona*: 'The man's as boss as a drum; he's just a wame and a wheen words.'

One hundred years after his death, it seems that time has not been kind to Stevenson. Immediately after his death, his family and friends set to work to fashion the legend of 'RLS' – one of the few writers instantly familiar from his initials alone. Works of hagiography turned him into a Christ-figure in the true sense, combining the earthly sufferings of Jesus with the divine status of a son of God; in accounts like Graham Balfour's authorised biography of 1901, his wife and her children played the role of ministering archangels. Arthur Quiller-Couch absurdly placed him in the same company as Shakespeare, Milton, Keats and Dickens: 'Surely another age will wonder over this curiosity of letters – that for five years the needle of literary endeavour in Great Britain has quivered towards a little island in the South Pacific, as to its magnetic pole . . . Put away books and paper and pen . . . Stevenson is dead, and now there is nobody left to write for.'[2] The reaction to this nonsense, when it came in the 1920s, was severe. Biographers like Steuart and Hellman first revealed the feet of clay of his wife, Fanny, and for this service have never ceased to be reviled by a certain faction of RLS-lovers. More seriously, Stevenson's own reputation as writer attracted the critical scalpel, and excerpts from three different adverse critics of the 1920s shows just how far the critical pendulum swung.

Frank Swinnerton, in the first great debunking book of criticism in 1924, accused Stevenson of being the literary equivalent of a singer who cannot hold a note: there were great moments in the Stevenson *oeuvre*, he claimed, but they were merely brilliant pieces in an indifferently executed mosaic, and it was because he had no central sustaining vision that RLS could never scale the heights of a Jane Austen, a Balzac or even an Alexandre Dumas *père*: 'It was because they offered no new effects that *The Great North Road* and *Heathercat* and *The Young Chevalier* dried suddenly upon his pen, dead before ever they were begun . . . he could not make romance out of chopped hay, such as *The Young Chevalier*, with its bald, hopeless attempts to galvanise the Master into life again.'[3]

Two years later, the American critic Thomas Beer joined the fray and flayed Stevenson for an alleged mixture of bogus bohemianism and picayune juvenilia:

> His intellect was not legitimately rebellious at all, and the wistful apology of the 'House of Eld' is the whole statement of his case . . . His levity impressed timid bookish folk as red rashness, and for fourteen years a heaving syrup of appreciation supported the gay invalid on its sweetness. His subjects were inoffensive – murder and more murder, fratricidal hate and madness, blood lust and piracy in seven forms. His prose chimes gently on, delicately echoing a hundred classic musics, gently dwindles from the recollection as do all imitations, and is now impressive only to people who think that a good prose is written to be read aloud.[4]

Between these two critiques appeared the most hostile blast of all. E.F.Benson, whose Marianas trench of deep moral seriousness was the *Mapp and Lucia* sequence, actually had the effrontery to criticise Stevenson because 'he lacks that deep stark tenderness for the sorrows of the world' and has 'too much of Mark Tapley in him'. Accusing Stevenson of turning his back on life and blowing a penny whistle, Benson refers sarcastically to

RLS's 'love of beauty as intense as any that the highest genius of the race have known' and, scraping the barrel for negative things to say about his *bête noire*, even criticises his sartorial appearance which 'cannot quite escape association with the type which we are accustomed to call "bounder"'.[5]

Despite the efforts of biographers like Furnas, Pope-Hennessy and Calder, Stevenson's reputation never really recovered from the critical buffeting it took in the twenties. Normally the critical pendulum can be relied on to swing back again, but there are five main aspects of Stevenson's work that have, until recently, militated against a proper adjustment to his literary reputation. First is the allegation that he was a mere master of stylistic pyrotechnics, a posturing emperor without moral clothes. George Moore accused him of, in effect, literary charlatanism, of employing a word-juggling fakery to strike effects that overawed an ignorant public, impressed with sound rather than sense. Others suggested he was no more than an aesthete and poseur, at best an accomplished mimic, and cited his long years of self-training against him, as if he were a rather dim product of a creative writing course. The most influential literary critic of the mid-century, F.R.Leavis, barred Stevenson from the esoteric circle of the 'Great Tradition' with this dismissive appreciation: 'Out of Scott a bad tradition came. It spoiled Fenimore Cooper, who had new and first-hand interests and the makings of a distinguished novelist. And with Stevenson it took on "literary" sophistication and fine writing.'[6] How anyone committed to a great tradition based on moral seriousness could have ignored *The Master of Ballantrae, The Beach of Falesá* or *Catriona* is a nice question; Leavis famously dismissed all of Dickens except *Hard Times* the first time round, then later recanted, but there were to be no revaluations of Robert Louis Stevenson.

Secondly, it has long been a popular perception that Stevenson was a mere 'boys' writer', and the tag has damaged him even more than it hurt Mark Twain; closely allied to this canard is the idea of RLS as a mere 'Peter Pan of Samoa', the *puer aeternus*, skimming the surface of life. Here one of Stevenson's greatest champions, G.K.Chesterton, must shoulder some of the blame, for he persistently plugged the line that Skelt's juvenile theatre was the key to the RLS *oeuvre*: '(his) sanity was madder than madness. He did not appeal to any ideal of the sort usually pursued by idealists; he did not try to construct an optimist philosophy like Spinoza or Emerson; he did not preach a good time coming like William Morris or Wells; he did not appeal to Imperialism or Socialism or Scotland: he appealed to Skelt.'[7] Despite his shrewdness, perceptiveness and originality, Chesterton was always an unreliable ally for an author, as when he singled out *Pickwick Papers* as Dickens's masterpiece. As it happens, we have an almost perfect 'control' by which to measure how far from a 'boys' author' Stevenson was, in the shape of fellow Scot R.M.Ballantyne. Ballantyne, who also died in 1894, created the Victorian child's classic *Coral Island* which, with its one-dimensional Panglossian optimism, is light years away from the sensibility of the deeply disturbing *Treasure Island*. And those who (falsely) lament the absence of a feminine principle in Stevenson's work, should investigate what happens when such a principle is truly absent by studying the astonishing sadism (in the true sense) of such Ballantyne works as *Coral Island, The Gorilla Hunters* and *Martin Rattler*.

Thirdly, there is the Jamesian prejudice against the adventure story as the proper medium for deep moral seriousness, which is still extremely influential today. It seems that we can accept that a motion picture can be 'great' if it uses the adventure story to express profound moral and psychological truths (John Ford's *The Searchers* is a good example), since excitement and forward momentum are appropriate to the visual medium, but we baulk at the idea in the novel. The absurdity of the idea in literature becomes apparent when we think of the *Odyssey, Morte d'Arthur* or *Moby-Dick*, to say nothing of Conrad, Jack London, Graham Greene or William Golding, but it is no use pretending that this bias against adventure is not part of our high culture. Stevenson tried to meet this prejudice head-on by arguing that the alleged 'romance' was actually superior to the naturalistic novel as a way of expressing profound truths about life, much as some respected students of the past argue that the historical novel is a better vehicle for this than scholarly history; primitive and archetypal forms of action 'such as fighting, sailing, adventure, death or child-birth . . . these aged things', he argued, 'have on them the dew of man's morning.'

Fourthly, Stevenson has often not found favour in his native land, as his Romantic Toryism so often collides with the very strong radical tradition in Scotland, for whom Burns is a much more acceptable exemplar. RLS has been accused of encouraging both escapist fantasy and 'the national propensity to wander' as means of camouflaging Scotland's real problems. The critic Leslie Fiedler argued that Scott and Stevenson were both romantic exotics but that Scott went back in time for his inspiration while RLS went outward in space.[8] This will scarcely do as an overall thesis, since Stevenson frequently went back in time – in his Jacobite novels – and had a more nuanced attitude to tradition and the British Empire than either Scott or Buchan, with whom he is often bracketed as an alleged trio of Jacobite-inspired reactionaries. However, it is true that Stevenson's position *vis-à-vis* Scotland has many weaknesses. The critic Andrew Noble has argued that Jacobitism was used by Scott in his novels as camouflage for problems to which *Jacobinism* was a real answer, and that the reason Stevenson did not engage with the real problems of the Scotland of his age was simply that he could not break the grip of the literary 'father', Scott.[9] There is some merit in this line of argument, for Stevenson always rejected socialism and other ameliorative creeds as a solution to human problems; like Dickens, he could be worked up into sympathetic outrage when contemplating an *individual* injustice, but always drew away if it was put to him that the individual case might be a mere instance of a general *structural* injustice.

Fifthly, and again in contrast with Scott, the high adventure of Stevenson's own life, his globetrotting, and above all his final phase in the Pacific, tended to make his own life a greater story than any he could devise; this may be termed the 'Byron syndrome' and it was precisely what RLS's friend Henry James feared would happen towards the end of his life. It may not have been the excellence of the life being bought at the expense of the excellence of the art, in Yeats's formulation, but it was a threat that the art might be overwhelmed by the brazen drama of life on Samoa. The American publisher Sam McClure summed this up well: 'One might say he was greater than what he wrote, or that what he wrote was greater than he; both is true; he was as great and noble as anything he ever wrote.'[10]

Since this is a biography and not a work of literary criticism, I have not attended to all the themes that a comprehensive study of Stevenson's work would entail. An interesting monograph could be written on the influences on Stevenson: Scott (obviously), James Hogg and the diabolic tradition in Scottish literature, Poe (even though his impact on RLS has been exaggerated), and Dumas *père*; in the case of Herman Melville, however, previous Stevenson scholarship has not sufficiently underlined his contribution to the 'formation' of the later Stevenson, so I have indicated some lines of enquiry. As an influence *himself*, Stevenson has been underrated. The early Yeats was an important disciple, as even the hostile George Moore conceded (we must remember that Moore's hostility was largely a function of RLS's own overdone and rather culpable hostility to Zola); Oscar Wilde was deeply influenced by Stevenson as both moralist and psychologist (can one imagine *The Picture of Dorian Gray* without *Jekyll and Hyde?*), even though he declared that RLS would have produced better work if he had lived in Gower Street rather than Samoa; while it fell to D.H.Lawrence to develop the sexual themes adumbrated by Stevenson in his fiction.

Then there is a group of writers who were almost explicitly his heirs. The Conrad of *Almayer's Folly, An Outcast of the Islands, Heart of Darkness* and *Victory* takes up and develops the motifs of *The Wrecker, The Beach of Falesá* and *Ebb-Tide*; Jack London, self-confessedly in his Pacific tales and *The Sea Wolf*, unconsciously perhaps in *The Star Rover* and the late 'Jungian' stories, takes up the RLS baton; J.M.Barrie worshipped Stevenson, and all his biographers have acknowledged the influence – Daphne du Maurier in fact referred to Captain Hook as being 'in the spirit of Stevenson and of Dumas'; while Buchan, of whom Andrew Noble has said, 'Most of John Buchan is to be found in Stevenson', resented the tag of epigone to RLS so much that he often sought to denigrate his literary 'father'.[11]

Stevenson tends to stick in the throat even of those who would like to spit him out. Shaw claimed to have learned from him that the Romantic hero is always mocked by reality, while Galsworthy, who began as a determined critic, later recanted and said that the superiority of Stevenson over Hardy was that Stevenson was all life while Hardy was all death.[12] The influence on Mark Twain, Conan Doyle and Chesterton would also repay detailed study. Of these possibly the most salient impact was that on Chesterton, for it was through Chesterton chiefly that RLS emerged as an influence on the modernist movement, especially on Nabokov and Borges and the entire Latin American school of 'magical realism'; what Faulkner is, as the U.S. influence on the Latin Americans, Stevenson is as the British analogue. I have paid less attention to RLS's verse as 'thing in itself' and used it mainly as a source for the life; I have no reason to dissent from the conventional view that the verse is a lesser achievement than the prose, though the idea of RLS the poet ending in a neo-Georgian cul-de-sac with the Sitwells is probably overstated – Robert Graves, always a trenchant critic of the Georgian strand in modern English poetry, drew particular attention to the merits of 'The Vagabond'.[14]

It would be too much to hope that in the Stevenson centenary year (1994) we might see a revival of critical and scholarly interest in this great Scottish writer, but if I persuade readers to go back to his magnificent writings and reassess this neglected genius, I shall be well content.

I

Early Years

Stevenson entertained many fantasies about his ancestors, most notably that he was descended from Rob Roy McGregor and that after the proscription of the clan some of the sept called themselves Stevenson. Another tradition, said to have been promoted by Stevenson's father Thomas, was that the first Stevenson came over from France as a barber-surgeon with Cardinal Beaton; Robert Louis, however, remained convinced that his family was originally Scandinavian. Yet all RLS's imaginings of possible Norse, Highland or French origins for his family were in vain.[1] He has been criticised for preferring the shadow of a Jacobite 'Family romance' – that his forefathers were 'out' in the risings of 1715 and 1745 – to the substance of the solid actual achievement of the Stevensons, but such criticism is beside the point, above all in the case of a creative writer. Moreover, with Stevenson nothing is simple, and there were times later in his life when he was to wonder whether the engineering feats of his father and grandfather were not actually to be ranked higher than his own scribblings. Applying Wren's motto *si monumentum requiris, circumspice* ('if you require a monument, look around you') to his own family, he noted proudly: 'I have often thought that to find a family to compare with my own in the promise of immortal memory, we must go back to the Egyptian Pharaohs.'[2]

The Stevensons can be traced to a man of that name who married Jean Keir in 1665. These early Stevensons were small-scale traders. The real story of the dynasty begins in the third quarter of the eighteenth century with the Stevenson brothers, Hugh and Alan, who established a business in the West Indies and died in their early twenties while pursuing a defaulting partner in an open boat. Alan, who had married Jean Lillie very young, left a son, Robert, born in 1772.[3] Robert's widowed mother remarried in 1787: her new husband was an Edinburgh man, Thomas Smith, aged 33, already twice a widower with five children (including two girls Jean and Janet), a shipowner and underwriter who had a solid business in lamps and oils.

The year before his marriage to Jean, Smith had been appointed engineer to the newly formed Board of Northern Lighthouses and at once replaced the old coal flares with his oil lamps and reflectors. Robert Stevenson (1772–1850) became his stepfather's pupil and eventually surpassed him in the construction of lighthouses on Scotland's rocky coast; he revelled in the outdoor life, working in what was then a virgin field. Familial duty could do no more, it seemed, but then in 1799, at the age of 27, three years after succeeding his stepfather as engineer to the Lighthouse Board, Robert married Jean Smith, his stepfather's daughter by an earlier marriage; as RLS later remarked with considerable understatement: 'the marriage of a man of 27 and a girl of 20, who had lived for twelve years as brother and sister, is difficult to conceive'.[4] To make sense of it, some have speculated that Robert Stevenson was a classic case of sublimation who opted for the line of least resistance and contracted a marriage of convenience; others more simply conjecture that Robert's mother Jean wanted to make sure that her son inherited Smith's money.

During Robert's forty-seven-year tenure of office as first engineer of the Lighthouse Board, he planned or built twenty-three lighthouses in Scotland, using the catoptric system of illumination and his own invention of 'intermittent' and 'flashing' lights, as well as acting as a consulting engineer for the construction of roads, bridges, harbours, canals and railways. It is possible that buried deep in this practical man was some literary talent, for his account of the building of the Bell Rock lighthouse in 1807–11 is nearly as outstanding as the achievement itself. He succeeded against the odds in using the primitive equipment of the time to construct 'a tower of masonry on a sunken reef far distant from land, covered at every tide to a depth of twelve feet or more'.[5] The dark side of the man manifested itself in his harsh treatment of strikers during the building of the lighthouse.

Robert Stevenson resigned in 1843 and died in 1850, four months before his grandson Robert Louis was born. His mantle as supreme lighthouse engineer was inherited by his sons Alan, who built the Skerryvore lighthouse in 1844, and Thomas. Born in 1818, the seventh and last son, Thomas Stevenson had twelve siblings, of whom eight died in infancy. His brother David carried on the great traditions of the Stevenson name, wrote his father's biography and sired David Alan Stevenson, the sixth in a line of Stevensons to bear that name. But it was Thomas who carried on the family skills of lighthouse engineering. He served first under his brother Alan in the building of Skerryvore then collaborated with him in the raising of Dhu Heartach lighthouse. Altogether Thomas and Alan built 27 shorelights and 25 beacons, and also constructed many harbours; the abandoned mole at Wick was one of their few failures. Thomas was also an outstanding theoretician: he studied waves and storms and pioneered the application of optics to lighthouse instruments. He made his name as an illuminator of lighthouses, bringing to perfection the revolving light his father had initiated; he invented the 'azimuthal condensing system' and the louvre-boarded screens used to protect meteorological instruments.

Superficially Thomas Stevenson was a simple man. He seldom visited London but when he did so put up at the same unprepossessing hotel as his father before him, refused to dine out and frequented the same church, restaurant and theatre year in and year out. In Edinburgh he had his own small circle and was much admired and esteemed there, not least because he had made Edinburgh the world centre for lighthouse engineering; in Germany he was dubbed 'the Nestor of lighthouse illumination', but it was different in France, where partisans of the optical physicist Augustin Jean Fresnel accused him of having simply applied their master's theories (Fresnel died of tuberculosis at thirty-nine in 1827). Yet Thomas's inventions surely entitle him to a place as one of mankind's benefactors, and it was not hyperbole that led Robert Louis to remark that in all parts of the world a safer landfall awaited the mariner because of his father. In later years he was fond of telling how a friend travelling through Latin America learned of the intense admiration in Peru for the works of Stevenson – but it turned out to be the engineer father, not the novelist son, whose works were being referred to.[6]

Thomas Stevenson was a man of patchy education. He knew no Greek but taught himself Latin, and was an omnivorous reader of theology: his favourite such reading was the work of Lactantius, the fanatical third-century convert to Christianity; the obscure Cardinal Bona; and a German Protestant theologian of the sixteenth century named Vossius. He had a deep attachment to the Calvinism of the Scottish Kirk, which was the cause of many later clashes with his son. When Robert Louis visited the convent of Our Lady of the Snows in the Cévennes in 1878, two of the inhabitants tried to convert him to Catholicism, adding that he would doubtless make his parents Catholic too. RLS commented: 'I think I see my father's face! I would rather tackle the Gaetulian lion in his den than embark on such an enterprise against the family theologian.'[7]

Another weakness in Thomas Stevenson's education was that he had never mastered pure mathematics, so he often had to call on the aid of friendly physicists like Professors Tait and Swan of St Andrews University. If this was a palpable weakness in a lighthouse engineer, an even greater one was his failure to take out a patent for his inventions; in this he emulated his father who had always declared that the Stevensons did what they did as a public duty and not for profit. He was taken at his word: the Stevensons never received money, titles or honours for their philanthropy. Thomas was content to collect furniture, prints and pictures, mull over his beloved theology or peruse one of his two favourite books for relaxation: Scott's *Guy Mannering* and the inspirational *Parent's Assistant*. In politics

he was a strong Tory, except that he had radical views – what RLS called
'hot-headed chivalrous sentiment' – on the 'woman question': he was in
favour of divorce on demand for women but thought no man should
ever be granted one, whatever the grounds. His clansman's loyalty to
the Church of Scotland was shot through with a pronounced sense of
his own unworthiness, a morbid interest in death and the typically Celtic
tendency towards melancholia. The 'no-nonsense' approach to life seemingly implicit in his engineering career masked a frustrated writer, and he
later admitted that he had suppressed some nascent stirrings towards the
literary life out of deference to his father; yet the impulse remained in
the form of the 'tushery' with which he liked to lull himself to sleep: his
own stories and serials invented around highwaymen, pirates, border raids
and the entire gallimauffry of the Scott and Harrison Ainsworth tradition:
'ships, roadside inns, robbers, old sailors, and commercial travellers before
the era of steam'. RLS summed him up thus:

> He was a man of somewhat antique strain; with a blended sternness and
> softness that was wholly Scottish, and at first somewhat bewildering; with a
> profound essential melancholy of disposition and (what often accompanies it) the
> most humorous geniality in company; shrewd and childish; passionately attached;
> passionately prejudiced; a man of many extremes, many faults of temper and no
> very stable foothold for himself among life's troubles. Yet he was a wise adviser;
> many men, and these not inconsiderable, took counsel with him habitually.[8]

In 1848 Thomas Stevenson married the nineteen-year-old youngest
daughter of the Revd Lewis Balfour of Colinton. Margaret Isabella Balfour,
tall, slender and graceful with bright grey eyes and a smiling mouth, was in
many ways the polar opposite of her husband: where he was emotionally
demonstrative, outspoken, dogmatic, despotic (though chivalrous and softhearted), with a gift of humorous and figurative speech but cursed by violent
mood swings that propelled him from gloom to austerity, to tenderness and
gaiety and back, she was cultivated, companionable, affectionate and a born
optimist, with a noticeable talent for shutting her eyes to trouble or ignoring
it rather than finding solutions. Sweet-natured, devout and with a penchant
for pouring oil on troubled waters, she was on the surface conventionally
minded – though her later life in the Pacific partly argues against this –
and suffered in early and middle life from nervous troubles and chest
complaints.

RLS's fantasies about having foreign blood were as far-fetched on
the Balfour side as his claim that the Stevensons descended from the
Macgregors. The nearest he came to finding an exotic connection was
that his maternal great-great-grandmother was Margaret Lizars, herself
the great-great-granddaughter of a French emigrant called Lisouris. His
mother's great-grandmother Celia Elphinstone, a descendant of the border-

raiding Elliots, married Professor James Balfour of Pilrig; for three centuries
the Balfours of Pilrig had produced judges, advocates and ministers of the
Gospel. It is true that there was a sprinkling of forebears more to the RLS
taste: somewhere in the background lurked a turbulent laird of Blairgowrie;
a Balfour had fought for the Covenanters against Charles II at Bothwell
Bridge in 1679; another was ruined in the Darien disaster in 1701. The
Revd Lewis Balfour, minister at Colinton since 1823, could match Robert
Stevenson in just one thing: he too produced thirteen children, but whereas
Thomas Stevenson grew up in the urban comfort of Baxter's Place, under
Calton Hill, alongside Leith Walk, his future wife Maggie was a daughter of
the manse, at Colinton, a village then outside Edinburgh on the Leith. For
the numerous Balfour progeny, the British Empire was indeed a species of
out-relief: many of Maggie's siblings went to India, and her brother John,
after many years in the subcontinent, came back to Fife as a physician and
an acknowledged expert on cholera. He had solid service with the East India
Company behind him and, so legend relates, was the last man out of Delhi
when the Indian Mutiny broke out in 1857; back in Scotland his medical
prestige soon rivalled that of his brother George, a royal physician.

The Revd Lewis Balfour was a notorious martinet who inspired his
children with terror but was also capable of a tenderness that would later
astonish his grandson. One of the last of a vanishing generation who spoke
broad Scots but was still considered a gentleman, the Revd Mr Balfour had
been a sickly youth who suffered from a weak chest; convalescence on the Isle
of Wight so far prevailed that he lived beyond eighty and begat thirteen children. But he bequeathed the pulmonary weakness to his daughter Margaret
Isabella, who in turn transmitted it to her only son, Robert Louis, born on
13 November 1850 at 8, Howard Place in Edinburgh, a sombre Georgian
terrace just north of Canonmill. The consequence was that the child never
enjoyed good health: from the age of two until eleven, apart from the usual
childhood ailments, he suffered from digestive upsets, feverish colds, gastric
fever, bronchitis and pneumonia. It is also likely that an illness he suffered
at twenty-nine months was diptheria, since he did not contract the disease
from Bob while nursing him in 1874 or in Silverado in 1880 from his wife
and stepson. The Balfours were not a particularly eugenic stock, and there
was also a dubious medical history on the Stevenson side, with an infant
mortality high even by the standards of the early nineteenth century.

Yet if RLS's notorious weakness of the lungs can be traced to his
parents, especially perhaps his mother, the facts of parentage do not
adequately explain his eccentric musculature and queer, thin and gangling
physical shape; Thomas after all was heavily built and Maggie normally
proportioned; nor can the problem be traced to nutrition, for the boy's
diet was far superior to that of most Victorian children. Medical diagnosis
nearly one hundred and fifty years on with no adequate medical records is

problematical, but some physicians have speculated from the oddity of his bone structure that there was an endocrinal problem: Stevenson's nervous problems and swellings when under medication later in life are consistent with a diagnosis of thyroid abnormality. The upper respiratory disease, with its associated haemorrhages, also presents interpretive puzzles, as we shall see later.

Summing up on the parental legacy to the child born on 13 November 1850, we may first of all contrast the pessimism of the Stevensons with the optimism of the Balfours. It is said that those thinking this the best of all possible worlds and those fearing that such may indeed be the case are invariably attracted to each other; whatever the truth of this paradigm, we certainly see the centripetal pull of opposites in the case of Thomas and Maggie. RLS's mother consistently put a brave face on things, even to the extent of behaving like the proverbial ostrich, and we may attribute to her influence the strain of facetious optimism for which the mature Robert Louis Stevenson was often criticised. But from his father came the countervailing tendency towards morbid gloom and melancholia. As RLS later put it: 'A profound underlying pessimism appears ... to be the last word of the Stevensons ... their sense of the tragedy of life is acute and unbroken.'[9]

The infant boy was baptised Robert Lewis Balfour Stevenson on Friday 13 December 1850. Three days before, the Revd Lewis Balfour wrote to tell Thomas Stevenson that he would be present and that 'I have not the smallest objection to the name you give to the boy.'[10] This is scarcely surprising, as the child was named after him. But the Revd Lewis died when RLS was ten, and it is significant that after this 'Lewis' became 'Louis'. In 1862 the boy's name appears on the Edinburgh Academy list as 'Robert Stevenson', but after 1863 the form 'Louis' was regularly used in the family. The poet William Henley, for a while RLS's best friend, later taunted him (posthumously) with affectation for using a spelling that once again seemed to hint at the longed-for foreign connection, and persisted in printing his second name as 'Lewis' as if to indict RLS of being a poseur for changing the orthography of his baptismal name. Yet it seems there is an altogether simpler and more prosaic explanation. Out of deference to the maternal grandfather, Thomas Stevenson had initially opted for the spelling favoured by the Balfours, but there was both a family tradition of using the form 'Louis' *and* there was a man named Lewis in Edinburgh whom Thomas Stevenson particularly disliked.[11]

There can be no doubting the love and devotion of Thomas and Maggie for their only son, especially as a decision was very soon taken by the couple that Maggie's frail constitution precluded any further childbearing. Infertility in the couple, each of whom was one of thirteen children, can scarcely have been an explanation, and the most likely hypothesis for RLS's status as only child is that Thomas, with his well-known solicitude for women, simply decided that his wife was not strong enough to be a childbearer in the classic Victorian mould. Maggie and Thomas were anyway temperamentally well suited to be the parents of an only child, as there was little of the forbidding paterfamilias about Louis's father or of the absentee mother about Maggie. There is a revealing story about his father's love. Once the little boy locked himself in a room, could not get out, and became hysterical at the thought of being trapped; while the staff went to fetch a locksmith, Thomas succeeded in calming his son by talking to him through the door. Yet Thomas's official duties took him away from the household for long periods, as the earliest extant RLS correspondence shows. When the boy was three, he scrawled, doubtless with considerable guidance: 'Dear Papa, do come home to see me.' Two years later we find a similar message: 'My dear Papa, I hope you are quite well and how do you like your voyage.' Other long absences are evinced by Maggie's rather arch letters to her husband: 'You are a very naughty boy for never writing to me ... Our little lamb is quite well and has written a letter to you today.' 'Smout (the parental nickname for RLS, denoting the small fry of the salmon) keeps well ... he is in the drawing room beside me just now writing down an imaginary note of your expenses.'[12]

While Thomas was away on business, Maggie herself was often *hors de combat* with illness and she suffered particularly badly from ill-health during 1850–62 – the precise time when her son most needed her. Further instability in the child's environment was caused by two changes of domicile by the Stevenson family. The house at Howard Place proved both too small and too near the polluted river, clogged with sewage and the effluent from a tannery, so in 1853 the family moved across the road to higher ground with a view across the New Town of Edinburgh to Arthur's Seat. This house in turn turned out damp and unsatisfactory, and in 1857 the Stevensons moved to the house most popularly associated with RLS – 17, Heriot Row, a south facing terrace in the heart of the New Town.

During these critical formative years stability and continuity were provided by the family nurse Alison Cunningham, the 'Cummy' of Stevenson legend. Born in Fife on 15 May 1822, the daughter of a fisherman, and a Calvinist of the severest stripe, Alison Cunningham entered the Stevensons' service when RLS was eighteen months old, having already served as nurse in the Free Church Manse at Pilrig to one of the boy's Balfour relations. Forty years later Stevenson drew on his memories of the speech-rhythms of Cummy in his portrait of the elder Kirstie in *Weir of Hermiston*:

Her feeling partook of the loyalty of a clanswoman; the hero-worship of a maiden aunt, and the idolatry due to a God. No matter what he had asked her, ridiculous or tragic, she would have done it and joyed to do it... Like so many people of her class, she was a brave narrator; her place was on the hearth-rug and she made it a rostrum, mimeing her stories as she told them, fitting them with vital detail, spinning them out with endless quo' he's and quo' she's, her voice sinking into a whisper over the supernatural or the horrific, until she would suddenly spring up in affected surprise, and pointing to the clock, 'Mercy, Mr Archie,' she would say, 'whatever a time o'night is this of it! God forgive me for a daft wife!'[13]

'Wife' is a peculiarly appropriate word: Stevenson later called Cummy 'my second mother, my first wife', implying that she was the first truly formative female influence in his life.[14] After three unsatisfactory nurses, the third of whom was found in an Edinburgh gin palace with the child left outside, Cummy would have shone out with simple normal competence. She proved a paragon beyond the Stevensons' dreams. She sat up with the child all night as he tossed feverishly with illness and lavished devoted care on him.

She was more patient than I can suppose of an angel; hours together she would help console me in my paroxysms; and I remember with particular distinctness how she would lift me out of bed and take me, rolled in blankets, to the window, whence I might look forth into the blue night starred with street lamps and see where the gas still burned behind the windows of other sickrooms ... where also, we told each other, there might be sick little boys and their nurses waiting, like us, for the morning.

But Cummy was also a religious maniac, fanatical in her hatred of 'Popery', who stuffed the child's head with the more unacceptable excesses of Calvinism and the Old Testament. An extract from her diary in 1863 when confronted with the iniquity of the Continent makes the point: 'Here there is everything to please the unconverted heart of man – worldly pleasure of every kind, operas too! Is it not *waesome* to see mankind thus turning his back on his best friend and *tramping* his honour in the dust? The great adversary does triumph here.'[15] When he was still an impressionable infant she read the entire Bible to him three or four times. She also read from the Shorter Catechism, a curious Scots doggerel metrical version of the Psalms, from Foxe's *Book of Martyrs*, from *Pilgrim's Progress* and from *The Remains of Robert Murray McCheyne* – a pietistic biography of a young Scottish clergyman who died at 28, which was then to be found in many Scottish homes and was said later to have comforted Gordon at Khartoum. Worst of all, she told stories handed down from her Covenanting ancestors in which hell-fire and the noonday demon seeking all whom he might devour were living realities. She encouraged Louis to buy 'cut-outs' of sanguinary melodramas, which the child coloured without cutting out. It is no exaggeration to say that she was forever frightening him with stories of ghosts, body-snatchers and Covenanters and it was from her perfervid imaginings that RLS drew one of his first short-story masterpieces, 'Thrawn Janet'.

The consequence was that by day the infant Robert Louis Stevenson was himself a tiny religious maniac. Someone who met Cummy and RLS at this stage in his life remembered that the child could repeat hymn after hymn in word-perfect fashion; another recalled that he was writing devotional stories for Cummy before he was four. The little boy liked to play at 'church' with his cousins and on one occasion when he was playing with the Blaikie children (for Cummy had also been nurse to the family of W.B.Blaikie) decked himself out as a Minister with mock clerical bands; Mrs Blaikie, horrified at the 'sacrilege', tore the bands from his neck.[16]

But by night the boy suffered the most exquisite nightmares, in which he wrestled with the themes of Hell, Evil and Damnation Cummy had inculcated during the day. He lay awake to weep for Jesus and was terrified that he would die in his sleep and go to Hell; he made no remark without adding: 'if I am spared.' At the age of thirty he remembered clearly how he woke from dreams of hell 'my knees and chin together, my soul shaken, my body convulsed with agony . . . Some of this feeling still remains upon me in my thirtieth year.'[17] Later he remarked laconically: 'I had an extreme terror of Hell, implanted in me, I suppose, by my good nurse, which used to haunt me terribly on stormy nights.'[18] Here RLS does less than justice to the acute night terrors that assailed him to the point where he dreaded the coming of dusk. In his poem 'Childhood' we encounter the following description of going to bed, suggesting Christian's coming battle with Appollinax:

> Must we to bed indeed? Well then,
> Let us arise and go like men,
> And face with an undaunted tread
> The long black passage up to bed.

On stormy nights the noises in his nightmare always focused on the sound of a horseman or succession of horsemen riding furiously past the bottom of the street and away up the hill into town. In 1874 he wrote to his friend Mrs Sitwell on this subject:

In those days the storm had to me a perfect impersonation as durable and unvarying as any heathen deity. I always heard it as a horseman riding past with his cloak about his head, and somehow always carried away, and riding past again, and being baffled yet once more, ad infinitum, all night long. I think I wanted him to get past, but I am not sure; I know only that I had some interest either for or against in the matter; and I used to lie and hold my breath, not quite frightened, but in a state of miserable exaltation.'[19]

In his poem 'Windy Nights' the experience is rendered simply:

> All night long in the dark and wet
> A man goes riding by
> Late in the night when the fires are out
> Why does he gallop and gallop about?

But in 'Stormy Nights' the experience has acquired a metaphysical patina:

> Do I not know, how, nightly, on my bed
> The palpable close darkness shutting round me,
> How my small heart went forth to evil things,
> How all the possibilities of sin
> That were yet present to my innocence
> Bound me too narrowly,
> And how my spirit beat
> The cage of its compulsive purity;
> How my eye, fixed,
> My shot lip tremulous between my fingers
> I fashioned for myself new modes of crime,
> Created for myself with pain and labour
> The evil that the cobwebs of society
> The comely secrecies of education
> Had made an itching mystery to meward.[20]

In bed at night the young Robert Louis declaimed his view of the universe in a sing-song voice. Typically he would treat of Satan and the fall of Man, and the following, which he was heard crooning in the half-state between waking and sleeping, is surely an astonishing effusion from a six-year old:

> Had not an angel got the pride of man,
> No evil thought, no hardened heart would have been seen
> No hell to go to, but a heaven so pure;
> That angel was the Devil.
> Had not that angel got the pride, there
> Would have been no need
> For Jesus Christ to die upon the cross.[21]

At three, RLS was so filled with piety that, hearing that sheep and horses knew nothing of God, he wanted the Bible read aloud to them. Yet even at such a young age, the child's formidable intelligence was making its mark. Told of Mary Magdalene's anointing Christ's feet, he asked why God had made her 'naughty'; he also asked Cummy pointedly, 'Why has God got a Hell?' (there is a particular dramatic irony here, since the two most famous storytellers of desert islands are Stevenson and Defoe, and it was Friday who similarly posed to Crusoe the unanswerable: 'Why God him not kill debil?').

Thomas Stevenson hardly helped matters by colluding with Cummy to fill the child's head alternately with themes of destiny and damnation or with the stories he himself invented between sleep and waking. In one of the nightmares that occurred after his father got him off to sleep, RLS dreamed it was his fate to swallow the world 'and the terror of the fancy arose from the complete conception I had of the hugeness and populousness of our sphere. Disproportion and a peculiar shade of brown something like that of sealskin, haunted me particularly during these visitations ... such agony of terror as, thank God, I have never suffered since.'[22] In another nightmare he dreamed that it was the Last Judgement and he had to recite a form of words on which his salvation depended; his tongue stuck, his memory went blank, hell gaped for him, and he woke up clinging to the curtain-rod with his knees up to his chin. The one advantage Thomas Stevenson had over Cummy was that he was able effectively to soothe the child in his worst terrors, which he did by reciting some of the lighter dialogue from his stories.

It was small wonder that RLS longed for morning and the time when the arrival of the country carts, accompanied by a babel of voices, yelling of the drovers, neighing of the horses, cracking of the whips announced the imminence of dawn. Stevenson always retained more of childhood in adult life than most people do, and he had virtually total recall of the terrors of childhood as well as the pleasures of the 'lost domain'.[23] Assessing the overall influence of his childhood on his life and work is difficult, for on the one hand many Victorians (Dickens, Charles Kingsley, Samuel Butler, George Eliot) went through similar traumas, and on the other Stevenson always claimed he was able to integrate these experiences into a balanced view of life. As he wrote to his friend William Archer in 1885:

'My childhood was in reality a very mixed experience, full of fever, nightmare, insomnia, painful days and interminable nights ... But to what end should we renew these sorrows? The sufferings of life may be handled by the very greatest in their hours of insight; it is of its pleasures that our common poems should be formed; these are the experiences that we should seek to recall or to provoke; and I say with Thoreau, "What right have I to complain, who have not ceased to wonder?" and, to add a rider of my own, who have no remedy to offer.'

On the other hand, to deny that Cummy's influence was morbid, as Edmund Gosse did, was both a denial of the obvious and a strange attitude for the author of *Father and Son* to strike.[24]

What of posterity's judgement on Cummy? At best she was a mixed blessing. Against the undoubted fact of her nursing and devotion has to be set her careless, ignorant and superstitious talk that exacerbated the child's night horrors. Her good intentions led straight to Hell in the most direct sense, but perhaps to understand her benighted inadequacy is to forgive all. RLS's parents too must share some of the blame for having given Cummy a remarkably free hand even by the standards of 'hands off' Victorian parents; his mother, virtually a permanent invalid in these years, 'was shocked when, in days long after, she heard what I had suffered'.[25] Superficially, too, Stevenson appeared to bear Cummy no grudge in later life for the miseries she had wrought in his childhood. In the essay 'Rosa quo locorum' he praised her for the rhythmic way she told her stories, which awakened his interest in the musicality of prose. He wrote to her in 1873:

> If you should happen to think that you might have had a child of your own, and that it was hard you should have spent so many years taking care of someone else's prodigal, just think this – you have been here for a great deal in my life; you have made much that there is in me, just as surely as if you had conceived me; and there are sons who are more ungrateful to their mothers than I am to you.[26]

Yet there are signs of anger and resentment elsewhere in the Stevenson *oeuvre*. In one early letter he writes to her: 'God will make good to you all the good you have done and mercifully forgive you all the evil.' Later, when working on his 'John Knox' essay, he relates that he is writing 'a horrible story of a nurse which I think almost too cruel to go on with'; he feels that the tale 'were a sort of crime against humanity – it is so cruel'. We may also ponder the significance of his remark at the end of 'Nurses' when he writes: 'I believe in a better state of things, that there will be no more nurses, and that every mother will nurse her own offspring.'[27]

Besides, RLS sometimes won small but significant victories against Cummy. He always maintained that children loved to do sinful things, that there was never again in life such a thrill, and he took his revenge on her religious mania from time to time by denying God just to see what would happen. On another occasion he had a pain in his side accompanied by visions of hell, which he attributed in his mind to his 'sin' in listening to a novel about the Crimean war which Cummy was reading to him; next day he turned the tables on her by saying that he had taken a vow not to listen any more. He tried to detach himself from Cummy by telling himself romances in which he played the hero which usually concluded with a heroic, and sometimes a cruel death: 'I never left myself till I was dead.' These fantasies were full of exotic travels and Homeric battles but 'as far back as I can remember, they bore always some relation to women, and Eros and Anteros must have almost equally divided my allegiance.' Stevenson's dreams also contain evidence of repressed anger towards Cummy, whom his unconscious dealt with by transmogrification. He was haunted in his dreams by a hunchback druggist he had seen at Bridge of Allan but also an old bearded woman who came in to do the washing. In few people have the boundaries between conscious and unconscious ever been so blurred as with Stevenson, and he was always half-aware of the latent meaning of his dreams. Hence the otherwise cryptic remarks: 'I hope and I do believe I am a better man than I was a child. With my respects to Wordsworth . . . the sight of deformed persons and above all hideous old women moved in me a sort of panic horror; yet I can well recall with what natural courtesy I strove to conceal my disaffection.'[28]

It is very clear that from Cummy and his father RLS derived a deep sense of guilt that would never leave him: it would have been entirely natural if he conflated his periods of physical illness with sinfulness and regarded his fevers as an outward sign of inner moral blemishes; the analogy between physical health and moral excellence is never far from the surface with the Victorians, and reached its *reductio ad absurdum* in *Erewhon* by Samuel Butler, another man with a 'sinful' childhood. The polarities of day/night, light/darkness, health/sickness, good/evil would have been reinforced for RLS by the daily life he saw around him; he observed his parents playing cards, giving dinner parties and going to the theatre even as Cummy dinned into him that such occupations were the work of the devil. Most of all, he was brought up to believe that 'there were but two camps in the world; one of the perfectly pious and respectable, one of the perfectly profane, mundane and vicious; one mostly on its knees and singing hymns, the other on the high road to the gallows and the bottomless pit.'[29]

More positively, both Cummy and his father encouraged his interest in drama, especially in the form of the then highly popular Skelt's toy theatre, later described so vividly in 'A Penny Plain and Twopence Coloured'. This was a collection of characters, scenery and mainly anonymous texts, given to Louis for his sixth birthday. Among the texts was 'The Battle of Waterloo: A Drama in Three Acts'; 'The Falls of Clyde: A Drama in Two Acts'; 'Pizarro: A Drama in Five Acts' and 'The Miller's Maid: A Drama in Two Acts'. The idea was to read the 12-page dramas and then enact them, using the 'set' and characters provided. Some excellent critics, G.K.Chesterton among them, have emphasised the influence of Skelt on the RLS world-view and in 'A Penny Plain and Twopence Coloured' Stevenson himself confirms this: 'What am I? What are life, art, letters, the world but what my Skelt has made them? He stamped himself upon my immaturity. The world was plain before I knew him, a poor penny world: but soon it was all coloured with romance.'

As for the further influence of his nurse, RLS's first biographer relates a conversation between Cummy and Stevenson when he was an adult.

'It's you that gave me the passion for the drama, Cummie.'

'Me, Master Lou? I never put foot inside a playhouse in my life.'

'Ay, woman, but it was the grand dramatic way ye had of reciting the hymns.'[30]

There is evidence in these early years of a longing for a more fully present mother than the invalid Maggie, who never arose from her bed until noon, allowed herself to be. 'Goodnight, my jewellest of mothers,' was one of his earliest recorded sayings. At the age of three, noticing that Cummy had covered his mother with a shawl, he took a doyley off the table, spread it over her and said, 'That's a wee bittie, Mama.' Later he decided to call her 'mother' sometimes 'just to remember to do it when I'm a big man.' Then there is the most famous of all the early Stevenson sayings, which conveniently draws together the omnipresent theme of religion and his maternal longings: 'Mama, I have drawed a man. Shall I draw his soul now?'[31] The irony was that Maggie loved her son much more intensely than most Victorian mothers, as her copious journals, with their minute observations of the young RLS, show. Yet it is clear that when RLS wanted strength he turned to his father for solace, and Thomas responded well to his beloved 'Smout'. In 1855 we find him writing from London about the breaking of an axle on the train on which he was travelling in letters full of soothing comments: 'My dearest Smouty. I was very glad to get your drawing of the soldier with the bullet box.'[32]

His mother was the dedicatee of his very first attempts at literature. Between 23 November and 21 December 1856 he dictated to her his juvenile composition *A History of Moses*, then, the following spring, followed up with *The Book of Joseph* and a short story, 'The American Travellers', a tale in the style of Mayne Reid. He illustrated *Moses* with his own drawings, in which every Israelite was featured with a pipe in his mouth.[33]

For much of his childhood, then, Stevenson lived in a closed universe of invalidism, religious bigotry and night terrors; some have even described him as being in a cage. The main escape route from this superheated atmosphere was to his grandfather's manse at Colinton, which represented normality. Since there had been thirteen Balfours and thirteen Stevensons, not surprisingly there were around fifty children of the in-laws, and when young Robert Louis went to Colinton, there were always at least half a dozen children to play with, some of them just returned from India with *ayahs*. The household was run by the Revd Lewis Balfour's daughter, Miss Jane Whyte Balfour, the 'Auntie' of RLS's poem: an accident on horseback as a girl had made her nearly deaf and blind but had transformed her from an imperious, managing and self-sufficient young woman into 'the most serviceable and amiable of women and the family maid of all work'. RLS's mother, who like the other two adult denizens of Heriot Row could relate anything to the Bible, was quick to spot a possible reference: 'the text, my mother says, must have been written for her and Aunt Jane: more are the children of the barren than the children of the married wife.'[34]

Aunt Jane, who had been the chatelaine of the manse since her mother's death in 1844, spoiled the young Robert Louis and bought him tin soldiers – always thereafter a passion with RLS. He enjoyed war gaming and later confessed that, had his health permitted it, he would have followed a military career. Proudly the boy showed his grandfather his armies as he sat over his port and nuts; the Revd Lewis responded with a long narrative about the battle of Coburg.

The long summer days at Colinton brought the boy a multitude of new impressions: the beeches, yews, hollies, chimney pots and slate roofs, all so different from the ambience at Heriot Row; the water-mill which inspired his later poem 'Keepsake Mill'. He and a playmate called Billy played at shipwrecked sailors having to live off the land and, finding no other food than buttercups, ate them and became violently ill. He wrote stories, including one set in the 'Witches Walk' with a spectral kitten as heroine, and it was at Colinton, from 20 February to 10 April 1857, that he dictated *The Book of Joseph* to his mother. In the Balfours' garden was a yew-tree under which RLS liked to hide and put his ear to the wall which divided the garden from the graveyard, declaring that he heard the spirits of the departed speaking to him. Another favourite trick was to run into the flowerbeds, which were forbidden to children, and then enlarge his footprint so that an elder cousin got the blame.

Most impressive of all, until his death in the boy's tenth year, was the terrifying patriarch himself, tall, upright and ruddy, with white hair, pale eyes and bloodshot eyes, who had suffered under the rod as a boy in the eighteenth century and believed in such Spartan treatment for the young; he seemed, however, to be clay in his grandson's hands and the only time RLS remembers his sternness was when he intervened to stop 'Auntie' giving the boy barleysugars, since he had declined to take Dr Gregory's powders (an old Scottish nostrum) first. Revd Balfour explained the family significance of his second name: all Balfour sons, it appeared, had a 'Lewis' appended and each had a distinctive adjunct, generally taken from their birthplace; so there was 'Delhi Lewis', 'Noona Lewis', 'Cramond Lewis', Lewis Charles and, of course, Robert Lewis, his favourite grandson. The young RLS apparently won the old man's heart on an early visit when he was sent into the library to recite a psalm to him; much moved, Revd Balfour took the boy in his arms with unwonted tenderness, kissed him and then returned a sermon as 'reward' for the psalm. Such a sermon was likely to have been of consummate dullness, for the Revd Balfour was considered feeble as a preacher even by the unexacting standards of Scottish Calvinism, and he often said things that were unintentionally hilarious: once during a sermon he dilated on the subject of Joseph and Potiphar's wife and declared that 'Mrs Potiphar's conduct was highly improper.'[35]

Of all the cousins with whom he played at Colinton, RLS's favourites were Willie and Henrietta Traquair, his mother's sister's children, whom he recalled fondly in the verses 'To Willie and Henrietta', 'The Hayloft' and 'Farewell to the Farm'. But in 1857, during the first winter at

Heriot Row, he was introduced to a cousin who was to be a major influence throughout his life. Robert Alan Mowbray Stevenson (always referred to as 'Bob' to distinguish him from 'Louis') and his sister Katharine were the children of Alan Stevenson, Thomas's older brother who, after his early brilliant work on the Skerryvore lighthouse, was struck down by a mysterious 'nervous illness' at the age of 45 and lived as an eccentric recluse for his remaining thirteen years. Since the illness was not a fast-wasting one of the motor neurone variety, and since Victorian families were always notoriously coy about strains of insanity in their family, it is to be presumed that what assailed Alan was some form of mental illness. At this stage, when Bob was ten and Louis eleven, Alan was still on the upward trajectory of his career.

Robert Louis was at once fascinated by Bob: 'an imaginative child who had lived in a dream with his sisters, his parents and the *Arabian Nights*, and more unfitted for the world, as was shown in the event, than an angel fresh from heaven'. The two boys lived together in a purely visionary state, coloured pictures, played tin soldiers, experimented with Skelt's theatre, continually dressed up to act out imaginary characters and invented rival kingdoms: Nosingtonia, shaped like Ireland, was Bob's, while RLS had domain over Encyclopedia 'which lay diagonally across the paper like a large tip-cat'. When they ate their porridge of a morning, they enlivened the meal by imagining fresh countries: Bob ate his with sugar and explained that this was a country continually buried under snow; RLS took his with milk and explained it to be a country suffering gradual inundations. On another occasion they sat down to calves' feet jelly and imagined that some part of it was hollow; sooner or later their spoons would uncover a miniature Red Beard or a bewildered Cassius or would come upon the treasure of the *Forty Thieves*.

From the intensity of these experiences with Bob, as much as from his own shrewd observations of others, RLS later distilled the acute observations in 'Child's Play' which mark him as a master of the psychology of childhood: he points out that children's perceptions are entirely subjective – they see rather than look – they cannot discriminate, and they accept the adult world as a mystery.

> Although the ways of children cross with those of their elders in a hundred places daily, they never go in the same direction nor so much as lie in the same element. So may telegraph-wires intersect the line of the high-road, or so might a landscape painter and a bagman visit the same country and yet move in different worlds ... Children think very much the same thoughts and dream the same dreams as bearded men and marriageable women. No one is more romantic ... "Art for art" is their motto; and the doings of

grown folk are only interesting as the raw material for play. Not Théophile Gautier, not Flaubert, can look more callously upon life, or rate the reproduction more highly over reality; and they will parody an execution, a deathbed or the funeral of the young man of Nain, with all the cheerfulness in the world.[36]

Bob encouraged Louis's flight into fantasy from the religious mania of the adult trio in the household. There were few external avenues to escape to, especially when the death of the Revd Lewis Balfour in 1860 sealed off the Eden of Colinton. Moreover, Louis was frequently ill and spent weeks sleepless and without appetite. In September 1858 for five weeks he was unable to sit up in bed; in 1859 he was down with chickenpox; he was bedridden again in the winter and spring of 1860–61 and in 1861 was ill for six weeks with whooping cough. Nevertheless the boy did sometimes manage to get out of his 'cage.' In 1857 the family went on a tour of the lakes, and in 1862 Thomas Stevenson's ill-health (he began to spit blood) brought the family south to London and the Isle of Wight; it was on this trip that RLS first saw Salisbury and Stonehenge. Later that same summer, again in pursuit of convalescence for Thomas, the family stayed in Hamburg for a month.

But otherwise escape from the cloying atmosphere of 17, Heriot Row had to be to the Scottish countryside or coast – on summer holidays at Peebles, or on the East Lothian coast and, above all, at North Berwick in the early 1860s. There it was that he learned to ride and raced ponies across the sands with Bob and Katharine; Bob's black pony was called 'Hell', Katharine's 'Heaven' while Louis's brown was 'Purgatory', and Katharine vividly recalled the three of them riding their mounts into the Tweed on the way to Innerleithen. There too it was that he first learned that a storyteller could, so to speak, jump the queue in hierarchies and pecking orders. At first he was excluded from games by the other boys, but gradually worked himself into a position of leadership by beguiling them with the enthralling products of his imagination. He used to organise secret meetings of his gang in a small cave in the rocks at Point Garry, whence he would dispatch his companions on elaborate games of pirates, smugglers and buried treasure. He loved 'crusoeing' with them and meeting them after dark with bulls-eye lanterns, and he later recalled some of these episodes in 'The Lantern Bearers'. Sometimes his imagination soared too high, literally: he had the idea of making a gigantic kite, but this lifted one of the boys off his feet and carried him in the air for about fifty yards before crashing. Louis's confidence was growing, as illustrated by an incident at Peebles when he fought a 'duel' with another boy from the Edinburgh Academy, in which they used real pistols and real powder but no bullets. There is also evidence from this period of a 'calf-love' friendship with a girl.

If his imagination was used in North Berwick to cajole other boys under the aegis of his charismatic leadership, it was also in its turn fired by the historical associations of the area; here were laid the foundations for many scenes in *Treasure Island, The Black Arrow, Kidnapped* and *Catriona*, most notably those set in Tantallon Castle, Point Garry and the Bass Rock, where he imprisoned David Balfour in *Catriona*. The same was true of his association with Bridge of Allan, then a health resort much frequented by Thomas Stevenson and his wife. In this area too Louis toured the historic sites: Falkirk, Sheriffmuir, Bannockburn, Stirling Castle; as an adult RLS often returned to Bridge of Allan or nearby Dunblane. In March 1861 he dictated to his mother descriptions of his excursions to Craigmillar Castle and Corstorphine Church. The foundations for *Weir of Hermiston* were also laid in 1863 when RLS visited the Lammermuirs. His mother later recalled this as the basis for Weir's place of exile and wrote: 'I have now made sure that in 1863 Louis paid a visit to his uncle Mr Traquair at a farm house called Overshiels in Stow parish among the Lammermuirs.'[37]

Stevenson's formal education was scrappy and perfunctory. He did not learn to read until he was seven, out of laziness he sometimes alleged, but really because he wanted to prolong the delights of the oral tradition – both hearing and telling stories. He went first to a local school at Canonmills, where he was teased for the oddity of his appearance and anyway suffered agonies from being away from a known environment, however much he later fulminated against his childhood incarceration. He always remembered his very first day at school.

> There came suddenly upon the face of all I saw – the long empty road, the lines of tall houses, the church upon the hill, the woody hillside garden – a look of such piercing sadness that my heart died; and seating myself on a doorstep, I shed tears of considerable sympathy. A benevolent cat cumbered me the while with consolations – we two were alone in all that was visible of the London road; two poor waifs who had each tasted sorrow – and she fawned upon the weeper and gambolled for his entertainment, watching the effect, it seemed, with motherly eyes.[38]

When he confessed this experience to his family, they decided he must be ill and needed a change of scene; he therefore went with his father to the Fife coast.

His next school was Mr Henderson's in India Street, just around the corner from Heriot Row. A fellow pupil, James Milne, remembered him as an eccentric boy who, taken on a day trip to North Berwick, continued to run around naked and play the fool when all the other boys were dressed after sea-bathing. He had two main problems. One was that he was frequently ill, so that even the walk to school taxed his constitution; once on a wintry walk from Howard Place to Danube Street he was so exhausted that he wanted to sit on every flight of steps. He found attendance for just two mornings a week beyond him, and was withdrawn, though he returned briefly in 1859. The other problem was that until he entered his teens he found it difficult to make friends with other boys. Once in Howe Street he asked a lame boy, who also seemed to be shunned by the herd, if he could play with him, but the lad repelled him with a volley of oaths. There are echoes of this difficulty in *Weir of Hermiston*. Frank Innes, supposedly Weir's friend, says disdainfully: 'I know Weir but I never met Archie', to which RLS adds: 'No one had met Archie, a malady most incident to only sons.'[39]

Later, at the age of eleven, RLS was at the Academy school in Henderson Row, from which he was often absent through illness. Later still he was at a private school in Frederick Street, kept by Mr Thompson, who detected no special literary talent in him. His schoolfriend David Lewis thought him (not surprisingly) more influenced by the Old Testament than any other book and recalls that young Louis was a keen naturalist with a talent for recognising birds and finding their nests; he once climbed a cliff to get to a kestrel's nest, ascending an incline that would have taxed an Alpinist.

It is hard to see what benefit Louis derived from these institutions. He never mastered the grammar of Latin nor any other language and was always a mediocre speller in English, possibly because of the confusing effect of the Scots dialect. His sporting prowess was no better: indifferent to golf, he was bored by football and to stimulate himself had to imagine the ball as a talisman bandied about in conflict between two Arab nations. Cricket merely left him bemused: 'Cricket, which is a mere matter of dexterity, palpably about nothing, and for no end, often fails to satisfy infantile craving. It is a game, if you like, but not a game to play. You cannot tell yourself a story about cricket; and the activity it calls forth can be justified on no rational theory.'[40]

The most dramatic interruption to this intermittent education came in 1863. Instead of returning to the Academy, RLS was sent south to Spring Grove, an English boarding school in Isleworth, Middlesex. Here he whiled his time away writing stories for the school magazine: one was about French soldiers in Belgium in 1818; another was a ghost story set in Lapland; a third was a tale of eighteenth-century wreckers; and a fourth an adventure story set in the Pacific in 1720. Yet once again Louis was deeply unhappy. His letters to his parents were full of references to illnesses and shortages of money, though he did send his father a specimen of a Latin exercise with the proud comment: 'I have done something! I have made a grand step!' But finally he threw off the mask. At the end of a letter written to his mother in atrocious French, he wrote despairingly: 'My dear Papa, you told me to tell you whenever I was miserable. I do not feel well and wish to get home. Do take me with you.' Thomas Stevenson, who had always had a rather insouciant attitude to formal education – he used to stop schoolboys in the street, examine their piles of books, then smilingly say it was all nonsense and they should read only what interested them – obliged, and took him on a continental trip lasting five months.[41]

This was RLS's second trip, for early in 1863 he had been with his family on a tour to Nice and Menton, starting in Paris, then through Italy, Austria and Germany, visiting Genoa, Naples, Rome, Florence, Venice, Innsbruck and the Rhine. The journey apparently made little impression on him, except that he retained a memory of the Brenner Pass for use in his short story 'Will o' the Mill', and in later life RLS's acquaintances were sometimes surprised to learn that he had ever been in Italy; the land that has meant so much to many British men of letters seems to have left Stevenson cold, and it was always France for which he had the overwhelming affection. The itinerary of the Stevenson family can be followed in minute detail in Cummy's diary, where her religious zealotry is again much in evidence; she constantly complains that Europeans do not keep the sabbath and even that it is impossible to get a good cup of tea abroad! RLS was ill on two occasions during the trip, once after climbing in the Alps, and the second occasion on the road between Viterbo and Orvieto after leaving Rome for Florence. Cummy made a bed for him in the coach with bags and a cushion and once in Florence wrote in typical manner: 'Dear Lew was very much knocked up, but he was able to appear at breakfast next morning. He is not well, poor boy, though he tries to brave it out, but I am thankful he is able to be out of bed. I stayed at home with him yesterday afternoon and read to him, at his own request, another lily gathered from Mr McCheyne.'

Yet if RLS was glad enough of the ministrations of the Janus-faced Cummy, he proved on this trip that he had already outgrown her influence and, reading between the lines, we can see the many ways in which he poked gentle fun at her. In a lemon grove at Menton Cummy was just about to stretch her hand out and pick one of the fruit but 'Lew said, in his old-fashioned way, that, though it was allowed, yet he did not think it altogether right, so I did not do it.' The inference that he was paying her back in her own bigoted coin becomes clearer from her description of an incident in a church in Nice. Cummy noticed some priests 'doing something in a corner curtained off' (i.e. hearing confessions). Louis could not resist the temptation to make fun of her. 'When we came out Lew said they were priests playing at cards for money. Is it not very melancholy?'[42]

On this trip through Europe Thomas Stevenson treated his 12-year old son as a grown-up, took him into smoking rooms to hear adult discussions, and discussed art and architecture with him as an equal. Later that year he also took him on a tour of the Fife lighthouses. In gratitude, Louis responded, when in Menton the following year, with some fulsomely loving letters to his father, who had to return early to Scotland. When Louis came home he was at Elibank Villa, Springhill, Peebles, for four months from early June to October 1864, where he wrote about Peebles in the manner of Thackeray's *Book of Snobs*.[43]

In 1865 RLS spent long periods of time with his mother and a private tutor in Torquay; here he spent most of his time writing an early story 'The Plague Seller' and working on an early draft of *Deacon Brodie*. Correspondence with his father took the form of arch requests for money. 'Respected paternal relative, I write to make a request of the moderate nature (for 2/6)'. Taxed with not having put away childish things and still being overfond of lead soldiers, Louis decided to defer to the parental wishes; secretly he vowed that as an adult he would make so much money that within a few years he could retire in peace with his soldiers, and even picked out his dream dwelling – a house he had once espied in the Esterel mountains between Cannes and Fréjus, 'a pretty house in an orange garden at the angle of the bay . . . this should be his Happy Valley. Astraea Redux; childhood was to come again!'

The desire to retreat from reality into fantasy was strengthened by a growing realisation that he was not robust as other boys were – already he was beginning to suffer from congestion of the lungs and bleeding – and that his original ambition to be a soldier could never be fulfilled. His first biographer Graham Balfour quotes RLS's schoolfriend H.B.Baildon on RLS's physical appearance at this time.

In body he was assuredly badly set up. His limbs were long, lean and spidery, and his chest flat, so as almost to suggest some malnutrition, such sharp corners did his joints make under his clothes. But in his face this was belied. His brow was oval and full, over soft brown eyes that seemed already to have drunk the sunlight under the southern vines. The whole face had a tendency to an oval Madonna-like type. But about the mouth and in the mirthful mocking light of the eyes there lingered ever a ready Autolycus mockery that rather suggested sly Hermes masquerading as a mortal. The eyes were always genial, however gaily the lights danced in them, but about the mouth there was something a little tricksy and mocking, as if of a spirit that already peeped behind the scenes of life's pageant and more than guessed its realities.[44]

Finally in 1866 he started at Mr Thompson's small school (just twenty pupils) for delicate and backward boys in Frederick Street, a short walk from home, where he remained until he went to university. Here he was allowed to pick and choose the subjects he wanted to study (French, Latin and Geometry); he spent most of his time working on a magazine with H.B.Baildon, and tried unsuccessfully to write on the Covenanters. At last, in 1866 he managed to cobble together a sketch of the seventeenth-century Pentland rising; in November his father paid to have one hundred copies of this 16-page pamphlet published.[45] But his schooling continued to be desultory and he was absent for long periods of time, either through illness or on holidays in Scotland with his parents. Bridge of Allan continued to be a great favourite; Louis's growing interest in women was stimulated by winter visits from a cousin, Jessie Warden, a young woman of eighteen or so who died in 1867. And there was a new Eden – Swanston Cottage, on the eastern spur of the Pentland Hills, five miles from the centre of Edinburgh, which Thomas Stevenson took for summer use in 1867. He retained the lease for fourteen years. Visible from the Castle – as Flora Gilchrist pointed out to the eponymous hero of *St Ives* – Swanston was to Stevenson's early youth what Colinton had been to his childhood. It was here that he met John Todd the shepherd and Robert Young the gardener, later immortalised in RLS essays. Young began by shouting angrily at the young Louis for disturbing the jittery sheep with his dog Coolin, but ended as a friend; Louis would often accompany him on 'sheep patrol' and lambing expeditions.[46]

The mid-sixties were memorable to Louis also for his meeting with R.M.Ballantyne – on the strength of his *Coral Island* the author the boyish RLS most wanted to meet. Stevenson waylaid Ballantyne one Sunday morning when he was emerging with his new bride at Colinton Kirk, introduced himself, and invited him to dinner with his uncle. Ballantyne chatted agreeably, asked the boy which of his books he most admired (*Coral Island*, naturally), and accepted the invitation; then and later at dinner the bearded Calvinistic author made a great impression on Louis. In his introductory verses to *Treasure Island*, RLS later hailed 'Ballantyne the brave' as one of his early inspirations though by the age of thirty he had begun to see his feet of clay and remarked drily that his sadistic boys' books 'scarce seem to me designed for immortality'.[47]

Every human being is profoundly influenced by childhood, and this is particularly so of those creative talents who can retain into adulthood a genuine capacity for empathy with the mental world of the child; such people have usually found it necessary to retreat into fantasy in childhood to an abnormal extent. As Andrew Lang remarked: 'Genius is the survival into maturity of the imagination of childhood, and Stevenson is not the only genius who has retained from childhood something more than its inspiration.' The legacy of a lonely childhood can produce great art, but also crippling periods of depression in adult life. How did it affect Stevenson? He was shrewd enough to see as a young adult that Cummy's categories of Heaven and Hell apply, not to an after-life, as she preached, but to the beginning of life. Was his early life, then, primarily Hell or primarily Eden? Appropriately for an ambivalent 'divided self', the only possible answer is: both. Stevenson's case was very different from that of someone like H.M.Stanley, who suffered a childhood so unrelievedly hellish that he spent a lifetime seeking vengeance for early nightmares. As RLS himself later remarked: 'Everything is true; only the opposite is true too: you must believe both equally or be damned.'

A decidedly negative aspect of his childhood was the legacy of Calvinism and superstition. Despite RLS's many personae – as Puckish sprite, amateur emigrant, bohemian invalid or Samoan laird – the quest for identity is not really a central theme in his life, as it would be for a more 'existential' hero. Scots Calvinism imposed its own identity, inculcating a sense of determinism and even predestination which pervades his work. The Jesuits used to boast that if they took a child by the age of seven, he was theirs for life, and the elders of the Kirk might have been entitled to make the same claim. That was why Henley's later strictures on RLS as the 'Shorter Catechist' were so unfair: he completely failed to understand how much strength and willpower was needed to surmount the daily barrage of religious propaganda in Heriot Row, coming at Louis from three different directions. How could anyone have remained completely impervious to such influences? A lesser man might have been immobilised by the contradictory impulses towards self-realisation and towards John Knox's God, and a negligible one could well have ended like Cummy, depositing Calvinistic tracts in Catholic churches abroad or denouncing the repairs to Colinton Kirk as 'Popish'.[48]

The supernatural, too, remained as an important element in his fiction. Its treatment suffered from lack of integration into the general universe of discourse of his novels and often featured as an 'intrusion', and here again we can see the influence of Cummy and Thomas Stevenson. It is true that the supernatural was used more readily by Victorian writers – Henry James, Dickens, Wilkie Collins, to name three very different authors – than would be the case a hundred years later, but even so there is a 'superplus' in Stevenson that goes beyond the normal conventions of a more superstitious age, when vogues for spiritualism and theosophy were quite respectable; significantly, his wife was also a believer in the occult, rounding off a trio with Cummy and his father. RLS himself claimed to have observed genuine supernatural phenomena in the Pacific islands, and his wife was to record an occasion when he fled from *aitus* (demons) in the woods of Samoa.[49]

On the positive side there can be no denying that Stevenson's childhood inspired his fiction in a direct and verifiable way, in contrast to, for instance, Henry James, where the experience is transmogrified. RLS himself made the point explicitly in his 'Humble Remonstrance' on the art of fiction addressed to James where he replies to 'the master's' statement, 'I have been a child, but have never been on a quest for buried treasure.' Stevenson answers: 'A Scottish child hears much of shipwreck, outlying iron skerries, pitiless breakers and great sealights; much of heathery mountains, wild clans and hunted Covenanters . . . Here indeed is a wilful paradox, for if he [James] has never been on a quest for buried treasure, it can be demonstrated that he has never been a child. There never was a child (unless Master James) but has hunted gold, and been a pirate, and a military commander, and a bandit of the mountains; but has fought and suffered shipwreck and prison, and imbued its little hands in gore, and gallantly retrieved the lost battle and triumphantly protected innocence and beauty.'[50] This debate in turn has engendered a controversy about which childhood, James's or Stevenson's, was the more common Victorian experience: there are those who say that RLS was universalising a specifically Scottish experience, and even those who say that he was extrapolating invalidly from the Stevenson milieu to *general* Scottish experience.

Again, there are grounds for believing that the fear, loneliness, anxiety of his childhood which, finding expression in such almost solipsistic poems as 'Travel', 'Going to Bed', 'The Land of Nod' and 'North West Passage' seem at times almost to denote an autistic child, are the deep impulses that led Stevenson to be a globetrotter. The psychological motivations of the true explorer and the traveller are different: an explorer like Stanley sought out new worlds as a resolution of childhood trauma, where the journey into the unknown comes to seem the actualisation of the childhood venture into darkness (hence the resonance of the 'Dark Continent'). In the case of the traveller, seeking out little-known but far from unknown areas – like the Pacific Islands – the impulse may well be adult compensation for the confinements of childhood. It is perhaps not hyperbole to say that the Samoa where Stevenson ended his days was the world already distantly glimpsed forty years before through the window of the nursery or sick-room.

2

The University Years

In November 1867 Stevenson began his studies at Edinburgh University. In Scotland a university education was open to people to whom it would have been closed in England – north of the border Hardy's Jude would not have needed to pen his pathetic letter to the master of the 'Christminster' college. 23% of Scottish university entrants in the 1860s came from working-class backgrounds, no doubt partly accounting for the higher literacy levels in Scotland (in 1850 these were 89% in Scotland and 70% in England).

Snobbish Oxbridge critics said of the nineteenth-century Scottish university much what they say of the twentieth-century American academy: that its standards were those of an English secondary school and its degrees the equivalent of English school-leaving certificates. It is hard to sustain this critique in the light of the distinguished individuals who held chairs at Edinburgh when RLS was a student there and a little later. The Professor of English was David Masson, biographer of Milton (whom RLS later described to J.M.Barrie as pompous and reactionary); presiding over Natural Philosophy was Peter Guthrie Tait, later Lord Levin; the chair of Latin was occupied by William Young Sellar, author of *The Roman Poets of the Republic*. Logic was represented by Campbell Fraser, Moral Philosophy by Henry Calderwood and Greek, memorably, by Professor Blackie, whose lectures ranged from Homer to Egyptian crocodiles and who liked to appear in Princes Street in tartan plaid and wide slouch hat. In RLS's lifetime other Edinburgh luminaries included the mathematician Professor Chrystal and the Greek scholar Samuel Henry Butcher, who collaborated with Andrew Lang on one of the best translations of the *Odyssey*. Best of all there were two distinguished scientists: Fleeming Jenkin, professor of engineering, and Philip Kelland, the mathematician, of whom Stevenson wrote: 'no man's education is complete or truly liberal who knew not Kelland . . . I have heard him drift into reminiscences in class-time, though not for long, and give me glimpses of old-world life in out-of-the-way English parishes when he was young.' RLS particularly marvelled at the way he could control the turbulent Edinburgh students by the firm but resolute exercise of kindness.[1]

Having been to school in both England and Scotland, Stevenson knew something of the great divide between the cultures so superficially bridged by the Act of Union, and there was no question which of them he preferred: in Scotland there were wider extremes of temperament and sensibility, while in England boys were much younger for their age, more interested in games, more concerned with the here and now, and in general less imaginative and romantic. Even on Sundays, where in contrast to the dark, dour Scottish Sabbath, England should have had the advantage, Stevenson found John Bull lacking alongside his beloved France: in, England the day of rest was an occasion for gorging on a huge lunch and sleeping off the repast like a boa. Always inclined to take a Montesquieu-like view of the influence of climate, Stevenson attributed to the winds and rains of Caledonia the ultimate causation for the observable fact that the Scots were metaphysical where the English were empirical. Necessarily, then, education was taken more seriously in Scotland, and it was grounded in a meritocratic principle of class mingling and the career open to talents.

> The English lad goes to Oxford or Cambridge; then, in an ideal world of gardens, to live in a semi-scenic life, costumed, disciplined and drilled by proctors. Nor is this to be regarded merely as a stage of education; it is a piece of privilege besides, and a step that separates him further from the bulk of his compatriots. At an earlier age the Scottish lad begins his greatly different experience of crowded class-rooms, of a gaunt quadrangle, of a bell hourly booming over the traffic of the city to recall him from the public-house where he has been lunching, or the streets where he has been wandering fancy-free. His college life has little of restraint, and nothing of necessary gentility. He will find no quiet clique of the exclusive, studious and cultured; no rotten boroughs of the arts. All classes rub shoulders on the greasy benches. The raffish young gentleman in gloves must measure his scholarship with the plain, clownish laddie from the parish school. They separate at the session's end, one to smoke cigars about a watering-place, the other to resume the labours of the field beside his peasant family. The first muster of a college class in Scotland is a scene of curious and painful interest; so many lads, fresh from the heather, hang around the stove in cloddish embarrassment, ruffled by the presence of their smarter comrades, and afraid of the sound of their own rustic voices. It was in these early days, I think, that Professor Blackie won the affection of his pupils, putting these uncouth umbrageous students at their ease with ready human geniality.[2]

It is in this differential post-lecture experience that the key to RLS's unpopularity with the other students – so insisted on in all memories and oral accounts of Louis's Edinburgh days as to be unimpeachable – must be sought. His status as a university student – at least as that word is commonly understood – was shaky, in that his attendance at classes was irregular, he followed no set curriculum, took little part in the work of the classes he did attend, and disrupted them when he became bored. On a good day he would sit at the back of a class with pencil and paper, pretending to take notes but in reality working on a private literary project; on a bad day he would simply storm out of the lecture, leaving the lecturer in no doubt about his (Louis's) opinion of his intellectual calibre. But this baiting, barracking and heckling took place only with those teachers RLS did not respect; if he respected someone, like Fleeming Jenkin or Blackie, he showed this by simply staying away. This behaviour was not exactly encouraged by his father but it was connived at, for Thomas Stevenson, with his cavalier attitude towards education, took the line that his son's future career as a lighthouse engineer was mapped out, and t⎯.at Edinburgh University was to be regarded as a kind of superior finishing school.

By and large Stevenson's fellow students regarded him as a poseur, a show-off, a phoney bohemian, with an almost English sense of 'effortless superiority', seeming to imply that university education was a farce and students who took it seriously merely dolts. The most critical contemporaries branded him crank, humbug and bounder, and there was particular bitterness about his iconoclasm at the expense of Edinburgh University on the part of those for whom the University was a genuine escape route from poverty; they regarded his sallies and squibs as simply the spoiled-brat tantrums of a pampered and self-indulgent youth who had his father's money to fall back on. He brushed aside talk of the 'necessity' of a degree and declared: 'I would sooner commit to memory the long bead-roll of names in the early chapters of the Book of the Chronicles than cram for a degree-exam.' Yet later, in *Lay Morals*, he evinced some guilt over the way he yawned and idled through lectures while his fellow students worked hard and had to follow the plough in the summer to make ends meet. He quickly decided that 'life was a handicap upon strange, wrong-sided principles; and not, as he had been told, a fair and equal race.' Taken aback by the number of avenues of opportunity closed to his academic equals and even superiors, he began to despise himself and flirt with socialism. The flirtation did not last long – Stevenson was by temperament a natural conservative – but for a time he was 'full of that trumpeting anger with which young men regard injustices in the first blush of youth; although in a few years they will tamely acquiesce in their existence, and knowingly profit by their complications'.[3]

Many physical descriptions survive which enable us to pin down the look of the student RLS like a butterfly in an album. He wore a pea-jacket and had long, shoulder-length hair (fair in his youth, it was gradually growing darker), which elicited hoots from the Edinburgh urchins; Stevenson, typically, hooted back. He had long spidery limbs, was narrow-chested, walked with a slight stoop and was so thin that his joints made sharp corners under his clothes. 5′10″ tall, he had fine bones, long sensitive hands, well-shaped feet about which he was vain, an oval face with high cheekbones, ruddy colouring, an aquiline nose like his mother's and a large and expressive mouth that was described as 'a little tricksy and mocking'. Yet his dark brown eyes were easily his most striking feature and invited a stream of epithets and descriptions: 'quick-glancing', 'observant', 'brimful of humour', 'gay of banter', 'luminous', 'gleaming', 'with the gypsy light behind', 'wonderful, dark, far-apart', 'unusually far apart with level eye-brows, one of which he often lifted in an odd Japanese sort of way'. His wife later recorded that his eyes were the kind of cool, frequently changing brown that is often labelled black and that he could smoulder and languish his orbs like any Polynesian.[4]

After nearly a year of desultory study, Stevenson spent the summer vacation of 1868 in north-eastern Scotland, about his father's business of marine construction. While learning the trade of lighthouse engineer in July, he spent a lot of time in the triple town of Anstruther Wester, Anstruther Easter and Cellardyke in Fife, which lay continuously along the strand of the Forth coast; his business lay particularly in the two Anstruthers, and it amused him that the 'twin town' was divided by no more than a tricklet and a small bridge. Lodging with Bailie Brown the carpenter seemed at first like a great adventure, but the 17-year old RLS was soon bored by the work: he complained that he drew badly and slowly and was more interested in a show given by a band of strolling players; he reported an accident when a truck overturned; and he lost patience with his father's workmen: 'Tell Papa that his boat-builders are the most illiterate writers with whom I have ever had any dealing. From beginning to end of their previous specification, there was no stop, whether comma, semicolon, colon, or point; and to tell whether the adjectives belonged to previous or subsequent noun, was work for five experienced boat-builders.' Finally he exploded with frustration: 'I am utterly sick of this grey, grim, sea-beaten hole' and announced that he was ill. His father took the hint and transferred him to an assignment at Wick in the far north, allowing him first a rambling, circuitous progress north via Oban.[5]

At first Stevenson was equally gloomy about the 'sub-arctic' town of Wick:

> You can never have dwelt in a country more unsightly than that part of Caithness, the land faintly swelling, faintly falling, not a tree, not a hedgerow, the fields divided by single slate stones set upon their edge, the wind always singing in your ears ... Only as you approached the coast was there anything to stir the heart ... It is one of the meanest of man's towns, and situate certainly on the baldest of God's bays ... In a bad year, the end of the herring-fishery

is therefore an exciting time; fights are common, riots often possible; an apple knocked from a child's hand was once the signal for something like war; and even when I was there, a gunboat lay in the bay to assist the authorities.

He complained of the boorishness of the fishermen and regretted that he did not see any fisticuffs: 'The riots were a hum. No more has been heard; and one of the war-steamers has deserted in disgust.' However, this temporary depression soon lifted and Louis hastened to apologise to his parents for his previous melancholy. Soon a new, more tolerant, mood was in evidence: one night his sleep was disturbed when a fellow-lodger came in, stood at the top of the stairs and preached from midnight to 1.30 a.m. at the top of his voice. Eventually RLS poked his head out of the door. 'Are we to have no sleep at all for that drunken brute?' he yelled. 'Drunken brute!' the man repeated indignantly. Then self-pity and contrition overcame him. 'Well,' he went on, 'if I am a drunken brute, it's only once in the twelve months!'

Louis's more eupeptic mood was a product of two influences. First, he entered into a sustained correspondence with Bob, so that he had a fellow-spirit to confide in. Then he entered more fully into the life of Wick by going to sea with the fishermen and then, as the crowning feat of his education as an engineer, by descending into the watery depths in the old-fashioned diving suit; the nineteenth-century diver in 'inner space' looked like a modern astronaut in the outer dimension. RLS made the descent during a fairly high swell, with lots of 'skipper's daughters' around; he was exhilarated by the experience and amazed by all the tricks gravity played on the human body underwater. 'It is bitter to return to infancy, and to be supported, and directed, and perpetually set upon your feet, by the hand of someone else. The air besides, as it is supplied to you by the busy millers on the platform, closes the eustachian tubes and keeps the neophyte perpetually swallowing, till his throat is grown so dry that he can swallow no longer.' The upward journey to the surface was therefore a relief: 'My ascending head passed into the trough of a swell. Out of the green I shot at once into a glory of rosy, almost of sanguine light – the multitudinous seas incarnadined, the heaven above a vault of crimson. And then the glory faded into the hard, ugly daylight of a Caithness autumn, with a low sky, a grey sea, and a whistling wind.'[6]

The euphoria of this experience doubtless explains the rather manic tone of his other letters to his mother from Wick, with their arch and bogus literariness. In September: 'Seven p.m. found me at Breadalbane Terrace, clad in spotless blacks, white tie, shirt etc and finished off below with a pair of navvies' boots. How true that the devil is betrayed by his feet! A message to Cummy at last. Why, O treacherous woman! were my dress boots withheld?' Then a month later: 'Ha my prophetic soul! how truly thou prophesied! or prophesiedest; but the latter is bad orthography and spoils the Alexandrine (Nota Bene: papa will again object to poetry).' But to Bob he was able to expand in truly romantic vein, as when he described a night ride on the top of the Thurso to Wick coach: the coach was crowded with Lewis fishermen going home, no tongue but Gaelic could be heard, and as they descended from the open moor to the shores of the roaring Pentland Firth, they came upon two gypsy boys aged about fourteen, gabbling in Italian as they walked and as out of place in those northern latitudes as a Roman legionary of old.[7]

The pattern of spending the summer vacation on remote stretches of the Scottish coast continued in 1869 and 1870. In June 1869 he accompanied his father on the yacht *Pharos* on a trip to Orkney and to Shetland to inspect the North Uist Lighthouse, the most northerly dwelling house in the realm. In 1870 he was in Argyllshire to view the early stages of the building of the lighthouse on the Dhu Heartach rock, on the Pentland Firth, and in the Hebrides; his trip was similar to one Sir Walter Scott had made just before writing *The Pirate*. During the travels in Argyll he made a detailed examination of the island of Earraid, off the south-west corner of the Ross of Mull, which he later used to good effect in *Kidnapped* and his short story 'The Merry Men'. There he swam in the sea and tried his hand at sailing a boat. Later he was to reflect that while he thus idled through the long hot summer, other young men were dying in the Franco-Prussian war. This gave rise to a typically 'guilty' RLS reflection: 'In that year cannon were roaring for days together on French battlefields; and I would sit in my isle (I call it mine, after the use of lovers) and think upon the war, and the loudness of these far-away battles, and the pain of men's wounds, and the weariness of their marching.' One significant encounter this summer, while he was aboard the ship *Clansman* off the Hebrides, was with a young man later to be a significant figure in his literary career: Edmund Gosse. On an August midnight the *Clansman* entered Portree harbour on the Isle of Skye to take a party of America-bound emigrants to Glasgow; Gosse remembered: 'As they came on board an eerie sound of wailing rose in the stillness of the night, which pierced my heart; it was a most extraordinary sound.'[8]

Stevenson's education as an engineer resulted in his seeing a great deal of Fife: Dunfermline, Inverkeithing, Aberdour, Burntisland, Kingshorn, Kirkcaldy, Dysart, Wemyss, Leven, Largo, Cellardyke, Fife Ness and St Andrews. Thereafter he played truant and the sum total of his knowledge, he sardonically remarked, was to discover that 'emphyteusis is not a disease nor stillicide a crime.' Here he sold himself somewhat short, for he did gather enough expertise to be able to deliver a paper about a new form of intermittent light for lighthouses before the Royal Scottish Society of Arts on 27 March 1871; this was considered a professional enough piece of work for him to receive one of the Society's five annual silver medals.

Yet this proved to be his last hurrah for, having demonstrated to his father that it was not lack of ability that stood in his way, he suddenly announced that he did not wish to proceed with this career. At this stage he did not dare lay all his cards on the table and admit that it was the avocation of letters that beckoned, so he agreed to switch courses at Edinburgh to Law. 'Tom wonderfully resigned' Maggie noted in her diary, and it may be that the pleadings of James Dick, head clerk of the Stevenson firm, had some effect: Dick pointed out that not only was Louis's heart not in it but that he was too fragile physically for such a robust career, with its risks of exposure in all kinds of weather.

The abandonment of the great tradition of his family left RLS with some guilt, which he later tried to expunge in his poem 'The Light Keeper' which suggests that the profession of literature is merely humanitarian lighthousekeeping by other means: both seek to bring light, the engineer literally, the artist in terms of creative enlightenment:

> This is the man
> Who gives up what is lovely in living
> For the means to live.

Yet in 'To the Commissioners of the Northern Lights' the tone is more jaunty and defiant:

> I thocht I'd serve wi' you, sirs, yince,
> But I've thocht better of it since;
> The maitter I will nowise mince
> But tell ye true.
> I'll service wi' some other prince,
> An no' wi' you.[9]

The one lasting legacy of RLS's time as a tiro engineer was his relationship with Fleeming Jenkin, the university's professor of engineering. Shortly after Jenkin's appointment to the chair in 1868, his wife Anne, then in her early thirties, in the course of making social contacts, took tea with the Stevensons at Heriot Row. Introduced to Thomas's young student son, she was bowled over by his sensitivity and intelligence: 'who was this son who talked as Charles Lamb wrote? this young Heine with the Scottish accent?' She invited him to lunch with her husband next day and told Fleeming that very evening that she had met a real poet. It was the beginning of a friendship marked by admiration and affection on their side but by something like idolatry on Louis's. For him the relationship was especially significant, for Jenkin (1833–85), who had the same dates and life span as another RLS hero, General Charles Gordon, was old enough to be a father figure, and it is of the essence of a surrogate father to project all the positive, caring features of paternity and none of its negative, authoritarian

ones; there was towards Jenkin none of the ambivalence Louis felt towards
Thomas and as he later confessed: 'I never knew a better man; nor one to
me more lovable.' His wife was almost as important, psychologically, since
she was the first of four significant older women with whom RLS forged
close emotional bonds. It is probably not an exaggeration to say that the
Jenkins were idealised parents, except that Stevenson's relations with older
women were always more complex than this simple statement implies.

Jenkin's was a fine intellect and, what is rarer, an original one. A
top-flight engineer, he had a range of intellectual interests and enthusiasms
that makes the inevitable clichéd comparison with Leonardo for once not
entirely hyperbolic. He reviewed for the influential *Saturday Review*; he
was a shrewd and insightful critic of drama and poetry and himself wrote
a prose play *Griselda*; he corrected the great Latinist Munro on Lucretius
and crossed swords with Darwin on the origin of species; his contribution
to science received the enthusiastic accolades of men like Sir Alfred Ewing
and Lord Kelvin; he had long discussions with RLS on the historical Jesus
and pointed out that the founder of Christianity never said anything witty
or amusing; he shared both RLS's love of the Highlands and his love of
arguing for the sake of it. He was a vastly entertaining talker, with a dry, brisk
and pertinacious manner, full of brand-new opinions and with a novel theory
for everything. In RLS's essay 'Talk and Talkers' he appears, perfunctorily
disguised, as 'Cockshot': 'He is possessed by a demoniac energy, welding the
elements for his life, and bending ideas as an athlete bends a horseshoe, with
a visible and lively effort . . . Cockshot is bottled effervescence, the sworn
enemy of sleep.'

Greater even than his intellectual impact on the young Louis was
his moral influence: he taught the young man not to strive for effect as
a critic and instead to aim for integrity. In the early 1870s RLS sent a
review of the actor Salvini's performance as Macbeth to *The Academy* and
showed Jenkin a copy; Jenkin read part of it, then flung it contemptuously
on the floor: 'That won't do. You were thinking of yourself, not Salvini.' It
was quite clear that Jenkin had detected RLS's fatal flaw – egoism.

Jenkin also put Stevenson in his place over his truancy. The only class
RLS ever attended with anything like assiduity was Kelland's, from whom
he once gained the one and only certificate of merit during his university
career. In five years he went to Blackie's Greek class no more than a dozen
times; later he claimed to regret the wasted opportunity but said that fear of
overworking and developing brain fever constrained him. 'I am sorry indeed
that I have no Greek, but I should be sorrier still if I were dead; nor do I know
the name of that branch of knowledge which is worth acquiring at the price of
a brain fever.' Stevenson compounded his casuistry with brazen effrontery,
by asking Blackie for a certificate of attendance for the classes he had cut.
'I don't seem to remember your face,' said Blackie. 'Probably not,' replied

Stevenson, 'but I hope that will not prevent you from giving me a certificate.'
Blackie shrugged and wrote out the certificate, humming a Highland air as
he did so; perhaps the scene is the basis for Alan Breck's humming ditties
during the fight in the roundhouse in *Kidnapped*.

Stevenson then decided to try the same approach on Jenkin, but the
professor pulled him up short. 'It is quite useless for *you* to come to me,
Mr Stevenson. There may be doubtful cases; there is no doubt about yours.
You simply have not attended my class.' There followed a barrage of equivocations and half-truths from RLS, to which Jenkin replied: 'You are no fool,
and you chose your own course. To comply would be to aid in a nefarious
attempt to steal a degree.' However, he was persuaded to examine other
certificates, Blackie's among them; on the strength of these, but probably
more for Thomas Stevenson's sake, the certificate was reluctantly given.
Nonetheless, there was a larger sense in which Jenkin had won the battle
and brought the young man to heel, for he cleverly used the incident of the
certificate to tap into RLS's Calvinistic sense of guilt. Such an interpretation
is borne out by Stevenson's words nearly twenty years later when he wrote
Jenkin's memoir after his early death at 52:

> I am still ashamed when I think of his shame in giving that paper. He made no
> reproach in speech, but his manner was more eloquent; it told me plainly what a
> dirty business we were in, and I went from his presence, with my certificate indeed
> in my possession, but with no answerable sense of triumph. That was the begin-
> ning of my love for Fleeming Jenkin. I never thought lightly of him afterwards.

However, there were bound to be more clashes between two such
highly talented men, each with the prickly sensitivity of a prima donna.
On one occasion Louis stormed out of Jenkin's house after the professor
took him to task in front of strangers. A month later they met at dinner,
and Jenkin was conciliatory. Again he showed a masterly understanding of
RLS's psychology by pitching the appeal precisely: 'You may have grounds of
quarrel with me; you have none against Mrs Jenkin; and before I say another
word, I want you to promise you will come to *her* house as usual.' On another
occasion he lectured Stevenson sanctimoniously but later recanted with the
words: 'You see at that time I was so much younger than you.'[10]

Given that Stevenson absented himself from so much formal instruction,
we are entitled to ask, exactly what did he derive from Edinburgh University?
The answer seems to be that, like most highly talented people, he used the
university years for an extended exercise in autodidacticism; such students
are the despair of their teachers for they 'tune in' to the ephemeral round
of undergraduate instruction only when something stimulates or takes their
fancy. Such an approach was even easier in the Edinburgh of the 1860s and
1870s, for when classes were ended

we of the North go forth as freemen into the humming, lamplit city. At 5

o'clock you may see the last of us hiving from the college gates, in the glare
of the shop-windows, under the green glimmer of the winter sunset. The frost
tingles in our blood; no proctor lies in wait to intercept us; till the bell sounds
again, we are the masters of the world; and some portion of our lives is always
Saturday.

Very occasionally Stevenson would make a sensible intervention at
classes. The Revd Archibald Bissett, a contemporary, recalls that at a
philosophy seminar he suddenly burst in with a question about Scott,
and in the ensuing conversation he turned out to have an encyclopaedic
grasp of Sir Walter and to be able to quote from him at will. He was not
much interested in the core questions raised by the great philosophers –
though he did read Hume's 'On Miracles' and J.S.Mill's *Examination of
Hamilton's Philosophy* right through – but was drawn to them for other
reasons: Berkeley he admired for the classical grace of his prose but,
despite his awe for Hume's lucidity as a thinker, he found his prose
'otiose'. In Latin classes RLS was much drawn to Virgil – and he always
retained his affection for him – but he was too impatient to knit up into a
first-class classical scholar and particularly hated using dictionaries or lexi-
cons: 'When I come to a word that puzzles me I just guess its meaning and
pass on; and my guesses are so often correct, that I think Latin must have
been my mother-tongue in some previous state of existence.' This system
worked well with simple Latin, as with Cicero's *De Oratore*, but Horace's
Ars Poetica and Juvenal's *Satires* were tougher nuts to crack; Bissett and
Stevenson therefore collaborated: the division of labour was that Bissett
would provide a correct literal translation and RLS would then polish it
up into more idiomatic form.

Like Shakespeare, then, RLS had little Latin and less Greek but,
again like the master, he worked tirelessly to turn himself into a master
of English. This was where the true education of Robert Louis Stevenson
took place. Although he had the reputation of an idler, in his chosen field
no one could have been more hardworking and painstaking. From an early
age he had determined to be a writer, and to this end he served a rigorous
apprenticeship: always equipped with two books, one to read from, the
other to write in, he wandered over the Pentland Hills and elsewhere fitting
appropriate words to what he saw; when he sat by the roadside he would
either read or write up his thoughts and impressions. He thus lived with
words, not imagining that he would ever publish these apprentice pieces,
but simply in order to practise his craft. 'It was not so much that I wished
to be an author (though I wished that too) as that I vowed I would learn to
write. That was a proficiency that tempted me; and I practised to acquire
it, as men learn to whittle, in a wager with myself.'

Yet practising descriptions of natural phenomena and writing down conversations from memory took him only so far, since it provided no standard of achievement. He therefore moved on to the second stage of his apprenticeship. Whenever he came across a passage in a book that particularly pleased him, he tried to reproduce its style and unique quality. He was frequently unsuccessful, but in time he learned invaluable lessons in rhythm, quantity, structure and coordination of parts. In a passage frequently derided by philistines, who thought that 'art' was 95% inspiration and only 5% perspiration, instead of the other way round, he wrote: 'I have thus played the sedulous ape to Hazlitt, to Lamb, to Wordsworth, to Sir Thomas Browne, to Defoe, to Hawthorne, to Montaigne, to Baudelaire, and to Obermann.' Other influences included Ruskin, Keats, Chaucer, Morris, Swinburne, Webster and Congreve. Stevenson showed superlative instinct and intelligence in putting himself through this training and the process was only ever suspect to those who worshipped at the shrine of 'originality' – a concept in any case much misunderstood; as Stevenson pointed out: 'There can be none more original than Montaigne, neither could any be more unlike Cicero, yet no craftsman can fail to see how the one must have tried in his time to imitate the other.' As his confidence increased, Louis began to plan a number of ambitious works: a biography of Carlyle, a modern murder drama, a collaboration with Bob on a tragedy about Monmouth.[11]

Unkind critics have sometimes suggested that the adult RLS was not a particularly well-read man, but the range and breadth of his undergraduate reading compels astonishment. He worked his way through Carlyle, Ruskin, Browning and Tennyson, reread *Pilgrim's Progress* and the New Testament, especially his favourite Gospel according to St Matthew, devoured Penn's aphorisms, Montaigne's essays, Wordsworth's poetry, Herbert Spencer's multifarious output and Mitford's *Tales of Old Japan*. Favourite classical authors were Virgil, Marcus Aurelius (whose stoicism in the *Meditations* struck a particular chord) and Martial, whose undeservedly bad reputation 'is among a thousand things that help to build up our distorted and hysterical conception of the great Roman empire'. Stevenson was always drawn to American literature, especially Thoreau and Whitman's *Leaves of Grass*, but perhaps there were four authors he loved most of all. One was Meredith, whose *The Egoist* he regarded as the one undoubted Victorian masterpiece, another Hazlitt, whose essay 'On the Spirit of Obligations' he regarded as the turning point in his life; then Shakespeare and Alexandre Dumas *père* completed the quartet. It is impossible to read Stevenson without becoming aware of his worship of Shakespeare: he made an early start with *Macbeth*, which his mother read to him in the nursery (taking care to omit the porter's speech), then in early adulthood he conceived a love for *As You Like It* which never died; *Hamlet* was another influence, and *Lear*, where 'Kent's speech over the dying Lear had a great effect on my mind.' Stevenson's praise for

Dumas and the *Viscomte de Bragelonne* has always raised eyebrows, but RLS regarded it as a moral tale that teaches us how to live well and how to die well, and he never felt any need to apologise for his taste:

> Perhaps my dearest and best friend outside of Shakespeare is D'Artagnan – the elderly d'Artagnan of the *Viscomte de Bragelonne*. I know not a more human soul, nor, in his way, a finer; I shall be very sorry for the man who is so much a pedant in morals that he cannot learn from the Captain of Musketeers . . . no part of the world has ever seemed to me so charming as these pages, and not even my friends are quite so real, perhaps quite so dear, as d'Artagnan.

In the main, RLS's literary tastes remained unchanged. Some ten years later he wrote an essay showing the mutations that had crept in. In the first league – those all-time favourites to which he returned again and again – he listed Shakespeare, Montaigne and two new entrants: Molière and three Scott novels: *Guy Mannering, Rob Roy* and *Redgauntlet*; towering above all, though, were *The Egoist*, which he had read five times, and *Bragelonne*, which he had read six times. In the class of second favourites were *Pilgrim's Progress* and Borrow's *The Bible in Spain*, but by this time Hazlitt, together with Wordsworth, Burns and Horace, had fallen away into a limbo of the once much-loved but now rarely read; finally there was a fourth category of those to which he thought he would one day return, principally Herrick and Virgil.[12]

Uneasily aware that he was pursuing two separate but parallel careers, Stevenson tried to integrate his secret project of authorship with his ostensible aim of qualifying for the professions, and this he did mainly by joining such university societies as appeared to dovetail the two. He was the prime mover in the formation of the D'Arcy Thompson Class Club, but this was a failure; Stevenson's verses were considered bad and his choice of claret worse. He joined the Conservative Club and made speeches but did not impress anyone with his oratory; at the Dialectic Society his remarks were considered wide of the mark and he was invariably ragged; at a Shakespearean Reading Society, he impressed with melodious, sonorous voice and he read without affectation – he was particularly fond of the part of Jaques in *As You Like It*. Later with Fleeming Jenkin, who had a passion for theatricals, RLS would play many roles but never scored a hit as an actor, probably because he was too physically frail; as with a later Scotsman who delighted in the 'dressing-up' aspect of the thespian life – David Niven – it could have been said of RLS: 'he's a very very bad actor, but he absolutely loves doing it.'

Only in the Speculative Society did Stevenson truly make his mark. Elected a member of the 'Spec' on 16 February 1869, Louis gave his valedictory address on 25 March 1873; in four years he delivered seven papers to the society, including subjects such as capital punishment, Communism (both of which he opposed) and the career of the Duke of Argyll. He was a poor debater, but his skill with words was noticed and his big chance came in December 1870 when he was invited to be one of four editors of the College Magazine; the others were George Ormond, James Walter Ferrier and Robert Glasgow Brown, of whom only Ferrier was to feature in the hard inner core of about half a dozen close friends; Brown and Ferrier both died tragically young. Thrilled as he was to be invited to be one of the four 'supremos', RLS showed himself to be his father's son in the pessimism that invaded his spirit as soon as he had accepted the invitation: 'Yet at the bottom of my heart, I knew that magazine would be a grim fiasco; I knew it would not be worth rereading; I knew, even if it were, that nobody would read it; and I kept wondering how I should be able, upon my compact income of £12 per annum, payable monthly, to meet my share of the expense. It was a comfortable thought to me that I had a father.' Indeed it was, for in the end RLS had to get his father to bale him out of the enterprise; not, however, before he had enhanced his literary career by contributing six essays to the magazine. All surviving accounts agree that the magazine was Stevenson's chief occupation during the winter of 1870–71; his co-editor Ormond remembers that Louis liked to stay up all night haranguing him and the other editors, and then at dawn would stalk off up Prince's Street, meerschaum pipe in mouth, to Arthur's Seat for a long walk and think.[13]

In the rumbustious, ragging aspect of student life Stevenson took no part, but did sometimes stumble into it by accident. During the election for rector he once came into the quad wearing a white Shakespearian collar pencilled with the name of the unpopular candidate in vivid black letters; partisans of the opposite faction then set on him and tried to tear the collar from his neck, and it was with difficulty that his friends rescued him 'half-choked and very mad'. On another occasion a snowball fight between town and gown became so violent that the police had to be called in; RLS had climbed to a vantage point above the Surgeon's Hall to watch the encounter and, clambering down hastily when the police arrived, ran straight into the arms of a constable. He was then arrested and released only when his father had given surety for his good behaviour.

Stevenson's student socialising took the form of careering round brothels and low-life pubs with three close friends: Charles Baxter, Walter Simpson and James Walter Ferrier. This trio was particularly important for RLS, as they plugged the huge gap left by Bob, separated from his soul-mate to be educated at Windermere College and Sidney Sussex, Cambridge and destined, it seemed, for a career as an artist. On the few occasions when Bob was in Edinburgh his cousin was aglow and a contemporary remembers RLS arriving to take Bob out to lunch, 'his alert face beaming with some story or huge joke which he had been reserving for his companion, and the two would depart chortling and laughing'. Meanwhile Louis desperately needed a Bob substitute and he found it in this unlikely trinity of Edinburgh friends. Ferrier, who lived round the corner from Heriot Row at Dean Terrace, had literary aspirations, but was already manifesting the overfondness for the bottle that would bring him to an early death in 1883; RLS remarked cryptically: 'the curse was on him. Even his friends did not know him but by fits.' Another near neighbour (in Queen Street, and later St Colme Street) was Walter Simpson, a baronet and son of the inventor of chloroform; shy, retiring, with a laconic sense of humour, Simpson's interests ran to sex rather than drink.

Closest friend of all was the law student Charles Baxter, always referred to as Louis's *fidus Achates*, two years Stevenson's senior and the only man who remained close from the Edinburgh days right through to the end. Described by Richard le Gallienne as a 'preposterously vital and imaginative talker, ample of frame, with a voice like a column of cavalry' and with a marked fondness for drink, Baxter played the physical role of Hardy to Stevenson's Laurel; their contemporary Thomas Barclay remembered two buffoons, one tall, fair, burly and aggressive-looking, the other willowy, immature, dark and gypsy-like, entering a law lecture late; after an unconscionable amount of time and noise spent settling themselves, the duo rose from their seats very rowdily two minutes later and stormed out again.

Louis was bowled over by Baxter's wit and charm and his positive, thrusting attitude to life. 'He is the only man I ever heard of who could give and take in conversation with the wit and polish of style that we find in Congreve's comedies.' Stevenson and his comrades invented their own language – a compound of slang and elements of known languages – and embraced the cult of 'jink', which meant doing the most absurd acts for the sake of their intrinsic absurdity and the consequent laughter. One of their wheezes was to pawn things under the name of John Libbel so as to achieve the following effect:

> at length, when some great German statist (sic) took it into his blockhead to examine the books of pawnbrokers, it would gradually dawn on him that, in all lands and for year after year, innumerable persons all answering to this one name of John Libbel were daily engaged in the act of pawning, and yet when he turned his eyes outward on the world to follow the conduct of these persons in a different sphere, behold there would be no John Libbel, no not one. We exulted over the mystification of the German statist.

To increase the circumstantial evidence for his existence, they had 'Mr Libbel's' visiting cards printed and distributed over wide areas of Edinburgh; they would ask for Libbel in hotels and guest-houses, and once tried to put an ad in the *Scotsman*, asking him to come forward to claim a vast fortune, but the clerk unfortunately scented a hoax. Louis's taste for practical jokes never really died, and in the mid-1880s as respectable married men, he and Baxter could still be found enticing the unwary; their particular love was to carry out confidence tricks on people who were themselves crooks or charlatans. They also invented two characters Johnston and Thomson, supposedly small-town hypocrites who employed a racy Scots dialect, and to the end of his life, Louis and Baxter slipped in and out of these personae in correspondence without being entirely clear which of them was supposed to be which.[14]

Even though the two young men appeared to be inseparable, there were many occasions when RLS prowled the mean streets and narrow entries of the city alone, marvelling at the bewildering variety of architectural styles: Gothic spires mingling with what seemed to be Egyptian and Greek temples and Venetian palaces and always the 'smoky beehives' of the ten-storey 'lands' or tenement buildings. His favourite time was when the lamps began to glitter along the streets at twilight; he felt that Edinburgh then was like a fairyland ruin and that real people, trams and trains were out of place. He seemed to sense the ghosts of John Knox, Claverhouse, Hume and Burns around him, but this was by no means his only 'metaphysical' intimation.

> One night I went along the Cowgate after everyone was a-bed but the policeman, and stopped by hazard before a tall land. The moon touched upon its chimneys and shone blankly on the upper windows. There was no light anywhere in the great bulk of the building; but as I stood there, it seemed to me that I could hear quite a body of quiet sounds from the interior; doubtless there were many clocks ticking, and people snoring on their backs. And thus, as I fancied, the dense life within made itself faintly audible in my ears, family after family contributing its quota to the general hum, and the whole pile beating in tune to its time-pieces, like a great disordered heart. Perhaps it was little more than a fancy altogether, but it was strangely impressive at the time, and gave me an imaginative measure of the disproportion between the quantity of living flesh and the trifling walls that separated and contained it.

Edinburgh had locations that matched Stevenson's every mood. When he was feeling positive and effervescent, his favourite vantage point was Arthur's Seat where he found 'a sight as stimulating as the hoariest summit of the Alps'. He loved to stand there on a frosty winter's evening when the clear night sky resembled an observatory dome and watch the lights of Edinburgh; the symbolism of light was always important to this scion of the family that provided so many stars for seamen. From Arthur's Seat, too, in summer he loved to stroll in the bracing combination of sunshine and east wind, watching the female prisoners in the New Jail taking exercise like a string of nuns, catching glimpses of Princes Street 'black with traffic' or looking north over the Firth of Forth. Of the world's major cities, only in San Francisco are there more prospects of the sea from so many different angles and from an early age RLS had a keen appreciation of the terrors of ocean that were to inform so much of his fiction: 'the sight of the sea, even from a city, will bring thoughts of storm and sea disaster ... Since Sir Patrick Spens sailed from Aberdour, what a multitude have gone down in the North Sea!'[15]

But when dejected and melancholic, Stevenson liked to feed his morbid fantasies in Greyfriars churchyard, walking upon the graves and disturbing the cats that overran the site, revolving thoughts of death while he watched children scattering crumbs to feed the sparrows. It was usually children, too, who wrenched Louis out of his sombre fancies and made him ashamed of the self-indulgence of his depressions. He remembered one occasion in midwinter when he was wandering the streets miserably and there came towards him, just after sundown when the lamps were enlarging their circles in the gathering dusk, two barefoot girls, one aged about nine, the other perhaps seven; though they were miserably clad and the pavement was cold, the pair came along waltzing and the elder sang a tune to provide the music.

Often, though, his depression was irremediable, and he would feed the *memento mori* motif by closely observing Greyfriars and its daily life. He learned to pity the working-class women who came with their snivelling babies to pay respects at some pauper's grave and overheard conversations in which they marvelled that anyone could afford to lay wreaths on tombs. He watched the gravediggers and sextons at work and concluded that Shakespeare was wrong (in *Hamlet*) in thinking them insensitive. His conclusions on the meaning of death have about them the ring of Lincoln's Gettysburg speech: 'They do not stand merely to the dead, these foolish monuments; they are pillars and legends set up to glorify the difficult but not desperate life of man. This ground is hallowed by the heroes of defeat.'

It has become a cliché to link sex with death and Eros with Thanatos, but most clichés are, after all, distillations of centuries of wisdom, and there is a particularly apt specimen of the association of sexuality and death in Stevenson's 'Old Mortality', of more than passing significance since it suggests that the youthful RLS's passionate interest in women was in part a means of warding off depression. The passage is unusual in its frank discussion of sex without love and in its awareness of mortality – for most young people consider themselves immortal. He stayed once in a hotel overlooking a graveyard as part of a programme for working through his unhappiness, and had the following experience:

A beautiful housemaid of the hotel once, for some days together, dumbly flirted with me from a window and kept my wild heart flying; and once – she possibly remembers it – the wise Eugenia followed me to that austere enclosure. Her hair came down, and in the shelter of a tomb my trembling hands helped her to repair the braid ... Even David Hume, as he lay composed beneath that 'circular idea', was fainter than a dream; and when the housemaid, broom in hand, smiled and beckoned from the shop window, the fame of that bewigged philosopher melted like a raindrop in the sea. And yet in soberness I cared as little for the housemaid as for David Hume.[16]

Everyone agrees that the impact of Edinburgh on RLS was enormous, but there is much dispute over its exact nature. Some have speculated that the division into Old and New towns reinforced Stevenson's deep conviction of the duality of things, and it is true that he often drew attention to this aspect of 'Auld Reekie'. In 1745 when Bonnie Prince Charlie entered Scotland's capital in short-lived triumph, there had only been the old town – a settlement of crowded tenements along a ridge extending from the Castle to Holyrood palace; in the days before a culture of privacy arose, even the wealthy lived in cramped and crowded conditions. By contrast, the New Town, begun at the end of the eighteenth century, was spacious and elegant. Although he lived in Heriot Row, in the heart of the New Town, and found it 'not only gay and airy, but highly picturesque', Stevenson tended to agree with Ruskin that this was an aberration, and that the soul of Edinburgh could be found only in the old sector, which he compared with Stirling, down to the castle. In the Old Town were the slums full of skulking jailbirds, unkempt, barefoot children and big-mouthed robust women in a sort of uniform of striped flannel petticoat and short tartan shawl. Stevenson remembered threading his way through the labyrinth of the Old Town, going under dark arches and down even darker stairs and alleys, where the way was so narrow that he could lay a hand on either wall and so steep that in greasy winter weather the pavement was almost as treacherous as ice. He would enter a court where layers of washing dangled from the windows and find ragged children at play and adults sitting on doorsteps. To be aware of this very different Edinburgh within a stone's throw of Holyrood or the Castle seemed like 'the Bedouin's camp within the Pharaoh's walls'.

It has sometimes been suggested that the division of Edinburgh into Old and New Towns imprinted itself on Stevenson's mind in such a way as, of itself, to produce a 'divided self'. Apart from the geographical determinism and 'fallacy of simple location' implied in such a proposition – why, one might ask, were not all burghers of Edinburgh, not just RLS, afflicted with a schizoid personality – it is anyway clear from Stevenson's writings on his native city that he took a more nuanced view of the situation. He was prepared to romanticise the Old Town but he was well aware that Victorian cultural expectations of privacy ruled out the eighteenth-century idea of having two score families in a single house, and was also concerned at the psychic damage to children from overcrowding; 'In the first room there is a birth, in another a death, in a third a sordid drinking bout, and the detective and the Bible-reader cross upon the stairs. High words are audible from dwelling to dwelling, and children have a strange experience from the first; only a robust soul, you would think, could grow up in such conditions without hurt.' Moreover, in his mind the contrast between Old and New Towns made for integration rather than division: 'the point is to see this embellished Stirling planted in the midst of a large, active and fantastic modern city, for there the two re-act in a picturesque sense and one is the making of the other.'

For Stevenson, too, the interpenetration of town and country was more important than the contrast between Old and New Towns; he liked to stand at the Dean Bridge, where the river ran to the bottom of a deep valley, among rocks and between gardens; the crest of either bank contained some of the finest streets and crescents in the city, where every afternoon carriages bowled along, carrying ladies on the social round. Down below, as a complete contrast, the little rural village of Dean could still be discerned, with its mills and foaming weir. This was typical of Edinburgh in general:

> Into no other city does the sight of the country enter so far; if you do not meet a butterfly, you shall certainly catch a glimpse of far-away fields upon your walk and the place is full of theatre tricks in the way of scenery. You peep under an arch, you descend stairs that look as if they would land you in a cellar, you turn to the back window of a grimy tenement in a lane: – and behold! you are face to face with distant and bright prospects. You turn a corner, and there is the sun going down into the Highland hills. You look down an alley and see ships tacking for the Baltic.

There were more important dualities in Edinburgh than that between Old and New towns, and Stevenson knew very well what they were. He thought that weather was a greater determinant on human behaviour than physical geography or architecture. He noticed that when winter came on, with its subarctic sunsets, which stamped the profile of the city in indigo upon a sky of luminous green, people 'fall into two divisions: one, the knight of the blue face and hollow paunch, whom Winter has gotten by the vitals; the other well lined with Newyear's fare, conscious of the touch of cold on his periphery, but stepping through it by the glow of his internal fires.'

Even more important was the clash between the ethos of Calvinism and the culture of the hard-drinking Scot, and the greatest blow to the nation came when New Year's Day fell on a Sunday, for then the pubs were closed and no singing or whistling was allowed. What a blow this was can be gauged from the normal celebration of New Year's Day in Edinburgh, where, except for the genteel classes, the streets were thronged with revellers; Auld Lang Syne was much in people's mouths, whisky and shortbread were staples. From an early hour an observer would be impressed by the number of drunken men, and by the afternoon the drunkenness had spread to the women; by the evening broken heads and empty pockets were being rested either in bed or in a police cell. Yet when New Year's Day and the Sabbath clashed, and the duty to go to church collided with the duty to drink gallons, the Scotsman was dejected: 'thus pulled about as if between two loyalties, the Scots have to decide many nice cases of conscience and ride the marches narrowly between the weekday and the annual observance.'[17]

Then again there was the duality produced by gross social inequality which, RLS thought, was 'nowhere more ostentatious than in Edinburgh ... to look over the South Bridge and see the Cowgate below full of crying hawkers is to view one rank of society from another in the twinkling of an eye.' It was this perception of the most blatant social stratification that turned Stevenson into a shortlived socialist.

It is not surprising to find in RLS an ambivalence towards Edinburgh fully matching the city's ambiguous profile. He combined a fervent desire to escape from its stifling influence with involuntary heartache at his self-imposed exile. Echoing Dr Johnson's remark that the finest sight a Scotsman sees is the high road that leads to England, Stevenson often thought that the passengers being borne south out of Waverley railway station were the happiest people in Edinburgh: 'Happy the passengers who shake off the dust of Edinburgh and have heard for the last time the cry of the east wind among her chimney-tops. And yet the place establishes an interest in people's hearts; go where they will, they find no city of the same distinction; go where they will, they take a pride in their old home.' The dislike that Stevenson undoubtedly felt for Edinburgh and its people is a compound of disparate elements. He felt that the dead hand of the past was on the city, not in the acceptable sense in which one could entertain nostalgic reveries about Bonnie Prince Charlie at Holyrood, but in the unacceptable way that the influence of the Scottish Enlightenment and its chief luminaries – Hume, Adam Smith, Fergusson etc – had petrified the burghers and made them complacent, content to rest on past laurels; the 'bourgeois' way in which even a genuine artist like Scott was read was a sign of this intellectual sluggishness – itself a grotesquely inadequate response to the disease, squalor, alcoholism and prostitution of the Old Town.

Then there was Calvinism, a gloomy religion seemingly in league with the depressing climate as if by pre-established harmony. Stevenson detested both the austere religion itself and, even more, the humbug and cant of the 'unco' guid', its practitioners, 'thronging by in their neat clothes and conscious moral rectitude'. His remarks on religion gave particular offence to the bourgeoisie of 'Auld Reekie' who objected that they were being attacked merely for churchgoing, keeping ledgers and wearing fine linen; 'we are wonderful patient haters for conscience sake up here in the

North ... Shakespeare wrote a comedy of "Much Ado about Nothing". The Scottish nation made a fantastic tragedy on the same subject.' Only Hawthorne, he thought, with his knowledge of the New England Puritans, could do justice to the peculiar odour of spiritual paraffin and the associated belief in the physical reality of the devil that was Scots Calvinism. Stevenson even assailed Ediburgh's church bells, pointing out that what was a symphony in Oxford was a mere discord in 'the Athens of the North': 'There are not many uproars in this world more dismal than that of the Sabbath bells in Edinburgh.' And he deplored the factionalism of Scottish religion: 'Surely there are few worse extremes than this extremity of zeal; and few more deplorable defections than this disloyalty to Christian love.'[18]

However, Stevenson later redeemed himself in Edinburgh eyes by his many nostalgic references to his native city and the conciliatory way he ended his penetrating essay *Edinburgh: Picturesque Notes*: 'There is no Edinburgh emigrant far or near, from China to Peru, but he or she carries some lively pictures of the mind, some sunset behind the Castle cliffs, some snow scene, some maze of city lamps, indelible in the memory and delightful to study in the intervals of toil.' And he never committed the unforgivable sin of preferring England; indeed his animadversions on the folk south of the border are all that the most fervent nationalist could desire. He found everything about England alien to a Scot: its flatness, its architecture, its people; 'the dull, neglected peasant, sunk in matter, insolent, gross and servile, makes a startling contrast with our own long-legged, long-headed, thoughtful, Bible-quoting ploughman. A week or two in such a place as Suffolk leaves the Scotsman gasping.' He contrasted the secretiveness, grudgingness and lack of generosity of the English proletarian with the openness of his Scottish counterpart; the Scotsman was vain, outgoing, original and eager for sympathy; the Englishman was egoistical, self-sufficient, superior, sneering and apt to talk in clichés. In the person of Burchell Fenn in his novel *St Ives*, we can see clearly Stevenson's opinion of the true Englishman: 'He gave me an opportunity of studying John Bull, as I may say, stuffed naked – his greed, his viciousness, his hypocrisy, his perfidy of the back-stairs, all swelled to the superlative.'[19]

It has sometimes been suggested that Stevenson's literary work suffers by comparison with, say, Meredith, Hardy and James, three distinguished acquaintances and contemporaries, in that it never really gets to grips with relations between the sexes. This is a complex issue, but at this stage it is worth recording both that Stevenson's early life was fraught with sexual tensions and anxieties, and that these appear, imperfectly disguised, in much of his early work. It may be an exaggeration to say that RLS's work is as saturated with sex as D.H.Lawrence's, but not by very much.

Ever since Louis wrote to Bob in October 1868 about his sexual longings and his feelings of guilt that a life of sensual pleasure would mean hypertrophied selfishness, he continued to wrestle with the tugs of the flesh and their moral implications. Stevenson was always a man of strong libido and was powerfully attracted by the physical beauty of women but he was also deeply sympathetic to the plight of the female sex, and these countervailing impulses both ruled out affairs with 'respectable' unmarried girls and caused deep sexual anxieties.

Of the physical attraction there can be no doubt. He wrote to Bob in 1875 after a visit to the Elgin Marbles at the British Museum: 'I don't know why; I just cried; these three women are so hellish calm and can see so far away can't they ... I'm glad they've lost their heads, I don't think any face could be worthy of those beautiful, *meaning bodies*.' Significantly, however, the strong vein of sexuality in Stevenson's *oeuvre* comes through most clearly in his poetry; Hardy claimed you could get away with things in verse that would have a hundred Mrs Grundys on your back if said in prose, and remarked sardonically that if Galileo had expressed his heliocentric view of the universe in hexameters he would have had no trouble with the Inquisition. In 'The Canoe Speaks' the boat tells us that it travels

> By meadows where at afternoon
> The growing maidens troop in June
> To loose their girdles on the grass

An even clearer statement of barely repressed sexuality comes in the following poem:

> Now bare to the beholder's eye,
> Your late denuded lendings lie,
> Subsiding slowly where they fell,
> A disinvested citadel;
> The obdurate corset, cupid's foe,
> The Dutchman's breeches frilled below.
> Hose that lover loves to note,
> And white and crackling petticoat
> From these, that on the ground repose,
> Their lady lately re-arose;
> And laying by the lady's name
> A living woman re-became.
> Of her, that from the public eye
> They do inclose and fortify,
> Now, lying scattered as they fell,
> An indiscreeter tale they tell;
> Of that more and secret her
> Whose daylong fortresses they were,

By fading warmth, by lingering print,
These now discarded scabbards hint.

A twofold change the ladies know.
First, in the morn the bugles blow,
And they, with floral hues and scents,
Man their be-ribboned battlements.
But let the stars appear, and they
Shed in humanities away;
And from the changeling fashion sees,
Through comic and through sweet degrees,
In nature's toilet unsurpassed,
Forth leaps the laughing girl at last.[20]

Alongside the physical desire was a deep sympathy for women which it is not anachronistic to call feminist. After his death his stepson Lloyd Osbourne recorded the following tribute:

> Women seemed to him the victims alike of man and nature. He often spoke of the chastity enforced on them under pain of starvation; he often said there would be no children had men been destined to bear them and that marriage itself would disappear. What man, he asked besides, would ever have the courage of a woman of the streets? In those days of large families the accepted right of men to their wives till they died filled him with loathing ... the obligation for women to be attractive at any age and in any circumstances appeared to him also as not the least of their many disabilities. I remember him saying: 'My God, Lloyd, think of all those poor old slab-sided, broken-backed frumps having to stick flowers in their hats and go through with the horrible affectation of pretending to be desirable.'

There needs no Lloyd to tell us of RLS's clear sympathy for women; it is present throughout his work. In 'Talk and Talkers' he remarks that women are better listeners than men as from an early age they have to bear with the 'tedious and infantile vanity of the other sex'. He found the female in general practical, down-to-earth and impatient with abstract argument which was why 'when a talk between men grows brighter and quicker and begins to promise to bear fruit, talk between the sexes is menaced with dissolution.' He knew better than to underrate women, as this gnomic sentence from *Weir of Hermiston* shows: 'Mr Weir must have supposed his bride to be somehow suitable; perhaps he belonged to that class of men who thinks a weak head the ornament of women – an opinion invariably punished in this life.'[21]

As so often happens, men with an instinctive sympathy for women attract the opposite sex, who sense the understanding. Much later in life Stevenson wrote half-jokingly that he seemed always to have an attraction for harridans, but the truth is that all kinds and classes of women were drawn to him. When he was on the Isle of Earraid in 1870, one of the men confided to him: 'Quite captivated my old woman, you did – she couldn't talk of anything else.' 1870 also saw an abortive romance with the daughter of a family acquaintance, sometimes referred to as 'Jenny', of which the details are obscure. Compton Mackenzie thought the girl came from Buckstane, just outside Edinburgh; whatever the case, there are clear traces of her in RLS's work. He records that he sent a copy of the university magazine he had edited to 'the lady with whom my heart was at that time somewhat engaged, and who did all that in her lay to break it; and she, with some tact, passed over the gift and my cherished contributions in silence'. This is almost certainly the girl referred to in his poem 'Duddingston'; there was a skating rink there which Stevenson often looked down on from his eyrie at Arthur's Seat and which he liked to frequent, even though he was an indifferent skater, and in 'Duddingston' he remembers a halcyon time there with his beloved:

> I swear had we been drowned that day
> We had been drowned in love.

There is strong circumstantial evidence that the Archie/Christine liaison in *Weir of Hermiston* echoes this adolescent romance. But the evidence for Stevenson's private life in these early years is tantalisingly exiguous and the girl at Duddingston may or may not be one referred to in a letter to Bob from Swanston in 1870 when RLS says he has been 'very much hit with a certain damsel who shall be nameless. He [Thomas Stevenson] detected a nasty overfriendliness towards me on the part of her relations, so when she was taken away by her parents, it was perhaps as well she left when she did.'[22]

It is tempting to pursue the theme of duality in Stevenson's private life for, side by side with this abortive romance with a 'respectable' girl there is evidence of another doomed affair, this time with a prostitute. Yet, as in the case of women in general, the deep impulse in Stevenson's attitude towards women of the night was towards integration rather than madonna/whore bifurcation. On the one hand there was a deep undercurrent of bawdy in Louis. In best 'know-all' saloon-bar manner, Sir Alfred Ewing was later adamant that the stories of RLS's student days among prostitutes and low-lives could not have been accurate since he (Ewing) had known many such types in South America and Stevenson was not one of them: 'I never saw a trace of laxity – vinous or other – nor heard from him a word that might suggest it.' But Louis was secretive and thus far a natural actor in that he would willingly play any role the observer cared to cast him in. Ewing would have been surprised if he could have read Stevenson's letters to Baxter or indeed any of the correspondence with Bob and Walter Simpson. A few excerpts from the letters to Baxter in the period 1874-81 may suffice to make the point: 'Do you twig, my lovely friend? if not you may retire up your own fundament?' . . . (when calling down a curse on someone) 'May he wallow in the underclothes of shopgirls.' From Menton in 1874 RLS wrote to Baxter that since one of their acquaintances had given up drink, he would take up buggery; attacking James Balfour, he said he would like to grab him by the testicles and bang his head against the wall; then he mentions that in a word game he had to finish a word beginning 'fou' and declined to finish it as he would have liked; he ended the letter: '*Baisez mon cul.*' RLS's friends gave as good as they got: in 1877 Walter Simpson wrote as follows: 'I was walking along the street the other night, passed two gents telling a story evidently and just heard (without appreciating for a moment) these words: "So", says she, "ye're no gawn to mak a foreign post office of my c--t." '23

There can be no doubting Stevenson's relish for low dives and brothels. It is celebrated clearly in his poem 'Brasheana' in which he recalls the many jousts he and Baxter had with the choleric publican, Brash. It is there in another verse, even if here there is a clear suspicion of *épater le bourgeois*:

> O fine, religious, decent folk
> In virtues flaunting gold and scarlet,
> I sneer between two puffs of smoke,
> Give me the publican and the harlot.
>
> Ye dainty spoken, stiff severe
> Seed of the migrated philistian
> One whispered question in your ear –
> Pray, what was Christ if you be Christian?
> If Christ were only here just now,
> Among the city's wynds and gables
> Teaching the life he taught us, how
> Would he be welcome at your tables?

And in 'The Light Keeper' he explicitly links his symbolic theme of light to the activities of 'Ladies of the night':

> I love night in the city
> The lighted streets and the swinging gaits of harlots
> I love cool pale morning
> In the empty bye-streets,
> With only here and there a female figure,
> A slavey with lifted dress and key in her hand,
> A girl or two at play in a corner of waste-land
> Tumbling and showing their legs and crying out to me loosely

But RLS's taste for prostitutes was no merely negative matter. Known as 'Velvet Jacket', he was a favourite of the *filles de joie*, whom he found gentle and honest, to the point where he would have trusted any of them with his money. His sympathy for them emerges clearly in his *Notebooks*:

Prostitution tends by a certain negative natural selection to reduce the tendency of the race to propagate; the men of the most violent sexual passions are, by prostitution, prevented to a large extent from having children, and so the race is left to be continued by the more sober and continent among whom chastity is the precursor of matrimony. The early marriages of the Irish prevent the action of this adjustment ... A Jew, a Christian, a Mormon, or a Thug were proud of the reproach, and wear the byeword as a distinction; while you may make many a prostitute cry by merely naming her trade to her.[24]

One of the great controversies in Stevenson studies concerns the reality of RLS's liaison with a certain prostitute, sometimes identified as 'Claire', sometimes as 'Kate Drummond'. The biographers of the 1920s, especially, fastened on this story. According to George Hellman, the girl was the daughter of a blacksmith from Swanston; according to John Steuart, she was a *fille de joie* who spent so much time in Stevenson's company that she was eventually beaten up by the brothel-keeper for neglecting her profitable duties. Both versions concur in maintaining that it was extreme pressure from the Stevenson parents and the threat to disown their son that dealt the *coup de grâce* to the relationship. It is supposed to be 'Claire' that Stevenson refers to in 'The Vanquished Knight' when he says:

> I have left all upon the shameful field,
> Honour and Hope, My God! and all but life.

The hunt for 'Claire' has been for Stevensonians like the search for Shakespeare's 'Dark Lady'. In 1950, the critic Malcolm Elwin instanced the statement made by Stevenson in 1873 to Mrs Sitwell – 'Of course I am not going on with Claire' – as definitive evidence that she existed. Roger Lancelyn Green and Graham Balfour took the view that 'Claire' was the name of an unfinished literary work, in which Stevenson tried to record his views on women, drawing on actual and imaginary females. Richard Aldington conjectured that the whole thing might be an elaborate RLS hoax along the lines of 'Libbel' or 'Thomson and Johnston'. The biographer J.C.Furnas found a letter in which Stevenson addressed Mrs Sitwell as 'Claire', promising to show all his favourite places in Edinburgh 'to you, Claire, some other night', and concluded that 'Claire' was merely one of his pseudonyms for Mrs Sitwell.[25]

It has been insufficiently realised that the specific issue of 'Claire' is logically independent from the question of whether or not the young Stevenson had a passionate liaison with a young prostitute. The fact that he addressed Fanny Sitwell as 'Claire' does not necessarily mean there was not a previous Claire or even more than one – he also addressed her as 'Madonna' and 'Consuelo' and there was certainly no patent on those names. Knowing Stevenson's penchant for *noms de guerre*, it is entirely possible that he attached the name 'Claire' to his current inamorata, whoever she happened to be, much as Dickensian employers used the name 'Richards' for housemaids, whatever their actual name. It would also be characteristic of RLS to transfer the name of a real lover to a fantasy one or to conflate what *did* happen with what might have happened – or even, what could still happen. To argue, as Furnas does, that Stevenson's use of 'Claire' to address Fanny Sitwell means there can have been no previous Claire, is a *non sequitur*. One can even imagine a scenario where Fanny Sitwell was unknown except for a single reference to time RLS had spent with her in Suffolk; a scholar might well imagine that this was a mythical extrapolation of an actual meeting with *Fanny Osbourne* to a Suffolk setting and declare imperiously that of course there was no other Fanny. I do not say there *was* a previous love called Claire; only that you cannot establish this by using Furnas's methods.

Yet even if there was no individual denoted as 'Claire' other than Fanny Sitwell, there was certainly at least one prostitute with whom RLS had close relations. This may or may not have been the 'Kate Drummond' of legend, whom critics and biographers have perhaps been too quick to dismiss as a chimera. Jenni Calder says: 'It is hard to believe that Stevenson's spontaneous self-dramatisation would not have provided us with better authenticated evidence.' This is to have it both ways: first you use the historian's 'archive fallacy' – that there is always written evidence of everything that has happened in the past – which amounts to a demand for *documentary* evidence; then you use inferential evidence ('it is hard to believe' etc) of the kind you damn in the second part of the sentence.[26]

The evidence that Stevenson had close relations with prostitutes is overwhelming. Working from the more general to the more specific, we may instance the following. First, Sidney Colvin, eventually the second closest friend after Charles Baxter, thought that the first Stevenson biography had omitted vital truths about the Edinburgh period and substituted idyllic fictions instead; perhaps significantly, when the 'Claire' controversy was first raging, he declined to enter the lists or clear the matter up. Secondly, it is clear that Stevenson contracted syphilis in these years; he speaks of 'the unblushing daughters of Venus' who 'did him a lasting injury' and boasts that no woman of easy virtue could ever resist him. When in New York in 1879, he wrote to Baxter that he was suffering terribly from the itch, and deleted the words 'very similar to syphilis', which imply personal knowledge. Thirdly, RLS's work is full of guilt about the harsh treatment meted out to prostitutes, and indeed there is good reason to think that his philippic against Burns because of his philandering is a disguised self-indictment. Like Wordsworth, Stevenson reacted in later life to his early sexual peccadilloes with a kind of prudish censoriousness. Writing to Trevor Haddon in 1881, he advised: 'Whatever you do, see that you don't sacrifice a woman; that is where all imperfect loves conduct us.

At the same time, if you can make it convenient to be chaste, for God's sake avoid the primness of your virtue; hardness to a poor harlot is a sin lower than the ugliest unchastity.' Finally, we actually have documentary evidence that Stevenson had known intimately a prostitute known as Mary H, for in 1923 Balfour conceded this in writing to Colvin.[27] All in all, then, the likelihood that there was a 'low life' relationship which threatened to turn serious and which required stern measures by Thomas Stevenson to thwart it is far from implausible. It would fit what we know of RLS's sympathy for the underdog, his quixotry, his toying with 'rescue fantasies', his strong feeling for women and the attraction he felt for redemption through suffering. The issue of 'Claire' is a red herring.

It is therefore interesting to find the noted Stevenson scholar, David Daiches, accepting the reality of 'Kate Drummond' and seeing Louis's early disappointment with her as a critical creative influence. Using 'Claire' as a shorthand tag for this early love, whoever she was, he interprets Miss Grant and the eponymous heroine of *Catriona* as two aspects of that formative passion:

> In Miss Grant he drew the wit and liveliness that one can be fairly sure was an important part of "Claire's" character; in Catriona he drew the purely feminine aspects, the tenderness, the dependence on male protection, the changing moods and passions . . . the comparative lack of reality of Catriona can be attributed to Stevenson's inability to speak frankly of his early love. The more masculine side of her character – the wit and vivacity and companionship – could be portrayed by Miss Grant; but Catriona represented the subtler feminine side, and here he could not speak freely. Catriona thus represents only one half of a split personality, and that one half portrayed under the limiting control of certain inhibitions.[28]

3

The Patriarch

Throughout his student days, having disappointed his father over the expected career as lighthouse engineer, Stevenson dared not admit that he was merely going through the motions of becoming a lawyer, that his real dream was to make a living by the pen. In 1872 he passed the preliminary examination for the Scottish Bar, but not before displaying his usual cavalier attitude towards academic study. During his Ethics and Metaphysics examination, when the examiner asked him a question, he replied: 'I beg your pardon, but I do not understand your phraseology.' 'It's in the textbook,' the examiner replied. 'Yes,' said Louis, 'but you couldn't possibly expect me to read so poor a book as that.' From 9 May to 5 July 1872 he worked as a law clerk, learning conveyancing and copying documents, in Skene's solicitors' office.

Meanwhile he kept scribbling and reading, sometimes even during classes. While taking notes on Professor James Muirhead's course on Public Law, he jotted down scraps of an essay on 'Imaginary Conversations and Intellectual Powers'. A letter to Maud Babington in 1871, written while perusing Clarendon's *History*, shows that he was already capable of putting his lucubrations to original use:

> It is a pet idea of mine that one gets more real truth out of one avowed partisan than out of a dozen of your sham impartialists – wolves in sheep's clothing – simpering honesty as they suppress documents. After all, what one wants to know is not what people did, but why they did it – or rather, why they *thought* they did it; and to learn that, you should go to the men themselves. Their very falsehood is often more than another man's truth.[1]

In the winter of 1872–73 there were experiments in team writing with friends with whom he intended to edit an amateur magazine, and jottings on meteorology, and early the next year he wrote on spiritualism for the Psychical Society of Edinburgh. By the autumn of 1872 he was leaning heavily for guidance on Bob, now back in Scotland. Charles Baxter had left

Edinburgh in pursuit of his legal career, and Walter Simpson was embroiled in an affair with a girl who later lived with him as his common-law wife, though RLS did manage to stay three weeks with him in Germany in the summer of 1872; Louis had wanted to spend the whole summer at a German university with his friend but his parents objected, so it was a mere three weeks with Simpson in Frankfurt, after which he had to join his parents at Baden-Baden. Meanwhile James Walter Ferrier, obsessed with Heine, increasingly seemed to lack the moral fibre to move from youth to adulthood. While applauding Ferrier's magnetism and charisma, RLS noted:

> with all his beauty, power, breeding, urbanity and mirth, there was in those days something soulless in our friend. He would astonish us by sallies, witty, innocent and inhumane; and by a misapplied Johnsonian pleasantry, demolish honest sentiment. I can still see and hear him, as he went his way along the lamplit streets, *la ci darem la mano* on his lips, a noble figure of a youth, but following vanity and incredulous of good; and sure enough somewhere, somewhere on the high seas of life, with his health, his hopes, his patrimony and his self-respect, miserably went down.[2]

Bob, then, was the major influence during the critical winter of 1872–73. Opinions have always divided on the relative talents of the two cousins. The usual view is that Bob was a genuine bohemian and rebel, while Louis merely played at being so, to annoy his parents. It is customary, too, to regard Bob as a brilliant flame that flared briefly, then guttered and died out, and it is true that his later achievement (a chair in fine arts and a biography of Velasquez) cannot begin to compare with Louis's. Yet there has always been a powerful undertow of opinion to the effect that Bob's intrinsic abilities were of a higher order than his more famous cousin. RLS's close friend William Ernest Henley certainly thought so ('a rarer brain, a more fanciful and daring humour, a richer gusto ... a far rarer spirit, a far more soaring and more personal genius than I found in his famous cousin'), while W.B.Yeats said that Bob 'gave as good entertainment in monologue as his cousin Robert Louis in poem or story'; Edmund Gosse, too, always inclined to a sliver of malice towards RLS, rated Bob higher. Some of his brilliance is apparent in Louis's affectionate portrait as 'Spring-Heel'd Jack' in 'Talk and Talkers':

> In the Spanish proverb, the fourth man necessary to compound a salad is a madman to mix it: Jack is that madman ... He doubles like the serpent, changes and flashes like the shaken kaleidoscope, transmigrates bodily into the views of others, and so, in the twinkling of an eye and with a heady rapture, turns questions inside out and flings them empty before you on the ground, like a triumphant conjurer.[3]

Certainly the two were at this time like intellectual and emotional Siamese twins. A year later, while studying art in Antwerp, Bob wrote to Louis: 'I have been so accustomed to see and do everything with, or with reference, to you that being unable to tell you everything day by day to hear what you say and to have you for public audience, world and everything, I am now quite stumped.' Louis replied in like vein, for Bob went on to tell a third party: 'He cannot get on at all without me, he writes; he finds that I have been the whole world for him; that he only talked to other people in order that he might tell me afterwards about the conversation.'

Whether it was the influence of Bob's cavalier bohemianism, with its implication of insouciant agnosticism, or whether the problematical affair with 'Kate Drummond' – whoever she was – led Louis to fume at the humbug of those who purported to subscribe to the teachings of a man who harboured Mary Magdalene, while turning from their doors the Magdalenes in their midst, RLS went through a crisis of belief in 1872. The storm can be seen approaching in October '72 when he wrote to Bob: 'A damn lot of waves and counterwaves have been breaking upon me of late . . . I want an object, a mission, a belief, a hope to be my wife; and please God, have it I shall.' The immediate result of his deliberations was an essay delivered to the 'Spec' in November on 'Two Questions on the relationship between Christ's teaching and Modern Christianity' in which, as later in 'Lay Morals', he discussed the difference between Christ's teaching and that of organised religion and suggested that the real attitude of Edinburgh's 'unco' guid' burghers to the historical Jesus would have been that of Dostoevsky's Grand Inquisitor. It is likely that Louis would have discussed all this with Bob, for the two spent an idyllic Christmas 1872 together at Bridge of Allan, Bob painting, RLS reading Thackeray.

It was also Bob who was the driving force behind the founding of the 'L.J.R.' (Liberty, Justice and Reverence) club, which advocated socialism, atheism and the abolition of the House of Lords. Its first rule was that you should disregard everything taught you by your parents. The situation in the Stevenson household in Heriot Row was that of a collision waiting to happen. Louis's mood was increasingly sour: taken on a trip to Malvern by his mother immediately after his time with Bob at Bridge of Allan, RLS wrote to Baxter despondently about the rain, about the fact that he spoke to his mother only at mealtimes, and that his one and only amusement was to play billiards with one of the waiters who, though intelligent, was too good-mannered and deferential to strike a spark with the young bohemian: 'I'm getting tired of this whole life business . . . let me get into a corner with a brandy bottle; or down on the hearthrug, full of laudanum grog; or as easily as may be, into the nice wormy grave.'4

On the last day of January the inevitable happened. Thomas Stevenson found a copy of the 'L.J.R' constitution and began to question Louis about his beliefs. Louis answered candidly that he no longer believed in the faith of his fathers but he reserved many points of belief until he had further information. The qualification did him no good: his father rained down imprecations on his head – 'careless infidel', 'horrible atheist' – until Louis had half a mind to retract. Although he hated lying, 'if I had foreseen the real hell of everything since, I think I should have lied.' Of course, had he done so, he would then have coiled himself in an infinite series of lies, prevarications and equivocations, so that he certainly did the right thing. The worst of it was that after the initial fury from his father and hysterics from his mother, the couple subsided into silence, depression and psychosomatic illness. His father told him he was a 'damned curse' to his parents and informed him: 'You have rendered my whole life a failure.' His mother weighed in with: 'This is the heaviest affliction that has ever befallen me.' RLS was devastated: 'O Lord, what a pleasant thing it is to have damned the happiness of (probably) the only two people who care a damn about you in the world.' Yet even in the midst of these woes he could discern black comedy and he confessed he scarcely knew whether to laugh or cry at his parents' naïveté: while his father sat in a chair gravely reading up Butler's *Analogy of Religion* in hopes of bringing his errant son back to the fold, his mother suggested he join the young men's class given by the Revd Maxwell Nicholson, minister of St Stephen's Church![5]

For two months the family lolled in the trough while the gigantic waves of discord beat above them. One immediate consequence was that Louis was sent into internal exile by being given a study next to his bedroom – which from his point of view was a consummation devoutly to be wished. Finally, in April, it was suggested that he visit a married cousin in Suffolk, a clergyman whose influence the Stevenson parents relied on to bring their son to his senses. The visit was a momentous one from Louis's point of view, but did not produce the consequences his parents wanted. Early in September he returned to Edinburgh to find that the plot of his 'atheism' had taken another twist. His cousin Lewis Balfour, who died young, warned his uncle Tom on his deathbed against the 'horrible atheists' in the Stevenson family. When pressed further as to whom he meant, Balfour denounced Bob as the serpent in paradise. Like many highly talented individuals, Bob had the capacity to inspire an insensate 'hate at first sight' as well as admiration and love, and it is quite clear that the pious Lewis Balfour detested Bob with a fanatical, superheated loathing. 'A blight', 'a mildew', 'how could God have made such a man.' The real serpent it seemed was Balfour, who pretended to be genuinely interested in all the 'L.J.R' ideas so as to entice Louis and Bob to reveal more and more of their inner thoughts, with a view to ultimate denunciation.

No doubt relieved to be able to conclude that his son was a mere dupe and not a protagonist in the 'atheist game', Thomas Stevenson took a decision that Bob was to be barred from Heriot Row and not allowed to see Louis again. Louis wrote: 'it is a Lord's mercy I was not at home, or things might really have come to a climax.' Yet three days later the hurricane burst over the unsuspecting Louis. Thomas Stevenson bumped into Bob in the street and took him severely to task. A nasty scene developed. It seems that at first Bob made the mistake of treating his uncle's remonstrations with Wildean repartee but at least RLS had the satisfaction that Bob had seen the full fury of the tyrant, just as Thomas was glad that Bob was the villain and not his son; the only one who lost out all round was poor Bob, as Louis's account shows:

> I was sitting up here working away at John Knox, when the door opened and Bob came in with his hands over his face and sank down on a chair and began to sob. He was scarcely able to speak at first, but he found voice at last, and I then found he had come to see me, had met my father in the way and had just brought to an end an interview with him. There is now at least one person in the world who knows what I have had to face and what a tempest of emotions my father can raise when he is really excited.

Next day he gave details of the encounter:

> The war began with my father accusing Bob of having ruined his house and his son. Bob answered that he didn't know where I had found out that the Christian religion was not true but that he hadn't told me. And I think from that point the conversation went off into emotion and never touched shore again . . . My views according to my father are a childish imitation of Bob, to cease the moment the mildew is removed; all that was said was that I had ceased to care for my father and that my father confessed he was ceasing, or had greatly ceased, to care for me . . . They shook hands; my father wished him all happiness, but prayed . . . that he should never see him between the eyes again . . . no practical issue except the ludicrous one that Bob promised never to talk religion to me any more . . . he had no idea that there was that sort of thing in the world, although I had told him often enough – my father on his knees and that sort of thing . . . I learn that my mother had hysterics last night over it all.[6]

Later that day RLS saw Bob again. It turned out that Bob had had a private letter from Louis's father, apologising for the tone of the interview but adhering to its substance. Despite its being marked 'Confidential' Bob let Louis read the letter, from which he learned of his father's 'writhings over a ruined life and hopes overthrown which are intolerable to think about'. Moreover, his mother was not helping matters; her idea of being an intermediary was to become hyperemotional with both males, pleading with each in turn for consideration for the other, which merely worsened matters. 'My mother had hysterics privately last night over it all,' Louis wrote on 10 September. On 12 September he reported:

> Tonight my father was talking of how he feared to do what he knew he ought; and I did I think some good to our deplorable condition in this home of ours by what I said. I spoke to my mother afterwards, telling her how I felt with my father and hoped all good from anything he could do; and only hoped

in that, that every man should do what he thought best, as best he could. But I had to stop, as she was growing hysterical.

The atmosphere at Heriot Row continued unbearable. On 13 September RLS wrote:

My father I believe has some of the satisfaction consequent upon a good auto-da-fé now he has finally quarrelled with Bob and banished him. And although it seems mean to profit by what my own heart feels anxious to resent, I am only too glad of any peace between us although every month of it were to cost me a finger. You will understand the wearying, despairing, sick heart that grows up within one, when things go on as sometimes they do; and how the whole of life seems blighted and hopeless and twilight.

A sane man would have allowed a cooling-off period at this stage, but once Thomas Stevenson's Calvinistic blood was up, he was like a terrier. In response, Louis's attitude started to harden and he ceased to try to enter his father's mental world and sympathise with him. On 17 September he wrote: 'It was really pathetic to hear my father praying pointedly for me today at family worship, and to think that the poor man's supplications were addressed to nothing better able to hear and answer than the chandelier.' The tempest simply would not blow itself out. At the end of September Louis was writing:

I am killing my father – he told me tonight (by the way) that I alienated utterly my mother . . . He said tonight, "He wished he had never married," and I could only echo what he said. "A poor end," he said, "for all my tenderness." And what was there to answer? "I have made all my life to suit you – I have worked for you and gone out of my way for you – and the end of it is that I find you in opposition to the Lord Jesus Christ – I find everything gone – I would ten times sooner have seen you lying in your grave than that you should be shaking the faith of other young men and bringing such ruin on other houses, as you have brought already upon this" that is a sort of abstract of one speech.

Maggie had gone away for a week to steady her nerves, but when she returned at the end of September, her contribution was even more unhelpful.

My father said no more than the truth about my mother's feelings to me; I see that now very clearly, although it does seem hard to have put it into words. She is quite cold and unresponsive, after all. I try to cheat myself with flimsies, but that's the hard kernel of fact. I tell you this is just a mere trial of strength between us. The weakest will die first, that is all. And I don't know whether to wish for the one alternative or the other. Both seem horrible; but not much more horrible than the unsightly, hopeless present.

On 3 October he saw Bob again, in defiance of the parental interdict. His father's latest outburst had been to the effect that as Louis was an infidel, he could not hope to inherit Christian money. Bob advised him to leave his parents on the grounds that the rows and miserable atmosphere were ruining his health; he declared with vehemence that if Louis became ill, he would tell Thomas some truths about his precious Christianity that 'he was not capable of thinking possible'. Louis demurred on the ground that the provision of the study at the top of the house showed a latent wish for compromise by his parents and that the burden of shame at having been unable to keep their son at home would be too great for them to bear. But he added a few days later: 'Bob has been, the few times I have been able to see him, a perfect God for me, all through my troubles.'[7]

The clash with his parents involved RLS in a double rejection of them, for in rejecting Christianity he was also rejecting the exact regime of redemption by suffering they tried to impose on him throughout September 1873. Yet there was a sense in which the rift over religion was the occasion rather than the cause of Louis's decisive break with his father. There are many signs, both before and after the drama of 1873, of a profound unconscious (and thus in Stevenson's case semi-conscious) antagonism of son towards father. Part of this was clearly an 'oedipal' struggle for Maggie's affections. Forbidden desires for the mother can often be sublimated by work (in Freudian theory an extremely powerful form of therapy), but then the repressed desire seeks another expression, classically finding an outlet in conflicts with the father over career and lifestyle or, in this case, over religion.

Thomas Stevenson, mutton-chop whiskers and Victorian paterfamilias stance notwithstanding, was no cardboard domestic tyrant. Emotionally demonstrative, outspoken, dogmatic and even despotic he could be, but he was also chivalrous and softhearted and suffered violent mood swings from gloom and austerity to tenderness and gaiety; it is quite clear that one of the seeds of *Dr Jekyll and Mr Hyde* was observation of the Janus face of Thomas Stevenson.

> His talk, compounded of so much sterling service and so much freakish humour, and clothed in language so apt, droll and emphatic, was a perpetual delight to all who knew him ... It was perhaps another Celtic trait that his affections and emotions, passionate as these were, and liable to passionate ups and downs, found the most eloquent expression both in words and gestures. Love, anger and indignation shone through him and broke forth in imagery, like what we read of Southern races.

Alexander Japp found Thomas to be both 'a quick, sensitive, in some ways even a fantastic-minded man' and a sincere and thoughtful one who had known sorrow and sleepless nights but who every now and then was touched by sudden humour. Japp actually preferred him to RLS and 'sometimes I have had a doubt whether the father was not, after all, the greater man of the two.'[8]

Yet if Thomas Stevenson was not the patriarch of Victorian melodrama, he was undoubtedly a difficult man for any free-spirited son to live with. The combination of austerity and humourlessness can be seen in his approach to his son's student finances: he gave him just two shillings and sixpence a week pocket money (about £13 a year), yet imposed a fine of a penny for each slang word Louis uttered. This was not just petty in itself but disastrous for an aspiring writer of fiction, who must perforce develop an ear for slang and idiom. As for the shortness of money itself, some have even speculated that it was being kept on such short commons that led Louis to seek out the prostitutes and other dispossessed of Edinburgh and to make common cause with them as fellow sufferers under the patriarchal lash. As Richard Aldington wondered: 'Did Stevenson seek out this "low company" because he had so little money, or was he deprived of money because his father knew what company the young man was keeping?' Thomas's humourlessness is further evinced in his intemperate response to the 'L.J.R' rule book; instead of treating this as an undergraduate joke, Thomas reacted in heavy-handed and minatory fashion and opened up a whole Pandora's box. Thomas was also angry that his son dressed in a slovenly or Bohemian way, especially when he appeared like a gypsy, with duck trousers, black shirt and tie described as being like a strip torn from a castaway carpet.

There were clashes between the two long before the 1873 débâcle. On one occasion at dinner Louis ventured some heterodox opinions on the Old Testament; his father replied that he would not have such opinions expressed at his table, and that if this was what he was learning at University, the sooner he left the better. On another Louis was praising Herbert Spencer. At length his father uttered, 'I think, Louis, you've got Evolution on the brain. I wish you would define what the word means.' 'Well,' said Louis, 'here it is verbatim. Evolution is a continuous change from indefinite incoherent homogeneity of structure and function through successive differentiations and integrations.' 'I think', said his father, 'your friend Mr Herbert Spencer must be a very skilful writer of polysyllabic nonsense.'[9]

There are also many passages in Louis's early letters that hint at an 'oedipal' antagonism towards his father and a desire to displace him in his mother's affections; by extension there are also gleeful memoirs of ousting the older generation of males. On 16 September 1873 – at the very moment the family rows over Bob were at their height, Louis reported the following to Mrs Sitwell: 'Today in Glasgow my father went off on some business, and my mother and I wandered about for two hours. We had lunch together, and were very merry over what people at the restaurant would think of us – mother and son they could not have supposed us to be.' An earlier incident reinforces this: 'Aboard a steamer mine eyes lighted on two girls, one of whom was sweet and pretty, talking to an old gentleman . . . so I sidled up to the old gentleman, got into conversation with him and so with the damsel; and thereupon, having used the patriarch as a ladder, I kicked him down behind me.'[10]

There is even more striking evidence of the tension between father and son in Stevenson's fiction. Stevenson, unlike Scott, shows patriarchy in moral and physical decay. This comes through clearly in the short stories 'The Pavilion on the Links' and 'The Merry Men'; the subtext of the novella *The Story of a Lie* is a transmogrified version of Stevenson's difficulties with Fanny Osbourne on one hand and his father on the other, and it is not hard to guess who was the model for Dick Van Tromp's father when we read these words: 'He would utter the word "boy" even more offensively than the average of fathers.' Fathers are absent, dead or ineffectual in *Treasure Island, Kidnapped* and *The Master of Ballantrae*, while in *The Misadventures of John Nicholson*, old Mr Nicholson is shown as rigid on temperance and the Sabbath but incapable of the Christian act of forgiveness; in this work the autobiographical elements are particularly clear, since John Nicholson's adventures in California are a clear parallel of Stevenson's time there in 1879–80. In *John Nicholson* a dialogue between father and son goes as follows: 'I rose this morning what the world calls a happy man – happy, at least, in a son of whom I thought I could reasonably be proud.' 'How could I tell you were proud of me? Oh! I wish, I wish that I had known!' *Dr Jekyll and Mr Hyde* has often been read as a struggle between father (Jekyll) and son (Hyde), and the slaying of Sir Conyers Carew the manifest form of a latent parricidal impulse in RLS, but perhaps the clearest indication of suppressed wishes towards the father comes in *A Child's Garden of Verses*, where the poet with a father named Tom throws his rival out:

> We built a ship upon the stairs
> All made of back-bedroom chairs
> And filled it full of sofa pillows
> To go a-sailing on the billows
>
> We sailed along for days and days
> And had the very best of plays;
> But Tom fell out and hurt his knee
> So there was no one left but me.

Stevenson's antagonism did not abate even when his father died, though there are signs in the later work of more understanding of the paternal position. In *The Wrecker*, Owen Nares regrets his quarrel with his dead father and says: 'I guess we're all beasts'; to which Loudon Dodd replies: 'All sons are, I guess . . . I have the same trouble on my conscience.' The attitude of Dodd's father reflects some of the words Thomas Stevenson used when remonstrating with Louis over his enthusiasm for Spencer and Walt Whitman: 'I am not afraid my boy will ever disgrace me; I am only vexed he should sometimes talk nonsense.' Loudon Dodd reflects: 'You can see for yourself how vain it was to argue with my father. The despair that seized upon me after such an interview was, besides, embittered with remorse.'

But perhaps the *locus classicus* for father-son rivalries is Stevenson's final work, *Weir of Hermiston*. Archie Weir opposed capital punishment, as Louis did, in both cases in flat defiance of their fathers and, like Archie, Louis 'made no attempt whatsoever to understand the man with whom he dined and breakfasted ... stayed as little as was possible in his father's presence; and when there, averted his eyes as much as was decent from his father's face.' In the unfinished section of the novel, Stevenson intended the hanging judge Hermiston to pronounce the death sentence on his son Archie and then die from the shock. Though assured this was impossible naturalistically, because of the requirements of Scottish law, Stevenson was determined to include the scene for reasons of poetic and dramatic truth – just as Schiller featured a non-historical meeting between Elizabeth I and Mary Queen of Scots in *Maria Stuart*. Psychologically, the point was to be that Archie's new life in the United States could only begin if the father died instead of the son, just as Stevenson's own new life began in the U.S.A. after *his* father's death.[11]

We have drawn evidence for RLS's antagonism to his father from his letters and from his fiction, but there is yet another source: his own unconscious as revealed in dreams. Fortunately there can be no doubt about the role of the unconscious in Stevenson's life as an artist, since he explicitly recognised it himself. A later observer, Katharine Osbourne, noted perceptively that in no other man was there so much of the unconscious in the conscious. In his childhood dreams two versions of evil were often confused: the banal (housework undone, the chaos principle) and the diabolic (questions of heaven and hell). As we have seen, these were often so intense that 'the night-hag would have him by the throat and pluck him, strangling and screaming from his sleep'; it was actually a relief to experience ordinary nightmares when he felt nothing worse than 'a flying heart, a freezing scalp, cold sweats and the speechless midnight fear'. As he grew older, nightmare was gradually displaced by fantasy; he had dreams in which he was a Jacobite engaged in adventures and the books he 'read' in his dreams were more vivid than the real books he read when awake.

The anxieties of university plunged him back into nightmare, and in his undergraduate days he had two recurring bad dreams. In one he was in a surgical theatre where the surgeons operated on 'monstrous malformations'; in another there was a long staircase which he was doomed to climb unendingly, 'stair after stair in endless series'. He consulted a doctor and was given pills, which had the effect of banishing the nightmares. But Stevenson never wanted to block the receptor to the unconscious entirely, for he recognised it as the true hidden spring of creativity. In one of his less troublesome recurrent dreams he was the son of a very rich and wicked man and lived abroad to avoid his father. Eventually he returned to England to find him married to a young wife, who loathed her fate and suffered his cruelty in silence. A quarrel arose between father and son, as a result of which the son struck the father dead. The son then lived at home, full of parricidal guilt, with the young woman, who knew nothing of the circumstances of her husband's death. Gradually, however, the son became convinced that she knew all about the murder, and finally she admitted that she loved him. At this point Stevenson awoke with a feeling of delight; what most amazed him, he said, was that he had no idea of the woman's motivation until the moment of her revelation. It scarcely takes a critic of much talent to see the obvious connection of this oedipal fantasy to RLS's waking predicament, and he himself recognised its relevance to the point where the dream was partially incorporated in the scene in *Dr Jekyll and Mr Hyde* where Hyde lethally assaults the elderly gentleman with a cane.[12]

At a conscious level Stevenson oscillated in his attitude towards his father. At times he showed understanding and even sympathy, but at others he confessed that Thomas's mere existence had a paralysing effect on him. He confessed to Edmund Gosse that 'a first child is a rival' to the father and (with obvious self-reference) 'the children of lovers are orphans.' In 'Reflections and Remarks on Human Life' he says that the love of parents for children is bound to be ill-starred since it begins before the child is born and is invested with imaginings which the reality is bound to disappoint; besides, the natural bond is stronger from parent to child than from child to parent. Yet at other times RLS takes the view that parents get too much sympathy from the world and children not enough, and he particularly took issue with Calvinism since large parts of the Old Testament, which the Calvinists revered, could be understood only in terms of the conflation of patriarchs or 'competition of Godheads' (i.e. one's own father and Yahweh): 'while we have plenty of praise for Abraham's faith, we hear not one syllable of comment on Isaac's obedience ... the whole of his conduct in the matter was too much *matter of course* for commendation ... a man was evidently expected to do much more for his parents than for his God.'[13]

On RLS's side the breach opened up in 1873 never really healed. When his father died in 1887 he regretted it but did not really mourn it. Instead he acted as if regenerated: 'I almost begin to feel as if I should care to live; I would by God! and so I begin to believe I shall!' If this sounds callous, it must be acknowledged that Thomas Stevenson's acceptance of his son's growing success in the late seventies and early eighties was grudging. Fundamentally, Thomas thought that literature was a pastime, not a serious occupation for a mature adult. When in 1879 Sir James Dewar prophesied that in time Louis's earnings as a writer would eclipse those of Stevenson's engineering firm, Thomas became extremely angry at the idea that a 'mere' writer could earn more than an engineer. Alexander Japp, who had a number of intimate conversations with Thomas in 1880–81, recorded that the father had never overcome his feelings of disappointment that the son had failed to pursue a legal career; however many times Japp pointed out that a successful writer could reach many more people than even the most successful lawyer or lighthouse engineer, Stevenson *père* still brooded wistfully on the might-have-been. RLS struck back in the early 1880s by cutting his father down to size through writing. When he edited Thomas's address to the Royal Society of Edinburgh he felt 'quite proud of the paper, as if it had been mine'. Being a writer allowed him to dominate his father psychologically, reverse the dynamics of interpersonal power, and convert his father into the dependent or 'son', even though Thomas still controlled the purse-strings. The complexity of his feelings for a man whose love he can never really have doubted comes through by implication in his remarks in the essay on Burns: since in indicting Burns RLS was also indicting part of himself (the lustful side), it is interesting to see how by transference he transmogrifies his darker self into his father, consoles the defeated self and then sets himself up as father to him: 'When I have beaten Burns, I am driven at once by my parental feelings to console him with a sugar plum.'[14]

What made 1873 such a traumatic year for Stevenson was that even as he was locked in combat with his father, he had to resolve problems on the maternal side of the oedipal equation; indeed, part of the furious dust of battle in September 1873 arose because of deep sexual frustration, and later confusion, on Louis's part. In short, he had fallen violently in love.

When Stevenson went to Cockfield Rectory in Suffolk in April for the 'cooling-off' period with his cousin Maud Balfour, wife to the Revd Churchill Babington, he had no reason to expect anything more than visits from fusty dons from Babington's Cambridge college. Yet the Babingtons' first important guest changed his life. She was Mrs Fanny Sitwell, twelve years his senior, a brunette with small hands and feet, a noted beauty who won the plaudits of discriminating judges as various as Henry James, Joseph Conrad, Osbert Sitwell, E.V. Lucas and John Garvin. It was said of her that she had more men in love with her than any other woman then living; all unwittingly, she left a trail of broken hearts behind her wherever she went. As if to complete this picture of an impossibly romantic heroine, she had in a mild form the weakness in the lung that carried off Violeta in *La Dame aux Camélias*.

Born Frances Jane Fetherstonhaugh into Irish Protestant gentry, she was brought up in genteel poverty as an itinerant tomboy; by the age of 17 she had lived extensively in Ireland, Germany and Australia, whence she returned in 1856 to marry the Revd Albert Sitwell of the Church of England. Sitwell obtained a chaplaincy in Calcutta and it was there that Fanny's son Bertie was born. Shortly afterwards, a cholera outbreak forced the family back to England where Sitwell secured assorted livings. But by this time severe marital breakdown, coyly attributed in the sources to his 'unfortunate temperament and uncongenial habits' – which certainly sets the imagination buzzing – led Fanny to walk out and take Bertie with her. Since divorce was a disaster for a respectable woman in Victorian England, and even separation was a very serious step – this was an age when a woman's body and money were supposed to be entirely at the disposal of the husband – something singular (as Conan Doyle would say) must have happened to cause the rift.[15]

Through her friends' contacts Fanny scraped a living as secretary to the London College for Men and Women, a revolutionary institution by the standards of the day as it instructed the sexes together. She became close friends with the art critic Sidney Colvin who, in this *annus mirabilis*, for Stevenson, of 1873 became Slade Professor of Fine Art at Cambridge at the age of 28 and, in 1884, Curator of Prints and Drawings at the British Museum.

Fanny, then, was the vision that burst on to Stevenson's besotted gaze at Cockfield rectory. Fanny Sitwell's first impression of Louis was much like that of the first older woman who had captivated him – Anne Jenkin – and Fanny's reaction to finding a young Heine was much the same: she sent for her male protector. In an uncanny rerun of the Fleeming Jenkin scenario, Colvin too took to the young man and quickly became a mixture of elder brother and father figure, to the point where, many years later, Stevenson would write: 'My dear Colvin, I owe you and Fleeming Jenkin, the two older men who took the trouble, and knew how to make a friend of me, everything that I have or am.' Louis was awestruck by Colvin's kudos as contributor to the *Fortnightly* and founder member of the Savile Club in 1868; but if anything it was Colvin who came away from the encounter reeling: 'He sped those summer nights and days for us all as I have scarce known any sped before or since. He seemed, this youngster, already to have lived and seen and felt and dreamed and laughed and longed more than others do in a lifetime.' Once he took the measure of his brilliant young protégé, Colvin was able to encourage him in his literary aspirations and activate his London publishing contacts on his behalf.[16]

It was when Colvin returned to Cambridge that the relationship between Louis and Fanny really caught fire. They had mutual needs based on their common desire to escape from oppressive situations – RLS from his parents, she from her marriage. Both were starved of love, and the mixture of vulnerability and courage in a woman was especially likely to appeal to Louis. They discussed books, shared jokes, told each other intimate secrets, and by the time of his departure for Edinburgh, Louis was already so close to her that he threw a prima donna tantrum when they disagreed on the worth of the young Robert Bridges. He was by now hopelessly in love and before he left he promised that he would produce a great work of literature now that he had found his Muse.

We are dependent for our knowledge of the course of the relationship on Stevenson's letters alone for, at her request, he destroyed hers to him, but there seems no question but that Fanny overplayed her hand and indulged in emotional brinkmanship, encouraging or at least conniving at a dangerous degree of infatuation by Louis. After his return to Edinburgh his letters to her were full of the crisis with his parents over Bob, but they also contained poignant and impassioned declarations of love which should have caused any circumspect Victorian lady to cry, 'Hold, enough!' The surviving evidence on Fanny does not suggest a coquette or a *capriciosa*; perhaps she allowed herself for a time to think that she too was in love, then had second thoughts later and requested Louis to destroy all traces of her earlier folly. Certainly no one reading the 21-year old Stevenson's letters could be in any doubt about the direction in which his mind was running.

> I hope more in the strong inspiration of your sympathy than ever Christian hoped out of his deity ... *meine schöne, liebe Freundin* ... you have spoiled a certain rough, vulgar and courageous volunteer in the war of life who went south some two months and a half ago and, since, you have put a new heart of flesh within him, you must help to keep it warm with sympathy...think how much you have been to me *alone* without thought of others, without thought of how many dark lands the white moon has looked healingly down into.

Such were the opening salvoes. On 10 September he wrote: 'My darling ... I have dreamed about you the last nights often.' There is no sign that Fanny tried to lower the temperature; given the significance of floral tributes for women, her gift of violets to her young admirer in mid-September had a meaning that Louis, with his feminine antennae, would not have been slow to pick up.[17]

Both because of the crisis with his parents and because Fanny was still in law a married woman, her letters to him were always addressed to the Spec, where he collected them from the porter. On one occasion the man mislaid the post and claimed there were no letters, which provoked the following epistolary outburst from Louis to Fanny:

> NO LETTER. Now this is very funny. I should have thought you would have answered my Tuesday's letter; I felt sure you would not have lost an hour in answering Monday's note; and yet, thank God, you are not ill, or Maud would have heard of that. What can this mean, old man? She could not be so brutal as to

give you no hint, as to let the whole correspondence cease without a word, and you go day after day up to the college and come back again with the heartache. And what can it be?

Then there are clear signs of the young man's cracking up as he writes, 'O God, God, God, God' in handwriting getting ever wilder. 'All that made me happy is at an end ... Now when it is gone, I do not quite know how I am to face the blank.'

The mislaid post soon surfaced and all was well, but the thought of what he had lived through temporarily inspired another effusion.

If I never saw you again, and lived all my days in Arabia, I should be reminded of you continually; you have gone all over the house of my mind and left everywhere sweet traces of your passage. It is not possible that our two minds should quite cease; I believe with Théophile Gautier – not a grain of dust that has ever been through my brain in these latter days, but will leap and thrill and waken to recollections if the wind should blow or the rain should wash it anywhere near you.'

There was much more in the same vein.

Your sympathy is the wind in my sails. You must live to help me and I must do honour to your help ... If some of us are spared there will be at least eternal honour to your name ... No, your name will never be quite forgotten but wherever there are humane men and noble women, the one will wish that they could have lived where they could have known you, and the others will set you before them as a model. *There.* If you don't believe that, it is because you doubt those whom you have inspired; and that would be rude.

But another emotion awakened by the 'rejection' of the 'unanswered letter' was remorse, and in one letter there is clear enough evidence to convince the sceptics who still claim there was nothing untoward in Louis's early romantic life.

I have been thinking a little of my wretchedness when your letters did not come; and the whole business knocked most unpleasantly at my conscience. I too left letters unanswered until they ceased to come, *from a person to whom the postage even must have been a matter of parsimony* [italics mine]; left them unanswered, on purpose that they might cease. O God! a thing comes back to me that hurts the heart very much. For the first letter, she had bought a piece of paper with a sort of flower-arabesque at the top of it. I wish you would write cruelly about this – I wish you would by God. I want something to make me take up arms in my own defence – no, I don't. Only I could not help writing this to you because it is in my mind – on my heart, and I hope you won't hate me for it. Only one thing gives me any little pleasure, and it is a very, very faint one. I never showed the letters to anyone, and some months ago they became insupportable to me and I burnt them. Don't I deserve the gallows?[18]

There had been a lull in the storms in the Stevenson household in

October: Thomas went to Ireland on business and took his wife with him. Hostilities were likely to break out again on their return, but then Louis had a stroke of luck. During a railway journey he and his father met the Law Advocate, Scotland's chief law officer, and he suggested that Louis should read for the English bar. Louis had been toying with the idea of persuading his father to let him read law at Cambridge – naturally he did not reveal his ulterior motive for wanting to be near Cockfield again – but this idea was even better.[19]

Thomas agreed, but soon found himself outmanoeuvred by the machiavellianism of his son. Few men were more ruthless than RLS when he really wanted something; as J.A.Steuart remarked, under the frothy surface Stevenson was flint. Knowing that in London he would still be within his parents' reach and therefore their control, he colluded with Colvin, Mrs Sitwell and some other friends to escape abroad. He had enough symptoms: sore throat, fever, pleurisy, rheumatism – to say nothing of anxiety about the formalities for admission as student to the London Inns of Court – to convince any doctor he was ailing, but just to make sure, his friends found a sympathetic physician in the shape of Dr (later Sir) Andrew Clark, who used the powerful circumstantial excuse that Louis weighed just 118 pounds to forbid him from taking law exams, and ordered him to seek rest, recuperation and convalescence in the sunnier climate of the south of France. Alarmed at this development, his parents sped to London. Maggie suggested taking him to convalesce in Torquay but Clark blocked that, and Thomas Stevenson, with his exaggerated respect for the opinion of professional men, was hoist by his own self-regarding petard. Maggie then suggested that she accompany her son to the south of France but Clark had anticipated that as well; it was true that Louis was in a poor state of health, but Clark knew very well what the real cause was and would not permit the export of the root cause of his sufferings. The agreement with his parents was that Louis would be away for just six weeks but, he remarked: 'Methinks I shall manage to disappoint them.'[20]

For ten days, until 5 November, Stevenson was almost continually in the company of his beloved, and his correspondence reveals that the flames of passion and adoration were further fanned by the face-to-face encounter. Fanny Sitwell met his parents, charmed Thomas and acted as intermediary to pour oil on some of the troubled waters. Maggie seems to have been less impressed by her son's goddess and was particularly annoyed that on his last Sunday in London he went to church with Mrs Sitwell rather than with her and Thomas – amazingly, throughout the entire imbroglio in Edinburgh RLS had continued to accompany his father to the Sabbath services on the meaninglessness of which he was so eloquent.

Stevenson's destination was the French resort of Menton, near the Italian border. He crossed from Dover on 6 November on a very rough sea. His impressions of the journey through France are contained in one of his very first publications 'Ordered South'. In Paris he was cold and lonely; in Sens what he noticed most was not the cathedral but a blind poet selling his books; he reached Avignon, enjoyed the view from the Rocher des Doms and remarked on the ferocity of the sun beating across the Rhône at Villeneuve.[21] Although Clark's prescription of a journey south contained some disingenuousness, there was no doubt that RLS was run down and in a state close to nervous collapse. He went to Nice to consult an English specialist but returned to his hotel at Menton in some confusion. 'I could not remember French, or at least I am afraid to go into any place lest I should not be able to remember it, and so could not tell when the train went. At last I crawled up to the station and sat down on the steps, and just steeped myself in the sunshine until the evening began to fall and the air to grow chilly.' A little later he wrote to Mrs Sitwell: 'if you knew how old I felt! I am sure this is what age brings with it – this carelessness, this disenchantment, this continued bodily weariness. I am a man of 70: O Medea, kill me or make me young again!'[22]

There are many such expressions of *taedium vitae* at this period of RLS's life, which one might be tempted to dismiss as the posing of a 'decadent' aesthete-bohemian. But there is much that points to the outbursts as being the symptoms of a deeper malaise. There were the sudden outpourings of anger, out of proportion to the stimulus, indicating at the very least nervous exhaustion. In Menton there was an upsetting altercation with a clergyman he rather liked, and later he had a furious row with an American who claimed that the British had not given sufficient satisfaction for the snub to U.S. honour over the *Alabama* affair. In that case, pay back the money your government accepted as compensation, snarled Stevenson, and the stage was set for a knock-down, drag-out verbal skrimmage. Many strands fed into his depression. First there was the failure of his relationship with Fanny to prosper in the way he wished. Then there was the conflict with his parents and consequent guilt. At some level he felt he was to blame for having escalated the family conflict: 'Generally it is my own blame, for I cannot help getting friendly with my father (whom I *do* love), and so speaking foolishly with my mouth.' He also felt guilty about the income he derived from his father and therefore believed he should live cheaply until he either died or recovered his health completely, so that he could earn money and 'pay off' his debt. He wrote: 'If I didn't hope to get well and do good work yet and more than repay my debts to the world, I should consider it right to invest an extra franc or two in laudanum. But I *will* repay it.' This breast-beating about privilege was exactly what Henley meant when he referred to the 'Shorter Catechist' element in RLS's personality, but there can be no doubting the hyperanxiety about money and – what in Louis's case amounted to the same thing – the possibilities of a lucrative literary career. As he said to Fanny Sitwell: 'If Colvin does not think that I shall be able to support myself soon by literature, I shall give it up and go (horrible as the thought is to me) into an office of some sort ... You do not know how much this money question begins to take more and more importance in my eyes every day.'[23]

That these expressions of despair were not simply an attempt to wring sympathy from Fanny or exert a form of emotional blackmail on her is clear from Louis's correspondence to Baxter in the same period. The despondent tone everywhere perceptible at this time has tempted those biographers who do not believe in psychological causes for nervous breakdown to speculate that Louis might still have been suffering from the venereal disease he undoubtedly contracted earlier in the Edinburgh stews. A letter on 15 November to Baxter is typical of his depression:

> I am awfully weary and nervous, I cannot read or write at all, and I am not able to walk much; all which put together leaves me a good deal of time in which I have no great pleasure or satisfaction. However, you must not suppose me discontented. I am away in my own beautiful Riviera, and I am free now from the horrible misery that was playing the devil with me at home.

To allay his anxieties he experimented with opium (laudanum and morphine, which his doctors had given him as a cough suppressant) and found the sensation pleasurable: when he went to bed, the bed itself seemed to oscillate softly, like a boat in a very gentle breeze; sadly the verses he wrote while under the influence were not the equal of Coleridge's *Kubla Khan*.

On his good days he tried to settle into the routine of Menton. In the nineteenth century medical science went through a vogue of recommending seaside resorts in hot, dry climates as refuges for consumptives and others with lung problems. On the Riviera, Menton was the favoured spot, and the small medieval town was spangled with hotels, pensions and guest-houses which played host to a vast international, polyglot population: Americans, Russians, Poles, Swedes and, above all, the British. In the third week of December Colvin came to stay a fortnight and ease him through the rites of passage in this expatriate community. They dined with Sir Charles Dilke and his wife, who, Louis discovered, was an excellent mimic, then visited the chocolate-box kingdom of Monaco, which neither of them liked: Colvin detested the Casino while Louis was disturbed by the constant pigeon-shooting and noise of gunfire.[24]

At the end of 1873, while Colvin departed for Paris, Stevenson took up residence in the Hôtel Mirabeau on Menton's East Bay. The residents were a very mixed bag: roistering Yankees, mild, milk-and-water English clergyman's daughters, M.Robinet, a bush-bearded French landscape painter of fervent clericalist and royalist views, a Francophile American couple with an eight-year old daughter whom Louis found first fascinating then tiresome and, most important of all, two 'brilliantly accomplished and cultivated' Russian (actually Georgian) sisters, the Princess Zassetsky and Madame Garschine. The Princess Zassetsky, the elder sister and the more vivacious of the two, had a lover in Russia, and a three-year old in tow called Nelitchka, but Madame Garschine, in her early thirties, was unattached though with an eight-year old girl, and soon set her cap at the young Scot. Sir Fitzroy Maclean, the diplomat and writer, tells us that there is a natural affinity between Georgians and Scots – both mountain people with a martial tradition – and certainly there seems to have been some spark of instant recognition in the two parties to the flirtation that followed. This was the third of Louis's significant relationships with older women.

Biographers have struggled to make sense of the clues, winks and nods used by Stevenson to describe his relationship with Madame Garschine, and in at least one case (J.C.Furnas) this has resulted in an ambiguous, opaque and virtually impenetrable account. The fault is Stevenson's, for anything less Jamesian than the sisters seems hard to imagine; they came from a very different culture, where the avowal of an emotional or sexual life did not have to be obfuscated under layers of circumlocution and insinuation; as Louis wrote of the sisters: 'They do what they want with perfect frankness.' What seems to have happened is that Madame Garschine made overtures to see whether there was a possibility of an affair with Louis; he declined, possibly out of loyalty to Fanny Sitwell, possibly because he already had sufficient ballast of guilt aboard and did not want to take on more, possibly because he felt himself out of his depth with a sophisticated and enigmatic Slav; it is likely that a combination of these feelings weighed in the balance. Louis himself used the experience to impress on Fanny his imperviousness to casual romances and also to make her jealous, and there is an element of *faux-naïveté* in the way he relates to her the successive stages of his relationship. 'I don't know what Mme G's little game is with regard to me. Certainly she has either made up her mind to make a fool of me in a somewhat coarse manner, or else she is in train to make a fool of herself.' Later: 'I had a good long talk with Mme G. I wish I could make up my mind to tell you what she said, for I should like to know if you would agree with it: I have been quite confused and upset every time I have thought of it since. If I am like what she says, I must be a very nice person!'

To be fair to Stevenson, perhaps, with his Calvinistic background, he could not entirely take it seriously when a woman put her cards on the table. Perhaps, too, there was a wider culture shock at work, for the Slav lack of inhibition sometimes took forms that were distinctly eccentric. What looks like a calculated snub towards Louis by Mme Zassetsky – and has sometimes been read by biographers as cold fury towards her younger sister – could have been simple *outré* hypomania. There was the occasion when she had Louis pose for a photographer, told the man that Louis was her son, was just nineteen and was proud of his newly sprouting moustache, and that therefore he should take care to highlight it in his snapshot. Another time Mme Zassetsky flew into a rage with the older girl and reprimanded her so severely as to suggest she had far outstripped her aunt-like role. Noting Louis's surprise, Mme Zassetsky told him that the child was actually hers and not Madame Garschine's, although the child did not know this; allegedly her younger sister had agreed to a 'motherhood of convenience' to assuage her own childlessness and allow the Princess greater freedom to conduct affairs. Later still, Madame Garschine told him that she had a husband in Russia from whom she was separated, that in Russia she was known as a woman in league with the devil but that in fact she was a fanatical lover of Jesus Christ: 'I have never loved any man I have seen,' she said. 'I want to have been one of those women who did love Him and followed Him.' It was not surprising that after this Louis could not be sure what was reality and what illusion in his dealings with the sisters.

Yet there is a suspicion of iron in the soul of RLS: we observe him telling Madame Garschine of his great love in England in order to put her off, while dangling titbits of his relationship with the Georgian lady before Fanny Sitwell, the whole expressed in cryptic innuendoes. On 25 January he wrote to Fanny: 'They are both of them the frankest of mortals and have explained to me, in one way or another, that I am to them as some undiscovered animal. They do not seem to cultivate RLS's [sic] in Muscovy ... Colvin must know nothing of this; it would be the deuce if he did; I'll take it as a real breach of confidence if you tell him.'

If his game of manipulation was as cold-blooded as one suspects, it was certainly effective with both women. Realising that the young man had no amatory intentions, Madame Garschine and her sister relaxed and began to behave towards him in an affectionate and maternal way. This was not quite the end of la Garschine, however. He later wrote a short poem in praise of her fairness of face and her love and constancy; later in 1874 she wrote a letter of some acerbity to him in Edinburgh demanding to know why he had not been in touch. But once he left Menton Louis never saw her again. Fanny meanwhile did not inform Colvin but she did alert Maggie, who wrote to Louis in some alarm. He stonewalled her with bromides about how the sisters knew their Mill and Spencer. Yet Fanny was evidently sufficiently piqued by the intriguing relationship to pen a hurt letter to Louis for we find him replying:

O my dear, don't misunderstand me; let me hear soon to tell me that you can't doubt me; I wanted to let you know really how the thing stood and perhaps I am wrong, perhaps doing that is impossible in some cases. At least, dear, believe me you have been as much in my heart these last few days as ever you have been, and the thought of you troubles my breathing with the sweetest trouble. I am only happy in the thought of you, my dear; this other woman is interesting to me as a hill might be, or a book, or a picture, but you have all my heart, my darling.[25]

As if to prove the point, he produced a new name for her: 'Consuelo' – after the heroine of George Sand, whose works he was then devouring.

As soon as Madame Garschine's attentions assumed a more moderate, quasi-maternal tenor, RLS devoted most of his attention to the two girls aged three and eight who, it now transpired – at least according to Mme Zassetsky's story – were sisters rather than cousins, though still unaware of the fact. Always fascinated by children, Louis noticed that the confusion of roles as between the sisters, with one the natural, and the other the adoptive mother (and how often this sort of confusion was to surround RLS!), meant that the three-year old was never disciplined properly; the child was so wild and out of control that he predicted a tragedy in the future. One of the greatest ironies – and tragedies – in the life of RLS was that this man with such a rare feeling for children should have been fated to be childless. To his mother he wrote, 'Kids are what is the matter with me.' To Fanny Sitwell he later elaborated: 'I sometimes hate the children I see in the street – you know what I mean by hate – wish they were somewhere else and not there to mock me; and sometimes again, I don't know how to go by them for love of them, especially the wee ones.'

The 'liaison' with Madame Garschine apart, little of note happened during RLS's three-month convalescence in Menton. Colvin returned from Paris and introduced him to Andrew Lang, who was later to be important in promoting Stevenson's literary career. Then Madame Garschine's cousin, Prince Galitzin, arrived and Louis got on so well with him that he made a half promise to go with him to the University of Göttingen and continue his studies there. But when April arrived and it was time to quit the warm south for home, Louis once again had to ponder the two great polarities of the previous year: his parents and Bob.

A continuing problem for Stevenson was that psychologically and morally he needed to be financially independent of his father but could not achieve this condition; not even after the success of *Treasure Island* and *Dr Jekyll and Mr Hyde* did he have enough money to stand on his own feet and when Thomas died in 1887 his son was still his pensioner. From time to time, additionally, RLS siphoned off money via his mother by sending her begging letters, and his guilt about this emerges clearly in 'Lay Morals'; it does not in his letters to Fanny Sitwell, for with her he was putting on a great show of being the rebel who fundamentally despised his parents. Malcolm Elwin sums up his ambivalence about money neatly:

> The Jekyll of conscience asserted that he was a social parasite in subsisting on his father's bounty, and urged him to secure independence by his own efforts as speedily as possible; but the Hyde of self-indulgent impulse resented the parsimony of his father's allowance, supplemented it by persuasively extracting subsidies from his mother, and did not scruple to play upon their concern for his health as a plea for prolongation of holidays.[26]

Some young men, it is true, would have cut loose from parents and taken a chance. This might have been Bob's way, but Louis was always a 'pretend' bohemian and much more circumspect and calculating than in the myth of the misunderstood aesthete. There were other considerations besides. He knew his health was not up to starvation in the proverbial garret; he knew too that he would in any case soon be inveigled homeward by his mother's hysterics; and above all, he was no fanatic: at root he did love his parents and showed the limits of his rebellion by not running up huge debts. His parents, for their part, were conciliatory while he was in Menton. A long rambling letter about moral independence from Louis convinced them that he was on the point of mental breakdown and they hastened to make reassuring noises to the invalid.

Early in April 1874 RLS left the warmth of Menton for the chill of Paris, eager to see Bob once again. The two were still inseparable spiritually: as Louis wrote to Colvin in January 1874: 'He has all the same elements of character that I have: no two people were ever more alike, only that the world has gone more unfortunately for him, although more evenly.' The tone of the letters he had received from Bob in Antwerp worried him, despite his cousin's bravado about the plethora of pretty girls there. He detected that Bob was lonely and depressed and that he was short of money and not spending enough on food. There was other dispiriting news from Bob's side of the Stevenson family. His father Alan had quarrelled with Thomas over the latter's imputation that Bob had led Louis astray, and the breach seemed irreparable; meanwhile his sister Katharine, who had scandalised her family by marrying a Cambridge atheist, Sydney de Mattos, was now finding her husband impossible to live with; she later divorced him and took their children with her, penniless though she was. One might remark *en passant* on the remarkably high incidence of divorce and separation – especially in this era – of all the women to whom RLS was close. However, when Louis settled into his berth at the Hôtel St Romain in Paris, he found Bob in good fettle, hankering after 'a nice woman to live with' and much improved in his craft; he told Louis he now regretted he had not studied in Antwerp from the start.

The fact that their son was, as they saw it, consorting with the enemy angered Louis's parents. His mother cabled that she did not approve of his going to Paris. He wrote back lamely: 'Well, I didn't approve of it particularly myself; I only did it to be sooner able to come home.' His actions belied his weasel words: he at once began to make plans to accompany Bob on a painting trip to Fontainebleau, prior to travelling to Göttingen to study Roman Law with Prince Galitzin. These preparations further angered his parents, who coldly did not answer his letter. In despair he wrote to Fanny Sitwell to protest: surely when one is 24 one can do what one wants without a quarrel with parents? 'If I get permission I shall probably go straight to Germany without delay: by permission I mean money.'

Once again illness struck, to make all such deliberations academic, as it did so often in his life. He went down with a raging headache, heavy sweating and nervous tics, which made his Paris doctor think he might be starting smallpox or typhoid. 'I am bronchial a bit and cough and I have mucous membrane raw over the best part of me and my eyes are the laughablest deformed loopholes you ever saw: and withal my lungs are all right.' When he recovered, parental pressure and simple prudence forced him home to recuperate; Bob departed alone to Fontainebleau and Barbizon, whence he reported with what could later be seen as dramatic irony: 'There are some very nice Californian men and women here.'[27]

Once in Edinburgh, RLS found himself the subject of both stick and carrot from his parents. They had been caught out once on the 'England dodge' and now insisted that Louis read for the examinations for the Scottish Bar; as a sop they increased his allowance to £7 a month – not a princely sum but a considerable improvement on the niggardly dole hitherto. All Stevenson's negative feelings about Edinburgh seemed multiplied and he retired, depressed, to Swanston. Yet by June he had slipped through the net again and was staying with Colvin in Hampstead, within easy reach of his 'Consuelo'. Remarkably, there seems to have been no overt rivalry between Louis and Colvin, though they were both in pursuit of the same woman.[28] Perhaps Colvin's calmness resulted from secret assurances he had been given by the lady, for it was on this visit to London that RLS learned that all his hopes of physical consummation of his passion for Fanny were vain.

Fanny had been finally forced to reveal her intentions by the sheer intensity of Louis's protestations. 'Only just tonight I cannot write any half-words. I can think of nothing but how much I love you and how happy it makes me that I do so. I would not give up my love of you for eternity.' Even more carnally explicit, with its hints of *la petite mort*, is the following, written after a visit with Fanny to the Elgin Marbles at the British Museum, where he bought photographs of three sensual female figures, which he used as the excuse to make overtly physical overtures to her: 'Think, if one could love a woman like that once, see her once grow pale with passion, and once wring your lips out on hers, would it not be a small thing to die?' Following the visit to the Elgin Marbles, his letters are full of paeans to the feminine principle and are orgasmic in their longing. No woman reading them could be unaware of the barely suppressed sexual desire and their implicit challenge to her to prove that this feminine ideal was not just a fantasy.

Details are unclear but it seems from the tone of Stevenson's subsequent letters that it was on this June visit that she warned him of the impossibility of a physical relationship. Perhaps she argued that such a liaison would be unfair to Colvin, who had a prior claim on her affections, while concealing the fact that the Slade Professor was anyway her chosen one. More likely she asked Louis patiently to think through what he was proposing. She was a married woman, and the scandal resulting from an affair could ruin her; moreover she had no money of her own, her scandalised employers would certainly dismiss her, and then where would they both be? Marriage with Louis after a divorce might conceivably have been a solution, but here she was likely to have urged, not so much the twelve-year gap in their ages as the fact that he was just twenty-three, far too young to cross the marital Rubicon in such a parlous context; moreover, his parents would certainly object and cut him off without a penny, and then they would both be destitute. Whatever she said, she let him down gently enough that he did not feel slighted or humiliated. It is a pity that Stevenson's letters immediately after the crucial interview do not give us more guidance, but for once in his life RLS elected to write in an opaque, Jamesian mode:

> Should I have been good enough, unselfish enough, to have let you follow without trammel the obvious way of your destiny, as the helper of all men, of the *Sun* (as I used to phrase it, do you remember, in old days) that is to shine on all, do good to all, encourage and support all? I fancy not; it is better as it is … I am afraid, had I been more fortunate, you had been less useful, and so, on the whole, the sum of help had been diminished.

Perhaps there were moments when RLS regretted he had been so steadfast in a love that, it now appeared, could never be consummated, for some intrusive thoughts of Madame Garschine would appear to have been triggered by the sight of children skipping in the lane outside Colvin's Hampstead house (where he was staying); there are clear reminiscences of the Russian children in the 'Notes on the movements of Young Children' that he wrote at this time. And perhaps he was still playing his games of manipulation when he wrote to Madame Garschine at Franzenbad, proposing a meeting. By then she had moved from that address, so Louis appealed to Fanny to discover her new address – an appeal which, not surprisingly, was ineffectual.

Momentary distraction from his disappointment was provided by the alarming news that Bob had gone down with diphtheria in France and, according to some reports, was likely to die. As Bob slowly recovered, he requested that Louis join him on a cruise through French waterways but, as it happened, Walter Simpson's mind had been working along similar lines, and Louis had already accepted an invitation to go sailing with him and Baxter on the lighthouse yacht *Heron*. As he cruised the Inner Hebrides, discussing with Simpson the 'irregular marriage' the baronet had contracted with what we should nowadays call a 'live-in lover', Louis sent Fanny a number of letters which constituted his 'testament of acceptance' of the new footing on which they stood to each other.

'I shall be a man yet, dear, and a good man, although day by day I see more clearly by how much I fall short of the mark of our high calling; in how much I am still a peevish and a spoiled child.' Later: 'Try to forget utterly the RLS you have known in the past; he is no more, he is dead; I shall try now to be strong and helpful, to be a good friend to you and no longer another limp dead-heavy burden on your weary arms. I think this is permanent: try to believe it yourself, that is the best means to make it so.' And later still: 'I don't know what to write either that will be agreeable to you, except the one fact that I have been and am very content. I do think the passion is over; I would not be too sanguine or fancy there would never be any momentary relapse; but in the meantime I am quite strong and satisfied.'

After the cruise through the Scottish islands, RLS was obliged to spend some time in August and early September with his parents, in Wales, at Barmouth and Llandudno. He used his acquaintance with Andrew Lang as an excuse to escape to Oxford, whence he proceeded on a walking tour of the Chilterns – via High Wycombe, Great Missenden and Wendover – and then in a dog-cart from Wendover to Tring, and by train to London to dine at the Savile, the new literary club (established in 1868) to which he had recently been elected on Colvin's proposal and on which he commented: 'I like my club very much: the table d'hôte dinner is very good: it costs three bobs (sic): two soup, two fish, two entrées, two joints and two puddings; so it is not dear, and one meets agreeable people.'[29]

Yet the real magnet in London continued to be Fanny Sitwell. Despite his promises, there was a certain amount of backsliding into erotic reverie, some of it marred by the ambivalent feelings of a deeply hurt and disappointed young man. One night he dreamed he saw her arriving at the Finchley Road Station 'as you did the afternoon before I left; and I never could catch more than a glimpse of your face before it turned into somebody else's – a horrible Scotch face, commonplace and bitter.' That sounds like the unconscious engaged in a civil war between yearning and aversion therapy, and there are some other signs of latent hostility towards the beloved by the rejected one. In November he wrote: 'I am not going to excuse myself formally for my long silence, the excuse for [which] one day will come out incidentally.' In December he mentioned a female cousin who wrote his father a distressing letter to ask for paid work, and added: 'Surely if there is one thing pure and lovely and of good report it is to find women work', which sounds gratuitous, as if he were ever so subtly reminding her of her own precarious financial position.

Still, as an emotional bulwark of another kind, RLS needed Fanny as much as ever, for there was continuing friction with his parents. On his first return in May his mother had thrown another of her hysterical fits, but his father had talked to him long and cordially. By autumn relations had turned sour with his father too, and Louis wrote despondently to Fanny:

> I have discovered why I get on always so ill, am always so nasty, so much worse than myself, with my parents; it is because they take me at my worst, seek out my faults, and never give me any credit. You remember, perhaps, at least I remember, I once wrote to you to tell how you should do with me; how it was only by getting on my weak side, looking for the best, and always taking it for granted that I should do the best before it is done, that you will ever get the best out of me. This is profoundly true; and I see it on the other side with my parents; I am always bad with them, because they always seem to expect me not to be very good; and I am never good, because they never seem to see me when I am good.

He found various excuses to go down to London for a few days so that he could be with his beloved, and just to talk to her seemed to give him strength. Yet the good effects were soon undone when he returned to Edinburgh to face the gloom and hysterical atmosphere of Heriot Row. One letter sums it all up. He begins by saying: 'I was never more sorry to leave you, but I never left you with a better heart than last night,' and goes on to say that although he had a long and cold journey back to Edinburgh 'I never was sick nor sorry the whole way.' This equanimity was then abruptly shattered when, on arrival at Waverley, he 'found my father waiting for me in the snow with a long face'. That winter of 1874 Thomas Stevenson rose to particularly steep crests and sank down into very deep troughs in the course of an acute attack of the depressive melancholia that always intermittently afflicted him, and some of his symptoms sound like manic depression. At one moment he would be skipping about and telling strange stories to the servants; at another he would become almost catatonic and immobilised with the 'black dog'. During one of these severe cyclonic storms of the mind, Thomas told his son that he could never hope to inherit a farthing of his money unless he embraced Christianity. This quickened Louis's resolve to become self-sufficient by writing and he told his father he accepted the situation completely, adding that any son who took his father's money in circumstances of such irreconcilable differences was a thief. 'And a damned thief, too,' added Thomas vehemently. 'I shall not let myself starve, of course,' Louis confided to Fanny, 'but beyond that must try to be an honest man.'

A lot of this was whistling in the dark. As yet RLS had put no more than a toe into the waters of literary journalism, and his general state of health, both physical and mental, did not bode well for one who aspired to spend a life in Grub Street. Sexual repression continued to gnaw at him, and he found the prescription of sublimation through work hard to swallow; his feelings found expression in a *cri de coeur* to Fanny:

> O, I do hate this damned life that I lead. Work–work–work; that's all right, it's amusing; but I want women and I want pleasure. John Knox had a better time of it than I, with his godly females all leaving their husbands to follow after him; I would I were John Knox; I hate living like a hermit . . . I wish to God I did not love you so much; but it's as well for my best interest as I know well enough. And it ought to be nice for you; for you need not fear any bother from this child except petulant moments. I am good now: I am, am I not?[30]

By December 1874 RLS had hit on a 'solution' for his turbulent emotions towards Fanny Sitwell. In terms of manifest content he simply converted her from a potential mistress into a mother figure. Instead of 'Consuelo' and 'My dearest friend' she becomes 'Madonna' and 'Dearest Mother' and the apparent tone of his letters is that of son to mother:

> You do not know, perhaps – I do not think I knew it myself, perhaps, until I thought it out today – how dear a hope, how sorry a want, this has been for me. For my mother is my father's wife; to have a French mother, there must be a French marriage; the children of lovers are orphans. I am very young at heart – or (God knows) very old – and what I want is a mother, and I have one now, have I not? Someone from whom I shall have no secrets; someone whom I shall love with a love as great as a lover's and yet more; with whom I shall have all a lover's tenderness and more of a lover's timidity; who shall be something fixed and certain and forever true.

By Christmas this theme has acquired other variations:

> I do not know what longing comes to me to go to you for two hours and tell you plainly you have another son. This letter will not speak to you plainly enough; and you must eke it out with what you know of me, madonna, and you do know that I love you dearly – and think of what I should say to you if I were there; and what I should look like as I saw you again out of the body with delight; and how childish I should be for very pleasure; and so, if you love me, this letter shall be to you as a son's Christmas kiss.[31]

As 1875 wore on, the intensity of Stevenson's feelings for Fanny Sitwell gradually faded, though she remained an important friend and confidante for some time to come. But there can be no doubt that in 1873–74 RLS was passionately in love with her; indeed, she was almost certainly the great love of his life. How are we to interpret the tangled web she and Louis wove in these two years?

From the virtual simultaneity of RLS's worst passages of arms with his father one might suspect *a priori* that there was some connection between the two processes. If we see Stevenson's violent and not entirely coherent emotions towards Fanny as mirroring a kind of 'oedipal confusion' – resulting from his mother's 'desertion' when she sided with his father in the family turmoil that made these years in Heriot Row a living hell (albeit intermittent) – we are surely in touch with part of the dynamic. Naturally, such an assumption immediately awakens the fury of biographers hostile to psychoanalytical methods. Jenni Calder argues: 'The surrogate parent will almost always feature in some form in any love affair, but to isolate this as the dominant characteristic in Louis's love for Frances Sitwell and Fanny Osbourne is misleading.' We are not told why it is 'misleading', and the answer to this facile attempt to dismiss a psychoanalytical interpretation is that not all men conduct passionate love affairs with women ten years their senior and still less marry them.

The oedipal confusion over Fanny Sitwell probably stemmed partly from Louis's sense of deprivation as an only child, which often perplexed him about roles – significantly, in *A Child's Garden of Verses* Cummy is called 'my second mother, my first wife' – partly from his mother's invalidism at critical points in his boyhood development, and partly from the hysterical way she reacted to the conflict between her husband and her son. Proper 'socialisation' into normal attraction to the female was further vitiated by the stern Victorian moral code which in effect did turn women into either whores ('Consuelos') or madonnas, and if Thomas Stevenson was indeed instrumental in ending an early relationship with a prostitute (Kate Drummond, or whoever she was) of his own age, this would both have increased oedipal antagonism between father and son – since Louis would, at least unconsciously, have seen Thomas as dog in the manger – and left him in a sexual cul-de-sac.

On this argument the transmogrification of Fanny from object of desire to sacred mother object would have been an attempt to separate in the conscious realm what was unitary in the unconscious – an early example of the disastrous mistake made by Dr Jekyll when he tried to drain all the evil in his nature into Mr Hyde. The ease with which Stevenson moved from sex-object to madonna masks the fact that the two were really one. Jenni Calder denies that RLS needed Fanny Sitwell as a mother figure on the grounds that he wanted her sexually, without seeing that this could actually be the exact reason why he wanted her in the first place. Sex without love, as with prostitutes, had proved a blind alley in more ways than one; on the other hand the love RLS felt for his mother could not be given conscious expression; the best way to integrate sex and love was therefore with an older woman, a mother surrogate. It is also interesting that in all three cases where he clearly felt sexual desire for a woman, with Fanny Sitwell, Madame Garschine and Fanny Osbourne, Louis first won the confidence of the woman by playing with her children, that is, in a sense becoming her child.

It is also intriguing that in his relationship with Fanny Sitwell, RLS tried to make her the 'good' mother, as opposed to the 'bad' one (Maggie) who had 'betrayed' him in Edinburgh. His letters are full of scornful complaints about his mother, as if he was hinting that Fanny might like to fill her place – and all this at a time when his orgasmic fantasies about her were at their height. In autumn 1874 he wrote to her: 'I have had a slight spar with my mother this afternoon about my movements tomorrow. She said, "You shall not have everything your own way, I can tell you." I said, "I don't expect it, but surely I may please myself as to where I am to sleep." She caved in incontinently and asked it as a favour, whereupon I facilely gave way and promised.'

Tentatively summing up on the bizarre events of 1873–74 we may perhaps hazard the following. Louis wanted to sleep with Fanny Sitwell as a solution to the impossible either/or of congress with prostitutes or marriage to a Victorian virgin; love meant avoiding the extremes of either hot lust or cold duty. A deeper reason for Louis's besotment may have been that he had just been 'orphaned' as a result of the feud with his father. Ordered south to Menton, he met another woman of roughly the same age as Fanny who seemed to offer a sexual relationship. Bewildered and still in thrall to Fanny, Stevenson turned her down. Returning to England, Louis finally made an unmistakeable sexual proposition, which Fanny in turn rebuffed. Wrestling with his confused emotions, RLS then converted her into a 'safe' mother figure, but the mask sometimes slipped, showing that in reality this was not a safe option at all but rather a more profound avowal of the latent content of his desire. He therefore ran the gamut in a single year from sexual attraction with love through sexual attraction without love (Madame Garschine) to love without sex, but all were coexistent manifestations of a single impulse. The idea that love for a mother precludes sexuality is anyway naïve, as Freud first realised in Italy when he observed the lubricious attitudes of suckling babes towards their mothers evident in one medieval painting after another. The final irony of RLS's relationship with Fanny Sitwell (his 'Madonna') was that it too was thwarted by a 'father', in this case Sidney Colvin. At the age of 23 Stevenson seemed to be in an emotional and sexual impasse.

4

Madonna

Amazingly, during all this emotional turmoil RLS kept up a steady pace of work. His routine during November 1874 may be taken as roughly typical of his working methods in general at this period of his life. He would take a leisurely breakfast, followed by a smoke at 8.30–10.00 a.m., then work from 10.00–12.45 p.m. He would take lunch from 1.00–2.00 p.m. while reading Schopenhauer and Comte and Spencer on Positivism. Then there was another hour of work followed by a free-wheeling period from 3–6 described by Stevenson as 'anything: if I am in before six I read about Japan'. At six there was dinner, after which he would smoke a pipe with his father until about 7.30 p.m. – and this went on even when their relations otherwise were very bad. Another two hours of work would follow, after which, at 9.30, he would go out to visit either Simpson or Baxter, or would take some supper and smoke another pipe before retiring. Other recreations included concerts – RLS was always very fond of music – especially of Mozart and Cherubini, though he shared the nineteenth-century prejudice that only the heavy Teutonic composers, like Beethoven and Wagner, deserved the label 'great'. If there was a hard frost he would go skating with the Jenkins – who were superior to him at this accomplishment as well as the Thespian craft – on Duddingston loch, scene of earlier delights. And he still liked to roam the streets of Edinburgh, playing 'God' to the beggars – which meant a kind of reverse pickpocketing whereby he collided with them and then slipped a coin into their pockets or dropped a coin in front of their feet while pretending not to notice. In his philanthropy towards the poor and needy he followed in his father's footsteps, though Thomas liked to give to charity anonymously, whereas the great pleasure for Louis was to observe the recipients of his largesse and take pleasure in their joy when they suddenly found a coin in their pocket or on the ground in front of them. One evening he encountered an urchin lost in the streets and spent the night trying to find his parents; he finally lodged him with a constable in the police station, and was staggered to hear later that the parents had not even reported him missing until ten o'clock the next morning.[1]

Most of all there were the amateur theatricals under Fleeming Jenkin's direction, which he loved. Although he was never more than a fair actor, hard work at his craft meant that Louis was sometimes considered competent enough to appear opposite his first madonna, Anne Jenkin, who was well respected as a brilliant actress. In 1875 he had the role of Orsino in *Twelfth Night* and at supper, after the play, he continued to impersonate Orsino in a superbly ducal manner, improvising quasi-Shakespearian lines. The imp of the perverse, observable with Mr Libbel and the other practical jokes with Baxter, sometimes got the better of him. On one occasion, while playing Puck in *Midsummer Night's Dream*, he raised the curtain on a scene not in the play. On another, he was working the curtain, and at the end of a Greek tragedy, the two principal actors, who had just received a tremendous ovation, somersaulted backwards with sheer euphoria on to a couch once the curtain was down and lay with their feet meeting in a kind of triumphal arch. Seeing an opportunity for fun, Stevenson pressed for the curtain to go up again, and a deeply moved audience had to overcome their initial astonishment at this buffoonery and change gear rapidly to applaud the unexpected comic antics.

These were the years when Fleeming Jenkin was still RLS's principal mentor, and it was through the professor that interest in Japan, mentioned in his journal of his daily routine, came about. The story of Yoshida Torajiro, which Stevenson included in his *Familiar Studies of Men and Books* – but who was the one name in the book completely unknown to English readers – was told to him when Jenkin introduced him to Taiso Masaki, who came to Edinburgh to recruit an occupant for a chair at Tokyo University – and found Alfred Ewing, later, as Sir James Alfred Ewing, principal of Edinburgh University and the most celebrated Scots engineer of his day. Anyone with a knowledge of RLS's private life would have known why Yoshida appealed. While in prison, awaiting execution, the Japanese hero took heart from a poem that can easily be read as an RLS motif:

> It is better to be crystal and be broken
> Than to remain perfect as a tile upon the housetop.

Thomas and Maggie Stevenson thoroughly approved of the relationship with the Fleemings. They were not an unknown quantity, like the cosmopolitan Sidney Colvin and Frances Sitwell in London, they were learned and respectable, and Fleeming, after all, was a professor of *engineering*. So the elder Stevensons did all they could to encourage their son in his amateur theatrical career and one eyewitness later recalled Maggie at the end of the *Twelfth Night* production 'radiant with maternal pride' with a 'look of adoration'. But at the dinners which Thomas and Maggie gave for the Jenkins and the cast, some of the tension between father and son was visible; 'father and son both talked, taking diametrically opposite points of view on all things under the sun . . . the father's face at certain moments was a study – an indescribable mixture of vexation, fatherly pride and admiration, and sheer bewilderment at the boy's brilliant flippancies, and the quick young thrusts of his wit and criticism.' One night the subject turned to the richness of the English language; Thomas and Louis debated with some heat the subject of neologisms and slang. Thomas upheld the orthodox doctrine of the 'well of English undefiled', which simply provoked Louis to rattle off with extraordinary ingenuity whole sentences composed of words of foreign origin which had been absorbed into English: from the East, from the classical languages, from the West Indies, and from the contemporary United States. By piling up the evidence he proved the absurdity of what Thomas was saying and thoroughly demolished him in front of an audience. One who was there recorded: 'I can see to this day his look of pale triumph. The father was silenced; but for a moment he had been almost tearfully in earnest. One could see it was not a matter of mere vocabulary with him.'[2]

Jenkin's position as mentor, however, was about to be seriously challenged. In autumn 1874 RLS had sent Mrs Sitwell a paper containing his 'desiderata:

1. Good Health
2. 2 to 3 hundred a year
3. *O du lieber Gott*, friends.

The first two desires were as far as ever from being granted, but he did get his third wish. On 13 February, in the Old Surgical Hospital, Edinburgh, Stevenson met the man who was to be the most turbulent male influence in his life. There were matters RLS could discuss with Bob, and others he could discuss with Baxter, hitherto his most important friends. But in William Ernest Henley it seemed, at last, that Louis might have found a comrade from whom nothing need be secret. It was Leslie Stephen, editor of the *Cornhill*, who was just beginning to appreciate the young RLS as 'one to note', who brought them together. Stephen came to Edinburgh to see both the 'young Heine' and a crippled colossus in the infirmary. He took RLS with him with the intention of introducing him to another aspiring literateur. Henley was larger than life even as an invalid. Stevenson noticed his understanding way with the two boys who shared his room as patients and his irrepressible brio: he 'sat up in bed with his hair and beard all tangled and talked as cheerfully as if he had been in a king's palace'.

What initially attracted RLS was the other man's stoicism and fortitude. Just a year older than Louis, Henley had been born into poverty. In addition, his early life had been full of hospitals: first Bart's in London, then the Royal Infirmary, Margate and finally Edinburgh, where he had been for nearly two years, working on the poetry that finally saw the light of day as *A Book of Verses*. Whether or not Louis had tuberculosis in his lung – we shall return to this later – Henley certainly had TB in his bones, had already had his left foot amputated and for a long time was in danger of losing the other one; it was the skill of Dr Joseph Lister, a pioneer of antisepsis, that saved him. Courage always impressed RLS and he at once took to the corpulent figure that lay on a bed playing tunes on a penny whistle. Friendship blossomed almost immediately. From February to April Louis made constant visits to the infirmary; as soon as Henley could sit up, he brought in an armchair, having exhausted himself by lugging it all the way from Heriot Row, unable to afford the cab fare. Soon Henley was well enough to accompany his friend on a carriage drive; in a letter to Fanny Sitwell RLS relates the sequel.

> I had a business to carry him down the long stair, and more of business to get him up again, but while he was in the carriage, it was splendid. It is now just the top of spring with us. The whole country is mad with green. To see the cherry-blossom bitten out upon the black firs, and the black firs bitten out of the blue sky, was a sight to set before a king. You can imagine what it was to a man who has been eighteen months in an hospital ward. The look on his face was wine to me.[3]

The next stage was for Louis to introduce his new friend to Baxter: Henley and Baxter were similar physical types, both heavily built, both pugnacious, both with a taste for alcohol, and the rapport was sealed there also; the three men now considered themselves Dumas's three musketeers come back to life. As the friendship deepened, RLS learned more. Henley came from a large family in Gloucestershire and his brothers also had artistic aspirations – Anthony became an artist and Edward an actor. Henley told Stevenson of the intense agony following the operations when Lister scraped his bone and went on to confide his own ambitions. Stevenson, a man of adamantine will himself, sensed a fellow spirit, and he was the least surprised when Henley later became a familiar figure on the London literary scene as editor, poet and critic. Hirsute, bearded, jovial, Falstaffian, loquacious, companionable, hard-drinking, a lover of pretty women, the extrovert Henley with his 'my dear lad' and 'my dear boy' seemed to dominate Stevenson. In some ways his relationship with RLS was almost paternal, which sounds absurd in light of the fact that he had been born in 1849 but, as a shrewd critic has noticed, 'at the precise moment Stevenson was fighting desperately to protect his romantic adolescence, Henley, healing but still uncured, was on the threshold of marriage, eager to assume the responsibilities of marriage.'

Stevenson adored this raffish roué, a welcome dash of cold water after his parents' priggish respectability; he would doubtless have embraced any life-loving colossus, regardless of his mental or creative stature, but Henley had the additional advantage that he was a genuine poet. Something of the flavour of Henley is conveyed in the essay on 'Talk and Talkers' where RLS portrays his new friend as 'Burly'.

> It has been said of him that his presence could be felt in a room you entered blindfold . . . There is something boisterous and piratic in Burly's manner of talk . . . He will roar you down, he will bury his face in his hands, he will undergo passions of revolt and agony; and meanwhile his attitude of mind is really both conciliatory and receptive . . . Throughout there has been the perfect sincerity, perfect intelligence, and a desire to hear, although not always to listen, and an unaffected eagerness to meet concessions.

Henley returned the compliment in his 'Apparition' which, especially in the following earlier draft, is one of the most perceptive psychological studies of RLS:

> Thin-legged, thin-chested, slight unspeakably
> Neat-footed, and weak-fingered: in his face –
> Lean, dark-boned, curved of beak and touched with race,
> Bold-lipped, rich-tinted, mutable as the sea,
> The brown eyes radiant with vivacity –
> There shines a brilliant and romantic grace,
> A spirit intense and rare, with trace on trace
> Of passion, impudence, and energy.
> Valiant in velvet, light in ragged luck,
> Most vain, most generous, sternly critical,
> Buffoon and lover, poet and sensualist:
> A deal of Ariel, just a streak of Puck,
> Much Antony, of Hamlet most of all,
> And something of the shorter catechist!

This poem caused some soul searching in Heriot Row when Henley sent it to Maggie with his compliments. Though pleased with the verses in general, Maggie predictably objected to 'most vain' and, especially, 'sensual'; Henley replied in a most obliging and conciliatory vein, but changed not a word.[4]

In some ways Stevenson's friendship with Henley was the most important of *all* his male relationships, but right from the start there were three different sources of latent tension that would later become manifest with disastrous consequences. Despite his excellence as a poet – and it must be conceded straight away that the best of the Stevenson verses could never match the best of 'Burly's' – Henley was a scattergun kind of craftsman where RLS was a precisian. This difference surfaced early in their differential attitude to writing letters, where Stevenson was meticulous and Henley dilatory and unmethodical; in letters to Fanny Sitwell RLS castigated both Colvin and

Henley for this fault, though in Colvin's case it had more to do with a general literary constipation. Failure to correspond regularly was a grave fault in the Stevenson moral canon, and he was even prepared to reprimand his 'madonna' for this, as a letter dated 28 December 1874 shows:

> I feel strangely as if all my letters were being suppressed. Colvin never answers, Appleton never answers and now you! ... Please communicate this to Colvin unless he has quarrelled with me by chance – he studiously will not answer my letters. I have been a bad correspondent, but he has been so much a *badder*! Indeed, if you don't think me getting insane, I think the world in a conspiracy against me; for devil a one will write to me except yourself. Even Bob sends me scraps only fit to light a pipe with.

Since Henley took poetry most seriously of the forms of literature, RLS directed his complaints on this point to 'Burly' in verse:

> All men are rot but there are two
> Sidney, obliviously 'Slade' and you –
> Who from that rabble stand confest,
> Ten million times rottenest.
>
> When I was sick, and safe in gaol,
> I thought my friends would never fail.
> One wrote me nothing; t'other bard
> Sent me an insolent post card.

The second apple of discord was that RLS had been born the son of a rich engineer, Henley the son of a poor bookseller. RLS was Henley's Maecenas; he introduced him to Baxter, Bob, Simpson and Ferrier and later to Colvin and Fanny Sitwell; through Louis's Edinburgh contacts Henley achieved the editorship of the *Scots Observer*. Then there was money. Stevenson was generous in the funds he siphoned off to Henley, both then and later, but he thought his subventions bought him loyalty and a willingness to pull critical punches; Henley thought that money was something to concern 'mere bankers', that artists should share and share alike, and that if RLS did not give in the right spirit, that was a problem for him and not the recipient. As with the beggars on the streets of Edinburgh, distributing largesse gave Stevenson a sense of philanthropic righteousness but he was not always sensitive to the pride and prickliness of those taking the handouts. Certainly Henley would not have liked the tone of the last sentence of his friend's letter to Fanny Sitwell on 13 February, when he says: 'I shall try to be of use to him.' A close student of Henley has observed: 'the relationship would never have developed had Henley known then of this patronising facet of his visitor's character.'[5]

The third tension was the most dangerous of all, for Henley, alone of RLS's male comrades, intuited and locked into the feminine side of

Stevenson. Henley described Louis as having 'feminine force' and Louis replied with 'I love you, Henley'. Both men were robustly heterosexual and it is not suggested that the attraction between them was homosexual in any ordinary sense; Furnas is quite right on this point in insisting that to take this as direct evidence of sexual chemistry is to misunderstand Victorian culture. But there are aspects of the relationship he has ignored or glossed over. The idea of RLS as a mere 'man's man' on the basis of his rugged adventure stories dies hard, but in fact there was a highly developed feminine side to Stevenson's sensibility. This emerges clearly in a letter to Fanny Sitwell in February 1875 – incredibly, in the very letter in which he describes the introduction to Henley: 'Oh I have such a longing for children of my own; and yet I do not think I could bear it if I had one. I fancy I must feel more like a woman than a man about that.'

Once again we see that RLS had drawn up more of the contents of the unconscious into the conscious than most men can. His self-knowledge is always striking and nowhere more than in his appreciation of the extent of 'anima', to use the Jungian term, in his make-up. In the portrait of him later done by John White Alexander he recognised 'a mixture of Aztec idol, a lion, an Indian rajah, and a woman'. In *Prince Otto*, RLS conceded that he gave to Princess Seraphina 'a trait taken from myself'. It was this aspect of him that Henley immediately sensed. In 'Apparition' the sections referring to

> trace on trace
> Of passion, impudence and energy
> . . .
> a streak of Puck
>
> Much Antony . . .

originally read as follows:

> with a subtle trace
> Of feminine force . . . a streak of Puck
> More Cleopatra, of Hamlet most of all

By his very suppression Henley confirms the 'feminine' appeal Stevenson exercised; 'Cleopatra' was changed to 'Antony' after Louis's marriage to Fanny Osbourne and he became Antony to someone else's Cleopatra.

This 'homoerotic' aspect of Stevenson has been increasingly noticed. Andrew Lang said that RLS had some uncanny power to make you jealous of all his other male friends and went on: 'Mr Stevenson possessed, more than any man I ever met, the power of making other men fall in love with him.' The American painter Will Low conceded this: 'Fascination and charm are not qualities which Anglo-Saxon youths are prone to acknowledge, in manly avoidance of their supposedly feminising effect, but it was undoubtedly this attractive power which RLS held so strongly through life.' Stevenson had a great appeal both for self-confessed homosexuals (like John Addington Symonds) and repressed ones (like Henry James and Edmund Gosse). Even Jenni Calder, usually hostile to psychoanalytical interpretations, concedes that the later rivalry between Fanny Osbourne and Henley may have contained an unconscious sexual element and writes: 'Henley's jealousy rivalled Fanny's ... like many others, Henley loved Louis... (Fanny) believed Louis's love for Colvin to equal his love for her. Colvin himself was not above jealousy.'[6]

In his life RLS was able to evoke strong responses – which it seems prissy not to recognise as sexual – in people of both sexes. It was this quality, transmuted by the alchemy of the creative process, that enabled him to write convincingly about women. If there are no entirely satisfactory heroines in the Stevenson *oeuvre*, this is not because he was unable to 'do women' but because he refused to do so if he could not portray them sexuality and all, as D.H.Lawrence was later to do; in the 1880s and 1890s Mrs Grundy would not permit this freedom unless the artist was prepared to risk banishment to 'art house' status, with the loss of income this entailed.

Problems of sexuality were again to the fore when Louis travelled to Paris in April to meet Bob. The year before, Bob had first ventured into the forests of Fontainebleau in pursuit of the artist's colonies at Barbizon, Grez and Marlotte. Bob was as fanatical a lover of women as Louis; his friend Will Low, the painter, noticed that he could never resist flirting with them even if he had no amorous intentions towards them. Bob's 1874 letters constantly express a desire to solve his sexual problems: 'Would like a nice woman to live with', and, from Barbizon: 'Everyone keeps a woman now. I begin to see the intrusion of Latin Quarter life.' At this stage Bob was inclined to refer to affairs with grisettes and '*hoc genus omne*' as tempting but meaningless – revealing that he, like Louis, was deeply inhibited by his Calvinistic upbringing, but by early 1875 he had changed his mind on the 'significance' of such liaisons and started to live with a model in Paris. She occurs in the correspondence with Louis as 'my Paris girl'; Bob could not resist teasing Louis with descriptions of her charms – 'the most sensual party I ever met'. Bob told Louis he felt guilty that she was dependable and considerate while he was a poverty-stricken artist who could offer her nothing in return; though not especially attractive as Bob described her, in point of sensuality she was 'a burning fiery furnace really'.[7]

RLS's first stop in Paris was Bob's studio on the Boulevard St Michel, from where he sortied to sample the delights of the artists' colonies at Montparnasse and the exquisite elegance of Lavenue's restaurant. Here he met Will Low, the American painter, who remembered the impact of Paris on RLS, and particularly that of the bohemian milieu, 'a situation strange to him, for in his short life he had known only the disquieting anxiety with which his most simple and casual action was interpreted that denotes misunderstanding; the family anxiety of the hen that has given birth to a duckling of Hans Christian Andersen, that was destined to become a swan'.[8]

Then Bob and Will took him down to Barbizon, a place that already had a niche in the history of art by virtue of its being the milieu of Corot and Millet. By 1875 there was no single commanding figure at Barbizon; at Grez there was Palizzi, at Cernay, Pelouse and at Marlotte, Olivier de Peune, and although Stevenson visited all these places in turn, it was Barbizon he particularly liked, precisely because there was no 'king'. What was important about Barbizon for RLS was that it was a *community* of artists rather than a court and could thus function both positively to provide organic solidarity and negatively as a bulwark against bourgeois philistinism; there was no such idyllic community available for British artists or writers, partly, RLS thought, because the roughness, the impatience, the selfishness and the more ardent friendships of the British would speedily dismember such a commonwealth. He was able to relate the experiment to what he had read about the Brook Farm experiment of a writers' colony in the U.S.A. and to the thoughts of Thoreau. Yet naïveté was never one of Stevenson's faults. He saw clearly the dangers of artists' colonies: that they became fashionable, that tourists moved in and forced prices up, and that eventually the original utopia became too expensive for the artists themselves – as had already happened at Trouville and St Raphael.

In Barbizon RLS and Bob stayed at Siron's inn. Here all artists entered into a communal spirit and were welcomed as comrades, no matter how personally unprepossessing they were. Room rent was five francs a day, and thereafter the landlord practised a form of primitive communism: he simply totted up his expenditure on meals and divided it by the number of guests, regardless of what they had eaten; the result was that the easygoing paid more and the tight-fisted less. Moreover, a bill was never presented unless one asked for it and it was possible to abscond without paying. In one of his many disquisitions at this time on the difference between the French and Anglo-Saxon character, RLS displayed his love of paradox: 'The Anglo-Saxon is essentially dishonest; the French is devoid by nature of the principle that we call "Fair Play". The Frenchman marvelled at the scruples of his guest, and when that defender of innocence retired over-seas and left his bills unpaid, he marvelled once again; the good and evil were, in his eyes, part and parcel of the same eccentricity; a shrug expressed his judgment upon both.' However, one Anglo-Saxon innovation the French could not shrug off so easily was the advent of English and American girl art-students, as Barbizon and environs were progressively abandoned to 'the fair invader': 'his French respectability, quite as precise as ours, though covering different provinces of life, recoiled aghast before the innovation.'

Stevenson loved to stroll alone in the vast forests of Fontainebleau,
so densely wooded that RLS swore he never heard a bird sing there.
Fontainebleau was for him an Arcadia – his Forest of Arden, perhaps,
when we remember his passion for *As You Like It*. It was here that he did
his reading for his biographical essays on Villon and Charles d'Orléans, and
discovered Théodore de Banville's modernisations of medieval verse forms;
Banville was peculiarly likely to appeal to RLS as he contained elements of
Musset, Verlaine and Heine, and to the interminable discussions with Bob
and Will Low about Balzac and Villon there was now added the subject of
Banville.

The primitive aspect of Barbizon struck a particular chord with RLS
– foreshadowing his later quest for the primitive in the Pacific – and he
explained why he preferred it to Grez (beloved of Sisley and, later, of
Delius) which, with its riverside setting out of the forest, its mill, bridge,
castle and ancient church, was the village particularly favoured by Parisian
artists. 'There is "something to do" at Grez. Perhaps, for that reason, I can
recall no such enduring ardours, no such glories of exhilaration, as among
the solemn groves and uneventful hours of Barbizon. This "something to
do" is a great enemy of joy; it is a way out of it; you wreak your high spirits
on some cut-and-dry employment, and behold them gone!'[9]

Louis returned to Paris in a state of euphoria which he masked with
an oblique letter to his mother: 'I am now a pauper once more. I have had
such a nice time and am very well, but more unintelligent than ever I was
before.' In fact he was already deeply intoxicated with France, and this visit
in 1875 was the beginning of a long love affair with the country. Long after
RLS's death, his stepson Lloyd Osbourne summed up as follows: 'France
had a profound influence on Stevenson; mentally he was half a Frenchman;
in taste, habits and prepossessions he was almost totally French. Not only
did he speak French admirably and read it like his mother-tongue, but he
loved both country and people, and was more really at home in France than
anywhere else.'

Yet Stevenson was no blinkered and doctrinaire Francophile. Although
he found the French fairly honest and free from hypocrisy – in contrast to
the canting, humbugging English, 'dishonest to the root', – he thought them
incapable of friendship and 'rather indecent to women', whereas the English
were praiseworthy on both these scores. Although no uncritical admirer of
French culture, he did relish their food and, especially, their wine, where
he became a connoisseur to match the most pedantic and discriminating
Gaul. Unlike the French, however, he most emphatically did not believe
that everything gastronomic that was worthwhile was contained in this one
country.

His command of the language was indeed impressive, but here he
emulated the methods of Richard Burton and picked up the demotic

French of the bar, the tavern and the marketplace; his written French is far from perfect. It was, however, exactly the sort of idiomatic tongue that the average Gascon, Norman or Savoyard would use, and it was this that so often led Frenchmen to identify him as one of their own. Once in Nice, dressed in typically tatterdemalion fashion, he stopped at a rough wayside inn and overheard two unsavoury characters express their detestation of Englishmen and their determination to rob the first one they encountered. They paused in the midst of their diatribe to take the measure of the newcomer, heard him order his drink, then relapsed into their fulminations and schemings, confident that the interloper was a local peasant. On another occasion, when the odds were more even, Stevenson took more decisive action. In a café he heard a local abusing perfidious Albion and all its works and was so stung that he sprang up and slapped him in the face. '*Mais vous m'avez frappé!*' exclaimed the astonished Frenchman. "*A ce qu'il paraît,*" replied Stevenson. The man was so astonished at finding this scarecrow to be a Briton in Gallic clothing that he did not retaliate.

Most striking of all aspects of RLS's francomania was his deep knowledge of the nation's literature. His love of Dumas has already been mentioned; he wrote a memorable study of Victor Hugo in *Men and Books*; and his *oeuvre* is studded with references to Balzac, Flaubert, Baudelaire, Musset, Daudet and other great names. In some ways his most intriguing literary engagement was that with his near-contemporary Zola. RLS detested the canons of naturalism adumbrated by Zola in *Le Roman Expérimental* and his essays on realism are designed to combat his 'pernicious' doctrines; but Zola, great genius that he was, often burst the theoretical straitjacket that he had put on himself, and when he did so, he found no more fervent admirer than Stevenson. On the subject of Zola's novel, *L'Oeuvre*, where the artist Claude is a transmogrified Cézanne – and which therefore had particular resonance for Bob – Louis wrote to Henley: 'The first four or five chapters are like being young again in Paris; they woke me like a trumpet. Does Bob remember the martyrdom of St Stephen with petits-pains? The man who insured his old mistress? The very model of him is here.' Stevenson also found Zola's beginnings better than his endings – a criticism he applied to the great novel of the Franco-Prussian war, *La Débâcle*; ironically, it was to be the thing most remarked on about his own work. Most of all, RLS disliked the so-called 'novels of the seamy side' like *L'Assommoir* and *La Bête Humaine*; here he and Henry James decisively parted company for though they were at one in detesting Hardy's *Tess*, generally Louis was prepared to defend Hardy against the fastidious snobbery of 'the master' ('the good little Thomas Hardy'), while James accepted Zola as a towering genius.[10]

Above all, the immediate influence of France was to convince RLS that he should no longer dissemble but openly embrace the life of a

Bohemian; he therefore made up his mind to tell his parents on his return from Paris that he would not practise law once he qualified as an advocate. His new-found confidence also found expression in some recidivism in his amour with Fanny Sitwell, for he appears, while passing through London on his way home, to have made another effort to convert the madonna/child relationship into a physical man/woman one. Evidently this overture was rebuffed, for we find him writing from Edinburgh:

> You need not be afraid, madonna. My dear, I will be as much to you as I can. I do not deny that I am glad of it. There is no longer anything that I am afraid to think of in my mind. But that is all; I will still be your son, dear, if you will still be my mother, or rather whether you will or not; it is very right. I will be as good as I can for your sake; remember that when I was in London I was just in the swing. I have settled down now, and feel very quiet and glad, glad of the past, and, quiet and somewhat careless of the future. Only as I say, I do not think I will be bad at all; I do not *feel* bad, not bad at all, dear; and I know I must be good for the love of you and my oath's sake.

The self-confidence of this made Fanny Sitwell wonder if she had over-played her hand; perhaps he had, after all, found another woman in France, and this was the real reason for the change she detected in him. She wrote to sound out the situation, only to be reassured that his feelings towards her had not changed a whit:

> Only I am changed to myself; all my *sham* goodness, I mean the orderliness, the citizenliness, and sort of respectability, that I had laid on, is going away and away down through wind into everlasting space. I cannot play thee games; I am made for the other thing; as I grow well, I fall back into it day by day ... No, dear, I have kept nothing from you. You know all my heart, I am sure. I wonder what could have made you think otherwise. It must have been my depression coming suddenly after so much good spirits. Be brave, my darling mother, or I shall not know what to do ... If there is any change, I think I love you better than ever. That is all. It is not at all a disquieting change, is it? You may be glad of it, dear. It is not love that will ever trouble you, for it is so clear: but it will endure all your life; and there will come days when I shall be able to help you better. They must come, darling; where there is so much love, there should be a way to help. O believe me, will you? thoroughly. I am not deceiving you or myself. I am keeping nothing back. You are the living soul of my body, dear mother, and I wish you not to be disquieted for me. I feel as if I was a little incoherent. But it's all right at bottom, right and sound and true.

Though he continued to have illusions of seeing her in the street and fantasised about turning the corner and bumping into her by chance, he tried to put thoughts of her to the back of his mind while he studied for the final examination as an advocate. He found cramming for this final hurdle stressful, not because of the intellectual difficulty the examination posed, but because it was tiresome to have to interrupt his literary labours for matters so picayune. However, on 14 July 1875 he took and passed the written papers and was then admitted as an advocate at the Scottish bar. It was a very cold day and Alexander Stuart, a fellow postulant, remembered that RLS looked the picture of misery. Stuart told him he looked like a drunken Irishman going to a funeral, to which Stevenson replied: 'I wish I were that Irishman, *coming from* that funeral.' When he heard he had passed out as a barrister, Stevenson drove around Edinburgh with his parents in an open barouche, waving his hat and shouting at bystanders. To Fanny Sitwell he wrote: 'Madonna. Passed. Ever Yours, RLS' – the signature written through a swirl of lines like isobars.

This success, earned at the urging of his parents, was a hollow one. It had cost £2,000 for him to acquire the title of 'Advocate at the Scottish Bar', and in his short and undistinguished legal career he earned just four guineas – and had his title disbelieved by a French policeman into the bargain. Moreover, Louis himself thoroughly despised the so-called 'achievement'. Speaking of Villon in *Familiar Studies*, he says: 'He passed his degrees, it is true; but some of us who have been to modern universities will make their own reflections on the value of the test.' A further disappointment was that Thomas Stevenson went back on his earlier commitment to give his son £1,000 when he had qualified as a lawyer, and now merely promised to review the situation when Louis had matured.[11]

However, it seems clear that Maggie slipped him some money as an unofficial 'reward' and with this unwonted bounty Stevenson first of all treated himself to another trip to Paris and the forests of Fontainebleau. Yet he resented the way the gift bound him closer to his parents and wrote despondently to Fanny Sitwell in the form of a paradox: 'I do so hunger and thirst after money (i.e. happiness); *and yet to get that, I must give up my hope of making myself strong and well (i.e. happiness).*' Yet once he was with Bob again, his spirits lifted. Once again he thrilled to the raptures of Barbizon, to which village he and Bob walked home one night in a thunderstorm from Grez, 23 miles away, 'which is not bad for the Advocate.'

The autumn and winter of 1875 passed uneventfully though there was continuing tension with Louis's parents, who only grudgingly, if at all, came to terms with the fact that their only son was to be a despised scribbler. RLS told Fanny Sitwell that the passing of his twenty-fifth birthday made him realise how little he had achieved, and that time was slipping away while he churned out obscure essays and reviews. Depressed and despondent, he escaped from Heriot Row as much as he could and on at least two occasions left his father's house at night after a row and sought refuge with Henley. He wrote to Fanny Sitwell: 'I feel I desire to go out of the house, and begin life anew in the cool, blue night; never to come back here; never, never.' A letter to his cousin Katharine (who married the Cambridge atheist Sydney de Mattos but soon got a judicial separation from him) in January 1876 is full of the death wish last fully evident in 1873. And in the same month he wrote to Fanny Sitwell: 'I am so dreadfully tired and stupid that I can say nothing. I was down at Leith in the afternoon. God bless me, what horrid women I saw. I was sick at heart with the looks of them. And the children, filthy and ragged! And the smells! And the fat, black mud! My soul was full of disgust ere I got back.'

In January 1876 he went on a walking tour in Carrick and Galloway, all the way from Ayr to Wigtown; this was the occasion when he passed through the village of Ballantrae and noted its name. Then he spent a month in London, refreshing himself intellectually in the company of Colvin, Lang and the man he had first met on his 1870 Hebridean trip, Edmund Gosse, now reintroduced by Colvin in the Savile Club. He did not contact Fanny Sitwell, possibly not trusting himself not to make yet another impassioned overture which would be rebuffed, but he later confessed to her that he hung around the areas she was known to frequent on her way to and from work – Queen's Square, Southampton Row and Casino Place – half hoping he would bump into her, half in trepidation about the same thing. He did bump into Lang one day in Bond Street, and was not thanked for the meeting. Stevenson was wearing a black shirt, red tie, black brigand cloak and velvet smoking cap. Appalled by this demonstration of eccentricity, Lang exclaimed: 'No, no, go away, Louis, go away! My character will stand a great deal, but it won't stand being seen talking to a "thing" like you in Bond Street!' RLS as eccentric became a London legend: two years later Lang and Gosse tried to persuade Louis to buy a new hat and got him as far as the shop; they were just asking the price when RLS bolted, unable to bear the thought of parting with the shapeless object he was wearing.

Gosse's initial impressions of RLS were not favourable, but he recalled an occasion when circumstances inculcated some worldly wisdom into the outré Scot. RLS was lecturing Gosse on the necessity of giving to beggars, while Gosse demurred. In Audley Street Stevenson saw a beggar and gave him sixpence. The man pocketed the coin, did not bother to thank his benefactor, glared at Gosse and cried loudly: 'And what is the other little gentleman going to give me?' Louis stormed off angrily. 'In future,' he said, 'I shall be the other little gentleman.' Gradually Gosse came to see something of his companion's talents: 'he was simply bubbling with quips and jests; his inherent earnestness or passion about abstract things was incessantly relieved by jocosity; and when he had built one of his intellectual castles in the sand, a wave of humour was certain to sweep in and destroy it.'

However, all the levity concealed continuing depression. In the late spring he wrote to Fanny Sitwell: 'I don't know where and how I have been living this while back ... but I have lost my hold of life; and so much the better perhaps; only as I did live earnestly for a while, the change is not easy.' In July 1876 he joined the Jenkins on their summer holiday near Loch Carron in the Highlands before proceeding to Barbizon with Bob, who had been living the artist's life in Chelsea. Louis had merely dreamed of colliding accidentally with Mrs Sitwell, but Bob had actually met the dreaded Thomas Stevenson – the man who had wished never to set eyes on him again – in a London street and the encounter had passed off surprisingly well.[12]

All through his early and middle twenties RLS had been making slow and painful progress up the literary ladder. Before the 1880s, Leslie Stephen (the editor of the *Cornhill*) was the only man in Britain of editorial status to be certain of Louis's genius, and this was all the more praiseworthy in Stephen as he profoundly disliked Stevenson at a personal level; RLS bound most men and women to him with silken cords but if ever his charm failed, it tended to fail in a catastrophic fashion. So it was with Stephen, and so it was to be with a handful of others; it is one of the mysteries of human behaviour that those who are saluted as emperors by the many can be so virulently detested as naked impostors by the few.

Admittedly, it is hard to see in Stevenson's early journeyman efforts much more than a promising minor talent; he made very little money and did not give the impression that he had anything startlingly original to say. In 1873 Colvin put his new young discovery in touch with Macmillans, who suggested that RLS write about Savonarola. Stevenson rejected the suggestion and instead began working hard on an essay on Walt Whitman; delayed when he lost his notes during the cruise on the *Heron* with Simpson in July-August 1874, this latter provided one of the best essays in *Familiar Studies*. In the Whitman essay RLS brings out the 'feminine' aspects of the great American poet: 'If verbal logic were sufficient, life would be as plain sailing as a piece of Euclid . . . Words are for communication, not for judgment . . . the majority of women, not learned in these scholastic refinements, live all-of-a-piece and unconsciously, as a tree grows, without caring to put a name upon their acts or motives.' On the 'experiment' of getting people to guess the sex of the author of Whitman's 'Civil War Memoranda' he says: 'More than one woman, on whom I tried the experiment, immediately claimed the writer for a fellow-woman.'

In the winter of 1873–74 RLS planned a play about Herostratus but, Colvin claims, his penchant for levity got the better of him and he spent much of the time devising a bilingual parody of hotel advertising cards. His next project was to write essays on great Scotsmen but his (mainly adverse) material on Scott was subsumed in the essay on Victor Hugo that eventually appeared in *Familiar Studies*. In his essay on Knox he tried to steer a middle course between him and Mary, Queen of Scots, but poked fun at Knox's lecherous attitudes to women, which he bore concurrently with his denunciation of the sex; Stevenson metaphorically shook his head in amazement at the masochism of the devout ladies who left their husbands to follow Knox's banner even as he denounced them as agents of the devil. The essay on Burns became notorious, for RLS dared to criticise this national icon and point out that the idol had feet of clay. Stevenson bitterly attacked Burns for his attitude to women and his philandering – and many have since read his philippic as a projection of his own guilt in sexual matters – and alleged that Burns's debt to the far greater poet Robert Fergusson was largely unacknowledged. Relishing the chance to settle many old scores – with his father, Calvinism, the 'unco' guid' and the whole Scottish tradition of bogus gentility – RLS pointed out, first, that no one was ever allowed to criticise Burns's promiscuity and his disastrous marriage; secondly, that in Scotland drunkenness was almost respectable when compared with 'irregularity between the sexes'; and thirdly – in a passage that could be cited by many Stevenson biographers in self-defence – that to point out the disastrous consequences of someone's marriage is not necessarily an attack on the institution of marriage itself.

But it was in the essay on Victor Hugo that RLS set down his most striking insights – on radicalism, the nature of the historical novel, nautical lore and much else. The genesis of this piece was Colvin's suggestion that his protégé should write something suitable for the *Cornhill Magazine*; its editor Leslie Stephen snapped 'Hugo' up at once. RLS was paid sixteen guineas but, more importantly, as he later told his biographer Graham Balfour, it 'marked, in his own judgment, the beginning of his command of style . . . in this essay he had first found himself able to say several things in the way in which he felt they should be said.'[13]

The account of the journey to Menton in December 1873 had meanwhile appeared as 'Ordered South' in *Macmillan's Magazine* – Stevenson received a fee of £5 – and a similar sum was earned for a review of Lytton's *Fables in Song* in the *Fortnightly Review*. Other incidental journalism included a piece on the mixed adult college where Mrs Sitwell worked – and which he wrote to please her – and some minor reviewing. For a very brief period – or perhaps this was a ploy to keep his parents quiet – he appears to have toyed with a career in ecclesiastical politics, for in late 1874 he wrote 'An Appeal to the Clergy of the Church of Scotland', but for much of 1874 he was trying his hand at fiction, and this produced a notable short story 'The House of Eld', which is deeply instructive on the murderous unconscious impulses that existed at this time towards his parents.

Jack, the hero, lives in a land where all children are shackled by the right ankle at birth. His parents tell him that all unfettered people are subhuman, but Jack nonetheless aspires to their condition. He learns that the shackling is ordered by a wizard who lives in the middle of a forest; he is virtually undetectable for, like Proteus, he can assume any other shape at will, but he betrays his identity when agitated by gobbling like a turkey. Jack tracks down the wizard who changes successively into Jack's uncle the catechist, his father and his mother. Only when Jack has dispatched all three manifestations does the wizard finally die. Jack returns to his country to find that the fetters have indeed gone from their right ankles but they are now shackled on the left. On entering his house, he finds his real father, mother and uncle dead of the wounds he dealt the wizard. Clearly Stevenson realised that to destroy his parents through an assault on their beliefs would merely leave him in another limbo, and the concluding moral rhyme is significant:

> Old is the tree and the fruit good,
> Very old and thick the wood.
> Woodman, is your courage stout?
> Beware! the root is wrapped about
> Your mother's heart, your father's bones;
> And like the mandrake comes with groans

That summer RLS also wrote some notes for a novel to be called *The Sea Board of Bohemia*, and there were even plans for a volume of short stories, but as yet Stevenson had not mastered the craft of fiction. As he told Bob in 1875: 'I have been working like Hell at stories and have, up to the present, failed. I have never hitherto given enough attention to the buggers speaking – my dialogue is as weak as soda water.' Nevertheless, he managed to complete 'When the Devil was Well' in the first two months of 1875.

1875 saw him wrestling with a variety of forms. There was the long experiment with prose-poems that summer, the first tentative collaboration on plays with Henley, the biographical sketch of Charles of Orléans, reviews of Poe, Jules Verne and Browning, and the fruit of his trips to Barbizon in the form of 'Forest Notes' and 'Fontainebleau', which were rejected for the *Cornhill* by Leslie Stephen who temporarily incurred Stevenson's extreme displeasure. He had not yet learned that Stephen admired his work without feeling any *personal* commitment, though the editor did make amends to RLS by trying to set up an interview with Carlyle; the great man, however, declined to oblige. In 1876 Stephen stepped up the rate of contribution from Stevenson by taking both his essay on the walking tour through Carrick and Galloway and the prophetic and revealing essay on marriage, 'Virginibus Puerisque'.[14]

After a dull first eight months in 1876 Stevenson decided to improve his mental health *and* sharpen up his talents as a travel writer by travelling by canoe through the river and canal system of north-eastern France. Walter Simpson, who had taken Stevenson yachting in the summer of 1874 and taught him canoeing in a two-seater on the Clyde, proposed to him that they make their way by water from Antwerp to Grez-sur-Loing and thence via the Loing, Loire, Saône and Rhône to the Mediterranean. Of all his friends, Simpson had, on paper, the least compatible temperament for a Stevenson travelling companion. As 'Athelred' in 'Talk and Talkers' he is portrayed as simple, rather dim, slow to make up his mind, all in all a bit of a bore. When they hiked together they were like hare and tortoise: RLS strode ahead at a great pace but soon tired, while the slow and ponderous Simpson slowly but surely made his superior stamina tell. Yet in some curious way Stevenson derived strength from his four-square stability; the mercurial Bob was fine for a quick 'sprint' at Barbizon, but for sustained plodding the saturnine Simpson was a better bet.

Heavy rains and flooding dogged them every inch of the trip. From Antwerp they set off up the Scheldt to Boom, then through Willebroek, Villevorde and Laeken. Beyond Brussels, where there were fifty-five locks between the Belgian capital and Charleroi, they crossed the French border by train. Already RLS was displaying the eye for women that would attract the priggish attention of critics when the book of his travels, *An Inland Voyage*, appeared. 'The sex likes to pick up knowledge and yet preserve its superiority . . . it is only by unintermittent snubbing that the pretty ones can keep us in our place . . . for my part I am body and soul with the women.'

They proceeded through Mabeuge and Hautmont, then on to the Sambre at Quartes to a stopover at Pont-sur-Sambre, where they experienced great difficulty finding anywhere to sleep because of the locals' suspicion that they were pedlars. After being asked half a dozen times whether they fitted this description, a weary Stevenson remarked: 'We began to think that we might be pedlars after all. I never knew a population with so narrow a range of conjecture as the innkeepers of Pont-sur-Sambre.' Stevenson got his own back on the suspicious innkeepers by ordering a dinner way beyond what the other guests could afford.

At Landrecies, after an unpleasant encounter with an old man whose sheer cynical malice took Stevenson's breath away, the two travellers had their one gratifying experience of the trip when the local judge invited the 'advocates' to dinner and laid on exquisite foods and wines. A drunken RLS discoursed on the Scots law of illegitimacy, of which he knew nothing, but spiced the conversation with personal innuendo, at which the judge seemed vaguely pleased. 'How strange,' mused Louis, 'that we should all, in our unguarded moments, rather like to be thought a bit of a rogue with women.'

They made their way down the Sambre and Oise canal, through Etreux, Tupigny, Vadencourt and Origny, where the motif of sex was again upper-most: 'the young ladies, the graces of Origny . . . picked up their skirts as if they were sure they had good ankles.' This may be partly the inspiration for the incident in his poem 'Storm':

> See – a girl passes
> Tripping gingerly over the pools,
> And under her lifted dress
> I catch the gleam of a comely stockinged leg.

Proceeding down the Oise to Moy, RLS purred contentedly: 'After a good woman, a good book and tobacco, there's nothing so agreeable on earth as a river.' He soon had all such thoughts of pastoral idylls knocked out of him, for at La Fère the landlady at the principal inn refused the travellers a bed; when RLS asked if they might eat there, the woman went purple with anger and threw them out. Such treatment always made Stevenson explode with rage and on this occasion he confessed that he would have set the temple of Diana on fire if it had been handy. They finally found shelter in a cheap lodging house whose landlord used to work as a house painter in Paris and loved going to the museums; this, Stevenson thought, sufficiently refuted the 'patronising' picture of the wedding party on the loose in the Louvre in Zola's *L'Assommoir*.

Beyond La Fère they descended the 'golden valley' of the Oise to Chauny and Noyon, where Stevenson visited the cathedral and found the clergy as deficient in reverence as they had been in Italy in 1864. They paddled on to the confluence of the Oise and the Aisne and thence to Compiègne, which they reached on 9 September. They found the streets of Louis Napoléon's favourite town thronged with military and reservists, for 1875–76 were the years of the threatened *revanche*, when it seemed likely that France would attempt to reverse the verdict of the Franco-Prussian war with Bismarck. Louis loved Compiègne with its ornate town hall and statue of Louis XII, and the spell of the river was broken additionally by the great packet of letters that awaited them at the post office. Despondently RLS penned a few lines to his mother: 'I do not know that I would have stuck to it as I have done, if it had not been for professional purposes: for an easy book may be written and sold.'

Gritting their teeth, he and Simpson continued along the upper Oise to L'Isle Adam and thence to Pont Sainte-Maxenée. In these places Stevenson always went into the churches, for he had discovered in France that there was always something worth seeing in them, even if it was only the fascinating sight of old women telling their beads in a state of religious ecstasy. The travellers pressed on through Creil to Précy and 'the worst inn in France' where they met a party of circus clowns and acrobats. By now both of them had had enough. 'To the civilised man, there must come, sooner or later, a desire for civilisation. I was weary of dipping the paddle. I was weary of living on the skirts of life; I wished to be in the thick of it once more; I wished to get to work. I wished to meet people who understood my own speech, and could meet with me on equal terms, as a man and no longer as a curiosity.'

A letter at Pontoise decided them; there and then they drew their paddles out of the Oise for the last time. But it was not quite the end of their adventures. They returned up the Loing valley through Château Renard to Chatillon-sur-Loing, amused by the peasants' tall stories of hair-breadth escapes from marauding *uhlans* in 1870. At Chatillon, they had two brushes with the notorious French officialdom, one humorous, the other less so. First the village postman mistook the portraits in Louis's knapsack for pornography and would not be deflected from his interest in buying them. Then Stevenson, temporarily separated from Simpson, was stopped by a gendarme and found not to have any papers; in all his rovings through the artists' colonies and the *quartiers* of Paris he had still not grasped the fundamental law of French life, that all persons, even beggars, must possess *papiers*, and that in 1876 all those not so equipped were under suspicion of being German spies. Hauled before the commissary, Stevenson's Anglo-Saxon love of liberty collided with the Gallic passion for order; tempers became heated, voices raised, and the upshot of the questioning of the young Heine by a semi-literate was arrest. Shortly afterwards, the lordly Simpson strolled and yawned his way into the *préfecture*; the commissary realised his mistake, and, with that exaggerated deference of all minor autocrats for the aristocracy, apologised humbly before releasing the 'vagabond'. The incident left a nasty taste; Simpson and RLS determined to shake the dust of Chatillon from their feet; they caught the train to Paris forthwith.

What had they achieved? RLS had 'copy' for his first book, and Simpson generously made over his own diary too. Stevenson had nearly drowned in the Oise while it was flooding. Otherwise very little had been accomplished and it is a tribute to Stevenson's literary skill that he was able to make an interesting book out of next to nothing. Nineteenth-century critics were upset by the amount of barely concealed sex in it; their twentieth-century counterparts have been far more dismayed by the Christmas-cracker homilies and the facile Panglossian reassurances to the dimmer kind of Victorian reader. It is significant that Thomas Stevenson admired the benevolent fantasy in this book ('I am sure I would rather be a bargee than occupy any position under heaven that required attendance at an office') but hated the hard-hitting naturalism of Stevenson's account of his American journey three years later. But the criticism of 'facile romanticism' can be overdone; one man's great adventure is another's aching yawn. 'To know what you prefer instead of humbly saying "Amen" to what the world tells you you ought to prefer, is to have kept your soul alive' – that sounds like a paean to self-respect. 'There is some life in humanity yet; and youth will now and again find a brave word in dispraise of riches, and throw up a situation to go strolling with a knapsack' – this could have been adopted as a maxim by the flower-power generation of the 1960s. Some of RLS's asides show an almost Freudian appreciation of journey as a metaphor for self-realisation: 'There is no coming back ... on the impetuous stream of life. And we must all set our pocket-watches by the clock of fate. There is a headlong, forthright tide, that bears away man with his fancies like a straw, and runs fast in time and space.' Yet generally the negative critics have had their way. Richard Aldington produced one of his best waspish flights when describing this journey.

> What in fact did they do? They went by dull canals and flooded rivers much of the time in rainy weather, seeing little but the towing paths or the banks; they made a long 'portage' by train from Brussels to Maubeuge; until they reached Compiègne they hardly saw a place worth recording; in their rain-soaked clothes carrying rubber knapsacks they were mistaken for pedlars and once rudely refused by a small hotel-keeper; and Stevenson nearly drowned himself.[15]

RLS's own conclusion was of the gnomic, moralising kind that so often drew the critical fire of those irked by the 'Shorter Catechist': 'You may paddle all day long; but it is when you come back at nightfall and look in at the familiar room, that you find Love or Death awaiting you beside the stove; and the most beautiful adventures are not those we go to seek.' This was prescient, for when he proceeded to Grez from Paris at the end of this journey he ran into unexpected adventure. Whether it was beautiful will have to be determined later.

5

Fanny Osbourne

Just before he set off with Simpson on the *Arethusa*, Stevenson had a casual meeting at Grez that changed his life, and at the conclusion of the ill-starred 'Inland Voyage' he was sufficiently intrigued to return to the Barbizon community for a second look. The object of his attentions was a 36-year old American woman named Fanny Osbourne. Frances Matilda Vandegrift Osbourne was born in Indianapolis on 10 March 1840 – she was thus a 'Hoosier', as natives of Indiana are called. Her father Jacob, a devout Presbyterian lumber-merchant who dabbled in real estate, was from a Philadelphia family of Dutch stock; her mother Esther Keen claimed descent from a Swedish military family and – in a scenario that was to set the pattern for three generations of Vandegrift women – had been married and divorced before becoming Vandegrift's wife. The couple had six children (five girls and a boy) of whom Fanny was the eldest. In 1842 Fanny and her mother were baptised as Presbyterians by the Rev. Henry Ward Beecher in a mass ceremony in the White River in which thousands participated. Fanny was brought up with a full complement of traditional feminine skills – cooking, gardening, seamstressing – but she was a tomboy, at her happiest in rough, outdoor pursuits or when frightening the other children with ghost stories. She had some talent for drawing and design, read voraciously and began to develop never-to-be-extinguished longings to be a writer. If higher education had been a possibility, 'hoydenish blue-stocking' might have summed up her profile.

Always a fantasist, Fanny liked to exaggerate the 'pioneering' aspects of her background, yet the sober truth is that Jacob Vandegrift was no Daniel Boone, but rather a city-dweller transplanted to a rather boring Mid-West 'new town'; founded in the 1830s, Indianapolis had a population of 3,000 and was in no sense a frontier town. The humiliation Fanny felt about her physical appearance was, however, real. In an age when fair skin was the talisman of beauty, she was dark and swarthy as a gypsy; probably she got her looks from her mother, about whom much is shrouded in mystery. There was a family legend that Fanny's grandmother once tried to wash out the darkness of her skin with an astringent soap but abandoned the hopeless task, saying: 'She's that colour by nature – God made her ugly.' Fanny was also short-legged and inclined to dumpiness, but against these physical drawbacks she combined small feet, beautiful hands, striking eyes, luxuriant hair and an all-round aura of sensuality. That she had sex-appeal was undoubted: when she was seventeen the local Lothario, Samuel Osbourne, by origin a Kentuckian, four years her senior and a man who could have had his pick of the young girls of Indianapolis, married her (on Christmas Eve, 1857). Sam Osbourne was considered locally to be a catch, for he was secretary to the governor of Indiana and seemed to be a young man with a glittering political future ahead. The Osbournes' first child, Isobel (Belle) was born the next year.

The coming of the Civil War destroyed the domestic idyll. Something happened to Sam Osbourne during the four years of fighting (1861–65), for ever afterwards he was a restless, troubled man, as unable to live a settled life in a fixed location as to stay long with any one woman. Ironically, in the late 1860s Fanny's life really was the pioneer existence she claimed as the estate of her childhood: in search of the 'quick buck' from silver-mining the permanently discontented Sam took his family first to San Francisco, then to Austin, Nevada and finally to Virginia City, which Mark Twain's writings had established as the wildest town in the wild west. These were the years when Fanny acquired many useful skills that later amazed RLS, such as her ability to slit the throat of a hog or to shoot down a row of bottles with a handgun from twenty yards' range. In Virginia City dreams of quick riches became dimmed, and for a while Sam returned to the occupation in which he had served his apprenticeship: clerk to the local court. His habitual adultery with, by all accounts, dozens of women, soon precipitated a clash with Fanny; the upshot was that Sam threw up his job and went prospecting again, while Fanny and Belle went to live in a hotel in San Francisco.

Then came news that Sam had been 'killed' in a fight with Indians. Osbourne was an early exponent of what we now know as the 'Stonehouse' effect; he was a past master at engineering mysterious disappearances when it suited his book. Obviously his money ran out and he could no longer wire subsistence dollars to San Francisco so, rather than go through rows and wrangles with Fanny, he dropped out of sight until he worked his current amour out of his system. It is little short of astonishing how often Stevenson biographers have been prepared to take Osbourne and his diaphanous 'explanations' seriously, and we may still read accounts written with great solemnity that assure us that Sam Osbourne 'narrowly escaped scalping', that 'he had left the main party before it was butchered'. Fanny, for one, was certainly not entirely surprised when one day Osbourne reappeared in the furnished room she rented with the produce of her labour as a seam-stress and calmly expressed wonderment that Belle had grown so tall. It is important to be clear that Fanny had no real illusions about Sam Osbourne but that she was in thrall to him sexually; libido was always an important element in the world of 'the Vandegrifter'. The couple were reconciled at once – it was as though Sam had merely been serving a prison sentence – and in 1868 a son, Samuel Lloyd Osbourne, was born.

Sam resumed his 'political' career, this time as court stenographer at ten dollars a day. With this comfortable middle-class income he bought a cottage across the bay in East Oakland, where for a time he and Fanny went through the motions of domesticity and normal marital bliss. The philandering continued, and Fanny seems to have connived at it as long as it did not become too blatant. Yet there were many rows about Sam's women, and Belle recalls an occasion when her father was reading *Vanity Fair* aloud to her. He reached the chapter dealing with George Osborne's betrayal of Amelia, whereat Fanny suddenly burst in with: 'I wonder, Captain Osbourne, you can read your own story!'

Finally the infidelities became too frequent and too insistent; a trial separation was agreed, and Fanny took her children to live with her parents. A year later a third reconciliation was arranged and it was during this period that the third Osbourne child, Hervey, was born. In the Oakland cottage Fanny appeared at her most typical. She had a taste for firearms and set up a rifle range in the 'yard' (garden); meanwhile she developed her literary and cultural interests with a range of friends in San Francisco, especially Virgil and Dora Williams, the painters, and the Irish lawyer Timothy Rearden, head of the mercantile library. She got to know the Williamses through Belle, who attended San Francisco's School of Design, which Williams had founded; Belle's glowing descriptions of the Bay area's artistic and bohemian life made Fanny eager to sample it herself, so she started to attend the school with her daughter.

In 1875, after further womanising had come to her notice, Fanny decided she could stand Sam's behaviour no longer. What she chose to do thereafter was the least imaginable course of action. Doubtless thinking that the Williams's flattery of her talent as a draughtswoman was a sober appreciation of her merit, she resolved to study art in Europe and to take with her the three children and a governess. Or perhaps it was more simple: that she was an adventuress, wanted to travel and knew that in those days women without a male escort could maintain the pretence of respectability only if they purported to be 'studying' something. Her exact motivation is as obscure as the source of the funds for the expedition; Sam Osbourne's salary as court stenographer would scarcely have sufficed to defray the expenses of a transatlantic crossing for five persons plus their upkeep for what turned out to be three years, and one is led to conjecture that one of his gambling or entrepreneurial projects must have paid off at about this time. It is certain that Sam *did* pay all the expenses, certainly for the first two years, despite Fanny's later absurd pretence that she had supported herself in Europe by writing magazine articles; *his* motivation – to get rid of his wife and family and enjoy unrestricted dalliance in the Oakland cottage – is clear, but a mystery attaches to the financial side of things.

Fanny travelled first to Antwerp, to seek admission at the Academy where Bob had studied. But the institute did not accept women and, besides, the infant Hervey was now showing disturbing symptoms of a mystery illness. After three months in Belgium, stick and carrot drove Fanny on, for she both feared the effect of an outbreak of 'Antwerp fever' and was recommended to take Hervey to a specialist in Paris. The French capital proved more welcoming: the Atelier Julian would admit any woman who could pay the fees, where others insisted on qualifications or entry requirements. She and Belle attended the life classes there daily; at home, in an apartment on the Rue de Naples, Montmartre, Lloyd, Hervey and the governess eked out on a diet of smoked herrings and black bread. The consequences of Fanny's headstrong and insufficiently thought-out flight to Europe were already becoming apparent: she found that she had grossly underestimated the cost of living in Europe and, even, to her stupefaction, that she missed Sam. To Rearden she wrote: 'His letters quite touch my heart . . . I don't like to be selfish, and it makes me feel so if he is unhappy at our absence. I didn't know I should miss him as I do.' That there was suffering all round because of her impulsiveness becomes clear from statements by her (then) and by Lloyd later. Lloyd spoke of the hardship thus: 'We were miserably poor. It seems to me that I was always hungry. I can remember yet how I used to glue myself to the baker's window.' Meanwhile Fanny wrote to the young Irish-American lawyer Timothy Rearden: 'I believe in women's rights in a general sense, so much despised by the "strong-minded" when they deservedly call us "the clinging vine". I do not want to be the oak and stand alone; it makes me loathsome to think of oak with no shelter, no support except what it provides for itself.'[2]

The harshest effects of the poverty and poor diet were visited on young Hervey, who began to ail and soon entered a terminal decline. He had convulsions, his eardrums were perforated, his joints cracked, and he lay in bed a perfect skeleton, with bones sticking out through his skin, crying plaintively, 'Blood, Mama!' The doctors spoke of 'scrofulous tuberculosis' but malnutrition was certainly a major precipitant. The child's illness was agonising and prolonged – long enough for Sam Osbourne to be summoned from the U.S.A. and to arrive in time to see his son die, at 5 a.m. on the morning of 5 April 1876.[3] Sam stayed to mourn for three or four weeks, but returned to California without his family; he paid off the governess, who found Fanny's regime impossibly spartan. Fanny meanwhile steadily went to pieces with grief and could gain no consolation from the physicians' assurances that, had he lived, Hervey would have been deaf, dumb and deformed. Further anguish was caused by the reflection that Hervey was buried in Père Lachaise in a pauper's grave, which meant that after five years all corpses were dug up and the bones flung into a common pit. Following the sleepless nights of nursing and the subsequent mourning and melancholia, she suffered giddy spells, memory lapses, blackouts and hallucinations. There is some evidence that Fanny was never the same person again, and her later deep neurosis and bouts of depressive illness, her hypochondria, mysterious illnesses and occasional lurches into actual psychosis must certainly have the death of Hervey as one of their causes, possibly even the principal one.

Warned that she faced nervous collapse if she did not convalesce, and that unless he got some country air Lloyd too might succumb, she went to Grez, of which she had heard at the Atelier Julian from an American student of sculpture, and put up at the Hôtel Chevillon, where the worst excesses of *la vie de bohème* were not permitted – no *grisettes* or mistresses admitted. Finding herself and Belle the only females among sixteen guests, Fanny liked the ambience so much that she decided to move down permanently; she returned to Paris, gave up the lease on the Montmartre apartment, and then moved back to Grez as the permanent base. In the hurly-burly of the Anglo-American artists' colony one of the first people she met was Bob. The story goes that Bob had always liked the club atmosphere of the Chevillon and was dismayed to hear that it had been invaded by two pushy women. Sceptical of the claims that these were in fact two 'beautiful Americans' Bob hastened down to Grez to roust the interlopers out – for it appears that he and Louis had earlier browbeaten the landlord into taking only selected guests into his establishment, with the threat that otherwise they could ruin his reputation with respectable clientèle. Fanny and Belle waited with trepidation for the visit from the two Stevensons, whose names were on everyone's lips in the colony; but when Bob arrived he was charm itself, a condition no doubt explained by his being bowled over by Belle, herself by now a dusky gypsy beauty of eighteen, the image of her mother at that age.[4]

Once he had decided to take Fanny and Belle under his wing, Bob introduced them to the rest of his 'crowd': Louis, Walter Simpson, his brother Willie who liked to get drunk on absinthe and feed it to his bull-terrier at the same time, so that man and dog reeled off precariously down the Loing towpath, the twenty-year old Irishman Frank O'Meara, Will Low, and many others. Fanny was a 'hit' with the young men, who vied among themselves to accompany her to her vantage point for painting in the forest or to take her canoeing on the river. It was in the summer of 1876 that Louis briefly made her acquaintance, when he appeared one July evening towards the end of dinner at the Chevillon and vaulted in from the street through the open window. The absurd later legend, abetted by Fanny, was that he had fallen in love with her then and there, at first sight. This was too much even for Belle, who colluded in much of the RLS hagiography, and she later remarked: 'It is romantic rubbish that Louis fell in love with my mother when he glimpsed her through a window.'[5]

Indeed, the Fanny Osbourne who emerges from the documentation for this period is light years away from the saintly, long-suffering Fanny of the Stevensonian myth. She comes across as a rather cold, unscrupulous and somewhat coarse coquette. The flirtatious element was always in her nature: at the Austin mining camp in the late sixties she had an English admirer, John Lloyd, after whom she called her son Samuel Lloyd, and whose attentions she had encouraged. Now she tried to churn Rearden up into waves of jealousy.

> I am known among the villagers as "the beautiful American" and they crowd round to look at me. I don't care so much. Isn't it funny that they should do that? It was a long time before I could believe but that I was mistaken. Only think! Some artists came from a distant town to see me. I never dared to ask what they thought. I don't mind, on the contrary I think it is all very nice.

And again:

> My chair by the fire and my chair at the table are always held sacred. I am taken out solemnly every afternoon for exercise ... Weekly pilgrimages are made to the city to get things to tempt my appetite ... Then to make me more vain they paint me, making me very beautiful, and make up sketches of my mouth, the back of my head and my nose, and model my arms in clay, and propose costumes for me and situations for me. Oh, I am awfully vain I do assure you.[6]

The golden days at Grez, the canoeing, painting and swimming – Fanny could not swim but she donned a bathing costume and splashed about in the river like a child – the games of consequences, the lolling about in hammocks, the food and wine, the general *dolce far niente*, all this masked some amatory tensions worthy of *A Midsummer Night's Dream*. The American sculptor Pardessus, who had recommended Grez to the Osbournes, was smitten with Belle, but she had eyes only for Frank O'Meara. Bob for his part was besotted with Belle, while Fanny's interest was wholly with Bob, with whom she could easily have fallen in love if given the least encouragement. Far from *coup de foudre*, Fanny's initial reaction to Louis was detached curiosity. This aspect of affairs at Grez was unknown to early biographers and is worth establishing in some detail.

Fanny was overwhelmed by Bob's wit and charm and talent. Many years later she wrote:

It seems incredible that a genius so unusual as that of Robert Alan Mowbray Stevenson should pass out of existence, leaving nothing more for posterity than a single brilliant volume [sc. his biography of Velasquez] and a few desultory papers on music and painting; but he was a dreamer of dreams, without ambition, who dwelt alone in a world of fantasy, from which he would sometimes merge [sic] to dazzle his friends with wild theories, sound philosophy, unexpected learning, and whimsical absurdities, all jumbled together and presented with such pertinent reasoning and certainty of the truth of his premises that his hearers would be swept off their feet.[7]

That is emotion recollected in tranquillity. The immediate actuality is conveyed in letters to Rearden. In an epistle soon after the first meeting when Bob came down to Grez to 'roust out' the American interlopers, she wrote: 'He is exactly like one of Ouida's heroes with the hand of steel in the glove of velvet ... He is the best painter here, a charming musician, speaks all languages, does all sorts of feats of strength, and has no ambition.' She went into rhapsodies about this 'Adonis' and 'Apollo' with the 'wonderful grace and perfect figure'. A jealous suitor among the painters tried to discredit Bob in her eyes by getting him so drunk that he had to be carried up to bed; Fanny merely remarked that Bob was the most charming drunk she had ever seen. Almost a year later, in April 1877, she wrote in a gallimauffry of nonsense: 'Bob Stevenson is the most beautiful creature I ever saw in my life, and yet, somehow, reminds me of you ... He spent a large fortune ... graduated at Cambridge with high honors ... took holy orders to please his mother, quit in disgust ... and now is dying from the effects of dissipation and is considered a little mad.'

The change in tone was occasioned by a walk in the forest in October 1876, when Bob, aware of the lady's admiration, had tried to steer her towards Louis. During the walk, which so absorbed them that they arrived back at the Hôtel Chevillon very late and set tongues wagging, Bob advised her which of the bohemians she should cultivate in Paris during the winter. Dismissing himself as a 'vulgar cad', he talked up the merits of his cousin whom Fanny had tended to dismiss because of his habit of fainting, weeping and throwing hysterical fits; Bob explained these were caused by 'ill health' and added: 'Louis is a gentleman and you can trust him and depend upon him.'[8]

Bob did not of course explain that his disinterested behaviour masked an ulterior motive. He wanted to be free of Fanny's attentions so that he could concentrate on wooing Belle. He evidently got his chance to press his suit, but Belle was her mother's daughter in mercenary as well as other ways and soon winkled out of her suitor the intelligence that he was virtually penniless. In January 1879 Bob wrote a revealing letter to Louis, from which the result of his passion for Belle can be inferred. Lamenting

his poverty and his inability to make painting pay, he went on: 'If I had
£500 or £1000 a year I dare say Belle would marry me but then I haven't.
I think I would go through the rest of my career moderately content if I
saw Belle for three hours once in a fortnight.' The implication is clear that
Belle's attraction for him was mainly sexual, and indeed he contrasted the
sensuality of Belle with the more sober attractions of his fiancée Louisa
Purland (whom he married in 1881); but he suggested that with Belle one
could combine sex and marriage, whereas with his 'Paris girl', who left him
in 1880 to make a new life in Brazil, sensuality was all. 'Live for sensuality.
How much our elders deceived us in saying that the pleasures of sense were
the most deceptive and fleeting,' he advised Louis. Belle remained Bob's
great passion. When Louis was in California in January 1880 and Belle had
already married the painter Joe Strong, Bob wrote from Chelsea: 'I never
think of Belle or look at letters or anything yet really I am always conscious
of her and of course if she really took to me I would go for her.'9

Fanny meanwhile took the hint and began looking at Bob's cousin Louis
with new eyes. The two became great friends but, hindsight notwithstanding, there is no evidence that, as yet, any grand passion had developed.
Initially, Fanny seems to have been bemused by Louis's eccentricity, his
habit of erupting into sudden laughter or bursting into tears and throwing
himself despairingly on the floor. He told her that his laughter could be
quenched if someone bent his fingers backwards; once in a carriage in Paris
he demonstrated and bent his fingers back so painfully that she had to bite
his hand to make him stop. The weeping was more difficult to deal with: 'I
do wish Louis wouldn't burst into tears in such an unexpected way; it is so
embarrassing. One doesn't know what to do, whether to offer him a pocket
handkerchief, or look out of the window.'

It is hard to know how much of the gallery touch informed these
exhibitions by Louis. It is quite clear that he liked always to be the
centre of attention and if he was not, he would do outrageous things to
have himself restored to his rightful place. Andrew Lang told A.E.W.Mason
that he once met Louis in an Edinburgh drawing room; when RLS thought
the other people were not concentrating on him sufficiently, he took off
his coat and sat sullenly in his shirt sleeves until his hostess reprimanded
him: 'You might as well put your coat on again, no one is taking any
notice of you.' On the other hand, Stevenson genuinely suffered from
violent mood swings, and could switch from charm to anger in a trice
if he suspected that someone was insulting him or trying to humiliate
him. He liked to impress Fanny with his knowledge of French wines,
and once in a Paris restaurant the waiter annoyed him by bringing a
bottle of wine that was corked. Irritatedly, Louis rejected the bottle,
but the management made the mistake of thinking he was an ignoramus
and simply sent back the wine disguised as a different bottle. In a fury

Stevenson strode across the room and smashed the bottle to pieces against the wall.[10]

For all that, Fanny regarded Louis as 'the wittiest man I have ever met'. He in turn basked in her admiration for, as he remarked in *An Inland Voyage* as if in intuition of things to come: 'If a man finds a woman admires him, were it only for his acquaintance with geography, he will begin at once to build upon the admiration.' At some stage that autumn, friendship deepened into something else. No precise chronology of the development of Stevenson's relationship with Fanny is possible, and the story has to be assembled from tantalising fragments, but when Fanny returned to Paris late in October 1876, RLS went with her; Will Low remarked that his daily trudges from their quarters in Montmartre to Fanny's lodgings told their own story. It is conceivable that physical consummation of the liaison did not occur until January 1878, but the Victorians believed in deferred gratification, and there is no reason why besotment should not have coexisted with chastity. Stevenson was in a difficult situation, for he was being plagued by demands from his parents that he should return to Edinburgh, even as he most wished to stay in Paris and promote his budding affair with Fanny. The pressure was extreme. On 18 January Thomas wrote to say that Maggie was pining for him: 'When are you coming home? The sooner the better.' On 5 February he followed this up with: 'Why don't you return to the bosom of your family? Why spend so much of your time among the "Mopons" [sic]. Life is short, at least mine is.'[11] Louis got his revenge on his parents by addressing his letters to them from Fanny's lodgings at 5, Rue Douay. In one of them he made a rather arch reference to Fanny and Belle by saying he had met a very beautiful woman and her pretty daughter at a party in the Rue Notre Dame des Champs. In another, written on 10 January 1877, he transmogrified the story of mother and daughter as follows: 'I am in a new quarter and flame about in a leisurely way. I dine every day in a *crèmerie* with a party of Americans, one Irishman and sometimes an English lady: elderly, very prim, a widow with a son in the army and married daughters. Poor woman! It is rather a pitiful story. She half quarrelled with all her family in order to come over here and study art; and now she can't do it, feels herself like a fish out of water in the life, and yet is ashamed to give in and go back.'[12]

At the beginning of February 1877 he and Fanny agreed that he should go back to Scotland. Fanny's financial position was grave, and her best hope was that Louis should finally get his hands on the £1,000 originally promised by his father when he passed his barrister's exams. Louis seems to have made it a condition to his parents that he would play the filial role they wanted from him if they in turn would treat him as an adult and let him have his money.

Since the relationship between Louis and Fanny is crucial to an understanding of the rest of his life, it is worth pausing to take stock of both of

them and to try to establish what was in their minds as they hovered on
the threshold of momentous decisions. A good guide to Louis's mental
state is in the two essays he wrote on relations between the sexes in 1876:
'Virginibus Puerisque' and 'On Falling in Love'. 'Virginibus Puerisque' tries
to assess the pros and cons of marriage as a solution to sexual temptation,
rates the rival attractions of solitude and companionship, establishes the
dialectic between truth and falsehood and, *en passant*, contains asides that
are revelatory on his relations with his parents. He is far from starry-eyed
about marriage, declares that in the wedded state a man becomes slack and
selfish and undergoes a fatty degeneration of his moral being, and remarks
that if people married only when they fell in love, most of the world would
die unwed ... The essay is studded with his usual perceptive insights on
women, who, he maintained (in a fairly exact anticipation of Shaw) benefited
from marriage as men did not; however, he was not blind to the problems of
mutual understanding between the sexes, which he likened to the incompatibility of the Latin and Teuton races. He condemned contemporary liberal
education as leading to greater confusion between the sexes, as it tended
to exaggerate the natural differences between them; he opposed a different
kind of education for men and women since 'when a horse has run away,
and two flustered people in the gig have each possessed themselves of a
rein, we know the end of that conveyance will be in the ditch.'

RLS was sceptical of the possibility of telling the truth in human
affairs, since the veridical was vitiated by considerations of power, and
in an obvious reference to the continuing tensions with his parents he
wrote:

> To speak truth there must be moral equality or else no respect and hence between
> parent and child intercourse is apt to degenerate into a verbal fencing-bout, and
> misapprehensions to become ingrained. And there is another side to this, for the
> parent begins with an imperfect notion of the child's character, formed in early
> years or during the equinoctial gales of youth; to this he adheres, noting only the
> facts which twit with his preconception; and whenever a person fancies himself
> unjustly judged, he at once and finally gives up the effort to speak truth.

Stevenson was also of the school that believes the best way to tell a
lie is to tell the truth, since the facts of social intercourse preclude the
possibility of answering questions without falsehood.

'Do you forgive me?'
'Madam and sweetheart, so far as I have done in life I have never yet
been able to understand what forgiveness means.'
'Is it still the same between us?'
'Why, how can it be? It is eternally different; and yet you are still the friend
of my heart.'
'Do you understand me?'

'God knows; I should think it highly improbable.'

The tone of Stevenson's attitude to wedlock suggests his usual ambivalence: marriage may provide a temporary escape from care but in the long run human beings are trapped in an endless struggle they cannot win.

> Times are changed with him who marries; there are no more by-path meadows where you may innocently linger but the road lies long and straight and dusty to the grave ... with what temerity you have chosen precisely *her* to be your spy, whose esteem you value highest, and whom you have already taught to think you better than you are. You may think you had a conscience and believed in God; but what is a conscience to a wife? ... To marry is to domesticate the Recording Angel. Once you are married, there is nothing left for you, not even suicide, but to be good ... And yet when all has been said, the man who should hold back from marriage is in the same case with him who runs away from battle ... ere you marry, you should have learned the mingled lesson of the world; that dolls are stuffed with sawdust and yet are excellent playthings; that hope and love address themselves to a perfection never realized, and yet, firmly held, become the salt and stuff of life.

Some of Stevenson's remarks are utterly incompatible with the persistent but totally false notion that he fell in love with Fanny on first glimpsing her through a window in the Hôtel Chevillon. *Coup de foudre?* 'One is almost tempted to hint that it does not matter whom you marry.' The 'niceness' of Fanny? 'That doctrine of the excellence of women, however chivalrous, is cowardly as well as false.' Irony? 'Certainly if I could help it, I would never marry a woman who wrote.'[13]

Even 'On Falling in Love', written when he was in Paris with Fanny in November–December 1877, scarcely suggests a grand passion. It is true that he calls falling in love 'the only event in life which really astonishes a man' and says it is 'the one illogical adventure, the one thing of which we are tempted to think as supernatural, in our trite and reasonable world'. But he ends the essay on a note which is at best melancholy and at worst cynical and even nihilistic.

> When the generation is gone, when the play is over, when the thirty years' panorama has been withdrawn in tatters from the stage of the world, we may ask what has become of those great, weighty and undying loves, and the sweethearts who despised mortal conditions in a fine credulity; and they can only show us a few songs in a byegone taste, a few actions worth remembering, and a few children who have retained some happy stamp from the disposition of their parents.[14]

How are we to interpret all this? It may be that, as sometimes happens, Louis did not spot Fanny's sensual attraction the first time round, that *this* occurred in the summer of 1877, and that had he written the essays then, he would have written differently – this of course would be yet another nail in the 'lovers at first sight' legend. It is more likely, however, that after the disappointment with Fanny Sitwell, RLS had given up on the idea of an all-encompassing integrating love, that the passion he felt for Fanny Osbourne was overwhelmingly sexual, and that he saw her deficiencies very clearly. The early stages of the affair with Fanny certainly sound uncannily like a rerun of the doomed romance with Mrs Sitwell. Apart from possessing the same given names and nicknames, the two Fannies were the same age, were both dark with pretty feet, both had intellectual and aesthetic leanings, had both survived disastrous marriages and both had young sons who died of respiratory illnesses. It is not inconceivable that the oedipal fixation earlier referred to played some part; it is interesting that in both cases RLS made his overture to the older woman by first winning over their sons by playing with them, thus in effect becoming a second son before making overt amorous advances. In seeking out a sexual relationship with Fanny Osbourne, RLS may have been hoping to gain in fantasy what he had been denied in reality – to 'possess' Fanny Sitwell.

A man with Stevenson's genius for apprehending the truth about people cannot have been unaware that Fanny was, from any angle, a very rum creature indeed. Because of the barnacles of legend that have become encrusted after hagiographers have done their work, it is almost impossible to retrieve the reality of the situation in 1876–78. Even the iconography is suspect, for the well-known photograph of Fanny, allegedly taken at the time of her meeting with RLS, in fact dates from years earlier, and this should really have been picked up by previous biographers, for the photographic study of Fanny at her wedding three years later shows a far older woman. If, on the other hand, these two images are to have the dates traditionally ascribed to them, Fanny must have deteriorated alarmingly in three years – at exactly the time when, according to the legend, she should have been at her most radiantly happy. The anecdotal evidence does not help us much either, for the faction sympathetic to Fanny – Will Low for example – describes her at the Grez period as being 'in full possession of the charm of womanhood', while the hostile faction describes her as having a squat figure, no neck, mannish shoulders, no waist and short legs. However, there can be no real argument as to how RLS *perceived* her physically. His poem 'Dark Women' says it all:

> The hue of heather honey,
> The hue of honey bees,
> Shall tinge her golden shoulder,
> Shall tinge her tawny knees.
>
> Dark as a wayside gypsy,
> Lithe as a hedgewood hare,
> She moves a glowing shadow

> Through the sunshine of the fair;
> And golden hue and orange,
> Bosom and hand and head
> She blooms, a tiger lily,
> In the snowdrifts of the bed.[15]

Fanny's deep character is another matter, as we shall see. Anyone coming to grips with her has to take into account her toughness and assertiveness, her bizarre earthy and visceral character, her profound interest in the occult, and her neurotic outbursts. Let us begin with the testimony of Sidney Colvin, who met her first at the end of 1877:

> Her personality was almost as vivid (as Stevenson's). She was small, dark-complexioned, eager, devoted; of squarish build – supple and elastic; her hands and feet were small and beautifully modelled, though busy; her head had a crop of close-waving thick black hair. She had a build and a character that somehow suggested Napoleon, with a firm setting of jaw and beautifully precise modelling of nose and lips; her eyes were full of sex and mystery as they changed from fire or fun to gloom or tenderness ... fine pearly set of small teeth, and the clear metallic accents of her intensely human and often quaintly independent speech.[16]

There was a mannish aspect to Fanny, alongside the feminine sexiness, which manifested itself most clearly in the pistol she took with her wherever she went. In Antwerp she took the piece to a gunsmith to have it cleaned, and the man, who had never seen an American firearm, went into raptures about this novelty. The Jungian psychoanalyst Barbara Hannah once described Fanny as the sort of woman who had a highly developed *animus*, and it was doubtless this aspect of Fanny RLS was intuiting when he wrote to her, with his usual role confusion, as 'My dear fellow', 'My dear Dutchman', 'My dearest little man'. It is true that Victorians went in for this kind of role confusion more than we relish – the eponymous hero of Melville's *Pierre*, for example, addresses his mother as 'sister' – but, as already noted, there is a 'superplus' of this kind of thing in Stevenson's case. With his antennae always quivering to detect signs of duality, Stevenson further underlined the 'male' side of Fanny's personality in his poem 'Dark Women':

> Tiger and tiger lily,
> She plays a double part,
> All woman in the body,
> And all the man at heart.
> She shall be brave and tender,
> She shall be soft and high,
> *She* to lie in my bosom
> And *he* to fight and die.

Fanny considered herself to possess 'second sight' and other psychic powers, believed implicitly in the supernatural and liked to dabble in the 'whiter' side of the occult. Birge Harrison, an American artist who knew her at Grez, referred to her 'mysterious sort of over-intelligence', implying some sort of paranormal faculty.[17] Just as RLS's taste for the uncanny had been fostered by Cummy's ghost stories, so too Fanny had childhood experiences to thank for aspects of her sensibility. As a girl she had been domiciled with other children for a while, in circumstances not entirely clear, in an undertaker's house, and had come to regard cadavers as part of the normal furniture of the world. There was a Vandegrift family story that the undertaker always ordered extra ice at the mourners' expense, ostensibly to deep-freeze the corpse, but really to make ice-cream for his young charges.

This primitive credulous side of Fanny was noticed by many. Birge Harrison declared: 'in no sense ordinary . . . she belonged to the quattrocento rather than to the nineteenth century.' Henry James famously referred to her as a 'poor, barbarous and merely *instinctive* lady'. His sister Alice worked in further variations on the 'primitive' theme: 'From her appearance Providence or Nature, whichever is responsible for her, designed her as an appendage to a hand organ . . . such egotism and so naked! giving me the strangest feeling of being in the presence of an unclothed being.'[18]

Yet the most full-blooded analysis of Fanny as barbarian comes from her daughter-in-law Katharine Osbourne. The Fanny hagiographers have always tried to dismiss Katharine Osbourne's testimony as the spite of a wronged woman, but recent scholarship shows it holding up much better than the pro-Fanny faction led by J.C.Furnas would have us believe. There were certainly many incidents in Fanny's later life with RLS which provide circumstantial backing for Katharine's story.

> She was a strong colorful character, with a will which could have conquered provinces, but all her ambition was turned to subjugating all the individuals about her. She was clairvoyant, uncannily so, she watched and studied everyone to turn anything her way or to thwart any of their plans and ambitions that were aside her use . . . I have sometimes thought that Fanny could have been another Anna [sic] Besant as far as clairvoyance and a love of the marvellous was concerned but she had not the proper industry nor ambition. She had an iron will but used it only to subjugate individuals . . . About her eyes: they were striking, but cattish, cruel, shifting, always moving in little quick jerks sideways . . . She never outgrew childhood and it seemed to me that she belonged to the childhood of the race – the first beginnings of the race – in some dark-skinned peoples. But she was not feminine, she was more a man. Her one great service to Stevenson was the pleasure she took in listening to his tales – and he always wanted a listener . . . I do not think she was mad, but of the year 10,000 B.C. and a pure romancer.[19]

James Pope-Hennessy argued that the spirit of romance was there when she wrote, allegedly disingenuously, to Timothy Rearden in April 1877, hoping to divert attention from the seriousness of her romance with Stevenson. But this rests on a misunderstanding of the chronology of events in 1877, which are admittedly confusing, to the point where even a careful biographer like J.C.Furnas states: 'She [Fanny] spent the summer of 1877 altogether at Grez. Louis was there a great deal until well into July.'[20] In fact RLS was seriously ill in Edinburgh from February to the end of May, made a brief visit to Grez in June–July and was back in Britain by August. During the period of Louis's illness in Edinburgh, Bob wrote to Fanny to ask her to send letters to his cousin, who was dying; Bob then fell ill, and Louis made the selfsame request of Fanny. The resulting confusion provoked the following from Fanny to Rearden on 11 April when, after paeans to the beauty of Bob, she continued:

> Louis, his cousin, the hysterical fellow, who wrote the article about Belle, is a tall gaunt Scotchman with a face like Raphael, and between over-education and dissipation has ruined his health, and is dying of consumption. Louis reformed his habits a couple of years ago, and Bob, this winter. Louis is the heir to an immense fortune which he will never live to inherit. His father and mother, cousins, are both threatened with insanity, and I am quite sure the son is. His article about Belle was written, as she says, for five pounds which she wanted to give a pensioner of his in hospital and was done when he had a headache, and badly enough we knew as well as he . . . the two mad Stevensons, who with all their suffering are men out of spirits, but so filled with the joyfulness of mere living, that their presence is exhilarating, I will never see them again. I never heard one of them say a cynical thing, nor knew them to do an unkind thing. With all the wild stories I have heard of them fresh in my mind, I still consider them the truest gentlemen and nothing can make them anything less.[21]

The 'black hole' from February to May 1877 may also hold the key to a further mystery in Stevenson's life. Almost certainly, at some time in the period 1877–79 he had an affair with a woman other than Fanny. Stevenson's moral code being what it was, it is unlikely that this occurred *after* he had slept with Fanny, for reasons that will become clear later. If Louis and Fanny became lovers in summer 1877 (or even if it was January 1878, as some authorities believe, given that RLS was almost continually in France from summer 1877 to January 1878), this pushes back the likely date for his other liaison to some time in early 1877. Of course it is *possible* that the other affair was a mirage, as Furnas and others think, but this is unlikely.

As with the earlier controversy over 'Claire', we must distinguish between solid evidence, and legend or hearsay. John Steuart alleged that in the late seventies Stevenson had *two* mistresses in addition to Fanny: one was the dark and slender daughter of an Aberdeen builder and carpenter who was working in Edinburgh; the second was tall, fair and well-built, the daughter

of a blacksmith. Some time around Christmas 1877, Steuart alleges, the two
rivals accidentally met outside Swanston cottage and came to blows; this
'battle of Swanston' was witnessed with stupefaction and disgust by Louis's
parents.[22] This story seems altogether too absurd to be true, but there may
be fire behind the smoke. The 'blacksmith's daughter' is too obviously a
harking back to the events of the early 1870s, but there may be more in
the builder's daughter than many have been prepared to concede.

It is certain that around Christmas 1877 Louis had another of his
'bare-knuckle' rows with his father, as a result of which he tried, briefly
and unsuccessfully, to maintain himself: hence his needing 'coin so badly'
in the New Year of 1878, as related to Colvin. Then there is a mysterious
reference in a letter to his father on 15 February 1878 of 'letters it hurt
me to write, and I fear it will hurt others to receive'. Finally, there is
an explicit reference in a letter to Henley in February 1880 to a letter
he has received 'from an enchanting young lady whom you have seen,
or rather from her inspiration, threatening letters, exposure, etc.' The
hypothesis of an unknown wronged mistress would also account for the
excessively censorious tone of the essay on Burns; in reproaching Burns
for his philandering, Stevenson was also indicting himself.

> It is the punishment of Don Juanism to create continually false positions –
> relations in life which are wrong in themselves and which it is equally wrong
> to break or to perpetuate ... If he had been strong enough to refrain or bad
> enough to persevere in evil; if he had only not been Don Juan at all, or been
> Don Juan altogether, there had been some possible road for him throughout this
> troublesome world; but a man, alas! who is equally at the call of his worse and
> better instincts, stands among changing events without foundation or resource.[23]

Biographers dedicated to the myth of Louis and Fanny Osbourne as
initials-in-the-heart lovers have tried to dispose of this evidence, and
in a singularly inept way. Furnas says: 'Whatever the now undiscoverable
facts, Henley left Edinburgh long before Louis met Fanny, so the affair
must have predated Louis's falling in love with his future wife.'[24] Only if
it can be shown that Henley *never* thereafter visited RLS in Edinburgh. Or
if it can be proved that it was impossible for an Edinburgh mistress to track
Stevenson down in London. Besides, why did the young lady referred to in
RLS's letter to Henley in 1880, who on the Furnas thesis would have been
discarded in 1876 at the latest, wait until 1880 before threatening exposure?

It is typical of the confusion and mystery that surrounds Stevenson's
private life that we cannot even be certain of the date when physical
consummation of his relationship with Fanny Osbourne took place. It
was certainly no later than January 1878, and many biographers have
indeed opted for that exact date. But I am inclined to think, from the
constant conjunction of Fanny and summer in Stevenson's verse, that

the period June–July 1877, when he returned to Fanny and the forests of Fontainebleau, was the critical one. A summer's day canoeing on the Loing with Fanny hints at watery dalliance:

> Deep, swift and clear, the lilies floated; fish
> Through the shadows ran. There thou and I
> Read kindness in our eyes and closed the match.

The idyll at Grez was brief, however. At this stage RLS, conscious that his £1,000 was rapidly diminishing the more he contributed to Fanny's coffers, was thinking ahead to the time he might need to touch his father for more, and was therefore trying to be conciliatory. Accordingly, by 25 July he was back in Edinburgh, answering questions about European politics from a Japanese correspondent. August he spent with his parents in Penzance but, as he told Mrs Sitwell: 'Cornwall is not much to my taste, being as bleak as the bleakest parts of Scotland, and nothing like so pointed and characteristic.' By this time, under pressure from Fanny Osbourne, the volume of his correspondence with his first love was running down, though he confided in her about each stage of his affair with the strange dark American; Fanny Sitwell, for her part, encouraged the blossoming romance (to get rid of him?).[25]

In September Fanny Osbourne moved back to autumn quarters in Paris, at 5, Rue Ravignan; Louis sped across the Channel to join her. At first he lived in lodgings nearby and spent a lot of his time fending off the epistolary assault from his parents, who by now must have suspected that it was a woman that drew their son constantly back to France and kept up an importunate barrage of letters to get him to return to Edinburgh. A letter from Thomas Stevenson on 7 October 1877 is typical: 'You say you want me to write to you. This is all very fine but you never write to me . . . Magnus Simpson says he can't find any fun in remaining so long at Gretz, neither can I . . . I said you should come home. I now say you *must* come home. If you don't you will be voted a humbug and be regarded as unpopular as the Colorado beetle.' There were other lectures on duty, morality and Christianity including a paternal warning against closing the mind 'against everything that cannot be explained by physical law'. RLS spent a lot of time and energy parrying these overtures, and he threw out a memorable sop: 'I don't believe you people know how much I care for you . . . I have been meditating a great deal about Christianity and I never saw it to be so wise and noble and consolatory as I do now.'[26]

Louis was a bad correspondent for other reasons, as he explained to his father on 10 October in a letter written in Maison Lavenue: 'What you say is quite true. I do not seem to be very anxious to write to you but it is not so easy to write with a bad eye; for my eye continues to be a little bit of a nuisance.' That was an understatement, for even as he cajoled his parents with mundane letters about the French elections and President MacMahon – whom he hated – he suffered near blindness through acute ophthalmia. Fanny creditably took him into her apartment, insouciant about her reputation, and nursed him. When November came and he was no better, she cabled Bob to come and take him home. There was no answer: she learned later that Bob was both away from Edinburgh *and* seriously ill himself, so he would have been no use to her. She then wired Sidney Colvin, whom she had never met, to say that she was bringing Louis to London.

Fanny enjoyed her first visit to England, and even had a minor operation successfully carried out on her foot, which she had injured at Grez. At first she stayed in cheap lodgings while Colvin and Mrs Sitwell looked after Stevenson's nursing, but the two Fannies surprisingly (or perhaps unsurprisingly) got on well and the upshot was that Mrs Sitwell invited Mrs Osbourne into her home at Chepstow Place. The American Fanny described the experience to Timothy Rearden thus:

> I was with very curious people in London, the leaders of the Purists, I was so out of place in their house that a corner was arranged, or disarranged, for me. They dishevelled my curls, tied up my head in a yellow silk handkerchief, wrapped me in yellow shawls and spread a tiger skin rug over my sofa, and another by me. Everything else was of a dull pale blue or green, so that I had quite the feeling of being a sort of Pocahontas in my corner. It seemed most incongruous to have the solemn Mr Colvin, a professor at Cambridge, and the stately beautiful Mrs Sitwell sit by me and talk in the most correct English about the progress of literature and the arts. I was rather afraid of them but they did not seem to mind but occasionally came down to my level and petted me as one would stroke a kitten. They called me Fanny directly . . . I had always been told that they were cold heartless people, but I didn't find them so. I wonder why people never are that to me. Perhaps because I am little and not so clever as they.[27]

Fanny certainly acquitted herself well. She and Louis were heavy smokers – Will Low reported that RLS could roll a cigarette thinner than any man alive (sympathetic magic?) – but Louis had warned her that on no account should she smoke in Mrs Sitwell's house. One day, however, she was so excited to find herself in animated conversation with Leslie Stephen and Henley – later to be a deadly enemy – that she absentmindedly lit up. Mrs Sitwell responded with tact and charm: she and Colvin went out and bought cigarette papers and tobacco and requested lessons on how to roll their own.

By the beginning of December Fanny was back in Paris while Louis returned to Edinburgh to convalesce. His mood was sour, possibly because at this time the crisis over the Scottish romance came to a head. Where previously he had praised George Eliot for having given us a woman, in Rosamond Vincy, who was not all peaches-and-cream niceness, he now wrote to Patchett Martin, who had sent him his first-ever fan letter from Australia, that Eliot was 'a high, but, may we not add, a rather dry lady. Did you . . . have a kick at the stern works of that melancholy puppy and humbug Daniel Deronda himself – the Prince of Prigs; the literary abomination of desolation in the way of manhood; a type which is enough to make a man foreswear the love of women.'

Whether the next breach with his parents came over theology or women, certain it is that on New Year's Day Louis was at Dieppe en route for Paris, and writing to Colvin about the pressing need for money. He was running through the £1,000 at an alarming rate, not just in support of Fanny but also on expenditure on ill-considered ventures: he and Simpson had at one time thought of taking a barge, to be named the *11,000 Virgins of Cologne*, cruising on European waterways, subsidising their journey by lecturing as they went. The absurd impracticability of this plan soon communicated itself to the pair, but by this time they had bought the barge and had to resell it at a loss.[28]

In Paris he rejoined Fanny, who had gone back with Bob to nurse him back to health; we are not told what Bob's illness was, so it is possible it was the family depression that plagued him later in life. By then Louis and Fanny were definitely lovers, as a letter to Henley, written in Edinburgh that spring, makes clear: 'I'm a miserable widower, but so long as I work I keep cheerful . . . And do I not love? and am I not loved? and have I not friends who are the pride of my heart? O, no, I'll have none of your blues; I'll be lonely, dead lonely, for I can't help it; and I'll hate to go to bed where there is no dear head on the pillow, for I can't help that either, God help me.'[29]

Evidently his first conversations with Fanny in Paris convinced him that a total breach with his father was a bad idea; Fanny knew better than most what survival on the breadline meant and talked her lover round to seeking a reconciliation. Louis wrote to his father to say that he was still grappling with the problems of Christianity and now realised that the problems he had were with St Paul rather than Jesus and with 'the Christian doctrine of revenge. And it appears that this came into the world through Paul.' He went on to assure his father that he was now a mature adult:

> I have had some sharp lessons and some very acute sufferings in these last seven and twenty years . . . I begin to grow an old man; a little sharp, I fear, and a little close and unfriendly; but still I have a good heart, and believe in myself and my fellow-man and God who made us all . . . There are not many sadder people in this world, perhaps than I . . . I have taken a step towards more intimate relations with you. But don't expect too much of me. Try to take me as I am. This is a rare moment, and I have profited by it; but take it as a rare moment. Usually I hate to speak of what I really feel, to that extent that when I find myself *cornered*, I have a tendency to say the reverse.[30]

It is most likely that RLS was being disingenuous here and was dangling the carrot of conversion to the faith of his fathers before Thomas's avid gaze. It has sometimes, naïvely, been objected that such a ploy could never have worked, as only complete acquiescence in Calvinist orthodoxy would satisfy Thomas. However, all the evidence suggests that Thomas was indeed the sort of man who could have been deceived by the lure of a black sheep supposedly on his way back to the fold; no one would have been more aware of this than his only son.

February 1878 brought shocks from three different directions. First, no sooner was Bob properly on his feet again than RLS himself went down with another of his enigmatic pulmonary illnesses. As he wrote to Maggie: 'Bob is home long ago; I only kept him till I could go about. I am much better indeed; but I cannot work too much time, I don't know why: I suppose I am still weak ... I am overclad, but fear to take off a stitch. I also fear to leave my greatcoat; yet I cannot wear it; and so have to trudge with it under my arm.' Then Fanny collapsed with a severe attack of depressive illness. Had Stevenson been a more cynical man, he might have noticed two things of great significance about Fanny even at this stage of their relationship. First, whenever Fanny was called upon to do any nursing she went down with a malady herself: it had happened in November and it happened again now in February; it was a pattern that was to repeat itself over and over again throughout their marriage. Secondly, Fanny revealed her mental imbalance only *after* she and Louis became lovers. There could certainly be no question about the gravity of her mental state. As RLS wrote to Mrs Sitwell from the Hôtel Canterbury on the Boulevard Haussmann: 'I wish I could say she is well; her nerves are quite gone; one day I find her in heaven, the next in hell. We have many strong reasons for getting her out of Paris in about a month.' Nor was Louis's composure improved by the news that Sam Osbourne, alarmed by rumours reaching him in California, intended to journey to Paris in May to see exactly how things stood with his wife: 'it makes me sick to write it,' Louis confided to Baxter. All in all, it was clear to Louis that his notion that he and Fanny could bear any hardship and stand four-square against the world was a non-starter. If he really wanted to help his severely mentally disturbed married mistress, he would have to bow his head under the paternal yoke.[31]

Reading between the lines, one can detect yet a third reason for despondency in RLS in February 1878. Fanny had urged on Louis that the time was not yet right for divulging their affair to Thomas, knowing that he would certainly regard her as a vulgar adventuress, interested only in the family money. But there is reason to believe that RLS's hand was forced, that the casual affair with the unknown Scots girl was threatening to become an open scandal, and that Thomas Stevenson was insisting that, if his son had really seduced this girl, he was honour bound to marry her. Invoking Mrs Sitwell as an intermediary – for he had not the stomach for another fight with his father – Louis had her point out to Thomas that such a marriage was impossible, as Louis's affections were already engaged to an American woman.

Such is the tangled background of Thomas Stevenson's visit to Paris in February. Furnas comments: 'Whether Thomas then met Fanny, whether he was made privy to the extent of the relationship, I do not know, but suspect that No answers both questions.' Thomas certainly did *not* meet Fanny before 1880, but it is absurd to imagine that Louis did not put him fully in the picture at this meeting. If he did not, what on earth was the urgent matter that brought Stevenson *père*, a man who loathed 'abroad', hot-foot to Paris? In fact, however, we know that it was Louis's relationship with Fanny that was the motive, since RLS tells us so himself, in a letter to Colvin. 'My father is coming, at my request, to Paris – don't be astonished, but admire my courage and Fanny's. We wish to be right with the world as far as we can; 'tis a big venture, wish us god speed.'[32]

There is no documentary evidence for what was said between father and son, but evidently some sort of compromise was hammered out, as a result of which Louis agreed to return to Scotland to spend the Easter holidays with his parents. The experience of staying with them at the Shandon Hydropathic Establishment at Gairloch, Clyde, was a miserable one. Louis wrote to Mrs Sitwell to tell her of his humiliation, depression and inability to work: 'I think I never feel so lonely as when I am too much with my father and mother, and I am ashamed of the feeling, which makes matters worse.' All the time he was getting messages from Paris about Fanny's mental illness which he confided to Mrs Sitwell, adding as a sweetener that the American Fanny adored her British namesake: 'I am afraid Fanny is not very bright in health but she says she is taking care. And Fate has handled us so lightly hitherto, that I almost begin to think it means us well in the main. Her letter to me was mainly about you.'[33]

Under the surface, guilt gnawed at him: guilt that he was in a liaison that his parents disapproved of, and guilt that, precisely because Fanny was a married woman, he had to play down the seriousness of the attachment and thus seemed to reduce her to the level of his other casual conquests. Once liberated from the parental yoke, RLS sped back to Paris and Fanny's arms. This time he had a good excuse for being in Paris, for Fleeming Jenkin was a juror at the 1878 Paris Exposition and employed Stevenson as his 'secretary'; this was the only paid post Louis ever had in his life, and as gainful employment was a polite fiction. Jenkin allowed him to draw salary as a sinecure and got others to write his letters for him, allowing Louis further precious moments in Fanny's embrace. Then in June came the day Louis had long dreaded: 'this is the last twenty days of my passion' he wrote to Baxter. Instead of travelling to Europe, Sam Osbourne suddenly ordered her to return forthwith or forego any further financial assistance. Fanny

...in an impossible position. To disobey her husband meant that she and ... only as lovers, thus alienating his parents and ... fortune she still thought him likely ... enson – and marriage was certainly ... consulted Baxter on the advisability ... y – she would have to get a divorce ... uis to support her financially, for the ... return to the U.S.A.[34]

... s and Fanny's erotic bliss, but had ... for Belle, as it aborted her budding ... an gave her a portrait of himself by ...) and a pug dog called Paddy as a ... ruined their romance: the lovers soon ..., her mental state at this time is well

...ing on the weight of a fanatic dedication to ... lf and her life to be. In some ways she was ... knew that she was no genius in painting or ... be. But she felt that she was noble, gifted and ... and values. She played this wishful role with ...ing actress, she conveyed it to at least half of ... respond were the more ruthless because they ...lse. It was a dream of self-hypnosis.[35]

...he transatlantic voyage. Bob met her at ...ly to his lodgings in Chelsea. Then Louis arrived and ... goodbye to them at the station where they took the train to the dockside, but Lloyd was disappointed that his beloved 'Luly' – as he called him – did not once look back as he walked away down the platform. Louis was depressed and angry: despondent at the wrench that took Fanny away and angry that Sam Osbourne still had the power to turn his life upside down. Ahead of him there seemed to loom nothing but a mountain range of work.

IMPORTANT - This ticket has been charged to your account. If ticket is not required this month, return both ticket and invoice intact immediately. If ticket is detached and returned, credit will be calculated according to LIRR refund policy.

MONTHLY TICKET

Conditions: The conditions under which this ticket is sold by the Long Island Rail Road and accepted by the purchaser are as follows:

1. Subject to all Passenger Tariff provisions and rules and regulations of the Long Island Rail Road.

2. Ticket is good only when signed by person for whom issued and is for his or her exclusive use and individual transportation during the period shown on the other side. Ticket must be officially stamped by selling agent.

3. If tendered for the transportation of any person other than the one whose signature appears on the face thereof, or if it bears any evidence of alteration, or is mutilated, or is permanently encased in any manner, ticket will be deemed forfeited and taken up by trainman. Person for whom ticket was issued expressly releases the Long Island Rail Road from any claim for reimbursement in case of forfeiture. Identification of holder as person for whom ticket was issued must be established to satisfaction of trainman whenever required. Misuse of this ticket may result in legal prosecution.

4. The sale of any ticket includes no assurance of a seat on a particular train.

5. Ticket must be displayed throughout ride and presented to trainman each time requested.

6. If ticket is not available for presentation to trainman, fare must be paid. No refund will be made of such fares nor will any adjustment be made for fares paid on account of lost, stolen or destroyed tickets.

7. Caution - Should you stop using the ticket during the month, submit it for refund immediately. Refunds will be determined, in accordance with Tariff, by deducting from the purchase price round-trip and/or weekly fares, for the days and weeks up to and including the date surrendered to ticket seller or mailed to LIRR, P.O. Box 383, Jamaica, New York 11435. The round-trip fare will be priced at two (2) times the full regular one-way fare for weekdays and at the off-peak round-trip fare for weekends and major holidays.

8. In the event of any conflict between the above provisions and the applicable Passenger Tariff in effect at the time, the Tariff shall prevail.

Name (please print) HOGG, Christopher

Address (please print) 1624 Stewart Lane Laurel Hollow (516) 6928221 MONTHLY TICKET

6

Uneasy Interlude

After the miserable parting with Fanny, Stevenson sped back to Paris. 'I feel pretty ill and pretty sad, as you can imagine,' he wrote to Baxter. The mood did not lift. A month later he informed the same friend: 'I find it damned hard work to keep up a good countenance in this world now-a-days, harder than anyone knows, and I hope you may never have cause to feel one half as sad as I feel.' The one slight consolation, as he told Mrs Sitwell, was that 'all's squared with my people'; his parents were relieved that their son would not be disgraced by living openly with Fanny.[1]

Louis was now working on the idea of a walking tour through the Cévennes mountains. Leaving his mail to accumulate at a *poste restante* at Montargis, he made his way to Le Puy in the Haute Loire and then to the upland town of Le Monastier, fifteen miles south, which he made his base for a month. Before he faced the austerity of the Cévennes, however, Louis gourmandised in Le Puy. For lunch he had a slice of melon, some ham and jelly, a *filet*, a plateful of gudgeon, the breast and leg of a partridge, green peas, eight crayfish, Mont d'or cheese, a peach, biscuits and macaroons, with table wine, all for just three francs – then about the equivalent of four shillings. At Le Monastier, where he was known to the local lacemakers as 'M.Steams', he worked on his 'Edinburgh Notes' and the stories which would eventually be published as *New Arabian Nights*. He found the town a 'mere mountain Poland' as it was riven by factionalism between the rival cliques of Legitimists, Orléanists, Imperialists and Republicans and the people 'gloomy rather, full of quarrels, bitter voluble, quarrelsome, cowardly, not a pleasant lot'.[2]

Stevenson planned a route that would take him over the mountains to Alais, whence he intended to visit the art critic P.G.Hamerton at his château in Autun. This meant crossing high, wild country on the marches of the Haute-Loire, Lozère, Ardèche and Gard and negotiating the 5,000' peaks of Goulet and Pic de Finiels. The locals reacted to the idea with consternation, urging on him the perils of cold, robbers, practical jokers, wolves and other nameless beasts. Louis brushed all this aside; he had more pressing practical problems. To carry his equipment over the mountains he needed a donkey and from 'Father Adam' at Monastier he purchased, for 65 francs and a glass of brandy, a female, Modestine, an animal the size of a large Newfoundland dog and the colour of 'an ideal mouse'. He loaded Modestine with a large home-made sleeping bag, capacious enough to accommodate two people: six square feet of green waterproof cart-cloth, lined with blue sheep's fur. The rest of his impedimenta included two changes of clothes, books, cooking-pot and spirit lamp, a lantern and candles, a Swiss pen-knife, tin-openers, a leather water-flask, a brandy-flask, a cache of tobacco and cigarette papers, a revolver and a lined exercise book in which he kept his journal. As food supply he took several packets of black chocolate, tins of Bologna sausage, and an egg-whisk to make his favourite egg-nog at breakfast, plus, on his first day out from Le Monastier as a special treat, a leg of cold mutton and a bottle of Beaujolais.

If the revolver and a silver gypsy ring he wore were reminders of Fanny, his decision to set out on a Sabbath can be read as deliberately cocking a snook at his parents' Calvinism. Yet initial progress on Sunday 22 September 1878 was so slow as almost to suggest the displeasure of the God of the Old Testament. The problem was Modestine. She refused to climb hills, shed her loads on a whim, and zigzagged off the straight path in search of shade. Stevenson was not to know that even seasoned explorers had the same problem in the heart of Africa, and feelings of inadequacy vied with reluctance to use force against a dumb animal. A local donkey-driver, taking pity on his incompetence, cut a switch and instructed him how to set about Modestine's flanks; the improvement in her behaviour was so dramatic that Stevenson became convinced her former recalcitrance was mere play-acting. Yet the necessary violence of driving beasts of burden sickened him – a feeling increased by the realisation that Modestine was female: 'The sound of my own blows sickened me. Once when I looked at Modestine, she had a faint resemblance to a lady of my acquaintance who once loaded me with kindness; and this increased my horror of my own cruelty.'

Thoughts of Fanny could not be banished, for everything Modestine did seemed to remind RLS of sex.

We encountered another donkey, ranging at will upon the roadside, and this other donkey chanced to be a gentleman. He and Modestine met nickering for joy, and I had to separate the pair and stamp out the nascent romance with a renewed and feverish bastinado. If the other donkey had had the heart of male under his hide, he would have fallen upon me tooth and nail; and this is a kind of consolation, he was plainly unworthy of Modestine's affections. But the incident saddened me, as did everything that reminded me of my donkey's sex.

Stevenson wanted to reach Lake Bouchet by sundown but, even after beating Modestine savagely, he got lost in a maze of country roads, the rope binding the bundle of possessions to her back snapped and spilled the contents on to the track, and in the end he found his way to his night's stopover only by following two dour peasants. At Le Bouchet he put up at the inn and shared a room with two beds, the other occupied by a cooper and his young wife. 'I kept my eyes to myself as much as I could, and I know nothing of the woman except that she had beautiful arms, full white and shapely; whether she slept naked or in her slip, I declare I know not; only her arms were bare.'

The first day's travel had not been auspicious: having paid too much for Modestine, RLS had compounded his carelessness by having to jettison the cold leg of mutton and the loaf of white bread. In the morning the genial innkeeper fashioned a proper goad for Modestine, while his much more abrasive but intelligent wife chatted to Stevenson about the proper contents for the journal he intended to publish. This marriage of opposites amused RLS, especially when the wife suddenly burst out angrily: 'My man knows nothing. He is like the beasts'; at which the husband nodded eagerly 'as if it were rather like a compliment'.

On the second day Stevenson headed due south, over the uplands of the Velay to Pradelles for lunch, then to Langogne on the river Allier, and across to the Gévaudan. This was the country of the famous 'Beast of Gévaudan', usually thought to be a giant wolf with a taste for human flesh, or even a pack of such maneaters, which terrorised these wild highlands in the 1760s. After Louis was received sluttishly and cheekily by two peasant children when he asked the way, he reflected: 'The Beast of Gévaudan ate about a hundred children of this district; I begin to think of him with sympathy.'

It was not just the children of the Gévaudan who were inhospitable. When he lost his way in the gloom, the peasants refused to put him on the right track; forced to sleep in a cave, he dined off his emergency supplies of chocolate and Bologna sausage, eating them piece by piece alternately and washing it all down with neat brandy. There could be no greater contrast to his reception next day at Cheylard, for here the locals fussed over him, dried his clothes and welcomed him to the inn, where he dined on a large omelette and drinking chocolate. It was typical of RLS, though, that the experience should have drawn merely an ambivalent response:

Why anyone should desire to go to Cheylard or to Luc is more than my much inventing spirit can embrace. For my part, I travel not to go anywhere, but to go; I travel for travel's sake. And to write about it afterwards, if only the public will be so condescending to read. But the great affair is to move; to feel the needs and hitches of life a little more nearly; to get down off this feather bed of civilisation, and to find the globe granite underfoot and strewn with cutting flints.

When the innkeeper pointed out that the sleeping bag was chafing Modestine and, on examination, sure enough, her forelegs were raw and the blood was running, Louis felt more irritation than compassion.

The road from Cheylard to Luc was the most desolate so far. Emerging from the wilderness by the ruins of Luc castle hard by the Allier, he decided to spend the night in a large clean inn. Then on Thursday 26 September he turned east from the Allier and set out along the valley, with the hills of the Gévaudan on the right and those of Vivarais on the left, intending to make for the Trappist monastery of Our Lady of the Snows. A kind of terror oppressed him as he approached the monastery – the fear of the born and bred Calvinist in close contact with the painted whore of Rome. Learning that he was not, as he appeared, a pedlar but a Scots author, the monks introduced him to Father Apollinaris, who assigned him a whitewashed cell in the guest quarters, provided him with a meal, took Modestine to the stables, and requested him to attend meals and services at will – the Trappists ate twice in every 24-hour period and just once in fast periods.

There were two other guests at Our Lady of the Snows at the time: a priest and an old soldier. At dinner these two sorely tried RLS's patience, especially as their actions consistently belied their words. Having agreed with the young Scotsman that it was impossible to say anything even mildly political in France without sparking off a tremendous row, and having deprecated such an attitude as unChristian, they waded into him the minute he praised Gambetta's moderation. The soldier at once went purple with fury and beat the table with his palms like a naughty child. '*Comment, monsieur?*' he shouted '*Comment?* Will you dare to justify those words?' The priest silenced the warrior with a glance, but next day it was the turn of the old trooper to play peacemaker. At breakfast RLS let slip that he was an unbeliever, at which the two descended on him with full proselytising zeal. Thinking to escape from the onslaught by mentioning that his parents were Calvinists, Louis merely precipitated a fresh tirade, in which it was suggested that having bowed his head to the Pope he should then try to convert his parents to Catholicism, for Calvinism was a mere sect and not even deserving of the title of religion. At this Stevenson exploded, went white with emotion and said to the priest with a glare in his eyes: 'I shall continue to answer your questions with all politeness; but I must ask you not to laugh. Your laughter seems to me misplaced; and you forget that I am describing the faith of my mother.'

The soldier smoothed over this altercation, and Louis left the monastery on friendly enough terms with his interlocutors. Here was an instance of the well-known phenomenon whereby an unbeliever will secretly curse the religion of his upbringing, but never allow criticism from a member of a rival dispensation. The monks saw him on his way, following the course of the Allier back into the Gévaudan towards its source in the Mercoire forest. He reached Chasserades by dusk and again put up at an inn, discussing the future of France over hot wine before retiring to a four-bedded room, of which he was the only occupant.

He was on the road again at 5 a.m. on Saturday 28 September, into the valley of the Chasserac, and now engaged with the great upland peaks of the Cévennes; first came the Montagne du Goulet at 4,700', and then he made his way briskly through Lestampes and Bleymard to the night's resting place among the pines of Lozère. The landscape was changing, and the moorlands, pine woods, rocky screes and gorges reminded him of the Scottish Highlands. Next day he crossed the Lozère, which lay east-west and cut the Gévaudan into two unequal parts, and began the ascent of the Pic de Finiels, at 5,600', which in clear weather commanded a view over the whole Languedoc. Although strictly speaking he had been in the Cévennes even at Le Monastier, this was the heartland, the 'Cévennes of the Cévennes', and the country of the Camisards, the Protestant rebels of the rising of 1702-03 whose defiance of Louis XIV had thrilled Stevenson since boyhood. With his mind reeling with images and associations of these 'Covenanters of the South' – about whom he wrote at length in the published version of *Travels with a Donkey* – RLS camped on the mountainside in a pine grove near a running stream. He was asleep at 9 p.m. but woke again five hours later. Modestine was gently cropping the grass, but there was no other sound. He lay on his back, smoked a cigarette and pondered the perfection of this experience under the stars. He fantasised the life of a lighthouse keeper by illuminating his gypsy ring every time he took a drag on his cigarette. He considered that now, for the first time, he was fully alive.

> In the whole of my life I have never tasted a more perfect hour of life ... O sancta solitudo! I was such a world away from the roaring streets, the delivery of cruel letters, and the saloons where people love to talk, that it seemed to me as if life had begun again afresh, and I knew no one in all the universe but the almighty maker. I promised myself, as Jacob set up an altar, that I should never again sleep under a roof when I could help it, so gentle, so cool, so singularly peaceful and large, were my sensations.

But next morning, when he wrote this passage in his journal, he realised that there was one thing wrong with his Eden: it lacked an Eve.

And yet even as I thought the words, I was aware of a strange lack. I could have wished for a companion, to be near me in the starlight, silent and not moving if you like, but ever near and within touch. For there is, after all, a sort of fellowship, more quiet even than solitude, and which, rightly understood, is solitude made perfect. And to live out of doors with the woman a man loves is of all lives the most complete and free ... The woman whom a man has learnt to love wholly, in and out, with utter comprehension, is no longer another person in the troublous sense. What there is of exacting in another companionship has disappeared, there is no need to speak; a look or a word stand for such a world of feeling; and where the two watches go so nicely together, beat for beat, thought for thought, there is no call to conform the minute hands and make an eternal trifling compromise of life.

On Sunday 29 September he crossed the Lozère into different terrain again and descended into the valley, following a watercourse to the river Tarn at Pont de Montvert. Here he had lunch with two pretty married women and flirted outrageously with a waitress named Clarisse. He left in the *Travels* some comments on Clarisse's physical charms that would have outraged a Victorian audience had they been made about anyone of higher social status than a chambermaid or 'serving wench' and this has snared the unwary into talking of Stevenson's 'elitism'. Yet if we accept that all the remarks about women in the *Travels* are coded messages to Fanny, then we can see the sexual desirability of Clarisse, which RLS clearly refers to, as being a transmogrified version of his feelings for Fanny.

After lunch he proceeded to Florac through the twisting road through the Gorges du Tarn and camped on the steep chestnut terraces above the river. This turned out to be a mistake: the 'shelves' were so narrow that he had to tether Modestine higher up in another cleft, and the dormitory was uncomfortably close to the road. Every sound, whether of frogs, mosquitoes, ants, rats or fallen leaves made him wonder if this was perhaps a band of brigands coming up from the road to rob him; consequently he spent a troubled, largely sleepless night, tossing and turning, waking abruptly from a light doze and reaching for his revolver. He was finally woken on the Monday morning by two peasants with pruning hooks, who asked roughly what he thought he was doing there; they watched with ill-concealed suspicion while he and Modestine stumbled back down to the road.

He proceeded to the hamlet of La Vernède and then to Florac, where lunch at the inn converted him to the locals, who seemed cordial and tolerant. Then he plunged into the valley of the Mimente and made his bed in a hollow underneath an oak. On the morning of 2 October he reached Cassagnas, at the separation of the watersheds: behind him the streams were bound for the Garonne and the Atlantic; ahead lay the basin of the Rhône. Determined now to press on the pace and get to Alais, he spent his longest day so far on the road, along the edge of Mont Mars, from where chain after chain and peak after peak of mountains stretched into the distance, finally, after nightfall, coming down into the village of St Germain-de-Calberte. He reached the only inn just ten minutes before it closed for the night and drank himself quickly to sleep with Volnay wine.

Next day he took the carriage road over the Col de St Pierre, fifteen miles over a very stiff hill, and came to St Jean du Gard after nightfall, having been slow to get under way in the morning. Here the local farrier found Modestine unfit to travel further; Stevenson promptly sold her for 35 francs and took the stage to Alais. It was typical of RLS to have regrets in retrospect. 'It was not until I was fairly seated by the driver, and rattling through a rocky valley with dwarf olives, that I became aware of Modestine. Up to that moment I had thought I hated her; but now she was gone – 'And oh! The difference to me!'[3]

From Alais Stevenson continued to Lyons and thence to Autun, where he had a very successful meeting with Hamerton, before returning to Paris. He pressed ahead quickly with publication of his journals, suitably written up. Henley read the finished manuscript at Swanston during the third week of January 1879; Hamerton, who had agreed to be Louis's agent, meanwhile secured an advance of £30 for the book.[4] When *Travels with a Donkey* appeared in book form, many of the critics noticed the ubiquity of sexuality – hardly surprisingly since, as RLS told Bob, it was a disguised ode to his new love: 'lots of it is mere protestations to Fanny.' This is particularly clear at the end of the book when he hears a woman sighing and wishes he could answer her: 'What could I have told her? Little enough; and yet all the heart requires. How the world gives and takes away and brings sweethearts near only to separate them again into distant and strange lands; but to love is the great amulet which makes the world a garden; and 'hope which comes to all', outwears the accident of life, and reaches with tremulous hands beyond the grave and death.' Maggie objected to the more 'sensual passages' and was shocked that Louis did not modify the offending words even when appealed to.[5] The critics, wearing the colours of Mrs Grundy, duly made their predictable appearance; the reviewer in the *Spectator* observed patronisingly: 'Until a man has passed out of the stage when women, with their love and their charms, make up all religion to him, his judgement upon the intellectual bearing of different creeds is worth as little as his love.'[6]

Obsessed by the sexual overtones, the critics largely missed the ambiguity, the irony and the humour; on the theme of duality what could be richer or more resonant than a man with the physical appearance of Don Quixote making a journey with the steed of Sancho Panza? Or the contrast between the superficially similar Covenanters and Camisards, the former shrouded in the darkness and gloom of Scotland, the latter deriving from a Mediterranean culture and a climate and landscape characterised by light? In his dedication to Colvin, RLS wrote: 'We are all travellers in what John Bunyan calls the wilderness of this world – all, too, travellers with a donkey, and the best that we find in our travels is an honest friend.' Yet it was abundantly clear that this was exactly what RLS had *not* found, and there is something deeply risible in the passage where, reluctant to brutalise Modestine, he ends up bearing her burden. Put in paradoxical form, the moral of this seems to be that in 'freedom' one is more burdened than in the 'bondage' of civilisation and that 'freedom' actually consists in shedding the onus of travel. This takes us back to a favourite RLS formulation: 'Everything is true; only the opposite is true too: you must believe both equally or be damned . . . A lie may be told by a truth, or a truth conveyed through a lie. The whole tenor of a conversation is part of the meaning of each separate statement; truth in the spirit, not truth to the letter, is the true veracity.'

From Paris Louis crossed to England in late October. He went first to visit Colvin at Trinity College, Cambridge, where he spent a few days but found he could not write: 'I can only write ditch-water,' he told Henley. ''Tis ghastly; but I am quite cheerful, and that is more important.' Like so many others, he found Oxbridge dons unreal and closer to phantoms or mythical creatures than to human beings: 'Have not spoken to a real person for about sixty hours,' he wrote to Henley. He returned to London, staying partly in Ealing and partly in the Savile Club. Here he worried about his friends; about the ructions in the Simpson family caused by Sir Walter's irregular marriage in 1874 to Anne Fitzgerald Mackay, but most of all about Katharine de Mattos, whose marriage had broken up and who now supported herself by journalism. The combination of knight-errantry and rescue fantasy, as well as his genuine liking for her, made Katharine a peculiarly suitable object of such charity as he could afford, but he exploded when Sydney de Mattos had the effrontery to write to him to complain that Katharine in Paris had not received a cheque for £10 that he (RLS) had promised. Ill at ease and fractious, Louis contemplated another walking tour in England and seems actually to have begun it, but this aborted in circumstances not entirely clear, as related to his mother: 'The walking tour broke down. My heel gave way and hurt horrid, and it was dull, cold and not singularly pretty on the road.' At a loss what to do next, the prodigal finally returned to Edinburgh, as set down thus by Maggie in her diary: '*At last* on the 21st [of December] after being more than six months away Louis came home.'[7]

During this gloomy period and into 1879, while he pined over the separation from Fanny, the sole slight consolation was the gradual consolidation of his literary career. For the first time he wrote, in 'Will o' the Mill', a short story of outstanding quality. The genesis for this was ideas contained in 'An Apology for Idlers', an essay written at Swanston and Queensferry in the dull early months of 1877, in which RLS defends himself against the reproaches of conscience and praises the wisdom of the idler and the opter-out: 'His way takes him along a by-road, not much frequented, but very even and pleasant, which is called commonplace lane and leads to the Belvedere of Commonsense. Thence he shall command an agreeable if no very noble prospect.'[8]

'Will o' the Mill' develops these ideas in a tour de force of the kind of pessimism and stoicism the young RLS so admired in Marcus Aurelius's *Meditations*. The critic Cope Cornford called it Stevenson's

> greatest achievement in literature ... to me, at least, that melancholy and beautiful fable is the best of Stevenson, and resumes his whole ideal philosophy of life ... the whole is informed with a sort of fatalism, hopeless yet courageous, which the English mind sets to the account of the Celtic temperament ... the night when Will o' the Mill goes at last upon his travels ... I venture to characterise as one of the finest pieces of pictorial narration in English literature.[9]

In 'Will', Stevenson repeats his conviction that marriage is not worthwhile, that travel is futile, that the kingdom of God is within. 'Romantic pessimism' best sums up lines like these: 'When I was a boy, I was a bit puzzled and hardly knew whether it was myself or the world that was curious and worth looking into. Now I know it is myself, and stick to that.' Pascal's idea that the world would be a better place if each man stayed quietly in his own room is here taken to the limit, and there is much flirting with the notion that death is a consummation devoutly to be wished. In the end, Will, who has never strayed outside his valley in his life, is confronted by Death in the guise of a mysterious visitor. At last the visitor reveals his identity.

> 'People call me Death.'
> 'Why did you not tell me so at first?' cried Will. 'I have been waiting for you these many years. Give me your hand and welcome.'[10]

Does this mean, as has sometimes been alleged, that Stevenson is guilty of a facile fatalism, that his optimistic style, full of sharp effects, is in conflict with a pessimistic world-view, that he portrays Man as pilgrim on a journey of illusory salvation, and that he praises the blessings of non-achievement? Hardly. Although an author's intentions are never conclusive – they could scarcely be, given the role of the unconscious in creativity – it is clear that such was not even RLS's *conscious* intention. In *Familiar Studies* he makes it clear that he thinks life should be confronted and its problems taken on; for this reason he praises Villon and Whitman for their courage and condemns Thoreau and Charles of Orléans for their cowardice and self-indulgence. He told his first biographer, Graham Balfour, that 'Will' was written 'as an experiment, in order to see what could be said in support of the opposite theory'.[11]

RLS later told Belle that he loved this work dearly and was disappointed that others did not share his view of its merits. That many critics were confused by his intentions was clear from Leslie Stephen's reaction: he accepted it for the *Cornhill Magazine* with reservations, objecting to the story's apparent fluctuation between allegory and realism. And 'Will' has probably not received its due in the Stevenson canon partly because RLS liked to jest about his work, to rib people and sell himself short. One night in the 1890s, at dinner in Samoa, Graham Balfour told the assembled company that Will had made a deep impression on him and affected his attitude to life. Stevenson replied brusquely: 'Will's sentiments about life are cat's meat.' Balfour persisted: 'It's the best thing on life that has been written in this age.' Fanny, always worried that Balfour did not fit in with the joshing and ribbing in the Stevenson ménage, quickly interjected: 'Edmund Gosse has told Louis that if he'd never written another thing, Will o' the Mill would have made his literary fame.'[12] However, there is some evidence that later in life RLS was unhappy even with his experimental endorsement of Will's fatalism. In the spring of 1884 he wrote to Trevor Haddon: 'I prefer galvinism to acquiescence in the grave. All do not; 'tis an affair of tastes; and mine are young. Those who like death have their innings today.' And in the last month of his life he rebuked 'Will's' champion Gosse: 'It is all very well to talk of renunciation and of course it has to be done. But, for my part, give me a roaring toothache.'[13]

The essay 'Crabbed Age and Youth', written in the summer of 1877, is a coded account of his turbulent relations with his father and is the first of a stream of essays that poured from his pen in the period just before and after Fanny's departure for California. 'Aes Triplex' and 'El Dorado' – a special favourite of Henley's – deal with death; 'The English Admirals' is a straightforward account of the island's great naval heroes from Drake to Nelson; 'Lay Morals', begun and substantially completed in early 1879 but published only posthumously, returns to the subject of the relationship between Christ's teaching and modern Christianity first raised by RLS in his 1872 essay for 'the Spec' and is to Stevenson's non-fictional output what Hume's *Dialogues concerning Natural Religion* are to *his oeuvre*.[14]

More interesting were Stevenson's other fictional endeavours: the short stories 'A Lodging for the Night' and 'The Sire de Maletroit's Door', where for the first time he grappled with the problems of writing historical fiction. 'A Lodging for the Night' deals with his hero Villon, but has always been criticised for losing its way in the second half, when RLS seems to switch from storytelling to the more familiar techniques of the essay, and certainly the ending is reminiscent of Browning. It does, however, provide a first outing for the gangs of cutthroats and degenerates who were to be so familiar in the later fiction (*Treasure Island, The Master of Ballantrae, The Ebb-Tide*, etc). As an allegory of human existence, 'The Sire of Maletroit's

Door' is a feeble follow-up to 'Will' and although there are some fine cameos and intriguing themes – the 'safeconduct' which provides no safety against the watch, the choice between marriage and death – it fails to convince in its wider ambitions.[15]

On the strength of these early ventures into fiction, Leslie Stephen tried to persuade RLS to attempt a full-length novel and virtually guaranteed its serial publication, whatever it turned out to be, but he can hardly have been expecting the stories that were eventually (1882) published in book form as *New Arabian Nights*, and which appeared in serial form throughout 1878. If 'Will' was Stevenson's *Pierre*, this book was surely his *Mardi*. Critics spotted the debt of 'Will' to the *Pentameron* and *Travels with a Donkey* to Sterne but, apart from noting that the 'Rajah's Diamond' story was a parody of Wilkie Collins's *The Moonstone*, this time they were bewildered. The volume has always had its champions, though. As Chesterton remarked: 'I will not say that the *New Arabian Nights* is the greatest of Stevenson's works; though a considerable case might be made for the challenge. But I will say that it is probably the most unique; there was nothing like it before, and, I think, nothing equal to it since.'[16]

Stevenson wanted to resolve feelings about death and the aesthetic life through a series of fictional stories and to this end produced a Ruritanian hero (popular in the Victorian age), Prince Florizel, as his protagonist. Another inspiration was Bob, who appears in barely disguised form as the young man with the cream tarts in the opening story, and would later go through other transmutations as aspects of the eponymous hero of *Prince Otto* and Paul Somerset in *The Dynamiter*. It was Bob too who first suggested the idea of a 'Suicide Club' where those tired to death could arrange for mutual destruction. *New Arabian Nights*, then, is many things: a meditation on death; a satire on fin-de-siècle pessimists like Wilde and Swinburne; an examination of Victorian England, with the Suicide Club as its microcosm; and, at the unconscious level, Stevenson's attempt to overcome the self-contempt he always felt about being an artist, alias prostitute, as he put it in 'To a young gentleman who proposes to embrace the career of Art'.

There has always been impassioned debate about whether RLS's physical debility did genuinely make him tired of life from time to time, or if it was merely self-pitying, self-conscious posturing. In 1875 he wrote: 'Only to go out forever by sunny day, and grey day, by bright night and foul, by highway and by-way, town and hamlet, until somewhere by a roadside or in some clean inn death opened its arms to me and took me to his quiet heart forever.' That sounds like the gallery touch or romantic play-acting; why a 'clean inn', for example? On the other hand, it is quite clear from a detailed examination of his correspondence that RLS did seriously contemplate suicide on at least three occasions: in 1873 during the violent wrangle with his parents; in early 1876 in despair over Fanny Sitwell; and

in 1887 when his friendship with Henley came to an end. Yet in the end
Stevenson's morality of strenuousness always overbore both the fantasies of
death and the genuine suicidal impulses, and in Florizel's remark about the
Suicide Club we surely discern RLS's own attitude: 'If a man has made up
his mind to kill himself, let him do it in God's name, like a gentleman. This
flutter and big talk is out of place.'[17]

New Arabian Nights is certainly excessively concerned with death, to
the point where the Thanatos of the new replaces the Eros of the old,
original Arabian Nights – with the translation of which Richard Burton
was to have such a success in the following decade – and since Victorian
audiences would not tolerate erotica, its displacement into violence was
not just fitting but almost inevitable, especially given that the banality of
Victorian London replaced the mysteries of the East, and melodrama had
to be substituted for magic. Stevenson has been criticised for beginning with
satire and then lurching into farce and melodrama, but this too reflects the
pattern and variety of the original stories; his own idiosyncratic contribution
is to layer his characteristic ambiguity and irony across the simple morals
of the Thousand and One Nights, mocking the pretensions of his effete
contemporaries in the shape of Mr Malthus and his associates, and pointing
up the ludicrous inability of humans to overcome their limitations. The real
problem is that an author is supposed to know his world as God knows this
one, but Stevenson is clearly at sea himself. The universe of New Arabian
Nights is the universe of chaos theory, changing as it does from the naturalistic to the fantastic to the whimsical, with an authorial voice pari passu
now satirical, now melodramatic, now farcical, now fantastical. Sometimes
RLS even misses the obvious tricks; it is surprising that he did not spot
the incompatibility between Florizel's fate and the much derided line in A
Child's Garden of Verses:

> The world is so full of a number of things
> I'm sure we should all be as happy as kings.

Florizel's reduction from monarch to tobacconist, which would have
made a good topic for a full-blown satire, gets lost in the whimsical
shuffle. Rather than darting in and out of different modes and different
universes of discourse. Stevenson could have produced a more effective tale
by showing how the Nietzchean Florizel, the ubermensch, ends by fumbling
in a greasy till, the pomp of European monarchy defeated by the banality
of a nation of shopkeepers.

The final months of 1878 saw the publication of one of RLS's few
stories in completely optimistic mood, 'Providence and the Guitar', based
on the plight of some strolling players he and Fanny had known at Grez.
He then began work on 'The Pavilion on the Links', an elaborate thriller,
finally completed in the U.S.A. and published in 1880; some of the Prince

Florizel stories had had a distinct flavour of Conan Doyle *avant la lettre* about them, but 'Pavilion' drew the explicit praises of Sherlock Holmes's creator when he encountered it in the early 1890s.[18]

Friendship and misplaced loyalty to Henley now led RLS temporarily into an artistic cul-de-sac. Ever since 1869, Louis had a draft of a play lying in his bottom drawer, dealing with the notorious eighteenth-century dual personality Deacon Brodie, a respectable businessman by day but a burglar by night – in short a perfect Stevensonian subject. Henley, who had married Anna Boyle in April 1878 and settled in Shepherd's Bush, was permanently short of money and thought that playwriting could bring him the crock of gold. He persuaded Louis to collaborate with him on a drama based on Brodie's life; from October–December 1878 Stevenson spent three hours every morning in the Savile Club writing second and third drafts, and then went over to Shepherd's Bush in the afternoon for a further three hours' polishing and discussion with Henley. Then in January 1879 Henley came up to the Swanston cottage for a final week's honing and shaping (incidentally, *pace* Furnas, here was an obvious occasion when he could have seen Stevenson's Scots mistress). Yet, if 'Burly', the elder brother surrogate, thought highly of their collaboration, neither of Louis's 'father figures' did. Colvin damned *Deacon Brodie* as a 'morally unintelligible, unconvincing and non-existent' work; Jenkin was even harsher, telling Louis that he and Henley had 'tried to do an impossible thing, and had not even tried it in a right way.'[19]

The collaborators stopped their ears against such jeremiahs and offered the play to Henry Irving; he prevaricated for almost a year before turning it down. While RLS was in the U.S.A., Henley, his faith in the 'masterpiece' undimmed, had it printed; it was performed in Bradford in 1882, in Aberdeen a year later, in London in 1884 at the Prince's Theatre, and finally in New York and the eastern seaboard in 1887–88, when it was taken on tour by Henley's bibulous younger brother Teddy, a thespian of limited talents. Undaunted by all the adverse criticism, RLS and Henley simply redoubled their efforts to conquer the stage, and on completion of *Brodie* immediately launched into a Cromwellian tragedy entitled *Hester Noble*, which RLS continued to work on in the U.S.A. in 1880, until a withering critique from Jenkin, opining that Louis had no talent as a playwright, halted him in his tracks.[20]

The failure of these attempts at dramaturgy left Henley, already despondent after his wife had given birth to a stillborn baby, nursing an obscure grudge against Louis, whom he blamed for not putting his back into the job and being distracted by other literary forms. He struck back by making carping criticisms at RLS's verses, to which Stevenson replied with mild irritation: 'If I don't rewrite them, it's because I don't see how to write them better, not because I don't think they should be.' From 1879 can be traced the snaking trail of gunpowder that would eventually blow the relationship sky-high: Henley thought that Stevenson approached playwriting in a cavalier and insouciant way, while Louis felt that his friend was trying, albeit unconsciously, to climb to fame and fortune on *his* back: as he told him later: 'You were not quite sincere with yourself; you were seeking arguments to make me devote myself to plays, unbeknown, of course, to yourself.'[21]

By the spring of 1879 RLS, now back in London and dismayed by the news from California, was beginning to unravel, and there are elements of Deacon Brodie in his own life at this time. By day he was the rising *littérateur*, clubbable at the Savile, renewing the acquaintance with George Meredith first made in March 1878 at Burford Bridge. Meredith now lived at Flint Cottage, Box Hill, and it was there in the spring of 1879 that RLS really got to know him. A wide-eyed admirer of *Harry Richmond, Richard Feverel* and, later, *The Egoist* (which he read six or seven times), Stevenson at first alarmed Meredith by the very vehemence of his enthusiasm but, once he had taken the measure of his young admirer, the older man prophesied a glittering future for him. Henry James once remarked on Stevenson's passion for Meredith: 'It is indeed my impression that he prefers the author of *The Three Musketeers* to any novelist except Mr George Meredith. I should go so far as to suspect that his ideal of the delightful work of fiction would be the adventures of Monte Cristo related by the author of *Richard Feverel*.'[22]

Yet by night RLS wandered the streets of London in ragged clothes, hoping to be arrested as a tramp; the depths of his misery and self-loathing can be gauged when his revulsion at being arrested by the French policeman in 1876 is remembered. His state of mind began to alarm friends like Edmund Gosse, who had always looked on RLS as 'the Great Exhilarator . . . my emblem of Life'. When taxed with this, Louis replied: 'I can do no work. I want – I want – I want – a holiday; I want to be happy; I want the moon or the sun or something. I want the object of my affections anyway . . . I envy you your wife, your home, your child – I was going to say your cat. There would be cats in my home too if I could but get it. I may seem to you "the impersonation of life", but my life is the impersonation of waiting, and that's a poor creature.'[23]

The problem of course was Fanny. When the lovers parted in the summer of 1878, there was clearly a tacit understanding between them that when Fanny returned to the U.S.A. she would petition for a divorce in the much freer climate there; Californian law permitted the civilised ending of marriages, and in this sense the lovers were lucky: they would not have to wait half a lifetime like Colvin and Fanny Sitwell. Yet when Fanny got back to California, she made no moves towards a divorce. Sam's charm once more did its work, the couple were partly reconciled, and Fanny resumed her marital role alongside Sam in the cottage at East Oakland. Lucy Orr Vahnenkamp, daughter of Cora Vandegrift and a close friend of Fanny's, said: 'She would never have left Sam Osbourne if she could have avoided it'; Louis was right to fear that once she got back to California she would backslide.[24] In the line of his career as court stenographer with the Bureau of Mines, Sam moved his family down to Monterey, where Belle promptly eloped with the young painter, Joe Strong, and Nellie, Fanny's sister, married Adolfo Sanchez, a Mexican saloon-keeper. RLS had insisted that Sam be put completely in the picture about his affair with Fanny, though her instincts were always towards discretion and secretiveness. Lloyd remembers an impassioned scene, which ended with Fanny's impassioned outburst: 'O Sam, forgive me!' Circumstantial evidence tends to indicate that Fanny confessed to the affair, and when Osbourne remonstrated defended her action as revenge for the short commons on which Sam had kept them in Europe, which was instrumental in the death of Hervey; but when Sam explained the full difficulties of his financial situation, she was struck with remorse.[25]

During 1878–79 Fanny, it seems, was tugged two ways: towards the physical appeal of Sam and towards the security that Louis, especially armed with his father's money, could provide for her. The resulting ambivalence and indecision paralysed her, so that she began to descend once more into the maelstrom of mental illness, always in her case triggered by stress. And here might be the place to point out that there is, after all, another side to the story of the Osbournes: that Sam's philandering might have been the effect rather than cause of Fanny's breakdowns, as in the dark hints thrown out by Sam's family that Fanny *drove* her first husband to infidelity. At any rate, the result of her breakdown this time was a series of wild letters to Louis, which so perturbed him that he confided in no one but Baxter. That Baxter, not Colvin, was the chosen confidant is clear from a depressed epistle sent by Stevenson to Colvin from Edinburgh in the summer of 1879: 'I like solitude and silence . . . Just now I have a perplexity, and do you know I can tell it to none of my friends . . . except Baxter.' To Colvin RLS kept up the fiction that he and Fanny were not in correspondence: 'To F. I never write letters. To begin with there's no good. All that people want by letters has been done between us. We are acquainted; why go on with more introductions? I cannot change so much, but she would still have the clue and recognize every thought. But between friends it is not so. Friendship is incomplete, and lives by conversation – on bits of knowledge not on faith.'[26]

Yet Baxter felt himself out of his depth in this supercharged world of violent emotions, and evidently passed on some of the confidences to Colvin, for on 6 February 1879 Colvin wrote to Gosse that Louis had 'been to pieces' recently, adding as the reason: 'He had got quite a sane letter from an intelligible address in Spanish California, where, after wild storms, intercepted flights and the Lord knows what more, she was for the present quiet among old friends of her own, away from the enemy, but with access to the children. What next, who shall tell?' Louis had eased his mind with a telegram, without, however, committing himself to anything. 'He won't go suddenly or without telling people. Which is as much as we can tell at present.' This tantalising fragment is all we have, since it is clear that Louis and Fanny later destroyed their correspondence. But it hints at very dark matters indeed, and James Pope-Hennessy hits the nail on the head when he comments: 'That what letters Fanny wrote to Louis during the months of separation must have been desperately odd seems to be shown by the fact that, in February 1879, Sidney Colvin bothers to comment on a "sane" one.'[27]

At times RLS seems to have considered giving Fanny up as a hopeless cause. Such at least seems the implication of a letter to Henley in spring 1879: 'I have parted company with half of man and nearly half of myself . . . I now know that I can suffer and not be permanently embittered or warped . . . God keep me brave and single-minded.' His confused state of mind seemed underlined when the 'Burns' essay appeared: on the one hand he was wracked with guilt by his earlier Don Juanism; on the other, he did not know which way to jump in the case of a woman to whom he owed a moral obligation because of sleeping with her while she was married. Perhaps, too, he was assailed by doubts about the purity of Fanny's emotions towards him: nearly a year had gone by, there was no sign of a divorce, only wild screeds from California, and requests for money; we know of these because in May RLS informed Baxter that he was sending £20 to Jacob Vandegrift, Fanny's only brother. It is of course logically possible that this was sent as a subvention to Jacob himself, who had recently migrated to California for his health, but since Louis had never clapped eyes on him, this seems implausible; a more likely explanation is that Jacob was the go-between and that Louis was thus sending money for the upkeep of a woman who was still another man's wife and, in theory at least, being maintained by him.[28]

Some of the confusion unwontedly seeped into his correspondence with his parents. In May he wrote from the Savile Club to his mother: 'I have been in such a muddle about my plans that I did not know what to write.' Trying to compose himself, he crossed to France and spent a couple of weeks relaxing at Lernay-la-Ville in the *département* of Seine-et-Oise. Money was very much on his mind: he had just £30 to his name plus £150 in credit that Baxter had managed to borrow for him against future literary earnings – itself a tall order in the light of Louis's recent earnings: an average of nine guineas for essays, £8 for short stories, £30 for *Travels with a Donkey* and £44.12s for the serial publication of *New Arabian Nights*. On his return to London in July he wrote to his mother: 'After a desperate struggle with the elements of every sort and principally money, I arrived last night in London the possessor of four shillings.'[29] He did not mention that he had foolishly spent £20 buying extra copies of *Travels with a Donkey* to give away to his friends.

By the end of July he was back in Edinburgh, chiefly at Swanston cottage. It was there that he received an urgent cable from Fanny, which has not survived, but is generally thought to have contained an almost hysterical appeal for help; the background to this appears to have been that Sam Osbourne had decamped to San Francisco with another of his long line of mistresses. It is important to be clear that Louis did not leave on a sudden impulse, and that the idea of a trip to California had been germinating since at least February, but Fanny's cable decided him once and for all. Interpreting Fanny's plea as an appeal to his honour, which his personal code would not allow him to deny, he at once purchased a steamship ticket for New York in secret, using the agents of the Anchor Steamship Line in Hanover Street, Edinburgh; his parents meanwhile were expecting him to accompany them to a spa in August. On 30 July he met his parents off a train at Waverley station and informed them he had to go to London on urgent business, so would not be going with them to take the waters at Gilsand. Then he sped down to London to discuss his trip to America with his friends.

To a man they were appalled and opposed the madcap scheme. Arguments about his poverty, his poor health, the loneliness and hardship he would endure crossing 3,000 miles of ocean and another 3,000 of North America's dreary wastes, the likelihood that he would alienate his parents, the damage he would do to his literary career, the fact that Fanny had given him no definite commitment were, from the rational standpoint, cumulatively irrefutable. Colvin and Henley both played the Dutch uncle, while Gosse told him bluntly that his proposed expedition was a mere freak and made a bet with himself that he would never see RLS again. All remonstration was in vain; on 7 August Henley bade his friend farewell at St Pancras, where he took the Glasgow train and then went down to Greenock to embark on the Atlantic steamer.[30]

If the circumstances of the appeal from Fanny are obscure, there is at least good evidence for Louis's state of mind as he set off across the Atlantic. To Colvin he wrote:

> No man is of any use until he has dared everything. I feel just now as if I had, and so might become a man ... I have never been so detached from life. I feel as if I cared for nobody, and as for myself I cannot believe fully in my own existence. I seem to have died last night ... The weather is threatening; I have a strange, rather horrible, sense of the sea before me, and can see no further into the future. I can say honestly I have at this moment neither a regret, a hope, a fear or an inclination ... I never was in such a state. I have just made my

will ... God bless you all and keep you, is the prayer of the husk which once contained – RLS.

As he approached New York he wrote again: 'At least if I fail in my great purpose, I shall see some wild life in the West ... But I don't know yet if I have the courage to stick to life without it. Man, I was sick, sick, sick of this last year.' To Bob he wrote: 'F. seems to be very ill. At least I must try and get her to do one of two things. I hope to be back in a month or two; but ... it is a wild world.'[31]

All of this sounds like a man weighed down by the world and realistically facing his moral obligations; it does *not* sound, as in the legend, like a man either desperately in love or determined to marry his lady. Louis's remark in 1878, in one of his now rare letters to Mrs Sitwell, praising *Clarissa* as a key work for understanding the problems of the sexes, suggests that his model for man-woman relations was conflictual rather than idyllic. And there is an important clue in 'The Story of a Lie' which he wrote while crossing the Atlantic and which is a transmogrified version of his difficulties with Fanny on one hand and his father – who even as Louis went through the greatest crisis of his life nagged him about taking the name of the Almighty in vain in *Travels with a Donkey* – on the other.

> All comprehension is creation; the woman I love is somewhat of my handiwork; and the great lover, like the great painter, is he that can so embellish his subject as to make her more than human, whilst yet by a cunning art he has so based his apotheosis on the nature of the case that the woman can go on being a true woman, and give her character free play, and show littleness, or cherish spite, or be greedy of common pleasures and he continue to worship without a thought of incongruity. To love a character is only the heroic way of understanding it. When we love, by some noble method of our own or some nobility of mien or nature in the other, we apprehend the loved one by what is noblest in ourselves. When we are merely studying an eccentricity, the method of our study is but a series of allowances. To begin to understand is to begin to sympathise; for comprehension comes only when we have stated another's faults and virtues in terms of our own. Hence the proverbial toleration of artists for their own evil creation.[32]

That sounds more like the solipsism of the romantic, with the woman as adventitious recipient of emotion, as in 'Virginibus Puerisque', than the *coup de foudre* of myth-makers.

That Fanny's appeal was always primarily sexual emerges from a reading of 'Lay Morals', written in March 1879.

> Thus, man is tormented by a very imperious physical desire; it spoils his rest, it is not to be denied; doctors will tell you, not I, how it is a physical need like the want of food or slumber. In the satisfaction of this desire, as it first appears, the soul sparingly takes part; nay, it oft unsparingly regrets and disapproves the satisfaction. But let a man love a woman as far as he is capable of love; and for

this random affection of the body there is substituted a steady determination, a consent of all his powers and faculties, which supersedes, adopts and commands all others. The desire survives, strengthened perhaps, but taught obedience and changed in scope and character. Life is no longer a tale of betrayals and regrets; for the man now lives as a whole; his consciousness now moves on uninterrupted like a river; through all the extremes and ups and downs of passion, he remains approvingly conscious of himself.[33]

At the very least there is confusion in this credo, and the 'amateur emigrant' who shipped out of Greenock in the *Devonia* on 7 August 1879 was certainly not a happy man.

7

A Year in America 1879–80

Despite the impression given by some RLS mythmakers, Stevenson did not ship out to America as a steerage passenger. The steerage fare was six guineas, but for just two guineas more one could attain 'second cabin' status: a higher level of comfort and accommodation, and with exemption from providing your own dishes and bedding; steerage passengers tended to be the Irish, the Scots and the English proletarians, but most 'second cabin' ticketholders were Scandinavians. In order to write, it was essential to have the extra comfort; this was the one and only reason Stevenson paid the extra two guineas.

Louis and his fellow passengers descended the Clyde in silence to Greenock where they boarded the *Devonia*. He found his quarters to be a kind of modified oasis in the very heart of the steerage. Through the thin partition he could hear the steerage passengers being sick, the rattle of their tin dishes as they sat at meals, the varied accents in which they conversed, the crying of the children terrified by this new experience, and the smack of the parental hand in chastisement. The diet of both steerage and second cabin was appalling: a thick brew doubling as both tea and coffee, porridge, Irish stew and a dinner of soup, roast beef, boiled salt 'junk' and potatoes. For 'tea' they were given pieces of meat that were obviously the scrapings from first-class plates. Five days a week the stewards doled out the same monotonous plum pudding, with a currant pudding thrown in as variety on the other two days.

The *Devonia* steamed out of the Clyde on Thursday night and on Friday morning took on the last batch of emigrants at Lough Foyle in Ireland. For the first time Louis appreciated the swathe that the great economic depression of the 1870s had cut through Britain. He quickly discovered that the cliché image of the U.S.-bound emigrant was false: most were men over thirty with families, and all were disposed to blame

their plight on Disraeli rather than some metaphysical trade cycle, and to
attribute their misfortunes in particular to the campaigns recently waged
in Afghanistan and Zululand. Always amused by the irrationality of his
fellow-humans, RLS noticed that during the improvised concerts which
were the only source of entertainment on board ship, such principles did
not prevent the anti-Disraeli artisans from joining with gusto in the singing
of the music-hall ditty which, in the 1870s, was virtually Disraeli's signature
tune: the anti-Russian 'jingoist' refrain, 'We don't want to fight, but, by Jingo,
if we do!'

Louis enjoyed these 'singalong' sessions but felt something of a fish out
of water and recorded ruefully: 'Humanly speaking it is a more important
matter to play the fiddle, even badly, than to write huge works upon recondite
subjects.' He was intrigued by the ambiguous profile of the Irish: 'The Irish
wenches combined the extreme of bashfulness about this innocent display
[dancing] with a surprising impudence and roughness of address.' This
aggression, he felt, masked great insecurity. From his reading and from
the lore and knowledge he had imbibed from his family, RLS had an
instinctive understanding of the sea, which most of his fellow emigrants
did not possess; where high seas and rough weather immediately induced
panic in the refugees from the slums of Glasgow, Dublin and Belfast, Louis
was insouciant and even spent the second night out on deck, as the second
cabin was so stuffy.

The voyage in the *Devonia* sharpened Louis's sense of class distinctions
and class conflict. His observations reinforced the conviction he had already
proved to his own satisfaction – that people judge others purely on sumptuary
appearance; he once tested the proposition by going round a London suburb
on successive days, the first time as a 'gentleman' the next as an artisan,
and noted that women, especially, reacted favourably to the first but with
extreme distaste to the second. Now on the *Devonia* he once again found
himself of the sharp end; his blood boiled at the way a young 'masher' from
first-class, with two young ladies in tow, picked his way through the steerage
as if visiting a zoo, and the experience triggered a momentary flashback to
the socialism of his youth. 'I have little of the radical in social questions,
and have always nourished an idea that one person was as good as another.
But I began to be troubled by this episode. It was astonishing what insults
these people managed to convey by their presence. They seemed to throw
their clothes in our faces.'

Despite his distaste for the mindless snobbery of the first-class passengers, and even more for the amused contempt of their lackeys, the
ship's officers, for the profession of writer, Louis was much too intelligent
to swing by reflex action into a sentimental glorification of the supposed
virtues of the proletariat. He found the British workman congenitally and
incorrigibly idle – 'it is not sufficiently recognised that our race detests work'

– and reckoned the hopes and dreams of most of the emigrants chimerical. As the three great causes of emigration, in his view, were drink, idleness and incompetence, it followed that a change of landscape could not cure these weaknesses. Ever a lover of Latin tags, RLS noted down scornfully: '*Coelum non animam*: a sea-voyage will not give a man the nerve to put aside cheap pleasure; emigration has to be done before we climb the vessel; an aim in life is the only fortune worth finding; and it is not to be found in foreign lands, but in the heart itself.' And he had nothing but contempt for the revolutionary opinions of the steerage passengers. 'They would not hear of improvement on their part, but wished the world made over again in a crack, so that they might remain improvident and idle and debauched, and yet enjoy the comfort and respect that should accompany the opposite virtues; and it was in this expectation, as far as I could see, that many of them were now on their way to America.'[1]

The horrors of the crossing as much as the account of Louis's lack of snobbery and preparedness to 'muck in' for the common good led Thomas Stevenson later – successfully – to request the suppression of RLS's account of the *Devonia* voyage. His truthfulness and naturalistic reportage did not appeal to a Victorian middle-class readership, both because they did not flatter it by underlining its supposed superiority to the lower orders, and because frankness was not a quality highly admired in a culture afflicted by neurosis and tunnel vision, capable of seeing nothing more in Zola than a 'pornographer'; as Henry James once remarked about Zola's critics: 'There are those who having once seen the alleged indecent, straightway see nothing else.' The following truthful remarks by RLS were judged 'coarse' and 'unacceptable' by Louis's friends and publishers. On going down into the steerage: 'the stench was atrocious, each respiration tasted in the throat like some horrible kind of cheese.' On the steerage in general: 'all who were here stewed together, in their own exhalations, were uncompromisingly unclean.' On a fellow passenger: 'he had been sick and his head was in his vomit.'

Amused by the lurid stories about New York that circulated in the steerage – 'you would have thought we were to land upon a cannibal island' – once ashore, RLS sometimes found the reality matching the reputation. He disembarked just before noon on the second Sunday of the voyage in teeming rain, which kept up its pelting continuously until he left the city on the following night. The tatterdemalion scarecrow that was RLS on embarkation was even more cadaverous when landing. In ten days he had lost a stone in weight despite having been unable to defecate during the entire voyage; additionally he had a syphilis-like itch on his skin that stung like a whiplash.[2] Having sustained himself all the way over with the thought of a proper meal at journey's end, he managed to find a 'reasonable' French restaurant where he dined with a fellow emigrant called

Jones. He and Jones rented a shilling room for the night from an Irishman named Mitchell – Jones had the bed and Louis the floor – but for RLS the night was virtually sleepless. He spent the night sitting up naked except for his trousers, scratching at the itch – possibly scabies, or eczema – which a pharmacist told him was the result of a liver complaint, leaving himself ill-prepared to deal with the violent mood-swings he encountered among New Yorkers; one minute he found himself being treated like an animal, and the next the selfsame people could not do enough for him.

Next morning was spent scurrying from bank to post-office, from bookseller to restaurant. The rain on Monday was so violent that his shoes, coat and trousers were drenched; they would not dry in time before he was due to take the train west and, if packed wet, would ruin the rest of his clothes, so with great reluctance Louis had to leave his only change of clothes behind in the lodging-house. It was typical of RLS to overspend on dinner in the French restaurant and then to lose further assets through carelessness. There were worse problems in store at the railway depot in New York. The train west was packed to the rafters with travellers, since no less than four emigrant ships had docked in New York harbour in the past thirty-six hours – one on Saturday night, another early on Sunday morning, then the *Devonia*, and finally a fourth vessel early on Monday – but no train departed west until Monday evening. The result was seemingly interminable waiting, first of all in a baggage room, then in a nightmare huddle of people and baggage in a long shed reaching from West Street to the river; finally, after a long, shambling procession taking hours, the emigrants were put in a river boat for the crossing to Jersey City.

After a slow river crossing, landing at Jersey City degenerated into a stampede, with everyone racing through the sluicing rain towards the train; all was in vain, as the cars were locked, so the passengers were forced to camp out on the platform. Louis sat down on his trunk in the downpour. There was no waiting room, no refreshment room, even cattle would have fared better. He managed to buy six oranges, but only two of them had contained any juice; when he threw the other four desiccated husks under the cars, both adults and children scrabbled for them.

In theory it was possible to sleep on an American railroad car – 'that long, narrow wooden box, like a flat-roofed Noah's ark, with a stove and a convenience, one at either end, a passage down the middle, and transverse benches upon either hand.' There was scarcely elbow room for two men to sit upright, so even if one adult had both spaces there was not really enough room to lie down and sleep. The railway company tried to solve the problem by trying to get each couple on a pair of benches facing each other to share two boards thrown across; the boards were sold together with three square cushions stuffed with straw and covered with thin cotton.

The benches could be made to face each other in pairs, for the backs were reversible. On the approach of night, the boards were laid from bench to bench, making a 'couch' wide enough for two and long enough for a man of middle height; there the 'partners' lay down side by side, with the head to the conductor's van and the feet to the engine.

Yet not even that uncomfortable manoeuvre was practicable when the train was full, as this one was. For the first forty hours RLS was unable to lie down, and was reduced to snatching fitful slumber in a sitting position. He remembered seeing the lights of Philadelphia before dozing off, and then spent a largely sleepless night before nodding off again just before dawn. He awoke on Tuesday morning to find the train at a halt in the middle of nowhere. All around him stretched green, undulating countryside: this was something very different from France or England and he was at once aware that sunrise was different in America; the purples, browns and oranges of the New World contrasted with the clear gold and scarlet in the old, and here in the Western hemisphere sunrise seemed less bracing and more like sunset, almost as if in some profounder sense, reinforced by the optical nerve, America was farther from the Orient.

Soon the train moved off again, the halt having been caused by an accident farther down the line, which threw everything into chaos. The chaos was not limited to track and rolling-stock: it proved impossible for Stevenson to buy any food except fruit; each time the train came to a station and he tried to elbow his way through to a coffee stall, the coffee ran out before he could get there. The combination of tiredness and hunger drove him close to the edge. He wrote to Colvin: 'I had no idea how easy it was to commit suicide. There seems nothing left of me; I died a while ago; I do not know who it is that is travelling.'

It was always characteristic of RLS to bounce back from despair to euphoria, and soon the sun-dappled Susquehanna valley was enchanting him – it was so much more preferable to seeing the sun glinting on the waving plains of the ocean. His spirits lifted, and he even turned to altruism, deadly enemy of depression, by looking after a small child out of one eye, while its mother slept, and reading with the other. '"If ye have faith like a grain of mustard seed". That is so true! Just now I have faith as big as a cigar-case; I will not say die, and do not fear man nor fortune.'

At Pittsburgh, Louis got his first meal in thirty hours and even found time to record a humorous incident. He was waited on by a black man who, he said, behaved towards him 'as a young, free and not very self-respecting master might have behaved to a good looking chambermaid'. RLS asked if it was etiquette to tip American waiters, to which the man replied with some passion that waiters in the New World considered themselves too highly to take tips and would even resent the offer. It was, of course, a different matter if a foreigner established a friendly, personal relationship and this particular instance was, he ventured to say, just such a rare conjunction. 'Without being very clear-seeing, I can still perceive the sun at noonday; and the coloured gentleman deftly pocketed a quarter.'

Trundling through Ohio and Indiana, RLS gallantly slept on the floor so that his neighbour, a Dutch widow, could sprawl over the two seats; but the woman requited this service with frigid reserve. At Chicago, passengers for the West alighted, took an omnibus and entrained again at a different station. Louis describes his feelings in the 'windy city':

> I can safely say, I have never been so dog-tired as that night in Chicago. When it was time to start, I descended the platform like a man in a dream. It was a long train, lighted from end to end; and car after car, as I came up with it, was not only filled, but overflowing. My valise, my knapsack, my rug, with those six ponderous tomes of Bancroft, weighed me double; I was hot, feverish, painfully athirst; and there was a great darkness over me, an internal darkness, not to be dispelled by gas. When at last I found an empty bench, I sank into it like a bundle of rags, the world seemed to swim away into the distance, and my consciousness dwindled within me to a mere pin's head, like a taper on a foggy night.

On Thursday, Stevenson woke up refreshed and at Burlington, Iowa, on the banks of the Mississippi, ate a hearty breakfast of porridge, sweet milk, coffee and hot cakes. That evening, just before nine, they reached the Pacific Transfer Station near Council Bluffs on the eastern bank of the Missouri river, where the travellers usually stayed at a kind of caravanserai for emigrants, but Louis checked into a hotel. At the Union Pacific Hotel, he got his first real experience of the consequences of two nations divided by a common language, and conceived a lasting dislike for the phoney egalitarianism of his unfavourite class of jacks-in-office: hotel clerks.

Next afternoon he joined a queue of emigrants to be sorted and separated for the journey to the Pacific coast, for the three cars on the train were strictly segregated as between women and children plus married men with families, single men or those travelling alone, with a third car for Chinese coolies. After coupling on a score of baggage wagons, at 6 p.m. the long train snaked out of the transfer station and crossed the wide Missouri to Omaha.

The rigours of the western journey were the most taxing of all. Meals were taken by the wayside: breakfast, dinner between 11–12, supper between 5–9, all leisurely affairs, since an emigrant train was always stopping and had to give way to expresses and all other locomotives on the track. On the other hand, there was no 'All Aboard' warning, so while you ate you had to keep an eye on the train, lest it suddenly moved off. To wash you had to fill a tin dish at a water filter opposite the stove, then you retired to the platform of the car, knelt down, held on to the woodwork or railing with one hand and tried to wash with the other – a cold, insufficient process and a dangerous one, especially when the train was moving fast. A primitive communalism was the norm: one man bought a towel, another soap, another a mug, and so on; on the stove, eggs were cooked, milk heated, coffee brewed. Appropriate social norms were imposed by majority opinion: group singing by raucous young men of 'In the Sweet Bye-and-Bye' was approved, but a cornet player offering the inappropriate 'Home, Sweet Home' was told to desist. Group solidarity was necessary in the teeth of the contemptuous hostility of the train conductors, who regarded themselves as superior to the emigrant rabble: on one occasion Louis asked a conductor three times when the train would stop for dinner, but the man refused to answer. The only reliable contact with the outside world was the newsboy; a friendly one could provide all the information necessary.

To RLS the great prairies of the mid-West were as boring as the great tracts of the Atlantic ocean. Crossing Nebraska, he wrote:

We were at sea – there is no other adequate expression – on the plains of Nebraska. It was a world almost without a feature; an empty sky, an empty earth; front and back, the line of the railway stretched from horizon to horizon, like a cue across a billiard board; on either hand, the green plain ran till it touched the skirts of heaven. Along the track, innumerable wild sunflowers, no bigger than a crown-piece, bloomed in a continuous flower-bed; grazing beasts were seen upon the prairie at all degrees of distance and diminution; and, now and again we might perceive a few dots beside the railroad which grew more and more distinct, as we drew nearer till they turned into wooden cabins, and then dwindled and dwindled in our wake until they melted into their surroundings, and we were once more alone upon the billiard board. The train toiled over this infinity like a snail; and being the one thing moving it was wonderful what huge proportions it began to assume in our regard. It seemed miles in length, and either end of it within but a step of the horizon. Even my own body or my own head seemed a great thing in that emptiness. I note the feeling the more readily as it is the contrary of what I have read in the experience of others. Day and night above the roar of the train, our ears were kept busy with the incessant chirp of grasshoppers – a noise like the winding up of countless clocks and watches, which began after a while to seem proper to that land.[3]

The journey across the vast open spaces of the American West would have taxed a man of robust constitution and Achillean stamina; Stevenson had neither attribute, and by the time he reached Wyoming his health was starting to crack. In the dog-eat-dog world of the cars, his plight attracted little sympathy; his fellow passengers seemed to think it very funny that he was ill but there were plenty of souls imbued with the spirit of gallows humour to tell him that he looked at death's door. He wrote to Henley: 'My illness is a subject of great mirth to some of my fellow-travellers, and I smile rather sickly at their jests.'[4]

The evening after leaving Laramie he was violently ill and of sympathy and compassion from his 'comrades' there was none. Sleep was impossible, and Louis gazed around him at the Dantean spectacle in the long, hollow box of the car: the sleepers in uneasy attitudes, some prone, some supine, some snoring, others groaning and murmuring in their sleep, all tossed and shaken roughly by the movement of the train, so that they twitched, stirred, turned or stretched out like children. To give himself something to do, he walked up and down, stepping across the uneasy, prostrate bodies, whose gasping and quaking gave him a measure of the worthlessness of sleep in such a situation. Although it was cold outside, and he already had a chill, the atmosphere was so airless and stifling that he was obliged to open the window to get fresh air. Outside in the glimmering night he saw the black amorphous hills shoot by into the wake of the train. 'They that long for morning have never longed for it more earnestly than I.'

At Ogden in Utah there was another change, from the Union Pacific to the Central Pacific line. This brought two advantages: first, the cars were twice as high on the new line and proportionately airier, and the seats drew out and joined in the centre, so that there was no more need for bed-boards, and there was an upper tier of berths which could be closed by day and opened by night; and secondly, it meant relief from the old cars which, after ninety hours of transporting human flesh, had begun to stink horribly. By this time RLS's views on his fellow-man were distinctly jaundiced. He could find no fellow-feeling with the only other Britishers on the cars – a knot of Cornish miners who kept themselves to themselves and spent the time reading the Bible. 'Not even a Red Indian seems more foreign in my eyes. This is one of the lessons of travel – that some of the strangest races dwell next door to you at home.' As for emigration itself, and its motives, here too all was vanity and illusion. 'There was no Eldorado anywhere; and till one could emigrate to the moon it seemed as well to stay patiently at home ... If in truth it were only for the sake of wages that men emigrate, how many thousands would regret the bargain! But wages, indeed, are only one consideration out of many; for we are a race of gipsies, and love change and travel for themselves.'

The mindless prejudice of his fellow travellers also affronted RLS: first it was their vile spite towards the Chinese who were actually cleaner and more salubrious than their American 'superiors'; then came the avalanches of bigotry towards the Red Man, for whose plight, cheated, exploited and massacred as they were, RLS had a strong visceral sympathy. It disappointed him that, just three years after the campaigns against Crazy Horse, Sitting Bull and Joseph, the Indian was already reduced. The only Plains Indians to be seen were pathetic broken creatures at wayside halts, stoically enduring the jibes from semi-literate emigrants of 'a truly Cockney baseness'.

After crossing Utah the Central Pacific train brought Louis on the Wednesday of his second week in the U.S.A. to Toano, then Elko, in

Nevada, where he caught his first glimpse of the train-riding hoboes later to be made famous by a man who in so many ways was his true spiritual heir – Jack London. Next day, after passing through a hot desert, the train began the climb to the summit of the Donner Pass in the high sierras, the gateway to California. The entry into California engendered in RLS's mind both joy at the prospect of journey's end and the inevitable association of ideas with Fanny.

> When I awoke next morning, I was puzzled for a while to know if it were day or night, for the illumination was unusual. I sat up at last, and found we were grading slowly downward through a long snowshed; and suddenly we shot into the open; and before we were swallowed into the next length of wooden tunnel, I had one glimpse of a huge pine-forested ravine upon my left, a foaming river, a sky already coloured with the fires of dawn. I am usually very calm over the displays of nature; but you will scarcely believe how my heart leaped at this. It was like meeting one's wife. I had come home again – home from unsightly deserts to the greens and habitable corners of the earth. Every spire of pine along the hill-top, every trouty pool along that mountain river, was more dear to me than a blood-relation. Few people have praised God more happily than I did.[5]

Soon they were dropping thousands of feet through the mining camps of the gold country. The whole train cheered with euphoria. The tired and huddled masses became new people again, all convinced this was the Promised Land. That California gave RLS new life is clear from a letter to Gosse in October: 'There is a wonderful callousness in human nature which enables us to live. I had no feeling one way or the other, from New York to California, until at Dutch Flat, a mining camp in the Sierra, I heard a cock crowing with a home voice; and then I fell to hope and regret both in the same moment.'[6]

That afternoon the train reached Sacramento and next morning before dawn came to journey's end at the Oakland side of San Francisco bay. The bay was perfect, with not a ripple or stain on its blue expanse, and the city of San Francisco, with its surrounding hills of golden corn, was lit from end to end with summer daylight. This was the beginning of RLS's love affair with the city, most eloquently celebrated in *The Wrecker*.

Stevenson sped down to Salinas on the narrow gauge railway and took the stage to Monterey, wearing a blue serge suit and bowler hat, but on arrival in the sleepy little Spanish town he needed a stiff drink to stave off physical collapse. Then he went at once to Fanny's cottage, a small two-storeyed rose-trellissed adobe fronting on Alvarado street, where he was expected. Some days before, Fanny had said to Lloyd: 'I have news for you. Luly's coming.' The hero-worshipping Lloyd remembered his idol's arrival: 'I remember him walking into the room and the outcry of delight that greeted him, the incoherence of laughter, the tears, the heart-swelling joy of reunion.'[7]

Lloyd Osbourne was, of course, part of the RLS mythmaking apparatus, and his account skates over the embarrassing details of the sequel to the 'joyful reunion'. Fanny, already undecided about which way to jump and far from committed to petitioning for a divorce from Sam Osbourne, became still more undecided once she took a good look at her Scottish suitor. He was a scarecrow, thin and pallid, with his clothes hanging loosely on his shrunken body, and his appearance conjured thoughts of funerals rather than weddings. Fanny knew instinctively that Louis would be a faithful husband, so that the anxieties she lived under with Sam would be lifted forever; it was possible, too, though less likely from the way Louis talked, that she would have the security of the Stevenson fortune; but what other inducement was there? When Stevenson pressed her on the progress of the divorce she stalled, and when pressed again admitted she had not started petitioning. Her indecision shook Louis and he in turn decided he needed time to think. He hired a horse and waggon to go wandering in the hills above Carmel – a kind of epigone to the *Donkey* journey, except that then he was hopeful and now cast down.

Those who persist in presenting the relationship of RLS and Fanny Osbourne as a storybook love story have a lot of explaining to do at this point; usually the solution is to 'cut' straight to the marriage. Yet there is a deal of evidence that the entire 'affair' was a good deal more cold-blooded than in the hagiographies. Belle claimed that Louis and Fanny were matter-of-fact and businesslike in their dealings with each other: 'Louis's conduct was not that of a romantic lover who had followed a sweetheart halfway round the world. Although he was gay and full of banter, he was almost coldly casual towards my mother and she to him . . . Maybe my mother saw in this contrast to my father the security from infidelity that had wrecked their marriage.' The tone used by RLS to Baxter in his first letter from Monterey, after the preliminary discussions with Fanny, when he refers curtly to having 'the itch and a broken heart' likewise scarcely suggests a fairy-tale idyll.[8]

Even odder is the tone used by Fanny about Louis at this juncture in her correspondence with her lawyer, Timothy Rearden, whom she regarded as a 'soul-mate'. Not many people would be capable of following an ironical statement of the exact truth about themselves with a falsehood of whopping proportions, but that is what Fanny did in her 'explanation' to Rearden. 'You always say that I never come to you except when I want something done . . . I hear that my literary friend from Scotland has accepted an engagement to come to America to lecture; which I think great nonsense . . . He has a line that belongs to him alone and would be an idiot to leave it for money and flattery.' After the meeting with Louis to discuss the divorce, she wrote archly: 'It is almost more than amusing to meet again the only person in the world who really cares anything for me. Though why should it be so amusing to you.'9

It was a disconsolate Stevenson who trekked into the Carmel hills, and the disappointment with Fanny, hard on the heels of the rigours of his transatlantic and transcontinental journeys, came close to finishing him off. In the wilderness, eighteen miles south of Monterey, he collapsed while camping and for two nights was in a stupor, doing nothing but fetching water for his horse, making innumerable cups of coffee, and going nearly mad with the noise of goat bells and tree frogs. While in this delirium, he was found by two backwoodsmen from an Angora goat ranch, one a 72-year old bear hunter, 'Captain' Smith, a veteran of the Mexican war of 1846-48, the other an Indian, Tom, who had travelled with Fremont in the early pioneering days. Smith pronounced the stranger 'real sick', took him back to the ranch and treated him with frontier remedies. For four days and nights Louis barely ate, slept or thought a coherent thought, but he obeyed his backwoods Aesculapius 'like an oracle' and at last threw off his fever. In return, he taught the children of the extended family at the ranch to read. Gradually he recovered his strength and was able to send word to Fanny. To Colvin he wrote: 'I will not deny that I feel lonely today; but I do not fear to go on, for I am doing right.'10

It was almost predictable that Fanny's response to hearing that Louis was ill was to go down with some mysterious psychosomatic illness herself, but the event did at least galvanise her in a more positive direction; learning that she had nearly lost her admirer, she at last made up her mind to marry him. When instructed to petition for a 'private divorce', Timothy Rearden was at first shocked and a sharp exchange, particularly as between counsel and client, ensued. In one letter Fanny said cryptically: 'The things you said to Belle show such injustice towards me that I shall write anyhow in spite of wounded pride.' Yet her description of Louis's near-fatal illness cannot be described as anything other than flip and cavalier: 'My literary friend is now in Monterey. He was off camping but had to come back to see the doctor. He was very ill but is better now . . . I think him the only really wise person in the world.'11

Californian law required a husband to support his wife during divorce proceedings. Sam Osbourne went down to Monterey to discuss matters with Fanny and agreed to maintain her and the children *provided* she did not rush things and allowed a decent interval to elapse for face-saving purposes. Shortly afterwards Rearden arrived to talk things over with Stevenson and was pleasantly surprised to find that he got on well with his 'rival'; it was agreed that for the sake of appearances Fanny and family would leave Monterey in mid-October and go to live in the Oakland cottage until the divorce was finalised. Louis was delighted at the turn of events and wrote elatedly to Colvin: 'By or before the end of January, there is some chance of all being well, in the fullest sense and most legitimate.' But the necessity for Fabian tactics caused Fanny further stress: there were more psychosomatic illnesses; she had dizzy spells and at times found herself almost blind and deaf.[12]

Louis meanwhile had to lie low. He was taken in by a French-Swiss hotelier who kept an old adobe inn on the hillside. In this long and low 'hotel' with shutters and climbing roses at the five windows of a huge airy room, Louis remained cooped up for three months. Every day he took coffee in the morning with his landlord Dr Heintz and his wife, then walked to the Post Office in Alvarado Street to collect his mail, bemused by the wooden boardwalks so different from European pavements. At midday he took a main meal in a little French restaurant in Monterey and sponged off friends and acquaintances, such as Bronson the local editor and Sanchez, the young saloon-keeper engaged to Fanny's sister Nellie, for the other two repasts. The assembly for the noon meal was cosmopolitan: a Frenchman, two Portuguese, an Italian, a Mexican, an American from Illinois, a naturalised Chinese, a full-blooded Indian woman, a Swiss and a German sat down to table with the penniless Scots scribbler. The friendly restaurateur, Jean Simoneau, once a wealthy merchant in Nantes but now an expatriate who had not seen his beloved France for thirty-five years, was delighted to play chess and discuss life, liberty and the pursuit of happiness with such a devoted francophile, gave him credit and got his other boarders to club together to provide a $2 a week 'salary', notionally earned by Stevenson's contributions to the local paper, *The Monterey Californian*. The fifteen articles Louis contributed to this organ – which in reality Bronson could not afford to pay for – gave him a feeling of solidarity with one faction in Monterey, and this was important, for Sam Osbourne was a popular figure locally and general opinion blamed Fanny for the breakdown of the marriage. Louis got his revenge on the pro-Osbourne faction by writing a broadsheet, of which two hundred copies were printed, blasting the meanness of the local priest, Padre Angelo Casanova, an old enemy of Bronson's.[13]

When not working or socialising, Stevenson liked to roam through the woods around Monterey, always surprising himself by new vistas of the Pacific, or trying out his fledgling Spanish on the mainly Mexican inhabitants of the town. In 1879, Monterey still overwhelmingly retained the flavour of Spanish California, with high adobe walls topped with tiles, behind which were secluded gardens alive with the heavy scent of floribundia and other subtropical flowers. It was a town of no more than three streets, paved with sea-sand, which became watercourses in the rainy season. There were no streetlights, which made nocturnal rambles dangerous, since the short sections of wooden boardwalk high above the level of the street ended abruptly, and there was no way for the walker to know where they ended. A smattering of Spanish was essential for the visitor, if only to make out the simple words to the Spanish love songs sung nightly by the serenaders who roamed the streets, strumming guitars and singing 'perhaps in a deep baritone, perhaps in that high-pitched womanish alto which is so common among Mexican men, and which strikes on the unaccustomed ear as something not entirely human, but altogether sad'.[14]

RLS noted the absence of real seasons in California and the small scale of everyday life: 'the population of Monterey is about that of a dissenting chapel on a wet Sunday in a strong church neighbourhood.' Smallness meant parochialism and he did not relish this aspect of the Carmel area; as he said to Henley: 'To live in such a hole, the one object of scandal, gossip, imaginative history – well it was not good.' Yet he preferred the Mexican openness, even in the form of its rather absurd 'code of honour', to the deviousness of the 'Yankee', and indeed he sometimes began to have doubts about the 'land of the free'; Fanny later admitted that Louis went to the U.S.A. with exaggerated ideas about the meaning of democracy, thinking he would find utopia there but ending by becoming sadly disabused. But Louis was always a gracious guest, and in a later verse 'In the States' he paid tribute to the American as the 'coming man':

> With half a heart I wander here
> As from an age gone by
> A brother – yet though young in years
> An elder brother I
>
> You speak another tongue than mine
> Though both were English born.
> I towards the night of time decline
> You mount into the morn
>
> You shall grow great and strong and free
> But age must still decay
> Tomorrow for the States, for me
> England and yesterday.[15]

Stevenson adored the Monterey coast and often took young Lloyd for hikes through the pines that ended so suddenly at the very edge of the Pacific. 'On no other coast that I know shall you enjoy, in calm, sunny weather, such a spectacle of Ocean's greatness, such beauty of changing colour, or such degrees of colour in the sound.' The impression of this ocean, with which his name will be forever linked, was later worked into the poem 'To My Name Child' that he dedicated to little Louis, the infant son of Adolfo and Nellie Sanchez:

> Seeking shells and seaweed on the sands of Monterey,
> Watching all the mighty whalebones, lying buried by the breeze,
> Tiny sandpipers and the huge Pacific seas.

Yet Louis's sense of Pacific folkways was not as acute as his feeling for nature. Forest fires were a permanent hazard on the Monterey peninsula, and on one occasion when such an inferno was raging nearby, the imp of the perverse got the better of him, and he applied a match to the moss on a great pine tree. The tree at once flared up like a torch, and the firefighters came running; Louis was frightened by their hatred of the blaze and was convinced that if anyone had seen what he had done, he would have been lynched.[16]

The greatest problem bedevilling Stevenson's daily life in Monterey during the last four months of 1879 was a dire shortage of money: in the year 1879 he made just £109 from his writings and on this he had to keep himself and pay all the incidentals of his American trip. He arrived from San Francisco with just £30 and wired Baxter to send him another £50. Baxter at once sent the money in 'circular notes' but added that his parents would give him all the money he required if he would just abandon his mad quixotry and come home; Louis refused on the ground that he could not abandon Fanny while she was ill – a universifiable prescription as she always was.

By the end of November Louis was optimistic that he could earn £300 by January, having spent £140 since leaving Scotland. But even as he ran his resources down to his last £80, Fanny told him that Sam Osbourne had 'lost' his job and could no longer support his family in Monterey; the responsibility for this would devolve on Louis. It is clear that Osbourne, resenting having to pay maintenance while another man waited in the wings to make off with his woman, simply got himself dismissed to avoid the burden. There is some bitterness in RLS's awareness of just what he had taken on in the shape of the Osbournes. He wrote to Baxter that it was a crushing burden to have to keep 'a wife [sc. to be], a sister-in-law, five cats, two dogs, three horses . . . and occasional descents of a son-in-law [Lloyd] from boarding school'.[17]

There was a sense in which shortage of money, nightmarish prospect though it was, was a rational or mechanical problem. Alas, for his health and state of mind, more intractable problems gnawed at Louis's soul. A letter to Gosse hints, in RLS's inimitably cryptic way, at some of them.

> My dear boy, I am having a rough time here; as indeed I begin to think it my way to have. Some people are so made, I fear, that their ahem brings down the avalanche; and step where they please they most always tread on other people's hearts. A combination of lapsing money, horrid feuds with threatening letters, telegrams requesting me to come home right away because my father was ill, sleepless nights waiting to run for the doctor here, doctors telling me that those who are most dear to me would not last the night . . . Your letter was like a warm shake of the hand in the midst of all these concerns. I try to tell myself that I am indifferent to people's judgments; but it is partly a pretence. I give you my word of honour, Gosse, I am trying to behave well, and in some sort, which is as much as one can say, succeeding.[18]

There are clear references here to Fanny's illnesses and to the mysterious Scottish love affair and its repercussions ('threatening letters'). It may be, however, that something even more disturbing was affecting Stevenson at this time. RLS told Baxter: 'there is to be a private divorce in January, after the girls are married'. He was referring to Nellie Vandegrift, about to marry Adolfo Sanchez, and Belle Osbourne, engaged to the painter Joseph Strong, a 'rebound' romance after the disappointment with O'Meara. Then in October Louis wrote to Colvin to ask that no more mail for him should be sent c/o Joe Strong in Monterey, as originally requested. 'No more to Strong, difficulties about Belle having hurt me a good deal. More hell with that young lady.'[19] What is this all about? Jenni Calder suggests a threefold explanation: that Belle resented Louis's 'stealing' Fanny from her father; that she found Louis too powerful a reminder of Bob; and that she married Joe Strong so as not to come under Louis's influence. But Belle, as Bob had eloquently testified, was not interested in him but in O'Meara; and she had shown no sign of solicitude for her father when Fanny and Louis were lovers in Paris – and Belle was the sort of woman who would have known the true situation between the lovers from the start. There seems to be something else going on here, and it is more than a little curious that Stevenson, who by November had written a large part of a novel entitled *A Vendetta in the West*, in which the principal female character was based on Belle, should suddenly have laid it aside and never taken it up again. For the next ten years, moreover, there was a tense and uneasy relationship between Louis and Belle, for which all the 'explanations' advanced hitherto seem inadequate.

In a context where we are at the mercy of circumstantial evidence and claim and counter-claim alone, all that can be done is to adopt the most plausible explanation for the known facts. It is thus that the much-derided testimony of Katharine Osbourne once again comes to assume great significance. Every time the allegedly wild statements of this 'wronged' woman are put under the microscope, one can see fire behind the smoke. In a letter to Gosse in 1922, Katharine alleged that in 1879, before her marriage to Joe Strong but while she was already living with the painter, Belle went to Louis and asked him to marry her instead of her mother, so that she would not have to fulfil her engagement to Joe Strong.[20] This has usually been dismissed as nonsense on the ground that Belle was already married to Strong at the time of the alleged overture, but the correspondence from RLS to Baxter shows clearly that the facts fit perfectly. From everything we know of Stevenson and his moral code, it is clear that he would have recoiled in horror from such a suggestion, and it would have left exactly the legacy of distaste for Fanny's daughter that is in fact observable. It is therefore not inconceivable that this episode, or something very like it, may well have taken place, thus explaining Louis's vehemence on the subject of Belle, as well as some of Colvin's later cryptic animadversions.

If Louis was by now starting to get some idea of what he had taken on in becoming head of the Osbourne household, he could look for little support from his own family. He had left Scotland, it will be recalled, without informing them of his mission, leaving a note with Colvin to be forwarded when he was safely launched on the Atlantic. When he read the note and realised what his son was about, Thomas Stevenson was stupefied and wrote to Colvin in anguish: 'My wife and I have exhausted all our powers of persuasion to get Louis to return home but without success . . . For God's sake use your influence. Is it fair that we should be half murdered by his conduct? I am unable to write more about this sinful mad business . . . I see nothing but destruction to himself as well as to all of us.' When he recovered his wits, Thomas tried other stratagems to bring his son home. First he offered to solve all his financial problems, to which Louis replied that he could not leave Fanny who was ill. Then he tried the trick of getting the family physician to cable and say that he (Thomas) was seriously ill and close to death; Louis replied that in that case it would be a mistake to travel back from California since his father would certainly be dead by the time he got home.[21]

Louis felt guilty about his parents, but not so guilty that he was prepared to alter his behaviour. As he put it to Henley: 'As for my poor people, I cannot help that, God knows; and I am glad that they mean to disinherit me; you know, Henley, I always had moral doubts about inherited money and this clears me of that forever.' By the end of the year he was reporting to Colvin: 'With my parents, all looks dead black.' By this time Colvin was heartily sick of his role as intermediary between Stevensons *père et fils* and wrote exasperatedly to Baxter about Thomas: 'When he talks of being obliged, by a purely private step of Louis's in regard to his own life, to leave Edinburgh and set up somewhere in England where he is not known, he seems to me to be talking unreasonably.'[22]

The only remedy for Louis in such a sea of troubles was work. He raced through the manuscript of his travels, later published as *The Amateur Emigrant* and *Across the Plains*, then sought fresh inspiration. At first he was deeply involved in the novel, *A Vendetta in the West*, but after he had abandoned it in mysterious and still unexplained circumstances, he turned to essay writing. The one book he took with him across the Atlantic was A.H.Japp's *Thoreau: His Life and Aims*, published the year before, and this stimulated him to his own interpretation of Thoreau. He began to proselytise for Thoreau among his friends and, learning that the rancher Edward Berwick had never heard of him, at once lent him a volume; however, the essay that RLS wrote that winter was later described as being merely 'frigidly appreciative' of the sage of Walden Pond.

As amanuensis during his writing Louis used Nellie Vandegrift, shortly to be married to Sanchez, Fanny's younger sister, not very much older than

Belle. The circumstances of her coming out from Indiana to join Fanny are obscure, but it is known that another sister in Indiana collapsed around this time with a more severe version of the mental illness that was periodically to disable Fanny. Nellie appears to have been the most normal of the Vandegrift girls: pretty, well-read and studious, she wore her blonde hair in a long plait and acted as 'chaperone' for Louis and Fanny. With Nellie Louis discussed a wide variety of tastes: she recalled that Francis Parkman was a favourite author but that he disliked Zola and made her promise never to read him; they also discussed popular music – he liked 'Marching Through Georgia' but disliked 'Home Sweet Home'. She also recalled anxieties about his health:

> While engaged in dictating, he had a habit of walking up and down the room, his pace growing faster and faster as his enthusiasms rose. We feared that this was not very good for him, so we quietly devised a scheme to prevent it, without his knowledge, by hemming him in with tables and chairs, so that each time he sprang up to walk he sank back discouraged at sight of the obstructions.[23]

RLS's literary efforts met with scant encouragement from his friends back home. Their project was to cajole him away from Fanny, whom they universally regarded as a bad influence, and to this end they employed a variety of stratagems. 'My own object', said Colvin, 'is to get Louis back, if without Mrs S [sic], so much the better; if with her, then as the best of a bad job.' Henley, who had never liked Fanny, put it more strongly: 'Come back he must, and that soon. Married or unmarried – *je m'en fiche*. If we can't have our Louis without the vice, we must have him with it.'[24] Both men at first showed their disapproval by complete silence and failure to react to Louis's literary endeavours; when he pressed to know their opinion they reacted with censure. Colvin pitched into 'A Pavilion on the Links' and criticised *The Amateur Emigrant* as a wordy and spiritless record of squalid experiences. It seems from Colvin's correspondence with Baxter that his dislike was real, and not just a ploy to pressurise RLS, and it is most likely that what offended conventional Victorians like Henley and Colvin – and later Thomas Stevenson – about Louis's accounts of his travels to and through the U.S.A. was the ease with which he slipped through class barriers; in their minds there was a lurking subversive classlessness about the works.

It is similarly hard to distinguish in the letters of Edmund Gosse to Louis how much was real anxiety about his health and financial situation, and how much play-acting; Henley certainly was outrightly sceptical about Louis's alleged financial plight, and of RLS's friends only Baxter believed that things were as black as they really were. Gosse's letters, with their jaunty 'Whether you live or die, you will live for ever in our hearts and in the roll of men of genius' suggest modish *fin-de-siècle* pessimism rather than real feeling. Louis was deeply upset about the tone of the letters reaching him from his friends. Responding to Colvin's criticism of *The Amateur Emigrant*, he said bitterly: 'You rolled such a lot of polysyllables over me that a better man than I might have been disheartened'; complaining that no one ever wrote to him with news or a light touch, he went on: 'If one of you could write me a letter with a jest in it, a letter like what is written to real people in the world – I am still flesh and blood – I should enjoy it.' To Henley he defended another of his books: 'If you despised the *Donkey*, dear boy, you should have told me so at the time, not reserved it for a sudden revelation just now when I am down in health, wealth and fortune. But I am glad you have said so at last. Never, please, delay such confidences any more. If they come quickly, they are a help; if they come after long silence, they feel almost like a taunt.'[25]

The one and only literary friend Louis could still rely on was Bob, and it was to him that he dedicated *The Amateur Emigrant*:

> Our friendship was not only founded before we were born by a community of blood, but is in itself near as old as my life. It began with our early ages, and, like a history, has been continued to the present time. Although we may not be old in the world, we are old to each other, having so long been intimates. We are now widely separated, a great sea and continent intervening; but memory, like care, mounts into iron ships and rides behind the horseman. Neither space nor time nor enmity can conquer old affection.

The strain of having to coax and sustain Fanny along towards the final hurdles in the divorce proceedings while she succumbed to fainting fits and headaches, of dealing with Belle and Sam, while warding off importunities from his parents and criticisms from his friends – all this in the midst of penury and financial insecurity – would have brought a much stronger man than Stevenson crashing down. Finally in December he succumbed to pleurisy and was reduced to staying in bed all day as the only way to keep warm enough to work, but as an additional scourge was wracked by toothache and could not afford to consult a dentist. Nursed by the devoted Simoneaus, he despaired of getting better and wrote to Gosse about his dilemma: 'I may be wrong, but if the writing is to continue, I believe I must go. It is a pity in one sense, for I believe the class of work I *might* yet give out is better and more real and solid than people fancy. But death is no bad friend; a few aches and gasps, and we are done.'[26]

Yet Louis came back from the brink, as he was to do so many times afterwards. In mid-December, when the divorce was finalised, he moved up to San Francisco to be near Fanny; in accordance with their promise to Sam Osbourne to allow a decent interval to elapse between divorce and remarriage, the two of them were reduced to meeting twice a week at a downtown restaurant. Fanny remained in Oakland, while Louis rented a workingman's room for six shillings a week at an Irish boarding house on

Bush Street; the Irish landlady, Mrs Carson, was initially suspicious of the Scottish scarecrow but both she and her husband gradually became friendly – Mr Carson even features in *The Wrecker* as Speedy. There he spent a dreary Christmas, while Fanny went through the farce of a family Christmas at Oakland with Sam and her children. On Boxing Day he wrote gloomily to Colvin: 'I am now writing to you in a café waiting for some music to begin. For four days I have spoken to no one but to my landlady or landlord or to restaurant waiters. This is not a gay way to pass Christmas is it? I must own the guts are a little knocked out of me.'[27] Fanny has been much criticised for the way she left her lover to languish over Christmas, but she can be defended on the need for discretion and the conflicting demands of her family; less defensible is her 'need' to pay for the upkeep of two horses so that she could go riding while Louis scrimped like a pauper across the bay – and this at a time when Sam had 'lost' his job, so that RLS was responsible for the expenses of the Oakland cottage as well as his room in Bush Street and daily subsistence.

The austerity of his daily existence was a trial for a naturally extravagant man. In his room at Bush Street he was hard at work on a novel, *The Adventures of John Carson*, based on the life of his landlord, who supplied him with enough reminiscences to fill seven pages of notes.[28] From this and the occasional reference in his letters to chopping sticks, one may infer that the Carsons let him have his room at a cut-price rate. He broke up the coal in his fireplace to make it last longer and wrote or read by candlelight in the cold winter evenings. Between 8–9 a.m. every morning he left his room and made for Powell Street where, in a branch of the Original Pine Street Coffee House, he spent five pence on a breakfast of roll and butter and coffee. After three hours writing back in his room, at midday, at the Donadieu restaurant (Dupont and Kearney), he ate a copious meal, with half a bottle of wine, brandy and coffee, for two shillings. In the afternoon he would walk or, if it was one of Fanny's visiting days, meet her off the Oakland ferry for a tryst. He usually liked to be back in his room at his books by 4.30. At 6 p.m. he returned to his breakfast café for another roll and coffee, and then worked until bedtime at 11 p.m. Yet by the end of January, his financial straits were such that he had to cut this daily expenditure of half a dollar on dinner (lunch) to twenty-five cents; living on 45 cents a day, he could no longer afford a single drink. Yet even as he was fainting with hunger himself, he was subventing Fanny: notes show two payments to her, of ten dollars and four dollars, during this dreadful January period. He wrote to Henley that he was staggering under an 'Alpine accumulation of ill news ... I have now £80 in the world and two houses to keep for an indefinite period ... My spirits have risen *contra fortunam*. I will fight this out and conquer.'[29]

What sustained him was the thought of the imminent marriage to Fanny, which would be his triumph over all the mockers and sceptics. He wrote to Gosse: 'I am now engaged to be married to the woman I have loved for three years and a half . . . as few people before marriage have known each other so long or made such trials of each other's tenderness and constancy . . . I do not think many wives are better loved than mine will be.' Yet the prospect of an early marriage faded the more he talked with Fanny: it now transpired that she needed time to prepare her family in Indiana, who were completely unaware of Stevenson's existence, and that care needed to be exercised because of her sister's mental illness. A further problem was that Fanny discovered that Sam Osbourne had no intention of paying her back her dowry or sharing with her the Oakland real estate held in his name. Writing to Colvin, Louis cursed his own naïveté and lack of cynicism about people. With Baxter he often allowed hope to triumph over experience.

> Osbourne is behaving better and seems to be going to keep his bargain. Whenever he shows symptoms of behaving well, I relapse into my wonderment. His whole conduct is an undecipherable riddle. But I suppose the truth of it is that he changes his mind and sometimes wants only money and sometimes both money and respect. I hope he will cherish this last inclination steadily as it tells upon my pocket when he varies, and indeed might plunge me under water altogether . . . He has made several attempts to find out how much I am worth, and for what reason I cannot fathom, keeps himself informed of my address.' A week later: 'The Osbourne continues to promise money, but as none comes, I suppose it is a mere flourish, and in the meantime we have to go on as best we can.[30]

Money continued to be Louis's biggest nightmare. Colvin claimed to have sent £100 from his own funds for Louis to a bank in San Francisco, but after exhaustive enquiries in all the city's banks, Louis could find no trace of any such transfer's having been made from England, and concluded ruefully that the whole thing was a fantasy in Colvin's mind. With some asperity he told Baxter that he now had the choice of two reputations in California: as an idiotic incompetent or as a lying swindler. Attempts by his parents to send him money foundered on one or other of the many mechanical and psychological shoals that lay between the space-time stretch of 6,000 miles and a six-week turn-round of letters. In October, alarmed that his son was travelling on the cheap, Thomas Stevenson sent £20 to New York to enable him to return first-class; the money lay in a New York office for months and was eventually returned. A further offer of £50 from his parents to Baxter was indignantly rebuffed by RLS because his friend passed on paternal comments about his 'spongeing', including a charge that the summoning of Thomas to Paris in February 1878 was a trumped-up excuse to squeeze money out of him.[31]

Tension with his parents continued. RLS told Gosse that his father was now a stranger to him and 'writes about how he has remarked my growing aversion to him all these years'. Thomas Stevenson for his part told Colvin that he had been genuinely ill with worry about his son and added: 'It is very sore upon a man come to my time of life and have all this to put up with . . . I lay all this at the door of Herbert Spencer. Upsetting a man's faith is indeed a *very* serious matter.' But Colvin thought he saw a chink of light in the tone of Thomas's letters, which seemed to suggest that he was disposed to take a gentler view of the matter, and he told Baxter he doubted Thomas's anger would long endure. Thomas hinted to Baxter that, now that Fanny was divorced and provided the marriage was delayed as long as possible, he was prepared to do what he could for his son. A change of tone is discernible in the letters to Louis from his parents; there is more sorrow than anger in Maggie's epistles that spring:

> We cannot understand why you have never attended to our request for information as to your plans. I must repeat again what we have said over and over before that *we can tell nothing because we know nothing*. We do not even know the names of any of your friends in San Francisco . . . You have behaved like a fool ever since you left us running risks which you were not fit for . . . We were much cast down by your letter . . . fain would I have started off at once to you but – there are many buts in the way.[32]

The six-week round-trip in correspondence meant that Louis was unaware of this softening of his father's attitude while he went through the eye of the storm. His dreary, penurious life continued. He tried to get work with the *San Francisco Bulletin*, without success. Fanny introduced him to Virgil and Dora Williams and they went to visit the newly-married Strongs in a flat in San Francisco's Latin Quarter, (Oscar Wilde later visited them here) where a sequence of young Chinese boys did the housework for a dollar a week until they had learned basic English. Through the Williamses Stevenson met Charles Warren Stoddard, author of *Cruising in the South Seas*, who fascinated him with tales of the Pacific and introduced him to the writings of Herman Melville. It was Stoddard who visited Louis at Bush Street and found him in bed immersed in a complete edition of Thoreau. Occasionally Louis's patience with the life of austerity would snap and he would take Fanny to his favourite restaurant, Frank Garcia's, which was normally way beyond his means. He was also elected an honorary member of a San Francisco club, but this failed to lift his spirits. 'I want to be married, not to belong to all the clubs in Christendie.' He also got to know some of the luminaries of San Francisco socialism.

> Were I stronger, I should try to sugar in with some of the leaders: a chield among 'em taking notes; one who kept a brothel, I reckon, before she started socialist,

particularly interests me. If I am right as to her early industry, you know she
would be sure to adore me. I have been all my days a dead hand at a harridan.
I never saw the one yet that could resist me. When I die of consumption you can
put that upon my tomb.[33]

For all his depressions and despondency, Stevenson always had a
warm feeling for the spirit of place, and few cities ever affected him more
than San Francisco; there are barely disguised paeans to it in *The Wrecker*.
He liked to talk to people who knew San Francisco bay before there was
a city there, and to distill the peculiar flavour of the Bay area. Some of
his observations, read more than a hundred years on, have a *plus ça change*
flavour, as when he notes that Californians seem to live on credit and even
to suspect cash. The symbiosis between entrepreneurship and capitalism
and high crime levels was much in evidence even in 1879: one newspaper
editor was shot dead while RLS was there, and another went everywhere
with an armed 'minder'. And already San Francisco had the cosmopolitan
ambience that has always impressed visitors:

> Choose a place on one of the huge throbbing ferry-boats, and when you are
> midway between the city and the suburb, look around. The air is fresh and salt, as
> if you were at sea. On the one hand is Oakland, gleaming white among its gardens.
> On the other, to seaward, hill after hill is crowded and crowned with the palaces
> of San Francisco; its long streets lie in regular bars of darkness, east and west,
> across the sparkling picture; a forest of masts bristles like bulrushes about its feet
> ... What enchantment of the Arabian Nights can equal this evocation of a roaring
> city, in a few years of a man's life, from the marshes and the blowing sand ...
> Such swiftness of increase, as with an overgrown youth, suggests a corresponding
> swiftness of destruction ... Next, perhaps, in order of strangeness to the rapidity
> of its appearance is the mingling of the races that combine to people it. The town
> is essentially not Anglo-Saxon; still more essentially not American. The Yankee
> and the Englishman find themselves alike in a strange country. There are none
> of those touches – not of nature, and I dare scarcely say of art, – by which the
> Anglo-Saxon feels himself at home in so great a diversity of lands. Here, on the
> contrary, are airs of Marseilles and of Pekin. The shops along the streets are like
> the consulates of different nations. The passers-by vary in features like the slides
> of a magic lantern.[34]

March 1880 saw RLS at the nadir. An attack of malaria brought him
very low, especially as this was a time when 'people rolled letters onto me
like boulders and then ran away and pelted me with notes like road metal.
I feared to open an envelope; there was sure to be some damned torpedo
or, at least, some Waterloo cracker that would singe my whiskers.' Then
came a crisis of a different kind. The Carsons' four-year old son, Robbie,
went down with pneumonia and seemed certain to die. Always susceptible
to children, Louis was fond of the boy and volunteered for a stint of sitting
up to nurse him; Robbie's plight seemed to be a symbol for all the evil in

the world and thus an objectification of all the ills that were oppressing him as well. The stress precipitated Louis at first into near-breakdown, and he wrote hysterically to Colvin: 'Oh what he has suffered! It has really affected my health. O never, never any family for me! I am cured of that . . . I did all I could to help; but all seems little, to the point of crime, when one of these poor innocents lies in such misery.'[35]

But the child survived and the pent-up stress in Louis brought on physical collapse and severe illness, at the height of which he sustained his first haemorrhage of the lungs. He suffered cold sweats, prostrating attacks of coughing, sinking fits in which he lost the power of speech, and violent fevers. The local physician Dr Bamford diagnosed galloping consumption and summoned Fanny over from Oakland to fight for the patient's life. Fanny took him first to a hotel in Oakland so that she could nurse him, but this soon proved too expensive so, defying gossip and scandal, she moved him into her own cottage. For six weeks Louis hovered between life and death, and he was undecided which the consummation was that was devoutly to be wished: 'I fear I am a vain man, for I thought it a pity I should die . . . although I still think life a business full of agreeable features I was not entirely unwilling to give it up.' When he came through the valley of death, however, in April, he felt triumphant: 'I won the toss, Sir, and Hades went off once more discomfited. This is not the first time, nor will it be the last, that I have a friendly game with that gentleman.'[36]

It is usually considered that this illness in San Francisco marked the definitive emergence of tuberculosis and that RLS was thereafter a victim of 'Bluidy Jack'. Stevenson himself certainly thought he was a consumptive, and this was the generic diagnosis of doctors in San Francisco, Edinburgh, Davos and Saranac Lake, though Dr Trudeau at Saranac thought that Louis's case was an arrested one and Dr Ruedi at Davos hedged his bets by talking of chronic pneumonia, infiltration of the lungs and enlargement of the spleen.[37] Yet there has always been a school of thought that doubts whether consumption really was what Stevenson suffered from. Some argue that his attacks were always and without exception brought on by stress of some kind, and that he did not die of T.B. Others contend that the aetiology of consumption is primarily functional (i.e. psychosomatic) and not organic at all, in effect returning the argument to square one. Still another piece of circumstantial evidence is that the Samoan chiefs – who knew tuberculosis well as it had been introduced by Europeans – were confident that Stevenson did not suffer from the disease. One plausible theory, toyed with by both Luzius Ruedi at Davos and E.L.Trudeau at Saranac (certainly the two most distinguished physicians to examine RLS), was that the cause of his haemorrhages might be a lung stone or fibroid which eroded the blood vessels from time to time and caused bleeding; Trudeau testified that he had never heard any abnormal sounds in Stevenson's chest, such as one would expect to find with consumption.

Another popular hypothesis is that RLS suffered from fibronous bronchitis – a disease of the supportive tissue of the lung, as opposed to the air cells – which creates no secretion of mucous as with tuberculosis; the haemorrhages would then occur as a result of tears in this supportive tissue. These lesions, scarred over the tissue as a result of frequent attacks, could come from a number of sources: hyperventilation, deep breathing from overexertion when walking or, most likely, nervous excitement engendered by emotional strain. Yet another possibility is congestion from a cold in the bronchial passages, resulting from lack of elasticity in the supportive tissue to permit expansion under stress of deep breathing. As each haemorrhage leaves its scar, there is then a distinct possibility of another to follow, with the likelihood that each successive attack will be more severe. Stevenson was caught in a dilemma. He was unable to breathe naturally, therefore the blood could not get enough oxygen, and therefore he had poor health. But he could not exercise his way out of ill-health, for the same symptoms impeded him, and oxygen starvation prevented his putting on weight.

Whether these differential diagnoses make much difference to the interpretation of Stevenson's behaviour is even less clear. Sufferers from fibronous bronchitis are often found to be irritable, but because of their lower body-temperature the old idea of a correlation between pulmonary impairment and high libido cannot be sustained; in any case the old idea of the highly-sexed consumptive seems to be a myth, based on a conflation of the medical fact of an increase in body temperature in a tubercular patient with the demotic meaning of 'hot-blooded'. With but a single exception, to be examined later, the old idea of consumption as being a psychological or creative determinant seems simplistic and reductive.

Once recovered from this near-fatal bout, RLS convalesced in the Oakland cottage. Used to stone structures, he was bemused by this wooden house which has been described as blowing in and out like a galleon in the wind, and amused to see that, poverty or no, four cats and two dogs still took daily meals. He strolled in the garden or sat in an armchair on the rose-canopied verandah, while Fanny alternated reading aloud to him with displaying her culinary expertise by producing multiple varieties of soup, eggs, cream, custard and preserved fruits. Louis was working on two projects at this time: one, a play called 'The Forest State' which was the embryo from which the novel *Prince Otto* grew; the other a novel entitled *What was on the Slate*, which he had begun in 1879; but he was increasingly dissatisfied with it and eventually told Colvin: 'The *Slate* both Fanny and I have damned utterly; it is too morbid, ugly and unkind; better starvation.'

It was now that he first truly appreciated the serendipitous consequences of the six-week communication lag. Seemingly out of the blue there arrived a cable from his father: 'COUNT ON 250 POUNDS ANNUALLY'. Shortly afterwards came a letter from his parents confirming that they would receive his wife. At last he was able to indulge in unwonted luxuries like going to the dentist. What had caused this sudden turn of fortune? Some allege that Fanny had abased herself and made an emotional appeal to the parents, but there is no evidence for this; more likely is the hypothesis that Baxter manipulated a father who was already softening anyway, and the letter from RLS to Baxter, which he 'inadvertently' allowed Thomas Stevenson to see, asking that all his books be sold and the proceeds remitted, was probably a cunning form of emotional blackmail.[38]

Soon relations with his parents were the best they had ever been. Jauntily he wrote that he would shortly be back in Scotland with Fanny: 'This is to inform you that the American Eagle is coming – the American Eagle I say – the British lion brings you this warning.' Thomas Stevenson entered into the jocose spirit: 'Most high and mighty American Eagle . . . I want you very badly indeed.' He even relaxed sufficiently to tell RLS an amusing comment from one of his senior associates, John Brown, who said to him: 'You should take him into a room when he gets home and give him a good whipping. What has he to do marrying?'[39]

Louis's friends were less pleased with the way things had turned out. Colvin continued to urge him, even at this late stage, to back out of the marriage, but his advice irritated RLS, who wrote back that Colvin's remarks had left him stupefied: 'I marry her certainly. What else should I do? Do I not want to have all rights to protect my darling? Perhaps you think there has been some scandal here; none.' Henley warned Colvin that he was wasting his time trying to dissuade Louis from marriage: 'He has gone too far to retract; he has acted and gushed and excited himself too nearly into the heroic spirit to be asked to forbear his point.' Henley was right. On receipt of his father's message, Louis wrote triumphantly to Gosse: 'I shall be married in May and then go to the mountains, a very withered bridegroom.'[40]

On 19 May 1880 Fanny crossed the bay to San Francisco on the Oakland Ferry, met Louis, who had sentimentally not spent his wedding eve with his bride, then took a cablecar uphill to the Williamses, where she and Louis picked up Dora for the walk to the Revd Dr William Scott's Presbyterian church. Dora Williams and the parson's wife were the only witnesses at the quiet ceremony, at which the couple exchanged two simple silver rings, as if they were French peasants; on the marriage certificate Fanny admitted her age (40) but claimed that she was 'widowed'. Louis always liked to reward people with books – Dr Bamford had been thanked with a copy of *Travels with a Donkey* – and to Dr Scott he presented a copy of his father's tract in defence of Christianity. Then they adjourned to the Viennese Bakery, 'a good restaurant in those days', for a celebratory lunch.

Against the insistence of the romancers, one must point out that both partners to the contract were singularly level-headed and down-to-earth. As RLS wrote to P.G.Hamerton: 'It was not my bliss I was interested in when I was married, it was a sort of marriage *in extremis*; and if I am where I am, it is thanks to the love of that lady, who married me when I was a mere complication of cough and bones, much fitter for an emblem of mortality than a bridegroom.' The tone of Louis's communication to Jacob Vandegrift, Fanny's brother, is similarly matter-of-fact:

> I know I am on trial; if I can keep well next winter, I have every reason to hope the best; but on the other hand, I may very well never see next spring. In view of this I am all the more anxious she should see my father and mother; they are well off, thank God, and even suppose that I die, Fanny will be better off than she had much chance of being otherwise ... I am an author but I am not very likely to make my fortune in that business, where better even than I are glad to get their daily bread.[41]

After staying two days in San Francisco in the same apartment block as the Strongs, they returned to the Oakland cottage to pack for the honeymoon. Louis had at first inclined to the idea of going to Shasta county in the far north of California but Fanny thought that his health required mountain air and hit on the idea of squatting in a deserted miner's shack in the hills above the Napa valley north-east of the Bay area. Life in the Bay area was not really suitable for a man with lung problems, for the noxious sea-fogs sweeping in from the Pacific sometimes came close to smothering the Oakland cottage. When Maggie Stevenson later queried the eccentricity of a life 'roughing it' in the Silverado hills in the case of a man who had just had a close brush from the wings of the angel of death, Fanny defended her corner vigorously: 'You wonder at my allowing Louis to go to such a place. Why, if you only knew how thankful I was to get there with him! I was told that nothing else would save his life, and I believe it was true. We could not afford to go to a "mountain resort" place, and there was no other chance.'[42]

They set out with Lloyd and Chuchu the setter-spaniel and stayed first at the big white hotel at Calistoga Hot Springs. Here Stevenson used a telephone for the first time in his life, and later visited a vineyard in the Napa Valley owned by the Schram family; Mrs Schram entertained Fanny on the verandah while the winefancier RLS tippled and tasted in the cellar. He was bemused by the Calistoga area: 'We are here in a land of stage-drivers and highwaymen: a land, in that sense, like England a hundred years ago.'[43]

At Calistoga the Russian-Jewish storekeeper who used the pseudonym Kelmar arranged for the Stevensons to be found a berth high in the Silverado Hills by one Rufe Hanson; he told them that they would not be impossibly far from civilisation, for quite close to Hanson's place was the Toll House, where the Lakeport stage called daily. Accordingly, on a Sunday morning at 8 a.m. Louis and Fanny set out in a double buggy, with Lloyd and Chuchu on horseback. After leaving the valley, they skirted the eastern foothills, then struck off to the right and entered the toll road on the gradient. The narrow stony road wound upwards among pines, oaks and madroñas: 'a rough smack of resin was in the air and a crystal purity.' Halfway up they stopped at the Toll House, a low wooden building where stagecoaches halted. After chatting with the landlord Corwin and a local engineer, Jennings, they set out on foot for Rufe Hanson's place and after two hours reached his shack which, somewhat inappropriately, bore the legend 'Silverado Hotel'. Hanson, like Corwin, Jennings and others in these hills, was a consumptive; 'in short the place was a kind of small Davos'; a poor white 'cracker', he was distinguished only by his claim to have shot one hundred and fifty deer the year before.[44]

At first Mrs Hanson swore up and down that there were no deserted miners' shacks in Silverado. There followed a comical Dickensian incident of finger-wagging negotiations out of earshot between husband and wife, at the end of which Mrs Hanson suddenly 'remembered' that there were still some dwellings at the end of a tunnel sunk by silver miners. The Stevensons proceeded to inspect the 'let'. At the head of a box canyon they ascended the hillside by a fixed wooden ladder. At the top were the deserted diggings; a line of iron rails, a truck in working order, a chaos of lumber, a blacksmith's forge; also an old brown, wooden house. 'It consisted of three rooms, and was so plastered against the hill, that one room was right atop of another, that the upper floor was more than twice as large as the lower, and that all three apartments must be entered from a different side and level. Not a window-sash remained. The door of the lower room was smashed and one panel hung in splinters.'[45]

Having inspected their honeymoon quarters, the Stevensons arranged with Hanson that he should come down to Calistoga and transport back their heavy baggage. They spent that night at the Toll House, stunned by the uproar of the wind among the trees on the other side of the valley and fascinated by all the characters and desperadoes who called at the waystation when the stage stopped there. Next day they returned to Calistoga, taking eight hours over the trip.

They were now ready for the move proper, and on their way up they again stopped at the Toll House, where they met Rufe Hanson's oafish brother-in-law, Irvine Lovelands, whom they at once dubbed 'the Caliban of Silverado'.

'Too lazy to spit' was the verdict on Lovelands by a local woman, but RLS's description of this 'redneck' was so devastating that in a later, pusillanimous era of draconian libel laws, he would doubtless have paid dearly for his portraiture.

He had a tangle of shock hair, colour of wool; his mouth was a grin; although as strong as a horse, he looked neither heavy nor yet adroit, only leggy, coltish and in the road ... he laughed frankly when we failed to accomplish anything we were about ... He prided himself on his intelligence ... He told us how a friend of his kept a school with a revolver, and chuckled mightily over that; his friend could teach school, he could. All the time he kept chewing gum and spitting ... A man, he told us, who bore a grudge against him had poisoned his dog. 'That was a low thing for a man to do, now, wasn't it? It wasn't like a man that, nohow. But I got even with him: I poisoned his dog.' His clumsy utterance, his rude embarrassed manner, set a fresh value on the stupidity of his remarks. I do not think I ever appreciated the meaning of two words until I knew Irvine – the verb, loaf, and the noun, oaf; between them they complete his portrait.[46]

At the 'Silverado Hotel' Mrs Hanson supplied the Stevensons with milk, eggs and venison, as agreed. Hanson himself was supposed to follow them up from Calistoga, bringing their boxes and a stove in his waggon, but he did not appear, having been inveigled into a game of poker. Fanny and Louis went on alone up the steep ravine by a rocky, overgrown perpendicular path, then scaled the ladder and took possession of their Silverado kingdom 'a world of wreck and rust, splinters and rolling gravel'. This time they had the leisure for a more thorough inspection. The ruin of the deserted mine was a labyrinth of tunnels and deep shafts, hard against the mountain. It was difficult to take a step on the rubble without the rocks shifting like quicksand, crunching underfoot and destroying shoes. A gale of wind howled over the hills; a clump of dwarf madroñas grew forlornly near the old forge; ahead of them a forest of giant firs and redwoods stretched out to the distant valley.

Silverado had once been a 'goldrush' settlement of hundreds, but all the wooden houses, stores and hotels had been towed away when the miners quit, and there remained just the tumbledown shack once used as assayer's office and miners' dormitory. The lower room, the quondam office, contained a barrel, a table, some yellowed papers, a plate-rack, some old boots and a hole in the leaky roof to allow the smoke from the fire to escape. The upper quarters, the one-time dormitory, held nothing but the skeletons of nine old three-tier bunks. To enter this room one had to walk the plank – a fitting experience for one so obsessed with pirates; this was a board balanced between the red rockface and the open door, and for support one had to clutch at poison oak. Fanny, always at her best when playing the role of pioneer, set to work to clear out all the rubbish, mine dust, dead leaves and saplings of poison oak.

By nightfall of their first day there was still no sign of Rufe Hanson; until he brought up their effects the hapless lodgers had nowhere to sit down except on a splintery table. With Fanny and Lloyd exhausted, and all of them famished, Louis volunteered to toil down to the Toll House to get some bread. He made the exhausting round trip with the bread, only to discover he had lost his watch. He lit the lantern, retraced his steps and found the watch in the middle of the path, within sight of the Toll House. By now it was 7.30 p.m. and the squatters were beginning to despair. Suddenly out of the gloom loomed Hanson and 'Caliban' with their effects, but as yet with no hay for bedding. It was not until 9 p.m. that the 'cracker' duo returned with the hay and it was possible to bed down. The Stevensons filled the bunks next to the door in the 'dormitory' and walked the plank to their beds.

Next morning they built a fire in the forge and Fanny cooked porridge, bacon and coffee. Partly because of his physical debility, partly because he was anyway useless at working with his hands, Fanny had to do all the hard manual labour – driving in nails and generally patching up their abode; Louis's chores were restricted to drawing water from a spring in the red wood and chopping wood. Soon the shanty was transformed 'with beds made, the plates on the rack, the pail of bright water behind the door, the stove crackling in a corner, and perhaps the table roughly laid against a meal'.

The rigours of this wild backwoods life soon proved too much for Fanny and Lloyd, who went down with diphtheria; since Louis was no more than convalescent, the Stevensons had to decamp to Calistoga, where they rented a cottage until fit enough to return. RLS told his friends in Britain what the pioneering experience had really been like.

> We have had a miserable time. We were six days in Silverado. The first night I had a cramp and was quite worn out after it; the second day Fanny mashed her thumb while carpentering, and had a nervous chill; the third day she had another from sleeplessness; the sixth day she and Sam [Lloyd] both began to have diphtheria. I got them down in an open cart; the cases are slight; Sam's especially, but Fanny has been pretty sick and a little lightheaded for forty-eight hours. You may fancy if I am tired. I am homesick for Europe; yet it is now a question if I shall be strong enough for the journey home this summer.[47]

To assist the invalids, Joe Strong, Belle and Nellie came up from San Francisco by stagecoach. When the Stevensons were well enough to move back to their Silverado eyrie, they made some improvements to lessen the strain of daily life. First they tried to hire as cook Kong Sam Kee, a Chinaman who lived in one of the other deserted shacks in the hills, but he declined the offer; finally they secured the services of an amateur painter who was also a good short-order cook. Returning to the squat, they found it sacked as if by Vandals: 'Wild cats, so the Hansons said, had broken in and carried off a side of bacon, a hatchet, and two knives.'

Fanny improvised by using the mouth of the old Silverado mine as an ice chest, where she hung sides of venison, pigeons, ducks and other game. They arranged to have cans of fresh milk brought up and from

Kalmar ordered quantities of wine, dried peaches, fresh fruit and tinned food, which they kept in the tunnel. Always first up in the morning and by now able to do a few more chores, Louis lit the stove, fetched the water, put it on to boil, then made coffee and porridge. As the rocky platform was furnace-hot during the day, he then took his books and writing materials under the shade of the madroñas and worked for four to five hours though, on his own admission, achieving very little. From time to time he made some half-hearted and futile attempts to teach Lloyd Euclid and Latin. At eleven in the morning and three in the afternoon Fanny would bring him a rum punch topped with cinnamon. Fanny's day was tiring, with no chairs and little shade to give her respite, so she was glad to join Louis in the evening on the platform and bask in the night scents of bay and nutmeg. They liked to toss stones down the chute and hear them land hundreds of feet below, but drew the line at venturing far into the tunnel. The onset of chilly night soon cut short their evening idyll.

When writing up the account of his sojourn in the Californian hills, RLS largely played down the misery and the squalor and put the emphasis on natural beauty, adventure and bohemian freedom, typically achieving the effect of a triumph of art over life, but there are times when the harsh truth peeps out: 'Our day was not very long, but it was very tiring. To trip along unsteady planks or wade among shifting stones, to go to and fro for water, to clamber down the glen to the Toll House after meat and letters, to cook, to make fires and beds, were all exhausting to the body.'

Louis knew all about the painful consequences of skin contact with poison oak but, unlike the dog who reacted with alarm, he was blissfully ignorant of the danger from rattlesnakes, which infested the area. From the earliest days he heard the rattling and the 'whizzing on every side like spinning wheels' but only later did he connect the noise with the presence of huge numbers of deadly snakes: 'we were told that in no part of the world did rattlesnakes attain to such a monstrous bigness as among the warm, flower-dotted rocks of Silverado.'[48] There were other even more subtle dangers, described by Fanny's biographer: 'During those two months, at any moment the dump might have slid down the hill, carrying the squatters along in an avalanche; or a crack of rotten wood might have been the only warning that the platform had caved in and fallen into the shaft underneath; or a wedge might have slipped, with the splintered camp disappearing under hundreds of tons of mountain.'[49]

As soon as he felt well enough to travel, Louis and family quit Silverado and made immediate preparations to return to Scotland. As with the journey in the Cévennes, a taste of freedom in the wilderness had the paradoxical effect of making the free spirit of RLS crave the creature comforts. All his utopias, whether Barbizon, Silverado or Samoa, ultimately disappointed him and he found his cabin in the sky in particular a long way from his dream of 'a clique of neighbourly houses on a village green ... all empty to be sure, but swept and varnished; a trout stream brawling by; great elms or chestnuts, humming with bees and vested in by song-birds'.[50]

Despite his gruelling westward experience on the 'cars', Stevenson elected to take his family across the continent by train, the experience doubtless cushioned eastward by first-class travel; the journey via Chicago was unmemorable and Louis left no records of it. The same was largely true of the Atlantic crossing in the Royal Mail liner *City of Chester*, in which he arrived on 17 August 1880 at Liverpool. But James Cunningham, who met him on this crossing, recalled nine or ten days of 'such talk as I had never before heard, and now do not expect ever to hear again. To the accompaniment of endless cigarettes, or sometimes, it might be, of a perilous cocktail which he compounded with such zest from a San Francisco recipe, the stream of his romantic and genial talk flowed on.'[51]

8

Davos

Acynic remarked that Stevenson returned from America with some admirable travel sketches, a fading middle-aged woman and tuberculosis. But he had something more: for the first time in his life he had access to real money. The first-class passage across the Atlantic was a sign of things to come, for it would certainly not have been affordable on the £250 per annum Thomas Stevenson promised his son. For seven years, from 1880 until Thomas Stevenson's death, Louis and Fanny refused to live within their means and looked to the patriarch of Heriot Row to bale them out.

Fanny worked out a subtle campaign to conciliate the Stevenson parents and she planned and executed it meticulously. As Jenni Calder has said, with memorable understatement: 'all the signs are that her moral sense was pragmatic rather than spiritual.'[1] She began while still in the States with a cleverly calculated appeal to Maggie. First she stressed (and exaggerated) the amount of loving, nursing care she had bestowed on Maggie's beloved only son: 'Taking care of Louis is, as you must know, very like angling for shy trout; one must understand when to pay out the line and exercise the greatest caution in drawing him in.' Then she played herself down in both a physical and mental sense, so that Maggie would feel no threat or rivalry. 'Your fancy that I may be a business person is a sad mistake, I am no better in that respect than Louis, and he has gifts that compensate for any lack. I fear it is only genius that is allowed to be stupid in ordinary things.' Even cleverer is this:

> Please remember that my photograph is flattering; unfortunately all photographs of me are; I can get no other. At the same time Louis thinks me, and to him I believe I am, the most beautiful creature in the world. It is because he loves me that he thinks that, so I am very glad. I do earnestly hope that you will like me, but that can only be for what I am to you after you know me, and I do not want you to be disappointed in the beginning in anything about me, even in so small a thing as my looks.[2]

Maggie took the bait and showed the flattering photograph of her daughter-in-law to all the friends on whom she called. The prophetic words RLS uttered in 'Virginibus Puerisque' were beginning to be fulfilled: 'The most masculine and direct of women will some day to your dire surprise, draw out like a telescope into successive lengths of personation.'

Yet Fanny realised that the real key to her future lay with Thomas Stevenson: this was where the power and the purse-strings lay; moreover Maggie would do very much as Thomas did, since what she desired most of all was harmony between her son and husband. When Fanny disembarked from the *City Of Chester* at Liverpool to find the Stevenson parents waiting with Colvin to whisk them away for an emotional hotel lunch, she at once began to charm, cajole and wheedle the older man to her utmost ability. People usually get on well with those who flatter them and agree with their every word; Thomas Stevenson was no exception. Even Maggie, not noticeably perceptive, jotted down in her diary: 'It was quite amusing how entirely she agreed with my husband on all subjects, even to looking on the dark side of most things, while Louis and I were inclined to take the cheery view.'[3] Fanny indulged Thomas's every foible and prejudice: when he objected crustily to the change in fashion whereby women wore black stockings instead of white, she went back to white to humour him. He responded with a compliment: 'I doot ye're a besom.' Louis's maternal uncle Dr George Balfour dissented and opined that Fanny *was* a besom, but sugared the pill by adding: 'I married a besom myself and I have never regretted it.'[4]

Flattery apart, Thomas had several solid reasons for being well disposed towards Fanny. After some of his son's earlier scandals with women, it would not have surprised him entirely if a painted harpy had walked down the gangplank off the steamer, yet here was a staid, almost grandmotherly woman with greying hair; it was likely that she would act as a brake on Louis's eccentricity and it seemed improbable that he could now return to the bad old ways of his youth. True, she was not the daughter-in-law he and Maggie had dreamed of, but then Louis was scarcely the ideal son. He also sensed almost at once that relations between him and Louis were better than they had ever been, and partly attributed the improvement to her influence. The truth is that under the lash of suffering father and son had grown closer and developed some mutual understanding. When the son lay at the point of death, he began to realise what really did matter to him; similarly when he thought he might never see Louis again, the father's natural love conquered his ideological principles and Calvinistic dogma. There is something poignant in the letter Thomas wrote to Dr Bamford, thanking him for saving his son's life; Louis, for his part, had already told Colvin: 'Since I have gone away, I have found out for the first time how I love that man; he is dearer to me than all, except Fanny.'[5]

As sometimes happens, a spurious, contrived or pretended emotion blossomed into something very much like the real thing. An easy relationship sprang up between Thomas and Fanny: he teased her by calling her 'The Vandegrifter' or 'Cassandra', following some gloomy prophecy; she talked back pertly to 'Uncle Tom', 'Mr Tommy' and sometimes 'Master Tommy' without ever making the mistake of being too familiar or presumptuous. She came to see that Maggie was more complex than she appeared at first sight and became convinced that Louis took after her. Her comments to Dora Williams on Thomas are especially warm.

> The father is a most lovely old person. He is much better looking than I fear Louis will ever be ... occasionally he comes in with twinkling eyes and reports a comic verse of his own making with infinite gusto ... He is a most delightful person; anyone else seems so sodden and dull at this hour, while his eyes are sparkling and he comes in with a sprig of heather in his hat looking so pert and wholesome that it does one good to see him.

Much later Fanny wrote:

> I shall always believe that something unusual and great was lost to the world in Thomas Stevenson. One could almost see the struggle between the creature of cramped hereditary conventions and environment, and the man nature had intended him to be. Fortunately for my husband, he inherited from his tragic father his genius and wide humanity alone. The natural gaiety of Margaret Stevenson, who lived as a bird lives, for the very joy of it, she passed down to her son.[6]

Back in Edinburgh, Thomas and Maggie showed their affection for Fanny by showering her with presents and turning her into a kind of 'dress-up doll'; Maggie opened trunks of once-worn clothes for her and even shared her own ample wardrobe. Fanny soon grew to have extravagant tastes, though 'gentility' always evaded her: she shocked Maggie by completing the embroidering on a piano cover in two days by fast and expert needlework; it was considered 'ladylike' to take an entire summer over such 'work'. The servants were bemused and baffled also. A maid told Fanny that she spoke English very well 'for a foreigner'; another was heard to say that Louis had 'merrit a black woman'. To please his parents, Fanny persuaded Louis to attend church in Edinburgh and then to go with them on holiday to Blair Atholl and Strathpeffer where he would have the benefit of mountain air.

It was on this excursion that Louis first conceived the idea of a history of the Highlands – yet another of his projects that went no further than the planning stage. Maggie noted in her diary: 'On this visit for the first time Louis acknowledged that the Highlands of Scotland were the most beautiful place in the world; before that he used to say it was too gloomy.' Yet if he liked the Highlands, he hated the tourists. RLS's negative reaction to the Ben Wyvis Hotel at Strathpeffer emerges in the verses 'On Some Ghastly Companions at a Spa':

> That was an evil day when I
> To Strathpeffer drew anigh,
> For I found no human soul,
> But Ogres occupied the whole.
>
> They had at first a human air
> In coats and flannel underwear.
> They rose and walked upon their feet,
> And filled their bellies full of meat.
> They wiped their lips when they had done –
> But they were ogres every one.[7]

Yet Louis was restless, suffering from catarrh and general debility: 'I must flee from Scotland,' he wrote. 'It is, for me, the mouth of the pit.' His maternal uncle George Balfour, the physician, examined him and diagnosed alarming congestion in his lungs; he recommended Dr Ruedi's sanatorium at Davos in south-eastern Switzerland, and it was soon agreed that RLS and family would leave Scotland for the South on 7 October.

It was in London that the fatal flaw of the Osbournes first revealed itself: gross extravagance. In one week at the Grosvenor Hotel Fanny and Louis ran up a bill of £46 – an immense sum in those days; Fanny's lame apology to the wealth suppliers in Heriot Row was that she had not known the ropes in English hotels. The truth was that inside the pioneering gun-toter was a bourgeois spendthrift struggling to get out; the two months in Scotland had given her a taste for luxury such as she had never experienced before, and she wanted more. To make matters worse, Lloyd and Belle were every bit as extravagant as she was: Colvin, who met the Stevensons at Liverpool on 17 August – he went out in the tug and climbed up the ship's ladder so as to be the first to greet them – was the first to get an inkling of the problem when in the hotel at lunch Lloyd put away 'the most enormous luncheon that ever descended a mortal gullet'. For the rest of RLS's life, Lloyd was a constant financial drain, requiring money for school fees, travel and, as a young man, all manner of fripperies and self-indulgences. The annual allowance of £250 granted by Thomas Stevenson to his son remained a polite fiction; in fact he provided his son each year with at least double that amount.

It might have been thought that, in return for the comfort and privilege she had secured for herself and her family, Fanny would have responded by being generous and complaisant towards his friends but, having secured her power base with the Stevenson parents, she moved on to phase two of her project: the alienation of Louis's friends. Of course she knew they had all opposed his marriage, and she was the last person in the world to be magnanimous in victory. The first stage in her 'divide and rule' policy was to make over Colvin and Baxter while excluding the others; once Henley, Bob, Gosse and the others were routed, she could decide what to do about Colvin and Baxter later.

Little suspecting what was afoot, RLS kicked off his one-week festival with his friends with a splendid lunch at the Savile, where Gosse, Lang, Henley and Walter Pollock were present, and proceedings were washed down with Stevenson's favourite among wines – Burgundy. As the week wore on and there were more meetings in the Grosvenor, perceptive onlookers noticed Fanny's eyes flashing angrily from one to another of Louis's interlocutors. The anger and resentment she felt emerges in a letter to Maggie:

> If we do not soon get away from London, I shall become an embittered woman. It is not good for my mind, or my body either, to sit smiling at Louis's friends until I feel like a hypocritical Cheshire cat, talking stiff nothings with one and another in order to let Louis have a chance with the one he cares the most for, and all the time furtively watching the clock and thirsting for their blood because they stay so late.[8]

Her defence for this posture was always that his friends did not realise how fragile his health was, but here she was disingenuous since in fact she was insanely jealous of his companions and hated it if Louis praised their qualities. This was doubtless justifiable if she could be all in all to him, but she could not, even had she wished to be, which is far from clear. Even a commentator sympathetic to Fanny, like Jenni Calder, remarks: 'There was no one person, and his wife was not to become that one person, with whom Louis felt he could share all aspects of his intimate life. This reinforces the sense that grows powerfully in his later years that the major dislocation in his life and career was that his art, his marriage, his love for friends, his parents could never coalesce.'

Fanny realised that the dynamics of power entailed driving a wedge between Colvin and Henley. It was Henley she resented most of all – D.H.Lawrence would have said that she apprehended his maleness in her blood and therefore recognised the enemy – and accordingly she decided to conciliate the more 'female' Colvin, whose character as an 'old woman' had in the past afforded so much mirth to Louis and Henley: in December 1881, for example, Louis wrote to Henley from Zurich: 'with every word you say of Colvin the dear and the good, I eagerly agree. I said the other day that he "introduced into literary life the chastity of an officer".' The antagonism between Henley and Fanny, always apparent from the very earliest days, may well have contained an

1. Thomas Stevenson, Louis's father
2. Margaret Stevenson, his mother
3. Margaret Stevenson with Louis, 1854

4. Louis (*right*), aged 8, with his cousin, Bob
5. Alison Cunningham ('Cummy') in later life
6. The Stevenson family with 'Cummy' (*right*) and two maids

WINDY·NIGHTS

WHENEVER the moon and stars
                    are set,
Whenever the wind is high,
All night long in the dark and wet,
    A man goes riding by.
Late in the night when the fires are out,
Why does he gallop and gallop about?

7. Charles Robinson's design for
'Windy Nights' in *A Child's Garden of
Verses*
8. Edinburgh: The Lawnmarket,
looking towards St Giles
9. Edinburgh: The shop on the corner
of Leith Walk and Antigua Street
where Louis bought stationery

10. Walter Crane's frontispiece illustration for *Travels with a Donkey*

11. RLS, aged 28. Etching by Wingman after a drawing by Fanny Stevenson

12. Siron's inn at Barbizon. A photograph taken in the 1870s

17 HERIOT ROW
EDINBURGH

My dear Henley,

The 1st 2 acts and a synopsis wanted before the 30th by Sidney S. Colvin, Woodbury Cottage, Riggin Hill Norwood. Hurry up our staff of copying clerks. I'll give you III. 3 and IV. 3. are end of week, I hope. Cold better, but I keep the house.

Yours ever
R. L. S.

13. RLS. A portrait inscribed 'To CB'
(Charles Baxter)
14. 17 Heriot Row
15. A letter to W. E. Henley

16. RLS. A portrait by Hawker of Bournemouth

17. Fanny Osbourne in 1880 before her marriage to RLS

18. RLS at Davos
19. Woodcut designed by Joe Strong for the frontispiece of *The Silverado Squatters* showing Louis and Fanny in their shack
20. Saranac Lake, New York State, 1887–88: (*from left*) Valentine, the French maid; a local 'help'; Lloyd Osbourne; Fanny, RLS

unconscious sexual element. As has been well said: 'Henley's jealousy rivalled Fanny's ... like many others, Henley loved Louis.' Henley's distaste for Fanny, in turn, may have been part of a generally misogynistic profile he presented to the world; it is certain that before his marriage Henley had had severely troubled relations with women. However, many of Fanny's overt criticisms of Henley were wide of the mark, as when she insinuated that he sponged off Louis via 'loans' when in fact he had refused a fee for acting as RLS's agent. Even J.C.Furnas, usually pro-Fanny in the many controversies surrounding her, noted: 'Such loans were no more than, as unpaid agent, Henley had earned twice over.'[9]

Colvin, however, whom she wanted to play off against Henley, was no particular admirer of hers. His report of meeting the Stevensons at Liverpool docks would scarcely have made reassuring reading. After describing RLS as 'looking better than I expected, and improved by his new teeth; but weak and easily fluttered', so frail that 'you could put your thumb and finger round his thigh', he went on to describe Maggie as looking the fresher of the two women and concluded by wondering: 'whether you [Henley] or I will ever get reconciled to the little determined brown face and white teeth and grizzling (for that's what it's up to) grizzling hair, which we are to see beside him in the future'. After the week in the Grosvenor, under the Gorgonian gaze, he wrote to Baxter of her love of 'harrowing her own and other people's feelings'.[10]

For the time being, needing Colvin on her side, Fanny could do little about Mrs Sitwell. There is some evidence, though, that Mrs Sitwell secretly resented Fanny's dominant position in the life of her former admirer, although superficially the correspondence between the two women was always cordial. Malcolm Elwin concluded: 'The reader of her "very affectionate" letters senses the presence of claws, hidden but none the less ready to strike, in the caressing velvet of her paws.' Certain it is that there are only three letters from Louis to Fanny Sitwell extant after his marriage, two of them clearly written under Fanny's eyes, and that Mrs Louis Stevenson exercised an unceasing internal and external censorship.

Gosse, too, fell foul of Fanny. His judgement on her, as given to Edward Marsh, was thus:

'She was one of the strangest people who have lived in our time, a sort of savage creature in some ways, but very lovable and extraordinarily passionate and unlike everyone else in her violent feelings and unrestrained way of expressing them – full of gaiety, and with a genius for expressing things picturesquely, but not literary. I think RLS must have caught some of his ways of feeling from her.'

Fanny soon detected Gosse's Achilles heel – an overweening narcissism and paranoid thin-skinnedness combined with a jealous watchfulness lest RLS's success overtop his. She encouraged her husband to jibe at Gosse for his shortcomings and to make common cause against him with Henley – who, Carlyle to his Thackeray, despised Gosse's penchant for celebrities and dining out in fashionable society. The consequence was a cooling in relations: in 1881 Gosse ceased to be 'dear Weg' and became merely 'my dear Gosse'.

Most discreditable of all Fanny's exercises in detaching RLS from his friends was the way she managed to marginalise Bob, once considered Stevenson's alter ego. By the autumn of 1880, Bob was going through a cycle of severe depressions and badly needed Louis's moral support: 'I have never got well again and never will be myself again,' he wrote forlornly. Yet four years later we find him writing with some acerbity to complain that he no longer knows his cousin's whereabouts and in January 1885, while he lived in Chelsea and Louis in Bournemouth – hardly the other side of the world – he was reduced to the following utterance: 'I hear through your mother that you had been ill.'[11]

The *obiter dicta* in RLS's essays are often prophetic, and perhaps none more so than this from 'Virginibus Puerisque': 'Marriage often puts old friends to the door.' Or as John Steuart thought about Fanny's unrelenting attitude to his friends: 'Possibly she did not think them worth conciliating; they had not the practical importance of Thomas Stevenson.' In a remarkably short time, Fanny had worked herself into a position where she controlled her husband's life: 'the old ebullient Stevenson was quickly subdued to her hand. . .in the immortal words of Sam Weller: "She's got him and what's more she has him now."' There are even those who claim that he bent his subsequent critical theories to her monetary desires: 'all his subsequent critical writings have to be regarded with suspicion, for he must always be suspected of making out a case for himself, embroidering theories which excused his own treatment of fiction and sprang from no honest conviction.'[12] This, however, is an exaggeration, as we shall see.

The Stevenson party that left for Davos in mid-October comprised, not just Louis, Fanny and Lloyd, but a black Skye terrier given as a wedding present by Sir Walter Simpson: this animal, a constant factor in the Stevenson household for the next six years, was to prove as much a monster as Thomas Hardy's notorious 'Wessex'. The curious thing is that RLS's essay on 'The Character of Dogs' describes the canine breed as an automaton, 'a machine working independently of his control, the heart, like the mill-wheel, keeping all in motion'. Yet RLS's bark was worse than his bite, in contrast to the dreadful 'Bogue'. As is doubtless fitting for a writer, problems of canine nomenclature long exercised Stevenson: at first he called the dog Wattie after Walter Simpson, but this later became corrupted to Woggs, Woggy and Wiggs before the final name was fixed upon.

Only a besotted owner could have endured the bad behaviour of this mutt. Fanny could not be bothered to house-train it, so it left a trail of faeces all over French hotels. 'The dog has bogged more than once upon this hostile soil,' he wrote from Troyes, 'with a preference for hostile carpets, than could be believed of a creature so inconsiderable in proportion ... Yet we all adore that dog.' If the epithet 'neurotic' can be applied to an animal, Bogue certainly qualified for the description. He was overexcitable, ill-tempered, obstinate, sly and suffered from fits and comatose spells; the exasperated staff at the Davos sanatorium dealt with him by giving him bromide. He bit Colvin in Davos and even bit Fanny, which dampened her ardour for the spoiled pet, but bit once too often at Bournemouth when he got into a fight with a stronger beast, from which encounter he died.[13]

Thus encumbered, the Stevensons took two weeks by slow stages to reach Davos. They broke the journey in Troyes, which RLS found 'stunning', and from where he dispatched an apology and explanation for the extravagance at the Grosvenor, blaming it on the exorbitant and prohibitive prices of London hotels.[14] At Landquart in the Alps ('the Alps are all there: they beat everything to smash') they began a slow eight-hour ascent through the snow to Davos, famously the setting for Thomas Mann's *The Magic Mountain*. At 5,000 feet above sea-level, Davos was an isolated town with three large hotels and a plethora of church-steeples, an unreal place like something out of a fairy-tale; the sense of a 'closed universe' or an island of the damned was reinforced by consumptive shopkeepers and tubercular hoteliers.

At the Hotel Belvedere, RLS made his introductions to Dr Ruedi, world famous as an expert on consumption. Ruedi ordered his patient to give up smoking and to restrict his writing to two hours a day; Louis responded by drinking three litres of wine a day. 'Guests' at the Hotel Belvedere were supposed to spend all day sitting out in the open air on a gravel terrace, or lying in a hammock in the woods behind. Ruedi was no respecter of persons and at once informed Fanny she was too fat and put her on a diet; the omens for Fanny were already bad, for on the day of their arrival, while she was upstairs inspecting the bedrooms, the châtelaine informed Louis that his 'mother' would be down shortly.[15]

At first RLS saw only the Alpine grandeur:

A world of black and white – black pine woods, and white snow ... and a few more invalids marching to and fro upon the snowy road, or skating on the ice rinks ... the place is half English to be sure, and the local sheet appearing in double columns ... but it still remains half German ... the row of sunburned faces can present the first surprise ... in the rare air, clear cold and blinding light of the Alpine winters, a man ... is stingingly alive ... (with) this sterile joyousness of spirits ... you can cast your shoe over the hill tops.

But soon he was deeply bored, complaining of the poor company, the bad food and the quasi-metaphysical *angst* engendered by the lowering Alps. His one recreation was billiards, at which he was a wild rather than skilful player. In despair at the lack of stimulating company, he made friends with Christian, the head waiter, something of an intellectual; together they would pace the empty dining room in wrapt discussions while the table was being spread for the next meal.[16]

In the evening things were better, for then he could enjoy deep conversations with the great Renaissance scholar John Addington Symonds, who had been a resident at Davos since 1877. Together they ranged over English and French literature, animatedly dissecting Dryden, Marvell, Tennyson, Milton, Sir Thomas Browne, Walt Whitman, Zola, Balzac and Flaubert, as well as the teachings of Christ and the music of Handel. It may be that, as Lloyd Osbourne remembered, Symonds, with his Balliol 'effortless superiority', treated RLS with condescension, and indeed the attitude is there in one of his letters: 'I have apprehensions about his power of intellectual last. The more I see of him, the less I find of solid mental stuff. He wants some years of study in tough subjects. After all a University education has some merits. One feels the want of it in men like him.' But he soon came to appreciate that RLS was an authentic genius and later in life looked back on the Davos period of 1880–82, when he saw so much of Stevenson, as the happiest time of his life. As to their respective merits, this was well summed up by Colvin, who was disposed to favour the academic and the scholar over the man who was creative and intellectual:

> Endless bouts of eager, ever courteous give-and-take over the dark Valtellina wine between Stevenson and J.A.Symonds, in whom he had found a talker almost as charming as himself, exceeding him by far in the range and accuracy of knowledge and culture, as was to be expected in the author of *The History of the Renaissance in Italy*, but nothing like his match, I thought, in essential sanity of human judgement or in the power of illumination by unforeseeable caprices of humour and fantasy.[17]

It is possible that what Lloyd Osbourne picked up was a trace of unconscious sexual hostility, for RLS confided the entire story of his romance with Fanny, which Symonds thought 'very curious and creditable to himself and her'. Yet he himself had no time for the 'illusion' of heterosexuality. Married, with four daughters, Symonds 'came out' as a homosexual in the 1870s to the extent of admitting his preferences to his wife. He put it to her that a man with an hereditary physical or mental disease ought not to procreate further and therefore they should abandon sexual relations while preserving the appearance of normal marriage; she, who disliked both childbirth and sexual intercourse, readily agreed. In 1889 Symonds wrote: 'This state of things has lasted now for twelve years, during which we have rarely shared the same bedroom, and never the same bed.' Released from the yoke of heterosexuality, Symonds quickly made friends among the young Swiss peasants. In 1877, when he was thirty-seven, he began a long affair with a nineteen-year old sledge driver named Christian Buol; they became lovers on a journey to Italy; he helped the Buol family out of financial difficulties; finally, he encouraged Buol, who was bisexual, to marry a local girl. There was another grand passion with the 24-year old Angelo Fusato – also a bisexual – in Venice in 1881, and thereafter Symonds made friends with a wide range of *braubunder* males – postillion drivers, carters, stagecoach conductors, carpenters, doctors, parsons, schoolmasters, hotel porters, herdsmen, masons, hunters, woodmen, guides, hotel-keepers, shopkeepers, stableboys and artisans. With hindsight, there is something comical about the way early RLS biographers censured him for holding himself aloof from the local Swiss and not getting to know them as Symonds and Powys did, as if he were a snob and they men with the common touch.[18]

Stevenson was aware of Symonds's proclivities, but this drew down on him and (especially) Fanny the unspoken wrath of Mrs Symonds. This was partly what he meant when he told Gosse that to associate with Symonds was 'to adventure in a thornbush'. He confided to Colvin the mutual dislike between the two wives: 'For Mrs Symonds I have much pity but little sympathy. A stupid woman, married above her, moving daily with people whose talk she doesn't understand'; Colvin, with his dislike of Fanny, doubtless silently mulled over the thought that this was a perfect description of Fanny herself. In 1885 the Symondses got their revenge for the humiliation involved in the Stevensons' knowledge of their private arrangements, when they regaled Margot Asquith with some petty stories:

'He [Symonds] said that Mrs Symonds suffered a great deal from the long visits which this distinguished man and his wife paid them at Davos; that Louis slept with his back to the light and Mrs Louis in the same bed with her face to it; that they wrote opposite each other till after lunch; but that they were not particular and that, what with hemorrhages, ink and cold mutton gravy, her sheets were often much spoilt.'[19]

During this winter of 1880–81 RLS worked away at his projected history of the Highlands since the 1715 Jacobite rising. But he was soon complaining that he found Davos 'a cage . . . the mountains are about you like a trap . . . you live in holes and corners, and can change only one for the other'. Irked by the high prices at the hotel, he and Fanny halfheartedly looked for a private house to rent, but she fell ill and had to drop out from the quest and RLS too lacked energy: 'I have no style and cannot write,' he told his parents. 'I dare say you will be glad of this but it galls me to the bone.' Even worse was the constant *memento mori* ambience at the Hotel Belvedere; for Louis the most unsupportable thing about his lungs was not that they caused him protracted and painful illnesses – with rare exceptions they did not – but they could usher in sudden death. The grim reaper was all round him in Davos: a great many of the sick died and sometimes at breakfast there would be an ominous emptiness in a chair where a friend sat yesterday.[20]

On top of this was the stupefying boredom: the usual stresses and strains of a closed society – jealousies, intrigues, love affairs, cliques – were enhanced by the imminence of death, which seemed to concentrate the mind only in malevolence towards fellow-man; elsewhere there was only banality: a woman would quarrel with her son's tutor, someone would lose a ring, there would be a snowstorm; otherwise – nothing. To complete the trio with death and boredom, anxiety arrived to plague Louis and the anxiety, predictably, derived from problems among the Osbournes. At the lowest level of seriousness was the question of what to do about the 12-year old Lloyd. For the first winter in Davos, RLS hired a tutor, but this cost £40 for five months, and thus made a large hole in the nominal annual allowance of £250; later Louis 'solved' the problem by sending the boy to a boarding school in Bournemouth. Yet, except when his patience became exhausted and he lost his temper (that is to say, rarely), Louis found it next to impossible to discipline the boy; the other inmates of the Hotel Belvedere often marvelled that he allowed his 'son' to address him as 'Louis'. He took the lad tobogganing in the moonlight, played tin soldiers with him, and let him into the secrets of arcane Stevensonian lore – his conviction, for instance, that gold spectacles were the badge of guile. As a final gesture of solidarity, RLS set up a handpress with the intention of producing editions of his own books, some to be illustrated by his own hand, and made Lloyd his 'co-editor'.[21]

Louis's perplexity about Lloyd's future partly arose because the spheres of influence between himself and Sam Osbourne ('that putrid windbag') had not been clearly drawn; as yet Osbourne still seemed to arrogate the right to decide on the boy's future and even on that of the married and now pregnant Belle, even though he contributed not a penny. Meanwhile RLS's allowance of £250 went nowhere near the cost of supporting three people, Lloyd's schooling and the astronomical medical bills he and his wife incurred; Fanny refused to economise, so there was no option but to 'touch' Thomas for further funds.' As RLS admitted ruefully: 'I always fall on my feet, but the legs are my father's. As for Sam Osbourne, an outburst to Baxter during this first winter in Davos expresses both the difficulty and Stevenson's angry reaction; 'His [Osbourne's] last wish was to send his daughter to a whore's lying-in hospital, where women go by numbers, no men are admitted, and kids are given for adoption. This he virtually proposed to the girl's husband; which, from a man who makes, I find, 2,400 a year is steep.'[22]

Most pressing of all dilemmas was that of Fanny. It quickly became apparent that he and she were in a Jack Sprat type of marriage, whereby whatever climate suited him did not suit her and vice versa. Davos did Louis a power of good, to the point where he was willing to swallow his reservations about Alpine exile: 'I think there is no doubt, on the whole, that I should stay here.' Yet Fanny claimed to find life at this altitude insupportable. Almost immediately after arriving in Davos, she succumbed to another cycle of mysterious illnesses, complete with fainting fits so alarming that some thought (and many still do) that she suffered from a minor form of epilepsy. As usual, Fanny's secretive and uninformative letters do not help us: Maggie received the following riddle: 'I have been so tired and worn out with so much to do that I broke down a little . . . living in Davos is like living in a well of desolation.' Despite her insistence that her illness had an organic cause, it seems certain to have been psychosomatic, if only because all the doctors she consulted could find nothing wrong with her. She was clearly depressed, and this was not an altogether irrational response to the situation she found herself in at Davos. All around her were the dead and the dying; the majority of the guests in the Hotel Belvedere were affluent Britons who looked askance at an American divorcee; and she was at this very moment the recipient of a violent attack from her old beau, John Lloyd, now a rising banker, accusing her of stringing him along while she secretly made plans to marry Louis.[23]

Her response to all this was to tighten her control over her husband. As her biographer explains: 'Gradually she took over part of his personal correspondence as well, and had unquestioned access to his desk. This sometimes altered the tone of his letters to and from his old friends, even the many letters which he himself penned.' In desperation, Louis even looked back fondly at the halcyon days with his parents, although they nagged him remorselessly about his failure to correspond regularly and deluged him with questions about the history of the Highlands. On Boxing Day he sent his mother a sentimental letter, reminding her that this was only the third Christmas he had spent away from home.[24]

Colvin went out to Davos in January 1881 to visit RLS and to accompany Mrs Sitwell, who looked to Davos for salvation for her consumptive 18-year old son Bertie, but found his friend depressed and melancholic, especially glum about Fanny's illness. Finally, in February it was decided that, cost or no cost, she would have to consult a specialist in Paris and she set off on an expensive ten-day trip to Paris. While she was away, Bertie Sitwell's health took a downward turn. Louis wrote to Colvin (who had returned to London at the end of January): 'Luck has failed; the weather has not been favourable; and in her true heart the mother hopes no more.' Fanny returned from Paris to find Louis and Mrs Sitwell clustered around the boy's deathbed; Bertie died on 3 April 1881, and the similarity in the maternal losses of the two Fannies was a further circumstance strengthening in Stevenson's mind the idea of a singular congruence in their careers. Louis remembered the dead boy in his 'In Memoriam F.A.S.'

> All that life contains of torture, toil and treason,
> Shame, dishonour, death, to him were but a name.
> Here, a boy, he dwelt through all the singing season,
> And ere the day of sorrow departed as he came.[25]

This death was the unkindest cut of all for Louis in his icy sarcophagus at Davos. Although Dr Ruedi had warned him initially he would have to stay in Switzerland for at least eighteen months, Louis now insisted he had to get away. Ruedi suggested that it might be possible, if he could get back to the Scottish Highlands in twenty-four hours, but neglected to explain how this was feasible with nineteenth-century technology. In the end he threw in the towel, merely warning his patient of the consequences. Stevenson had at one time toyed with spending the spring in Italy to economise. Later there was talk of meeting his parents in Fontainebleau; but in the end Fanny went on ahead to France, having arranged to rendezvous with her husband at their old trysting ground at Siron's inn in Barbizon.[26]

In mid-April, Louis and Fanny were reunited in Barbizon, but their sojourn there was brief; the smell from the open drains induced in the increasingly hypochondriacal Fanny fear of an imminent cholera outbreak, so they pressed on to Paris. Here they checked into the Hôtel St Romain on the Rue Saint-Hoch and, as usual whenever in a large city, overspent hugely. Combing through the bric-à-brac and antique shops, they bought up a number of pieces, including an antique watch which Fanny admired, and which cost them virtually their last *sou*. 'Now we'll starve,' said Fanny melodramatically, knowing perfectly well that Thomas Stevenson would bale them out; as it happened, when they got back to the hotel Louis found an uncashed cheque in the pocket of an old coat, so did not need to cable his father. But the tourism in Paris wore Louis out; one night he had a haemorrhage and a doctor had to be summoned at 2 a.m.; 'a week in Paris reduced me to the limpness and lack of appetite peculiar to a kid-glove,' he wrote. He and Fanny agreed that the climate in Paris was affecting him adversely, so they moved out to St Germain-en-Laye, where he heard his first nightingale. Here again RLS fell foul of the French *petit-commerçant* mentality: the landlord at the Hôtel du Pavillon Henry IV became insolent and insulting when they requested time to pay the bill for the first two nights – an attitude doubtless encouraged by the sight of Louis's red flannel shirt – but then lurched back into baffled deference when a large money-order arrived from Scotland, leaving the mercenary innkeeper with the regretful knowledge that he had been harbouring the son of a Scottish 'milord'.[27]

At the end of May 1881 the travellers arrived back in Edinburgh. Louis had made it a condition of his return that he would not live in hotels in the Highlands but wanted a house near heather, pine trees and running water; accordingly his father had taken a two-month lease on Kinnaird Cottage at Pitlochry in the Atholl valley. The modern cottage (though without a bath and lit by oil lamps) was divided into two apartments and had a long garden, at the end of which one could emerge on to unspoiled glens. Here Louis and Fanny at once decamped, together with Maggie and Lloyd, whom they had collected from the clergyman's school in Bournemouth. The widowed owner, Mrs Sim, did the cooking and her daughter acted as waitress, but living in the cottage was akin to life in Lilliput, for when they were all seated at the dining table, Helen Sim (the daughter) could not hand the dishes round; James Cunningham, commenting on the tiny sitting room with just one window, exclaimed that it 'might have been the window in Thrums as regards size'. Occasionally Thomas came up from Edinburgh to visit them, but he scarcely helped the atmosphere. The only reading matter in the cottage was a two-volume life of Voltaire, which was removed one Sunday by the patriarch on the ground that it was not suitable Sabbath reading.

They all ate well and slept like tops and everything was satisfactory except the weather; the biting winds and cold rains barely ceased for the two months they were there. Maggie seldom arose before eleven, when she and Fanny would take Bogue for a walk; the dreaded cur at last got its come-uppance in Scotland for, having been used to the muzzled dogs of Davos and the cowardly ones in France, it thought to rule the Highland roost, took on a couple of tough Highland sheepdogs and was savagely bitten for its pains. Thereafter Fanny and Maggie walked him on a leash; very occasionally Louis accompanied them, and once this led to a memorable altercation with a Highlander who was beating his dog. When RLS remonstrated vehemently, the owner replied; 'It's not your dog.' 'No,' replied Stevenson angrily, 'but it's God's dog and I'm not going to see you ill-use it.'

More usually, cooped up in the cottage near the fire lest the rains affect his lungs, RLS expended his anger on other targets: the Fenian bombings, and the British war against the Boers in South Africa, which ended so ingloriously at Majuba hill; his vehement opposition to what he saw as blatant British aggression was such that Fanny suppressed an essay for fear it would damage his reputation.[28] He worked away on a number of projects: first a speculative biography of Jean Cavalier, the Protestant leader of the Camisards in the Cévennes, of which he managed no more than the opening paragraph; then the Poe-like chiller 'The Body Snatcher'; finally two undoubted masterpieces of the short story genre: 'Thrawn Janet' and 'The Merry Men'.

'The Body Snatcher' was based on the career of Robert Knox the anatomist, to whom the notorious Burke and Hare supplied for dissection the newly slain bodies of their victims, yet, despite Compton Mackenzie's advocacy, it is a slight piece alongside the other two products of this period. 'Thrawn Janet', however, is, as Henry James put it, 'a master-piece in thirteen pages'. A story of literal diabolic possession, influenced both by Cummy's horrifying stories told to Louis in infancy, and the seventeenth-century George Sinclair's *Satan's Invisible World Discovered* (1685), and triggered by the macabre tales told him by Mrs Sim out of her thesaurus of uncanny and supernatural tales, which he would coax from her around the fireside, 'Thrawn Janet' has not received the acclaim given to far inferior stories in this genre by Poe, Conan Doyle and others, almost certainly because it is written in broad dia-lect.

Something of the same problem attaches to 'The Merry Men', a complex tale in which many favourite Stevenson themes are integrated: superstition (the devil as a black man); fear of the awesome power of the sea (a motif ever present in the RLS *oeuvre*); the quest for treasure; and above all the problem of evil. RLS made good use of his 1870 visit to the island of Earraid, of his father's eyewitness account of a wreck in the Pentland Firth, and his own knowledge of the Spanish Armada. What is distinctive is the style and the power of the writing, marking an advance beyond anything achieved by Stevenson hitherto; the description of the storm is superior even to that in *David Copperfield*, and it is not surprising that even the curmudgeonly Henley loved it. 'It is a fantastic sonata about the sea and wrecks,' Stevenson told Colvin, 'and I like it much above all my other attempts at story-telling; I think it is strange; if ever I shall make a hit, I have the line now, as I believe.'[29]

'The Merry Men' is Stevenson's first serious attempt to wrestle with the problem of evil – 'Thrawn Janet' is at this level merely a superior ghost story – and the influence of Herman Melville, to whose work he had been introduced in San Francisco by Stoddard, is palpable. Gordon Darnaway, a fanatically pious Presbyterian Lowlander, throws himself enthusiastically into the embrace of the world's evil – or at least what he conceives to be such. He rationalises his guilt by worshipping the malevolent force of the sea.

If it wasna prentit in the Bible I had whiles be tempit to think it wasna the Lord but the muckle black deil that made the sea ... If ye had sailed it for as lang as me, ye would hate the thocht of it as I do. If ye had but used the een God gave ye, ye would have learned the wickedness of that fause, saut, cauld, bullering creature, and of a' that's in it by the Lord's permission; labsters and partans an' sic like, howking in the deid, muckle, gusty, blawin' whales; an' fish

– the hale clan 'o them – cauld-warmed, blind-eed uncanny ferlies. O sirs, the horror – the horror o' the sea!

There are two distinct themes here. One is the pervasive Stevensonian fear of the sea, perhaps traceable to a Calvinistic upbringing which tended to see gigantic forces of nature as the agents of supernatural intervention: RLS's words to Colvin in 1890 are significant: 'I . . . had always feared the sound of the wind beyond anything. In my hell it would always blow a gale.' In 'The Merry Men', at a fantasy level, RLS dealt with fears he would actually experience in the Pacific. The other is the Mevillean theme of defiance of God, resting in turn on the mistaken view that the universe has meaning, for good or evil; whereas for RLS the meaning (as for Melville) is either non-existent or ambiguous. This is why a popular critical view of 'The Merry Men' – as a diabolical version of Hopkins's 'The Wreck of the Deutschland' – does not convince. However, Darnaway *is* guilty of the same kind of hubris as Ahab: he sees the destruction of ships by the 'Merry Men' as an aspect of his will or consciousness and thus as revenge on God. This confidence that he can set God at naught is shattered when a black man emerges from the sea, precipitating the final disaster. The black man is of course a very weak dramatic device, and this wrenches the tale off its metaphysical course back on to the merely superstitious tracks of 'Thrawn Janet'; however satisfying Darnaway's death is in dramatic terms, it serves to fudge the profounder issues Stevenson has raised earlier.[30]

The ghost stories with which Fanny and Louis terrified each other nightly – and which once provoked screams from Fanny that brought Mrs Sim knocking on their door – were not the only intimations of the uncanny vouchsafed to the 'psychic' Hoosier. One day she was sketching Ben Vrachie when the ground suddenly began to swim before her eyes and she felt faint. She made an effort to rise and reach the road, and had just managed to snatch up her sketching materials and move from the place when a tree crashed down on the exact spot where she had been standing. The naturalistic explanation was that the waving motion of the turf caused by the loosening of the shallow spreading roots of the falling larch produced the illusion of fainting that saved her life; with her belief in the occult, Fanny naturally opted for more far-fetched explanations.[31]

While cooped up in the Kinnaird cottage, RLS conceived one of his stranger ambitions: to occupy a chair at Edinburgh University. The professorship of History and Constitutional Law became vacant; it was an attractive post that carried a salary of £250 for just three months lecturing in the summer months, when Stevenson would very likely be in Scotland anyway. Henley, Bob and Baxter all expressed amazement that one who had always been so scathing about academic life should be offering himself as a candidate for a prestigious chair, but Louis stressed that with the salary, his allowance and the earnings from his writings, he might finally attain financial independence. In a white heat of enthusiasm he wrote to friends and sympathisers for testimonials: Leslie Stephen, J.A.Symonds, Colvin, Gosse, Andrew Lang all supported him, as did Professors Lewis Campbell, Meikeljohn, Sellar, Babington and P.G.Hamerton, albeit tepidly; significantly, though, Fleeming Jenkin was noticeable by his absence from the glossy fourteen-page pamphlet containing professorial encomia Stevenson submitted in support of his application. The outcome was scarcely a surprise, though it seems to have shocked the Stevenson family, showing how little their son was esteemed by bourgeois society there. There were four candidates, of whom the two leading ones secured 133 votes between them; Louis received just nine although, as Lord Sands later pointed out: 'had the distinction he was to achieve been generally foreseen, there would have been not nine but ninety and nine eager to vote for him.' RLS was momentarily cast down, but Fanny was jubilant, as she had already confided to Dora Williams how little she wanted to be a professor's wife. On reflection, too, the Stevenson parents thought all had been for the best: Maggie wrote to her son: 'I am on the whole relieved that you have not got the chair as I am sure it would have worried you.'[32]

Although Gosse and Colvin visited the Stevensons at Pitlochry (Henley, wisely, did not), this exacerbated rather than improved Fanny's depressed and irritable mood; RLS meanwhile was thriving and declared: 'I never thought I should have been as well again, I really enjoyed life and work.' But Fanny and Maggie, who daily had to brave the hostile elements, hoped for better weather elsewhere and were eager to move on. At the end of July the ménage moved north to another cottage at Braemar where, however, the rain and wind were even worse; since they were just off the road to Balmoral, the women had to be content with frequent sightings of Queen Victoria as she drove past in an open carriage, her ladies in waiting chafed and chapped with the cold. Louis remarked to Mrs Sitwell: 'The Queen knows a thing or two, I perceive she has picked out the finest habitable spot in Britain.' However, when Gosse proposed another trip to Scotland, Louis warned him: 'If you had an uncle who was a sea captain and went to the North Pole, you had better bring his outfit. Verb. sap.'[33]

Another trial about Braemar was that Thomas came up more regularly. If ever father and son saw too much of each other, they started to grate, and the tension of having to please his father by Sabbath observance and general biting of the tongue to please Fanny gradually wore Louis out; his father, too, did not requite restraint with restraint but, as was customary, interpreted the lack of overt clashes as licence to continue his niggling. He criticised Louis for smoking too many cigarettes and even for the way he smoked them; he insisted that *The Amateur Emigrant* be withdrawn from publication and suppressed because 'I think it not only the worst thing you have done, but altogether unworthy of you'; and he reprimanded him explicitly for extravagance and implicitly for mental illness: 'I am quite satisfied that one of the great causes of your condition is just what occasioned the same state in Alan [his brother] – a total want of business habits.' In despair at this nagging, Louis wrote to Colvin: 'If you knew all that I have had on my hands, what with being ill, living in an atmosphere of personal quarrel, apologies and (God save the mark – what has become of all my themes) imminent dwelling . . . I am in a great hurry to leave this hell of a place.'[34]

However, Braemar was notable in RLS's life for giving him the inspiration and leisure to write the book which, though not his best, is the one for which he will always be famous: *Treasure Island*. In fifteen days he raced through fifteen chapters of the novel he originally called *The Sea Cook* but became bogged down in the sixteenth, lost his touch, and was not able to complete until the winter of 1881 in Davos. In the evenings, he delighted his family, especially Thomas Stevenson, by reading aloud from the completed chapters. Opinions were always divided about RLS's actorly qualities, but Fanny later wrote: 'My husband's voice was extraordinarily thrilling and sympathetic, with a fine dramatic quality.' Gosse and Colvin, who visited at Braemar, were also encouraging. Gosse wrote to his wife on 3 September: 'Louis has been writing, all the time I have been here, a novel of pirates and hidden treasure, in the highest degree exciting.' Alexander Japp, the third of the visitors to Braemar, agreed that the story was exciting and that Stevenson read it beautifully: recalling how he swayed rhythmatically while reading it aloud, he recalled: 'His fine voice, clear and keen in some of its notes, had a wonderful power of inflection and variation.'

It is typical of the Osbourne sept that in later years they should have tried to appropriate the credit for the genesis of *Treasure Island*. Louis himself was quite clear that the principal motor in the writing was the desire to write something that his father would approve of, and indeed the book acted as a powerful therapeutic bond, even though there is a subtext implicitly critical of patriarchy, and despite the fact that the religious fanatic of a patriarch later tried to have a long religious passage inserted into his quintessential adventure story. Fanny initially turned up her nose at the entire project, grudgingly agreed to its serialisation in *Young Folks* on condition that it would never appear in book form, and wrote to Gosse's wife: 'I am glad Mr Gosse liked "Treasure Island." I don't. I liked the beginning but after that the life seemed to go out of it and it became tedious.' Later, of course, when she and her family were living sumptuously on Louis's posthumous royalties, and *Treasure Island* was his best-loved, and therefore most lucrative, book, she changed her tune and claimed to have been a partisan from the earliest days.

Similar mendacity comes from Lloyd, who claims that it was his drawing and colouring of an imaginary island that gave Louis the idea, and that his original map was used – all of which was later denied by RLS. How reliable a witness Lloyd is can perhaps be gauged from the fact that his other memory of 1881 has RLS applying for a chair of *English* at Edinburgh, and there is something distastefully vainglorious about the following: 'Had it not been for me, and my childish box of paints, there would have been no such book as *Treasure Island*.'[35]

All available evidence backs the hypothesis that it was the sixty-three-year old Thomas, not the thirteen-year old Lloyd who was the true inspirer. Instrumental in getting the work placed for serialisation with *Young Folks* was Dr Alexander Japp, scholar and journalist, biographer of De Quincey and friend of Mrs Henry Wood, a man with a legion of contacts in London literary cicles. RLS had corresponded with him on their very different attitudes to Thoreau, following which he invited him up to Braemar for further talks. When Japp arrived he was greeted cordially and told by Louis not to stand on ceremony: 'It's laugh and be thankful here.' Japp took to Thomas Stevenson and used to go on long walks with him, even wondering whether he was not more impressive than his son. A kind of rivalry for the older man's attentions developed between Japp and Gosse, who similarly went on long morning walks with him; Gosse found Thomas a vigorous and singularly charming personality, indignant at coming of the old age, and he reported the following snatch of monologue: '63, sir, this year; and, deuce take it; am I to be called "an old gentleman" by a cab-driver in the streets of Aberdeen?'[36]

Japp took the manuscript away with him and soon reported that he had placed the serialisation with *Young Folks* and that the expected receipts were £100, or £2.10s per page of 450 words; however the actual receipts were nearer £30 than £100. It was the editor, Robert Leighton, who discarded the title *The Sea Cook* in place of *Treasure Island*, and he claimed that this title alone was the bit that hooked the young readers, since the story was really too 'arty' for juvenile taste, which did not appreciate slow build up and the subtle accumulation of atmosphere; the juvenile mind ran rather to that sensibility famously appealed to by Hollywood's Samuel Goldwyn when he ordered one of his producers to start with an earthquake and build up to a climax. *Treasure Island* was not even *Young Folks*'s principal feature – that honour was given to the instantly forgettable tushery *Don Zalva the Brave*.

Louis, however, had no doubt of the tale's merits. He wrote to Henley on 25 August:

> If this don't fetch the kids, why, they have gone rotten since my day. Will you be surprised to hear that it is about Buccaneers, that it begins in the 'Admiral Benbow' public-house on the Devon coast, that it's all about a map, and a treasure, and a mutiny, and a derelict ship, and a fine old Squire Trelawny (the real Tre, purged of literature and sin, to suit the infant mind), and a doctor, and another doctor, and a sea-cook with one leg, and a sea-song with the chorus 'Yo-ho-ho

and a bottle of rum' (at the third Ho you heave at the capstan bars), which is a real buccaneer's song, only known to the crew of the late Captain Flint (died of rum at Key West, much regretted) . . . Buccaneers without oaths – bricks without straw. But youth and the fond parent have to be consulted.[37]

RLS's sources for *Treasure Island* make a fascinating study, indicating both the complexity of this apparently straightforward 'boy's book' and the way in which the alchemy of Stevenson's genius could transmute base metal into gold; in this sense the book was his own 'treasure'. Major influences include Washington Irving's *Tales of a Traveller*, Defoe's *Robinson Crusoe*, Captain Johnson's *History of Notorious Pirates*, Kingsley's *At Last* (from which he got the name of the Dead Man's Chest), Poe's short story 'The Gold Bug' and Fenimore Cooper's *The Sea Lions*.[38]

Treasure Island can be read in a number of ways, each of them shedding light on Stevenson's unconscious. At the simplest level is the 'sentimental education' theme of a boy growing to maturity and learning new values. RLS's protagonists are often children or infantile adults at odds with authority; either literal orphans (David Balfour in *Kidnapped*, Richard Shelton in *The Black Arrow*) or emotional ones (Archie in *Weir of Hermiston*), or are separated from their remaining parents (Jim Hawkins and Loudon Dodd in *The Wrecker*). Even as adults they tend to be estranged from their family or burdened with family responsibilities for which they are unprepared (the eponymous hero of *St Ives* and Henry Durie in *The Master of Ballantrae*). Yet it is typical of Stevenson's ambivalence that the process of reaching maturity should be viewed with jaundiced eyes; at the end of *Treasure Island* Jim Hawkins, with the treasure in his grasp, is set for a life of boring and inglorious retirement; only with and through Long John Silver has he truly lived, so that the rejection of Silver, like that of Falstaff by Hal, entails the rejection of what is best in the hero's nature.

Yet there is a disturbing darkness about *Treasure Island* absurdly glossed over by those who continued to treat it as a mere 'boy's book.' It is not often pointed out that Jim Hawkins finds the whole experience a nightmare, and Stevenson could certainly not be accused of sentimentalising the sordid world he depicts. Most of Stevenson's novels (*Treasure Island, The Black Arrow, Kidnapped, Catriona, The Master of Ballantrae, The Ebb-Tide*) hint in a Shakespearean way at a chaos beneath the superficial order of the universe, where civilisation is displaced by the law of the jungle and the survival of the fittest, leading to an amoral world of betrayal, primitive passion and sudden death. One of the most disturbing aspects of *Treasure Island* is its lack of a moral centre. Money is the ruling principle and even Dr Livesey and Squire Trelawny are corrupted by it, leave their bucolic pastures and rush off to the Caribbean with unseemly haste in the hopes of getting rich quick. This in effect reduces the morality to the Nietzchean one of strenuousness, where

Silver is head and shoulders above the others; he at least has no illusions, is pragmatic, openly selfish and in no way self-deceiving, unlike the others. In a novel like B.Traven's *The Treasure of the Sierra Madre* the worth and the morality of money are questioned, and the quest for it shown to be an illusion. This never happens in *Treasure Island* and indeed the fact that the treasure itself, when found, contains items from all the world's currencies seems to suggest that it is indeed a source of universal, overarching value. The Marxist critic would accuse Stevenson of being as much in thrall to Victorian attitudes to Mammon as Defoe in *Robinson Crusoe* was to eighteenth-century mercantilism.

At another level the theme of the island has a profound significance. There has been much scholarly discussion about Stevenson's island: was it primarily based on Edinburgh as seen from the Pentland hills or was it the Isle of Pines near Cuba? Clearly it was a montage: partly based on islands visited in the *Pharos* in 1869, partly on the Caribbean island described by Kingsley in *At Last*, and partly on the Californian scenery of Napa and Monterey.[39] Less discussed has been the general significance of islands in Stevenson's psychic world. That islands fascinate writers is clear: Ballantyne's *Coral Island*, Wells's *The Island of Dr Moreau*, the half dozen islands in J.M.Barrie's *oeuvre*, to say nothing of modern examples like those in Golding's *Lord of the Flies* and John Fowles's *The Magus* show the power they exert on the imagination. A metaphor for alienation and for the principle of imagination as against reality, an island is the perfect spatial focus for the anxiety of the lonely parentless youth. Ever since John Donne, the idea of the individual as island has been a cliché, but if by metaphorical extension the island features as wise alter ego, this offers the youth the possibility of spiritual growth, and it is plain, from Plato's Atlantis to More's Utopia to Crusoe's island, that any sea-girt isolated territory represents the ideal, the best of which the individual is capable. But since islands satisfy most major fantasies – escape from parents, domestic responsibilities, illness, consumption – they also connote a regression to the certainties of childhood: in some psychoanalytical literature the foetus is interpreted as an island surrounded by an amniotic moat – and the playpen continues the idea of a closed private space. In other words, there is a case for saying that in *Treasure Island* RLS was working out the dialectic between good and bad islands, between regression and responsibility, anxiety and liberation.

A third important theme is that of treasure; always a Stevenson favourite, it features in *The Master of Ballantrae* and was to have been the centrepiece of the abandoned work *The Young Chevalier*. Treasure is the symbol for perfect happiness – in whose possibility Stevenson did not believe – and Jim Hawkins's finding of the trove was superficially like Heinrich Schliemann's discovery of Troy – hailed by Freud as an example of the only kind of happiness possible on earth. That treasure is itself an ambivalent symbol can be discerned in those psychoanalytical studies that see Long John Silver's loss of a leg as symbolic gelding and the hunt for treasure as being couched in terms of castration anxiety: 'Long John' is a phallic pseudonym indicating kinship with the later Mr Hyde; the deluded men stand in horror before an empty pit (vagina); George Merry is pitched into it, and so on. Sexual interpreters of *Treasure Island* are fond of including the passage from RLS's short story 'The Treasure of Franchard' where the loot is found in the cleft of a rock covered with moss.[40]

Inevitably this brings us to the fourth motif: that of the wooden-legged Long John Silver. To see his disablement as symbolic castration ignores the long line of sea heroes (Ahab in *Moby-Dick* and Captain Hook in *Peter Pan* are the best known examples) who suffer their wounds as a result of their Promethean ambitions; in the old legends the great heroes were often so disabled as the cost of their ambition to harrow hell (Tyr with the Fenris-wolf in Norse mythology, for example), and in the early non-Gospel sources Jesus had to undergo ritual laming on Mount Tabor. However, Silver clearly *is* a focus for displaced childhood trauma and for Stevenson's continuing struggle with male figures of authority. Jim Hawkins's nightmares recall Pip's about Magwitch in *Great Expectations*:

> How that personage haunted my dreams. On stormy nights, when the wind shook the four corners of the house, and the surf roared along the cove and up the cliffs, I would see him in a thousand forms, and with a thousand diabolical expressions. Now the leg would be cut off at the knee, now at the hip; now he was a monstrous kind of creature who had never had but one leg and that in the middle of his body. To see him leap and run and pursue me over hedge and ditch was the worst of nightmares.

The Janus-face of Silver is built up by keeping him in reserve until the subsidiary characters of Billy Bones and Blind Pew (blustering buccaneer and vicious, psychopathic cripple) – both aspects of Silver – have been disposed of. The blindness of Pew is a prefiguring of Silver's disablement, and to juxtapose the description of his tapping and groping with Jim's description of Silver in the nightmare is to produce at once the diabolic manifestation in M.R.James's 'O Whistle and I'll Come to You, My Lad'. The scene where Jim is appalled at the athleticism of the cripple who can dispatch Tom Morgan at such lightning speed reflected Louis's awe in face of Henley's combination of infirmity and power and he told Henley: 'It was the sight of your maimed strength and masterfulness that begot John Silver in *Treasure Island* . . . the idea of the maimed man, ruling and dreaded by the sound, was entirely taken from you.'[41]

Whether, at the unconscious level, the relationship between Jim Hawkins and Long John Silver was really about RLS's feelings for Henley may be doubted, even though critics like Leslie Fiedler have used this thesis to argue that the Hawkins/Silver relationship is covertly homosexual. At the other end of the hermeneutic scale, Professor Kiely attempts to dismiss the connection between Jim Hawkins's absent father and Thomas Stevenson by arguing that no boy's adventure story can get going if a figure of male authority is present; a father has to give way so that a Nigger Jim, Queequeg or Silver can take his place alongside the Huck Finns, Ishmaels and Jim Hawkinses.[42] The problem with this argument is that it ignores the absence of fathers in Stevenson's 'adult' books and concentrates on the wrong paternal connection; the significant correlation is not between Thomas Stevenson and Jim Hawkins's father, nor between Jim and Silver as transmogrified RLS and Henley, but between RLS and his father.

Jim's nightmare above, complete with the reference to stormy nights, is a clear reference to Louis's own childhood nightmares; the 'middle leg' suggests an almost textbook oedipal anxiety; and since Henley was already 'father figure', with all the attributes of maleness that RLS truly admired, it was natural that Stevenson's creative imagination – the 'Brownies', to use his own term – should have performed a double mutation: first Thomas to Henley, then Henley to Silver. It is now that the island theme assumes great significance, for the dark side of islands is the way they have so often been used as prisons: Devil's Island, St Helena, Robben Island, Blood Island, Shark Island. The desire to return to the pleasure principle of childhood and evade the onus of the Osbournes and the humiliation of daily contact at Braemar with the paternal Maecenas is blocked by the realisation that the oppressor lurks back in childhood as well. In symbolic terms the island is both a means of liberation and a new form of incarceration. The realisation that there is no escape from the stubborn and irreducible facts of life throws dark splashes over the brightly coloured tropical canvas of Stevenson's island.

All this is speculation. What is hard fact is the disappointing way Louis's critical friends reacted to the book, seeing only the 'rattling good yarn' and affecting to disdain such pot-boiling. When Henley passed these reactions on to him, Louis reacted vehemently:

> To those who ask me (as you say they do) to do nothing but refined, high-toned, bejay-bedamn masterpieces, I will offer the following bargain: I agree to their proposal if they give me £1,000, at which I value *mon possible*, and at the same time effect such a change in my nature that I shall be content to take it from them instead of earning it. If they cannot manage these trifling matters, by God I'll trouble them to hold their tongues, by God ... I will swallow no more of that gruel. Let them write their damn masterpieces for themselves and let me alone ... I am ever yours, the infuriated victim of his early books, who

begs clearly to announce that he will be so no longer, that he did what he has done by following his nose to the best of his ability, and, please God Almighty, will continue to pursue the same till he die.

Of course, from some people RLS did not expect sympathy. When he was adding the finishing touches to the book in Davos in the winter of 1881–82,

> John Addington Symonds (to whom I timidly mentioned what I was engaged on) looked on me askance. He was at that time very eager I should write on the *Characters* of Theophrastus, so far out may be judgements of the wisest man. But Symonds (to be sure) was scarce the confidant to go to for sympathy in a boy's story. He was large-minded; 'a full man' if ever there was one; but the name of my enterprise would suggest to him only capitulations of sincerity and solecisms of style.[43]

Gradually, however, *Treasure Island* established itself as a classic, drawing plaudits from the widest range of literary sensibilities. In 1890 W.B.Yeats wrote to tell him that the book was the only one in which his seafaring grandfather had ever taken any pleasure and that he reread it on his deathbed with infinite satisfaction. Jack London, in so many ways RLS's true spiritual heir, declared: 'His *Treasure Island* will be a classic to go down with *Robinson Crusoe, Through the Looking Glass* and *The Jungle Books*.' However, RLS did not necessarily welcome all his admirers. He particularly detested Gladstone, both because he himself was a Scottish Tory and the 'GOM' a Liberal, but also because he typified the kind of bourgeois respectability he most despised (unconsciously, who knows?: there is certainly a striking physical similarity between Gladstone and Thomas Stevenson); when he heard that the Prime Minister had been up till two in the morning, unable to put *Treasure Island* down, RLS scornfully remarked: 'he would do better to attend to the imperial affairs of England.'[44]

On 23 September 1881 the Stevensons returned to Edinburgh and then departed almost immediately for London. There was another typical RLS fiasco when he called to see Robert Leighton, editor of *Young Folks*, at his office but, because of his bohemian and tatterdemalion appearance, was at first refused admission by the clerks. Reluctantly, he and Fanny then set their course for Davos and another winter among the Alps. This time they rented the Chalet am Stein, a small bleak wooden house on the mountainside, more expensive even than the Hotel Belvedere, about whose prices RLS had complained so bitterly the winter before, but well away from the Belvedere's hothouse atmosphere of gossip and intrigue. From Louis's point of view, the second winter was far more successful than the first, and with his unparalleled sensitivity for the latent significance of things, he sensed that life as an invalid in Davos was in one sense a regression to childhood.

'In the rare air, clear, cold and blinding light of Alpine winters, a man takes a certain troubled delight in his existence, which can nowhere else be paralleled. He is perhaps no happier, but he is stingingly alive. It does not, perhaps, come out of him in work or exercise, yet he feels an enthusiasm of blood unknown in more temperate climates. It may not be health, but it is fun.

'There is nothing more difficult to communicate on paper than this baseless ardour, this stimulation of the brain, this sterile joyousness of spirits. You wake every morning, see the gold upon the snow-peaks, become filled with courage, and bless God for your prolonged existence. Is it a return of youth, or is it a congestion of the brain? It is a sort of congestion, perhaps, that leads the invalid, when all goes well, to face the new day with such a bubbling cheerfulness . . . But on the other hand, the peculiar blessedness of boyhood may itself be but a symptom of the same complaint, for the two effects are strangely similar; and the frame of mind of the invalid upon the Alps is a sort of intermittent youth, with periods of lassitude.'[45]

In six months of generally improving health Louis wrote 35,000 words: *The Silverado Squatters*, some sketches for *Prince Otto*, and some essays, especially the studies of his father, Bob, Fleeming Jenkin and Symonds later published as 'Talk and Talkers'. He even began a western, *The Squaw Man*, and wrote the first chapter and half of the second before abandoning it. With his mind still on American subjects, he also considered writing a biography of Benjamin Franklin; Colvin thought this a good idea and approached the American editor of *Century Magazine*, but he thought that Franklin was already written into the ground. He was also hoping to write a book on Hazlitt, one of his long-time favourites, but abandoned it, and a long short story 'The Adventures of John Delafield' met the same fate. Another project germinating at this time was 'The Murder of Red Colin', the seed from which *Kidnapped* would grow. Meanwhile he had had the satisfaction of seeing the last of the portraits that would eventually comprise *Familiar Studies* – the essay on Samuel Pepys – appear in the *Cornhill Magazine*; he was taken to task for assuming that Pepys's diaries were mere posing and posturing for a putative reader, when in fact they were designed to be read only by himself. Still, his reputation was growing all the time, he had offers for books from two London publishers and he told his father: 'Really I ought to make money now.'[46]

Another literary pastime – a product of the continuing friendship with J.A.Symonds – was a temporarily obsessive interest in translating Latin poetry, principally Horace and Martial, into English verse. With Symonds and his friend Horatio Brown RLS spent long evenings discussing classical metre and principles of prosody, and the result was some distinguished, if little-known, verses. So great was the obsession for a time that an English parson was once summoned to attend RLS at 6 a.m., went along fearing the worst, but found only a haggard face peering from the bedclothes and an agonised voice that exclaimed: 'For God's sake, have you got a Horace?'[47]

Symonds confessed that he liked RLS more and more each time he saw him, and that the 'improvement' was because he himself felt more relaxed and less patronising than in the winter of 1880–81. At first he reported that Stevenson was very ill and that Dr Ruedi, hovering between a diagnosis of consumption and bronchiectasis or erosion of the lungs, thought his disease had advanced since the previous winter. 'Somehow, I am not hopeful about him. He does not seem to me to have the sort of toughness or instinctive energy of self-control, the faculty which I possess, of lying still when I feel my centre of vitality attacked.' Later he commented: 'Stevenson is better. He is certainly not going to die yet. But I do not like his habit as an invalid. One thing is in his favour – his serenity of soul about what is called comfort. But the *défaut de cette qualité* is that he is, as a Bohemian, ever restless in mind.' In other words, Symonds was shaking his head over RLS's inability to keep to the regime prescribed for a consumptive: he tobogganed when he should have rested and sat in bed writing when he should have been taking the air. Horatio Brown concurred in this estimate:

> I saw a good (a great) deal of RLS in the winters he was there [Davos] and I feel pretty sure that he never did any systematic open-air cure, or systematic anything. He lived a far from invalid life, except when he broke down and retired to bed. I have vivid recollections of long talks with him all through snowy afternoons, when we drank old Valtelline wine and smoked, and eventually I got the impression that there was nothing of him in the room but his bright eyes moving about, and his voice. This sounds as though I were in a not unknown condition; but it was not so; at least not from the wine; perhaps from the words.[48]

In his cups Stevenson was not always discreet and he blurted out a secret told him by Gosse in Braemar, that Gosse felt resentful about some alleged breach of hospitality on the part of the Symondses; much mortified, Symonds wrote to Gosse to clear matters up, and then Louis had to explain to Gosse that he had inadvertently divulged a confidence.[49]

In general, RLS's daily life at Davos in 1881–82 was as boring and humdrum as the winter before. When not writing or translating, he read Dickens – *Our Mutual Friend* helped him through the Alpine winter – but in general Stevenson was not a great admirer of Dickens, and Esther Summerson and the Cheerybles were among his particular *bêtes noires*. To alleviate the tedium he liked to play jokes and rib and tease, but Teutonic audiences were not fertile soil for his 'Mr Libbel' fooleries. It was all right as long as he restricted his activities to Britons, as when he staged a mock trial of a Mr Cornish, one of his Davos acquaintances, but tensions invariably arose with the Germans. Once a stuffy German professor was inveighing against the 'weakness' of English women, in contrast to the sturdiness of their German sisters. RLS at once cut in: 'What?' he exclaimed, flinging his arms out histrionically, 'do you talk of German women? I tell you, this neck of mine is wet with the tears of German women!'[50]

Such jests show RLS in good heart, and indeed he throve mightily in the climate of Davos: both climate and Dr Ruedi's treatment suited him, but both were undone by the swallow-like migration when spring came. For this the impetus came from Fanny, who was almost permanently ill at Davos. The mysterious 'disease of the stomach' that had prostrated her in 1880–81 was now compounded with spotted throat, diarrhoea, 'drain-fever' and much else. None of this is mentioned in the legend of Fanny as Florence Nightingale built up by her sister Nellie Sanchez and, as Malcolm Elwin has well said: 'Her sister's omission to mention her state of health at this time gathers significance; hints in the letters build up a picture oddly at variance with the legend of the stoical nurse, devotedly tending the querulous consumptive.' Stevenson scholarship has moved on since Elwin and the 'hints' are now well documented, not least by Fanny herself; when Maggie mentioned that her symptoms sounded rather like those Thomas Stevenson suffered from, Fanny wrote back: 'I take it as a compliment that I am thought like him.'[51]

There is an element of black comedy in the miserable letter Louis wrote to Baxter in mid-November, explaining that he and Fanny were both ill in bed together, with a sick nurse in attendance and the dog Bogue howling miserably outside with an abscess in its ear; Louis's cough was so bad that the only way he could sleep was to keep a little flask of chloral and haschisch at the bedside. Finally, at the end of November, Fanny departed for four weeks of rest cure and medical consultations in Zurich and Berne; the doctors found bloody stools, thought she might have passed a gallstone and feared ulceration of the bowel. Despondently Louis wrote again to Baxter: 'We have been in miserable case here, my wife worse and worse, and now sent away, with Sam [i.e. Lloyd] for sick nurse, I not being allowed to go down ... I don't care so much for solitude as I used to; results, I suppose, of marriage.'

Fanny's illness, the bowel condition apart, was again largely psychosomatic, doubtless a revolt against the confinement in Davos which she could not consciously acknowledge. That she was in a most precarious mental state is clear from her obsession this winter with two running themes: the impertinence of servants; and the ingratitude of Belle. Not having been brought up in an environment where domestic service was taken for granted, and therefore uncertain how to deal with maids, cooks and butler, Fanny always had problems with servants, largely, it seems, because she oscillated between over-familiarity and authoritarianism instead of maintaining a firm but polite middle course. When she and Louis moved into the Chalet am Stein, they engaged a German maid who turned out 'disagreeable'; when she was discharged, more of the same appeared to fill the breach – first a pretty one (too pretty perhaps), then an old reliable one whom they could not understand – and Fanny's letters to her female correspondents were full of lamentations on the old theme of the impossibility of obtaining proper staff. A more acute cause of anger was Belle, who was ungrateful for the financial subventions Louis sent her, wrote letters full of coarseness and angered Fanny by sharing a house in San Francisco with people she did not approve of: 'those vulgar improvident bohemians, the Taverniers'.[52]

Fanny's uncertain mood, her permanent illness and the worry about the cost of a month's treatment in Switzerland's cities affected Louis adversely, as did the increasing signs that Lloyd was a pampered mother's boy at heart; he refused to return to the clergyman's school at Bournemouth and had to be expensively tutored in Davos – for fairly basic instruction in Latin, French and mathematics by a consumptive Oxford man, Charles Garrard, Louis had to pay 1,062 francs for the period 15 November 1881–5 April 1882. The stresses in the household sometimes led to rows, typically triggered by subjects a long way from their real cause. Louis confided in Bob: 'Anxious to stop something said I had the extreme politeness to tell Fanny that she lied. She was naturally annoyed; because all she said was true. But, as I say, I am sure you knew what I meant, which was, in my heated, drunken way, to choke off a matter I thought unpleasant and unnecessary.'[53]

Nonetheless, Louis missed Fanny during her month's absence in Zurich and Berne. On Christmas Day he went down to Berne to fetch Fanny and Lloyd, who had absconded from his lessons to be with her. They then had a seven-hour drive back up steep ridges through forests of Christmas trees in the snow in an open sleigh – the only carriage available over the holiday. The cold was so intense that Louis confessed to having often suffered less at the dentist and dreaded that Fanny might ask him for brandy or laudanum, as this would mean taking his hands out of his gloves; such a journey was scarcely ideal therapy for a consumptive. Almost immediately thereafter, the couple took to their beds, and for the rest of that mild winter were rarely seen by the inhabitants of Davos; at the beginning of March Symonds wrote to Horatio Brown: 'the Stevensons still go on in the same wretched way. He says they have not been out of the house since the first of January.' Louis was in despair: 'I wish to God I or anybody knew what was the matter with my wife ... I am in the blackness of low spirits tonight, for Fanny has had a sharp relapse, and I have hurt my dog and bust my own knee. We have both been in bed for near a week ... I will not write much more for I should fear to say what I really felt.[54]

Continuing lame, and with occasional attacks, Louis alternated his illnesses with Fanny; if ever both of them were well for a day, the dog would be ill. While confined to bed, Louis tried to distract himself by addressing himself to the problems of his friends: Bob, who had married the year before; Katharine de Mattos, who was living in poverty; and Walter

Simpson, whose marriage had turned into a disaster. He asked Baxter to examine the de Mattos marriage contract to see if she could either get de Mattos to increase his maintenance payments or escape to divorce through a loophole, and warned that Simpson would pay dearly for his choice of wife. Between Anne Simpson and RLS there was the same kind of tension as between Henley and Fanny, and Louis's remarks about Lady Simpson have an ironical ring in the light of Fanny's plans: 'A lady of title will not rest (and at present is not resting by any means) till she has cleared every manjack of her husband's friends out of the boutique.'[55]

Only the steadily deepening friendship with Symonds sustained them through the first three months of 1882. There are signs too that Fanny's slow poisoning of her husband's mind against his old friends was beginning to do its work, for in March Louis sent this ominous missive to Colvin: 'I brought home with me from my bad times in America two strains of unsoundness of mind, the first, a perpetual fear that I can do no more work – the second, a perpetual fear that my friends have quarrelled with me. I struggle as hard as I know against both, but a judicious postcard would sometimes save me the expense of the second.' Fanny had also made her point in other ways, and a marginal improvement in her health provided the motive and opportunity to decamp. It was clearly impossible for them to continue to live in Davos, and when Dr Ruedi after examination (what Henry James would call 'auscultation') told Louis that his lungs had improved, despite the many bedridden days, and reluctantly gave the nod for his patient to live experimentally in the south of France – provided he lived near a fir wood and no farther than fifteen miles from the sea – the Stevensons set course for Scotland. A jubilant Louis wrote to Henley as if he were Silver himself: 'My lungs are said to be in a splendid state . . . Taiut! Hillo! Hey! Stand by! Avast! Hurrah!' After a short spell with the parents, the Midi would beckon and it was farewell for ever to the icy cage of Davos.[56]

9

French Interlude

According to Symonds, Fanny and Louis intended to settle initially in Normandy – which would be more convenient for London publishers and enable Fanny to cross the Channel regularly to conciliate Thomas Stevenson. The plan came to nothing. First Thomas and Maggie met them in London and they all stayed together in hotels for a few days, which enabled Louis and Fanny to meet Bob and his new bride, Louisa Purland. Then they stayed for a short time with Katharine de Mattos in Surrey, but were careful not to overstay their welcome, since Katharine had been reduced to genteel poverty by the separation from her husband. Always keen to renew his acquaintance with George Meredith – he had seen him again in Weybridge in September 1881 – RLS managed another visit to Burford Bridge; as was the case with Symonds, Meredith found Louis more and more impressive each time he saw him, and he would base Gower Woodseer in *The Amazing Marriage* on his enthusiastic Scots visitor.

After a month in Edinburgh, Fanny and Louis departed for Stobo Manse in Peebleshire, intending to spend the summer there, but within two weeks Louis was coughing up blood; he went down to London to see Sir Andrew Clark, the same doctor who had originally ordered him south in 1873, and was recommended to try a location farther north in Scotland. At the beginning of August the Stevensons rented a cottage at Kingussie on Speyside – this was to be the last full month RLS ever spent in Scotland.[1] Throughout this summer of 1882 he continued to gather material for his intended book on the Appin murder, but gradually the project began to languish. At the end of his time in Scotland his energies were devoted to the short story 'The Treasure of Franchard', sometimes hailed as a portrait of the French bourgeoisie to rival Zola's.[2]

The Osbournes continued to gnaw at his vitals. He found himself continuing to send money to Belle and Joe Strong, even though Belle was overtly hostile to him; the Strongs took everything they could get while ignoring their benefactor and not even bothering to correspond with Fanny. Joe Strong was at the time a prosperous painter who got plenty of money from commissions, yet squandered it on wild parties and riotous living; Belle's stance was that her mother and stepfather should pay for the necessities of life, while Joe's income was to go only on luxuries. All Louis's friends were scandalised that, in his difficult circumstances, he was still expected to send money to such a couple, yet Fanny did not put her husband first to the extent of staunching the outflow; her 'primitiveness' manifested itself in a perennial commitment to her brood first, husband second. Yet the more Louis sent, the more Belle in her occasional letters to her mother complained that he had not sent more. As Fanny's biographer has written: 'Belle seemed to feel that since Louis had broken up the Osbourne family, it was the least he could do to subsidize them all. As for Joe, he had no sense of financial pride or obligation; he merely grabbed money – any money – like a small child.'3

At Kingussie, Louis suffered a second haemorrhage, which raised fears in Fanny's mind that he might be ordered back to Davos. She at once fell ill, and this time sent Lloyd back to the school in Bournemouth. In London, Sir Andrew Clark, after examining Louis and listening to his reservations about Switzerland, suggested abandoning both Davos and the Highlands; treatment of consumptives divided specialists between the sea air and mountain air schools; if Ruedi at Davos was clearly of the mountain faction, Clark, as his penchant for Menton indicated, was a 'seaside' man. Since Fanny was now too ill to accompany him, Stevenson set off for the south of France with Bob.

First they tried Montpellier, but Louis had another haemorrhage and was advised not to settle there. He wrote a singular letter to Fanny, indicating both that the real 'divided self' in RLS was between the tubercular person he was and the healthy person he wanted to be, and that Fanny's much-vaunted nursing skills (as in the Fanny legend) had left her husband unimpressed: 'I don't want you when I am ill. At least, it's only half of me that wants you, and I don't like to think of your coming back and not finding me better than when we parted. That is why I would rather be miserable than send for you.' A further haemorrhage found him spending the afternoon in Dr Caisso's waiting room, chatting and making friends with the local peasants. Caisso advised rest and silence and cautioned against travel, but Stevenson's importunities wore him down. The black dog is evident in Louis's next letter to Fanny:

> I do not ask you to love me any more. I am too much trouble. Besides, I thought myself all over last night; and, my dear, such rubbage. You cannot put up with such a man. In one way, I see you act on these principles, for I hear from you very rarely. Indeed, I suspect you of being very ill. If you are I shall forgive you, my dear, you are provoked to it, I know. If you are not, you might write oftener, I think, to one who is devoted to silence and repose.4

While Bob returned to England, Louis shifted his base of operations to Marseilles, where a valetudinarian Fanny joined him in mid-October: 'The wreck was towed into port yesterday evening,' Louis told his mother. Within three days he had fallen in love with a spacious house in the suburb of St Marcel, to the east of Marseilles. Campagne Defli, as the house was called, was set in a large estate and overlooked a picturesque valley of cliffs and woods; the rental, just £48 a year, was low for the south of France, and the place seemed the ideal headquarters for a three-year writing campaign. RLS cabled Colvin (then acting as his agent) to send out £54 to cover the rent and incidentals. Fanny sent for the heavy luggage and engaged servants for the task of springcleaning and refurbishing, but she had her usual contretemps with the serving class. As she was standing on a ladder, hammering a nail into the wall to hang a picture, she overheard one maid whisper to the other: '*Elle est folle.*' Doubtless the maid thought she was safe, for Fanny never mastered more than a smattering of French, but the maids reckoned without her witchlike antennae for snubs real or unintentional. She shook the hammer at them and exclaimed indignantly: '*Pas folle. Beaucoup d'intelligence!*' However, the effect of this riposte was somewhat spoiled when she overbalanced and fell off the ladder, to the ululations of the fleeing maids.[5]

From the very beginning, Campagne Defli seemed ill-starred. First, news came from Scotland that Baxter's infant child had died. Baxter was a difficult man to deal with and early in 1882 Louis had fallen foul of him during some routine business when Baxter took offence at an expression used in the correspondence. Fanny was normally the very last person, from the viewpoint of tact, to deal successfully with Baxter, but this time she knew just what to say: 'I have lost a child myself, and I have no word of consolation to offer. I know too well that there is nothing to be said. I thought once that I could not lose my child and live: such sorrow seemed impossible to bear. But I had to bear it, and I lived.'

Louis had also been in touch with William Dean Howells and invited him to St Marcel; then he read Howells's *A Modern Instance* and realised how strict the author's views on marriage and divorce were. He at once dashed off a letter explaining that Fanny was divorced and threw down the gauntlet in typically Stevensonian manner: 'It will be my sincere disappointment to find that you cannot be my guest. I shall bear up, however; for I assure you I desire to know no one who considers himself holier than my wife.'

Then the dream house itself started to turn into a nightmare. A residence situated in an area where the mistral blew 175 days of the year was scarcely ideal for a man with pulmonary complaints; Louis had several haemorrhages within a matter of weeks, and on top of this came a typhoid outbreak in Marseilles – some say it was an epidemic of enteric

fever that Fanny took to be typhus. RLS summed up his feelings on the
disappointment of his hopes:

> Campagne De-fli:
> O me!
> Campagne De-bug:
> There comes the tug!
> Campagne De-mosquito
> It's eneuch to gar me greet, O!
> Campagne De-louse:
> O God damn the house![6]

They quickly decided that Louis should seek refuge in Nice, and Fanny
would join him there as soon as the money arrived from Colvin and after
she had met Lloyd, due in Marseilles for the Christmas holidays.[6] When the
time came for Fanny to join him there, what happened was at best a ludicrous
confusion from *The Comedy of Errors* and at worst one of Fanny's neurotic
fantasies. Instead of a single exchange of telegrams between Nice and
Marseilles, Fanny found herself scurrying between Marseilles and Toulon,
looking for her husband, who was all the time in Nice. Apparently she got
it into her head that an epidemic of plague had hit the French Riviera,
that people were dying like flies and being buried unidentified in mass
graves for sanitary reasons, and that Louis had succumbed to just such
a fate. Two judgements on all this will suffice. Richard Aldington remarks
curtly: 'Fanny's account shows her usual exaggeration and inaccuracy.' And
J.C.Furnas, usually on Fanny's side in the many controversies attached to
her name, concludes:

> Her letter to the Symondses about her subsequent experiences sounds like
> a bad dream; I suspect that much of it was just that ... Any of it is
> conceivable, but all of it sounds too much like the authoress of certain tales
> in *The Dynamiter*. Though she never lied for practical advantage, Fanny
> sometimes justified her dreads with details that happened never to have
> existed – what psychiatry calls "retrospective falsification".[7]

In her hysteria Fanny cabled Louis's friends in England that he was
dead or dying. When the truth emerged, it seemed to confirm all the worst
fears about Fanny entertained in RLS's old circles. 'I will never let myself
be frightened by that maniac partner of his again,' Colvin wrote angrily to
Baxter, 'and she may cry wolf till she is hoarse.' Thomas and Maggie were
also far from pleased, and Louis had to fudge the issue and obfuscate it to
save Fanny's blushes, as can be inferred from a letter to his parents when
he pleads that, with his weight down to 7 stone 12lbs, Fanny's fears were
justified: 'No, Cassandra was Cassandra, as you imagine. I have just come
from being weighed and I am down to 7 stone 11¼, far lower than I
have ever been in my recollection.' Further letters from his parents must

have hinted that Fanny's neurotic outbursts were bad for him, for a week later he wrote unhappily to expostulate against their criticisms: 'What she is to me, no language can describe, and she can never learn.' Yet he found it necessary to apologise to Colvin for a peremptory telegram fired off in the heat of the crisis, in which he cancelled a previous invitation to visit them at St Marcel: 'My dear Colvin, I am aware I must appear like a kind of lunatic to you ... I felt so sure Fanny and I had put unfair pressure on you.'[8]

The first two months of 1883 Stevenson spent recuperating in Nice, first at the Grand Hôtel, later at the Hôtel du Petit Louvre, and commuting between Nice and Marseilles while he tried to dispose of Campagne Defli without incurring the hefty charges consequent upon breaking a long lease. Eventually, on 15 February, he was able to tell his family and friends that he had got out of the lease and escaped paying compensation by threatening to countersue on the grounds of exorbitant rent charged for a known health hazard. As he wrote to his parents: 'Hooray! hooray! hooray! Got rid of the house, grrrrrrrrrreat success!' This made up to some extent for his continuing despondency about not being able to afford a suitable billet. The ideas flew thick and fast and became wilder and wilder: first Nice, then Cannes, St Raphael and Lake Geneva. It was well into March before they found what they were looking for and rented a new house at Hyères.[9]

During this interim period of living in hotels, there were two very different developments, illustrating the constant yin and yang in the life of this double man. On the negative side came the devastating news that Ferrier was dying of an alcohol-related disease (probably cirrhosis). The news of his impending demise was broken by Mrs Ferrier at the beginning of 1883 in a distraught letter which virtually accused Louis of being responsible for her son's alcoholism: 'He now exists among the number of those degraded ones whose society on earth is shunned by the moral and virtuous among mankind.' In the autumn of 1883 came news of the inevitable end. Louis was devastated: he told Ferrier's sister, Elizabeth ('Coggie') that he 'could not see for crying'; Steuart commented: 'Stevenson mourned him as David mourned Jonathan.' With his brain bursting with mournful thoughts of Ferrier, RLS wrote to Will Low that he was preoccupied with 'new thoughts of death. Up to now I had rather thought of him as a mere personal enemy of my own; but now that I see him hunting after my friends he looks altogether darker.'[10]

On the positive side, Louis completed his first book of verse, that prime source for his childhood: *A Child's Garden of Verses*. A vivid, barely disguised self portrait introduces us to the child of well-to-do parents, who is cared for by a nurse ('My Kingdom') and lives in a large house ('North West Passage'). Ill and lonely, he is confined to the walled family garden and is frequently in bed ('The Land of Counterpane', 'My Bed is a Boat'). Imaginative, curious and introspective, he often compares his life with that of other children, real and imagined ('The Sun Travels', 'Where Go the Boats?', 'Foreign Children'). Avoiding the traps of mawkishness, whimsy and didacticism of other 'children's versifiers' such as Isaac Watts and Walter de la Mare, Stevenson provided an outstanding picture of the suppressed wishes, loneliness, anxiety and uncertainty of childhood. The dialectic between pleasure and reality principles, between childhood as lost domain or vanished Eden and Purgatory, has not always pleased critics who argue that the very 'dialectical' quality is what is false about *Child's Garden*: on the one hand the child wishes to escape his physical and spiritual prison, but on the other the adult creator, by exorcising his own childhood demons, has already escaped from the cage he is complaining of.[11]

After a few weeks of hotel living at Hyères, in March the Stevensons signed a long-term lease – somewhat reluctantly as they would have preferred an experimental monthly rental – for the Chalet de la Solitude, situated halfway up a hillside between the high old town with its Saracen citadel and the low-lying new town. Perhaps the superficial similarity of the layout of Hyères with that of Edinburgh was why Louis's correspondence with Baxter underwent an exponential increase and why there are so many nostalgic lamentations for the wild days of his youth. Described in a letter to Mrs Sitwell as 'the loveliest house you ever saw, with a garden like a fairy story and a view like a classical landscape', the Chalet de la Solitude had been a model chalet at the Paris Exposition; it was supposed to have been reproduced on a larger scale for actual living but had not been so; with its three small rooms downstairs and four upstairs, it gave Louis his second taste of living in Lilliput (the first had been at Pitlochry in 1881).[12]

Delighted with his new house – he later claimed he spent the happiest time of his life here – Louis also had the good fortune of acquiring the perfect maid, in the form of Valentine Roch. Born in Switzerland into a large French family now domiciled in Hyères, where her father worked on the railways, Valentine had intelligence and humour far beyond those usually found in servants. Young, blonde and a charmer, she had no previous experience as a maid, but quickly made herself indispensable and held the household enthralled at night when she gave her review of neighbourhood gossip. Louis was very fond of her and usually called her Joe – denoting her extrovert high spirits. But when she had had a bruising encounter with Fanny – for Fanny was incapable of behaving correctly with servants even when she had the good luck to find a 'treasure' like Valentine – Valentine turned moody and then Louis called her Thomasina. The bonds between them were strengthened in mid-May when RLS went down with flu and again hovered between life and death. Valentine, properly instructed by Fanny, took turns nursing the patient and made a great success of it. Once she had seen the master through the crisis, Valentine decided she had had

enough of Fanny and announced she was leaving. Then she herself went
down with flu, was nursed through it by Fanny, and in gratitude decided
to stay on; she remained with the Stevensons for six years and quit only
when unjustly accused of theft by her mistress.[13]

There is much evidence that Louis was physically attracted by Valentine
– he always had a wonderful eye for the charms of women – though it is
false to suggest, as has sometimes been alleged, that he had an affair with
her. Over the years there has been a quite futile scholarly debate about
whether his poem 'Ne Sit Ancillae Tibi Amor Pudori' ('Don't be ashamed
of your love for a maid') is about his feelings for Valentine or for some other
maid encountered in the early 1870s. Whatever the case, the verses can stand
as indicating RLS's *likely* reponse to Valentine Roch:

> There's just a twinkle in your eye
> That seems to say I might, if I
> Were only bold enough to try
> An arm about your waist.
>
> I hear, too, as you come and go,
> That pretty nervous laugh, you know;
> And then your cap is always so
> Coquettishly displaced.
>
> Your cap! the word's profanely said,
> That little topknot, white and red,
> That quaintly crowns your graceful head,
> No bigger than a flower,
>
> You set with such a bewitching art,
> And so provocatively smart,
> I'd like to wear it on my heart,
> And order for an hour.
>
> O graceful housemaid, full and fair,
> I love your shy imperial air,
> And always loiter on the stair,
> When you are going by.
>
> A strict reserve the fates demand;
> But, when to let you pass I stand,
> Sometimes by chance I touch your hand
> And sometimes catch your eye.[14]

The days at Hyères, when Louis was not ill, were idyllic. After a
morning's writing, there would be a light lunch, with salad and a *vin du
pays*; Fanny and Louis would discuss the morning's work and then stroll
up to the castle or enjoy the simple pleasures of the garden, which was the
really outstanding feature of the Chalet de la Solitude: Louis told Will Low

that at night there was the most wonderful view into the moonlit garden, with the sensuous paradise completed by aromatic scents and 'flutes of silence'. After dinner Louis read voraciously: Seeley's *The Expansion of England*, the publishing sensation of 1883, with its assertion that the British empire was acquired in a fit of absence of mind; St Augustine's *Confessions*, Tacitus, Petronius, Barbey d'Aurevilly, Dickens, Balzac. At one time he thought of turning *Great Expectations* into a play and wrote to his father with his comments: 'Miss Havisham is probably the worst thing in human fiction. But Wemmick I like; and I like Trabb's boy.' His father replied some time later to say that he found *Dombey and Son* the worst novel in the English language, no doubt because of its devastating portrayal of a patriarch.

His thoughts on Balzac were confided to Bob, and they sparked off wider thoughts on aesthetics and the art of writing:

> Were you to reread some Balzac as I have been doing, it would greatly help to clear your eyes. He was a man who never found his method. An inarticulate Shakespeare, smothered under forcible-feeble detail. It is astonishing to the ripe mind how bad he is, how feeble, how untrue, how tedious; and of course, when he surrendered to his temperament, how good and powerful. And yet never plain or clear. He could not consent to be dull, and thus became so. He would leave nothing undeveloped, and thus drowned out of sight of land amid the multitude of crying and incongruous details.

This is revealing, as it shows how far out of line Stevenson was with the main currents in nineteenth-century fiction, with its bias towards the ornate periphrasis, the elegant circumlocution, the overclotted prose. RLS thought many of his contemporaries deficient in craftsmanship, which was why, despite his brilliance at first drafts, he forced himself to redraft and rewrite. His credo was: 'Perfect sentences have often been written; perfect paragraphs at times – but never a perfect page.' As he wrote to Bob in the 'Balzac letter': 'There is but one art, to omit! O if I knew how to omit, I would ask no other knowledge. A man who knew how to omit would make an Iliad of a daily paper.'[15]

Illness continued to dog both Louis and Fanny. After the near-fatal flu came fever and, perhaps not coincidentally, the discovery that the ground under the chalet was riddled with cesspools, which had to be cleared out at great expense. Fanny continued to ail with mysterious maladies – pleurisy was mentioned – and now her hypochondria found a new focus; she became a subscriber to the *Lancet* and found fresh theories to support her suspicions of a wide range of foods. Vinegar, it now transpired, was detrimental to health, salads were full of tapeworm's eggs, wines of different areas had different febrifugal qualities, and so on. She announced successively that Louis had 'Roman fever' and 'drain poison' and even claimed to see something sinister in his visit to the dentist in Marseilles.[16] By midsummer she had persuaded her husband that it would be better to 'estivate' in the Auvergne rather than face the 'miasmata' of the Midi. They travelled north, spent a couple of days in Lyons, then travelled by easy stages to Vichy, but everywhere they went the climate was unsuitable or the hotels were unable to provide meals suitable for people with weak lungs. They moved on to Clermont-Ferrand, which was better than Vichy, though they still had doubts about its general salubriousness; the picturesque streets were narrow and likely to become airless as the summer wore on.

At Clermont, RLS had yet another brush with French officialdom. Smarting from a recent experience when he had been refused admission, without reason but almost certainly because of his eccentric appearance, to the casino at Monte Carlo – which particularly piqued him since it was quite prepared to welcome the canaille of Europe, he now fell foul of a different class of jack-in-office. Attempting to cash a cheque drawn on the British Linen Company of Edinburgh, he so appalled the cashiers by his slovenly appearance that they threatened to call the police, on the grounds that they had never heard of a British Linen Company. This time RLS won a notable victory. He insisted that the police indeed be sent for and, while he was waiting, ransacked a pigeonhole in the bank. Here he found not just a cache of correspondence from the allegedly unknown British Linen Company, but the actual letter of credit authorising Stevenson's cheque to be cashed. RLS then demanded to see the manager; when the man was brought out he poured invective on his head. When the police arrived, both constables and manager escorted him from the premises with much apology, fawning and grovelling.[17]

While RLS stayed in Clermont-Ferrand to write, Fanny and Lloyd – who had not returned to school in England but was being coached by a tutor in Toulon and was now on holiday – scouted possible ideal locations in the environs. A short distance away they lit on Royat, a spa on high ground overlooked by the Puy de Dôme, with comfortable hotels and set in pleasant countryside; at that time unknown to British tourists, Royat was said to have played host to Julius Caesar, who bathed in the hot springs. Louis was delighted with the find, for Royat offered him three different attractions. There was the medieval cathedral, with sentry posts on the towers, walls full of loopholes and embrasures and iron-bound doors built to withstand battering rams, the whole redolent of the warfare of the Middle Ages in which he was then steeped, as he was in the middle of *The Black Arrow*. There was the panoramic road leading to the Puy de Dôme through wooded ravines and hills where the sound of waterfalls was continuous.

Most of all there were the baths. Though the springs had a high arsenic content and could be drunk only in small quantities, they impressed with their variety, one tasting like chicken broth, another fizzing like champagne. Guests were treated royally: a sedan chair came to your bedroom, you stepped inside in a dressing gown, the door was closed, and you emerged only at the bath-tub. Yet if the privacy was welcome, less so was the jolting progress to the baths from the hotel. The bearers were supposed to take the sedan chairs down to the baths by a zigzag route, but seldom kept time as they walked, so that the chair swayed from side to side. There was, however, an even greater risk. An immense flight of steps led down from the town to the baths, but there had been so many fatal accidents when the bearers lost their footing that it had been illegal for porters to take their charges that way. But sometimes the porters were in heavy demand and to save time would descend by the illegal route, taking advantage of the fact that the person within could not see where he was going. Both Louis and Fanny claimed to have been the victim of this perilous short cut.

However, Royat certainly agreed with Louis's health which so far improved that he was able to take long drives to the Puy de Dôme and then spend the evening listening to the string band in the Casino. It was in Royat that Louis polished off *The Black Arrow*, and his feelings about Royat were so favourable that he notified his parents of the *trouvaille*; they came out, were also enchanted and spent the whole summer there. In September, they departed for Edinburgh, while son and daughter-in-law headed south for Hyères. It was becoming increasingly clear that the Midi was the wrong place for Louis, for he spent most of the rest of the year as an off-and-on invalid.[18]

During 1883 the three perennial problems in Stevenson's life – money, his father, and the Osbournes – presented themselves in acute form. In 1882 he made £268 from his writings but, as he told Henley: 'it might do for an exceptionally chaste bachelor. But for a married man, who is sick, and has a sick wife, and a boy at school, it is scrimp.' Louis constantly expressed the hope that he could become self-sufficient from his earnings if only his health would hold up, but always another illness or another expense would supervene to cast him down, raising the question whether his ill-health was cause or effect of the strain he lived under. As he told Henley at the time of the clearing out of the cesspools: 'A word in your ear. I don't like trying to support myself. I hate the strain and anxiety and when unexpected expenses are foisted on me, I feel the world is playing with false dice.'[19]

He was greatly cheered by the news that he was to receive £100 for *Treasure Island* in book form, though this book never gained him the rewards it should have done; by 1901, largely because of the many pirated editions in the U.S.A., it had still brought only £2,000 into the Stevenson estate. In some ways the £40 he received for *The Silverado Squatters* was more important, for this led in the autumn of 1883 to an offer from Lippincott's of Philadelphia for him to write a travel book on the Aegean islands, the travel to be done in autumn 1884; he was to be paid £450, with £100 as advance payment. Louis's health did not permit him to take up the offer, but Fanny disingenuously used it to wrongfoot Baxter; when Baxter tried to cancel a meeting with RLS in Nice at the end of 1883, Fanny upbraided him on the grounds that Louis had given up his Aegean trip 'just to meet' his old friend; she did not mention that the trip had been scheduled for autumn 1884.[20]

Gradually, Louis allowed his financial hopes to build. 'This year for the first time I shall pass £300,' he wrote to Gosse, and his prediction was fulfilled. On 1 January 1884 he was in exultant mood: 'The year closes, leaving me with £50 in the bank, owing no man nothing, £100 more due me in a week or so, and £150 more in the course of a month; and I can look back on a total receipt of £465.0s.6d for the last twelve months.' Yet there was always an association of ideas between his general anxieties and money. He became so disillusioned with the paucity of letters from Colvin that he sardonically offered £10,000 for news of his whereabouts. To Henley, by now jealous of RLS's growing critical and financial success, who passed on to him petty quibbles about the accuracy of the seamanship and marine lore in *Treasure Island*, Louis was blunt. *Treasure Island* was not a work of realism, so that Henley's picayune criticisms confused facts with truth: 'the next thing I shall hear is that the etiquette is wrong in *Otto*'s court!'[21]

Conflict between Louis and Thomas Stevenson continued, even though the balance of power was by now subtly shifting in favour of the younger man. There were three main reasons for this. In the first place. Thomas had become reconciled to his son's literary career, admired him for his success with *Treasure Island*, and was inclined to feel guilty about his earlier opposition. Secondly, Fanny's flattery and manipulation of the old man was having its effect. Thirdly, Louis was becoming more viable financially, even though he did not begin to make any profit on his writings until 1886 and was still financially dependent on him when his father died in 1887. The result of the changing balance of power was that Louis felt able to express his anger and resentment more clearly. As Thomas slipped more often into melancholia and brooding, Louis became more and more critical of him. Thomas wrote to Fanny in September to say that he had resolved 'to enter on a most determined battle to attain to a more complete resignation to God's will'. Louis cut in very brusquely in clear 'so you ought' vein:

What you say about yourself I was glad to hear; a little decent resignation is not only becoming in a Christian, but is likely to be excellent for the health of a Stevenson. To fret and fume is undistinguished, suicidally foolish, and theologically unpardonable; we are not here to make, but to tread predestined pathways; we are the foam of a wave, and to preserve a proper equanimity is not merely the first part of submission to God, but the chief of possible kindnesses to those about us.

Yet this was mild stuff alongside RLS's 'Christmas message' to his parents. On 25 December he indited a letter to Thomas reproving him for not counting his blessings – the fact that he had gained a stone in weight, had an enduring marriage and a son who was healthy, successful and a credit to him. His signing-off was relatively jovial: 'And now, you dear old pious ingrate, on this Christmas morning, think what your mercies have been.' But to Maggie he wrote a letter which, equating as it does his mother with a dog, made it plain that the 'enduring marriage' was no more than the relationship between master and pet; written *to his mother and on Christmas day*, this extraordinary missive is surely a candidate for the much overused description 'oedipal rage':

> My dear Mother – I give my father up. I give him a parable ... and he takes it backside foremost, and shakes his head, and is gloomier than ever. Tell him that I give him up. I don't want such a parent. This is not the man for my money ... Here I am on the threshold of another year, when, according to all human foresight, I should long ago have been resolved into my elements; here am I, who you were persuaded was born to disgrace you – and, I will do you the justice to add, on no insufficient grounds – no very burning discredit when all is done ... There is he [Thomas], at his not first youth, able to take more exercise than I at 33, and gaining a stone's weight, a thing of which I am incapable. There are you: has the man no gratitude? There is Smeoroch (the dog): is he blind? Tell him for me that all this is NOT THE TRUE BLUE![22]

What made this outburst particularly steep was that Louis had not long before written a long letter, listing Fanny's symptoms, as she had once more 'bust up' – this time complaining of unbearable pains in her ear – and requesting a further supply of funds for her rapidly lengthening medical bills. The problems with the Osbournes were fourfold: the Strongs continued to solicit vociferously for funds; Lloyd was getting more and more out of hand; Sam Osbourne had reappeared to muddy the situation; and Fanny's depressive illness was taking more and more of a toll.

Belle suddenly wrote to Fanny from the Strongs' new home in Honolulu to say that her husband was seriously ill and unable to earn anything; Louis thought it strange that he had just seen some Strong sketches in *Harper's* and became suspicious. 'Do please', Fanny wrote to Dora Williams, 'try and find out if Joe Strong is really ill.' Lloyd meanwhile was showing signs of the character defect that came through fully as an adult; he would turn his hand only to what pleased him and only when it pleased him; for much of 1883 he successfully resisted pressure either to return to the tutor in Toulon or the school in Bournemouth, so that Louis, on top of all his other worries, was reduced to teaching the boy some Latin and French if he was to receive any education at all. Why was Louis so complaisant, why did he spoil the boy? Richard Aldington suggests one possible answer, which also helps to explain the deep antagonism between Fanny and Henley: 'Stevenson was not a homosexual, but he had played about so much with women in his youth that he could not give himself entirely to a woman, and kept some of the best of himself for men ... There are times when one stands a little aghast at suspecting that he really loved Lloyd more than Fanny.'

Lloyd's principal interest was to ride the cycle that his father had sent him, without a word of consultation with Fanny or Louis. Now, in 1883, Sam Osbourne made an even more disruptive entry on to the scene. First he wrote to urge – naturally dissociating himself from any of the necessary costs – that Lloyd should be given intensive tuition in chemistry and metallurgy so that he could become a mining engineer in California. Then in August he cut across Louis's plans for sending Lloyd back for some formal education by coming to Europe with his new wife 'Paulie' – Miss Rebecca Paul, a slim, black-eyed curly-haired woman who seemed besotted with him. By this time the restless Sam had gone into wine production in Sonoma county but, though struggling to pay the mortgage on his vineyard, still somehow found the funds to take his new bride to Europe. He then demanded that Lloyd be released to go on a walking tour with him and 'Aunt Paulie' in the south of France.[23]

In the light of Louis's problems with Fanny in 1883, a description of Rebecca Paul is of more than passing interest, showing what it was that Sam Osbourne had both liked and disliked about Fanny. Sam's sister, Cynthia, wrote to her son: 'He and Aunt Paulie visited our house soon after their marriage. I have heard Mama say that it seemed that he chose a wife as much like Fanny as he could find. There was a strong resemblance between them. But while Aunt Paulie was sweeter, she lacked the keen-mindedness of Aunt Fan.' Keen-mindedness would be a considerable euphemism for Fanny's behaviour in 1883, for it was then that she first exhibited her tendency to browbeat RLS into destroying, abandoning or burning manuscripts on subjects of which she did not approve. At around this time RLS completed enough of a novel entitled *The Travelling Companion* – about a prostitute and partly set in North Italy – to submit it to a publisher. Colvin later remembered that the publisher to whom it was shown declared it a work of genius, but indecent; after its rejection Fanny persuaded Louis to consign it to the flames. At least one other manuscript found its way into the fireplace following angry rows between RLS and his wife, who cared nothing for artistic truth and integrity but everything about commercial success; she feared that hard-hitting novels like these would get her husband the reputation of being an English Zola. What a serious step this was to take for Louis's spouse can perhaps be inferred from a letter to Henley at this time, in which RLS set out his artistic credo: 'I sleep upon my art for a pillow; I waken in my art; I am unready for death, because I hate to leave it. I love my wife, I do not know how much, nor can, nor shall, unless I lost her; but while I can conceive my being widowed, I refuse the offering of life without my art. I *am* not but in my art, it is me; I am the body of it merely.'

That there were many highly charged moments in the Stevenson house-hold at this time emerges not just from Valentine Roch's later testimony but from hints in the family correspondence. 'Dear wierd [sic] woman. You have made a slight confusion by not properly explaining the arrangement you made at Hyères,' Louis wrote. Meanwhile Fanny wrote obliquely to Maggie: 'I think it is not often that a Stevenson steers the safe middle course. They keep such a head of steam on.'24

Perhaps there is a hint of the wrangles with Fanny in the novel *Prince Otto*, written in five months between April and December 1883, but intermittently, since RLS was working at the same time on *The Black Arrow*. Once again RLS returned to the world of Ruritania for his inspiration: Otto is clearly first cousin (spiritually) to Prince Florizel of *The New Arabian Nights*; like him he becomes a royal outcast, loses his throne and retreats to the forest to compose poetry, just like his historical model and counterpart, Charles of Orléans. Yet in another sense Prince Otto is in the mainstream of Hamlet-like Stevenson heroes: 'Stevensonian man elevated to the throne, a Will o' the Mill given regal authority.' The writing of this work particularly points up Stevenson as perfectionist: entire chapters were written five or six times and one, 'The Countess and the Princess', went through no less than nine drafts, one by Fanny and eight by Louis. Ostensibly a parable about marriage and the relative claims of action and resignation, *Prince Otto* is one of the most self-revealing of all Stevenson's works and it may be that this is why, after *The Master of Ballantrae* and *Weir of Hermiston*, it was the closest of his novels to his heart. In one form or another, the three greatest influences in his life – Bob, Fanny and his father – all make an appearance.

In his censure of Princess Serafina for her meddling, RLS made a barely-veiled attack on Fanny. For the more important character of the Countess von Rosen, the dangerous and indefatigable intriguer, he drew on the elder of the two sisters at Menton, Madame Zassetsky; the manner of the countess's advances to Otto are generally thought to be a reproduction of la Zassetsky's attempts at flirtation with the young RLS before she bowed out in favour of her sister, Madame Garschine. Fanny hated the character of Princess Serafina, probably seeing all too clearly what her husband's intention was, but she praised Countess von Rosen; as Louis wrote to Henley: 'My wife who hates and loathes and slates my women – admits a great part of my countess to be on the spot.' He himself thought that the Countess Rosen and Madame Desprez in

The Treasure of Franchard' were his only successful female characters before the 1890s. The portrait is certainly a devastating one and shows that, for all his feminism, RLS never subscribed to the absurd doctrine of the intrinsic 'niceness' of all women. As he explained to Henley when admitting his fears of a visit from Mrs Grundy: 'To be quite frank, there is a risqué character, the Countess von Rosen, a jolly, elderly – how shall I say – f-stress, whom I try to handle so as to please this rotten public, and damn myself the while for ruining good material. I could, if I dared make her jump.[25]

Any facile notion that the depressing characters of Countess von Rosen and Princess Serafina indicate misogynism is quickly dispelled by the even more devastating indictment of Prince Otto himself. Otto is another Florizel, down to the disguises he employs, and is similarly self-deceiving. Just as Florizel, having lost the suicide game and feeling honour bound to keep his appointment with the murderer from the Suicide Club, nonetheless allows himself to be 'persuaded' out of the rendezvous by Colonel Geraldine, so Otto abdicates from the exercise of courage, will or responsibility by greeting the arresting officer as Will o' the Mill greeted Death. In his *Familiar Studies* RLS attacked Charles d'Orléans for his ineptitude and weakness, for failing to succeed in any purpose he set himself and for an incapacity to see the world with any spark of greatness. The indictment was the more telling as this was the very fault Stevenson feared in himself, and in his self-portrait as Otto he pulls no punches. His self-loathing will not permit any escape into 'scepticism' or 'stoicism' as solutions: 'Coward is the word. A springless, putty-hearted cowering coward.' The problem of action versus inertia informs so much of Stevenson's fiction (Allan Breck versus David Balfour, Henry versus James Durie), and the 'divided self' often manifests itself in an inactive hero and strenuous anti-hero. In *Prince Otto* the active character is the one who would in conventional terms be considered 'evil' (Countess von Rosen), but it is typical of Stevenson's ambiguity to suggest that the faults of Otto may be even worse; at least von Rosen stands for something, even if it is merely the exercise of power, and this sets her above the quietism and nihilism of Otto.

Yet such was RLS's passion for ambivalence that the moral ambiguity as between Otto and the Countess von Rosen is compounded by a duality within Otto himself. Otto began by being based on Bob, but ended as a portrait of Louis, and in this connection it is fascinating to ponder Fanny's statement in 1905 that Louis and Bob were 'the component parts of one individual somehow disrupted by a cataclysm of nature'. Gosse confirmed this 'dialectical' aspect of the relation between the cousins and the nuanced fictional personalities it engendered when he wrote in 1906:

There are now but few of us who can look back upon "those days of wild discussions that embraced everything known and unknown in the universe" when it was our happiness to listen, in a dazed condition of rapture, to the alternate and inexhaustible extravagances of R.A.M.S and RLS, each outdoing the other in feats of amoebean audacity. Certainly, brilliant as each might be alone, they shone with redoubled splendour when their wit, diverse in its nature and form, clashed through the course of these magnificent combats.[26]

Prince Otto addresses itself to the Tolstoyan question RLS was increasingly to wrestle with: what should the good man do? Is the response of Jaques in *As You Like It* or his own Will o' the Mill adequate? Is not resignation and quietism merely a form of cowardice? On the other hand, the Nietzchean morality of strenuousness can lead to blind alleys, like those taken by the Jacobites Lord George Murray and Cameron of Lochiel, who rose for Prince Charlie in 1745 while convinced the attempt to restore the Stuarts was foredoomed to failure. And what of unintended consequences or heroic activity for dubious ends? The problem of moral acts for dubious ends had already been posed in 'The Pavilion on the Links' when Cassilis says: 'We were here three very noble human beings to perish in defence of a thieving banker.' While Stevenson was convinced that resignation and quietism were cowardice, he was far from convinced that action *per se* provided any solution, and the dilemma immobilised him. This was why he was prepared to enter a partial defence of Otto, as he explained to Miss Monroe in June 1886:

> You are not pleased with Otto; since I judge you do not like weakness; and no more do I. And yet I have more than tolerance for Otto, whose faults are the faults of weakness, but never of ignoble weakness, and who seeks before all to be both kind and just. Seeks, not succeeds. But what is man? So much of cynicism to recognise that nobody does right is the best equipment for those who do not wish to be cynics in good earnest.

And to Trevor Haddon in 1884 he provided a further clue to his thinking: 'I prefer galvinism to acquiescence in the grave. All do not; 'tis an affair of tastes; and mine are young. Those who like death have their innings today.'[27]

The usual reading of such themes in Stevenson is to stress that RLS chose imprisonment and retirement on a South Sea island as a way of dealing with the fact that he could never be what he wanted to be: a great soldier like Gordon or a man of action like Burton, and that the fictional interweaving of the inactive hero and active anti-hero shows the conflict between RLS as he was, and as he wanted to be. Yet, given the fact that Louis refers to Hamlet more often than any other play by Shakespeare, that characters like Will, Florizel and Otto are 'Hamletic', and that Freud convincingly argued that the true source of Hamlet's indecision was his ambivalence towards the father he was supposed to avenge, one wonders whether the true psychological force immobilising RLS and inclining him towards retirement was not always his father. It is certainly interesting to note that the Christmas Day outburst against Thomas occurred immediately after he had completed *Prince Otto*.

Stevenson thought very highly of *Prince Otto*, and it has sometimes been held that the acid test for the true Stevensonian is a devotion to this book, but few then or now have been prepared to accord it a high place in his *oeuvre*. Andrew Lang, who after *Treasure Island* became and remained a doughty champion for Stevenson in the critical lists, thought that the women in *Otto* had escaped from Meredith, *Harry Richmond* especially, and had no place in the world of RLS. Professor Eigner has detected a malign influence from Trollope, of whose Plantagenet Palliser novels Louis was so fond. Henry James paid the work a backhanded compliment: 'As in his extreme artistic vivacity he seems really disposed to try everything, he has tried once, by way of a change, to be inhuman, and there is a hard glitter about *Prince Otto* which seems to indicate that in this case, too, he has succeeded, as he has done in most of the feats that he has attempted.'[28]

Some of the same themes appear in the historical novel, *The Black Arrow*, written in tandem with *Prince Otto* but completed earlier, in Royat in August 1883, and concerned with: 'the desperate game that we play in life, and how a thing once done is not to be changed or remedied by any penitence.' Superficially a boy's adventure story set among the shifting alliances of the bloody dynastic struggle of the fifteenth-century Wars of the Roses, *The Black Arrow* shares with *Treasure Island* the theme of a descent into a chaos world. The inadequacies of the Hamlet-like hero are never more fully exposed. It is impossible to find a point of moral leverage, for the adherents of the House of York are just as brutal and villainous as those of the House of Lancaster; such a world, in which he who hesitates is lost indeed, calls for a commitment to action without any certainty that one is on the right side, or even that there is a right side. In this book Stevenson's palette is so severely restricted that he seems to paint only in black: a shipboard rescue goes horribly wrong, the hero Dick Skelton's followers are slaughtered mercilessly, his ship is piled up on the rocks. In this amoral world, when Dick intervenes with Richard of Gloucester to save a man's life, the man is completely ungrateful and moans about the loss of his ship.

If *The Black Arrow* in one aspect links with *Prince Otto*, in another it is a return to the world of *Treasure Island*, not just because evil is ubiquitous, but because the familiar Stevensonian themes of pirates and treasure are also present. Dick gulls the sailors into the seaborne rescue attempt by telling them they are going to uplift treasure, and when they are being skewered with arrows after the shipwreck, the following explanation is given: '"They take us to be French pirates," answered Lord Foxham. "In these most troublesome and desperate days we cannot keep our own shores of England; but our old enemies whom we once chased on seas and

land, do now rage at pleasure, robbing and slaughtering and burning. It is
the pity and reproach of this poor land.'''[29]

The Black Arrow, like its back-to-back partner of 1883, *Prince Otto*, has
never enjoyed a very favourable critical press. It has been criticised for its
use of archaic language, its facile and dilettante goriness, for being too much
a prisoner of its sources, for its poor construction, with too much blood-and-
thunder action and too many mini-climaxes, and for the unsatisfactory nature
of its hero. It may be implausible that Jim Hawkins could match wits with
Silver, steer a ship singlehanded and dispatch Israel Hands, but at least he
breasts the flood whereas Richard Skelton is for much of the time frozen into
inaction by the mere contemplation of egregious evil. Whenever Stevenson set
novels in the eighteenth century, the epoch seemed to give him the freedom
he needed, as well as providing him what is self-confessedly his favourite
trio – pirate, highwayman and Jacobite. In *The Black Arrow* he appeared
bound down by the historical specificity of the fifteenth century, and by
fidelity and respect for his main source, the Paston letters. Moreover, it
is clear that Stevenson's heart was not wholly in the project: he dismissed
the book as mere 'tushery', forgot what had happened to the characters and
had to wait for proofs of a previous episode before he could complete the
next instalment for *Young Folks*; and completely neglected a point crucial to
the plot – the fourth arrow and the fate of Sir Oliver – until a proofreader
drew his attention to it.[30] It is incontestably an inferior book to *Treasure
Island*, lacking the latter's timelessness and mythical dimension. There is
a unity of meaning and action in *Treasure Island*, where in *The Black Arrow*
the two work against each other; most of all, as Aldington argued, *The Black
Arrow* never transcends the limitations of the historical novel genre, whereas
Treasure Island is a fantasy of the unconscious.[30]

Nevertheless, a partial rehabilitation is possible. As a historical novel
it is very distinguished, and was praised by G.M.Trevelyan in 1919 as
reproducing 'a real state of society in the past'. Moreover, it is the first
Stevenson novel to make explicit use of the 'double' – the device for which
RLS would achieve everlasting fame in *Dr Jekyll and Mr Hyde*. Richard of
Gloucester is Dick Skelton's *alter ego* and represents the side of himself he
dare not acknowledge consciously. Richard 'Crookback' Gloucester tells
Dick he has a fondness for people with the same name, calls him his
'namesake' and finally makes his meaning unambiguous: 'two Richards are
one.' With his fondness for overlapping and overdetermining dualities, RLS
provides a double motive for Dick Skelton's lack of enthusiasm for action:
both because he is convinced it is futile and because his own actions have
helped his 'double' to success – a thought that so repels him that, like Jim
Hawkins with Silver, he is shocked into rejecting a part of his own nature;
the Richard of Gloucester seen by Skelton in the Wars of the Roses is the
fictional extension of the devil seen by the infant RLS in his nightmares.[31]

Publication of *The Black Arrow* in book form had to wait until 1888, but Louis scored a great commercial triumph with *Prince Otto*. Asked to put a price on it for serialisation in *Longman's* magazine, he daringly asked for £250 at Fanny's urging. The reply took a long time to come, and Louis was just on the point of sending out a cable halving his demand when a message arrived from *Longman's* to say they considered £250 a very reasonable price and would go to press at once.

The year 1884, which had opened so promisingly with the prospects of RLS's self-sufficiency, was nearly his last on earth. The first in a series of haemorrhages that went on for six months and led eventually to the abandonment of Chalet de La Solitude occurred in January, after a visit from Henley and Baxter. Fanny was in sour mood throughout the visit, resentful that Louis had paid Henley's expenses out to France and ignoring his status as unpaid literary agent; she winced at Henley's hard drinking, Falstaffian bellows of laughter and his general rollicking rambunctiousness. The three friends spent a couple of roistering days on the Promenade des Anglais, at the end of which RLS caught cold. The illness did not seem severe, so Henley and Baxter departed for England. Immediately after their departure, the cold turned into an infection of the lungs and kidneys and Louis was stranded in Nice, laid up in the Pension Louis Rose; Fanny was warned that her husband might not survive. Furious with Henley for having 'caused' this potentially fatal outbreak by taking Louis on a round of the bars and hotels of Nice when his health could not stand it, she declined to summon him back for moral support, but instead cabled Simpson to start for France at once if he wanted to see his old friend alive. The snag was that Stevenson's friends had by now heard the cry of 'wolf' once too often; to Fanny's inexpressible fury Simpson declined to come.

She next cabled Bob, who did respond, came to Nice and performed prodigies of encouragement and moral support for patient and wife. While Bob was on his way out, Louis commenced a genuine fight for life. The virtual daily bulletins from Fanny to Baxter tell their own story. 22 January: 'Louis is much worse, the doctor says in great danger, almost no hope ... I know Louis better than doctors and I do not give him up yet.' 26 January: 'Louis is worse again today, and my faith is at a low ebb. The fever is frightful and the cough excruciating.' 27 January: 'This morning Louis very nearly passed away. He fainted, and it was just a chance that he came through it.' Once, in a delirium, he seized Fanny and shook her as a terrier would a rat. Fanny received conflicting medical advice: one of the physicians she used said Louis was certain to die; but a British doctor called Dr Drummond thought that he could live to be seventy provided he looked after himself and did not travel about so much.[32]

In her panic Fanny called in too many doctors and this led to multiple embarrassments. She engaged a Dr Wakefield, who spent two weeks in close attendance on the patient, but this was too much for Dr Drummond; he did not mind working with a French colleague, as this eased all kinds of local administrative bottlenecks, but for Fanny to take on a second English doctor looked as though she were impugning his competence. When Louis's parents, who had been given his name initially as the supervising physician, wrote to him, they received the dusty answer that as Dr Wakefield appeared to have taken over, he (Drummond) would answer no questions about the case. Fanny then went behind Wakefield's back to solicit Drummond's opinion privately; the eventual upshot was that Dr Wakefield agreed to work under Drummond's orders. Yet both physicians considered they had been badly treated; when Fanny finally got Louis back to Hyères she wrote to Baxter: 'We had the most *awful* time with the doctors before we left. They both consider that they have been bitterly insulted by Louis's people.' By the time Louis was well enough to travel, the English doctors were no longer on speaking terms with Fanny and in Hyères she would be reduced to using the local quack, Dr Vidal. She tried to put the blame on the elder Stevensons for cabling the doctors direct, but the initial confusion about whose case it was must rest squarely at her door.[33]

When Louis returned to Hyères, he had to lie in bed with his right arm strapped to his side, under strict orders not to talk. Speechless, he could neither read nor play games and had the choice of lying comatose but sleepless or slumbering under a heavy drug. As he slowly recovered, the 'post-mortem' judgements began. Louis was aware how close he had been to death – he talked of 'the creak of Charon's rowlocks and the miasmas of the Styx'. Yet he refused to mend his ways, even though fully conscious of the possible consequences:

> I survived, where a stronger man would not ... 'pain, pain, forever pain' played a loathesome solo. Now I dislike pain. I am not one of those who triumph over the carrion body, frail tabernacle, wicked carcase or what you please; but when Pain draws a lingering fiddle-bow, and all the nerves begin to sing, I am conscious of an almost irresistible temptation to chime in ... I am now shorn of my grog forever. My last habit – my last pleasure – gone. I am myself no more. Of that lean, feverish, voluble and whiskyfied zany Scot who once sparked through Britain, bent on art and the pleasures of the flesh, there now remains no quality but the strong language ... [the doctor] told me to leave off wine, to regard myself as 'an old man' and to sit by my fire. None of which I wish to do.[34]

Louis also thought that, Bob excepted, his friends had let him down: they had either declined to come out and visit him during his near-fatal illness or had used the excuse of his long periods of unconsciousness not to write to him. Although Henley was indicted along with the others, and excused himself to Baxter by saying that 'Mrs Louis is certainly the best alarmist living', when it came to her husband's health, he thought that Fanny had a point for once and that Walter Simpson's conduct was reprehensible. Curiously, Louis made light of Simpson's cavalier attitude to his brush with death and was soon corresponding with him on the same old intimate terms.[35]

Fanny meanwhile contrasted the heroic attitude of Bob with the supremely unhelpful antics of the Stevenson parents. At the end of February she wrote to Baxter: 'Bob leaves us tomorrow to my infinite regret. Had he not come I should never have got Louis home again.' She was convinced that Bob's brilliant witty talk had materially assisted in Louis's convalescence and declared that a Bob soliloquy was worth more than all the drugs in the chemist's shop. Her conviction that Bob and Louis were two halves of one person, forever seeking union like the male and female souls in Plato's *Symposium*, received an unwelcome confirmation when Bob, on a visit from Nice to Monte Carlo, was forbidden entrance to the casino, just as Louis had been the year before. Angrily she wrote to Baxter: 'What is it that is stamped upon the Stevenson brow that makes them seem unfit to enter even the lowest gambling house?' She was exasperated too with the elder Stevensons, who began by dismissing his illness as 'just nerves' even in the face of her repeated cables, then suddenly woke up to the situation, panicked, deluged Dr Drummond with incoherent telegrams, and had to be silenced by a 'Louis much better' cable she sent them, which was not strictly true.[36]

There was a brief period of about two weeks in late March when Louis was up and about. To Simpson he wrote with astonishing news: 'A month or two ago there was an alarm; it looked like family. Prostration: I saw myself financially ruined. I saw the child born sickly etc. Then, said I, I must look at this thing on the good side; proceeded to do so studiously; and with such result that when the alarm passed off – I was inconsolable.' A pregnancy at forty-four, with all the well-known risks to the foetus, was not a welcome prospect, and it is clear from the general tone of RLS's remarks that he and Fanny had long since taken the decision not to have children, despite his own special affinity for them. Stevenson's attitude to paternity was complex: he acknowledged having fatherly feelings but doubted that his physical constitution and slender financial resources would stand up to the strains of parenthood; besides, having witnessed the death of Fanny Sitwell's son in Davos, he knew how much potential sorrow a parent stood to inherit. The frustrated paternal feelings found expression in extra protectiveness towards Fanny, clearly evinced at this very time. Louis wrote to his mother: 'My marriage has been the most successful in the world . . . She is every-thing to me: wife, mother, sister, daughter and dear companion.' Basking in the warmth of her husband's caring and attentive attitude, Fanny wrote rather smugly (and, significantly, to her 'rival', Fanny Sitwell) that Bob on his recent visit declared that he, Louis and Thomas Stevenson all had one thing in common: 'some special guidance that kept us from marrying the wrong women.'[37]

Louis's period of uncertain convalescence did not last long. Hyères, with its crooked, narrow, foul-smelling lanes and sunless old houses, was no place for an invalid; it was rather a hotbed of disease, with typhus, smallpox and cholera prevalent. Complaints to the town's officials to do something about the unsanitary conditions were counterproductive. The first time the Stevensons wrote to the mayor, he had the town swept and cleansed but then deposited all the rubbish outside Rosemount – a cottage belonging to an absentee English couple, past which ran the main road into Hyères from La Solitude. When RLS wrote again to ask that the road outside La Solitude be made up, so as to make conditions more hygienic, the mayor sent out a road gang which 'tarmacced' the road outside the chalet with impacted refuse brought from the dump outside Rosemount. Having to his own satisfaction discharged his civic responsibilities, the mayor then ignored all further representations from the 'troublemaking' foreigners.

One immediate result of the swirling of filthy dust outside his home was that Stevenson went down with ophthalmia: he had to stay in the shade or venture out into sunlight only with double green goggles and a shade; indoors he wore a pair of blue glasses. He told his father: 'I have now read nothing, book, letter, paper, for about a month, and I think reading a mighty small privation. A man can do without anything except tobacco and his wife, and even these for a while.' Yet his eyes were the least of his problems. When he heard that Edmund Yates, a venomous gossip columnist of the yellow press, whose most famous vitriolic assault had been on Thackeray, had been imprisoned for two months for criminal libel, Louis celebrated with candles in the window and a bonfire in the garden. He, Fanny and Valentine danced around the bonfire – a piece of triumphalism he later deplored – and did not notice the mistral until they suddenly found themselves chilled to the bone. There followed an illness even worse than that in Nice. First came haemorrhage, then immobilisation once more: he lay helpless in bed with sciatica, his right arm bound to his side, lest an inadvertent movement trigger a return of the haemorrhage; he could not speak and since the ophthalmia worsened with his general physical decline, he had to wear a bandage over his eyes. Too blind to read, too weak to walk, too tired to talk, he took it all stoically and even found the reserves of energy to cheer up the despondent Fanny. 'Now if you would only look at it in the right light,' he told her, 'you would see that this is the best thing that could have happened.'[38]

Lying flat and silent in a darkened room, with his right arm bound, Louis still forced himself to communicate with the outside world. A board was laid across his bed on which two large sheets of paper were pinned; on these, or on a slate attached to the board, he wrote in the darkness with his left hand for Fanny to transcribe. A letter to Gosse is typical of this period: 'A month in bed; a month of silence; a fortnight of not moving without being lifted . . . devilish like being dead.' Fanny kept a small bottle of ergotin and a minim glass at the bedside in case of sudden haemorrhage. One night early in May, strike it did, the worst yet: Louis suddenly coughed and was choked with a rapid flow of blood. Fanny was too distraught to pour out his ergotin, so he did it himself, signed to her to bring him paper and pencil, and wrote laboriously: 'Don't be frightened. If this is death, it is an easy one.' Having no confidence in Dr Vidal, Fanny sent for an eminent physician from England, Dr Mennell. He recommended perfect tranquillity, complete freedom from stress, shocks or surprises, even pleasant ones, very little food and drink, and the bare minimum of walking, talking and writing.[39]

Fanny was in despair: 'Louis is very low and seems growing weaker and paler,' she told Henley. 'His courage is wonderful. I never saw anything like it.' To his mother she wrote more cheerfully: 'I am not very good at letter writing since I have been doing blind man's eyes, but here is a note to say that the blind man is doing very well, and I consider the blindness a real providence. Since he has been unable to read or do anything at all a wonderful change has come over his health, spirits and temper, all for the better.'[40]

By June Louis was making a steady recovery. But now came another danger. An epidemic of cholera along the Riviera had reached Hyères – at least that was Fanny's story; her son Lloyd who came out to Hyères in June for holidays attributed it to his mother's habit of imagining illness and disease everywhere – a habit reinforced by her assiduous reading of *The Lancet* – which caused her to overreact to a mild and routine outbreak of cholera in the slum area of Hyères. Whatever the real reason, by the end of June a valetudinarian RLS was on the road to Royat; he described himself to Colvin as 'a blind, bloodspitting, somnolent, superannuated son of a bedpost, rotten-ripe'.[41] At Royat his health improved, just as it had the year before; he corresponded about the production of *Deacon Brodie*, to be staged in London that summer, and devoured Defoe's work. To decide on their future plans Fanny and Louis decided to go to England to consult specialists and take soundings on where to live next. He did not know it, but he was never to see his beloved rural France again.

Bournemouth

Richmond-upon-Thames, a few miles west of London, was the unlikely venue for Louis's reunion with his parents but it enabled Fanny to attend the first night of *Deacon Brodie*, which was quite well received. On consulting specialists in London about his lungs, Louis found them divided about this disease which in turn led to division within himself – another example of Stevensonian ambivalence within ambiguity: two (Dr Mennell and Louis's uncle, Dr George Balfour) said residence in the south of England was a mistake, two others that it would be beneficial. Since the lingering cholera in Hyères barred his return there, he exercised his own casting vote and opted to stay in England for a while; the actual choice of Bournemouth as a residence was an aleatory affair: Lloyd was at school there and Fanny wanted to be with her beloved son. The Stevensons first took lodgings above the beach, tried twice to rent a house only to see the deal fall through at the last minute, but eventually rented a house, 'Bonallie Tower' (though, as he told Baxter, 'the deevil a tower ava' can be perceived'), in the sylvan Branksome Park area.

Throughout most of the autumn and winter of 1884 Louis's health was poor. He underwent one operation for the removal of a tapeworm and resisted pressure from his physicians for a second, to alleviate a persistent cough. Lloyd, who had asked to be trained as a lighthouse engineer under the tutelage of Thomas Stevenson, departed for Heriot Row. Left on their own with Valentine, the Stevensons lived quietly except when friends came down; unfortunately for the peace of mind of Fanny, who suspected all comers of harbouring dangerous germs, this was a frequent occurrence.[1]

Almost his first visitor at Bonallie Tower was Bob. He had made the acquaintance of Lord Rosebery, who lived nearby, and he wanted to introduce his illustrious cousin, but Louis was less than keen on the idea. Far less welcome to Fanny was the red-bearded Henley, swinging his crutch around Bonallie Tower with all the gusto of John Silver, promising his friends that his playwriting ideas would make them rich. His first

Bournemouth collaboration with RLS was *Admiral Guinea*, of interest mainly in that it resurrects Blind Pew from *Treasure Island*. Stevenson himself did not think much of it and told Henley that reading it again 'was a sore blow, eh, God, man, it is a low, black, dirty, blackguard, ragged piece, vomitable in many parts. Pew is in places a reproach of both art and man.' But when Thomas Stevenson tried to put his critical oar in, accusing *Admiral Guinea* of obscenity and vulgarity – much the same indictment his son brought against it – Louis was having none of it and defended his creation doughtily: 'Allow me to say, in a strictly Pickwickian sense, that you are a silly fellow.'[2]

More successful was *Beau Austin*, written in four days at Bournemouth, where the typically Stevensonian theme of Eden as an illusion takes the form of the loss of virginity by the naïve, innocent Dorothy Musgrave to the eponymous hero. The usual criticism of this play is that it is neither fish nor fowl, neither Georgian nor Victorian in spirit but a kind of cynical halfway house: the lady does not merely have her reputation compromised but is seduced – thus alienating Mrs Grundy – but the authors do not then have the courage to go on to indict Victorian hypocrisy – thus failing to satisfy a radical audience. Theatrical impresarios seemed to take the point, for it was not until 1890 that the play received a London première, with Beerbohm Tree in the title role. The best Henley-RLS collaboration came in *Macaire*, written in January 1885, for here the authors managed a judicious mixture of farce and melodrama and had a hero, Macaire – a master of disguise and a sort of more successful Deacon Brodie – of the kind that particularly appealed to Stevenson. However, Beerbohm Tree almost at once dashed their hopes of riches by replying to the authors, when they asked him to read it, that they knew nothing of stagecraft.[3]

By March 1885 RLS had become disillusioned and he wrote to Henley: 'I have come unhesitatingly to the opinion that the stage is only a lottery ... It is bad enough to have to live by an art – but to think to live by an art combined with commercial speculation – that way madness lies ... If money comes from any play, let us regard it as a legacy, but never count upon it in our income for the year.' There were two main reasons for the failure of the dramaturgical Henley-RLS collaboration, one contingent, the other more deeply rooted in temperamental and artistic incompatibility between the partners. The contingent reason was Fanny. Try as she and Henley might they could not bridge the gap of visceral antagonism that separated them. At first they both tried hard. She teasingly called him Buffalo William (as he reminded her of Buffalo Bill Cody) and in August she told him: 'You know we love you in spite of your many faults, so try to bear with our few.' On his side he promised her a ruby bracelet on the expected proceeds of *Admiral Guinea*. But the truce did not long endure: Fanny thought that many of her husband's lapses into illness were caused by Henley, that he tried to push him too hard, too far and too fast in the direction of the mirage of theatrical riches. She wrote to him that autumn: 'When you come, which I hope will be soon, you must not expect Louis to do any work.' Needless to say, Henley ignored the advice; Fanny retaliated by being an ungracious hostess, doling out tiny measures of alcohol to the hard-drinking Henley and generally being obstructive. To some extent she had right on her side: Lloyd Osbourne, who often saw the two men working together, said that RLS was most interested in getting on with his own fiction and as a playwright 'had to be resuscitated by his unshaken collaborator'.[4]

Additionally, Fanny pushed herself more and more to the fore as an active partner in the playwriting projects; she lay awake at night memorising every line of *Admiral Guinea* and suggesting revisions. This irritated Henley, who had no great opinion of her creative talents; in a letter to Baxter, he unerringly put his finger on the real problem in his collaboration with RLS: 'The match is no longer equal. Louis has grown faster than I have; and then there's the Bedlamite [Fanny]. I love her; but I won't collaborate with her and her husband, as I begin to feel that one means both.' The rift became more overt. After various epistolary jousts he wrote to her: 'I think, Mrs Louis, that we'd better give up corresponding on any save the commonest subjects.' She retaliated by writing to Fanny Sitwell: 'Henley must not come to him [RLS] now with either work or business unless he wishes to kill him.'[5] However, there was a strong vein of disingenuousness in Fanny's ostensible reasons for being annoyed with Henley. She pretended that Henley had gulled RLS into overwork by painting an illusory picture of the likely financial rewards from writing plays; but her letters show her just as keen as Henley to egg her husband on to achieve the crock of gold, and her charge that Louis wrote plays only because seduced or browbeaten into it by Henley looks hollow in the light of her own (later) collaboration with him on *The Hanging Judge*.

The more fundamental problem besetting the Henley-RLS collaboration was that both authors were pulling in different directions. Henley knew more about the technicalities of stagecraft and the academic theories of drama but was frozen by the traditional constraints of the genre: he thought that in drama emotion was all-important and liked the grand style which aimed at effect through exaggeration; he also wanted to stick to the time-hallowed themes of tragedy and to write parts for larger-than-life villains, on the ground that this was what the public now wanted. As he wrote to RLS in 1883:

The Shakespeare of tomorrow will take for his hero, not Othello but Iago. The heroes of iniquity, the epic of immorality, the drama of vice – *voilà la vraie affaire*. In fifty years, the Deacon, if we had but done it, might be a great work. We are syphilised to the core, and we don't know it. Zola is our popular eruption, as Balzac was our primary sore. Presently we shall get to our tertiarism; and the Ugly will be as the Beautiful.

RLS, however, parted company with Henley on just about every single item in his collaborator's dramatic agenda; they even disagreed on basic issues of morality, as when Louis wanted to repay £40 to the *Pall Mall Gazette* on the grounds that he had not been able to produce his best work, and Henley contemptuously dismissed the idea, alleging the well-known wealth of publishers.[6] For Stevenson, evil was not the simple matter it seemed to be to Henley; characteristically, he wished to portray *ambiguity* in his plays: not just the moral ambiguity of a Shaw play, but an ambiguity rooted in the very structure of the drama. He was always deeply drawn to the 'problem comedies' of Shakespeare, where the elements of traditional tragedy and comedy were fused, where the combination of laughter and tears transcended the obvious either/or polarities, and a dialectical fusion between the determinism of tragedy and the voluntarism of comedy was achieved. This made him, as playwright, infinitely more imaginative and ambitious than Henley. Drama was not the right medium for a writer whose speciality was striking incident, elegance of style and broad symbolic patterns, nor was Henley the right collaborator even given these limitations. Yet the failure of the experiment at dramatic collaboration left Henley bitter, feeling both that Louis had not put his back into the experiment and that Fanny had systematically sabotaged it by her meddling and intriguing. The seeds were sown for the later dramatic quarrel in 1887.

That Fanny was indeed developing delusions of grandeur about her status as a writer is clear from *The Dynamiter*, on which she and Louis collaborated in the winter of 1884–85. *The Dynamiter* would have marked a retrograde step even from the author of *The New Arabian Nights*, but from the master storyteller of *Treasure Island*, it was mediocre stuff indeed, so much so that some scholars think it almost entirely Fanny's work. Her biographer sums up her literary talent as follows: 'Though in letter-writing her style was often attractive and even graceful, when she laid her hand on fiction it had a coarse texture and synthetic manner which one does not find in those of her husband's works in which she was not a collaborator.' The feminine hand is surely detectable in the portrait of the anarchists, where the women are much better at telling stories than their men are at making bombs. On the other hand, there is the occasional sign of the authentic RLS presence: 'There fell upon his mind a perfect *hurricane* of horror and wonder' continues the storm motif observable in RLS's *oeuvre* since before he met Fanny; and Clara Luxmore, the female deceiver of *The Dynamiter*, looks like a transmogrified picture of Fanny: '"Harry," she began, "I am not what I seem. I was never nearer Cuba than Penzance. From first to last I have cheated and played with you."'[7] To which one might add, in Melvillean mode, that Fanny was never nearer the Cuba of real artistic aspiration than the Penzance of the would-be bestseller.

Originally sketched at Hyères in 1883, *The Dynamiter* takes as its point of departure the Fenian bombings in England that year, but this sets a tone that rubs uneasily against the fantastic elements that follow. One of the shrewdest and most perceptive of all Stevensonians, G.K.Chesterton, saw what was wrong with this work: 'It is really impossible to use a story in which everything is ridiculous to prove that certain particular Fenians or anarchist agitators are ridiculous. Nor indeed is it tenable that men who risk their lives to commit such crimes are quite so ridiculous as that.' The serious idea in *The Dynamiter* is that religion is not necessary as a buttress for morality; the absurd Nietzchean idea that, with the 'death of God', normal morality is the province of fools or cowards is light years away from the sensibility of RLS, one of whose abiding purposes was to demonstrate that agnosticism did *not* imply a lack of concern with right and wrong. Yet there is clearly a disjuncture between this serious idea and the means employed to get it across in this novel; a fantastic universe in which men and women with tendencies towards nihilism, suicide, seduction, murder, theft, madness and anarchy are all silly and ineffectual and have to lie and wear false whiskers to bolster their own absurd images of themselves. This kind of flabby thinking is uncharacteristic of RLS, so once again we may suspect the hand of Fanny.

Nevertheless the novel was influential in many ways: the theme of the Mormons as a sinister, murderous sept was taken up in Conan Doyle's *A Study in Scarlet* and Jack London's *The Star Rover*. As a detective story, *The Dynamiter* looks back to the Dupon stories of Poe and forward to Conan Doyle, and there is a paean of praise to the detective as a kind of urban lighthouse keeper, bringing light into darkness.

> Chance will continually drag before our careless eyes a thousand eloquent clues, not to this mystery only, but to the countless mysteries by which we live surrounded. Then comes the part of the man of the world, of the detective born and bred. This clue, which the whole town beholds without comprehension, swift as a cat he leaps upon it, and makes it his, follows it up with craft and passion, and from one trifling circumstance divines a world.

However, perhaps RLS's most significant input into *The Dynamiter* came in the introduction, where he praised the two policemen involved in heroic action in 1883 against the Fenian bombers as heroes in the mould of General Gordon. Gordon was much on Stevenson's mind in the winter of 1884–85. On his father's advice he toyed with the idea of writing a biography of the Duke of Wellington and thought of writing to Gladstone about his memories of the Iron Duke. Yet when Garnett Wolseley's relieving force arrived in Khartoum too late to prevent the murder of Gordon by the Mahdists in January 1885, RLS joined vociferously with those who reversed the initials conventionally applied to Gladstone (G.O.M. – Grand Old Man) to read M.O.G. – Murderer of Gordon. He decided not to write to the Prime

Minister after all, explaining to Colvin that the only appropriate mode of address would be 'your fellow criminal in the eyes of God'. His vehement animadversions on the subject of Gladstone and his glorification of the two policemen, Cole and Cox, drew a surprised and baffled query from Symonds in Davos, to which Stevenson replied with astonishing vehemence:

But why should I blame Gladstone, when I too am a bourgeois? when I have held my peace? Because I am sceptic: i.e. a Bourgeois. We believe in nothing, Symonds; you don't and I don't; and there are two reasons, out of a handful of millions, why England stands before the world dripping with blood and daubed with dishonour ... See, for example, if England has shown ... one spark of manly sensitivity, they have been shamed into it by the spectacle of Gordon. Police-Officer Cole is the only man that I see to admire. I dedicate my New Arabs [sc. The Dynamiter] to him and Cox, in default of other great public characters.[8]

RLS's periods of collaboration in 1884–85 aggravated Fanny's shaky mental state. First there had been the tension with Henley who, when he stayed in Bonallie Towers to work, thought he had the right to elementary courtesy from his hostess, but found the decanter whisked away as Fanny's signal that it was time to go to bed or himself banished from Stevenson's presence if he had a cold. Then when she herself was the collaborator on The Dynamiter, she was bitterly resentful that her contribution was downgraded, that the critics did not give her her due. Furious when one critic referred to her, on The Dynamiter's appearance as 'undoubtedly Mr Stevenson's sister', she wrote to Maggie: 'I thought in the beginning that I wouldn't mind being Louis's scapegoat, but it is rather hard to be treated as a comma, and a superfluous one at that.' RLS must sometimes have thought back to his words in 'Virginibus Puerisque' and realised that he was the Cassandra: 'Certainly, if I could help it, I would never marry a wife who wrote. The practice of letters is miserably harassing to the mind, and after an hour or two's work, all the more human portion of the author is extinct.'[9]

The winter of 1884–85 was not a satisfactory one for RLS from any point of view. He was almost continuously ill: haemorrhages, influenza, fever, colds, backache, rheumatism all assailed him; in addition the weather was so cold that he spent a lot of time in bed just to keep warm. Astonishingly, except when seriously ill, he maintained a daily regime of five to seven hours' work, and his thirty-fourth birthday, when Bob came down again, was a great success. But around Christmas 1884, he had another severe haemorrhage: he and Fanny were both ill in bed, and outside the dog Bogue was yapping; when let in, the cur bit Fanny, which so enraged Louis that he beat the animal; however, the exertion precipitated another flow of blood.

From his friends there came nothing but bad news. Both Bob's wife,

Louisa, and Walter Simpson's wife, Anne, it now transpired, disliked him, as did Simpson's sister, Eve, of whose unconventional private life Louis in turn disapproved. Louis and Simpson, however, still retained something of their old intimacy; when Walter's brother Magnus died at 32, adding another strand to the estrangement between Walter and Eve, Louis commiserated with the brother, but declined to write to the sister so as to make his sympathies quite clear. After Louis's death, in 1898, Eve Simpson published an uncomplimentary memoir; the cause of the animus is obscure but a clue may be sought in a letter from Louis to Baxter in 1892 when he says: 'The animosity of women is always an extraordinary study. And when I remember that I once seriously dreamed of marrying that underhand virago my heart wells over with gratitude.'[10]

The one consoling fact of private life was that relations with his father were better, on the surface at least. Louis told Simpson in early November: 'My father is in a gloomy state and has the yellow flag at the peak, or the fore, or wherever it should be; and he has just emptied some melancholy vials on me.' Yet relations improved when Thomas confided in his son his hopes of being elected president of the Royal Society of Edinburgh; Louis encouraged him to let his name go forward, and Thomas was duly elected. Stevenson *père* was also touched by Louis's defence of the family honour when he wrote to *The Athenaeum* on the subject of the Bell Rock Lighthouse: a recent book by Frederick Whymper, *The Sea: its Stirring Story of Adventure, Peril and Heroism* had done his grandfather Robert Stevenson less than justice and asserted that one Robert Rennie had been the chief engineer.[11]

The area of conflict between the generations temporarily shifted to the distaff side. Maggie naturally objected to Fanny's draconian policy whereby anyone with a cold was kept away from Louis, considering that such a prescription should not affect relations between mother and son. The upshot was a complaining letter from Fanny to Colvin, (both him and Mrs Sitwell she took in and out of her confidence as the mood took her): 'Louis is ill again, *not* this time with haemorrhages, but a cold, a present from his mother . . . in spite of all my entreaties . . . and [she] went off saying, "Now that Louis has entirely recovered his health, we shall expect him to spend his summers in Scotland with us."' Colvin confided to Henley that, judging from letters he and Mrs Sitwell had received, Fanny was 'evidently nearly off her head'.

Her irritation with Maggie did not prevent Fanny from using the elder Stevensons whenever it suited her. At sixteen, Lloyd Osbourne was already demonstrating the 'take the easy path to riches' attitude that marked him as an adult. Idle, snobbish, vain and encouraged by his mother to think himself the centre of the universe, Lloyd at first thought that money and status would be conferred by a training as a lighthouse engineer, so went to Heriot Row to live with Thomas Stevenson and enrolled as a science student at Edinburgh University. Though she could never admit it, it is clear that in her heart Fanny realised her son's weakness for quick and easy luxury, which was why she was so enraged when Sam Osbourne suddenly wrote from California to say he would like Lloyd to run the ranch in Sonoma county, holding out mouth-watering prospects of the money to be made. Fanny told Dora Williams that she would allow Lloyd to go only if Sam entered into a written contract to be legally responsible for his son's maintenance at the level to which he had grown accustomed; she shrewdly saw that this would deter Sam and, when she explained the hard work involved in running a Californian ranch, Lloyd also. Everything turned out as she hoped, and Lloyd remained tied to her apron-strings.[12]

That Fanny was slowly but surely gaining the upper hand in her scheme to make over the Stevenson parents became clear when Thomas decided to buy her a house in Bournemouth, plus £500 with which to furnish it; Thomas was beginning to ail, wanted his son near him during his last years, and feared that unless he provided a solid anchor, Fanny and Louis would soon be globetrotting again. The new house, purchased in February 1885, was located in a highly desirable area above the chalk cliffs on the outskirts of Westbourne: a tall, yellow-bricked, ivy-covered villa with a blue slate roof, it stood in an acre of ground; the lawn ran down to a sort of ravine, with a stream in the 'valley' and on the slopes grew laurel, rhododendron, heather, gorse and pine, which reminded Louis of Scotland. In the gardens were stables, a kennel and a dovecote. Fanny wrote excitedly to Dora Williams: 'We have just moved into our lovely house . . . It is very comfortable to know that we have a home really and truly and will no more be like Noah's dove, flying about with an olive branch.'

The move took place at Easter 1885. Louis renamed the house 'Skerryvore' after the lighthouse erected by his family, and at the street entrance he had a model of the original Skerryvore built, with a light that shone every evening and a ship's bell in the garden. Always a fanatical gardener, Fanny planted fruit trees, hydrangeas, roses and tiger lilies and sowed Indian corn and tomatoes. On the slopes of the chine she worked out a maze of paths, stairs and arbours, with seats where RLS could write. Louis's own comment on his good fortune was wry: 'It is fortunate for me I have a father or I should long ago have died.'[13]

Fanny had to make a brief visit to France to wind up their affairs at Hyères; in her absence Valentine slept in RLS's room by the fire, to be on hand in case he haemorrhaged. From this simple fact of expediency scandalmongers later created a myth of an affair between Louis and Valentine, though the rumour was given circumstantial cogency by his well-known liking for Valentine and the fact that he found her physically attractive. Henley, in particular, liked to keep this rumour buzzing, as a means of revenge against Fanny, and because he thought of himself and Louis as musketeers, free spirits, untrammelled by bourgeois conventions; there is a revealing letter of April 1884 when he writes to Baxter: 'Louis has confessed that female underclothing ... are his fate', though whether this refers to Fanny, Valentine or lingerie in general is not clear. However, RLS had a strict moral code once married, and it is inconceivable that he would have had an affair with Valentine. Their relationship was affectionate, with none of the tension of carnality, and most of Louis's casual references to her concern trivia such as her meagre skills as a pastrycook and her jousts in the kitchen with the parlourmaid Mary Anne. Once when he summoned her, she was late arriving and tried to justify herself. 'Hush, Joe!' he cried. 'You know when one tries to justify oneself, one puts someone else in the wrong and life is not possible under these conditions.' Valentine, who later in life became a professional nurse and in retrospect regretted that her care of Stevenson had been so amateurish, remembered the days at Skerryvore as a time of great happiness and thought Louis a supremely wise man: 'From him I learned that life is not for self if we want happiness – and that it is only in service that we fulfil our destiny.'[14]

Ensconced as a bourgeois couple in this uneasy 'revolt into respectability', the Stevensons became the object of attention from the vicar and from people who left calling cards. Among those they took to were two elderly couples: the poet's son Sir Percy Shelley and his wife, and Sir Henry and Lady Taylor, who presented RLS with the dark red poncho that became as much part of the sartorial Stevenson legend in Bournemouth as the velvet coat had been in Edinburgh or the red flannel shirt in France. Fanny liked both the titled dames: Lady Shelley, who was old and eccentric (and that may have been *why* Fanny liked her), and on one famous occasion caused uproar by upbraiding Maggie 'for daring to purloin a son who was really hers'; and Lady Taylor, who shared her taste for hypochondria.

A more enterprising caller was a young woman named Adelaide Boodle, who had a star-struck attitude to writers, and persuaded her mother to accompany her on an unsolicited visit to Skerryvore. The bell-wire was out of order, so the Boodles knocked on the door; after a long time without an answer, and fearing that she had committed a social gaffe, Mrs Boodle began to cry, winning for the front porch thereafter from RLS the Homeric descriptive phrase 'The Pool of Tears'. Confusion piled on confusion, for Valentine came to the door flustered and admitted the visitors without enquiring whether the Stevensons were 'in'; the end result was that the Boodles found themselves taking tea with Louis in his velvet coat and Fanny in a painting apron, the four of them perched on packing cases. Adelaide Boodle was duly admitted into the inner circle, though allowed only limited access to Louis; in compensation she spent long hours with Fanny, observing her every mood. In time the relationship bore fruit in the form of a hagiography, *RLS and His Sine Qua Non*, in which, however, the dark side of Fanny is clearly visible beneath the idolatry.[15]

The Boodles were not the only admirers. The painter, John Singer Sargent, had first come down to Bournemouth when the Stevensons were still at Bonallie Tower, in response to a commission from the wealthy RLS fans Mr and Mrs Charles Fairchild of Boston. Louis liked Sargent at once but strongly disliked his first attempt at a portrait, as did Fanny; he told Will Low: 'It is a practical but very chicken-boned figurehead.' In the summer of 1885 Sargent came down to Skerryvore and this time painted a portrait that gave RLS great satisfaction. Fanny, however, again took exception to Sargent's work, but she had herself mainly to blame; employing her arch 'little me' persona, she said to Sargent that she was but the cipher under the shadow, not expecting or wishing to be taken seriously; Sargent, though, took her at her word and relegated her to a shadowy figure in the corner, her bare foot peeking from beneath an Indian sari (included purely for colour), and from this sprang the legend that she used to go barefoot to London parties.[16]

As well as introducing RLS to new friends, Bournemouth permitted his old ones to see more of him, to Fanny's intense irritation and displeasure. She tolerated Bob, because of his behaviour at Hyères, and he and his sister (not his wife) were frequent visitors. Louis always had a soft spot for Katharine de Mattos – of all his women friends and acquaintances he admired her mind most – and was susceptible to her magnetism and charisma. He singled her out as the dedicatee who would most appreciate *Dr Jekyll and Mr Hyde*, and dedicated his poem 'Katharine' from the *Under-woods* collection, in which he looked back to the idyllic childhood scenes in Scotland, to her; the inference from this poem is that her moods were as changeable as April weather. As for Bob, Louis's sojourn in Bournemouth permitted a brief résumé of their earlier intimacy; when deep into *Jekyll*, Louis told Will Low: 'I will announce the coming *Lamia* to Bob; he steams away at literature like smoke. I have a beautiful Bob on my walls, and a good Sargent, and a delightful Lemon; and your etching now hangs framed in the dining-room.' Bob was 'good value' in every sense, sharing Louis's admiration for Valentine and 'entering into the spirit' when Fanny claimed Skerryvore was haunted.[17]

Another great female favourite was Elizabeth 'Coggie' Ferrier, sister of the tragic James Walter; the intimacy with her had blossomed in France when the Stevensons invited her to stay at Chalet La Solitude to get over the loss of her brother. Almost as intelligent as Katharine de Mattos, she was even more liberally endowed with a sense of humour; RLS often wrote to her in the person of Thomson, the imaginary querulous Scots ne'er-do-well persona – the only soul except Baxter to whom he accorded the privilege – complete with the risqué repertoire he used when talking to Johnston, which Coggie found delightful.[18]

The two friends notable for their absence from Skerryvore were Henley and Gosse. A typical Fanny ploy when Henley intended to visit was to invite Colvin down first and then 'reluctantly' conclude that two visitors at any one time would be too much for her husband; the fact that Colvin and Henley did not really get on helped her case. Henley took the hint and retaliated by not answering Louis's letters for a time; from the injured tone of RLS's correspondence, one infers that he had not yet taken the measure of his wife's machiavellianism in this regard. She played the role of stupefied innocent perfectly and even had the effrontery to write to Baxter as follows: 'A good deal of feeling has been occasioned by the disappearance of an individual known by several aliases, but passing in London under the name of William Ernest Henley.' Gosse, who thought that Louis's grave illness of January 1884 marked a watershed in his life, after which his debonair talents gave way to a more sombre sensibility, gave a broad hint that it was Fanny as Cerberus that kept him away from Bournemouth: 'this was a pleasure that was apt to tantalise and evade the visitor, so constantly was the invalid unable, at the last, to see the friend who had travelled a hundred miles to see him.'[19]

A newcomer to the Skerryvore milieu was the critic, William Archer, to whom RLS confided his continuing love of *Bragelonne* and with whom he discussed exhaustively the merits of pessimism and optimism. After his first visit to Skerryvore, Archer left a memorable portrait of his host:

> He now sits at the foot of the table rolling a limp cigarette in his long, limp fingers, and talking eagerly all the while, with just enough trace of a Scottish intonation to remind one that he is the author of *Thrawn Janet* . . . He has still the air and manner of a young man, for illness has neither tamed his mind nor aged his body. It has left its mark, however, in the pallor of his long oval face, with its wide-set eyes, straight nose, and thin-lipped sensitive mouth, scarcely shaded by a light moustache, the jest and scorn of his ribald intimates. His long hair straggles with an irregular wave down his neck, a wisp of it occasionally falling over his ear, and having to be replaced with a light gesture of the hand. He is dressed in a black velvet jacket, showing at the throat the loose rolling collar of a white flannel shirt; and if it is at all cold, he has probably thrown over his shoulders an ancient maroon-coloured shawl, draped something after the fashion of a Mexican poncho. When he stands up you see he is well above the middle height, and of a naturally lithe and agile figure. He still moves with freedom and grace, but the stoop of his shoulders tells a tale of suffering.[20]

The most unlikely relationship, on paper, was that which developed in 1885 with Henry James. The two had met in 1879, just before Louis's departure for the U.S.A., without striking any sparks of artistic recognition. James wrote patronisingly: 'He is a pleasant fellow, but a shirt-collarless Bohemian and a good deal (in an inoffensive way) of a poseur.' Stevenson in response, while at Davos, wrote some private verses for Henley, in which he expressed his contempt for James's fastidious snobbishness, and agreed with James's critics who said he had turned his back on a great historical experiment in the New World to listen to tittle-tattle over the clink of tea cups in the Old:

> Not clad in transatlantic furs
> But clinking English pence
> The young republic claims me hers
> In no parochial sense.
>
> A bland colossus, mark me stride
> From land to land, the sea
> And patronize on every side
> Far better men than me.
>
> My books that models are of wit
> And masterworks of art
> From occident to orient flit
> And please in every part.
>
> Yet I'm a sentimental lot
> And freely weep to see
> Poor Hawthorne and the rest who've not
> To Europe been like me.

The trigger for the entente that developed in 1885 was an attack on Walter Besant's theory of the novel that James published in the September 1884 *Longman's Magazine* as 'The Art of Fiction', which argued that art must be in competition with life and that great fiction was, therefore, history. To RLS, who had long pondered the relationship of life to art, this was wrongheaded, and he set about demolishing James's arguments, his caustic pen swayed only by James's description of *Treasure Island* as a 'delightful story'.

Stevenson argued that literature, a metaphor for life, inhabiting the realm of necessity, must be distinct from life itself, which was contingent and aleatory.

Life is monstrous, infinite, illogical, abrupt and poignant; a work of art, in comparison, is neat, finite, self-contained, rational, flowing and emasculate . . . To 'compete with life', whose sun we cannot look upon, whose passions and diseases waste and slay us – to compete with the flavour of wine, the beauty of the dawn, the scorching of fire, the bitterness of death and separation – here is, indeed, a projected escalade of heaven; here are, indeed, labours for a Hercules in a dress coat, armed with a pen and a dictionary to depict the passions, armed with a tube of superior flake-white to paint the portrait of the insufferable sun. No art is true in this sense; none can 'compete with life'; not even history, built indeed of indisputable facts, but these facts robbed of their vivacity and sting; so that even when we read of the sack of a city or the fall of an empire, we are surprised, and justly commend the author's talent, if our pulse be quickened. And mark, for a last differentia, that this quickening of the pulse is, in almost every case, purely agreeable; that these phantom reproductions of experience, even at their most acute, convey decided pleasure; while experience itself, in the cockpit of life, can torture and slay.

James wrote magnanimously to acknowledge the force of much of what Louis had said but most of all to congratulate him on his talent as a writer: 'The current of your admirable style floats pearls and diamonds ... The native *gaiety* of all you write is delightful to me, and when I reflect that it proceeds from a man whom life has laid so much of the time on his back (as I understand it) I find you a genius indeed.' RLS, conscious by now that he and James did after all share common ground – their concern for prose style, their perfectionism, their serious engagement with the technical and philosophical problems of writing fiction, their contempt for the lowest common denominator of public taste and readership – invited James to visit Skerryvore if he ever found himself in the neighbourhood.

In the spring of 1885 James came to Bournemouth to spend some weeks with his invalid sister Alice and took up RLS's invitation. Valentine mistook the portly bearded man on the porch for a tradesman who was supposed to be calling to apologise for a sin of omission, and kept 'the Master' waiting. Once the mistake was rectified, a splendid evening ensued; RLS and James were so entranced with each other's company that they arranged a further session the following evening, and thereafter James made a habit of dropping round almost every evening after dinner and staying as late as he could. They ranged far and wide through literature, arguing about Zola – whom James admired and Stevenson largely disliked – and Hardy, where the admiration and dislike were the other way around. James's influence on RLS was to encourage him to continue along the Meredithian path of complex individual psychology while avoiding Meredith's political radicalism; RLS's on James was to urge him to cast his characters in a less academic mould and to pitch the incidents as if from old-style adventure. James, though, was not really one for 'adventure': he despised *She* and *King Solomon's Mines* and all other work by 'the unspeakable Haggard' even as RLS's staunch literary supporter Andrew Lang – who had by now forgiven him for marrying against his advice and not writing to him from America – urged the merits of Haggard on Stevenson.[21]

The coalescing of the mutual James-RLS influences can be seen in James's *Princess Casamassima*, published the following year. *Casamassima*, which is to the James *oeuvre* what *Prince Otto* is to RLS's, similarly deals with the prospects of social revolution but in a pessimistic way, suggesting that the survival of civilisation depends on the existence of a cultured elite; *Otto*, influenced by Meredith even to the extent of being set, like his *Vittoria*, in the *annus mirabilis* 1848, had been more optimistic about the dispensation that would replace the ousted prince. Yet *Casamassima*, uniquely for James, shows him taking the road recommended by Stevenson, and RLS duly praised it: 'Yes, sir, you can do low life, I believe.' It is significant that RLS always liked James at his most positive and approachable (*Roderick Hudson*, *The Bostonians*, *Casamassima*) and disliked the works that showed the subjugation of women (*Washington Square*, *The Portrait of a Lady*); he would certainly have disapproved of the esoteric late novels, *The Wings of a Dove* and *The Golden Bowl*.[22]

RLS's liking and admiration for James soon found expression in verse, in a sonnet which suggests, by its reference to his heroines, that it is the man rather than the artist that Stevenson especially prized:

> Who comes tonight? We bar the door in vain.
> My bursting walls, can you contain
> The presences that now together throng
> Your narrow entry, as with flowers and song,
> As with the air of life, the breath of talk?
> Lo how these fair immaculate women walk
> Behind their jocund maker; and we see
> Slighted *De Mauves*, and that far different she,
> *Gressie*, the trivial sphinx; and to our feast
> *Daisy* and *Barb* and *Chancellor* (she not least!)
> With all their silken, all their airy kin,
> Do like unbidden angels enter in.
> But he, attended by these shining names,
> Comes (best of all) himself – our welcome James.

On this far the best comment comes from James Pope-Hennessy: 'In these verses Louis used a certain poetic licence, for by no stretch of the imagination could Olive Chancellor, the bleak Sapphist of *The Bostonians*, be called "fair, immaculate" or "silken" or "airy".'

James became a regular visitor at Skerryvore and liked to sit in the big blue armchair brought down from Heriot Row that used to belong to Louis's grandfather; it quickly became known as 'Henry James's chair'. RLS grew more and more fond of him: 'Character, character is what he has!' he exclaimed. 'His feelings are always his reasons.' A present from James in February 1886 – a Venetian mirror – inspired more verses ('The Mirror Speaks'):

> Now with an outlandish grace,
> To the sparkling fire I face
> In the blue room at Skerryvore;
> And I wait until the door
> Open, and the Prince of Men,
> Henry James shall come again.[23]

James was masterly in his handling of Fanny, never overstaying his welcome, tiring Louis or remaining at Skerryvore too late; perhaps as an American, used to matriarchy, he had an instinctive understanding of the type of woman Fanny was. He was fascinated by the Stevenson marriage, and achieved the unique distinction of being the only one of RLS's friends with whom Fanny never quarrelled, though it is untrue to say, as often has been, that he based *The Author of Beltraffio* – which shows the deleterious effect of a domineering wife on a writer – on the Stevensons. For the managing wife, James used as model Fanny's old enemy Mrs J.A.Symonds and, prickly, paranoid and suspicious as she was, Fanny would certainly have objected vociferously when she read *Beltraffio* if she had recognised herself; instead she gave the book unqualified praise. There may, however, be firmer ground for the assertion that the Stevensons inspired his short story 'The Lesson of the Master' in which Mrs St George burns her husband's autobiographical novel.

Fanny thoroughly approved of Henry James, not suspecting his 'poor, barbarous and merely instinctive lady' reservations about her: she told Colvin that 'after ten weeks of Henry James the evenings seem very empty, though the room is always full of people.' She did, however, object to the way Louis excluded her from his conversations with 'the Master': 'naturally I have hardly been allowed to speak to him, though I fain would. He seems very gentle and comfortable, and I worship in silence – enforced silence.' And she would have been devastated had she known of Alice James's strictures on her – interesting as underlining once again the 'primitive' element in Fanny that so many observers perceived: 'From her appearance Providence or Nature, whichever is responsible for her, designed her as an appendage to a hand organ, but I believe she is possessed of wifely virtues . . . but such egotism and so naked! giving one the strangest feeling of being in the presence of an unclothed being.'[24]

Fanny especially valued James's presence as a means of diluting the impact of the in-laws. There was a particularly disastrous visit by the Stevenson parents in the autumn of 1885, at the end of which 'three weeks of chilling selfishness' Fanny confided to Colvin that she would even welcome a visit from Henley. As Thomas's mental powers declined, he grew increasingly subject to moods of morbid gloom and superstitious foreboding; Maggie meanwhile would flutter around him helplessly in hysterical agitation. Additionally, Thomas found Bournemouth grey and cold and fell ill; in her letters to Colvin, Fanny censured Maggie for lack of wifely concern: 'It is very unfair to that poor old man to keep him in a climate that is bad for him'; later she wrote: 'The dear old father has been very bad and yesterday was sent off home which I think he will never leave again.' The real sufferer in terms of nervous exhaustion was Louis: Fanny reported that Maggie 'having crushed and exhausted him . . . left him the legacy of an influenza cold ... If Louis dies it will be murder.' For once Fanny had someone to concur in her hyperbolic estimates, for Henry James told Colvin: 'My visit had the gilt taken off by the somewhat ponderous presence of the parents – who sit on him much too long at once. (They are to remain another week, and I can't see why *they* don't see how much they take out of him) ... If he could be quite alone on alternate, or occasional weeks, it would be a blessing.'[25]

Throughout 1885 Stevenson's mood was darkening, as he prepared to unleash on the world his definitive statement on the evil in man, contained in *Dr Jekyll and Mr Hyde*. The short stories 'Markheim', written early in the year, and 'Olalla', written in the autumn, can almost be seen as the male and female components of the diseased carrion, Mankind. 'Markheim' is in some ways a cameo version of Dostoevsky's *Crime and Punishment*, of which RLS remarked to Symonds that it was 'easily the greatest book I have read in ten years'. Like Dostoevsky, Stevenson uses the *doppelgänger* tradition to suggest the psychology of a tormented soul; the alter ego is a projection of unconscious drives; the mysterious visitant is either a product of Markheim's deranged mind or of his conscience.[26]

To set a murder by *acte gratuit* at Christmas time turns the idea of Christian resignation on its head and marks a clear denial of the possibility of redemption; here is Stevenson, at 36, the same age as Markheim, stating clearly that he does not believe in salvation, that all is hopeless, and yet he will endure stoically and even cheerfully. The conversation with the stranger uncannily echoes the interior monologue in RLS's philosophical essays, and there is the characteristic idea of evil as a mixed or ambiguous category: 'Do I say that I follow sin? I follow virtues also; they differ not by the thickness of a nail ... Evil, for which I live, consists not in action but in character.' The possibilities of escape for the artist via fantasy seem so limited that actual or metaphorical suicide now seems the answer; where the Stevensonian child of the *Child's Garden* wished to escape from his cage, RLS/Markheim seems to accept that such an escape route is no longer possible and seeks to flee from existence by surrendering to the police. 'Markheim' is a pessimistic version of *Crime and Punishment*, for surrender to the police after a murder in 1885 meant the death penalty; the suicide is not merely metaphorical as in Dostoevsky. Moreover, in Dostoevsky Christianity offers Raskolnikov the possibility of redemption through suffering, but for Stevenson Christianity is a merely negative force which justifies inaction and encourages suicide. That Stevenson's vision was darkening can be seen even by comparison with such sombre products of the early 1880s as 'Thrawn Janet' and 'The Merry Men'. There it was possible to interpret the stories in terms of the normal conventions of supernatural fiction, with either an actual devil or a supposed devil in the form of a black man; but in 'Markheim' it is impossible to interpret the mysterious visitor ('at times he thought he knew him; and at times he thought he bore a likeness to himself') as devil (or angel); he can only be a double, the externalisation of conscience or the figment of a fevered imagination. In the Poe story 'William Wilton' the narrator is confronted by his better self; but in 'Markheim' it is the dark self that compels the surrender.

An even darker and more complex tale – with his taste for economy and simplicity RLS thought that the complexity finally dragged it down, which is why he preferred 'Markheim' – is 'Olalla', one of the works inspired by his dreams. From the 'Brownies' (the unconscious as revealed in dreams) came the idea of the mother, the court, Olalla herself, the mother's niche, the broken window, the biting scene. In one way, 'Olalla' is clearly a companion piece to 'Markheim' and Olalla's withdrawal into her cloister is a kind of parallel to Markheim's surrender to the police. It is legitimate to ask why Olalla should sacrifice herself for the diseased blood of her family when she herself has escaped the taint, and the obvious answer is in terms of RLS's own sense of guilt, calling for self-immolation. The withdrawal into the cloister is certainly not Christian in any recognisable sense – more nihilism – since a refusal to engage with life on any terms is by no means the same as expiation of sin.

Yet there is much more to 'Olalla' than this. Taking as his point of departure Bulwer Lytton's *A Strange Story* (1861) – from which he got the idea for Felipe's torture of the squirrel – and the knowledge of the Peninsular wars he acquired during his short-lived researches for the book on Wellington, RLS interwove influences from a variety of sources: Poe (especially 'The Fall of the House of Usher'), Keats's 'Lamia' and Henry James's *The Aspen Papers*, to produce a High Romantic nightmare, in some ways the perfect neurotic fantasy with its blending of atavism, the power of the past, sexual anxiety and the Gnostic idea of a vital secret underlying the appearance of normality. The decay in the house is the strain of diseased sexuality that seems to permeate the very rafters. 'The spider swung there; the bloated tarantulas scampered on the cornices; ants had their crowded highways on the floor of halls of audience; the big and foul fly, that lives on carrion and is often the messenger of death, had set up his nest in the rotten woodwork and buzzed heavily about the rooms.'

At its simplest level, this tale of the adventures of a Peninsular war veteran in the mountains of Spain can be read as the conflict of Calvinism and Catholicism, of civilisation (the plain) against barbarism (the mountain). Yet behind this lies a clash of id and ego or, if Lawrentian categories are preferred, of the 'red blood self' and 'white mental consciousness'. Even more redolent of D.H.Lawrence than the triumph of unreason over reason is the ubiquitous and ambiguous motif of blood, which has led some critics to speak of Stevenson's attempt to deal with the gore of his haemorrhages by projection: the blood of Christ as the symbol of salvation and the blood the vampire sucks as the token of damnation. Even more perplexing is the confusion between blood as emblem of passion ('hot blood') and symbol of death, as in the hero's conviction that Olalla's love and her mother's vampiric bite are two aspects of a single impulse. This confusion of Eros and Thanatos is clear in Olalla's statement: 'the hands of the dead are in my bosom; they move me, they pluck me, they guide me.' One can quite understand RLS's fears that his multi-layered allegory had overwhelmed the story.[27]

There was a frenetic quality to the work rate of RLS in 1885–86, virtually imprisoned as he was in Bournemouth. There were many false starts, many unfinished fragments, this time of the life of Wellington and *The Great North Road* – a novel that was to have combined the Hamlet theme with a tale of highwaymen; in what survives, both the principal characters, Archer and Holdaway, appear to be 'Hamletic' failures. No single explanation will suffice for why RLS left so many projects unfinished: sometimes the explanation lies deep in the psyche, but in these cases there is some merit in Frank Swinnerton's suggestion that Stevenson had not thought through meticulously enough what it was he was trying to achieve: 'He was not sufficiently critical of a theme, so long as it seemed superficially to offer some scope for his skill.'[28]

A blow second only to the loss of Ferrier two years before was the sudden death of Fleeming Jenkin at 52 in June 1885. Grief-stricken at the loss of his very first mentor, Louis wrote to Anne Jenkin to offer to write his biography; she accepted, on condition that he stress Fleeming's essential greatness and not stress *her* influence. This was not an injunction Louis found hard to obey, for it was Jenkin who had written to him when he was in the depths of despair in California: 'even if you acted more foolishly and worse than other men you did so from much wiser and better motives than theirs.' Anne Jenkin came down to Skerryvore to help Louis in the preparation of the biography. The appearance of the first of the 'older women' to have influenced her husband caused the ever-jealous Fanny some misgivings to which she gave expression in an oblique way; in the teeth of the fact that Anne Jenkin was one of the darlings of Edinburgh society, Fanny reported to Dora Williams that although Anne Jenkin was not a popular figure, she (Fanny) personally liked her!

Louis found the writing of the memoir difficult, doubtless because of the complex emotions involved: work proceeded slowly and the biography was not completed until the summer of 1887. It is not a work that has ever found favour with the critics, the odd revealing anecdote and the account of Jenkin's parents and wife apart; Swinnerton remarked scathingly: 'Jenkin is poorly drawn, so that he might be anybody.'[29]

The ambiguity of RLS is perhaps nowhere better illustrated in a concrete situation than in the overtures he made to Thomas Hardy in the summer of 1885, when the relationship with Henry James, who detested Hardy, was at its apogee. In August he and Fanny travelled to Dorchester to meet the celebrated novelist, whom Louis had met once briefly at Colvin's. There are two accounts of the meeting: Hardy's and Fanny's. Here is Hardy: 'He [RLS] appeared in a velveteen jacket with one hand in a sling. I asked him why he wore the sling, as there seemed nothing the matter with his hand; his answer (I am almost certain) was that he had been advised to do it to lessen the effort of his heart in its beats.' And this is Fanny, in a letter to Maggie: 'We saw Hardy the novelist at Dorchester . . . a pale, gentle, frightened little man, that one felt an instinctive sympathy for.' To Colvin she wrote: 'We saw Hardy the novelist and liked him exceedingly.' Emma Hardy, however, she found less impressive and dismissed her in an ironically boomeranging judgement: 'What very strange marriages literary men seem to make!'[30]

At first the entente between Hardy and RLS seemed especially cordial. Ten months later Louis wrote to Hardy: 'I have read the Mayor of Casterbridge with sincere admiration: Henchard is a fine fellow, and Dorchester is touched with the hand of a master. Do you think you would let me try and dramatise it?' Hardy was delighted: 'I feel several inches taller at the idea of your thinking of dramatising the Mayor. Yes, by all means,' he told Louis in June. This idea went the way of so many of Stevenson's short-lived enthusiasms, and perhaps there was some personal difficulty in the next meeting at the Colvins' in 1886, for in December that year, after a long conversation with Bob Stevenson at the Savile Club, Hardy declared him to be 'a more solid character than Louis'. Later, after reading *Tess of the D'Urbervilles*, Louis changed his mind about Hardy's excellence and agreed with Henry James that it was a 'vile' book. Hardy struck back by dubbing James and Stevenson the 'Polonius and Osric' of literature; when after James's death the full text of his interchange with RLS on Hardy was published, the grand old man of Dorchester, notoriously sensitive to the slightest criticism, remarked witheringly: 'How indecent of those two virtuous females to expose their mental nakedness in such a manner.'[31]

The visit to Dorchester in August 1885 produced more immediate unfortunate consequences. On the way back from visiting Hardy, the Stevensons stayed overnight at a hotel in Exeter; Louis had another haemorrhage and they ended up marooned in the hotel bedroom, unable to get back to Bournemouth until 12 September. Worn out by the mental stress and the physical exertion of lifting her husband in and out of bed ten times during his delirium, Fanny also took to her bed once back at Skerryvore, but was catapulted out of it at the end of September when Louis had yet another haemorrhage. Although it was not as severe as the one in Exeter, the proximity of the two attacks was deeply worrying and Fanny wrote to

Baxter: 'He is very cheerful now, though he was, for the first time, inclined to give up the fight, and thought of Davos. I hope England is not a fatal mistake. I could see nothing else to do with cholera yonder.'[32]

Here the lady was protesting too much, for the 'something else' to do was obvious, as she admitted: Davos. This was ruled out because *she* could not tolerate it; it had little to do with RLS. It becomes clearer and clearer that the sojourn in Bournemouth during 1884–87 was a victory won by Fanny in a battle of wills against Louis: she relished, as he did not, being the centre of a bourgeois circle comprising the Taylors, Shelleys and others. The price she had to pay was that Bournemouth was accessible to Louis's friends, but she did her best to control them and deter them from visiting: Gosse and Henley she managed to banish almost completely; she even begrudged visits from the Stevenson parents whose largesse had made her status as Bournemouth property owner possible in the first place. Louis, by contrast, wanted to be on the move, to visit foreign lands, and to travel hopefully; in this respect the haemorrhage at Exeter played beautifully into Fanny's hands, since it demonstrated the 'impossibility' of living anywhere other than at Bournemouth.

Of RLS's unhappiness during these three years in Bournemouth there can be no serious doubt; the one beneficial 'spin-off' was that he worked well, as he did whenever he was ill or miserable. He felt that he was a prisoner, both in the sense that he was physically restricted, and that he seemed to have joined the bourgeoisie against whose values he had stood out so long. To Henley he wrote: 'What in the name of fate is to become of an RLS who can no longer 1) spree 2) walk 3) cruise 4) drink 5) or smoke? Yet that is the state of affairs.' Dubbing himself 'the hermit of Skerryvore', in a letter to Gosse he hinted sadly at the Bohemian circumstances in which he had first met Fanny and how far a cry it was from Barbizon to the gentility of Bournemouth. Many years later he asked Colvin to 'remember the pallid brute that lived in Skerryvore like a weevil in a biscuit'. The guilt and self-disgust that seeps into 'Olalla' and 'Markheim' are a reflection of his quotidian state of mind in Skerryvore. To Archer he wrote: 'Can you imagine that he [i.e. himself] is a backslidden communist, and is sure he will go to hell (if there be such an excellent institution) for the luxury in which he lives?' Even earlier, when at Bonallie Towers, he wrote to Gosse: 'I am now a beastly householder, but have not yet entered on my domain. When I do, the social revolution will probably cast me back upon my dung heap. There is a person called Hyndman [sc. the socialist H.M.Hyndman] whose eye is on me; his step is beHynd me as I go.'

Fanny gradually tightened her grip, controlling the movement of persons into Skerryvore, playing more and more of a role as Louis's editor, steering it away from what meant most to him towards what would earn most. Malcolm Elwin went so far as to say that Stevenson's marriage 'introduced to his domestic hearth a watchful ambassadress of respectability, a spiritual god-daughter of Mr Mudie and Mr Gladstone'. Some have interpreted this as the 'mannish' Fanny imposing on the 'feminine' RLS – introducing yet another twist into the confusion of sexual roles that always seemed to bedevil Stevenson – and the words of a recent critic are eloquent in this regard: 'He sends his text out towards the market from a sickbed where he continually bleeds from within, almost in a menstrual fashion.' The appearance of RLS as both 'Markheim' and 'Olalla' in 1885, especially the latter, takes on another layer of meaning. Fanny even tried to control her husband in 'inner-directed' matters. One result of his work on Fleeming Jenkin was to rekindle the old interest in music, and he attempted to learn the piano. For Fanny, as Nellie Sanchez reported, music was a closed book: 'she could not sing a note nor hardly tell one tune from another'; evidently she felt threatened by music and so she put a stop to her husband's experimentations, using, as usual, the 'catch-all' excuse of his health. She told Colvin: 'I am afraid the piano is *not* good for him. In the morning he gets up feeling very well indeed, and at about ten sits to the piano, where he stays till three or after, drinking his coffee, even, at the instrument. At three or thereabouts he breaks down altogether, gets very white and is extremely wretched with exhaustion until the next morning again.' RLS's rebellion was mild; he contented himself with strolling round the grounds with a red parasol, watching Fanny working in the garden but without taking part; the contrast with his later energy at gardening in the South Seas was *not* simply a function of his differential health.[33]

Inevitably the tensions between the nest-building, comfort-seeking, aspiring bourgeoise, her eye always on the commercial possibilities of the literary marketplace, and the restless, driven, Magian rover whose commitment to his art was, as he admitted, greater than that to wife and adopted family, often burst into the open in the form of rows, of which there were many in Bournemouth. Those who claim that the turbulent relationship between Fanny and Louis in Skerryvore was simply part of an ongoing dynamic between two highly-strung, passionate people, need to explain why these conflicts were almost wholly absent during the period of the rovings in the Pacific, when the balance of marital power shifted to Louis.

In the unconscious is truth, so that we should be alerted when told by Fanny's biographer that 'sometimes, almost out of his head with fever or haemorrhage or both, he swore at Fanny when she tried to nurse him'. But there was enough tension at the conscious level. Adelaide Boodle testified that there were times 'when the casual looker-on might have felt it his duty to shout for the police with cries of "Murder!"' These were the times when Louis would openly express his contempt for Fanny's ideas and opinions; he quoted disparagingly to Baxter the Old French proverb about the self-delusion of women: '*Ce que femme veult, Dieu le veult.*' That the rows were frequent emerges from a number of casual references in RLS's letters to passages of arms with his wife – how often would a normal man see fit to record normal marital tiffs in letters to his friends, unless they were of egregious seriousness? The only alternative is to see Louis as a poseur, using all experiences, even the most intimate, as 'copy' for literary correspondence.

Louis tended to divulge these domestic uproars either to those he suspected of having an uncritical view of Fanny, or to those he knew would be automatically sympathetic. So, for instance, he told his father that they had had a 'dreadful overhauling' on the subject of whether or not he had been a good son, with Fanny vociferously expressing the opinion that he had been a 'detestable bad one'. To Henry James he wrote:

> My wife is peepy and dowie ... she is a woman (as you know) not without art: the art of extracting the gloom of the eclipse from the sunshine; and she has recently laboured in this field not without success or (as we used to say) not without a blessing. It is strange: "we fell out my wife and I" the other night; she tackled me savagely for being a canary-bird; I replied (bleatingly) protesting that there was no use in turning life into *King Lear*; presently it was discovered that there were two dead combatants upon the field, each slain by the arrow of truth, and we tenderly carried off each other's corpses. Here is a little comedy for Henry James to write! The beauty was that each thought the other quite unscathed at first. But we had dealt shrewd stabs.

But to Fanny's enemy, Henley, he wrote with real and disloyal passion: 'I got my little finger into a steam press called the Vandegrifter (patent) and my whole body and soul had to go through after it. I came out as limp as a lady's novel, but the Vandegrifter suffered in the process, and is fairly knocked about ... I am what *she has made me*, the embers of the once gay RLS.'[34] Worst of all rows, however, was the one that occurred when Fanny read the first draft of *Dr Jekyll and Mr Hyde*: this brought to a head the conflict between Louis's desire to tell the truth as he saw it and Fanny's wish for commercial success. The altercation ended with Louis's throwing the manuscript on the fire as 'the only way to put temptation beyond my reach'. This was an act of momentous significance, whose importance can only be gauged by entering more closely into the dark world of *Jekyll and Hyde*.[34]

Bournemouth: Prometheus Unbound

In *Dr Jekyll and Mr Hyde* Stevenson delved deeper into the unconscious than in any other work. The book has become one of those universal texts into which every conceivable meaning can be read, but ambiguities and controversies attend even the circumstances of its composition. The period of gestation and writing occupied September and October 1885: '*Jekyll* was conceived, written, rewritten, re-rewritten, and printed inside ten weeks,' RLS told F.W.H.Myers in March 1886, excusing the great speed on the grounds of pressing money problems and the need to pay 'Byles the butcher' – his generic name for tradesmen. According to Lloyd, RLS wrote the first draft in three days, then burnt it and started again after Fanny had given it a dreadful critical mauling. Biographers have objected that a work rate of 8,000 words a day for an invalid sounds like a tall story; Dr Myron Schultz has conjectured that such prodigious energy may have been the result of taking cocaine for respiratory complaints; whatever the truth, it is certain that *both* versions were written at great speed.

Why did Stevenson destroy a manuscript which was, as he told Nellie Sanchez, 'the best thing he had ever done'; why did he ever afterwards assert that *Jekyll* was a negligible achievement, because Fanny had ruined the version he wanted to publish? Almost certainly because in the first draft he finally fired himself up to present an adult view of sexuality, at which Fanny panicked, fearing the effect on her husband's public image as a writer of adventure stories and books for children; it has been suggested that the 'disgraceful pleasures' indulged in 'from a very early age', to which Jekyll refers, may have been masturbation and that this was made clear in the pilot version. It has even been suggested that it was this first draft, not 'The Travelling Companion', which was submitted to a publisher and returned by an editor 'on the plea that it was a work of genius and indecent'; others argue that the 'editor' who made those comments was none other than Fanny herself. The plot thickens in the light of Stevenson's statement that he burned 'The Travelling Companion' on the grounds that 'it was not a work of genius and that Jekyll had supplanted it.' Is one burning being extended into two, or could it be, as Hellman suggests, that the pyromania common to the wives of eminent Victorians was rampant in the Stevenson household? 'How many manuscripts, in addition to the novel and *Dr Jekyll* did Stevenson, one wonders, destroy in anger after such discussions with his wife?'[1]

What is clearly nonsense – and a transparent attempt to explain away Fanny's philistinism – is Nellie Sanchez's statement that RLS burned the first draft and started again because Fanny pointed out that he had 'missed the point of the allegory'. The idea of a singularly perceptive critic like Stevenson missing what was obvious to any intelligent reader would be laughable, even if we did not have RLS's quite different, and convincing, account of the genesis of the book. Fully to make sense of this we have to return to that dream world which had been so potent a source of inspiration to him since childhood.

The use of dreams as a direct inspiration to storytelling is unique to Stevenson among writers – Coleridge and de Quincey induced them by opium – and the Shakespearean adage that we are 'such stuff as dreams are made on' is appropriate to Stevenson as to no other novelist. The presence of Jacobitism as a theme in three of Stevenson's books (*Kidnapped, Catriona, The Master of Ballantrae*) as well as the unfinished *The Young Chevalier* is largely due to his dreams, for at one stage in his life he used to dream nightly that he was involved in Jacobite conspiracies. As a student he began to dream in sequence and lead a double life, one of the day and one of the night, with no means of distinguishing reality from illusion. One of his dreams gains added significance when we remember that Dr Jekyll's laboratory used to be a dissecting room for surgeons.

He passed a long day in the surgical theatre, his heart in his mouth, his teeth on edge, seeing monstrous malformations and the abhorred dexterity of surgeons. In a heavy, rainy, foggy evening he came forth into the South Bridge, turned up the High Street, and entered the door of a tall land, at the top of which he supposed himself to lodge. All night long, in his wet clothes, he climbed the stairs, stair after stair in endless series, and at every second flight a flaring lamp with a reflector. All night long, he brushed by single persons passing downward – beggarly women of the street, great, weary, muddy labourers, poor scarecrows of men, pale parodies of women – but all drowsy and weary like himself, and all single, and all brushing against him as they passed. In the end, out of a northern window, he would see the day beginning to whiten over the Firth, give up the ascent, turn to descend, and in a breath be back again upon the streets in his wet clothes, in the wet, haggard dawn, trudging to another day of monstrosities and operations. Time went quicker in the life of dreams, some seven hours (as near as he can guess) to one; and it went, besides, more intensely, so that the gloom of these fancied experiences clouded the day, and he had not shaken off their shadow ere it was time to lie down and renew them.

In some ways even more suggestive than that dream, with its constant dualism and polarities, was the vision of evil ('the lord of the flies') he experienced in another recurring nightmare.

It seemed to him that he was in the first floor of a rough hill-farm. The room showed some poor efforts at gentility, a carpet on the floor, a piano, I think, against the wall; but, for all these refinements, there was no mistaking he was in a moorland place, among hillside people, and set in miles of heather. He looked down from the window upon a bare farmyard, that seemed to have been long disused. A great uneasy stillness lay upon the world. There was no sign of the farm-folk, or of any live stock, save for an old brown dog of the retriever breed, who sat close in against the wall of the house and seemed to be dozing. Something about this dog disquieted the dreamer; it was quite a nameless feeling, for the beast looked right enough – indeed he was so old and dull and dusty and broken-down, that he should rather have awakened pity; and yet the conviction came and grew upon the dreamer that this was no proper dog at all, but something hellish. A great many dozing summer flies hummed about the yard; and presently the dog thrust forth his paw, caught a fly in his open palm, carried it to his mouth like an ape, and looking suddenly up at the dreamer in the window, winked up at him with one eye.

Gradually RLS learned to impose a structure on his dreams: the very discipline and craftsmanship that enabled him to write fed back into the unconscious and affected the resolution of the dreams; he later regretted not having been able to bring the dream about the brown dog to a satisfactory end and said (of himself as the dreamer): 'It would be different now; he knows his business better.' Stevenson called the springs of his unconscious inspiration 'the Brownies', which he imagined as underground creatures like the dwarves of the Nibelung, engaged in fashioning stories instead of gold, and he claimed that once he became a professional writer, the Brownies understood the change: hitherto 'the little people who manage man's internal theatre had not as yet received a very rigorous training; and played upon their stage like children who should have slipped into the house and found it empty, rather than like drilled actors performing a set piece to a huge hall of faces'. Now he would start devising a story, and the unconscious would take over once he was asleep; the only dreams he had thereafter were of reading delightful books and visiting delightful places. The rest of his dream life was taken up by the fashioning of his stories; sometimes, of course, on waking he could not recapture the high drama of the night's dreams.

And yet how often have these sleepless Brownies done him honest service, and given him, as he sat idly taking his pleasure in the boxes, better tales than he could fashion for himslef . . . My Brownies, God bless them! who do half my work for me while I am fast asleep, and in all human likelihood, do the rest for me as well, when I am wide awake and fondly suppose I do it myself.[2]

It was the Brownies who suggested to RLS most of the key incidents in *Jekyll and Hyde*: the scene at the window; Hyde taking the powders; the spontaneous transformation of Jekyll on the park bench. When critics objected to the powders as being, in Henry James's words, 'too material an agency', RLS explained that he too had his reservations about this device but felt compelled to leave it in as it came from the dream world: 'Will it be thought ungenerous, after I have been so liberally ladling out praise to my unseen collaborators, if I here toss them over, bound hand and foot, into the arena of the critics. For the business of the powders, which so many have censured, is, I am relieved to say, not mine at all but the Brownies'.'

Two things become clear from this description of the 'Brownies': first the absurdity of the suggestion that RLS missed the point of *Jekyll and Hyde* in the first draft until alerted to it by Fanny; and the symbolic importance of the colour brown. An interesting study could be made of writers' simultaneous fascination with and aversion to certain colours: with Sir Richard Burton, it was the green of the jungle, so alien to one who preferred the yellows and creams of the Arabian desert; with Melville it was the whiteness of the whale, with Jack London the blankness of the white silence and its analogue 'white logic'; with D.H.Lawrence the deadness of the white mental consciousness in its struggle with the red blood-self. For Stevenson the key colour was brown: this was the colour that terrified him in his childhood nightmares, it was the colour of the diabolical dog in the dream, of the 'Brownies' and of the fog in *Jekyll and Hyde*. It would no doubt be stretching a point to make a big issue of Fanny's colouring, but it is more than a little interesting that Stevenson often dwells at length on her 'gypsy' pigmentation; a description of his wife in May 1885 sounds like something from one of his dreams: 'There came here a lean, Brown, bloodshot woman, claiming to be Fanny.'[3]

Fortunately, it is not our task here to tease out all the layers of meaning in *Jekyll and Hyde*, nor to attend to the myriad 'readings' of the text which purport to show it as homosexualist, misogynistic, a tract on sibling rivalry, a statement of position by a political reactionary, and much else. Yet some attempt must be made to establish the meaning of the dualities in the novel for Stevenson *personally* – which is not, of course, to exhaust the range of its possible resonances *in general*. Two questions suggest themselves: to what extent was the notion of the essential duality of man original to Stevenson; and in what ways did he consider himself, or can he be considered by others, as a 'divided self' or dual man?

'Doubles' were an aspect of the nineteenth-century *zeitgeist*; there is also a sense in which 'the beast in man' was a theme with a special relevance for the 1880s. Antithesis, or dualism, can be seen at the exalted level in the philosophy of Kant and Hegel and at the more sensational literary level of the doppelgänger in a host of works: there are 'doubles' in Poe's 'William Wilson', Hogg's *Confessions of a Justified Sinner*, Musset's *La nuit de décembre*, Balzac's *La Peau de chagrin*, Dostoevsky's 'The Double', Chamisso's *Peter Schlemihl*, and Hawthorne's 'Monsieur du Miroir'. By the nineteenth century, the concept of the self had become binary or double-decked, and by the 1880s it would not have been unusual to anthropomorphise each part, as Wilde did later in *The Picture of Dorian Gray*, Conrad in *The Secret Sharer*, James in 'The Jolly Corner'; a similar process can be observed in the work of Valéry and Beerbohm. In this tradition, RLS drew particularly on his Scottish predecessor, James Hogg, to the point where Chesterton later objected that, though set in London, *Jekyll and Hyde* was everywhere redolent of *Scottish* experience – to which other critics in turn objected that the divided social self of Edinburgh was that between Old and New Towns, but in London it was between the rich and the poor.[4]

Another powerful influence, alongside Hogg, was Mary Shelley's *Frankenstein*, especially for its Gothic atmosphere. The Gothic tradition at the psychological level depends on the sensation of forbidden, repressed desires, creating an atmosphere that has been dubbed 'psychosexual'. Structurally, it throws up multiple narrators, fragmented points of view, dissolution of hero into anti-hero, narcissism into depression, the self into its shadow, as well as providing a 'monster' full of symbolic resonance. Yet no great artist writes to a formula, and in the creation of Jekyll and Hyde one can detect other influences: the shadow about whose utility Stevenson wondered as a child and which appears in the *Child's Garden*; Victorian man alienated between his role as worker and his life as a private citizen, as in the portrait of Wemmick in *Great Expectations* that RLS so admired.

Quite apart from the overall nineteenth-century *zeitgeist*, there were in the 1880s specific anxieties that help in the 'placing' of *Jekyll and Hyde*. That it was a decade of *angst* emerges in many strange ways: the 'scramble for Africa' for example, which the sociologist Joseph Schumpeter analysed as 'social atavism' or displaced anxiety neurosis. In 1886 appeared Nietzche's *Beyond Good and Evil*, with its plea for a new morality now that God was 'dead'. In 1887 Maupassant produced his version of *Jekyll and Hyde* in 'The Horla' and two years later Zola's 'divided self' made its appearance in *La Bête Humaine*. And those who like parallels between art and life have always been fond of pointing out that, even as a dramatic version of *Jekyll and Hyde* was being put on in London's theatreland in 1888, a real Hyde was stalking the East End in the form of Jack the Ripper.

Naturally, it is not suggested that *Jekyll and Hyde* can somehow be reduced to the sum of all these influences: its originality lies not in theme but in treatment. For instance, Stevenson suggests that in the end we may discover that each human individual is not just one, or even two, but many. The terror expressed in the novel at the loss of identity clearly reflects RLS's own anxieties, and the idea of a multiple personality may be explained psychologically as the result of RLS's protean talents – the scope of his fiction, his poetry, his essays, his aspirations as an historian, which in turn led to his leaving so many projects unfinished – and the multiple roles he had to play in the complex relationships with his parents, Fanny, the other Osbournes, Mrs Sitwell, and so on. In the history of literature we can see the prophecy of multiple personality becoming fulfilled in the work of Nabokov and even more clearly in the Beckett trilogy of novels: *Molloy, Malone Dies* and *The Unnameable*. Some critics have even suggested that the text of *Jekyll and Hyde* is itself schizoid, since it extends backward in time to James Hogg and forward to Beckett.

The originality of Stevenson's conception of the self is seen most clearly if we emphasise *Jekyll and Hyde*'s place in the Gothic tradition rather than that of the *doppelgänger*. In RLS's novel the progress is all towards disintegration, not integration, as is usually the case. In all the previous works in which doubles appear – *Melmoth the Wanderer, Frankenstein, Caleb Williams, The Confessions of a Justified Sinner* – confidence is retained in the ideal of a unified self, however threatened; but in *Jekyll and Hyde* there is an explicit denial of the unity of the self. To put it in more general terms, in Mary Shelley's *Frankenstein* there is chaos but the overriding tendency of the universe is back towards order; in *Jekyll and Hyde*, possibly influenced by some of the apocalyptical talk among 'entropy' scientists of the time, RLS postulates in the future a 'normal' situation of permanent unending chaos, where even 'certainties' like the endurance of the individual human personality will be dissolved.[5]

The dual personality of Jekyll-Hyde represents the many contradictory impulses in the mind and psyche of RLS. Everything about him seemed ambiguous: 'I have a genius for morality and no talent for it,' he told Fleeming Jenkin in 1882. Fanny spoke of two photographs taken of him by the Taylors, in one of which he looked like an angel and in the other a devil.[6] RLS always tried to incorporate the yin and yang of both conscious and unconscious drives in his work, and in this sense *Jekyll and Hyde* represents the culmination to date of the themes of a lifetime. The key texts are not the obvious ones where he adumbrates the theme of dual personality – Deacon Brodie after all seems a parochial amateur involved in the banality of evil alongside Henry Jekyll – but those where RLS wrestles with the god Janus in a deeper, metaphysical sense. The essay 'Pulvis et Umbra' can be read superficially as Panglossian optimism, but is in fact full of a barely disguised pessimism: there is a Zolaesque description of the origins of life, a Darwinesque picture of the survival of the fittest and a Swiftian savage indignation about Man himself. 'The House of Eld' shows the futility of murdering parents and what they stand for, since you will merely replace the shackles on the right leg with shackles on the left; this points forward to the key idea in *Jekyll and Hyde*: that you cannot drain evil out of a personality and leave just the good, since the two are inextricably mixed.

The same themes are evident in Stevenson's poetry. In some of the early poems, dealing with sexual anxieties, RLS sees his body as part dungeon, part pleasure garden, and in 'Et Tu in Arcadia Vixisti' he envied Bob's ability to integrate the two halves of centaur-like Man – half animal, half divine. Of the later poems, *Moral Emblems and Tales* were dedicated to the proposition that things are seldom what they seem, and that all the conventional homiletic wisdom is false: crime *does* pay, cheats *do* prosper, etc. In 'Robin and Ben, or, the Pirate and the Apothecary' he illustrates the interpenetration of opposites. Robin runs away to sea and becomes a pirate, yet behaves according to a strict idiosyncratic moral code; Ben becomes a respectable bourgeois chemist but is in fact morally depraved. Although this points to the familiar RLS theme that honest villainy is always to be preferred to the humbug of the 'unco' guid', yet no simple moral can ever be extracted from RLS's work. In 'The Builder's Doom', a Samson-like fable, the hero compasses his own destruction along with that of the innocent which, to Stevenson, points up the inscrutability of the universe, where it is pointless to look for justice. As he put it in 'Virginibus Puerisque':

Hope is the boy, a blind, headlong, pleasant fellow, good to chase swallows with the salt; Faith is the grave, experienced, yet smiling man. Hope lives on ignorance; open-eyed Faith is built upon a knowledge of our life, of the tyranny of circumstances and the frailty of human resolution. Hope looks for unqualified success, but Faith counts certainly on failure, and takes honourable defeat to be a form of victory.

In 'Ticonderoga' a Stewart clansman kills a Cameron, then flees to the murdered man's brother to claim the inviolable right of sanctuary. The Cameron brother, unaware of the murder, grants the boon and then finds himself caught in an impossible dilemma, constrained on the one hand by the laws of hospitality, yet urged forward by the law of vendetta on the other.[6] Trapped between these two fires, the Cameron goes to America to meet his double and his death. A typical Stevenson character is always doomed to failure whichever way he jumps; RLS likes to place his characters in 'Hamletic' situations from which there is no escape: in 'Ticonderoga' the New World is simply the cemetery of the old. This 'no escape' motif was a feature of Stevenson's own life, for the places he needed to go to for his health (e.g. Davos) were not those where he got spiritual solace (e.g. Barbizon) and this contradiction continued throughout his life. Even in the cold Adirondack Mountains of New York state in 1887, he longed for Scotland; the yearning continued in Samoa, but on the other hand to return to Scotland meant virtually certain death.

Some critics have therefore concluded that the entire optimism/pessimism debate about Stevenson's work – whether an optimistic style, full of sharp effects, was really in conflict with a partly repressed pessimistic world-view, and so on – is misplaced and conclude that the fundamental vein in RLS was nihilistic. 'Nihilism' is too strong, 'futility' is better. Stevenson sometimes appeared sanguine and eupeptic, but only when he wanted to combat the rather facile and spurious *fin de siècle* pessimism, which was merely a decadent pose. Yet his overall stance is Melvillean: he believed that the world was likely to be 'a labyrinth without end or issue' and that 'Man is indeed marked for failure in his efforts to do right.' His moral advice was always sceptical: 'You will always do wrong: you must try to get used to that, my son. It is a small matter to make a work about, when all the world is in the same case. I meant when I was a young man to write a great poem; and now I am cobbling little prose articles ... Our business in this world is not to succeed, but to continue to fail in good spirits.'[7]

Stevenson was paralysed by his conflicting views on the morality of strenuousness: on the one hand he described the attitudes of Will o' the Mill as 'catsmeat' and thought that the philosophy of quietism was the coward's way out – you can only be emotionally numb to death if you are also indifferent to life; on the other he regarded action as futile – 'to travel hopefully is better than to arrive' and was always drawn to poems of resignation and retirement like Tennyson's 'Lotus Eaters' or Yeats's 'The Lake Isle of Innisfree'. The futility of action is best expressed at the end of *An Inland Voyage* when he says that the poorest actor is like an artist because 'he has gone upon a pilgrimage that will last him his life long, because there is no end to it short of perfection'. Drawn to Rousseau and the Romantic movement, Stevenson nevertheless thought that Wordsworth and his school had ended in a neurotic world of illusion, and Will, referring to the impasse of Schopenhauer and his followers, is not an idly chosen name. As Professor Kiely has remarked of RLS: 'His first impulse may be romantic, but his second thought is almost always classical.' Stevenson's ferocious animadversions on Zola, too, may be read as an externalised internal dialogue, in which Stevenson tries to rid himself of some of his doubts about the claims of romance against realism. His own fiction in fact splits between the two, and in this respect looks forward to the 'schizoid' Conrad novel, with its unresolved tension between the mass cultural romance and the methods of high cultural modernism.[8]

Ambivalence, ambiguity, duality, dichotomy, bifurcation – these are the kinds of nouns customary when analysing Stevenson. *Jekyll and Hyde*, then, provides a kind of overarching summation of the themes in his thirty-six-year old life. The Stevensonian 'divided self' is overdetermined at a number of levels. We may begin by briefly considering the argument from medical aetiology – that there is something about consumption *of itself* that produces a 'divided self' perception. At first sight this looks attractive: there are the multiple ambiguities of Keats's poetry, the crisscrossing dualities of D.H.Lawrence, and the tormented ambivalence of George Orwell, who accepted that British imperial rule in Burma was wrong, but wanted to chastise the Burmese who pointed this out. Yet, quite apart from the open question whether Stevenson was a consumptive, this argument is uselessly reductive – it does not explain, for example, why Stevenson wrote *Jekyll and Hyde* rather than 'La Belle Dame sans Merci'.

More convincing is the contrast between the two main strands in traditional Scottish culture, the Calvinistic and the Jacobite, representing in RLS's case the competing tugs of the conscious and the unconscious, the determined and the voluntaristic, the life-denying Thanatos principle and the life-enhancing Eros. Though brought up in the Calvinistic tradition, Stevenson preferred the Jacobite sensibility, which can be seen in psychic terms as a bid to achieve 'wholeness'. Chesterton argued, convincingly, that Puritanism in Scotland involved too great a disjuncture between the world of childhood and imagination and the real world; the Jacobite/Catholic tradition, on the other hand, provided a cult of the Holy Child, a feast of the Holy Innocents, a celebration of the little brothers of St Francis to allow continuity between childhood and the rest of life. Chesterton's general argument was that the Catholic sensibility was monistic, the Protestant dualistic; RLS was therefore someone who 'knew the worst too young' because of a system (Calvinism) that saw no difference between the worst and the moderately bad.[9]

Another division in Stevenson was between the man he was – an invalid with pulmonary impairment, possibly tuberculosis, possibly some other erosion of the lungs – and the man of action he wanted to be. Whenever he looked in a mirror – and Henley assures us that this was often – he saw 'the other': a bronchitic/consumptive specimen, not the hero he imagined himself to be. It would not be surprising if in the end he came to see his body as the sworn enemy of his intellect and imagination and elaborated a Gnostic equation whereby matter was evil and mind good; Jekyll's foolhardy attempt to drain all the evil out of himself into Hyde would be a symbolic enactment of the desire to vault free from the prison of the body. At the same time, as *Jekyll and Hyde* makes clear, he knew the ambition to be illusory, not just in the sense of physical determinism, but because ultimately he was convinced 'the kingdom of God' lay within, not in being a Burton or a Stanley. Yet he was aware that to act out this conviction would take him into Will's cul-de-sac, so he oscillated uneasily between the Nietzschean worship of action and the Jacobite gloom of a Lord George Murray, accepting the existential need for action while being sceptical as to its utility. The analogy between the life of the healthy man and that of the invalid suggested an analogy between art and life, yet Stevenson could never decide which of the two should be given paramountcy: his credo to Henley – that art was his pillow, that he could live without his wife but not his art – conflicts head on with other utterances, where he implied that only a fool would prefer art to life. In the very year of *Jekyll and Hyde's* publication (1886) he described himself to an American reviewer as a person 'who prefers life to art, and who knows it is a far finer thing to be in love, or to risk a danger, than to paint the finest picture or write the noblest book'.[10]

Yet another ambivalence – which has particularly attracted critics because it draws Fanny and Thomas Stevenson into the picture – is that between RLS as uncontaminated artist, a man who has not truckled or sacrificed his integrity, and the commercially successful author that his wife and father wanted him to be. Published in January 1886, *Jekyll and Hyde* was a superseller, which sold 40,000 copies in six months in Britain and another 250,000 in pirated editions in the U.S.A. The success brought financial rewards but left Stevenson troubled: it was, after all, the version sanctioned by Fanny that had found public favour, not the 'real' story she had made him burn. He was convinced that a true artist would not gain public acceptance except accidentally, and that success involved prostitution. He wrote to Gosse in 1886 as follows:

> What the public likes is work (of any kind) a little loosely executed . . . I know that good work sometimes hits; but with my hand on my heart, I think it is by an accident. And I know that good work must succeed at last; but that is not the doing of the public; they are only shamed into silence or affectation. I do not write for the public; I do write for money, a nobler deity; and most of all for myself, not perhaps any more noble, but both intelligent and nearer home.
>
> Let us tell each other sad stories of the bestiality of the beast whom we feed. What he likes is the newspaper; and to me the press is the mouth of a sewer, where lying is professed as from a university chair, and everything prurient, and ignoble, and essentially dull, finds its abode and pulpit. I do not like mankind; but men, and not all of these – and fewer women. As for respecting the race, and, above all, that fatuous rabble of burgesses called 'the public', God save me from such irreligion – that way lies disgrace and dishonour. There must be something wrong in me or I would not be popular.[11]

It gradually becomes clear that the principal sources of Stevenson's anxieties – his father and his wife – are present in disguised form in *Jekyll and Hyde*. It has often been noticed that, the maid and the little girl apart, there are no women in the novel. Stevenson's own explanation was that he never included women in his work unless there was a chance that he could treat them realistically, untrammelled by Mrs Grundy; clearly in a sensational novel like this, there was a danger that he might have to deal with sexuality in a way unacceptable to a Victorian readership. Yet it is also likely that he was not on this occasion unhappy with the absence of women, as this could be construed, in its own way, as a snub to Fanny for forcing him to destroy the version of the story in which he told the truth.

However, the final version certainly did not banish sexuality, in its many latent forms, from the text. Stevenson was adamant that the book was not about sex, but he is often misunderstood on this point. What he meant was that Hyde should not be read, to use the language coming into fashion twenty years later, as id to Jekyll's ego or, at least, that this was only a small part of his message. It has to be conceded that there was some confusion even in RLS's mind on this point. In 1887 he wrote to John Paul Bocock that Hyde was

> not, Great Gods! a mere voluptuary. There is no harm in voluptuaries; and none, with my hand on my heart and in the sight of God, none – no harm whatsoever in what prurient fools call "immorality". The harm was in Jekyll, because he was a hypocrite – not because he was fond of women; he says so himself; but people are so filled full of folly and inherited lust, that they think of nothing but sexuality. The hypocrite let out the beast of Hyde – who is no more sexual than another, but who is the essence of cruelty and malice and selfishness and cowardice, and these are diabolic in man – not this poor wish to love a woman that they make such a cry about.

Yet to J.A.Symonds RLS wrote rather differently: '*Jekyll* is a dreadful thing, I own, but the only thing I feel dreadful about is that damned old business of the war of the members. This time it came out; I hope it will stay in, in future.'[12]

We know, of course, that an author's intentions can never exhaust the meaning of a work of art but it is interesting that Stevenson, far more in touch with the receptors to the unconscious than most artists, should have fallen into confusion on this point. The fact that sexuality is palpable in the texture of *Jekyll and Hyde*, coupled with the absence of women, has led some unwary, penny-in-the-slot critics to talk of 'misogynism' and 'patriarchy'. In fact the clearest message that can be read from this book is a critique of the alleged patriarchy. The failure of the potions symbolises the failure of nineteenth-century science – the *locus classicus* of the 'patriarchy', to lapse into the jargon for a moment – to provide a solution to the human condition. The (male) Victorian notion of human perfectibility is also a target of *Jekyll and Hyde*; the tragedy at the end is caused at root by an unwillingness to face the reality of the mixed heritage of human beings and to worship instead at the altar of the false god of perfectibility. Jekyll admits he was 'made to learn that the doom and burthen of our life is bound forever on man's shoulders, and when the attempt is made to cast it off, it but returns upon us with more familiar and more awful pressure'. Dr Lanyon, an exemplar of complacent Victorian man, is unable to stand the shock of seeing Hyde turn into Jekyll since it is an affront to all conventional reason and logic – as indeed is the notion that two men are really one, or that one man could be a multitude. Such an idea comes more easily under the purview of feminine discourse, and one remembers Jung's insight that if the matchbox he held in his hands were suddenly to float in the air, all the women in the audience would applaud joyfully, while the men would deny the evidence of their eyes or flee in terror.

Feminine sensibility, then, is by no means banished from *Jekyll and Hyde* but, significantly, what remains is, again to use Jungian terms, the *anima* kind; it is Fanny and the kind of woman that stands for assertive sexuality that is absent. According to Barbara Hannah, it was Fanny's banishing of a true female figure that made the work entropic, turned towards chaos rather than order, and reduced the chance of reconciliation and integration offered to Stevenson by his 'Brownies': 'the dream of the incident at the window gave Stevenson a glimpse of the original wholeness of man. There are four figures: Utterson and Enfield below, the dual figure of Jekyll-Hyde above.'[13]

As for Thomas Stevenson, almost without exception critics of *Jekyll and Hyde* have pointed out that the true relationship of Hyde to Jekyll is not that of brother; Hyde is Jekyll's creation and as such, symbolically, is his son. If the thesis of oedipal conflict between RLS and his father is correct, then the slaying of Sir Danvers Carew by Hyde looks like disguised parricide. It is well known that the fantasies of childhood can be preserved in the memory and then returned to consciousness through the avenue of dreams, and since RLS himself expressly linked the work of the Brownies on this book to his recurring dreams, it is by no means fanciful to relate Hyde's lethal assault with a cane to the slaying of the father in the dream where the stepmother declared her love for the stepson. It is also possible that one unconscious motive for the omnipresence of the treasure theme in the Stevenson *oeuvre* is shortage of money – a very good reason why, unconsciously, Louis might want to see the death of his father. The psychoanalyst, Dr Mark Kanzer, concluded: 'Hyde, the guilty heir, was permitted to achieve his impulses in the dream, while Stevenson, punishing the criminal with death in his narrative, could salve his own conscience while at the same time satisfying his creditors and easing his parricidal tensions by gaining access to new funds.'[14]

Jekyll and Hyde was the book with which Stevenson broke through into fame (if not yet quite fortune). It also evinces the maturing of many persistent themes in his *oeuvre* hitherto, as well as providing interesting clues to his deep anxieties. Most impressively of all, RLS moved the problem of evil in mankind on to a new plane. It is no longer a question of diabolic possession as in Hogg's *Confessions* or 'Thrawn Janet' or even, as Stevenson himself noted, a simple matter of unchained libido, but of the kind of darkness in the heart of human beings that would produce the death camps of the twentieth century. When all its implications were teased out, no more devastating blow to Victorian optimism could be imagined. That is what RLS meant when, referring to Dr Jekyll in a letter to Will Low, he said: 'I believe you will find he is ... quite willing to answer to the name of Low or Stevenson.' It was what Gerard Manley Hopkins meant when he claimed to recognise the Hyde in himself and declared: 'I think Robert Lewis [sic] Stevenson shows more genius in a page than Scott in a volume.'

Most perceptive of all the contemporary critics was Louis's old friend J.A. Symonds, who noted that *Jekyll and Hyde* was a genuine heart of darkness: Man was in thrall to biological determinism; a yawning moral chaos world opened up, which Symonds compared to the Cave of Despair in *The Faerie Queen*; the reader was left deeply disturbed because there was no comfortable dénouement, as in *Crime and Punishment*, with Raskolnikov answering for his sins and being given the chance of redemption.

> It makes me wonder whether a man has the right to scrutinise 'the abysmal deeps' of personality. It is indeed a dreadful book, most dreadful because of a certain moral callousness, a want of sympathy, a shutting out of hope. The art is burning and intense. *Peau de Chagrin* disappears; Poe is as water. As a piece of literary work, this seems to me the finest you have done – in all that regards style, invention, psychological analysis, exquisite fitting of parts and an admirable employment of motives to realise the abnormal. But it has left such a deeply painful impression on my heart that I do not know how I am ever to turn to it again. The fact is that, viewed as an allegory, it touches one too deeply. Most of us at some epoch of our lives have been upon the verge of developing a Mr Hyde.[15]

The year of 1886 was truly Stevenson's *annus mirabilis*, for between January and May that year he wrote another masterpiece. Serialised in May in *Young Folks* and published in book form in July, *Kidnapped* was later hailed by Henry James – who himself enjoyed a wondrous year in 1886 with the publication of *The Bostonians* and *The Princess Casamassima* – as the greatest of Louis's books. It contains some of Stevenson's most memorable scenes: the fight in the roundhouse, the flight in the heather, the encounter in 'Cluny's cage' and, most of all, the quarrel between David Balfour and Alan Breck Stewart. Although it does not probe so deeply into the nature of duality as *Jekyll and Hyde* and yields fewer clues to the author's life, *Kidnapped* is far more satisfying as a novel, and is let down only by the 'framing action' with the wicked uncle at the beginning and end. If in *Jekyll and Hyde* Stevenson finally wove together all the philosophical threads of his mental life, in *Kidnapped* for the first time he managed wholly successfully to dovetail high adventure with deep psychology.

It is a commonplace of Stevenson criticism that David Balfour and Alan

Breck are two aspects of RLS himself: David the limited Lowlander RLS felt himself to be; Alan Breck the hero he would like to be. Like Whitman who contradicted himself because he contained multitudes, Stevenson also felt that the two halves of his own sensibility represented the gulf that separated the Scots of the cities and the Lowlands from their brethren in the Highlands. So David Balfour versus Alan Breck comes to symbolise the Covenanter tradition against the Jacobite, realism against romance, the Edinburgh of the Enlightenment against the old Scotia of the clans. Chesterton said that RLS was 'intellectually on the side of the Whigs and morally on the side of the Jacobites', to which Sidney Dark added the gloss: 'the artist in him was inevitably with Bonnie Prince Charlie, the Shorter Catechist was with the Covenanters'. David Balfour is a naturalistic hero, unlike Jim Hawkins who is a creature of fantasy; where young Jim could shoot and handle a schooner, David has never learned to use a sword. Yet beyond these 'naturalistic' features is a disturbing inertia or inaction, which Stevenson clearly sees as a Lowland trait; David reacts but never initiates action, and this lack of willed action RLS is inclined to attribute to the dead hand of Calvinism and the doctrine of predestination. The dilemmas of David represent the guilt and self-questionings of Louis, the feeling that scepticism was always another name for cowardice, and that Calvinism, the legitimating ideology of the Lowland bourgeoisie, represents, as he expressed it in his essay on John Knox:

> that passive obedience, that toleration of injustice and absurdity, that holding back of the hand from political affairs as from something unclean, which lost France, if we are to believe M.Michelet, for the Reformation; a spirit necessarily fatal in the long run to the existence of any sect that may profess it; a suicidal doctrine that survives among us to this day in narrow views of personal duty, and the low political morality of many virtuous men.[16]

Alan Breck is more complex: martial and courageous yet boastful and undependable, both a warrior and a fop. In one way the extreme of the masculine principle, as when he slaughters men in the roundhouse without compunction, he shows a feminine concern for his appearance and brushes his coat 'with such care and labour as I supposed to have been only usual with women'. The brilliance of the quarrel scene, which Henry James fastened on, is that David and Alan, as opposites, interpenetrate and show that in certain spheres – relating to life in the Highlands and Lowlands respectively – each is helpless without the other. Using his favourite device of ambivalence within an existing ambiguity, Stevenson shows both the strength of the bonds that mesh the pair *and* the crevasse that divides them.

Louis was well pleased with his creation and wrote to Gosse: 'It is my own favourite of my works, not for craftsmanship, but for the

human niceness in which I have been wanting hitherto.' Gosse agreed that
it was Louis's best work to date: 'Pages and pages might have come out of
some lost book of Smollett's. You are very close to the Smollett manner
sometimes, but better, because you have none of Smollett's violence. Your
eighteenth century is extraordinarily good.' Coming hard on the heels of the
Jekyll and Hyde sensation, which had been the subject of Sunday sermons in
London churches, *Kidnapped* drew the attention of heavyweight members of
the Victorian intellectual elite and firmly established RLS as a major British
literary figure. William Morris wrote to George Bernard Shaw in October 1886
as follows.

> I haven't written anything about Stevenson's books: I have read *Treasure Island*
> and *Kidnapt* [sic] and was much pleased by both: to be critical and disagreeable
> I thought that in the first I could see the influence of three books, in the first
> part *Lorna Doon* [sic], in the second *Arthur Gordon Pym* mingled with *Masterman
> Ready*, but I see no harm in that after all *Kidnapt* is a much more artistic book
> I think; the defects (to be again nasty) being that he has failed to interest one
> in the wicked uncle's scheme, and that the book doesn't end properly: however
> nobodies [sic] books do now-a-days. For the rest the book is full of admirable
> pictures: there is one particularly of when they are hiding on the big stone, and
> turn in with the valley solitary and make up with it full of soldiers – Item the
> cowardly revolutionist kinsman (James I think) touched me home.[17]

Kidnapped was particularly impressive, since it was written in extremely
difficult conditions. The first six months of 1886 found Louis ill most of
the time and, in addition, having to deal with his father who was rapidly
declining into senility. The year's correspondence is full of complaints:
'I am in bed again – bloodie jackery and be damned to it.' 'I have lost
my spectacles and write vaguely and with itching eyeballs.' He meant to
complete the adventures of David and Alan (finally achieved six years
later in *Catriona*) immediately, but lack of stamina forced him to hold
them over for a later sequel; he rationalised the delay by claiming that he
did not yet know how the public would receive *Kidnapped*. Meanwhile his
father snapped at his heels, becoming ever more tiresome as his mental
condition deteriorated. He asked his son to infuse some religion into the
book and meanwhile added a vintage sliver of criticism on *Jekyll and Hyde*:
'I confess I can make nothing of the said work however it seems to have
made its mark.' To humour his father, Louis took over a couple of his
minor suggestions for the plot, but as he worked away in the white heat
of inspiration, it cannot have helped him when the redoubtable Thomas
informed him with a whoop of triumph that he had detected a 'vulgarism'
when rereading *Travels with a Donkey*.[18]

The pressures were building on Thomas Stevenson, for his mind
was giving way just when his business affairs were beginning to falter.

Louis felt responsible for the ageing parent but got no help from Fanny, her oft-protested fondness for Thomas notwithstanding. When Louis, in the middle of writing *Kidnapped*, announced that something would have to be done for his father, Fanny's response was to decamp to Bath to consult specialists over her 'broken health'. The luckless Louis, who had previously been told by his wife that it would be fatal to stray outside the confines of Bournemouth, was, however, let off the leash for the purpose of accompanying Thomas to the baths at Matlock -a task Fanny was 'too ill' to accomplish. The weeks Louis spent with his father at Smedley's Hydropathic Institute in Matlock were a nightmare. They arrived in a dreadful Derbyshire spring snowstorm, and Louis was bored from the very first day: 'I have no plans,' he wrote to Fanny, 'but to keep my father in patience for as long as I can and then streak for home like a swallow.' Yet keeping his father 'in patience' was an ordeal, for in his dementia the old man was experiencing violent mood swings of a kind that turned him at times into an incarnation of Louis's diabolic creation: Louis complained to his mother about the futility of the sojourn at Matlock:

> My father, I am sorry to say, gave me a full dose of Hyde this morning. He began about breakfast as usual; and then to prove himself in the right that he did well to be angry, carried on a long time (obviously on purpose) about the moon. I was very severe with him, and refused to speak again till he was quiet; after which he admitted he had been silly; and yet when I, to let him down gently, took the thing humorously, he began to start it again. He is certainly hard to manage. I half thought he was looking worse; but I have applied to several people who do not think so ... the dose of Hyde at breakfast finished me (Jekyll has been in the ascendant till now).[19]

The depressing experience with his father at Matlock led Louis, once back in Bournemouth, to more gloomy and guilty introspection. Was he really a moral coward in taking on the 'easy' life of a writer and battening off his father? Louis tried to answer the question in two poems he wrote at this time about the Skerryvore Lighthouse; the last stanza of 'Skerryvore. The Parallel' is particularly striking:

> Say not of me that weakly I declined
> The labours of my sires, and fled the sea,
> The towers we founded and the lamps we lit,
> To play at home with paper like a child.
> But rather say: In the afternoon of time
> A strenuous family dusted from its hands
> The sand of granite, and beholding far
> Along the sounding coasts its pyramids
> And tall memorials catch the dying sun,
> Smiled well content, and to this childish task
> Around the fire addressed its evening hours.

In lighter vein Louis celebrated the acquisition of a butler – an attempt
to solve Fanny's continuing problems with female servants. To Colvin he
wrote: 'We have a butler! He doesn't buttle, but the point of the thing is the
style. When Fanny gardens, he stands over her and looks genteel. He opens
the door, and I am told waits at the table. Well, what's the odds. I shall have
it on my tomb – "He ran a butler".' Inspired by the humour of the situation,
Louis composed some more verses 'On Himself':

> He may have been this or that,
> A drunkard or a guttler;
> He may have been bald and fat –
> At least he kept a butler.
>
> He may have sprung from ill or well,
> From emperor or sutler;
> He may be burning now in Hell –
> On earth he kept a butler.[20]

Temporary respite from the cycle of illness and boredom in Bournemouth came in the summer of 1886, when Louis's physicians, alarmed
at the number of small haemorrhages earlier that year and the continual
'leaking' from his lungs, advised a change of climate. Ironically, under
pressure from Fanny, Louis had just turned down an excellent chance
of fresh foreign vistas. The American *Century Magazine* made a generous
offer for a travel book based on an expenses-paid cruise down the Rhone;
the book was to be illustrated by Will Low and as a third companion they
were to take the critic P.G.Hamerton. Louis was keen but Fanny argued
that France was hot and unhealthy in the summer. Having perforce turned
down that opportunity, Louis cast around for other opportunities. At one
time he and Fanny planned to take ship to Bordeaux and then cross the
Pyrenees to their old haunts on the Riviera, but Fanny intervened again,
to point out how strenuous such a trip would be. She also vetoed the idea
of Norway and when Louis in desperation talked of the Highlands as a
kind of accessible Scandinavia she wrote negatively to Mrs Sitwell: 'The
Highlands are suggested, but we are cut off from that refuge, as Louis's
father would instantly join us, which would kill Louis.'

Eventually Louis made his way to London, hoping Micawber-like that
something would turn up. He stayed with Colvin, dined out as much as
possible, thereby meeting Robert Browning and the painter Sir Edward
Burne-Jones, had his portrait painted by George Richmond, but declined
to visit Balliol College, Oxford, when invited, for fear of falling ill in the
'miasmic' climate of Oxford. Then Henley persuaded him to accompany him
to Paris, where he spent an enjoyable two weeks in August in the company
of Auguste Rodin; both men were flattered by each other's attentions, and

Louis planned to write an extended essay on the great sculptor. He began his championship of Rodin by writing to *The Times* to protest about their characterisation of Rodin as 'the Zola of sculpture'; Louis resented having his new friend's name bracketed with that of a novelist for whom he had scant respect. The fortnight in Paris did him good: he was alone, since Fanny had gone off on her own to spend time under Swedish doctors at a new-fangled sanatorium, and he returned to Skerryvore alone to find his valetudinarian wife still absent.[21]

If anything, Fanny's hypochondria worsened at Bournemouth, and the household at Skerryvore habitually presented a kind of musical chairs look, whereby the whole family was never well at the same time; as one rose from the sickbed, the other would dive into it; sometimes they would both be ill together and sometimes Valentine, too, would take a turn as an invalid (she suffered from jaundice in this period). Louis's letters to his parents gave all the appearance of continuous medical bulletins: 'Fanny (who is far from well) would do well to go to Bath'; 'We are all on the mend and mean soon to be quite well'; 'Today I am up but the Vandegrifter (that heraldic animal) still couchant'. Fanny continued to consult the *Lancet* and to embrace (temporarily) the latest would-be panacea: at one time in 1886 she opted for a Gallic 'holistic' interpretation of the body as governed by the liver; at another she opted for teetotalism as the solution; by autumn she was reduced to fulminations against Dr Mennell, whom she considered to have entrapped by his constant misdiagnosis not just herself and Louis but Bob, Henley and many of their other friends. At the same time she complained that she was being used as a buffer between Louis and his parents and was resentful that Louis's care for his father cut down on his work rate. The news from California that Virgil Williams had died led her to confide to his widow that she had had a premonition of this (naturally); it also sparked off a new hypochondriacal neurosis, this time to the effect that she was certain to suffer an early death from neuralgic rheumatism of the heart. Not surprisingly, the refreshing effect of Louis's Paris sojourn with Rodin did not last long in such an atmosphere; on a visit to Colvin in November 1886, he suffered another haemorrhage; Fanny had to hurry up from Bournemouth in company with Louis's regular physician Dr Scott.[22]

In the rare intervals when she was not bedridden, visiting sanatoria or consulting specialists, Fanny tried her hand at reviving *The Hanging Judge* – the play Louis and Henley had earlier laid aside as being unstageable – they were right, as it turned out. The reason she was so keen on the play was that Louis had written a defence of loyalty to one's married partner as the supreme value – beyond honour, truth, justice and virtue – and she was often to seek consolation in the words during the bitter quarrel with Henley in 1887. Justice Harlowe condemns a man to death unjustly in order to save his wife and rationalises his action thus: 'I will defend my wife, she is ill, her days are threatened; I will defend her. What do I care for laws? I love my wife! A beast – a senseless beast would do as I do; shall a man do less? Oh, this talk of crime and sin, right and wrong, what dross it is, what dust to any creature that lives!' Commitment to one's kin, *whatever moral laws they have transgressed* is the sign *par excellence* of the undercivilised human – it is after all peculiarly associated with *mafiosi* and exponents of the blood feud – and Fanny's endorsement of this posture provides powerful circumstantial backing for those who labelled her 'primitive'.[23]

Fanny was not the only member of the Osbourne clan to pile the stress on RLS. While Stevenson sometimes came close to nihilism, he was never cynical, but his stepson was seldom anything else. 'No man ever believed less in heroical good or bad than Lloyd Osbourne' is Professor Eigner's understated comment. By 1886 the eighteen-year old Lloyd was a tall, blond, blue-eyed young man, big-boned, with his mother's curly hair, but with a heart of ice. He began his adult life by thinking that study in Edinburgh would quickly win him a senior partnership in the Stevenson engineering firm, but soon realised that years of hard slog lay ahead of him; he therefore emulated his mother by claiming that he was 'too ill' to continue his studies. An important examination loomed at the end of 1885, but Lloyd claimed he was going blind, so could not sit the papers. It is true that Lloyd had always suffered from poor eyesight – Henry James noticed this on one of his visits to Skerryvore – but his was the selective myopia that was always aggravated by having to do a day's work. His future wife, Katharine, later testified that the period in Bournemouth was the one time when RLS actually lost his patience with the boy he normally spoiled outrageously. At first, he insisted that Lloyd take the exams, then backtracked under pressure from Fanny, but confessed to Maggie that he was sure he had made a mistake.[24]

The 'problem' with Lloyd's eyes (doubtless an inability to focus on engineering books) which led Fanny to express fears that he might eventually go blind soon cleared up when his mother suggested he go on a tour of the West Indies to recuperate – at RLS's expense, of course. Soon she was getting letters from Venezuela and the Windward and Leeward Islands, full of the joys of tropical living. By the spring of 1886 Lloyd was back in Bournemouth, having announced that his new career would be that of professional writer. Instead of sending the young upstart packing, Louis magnanimously took him under his wing and began to teach him some of the skills of his craft. The change in Louis's attitude was probably caused by a desire to escape Fanny's domination, but he himself scarcely penetrated his own motivation: he understood that there was a frustrated paternal urge in his 'present and crescent infatuation for the youth Lloyd ... a damn fine youth' but not the unwitting role of Fanny in making him seek other forms of bonding. Occasionally there were glimmerings of the truth, as when he wrote to

Thomas Stevenson: 'The Cassandra woman being fled I have been alone with Sam [i.e. Lloyd].' The entente between the two is puzzling: Lloyd was lazy, self-regarding, snobbish, venal, amoral and corrupt; even Fanny once conceded to Dora Williams that her son was 'something of a born prig'. It is said that every great man has a glaring blind spot and in Stevenson's case it was Lloyd Osbourne. Even with Fanny he sometimes saw the harsh truth, but with Lloyd, until the very end, almost never. The Osbourne family had a gift for condemnatory phraseology which we can now read as dramatic irony, so that Lloyd's jealousy that anyone other than himself or his family should ever benefit from Louis's generosity sounds to present-day ears like a famous self-indictment: 'He often championed people who were not worth championing, impulsively believing in them and getting himself, in consequence, in a false position. He was unduly quick to accept responsibilities or tasks that soon grew extremely irksome, and which, with a moment's reflection, might easily have been avoided. He gave away money with a royal hand, and often to arrant impostors.'[25]

In his memoirs Lloyd Osbourne makes no mention of the circumstances in which he abandoned his studies but merely states that he returned to Skerryvore to write 'after college', as if RLS had been pressing him to do so. He does, however, concede his dismay at finding that Stevenson had 'got religion' – or rather that he had temporarily embraced a Tolstoyan version of Christianity, based on the simple morality of the law of love and the Sermon on the Mount. The cynical Lloyd, who had so resented attending Sunday services in Edinburgh with the elder Stevensons, blenched as Louis repeated to him the Tolstoyan dictum: 'Do nothing to increase the area of suffering, and in time all suffering will disappear.' This was not at all what Lloyd wanted to hear: he did not care who suffered as long as he was not required to lift a hand or do anything other than what was occasioned by the self-indulgent whim of the moment.

However, he was forced to tread carefully, for even as Louis read him another homily, his putative escape route was cut off. His father, Sam, had been to England twice during 1884–86, on trips where he had 'access' to his son, much to Fanny's disgust and annoyance (she claimed Sam 'vulgarized' the boy), but the situation suited Lloyd as he could play one parent off against another and thus eventually get his own way. Suddenly the ground was cut from under his feet. Sam, who had disappeared so mysteriously fifteen years before while 'fighting Indians', now vanished for good, complete with the pile of clothing abandoned on the beach (in the manner of Sergeant Troy or John Stonehouse). A popular theory was that he had committed suicide or been the victim of gang warfare in San Francisco's waterfront area, but he was later definitely sighted in South Africa. Fanny and Louis knew the truth: Fanny, when later told that he was alive, replied impatiently that she wanted to hear nothing about him; while Louis felt honour bound· to settle some of the more embarrassing debts Osbourne had left behind, including a bill for 450 francs left unpaid by 'that really disgusting person' (Louis's phrase) at the hotel at Grez in 1876. Almost certainly, Sam Osbourne had decamped with a younger woman, as was his wont. His wife 'Paulie' was left devastated, destitute and in debt. Lloyd for his part now shut his father out of his life, dropped his given name of Samuel, and swung decisively into Louis's orbit; Fanny told Dora Williams: 'the thought of his father is a nightmare horror to him.'[26]

During the first six months of 1887 Louis was increasingly depressed and ill. Confined in Bournemouth, by now he was sometimes deprived also of his wife's company at night, since she found it difficult to sleep unless she was alone: 'Dear fellow,' he wrote to her while she was away at Bath, 'I am just the reverse of you, and sleep better when I am with you.' He could barely raise a smile at the old ribaldries from Simpson, as when 'the Bart' informed him from Edinburgh: 'There is a young girl staying here (Florence Fitzgerald) who has an insatiable appetite for young men.' When J.A.Symonds visited the Stevensons at Skerryvore early in 1887 during one of his brief truancies from the icy cage of Davos, he wrote to Horatio Brown that RLS had 'gone downhill terribly'.[27]

The worst of all Louis's problems was his father – both his declining mental health and the alarming downward spiral in the Stevenson family business, whose limbs were beginning to be torn apart by the jackals as the old lion started to fail. As soon as it became clear that Thomas no longer had a clear memory for past events, his brother David Stevenson, with the help and connivance of James Dick, Thomas's head clerk, put in a bid for part of the family fortunes on the basis of 'verbal commitments' made by the ailing patriarch. Since his mother became increasingly hysterical as Thomas Stevenson fell apart, Louis suggested that his parents rent a house in Bournemouth for the winter of 1886–87 so that he could be near them; meanwhile he bent all his energies (in vain) to try to get him a knighthood. By the New Year of 1887, Thomas Stevenson's calamitous mental collapse could no longer be disguised, and Louis wrote of him: 'Very changeable; at times he seems only a slow, quiet edition of himself; again, he will be heavy and blank; but never so violent as last spring; and therefore, to my mind, better on the whole.' Maggie's experience was the worst, as her husband kept her awake at night to share his relentless depression; one night they finally both fell asleep but within minutes he awoke her to say: 'My dear, the end is now come; I have lost the power of speech.'[28]

Perhaps an unconscious wish for extinction, to be rid of the burden of an insane father, a hysterical mother, a neurotic wife and a feckless *fainéant* stepson, underlay Louis's most dramatic bid to escape from his prison at Skerryvore. The quixotic streak in his personality that had led him to support the Boers during the war of 1880–81, Gordon during the Khartoum crisis of 1884–85, and which would be much in evidence during his later years, erupted in the form of a suicidal plan to defy the Irish nationalists. RLS had a history of anti-Irish sentiment, from his vehement denunciation of the Fenians to his vociferous opposition to Gladstone's 1886 Home Rule Bill, and now he found a cause that expressed both his contempt for Irish independence and his desire for martyrdom. During the Land League agitation of the 1880s a Protestant farmer named Curtin had been killed, plus a member of the crowd that had been mobbing him. The Land League in retaliation then mobilised its favourite weapon of boycott; the British press, as ever when faced with Irish questions, left logic and reason behind and concentrated on the emotive issue of the plight of Curtin's surviving wife and daughters. When Stevenson's blood was up, his critical faculties tended to desert him, and so it was on this occasion. To the horror of Fanny, and even more of Lloyd, who never did a selfless deed in his life, Louis now proposed that the entire household be transferred lock, stock and barrel from the ease of Skerryvore to the turbulence of the boycotted Curtin farm in Ireland; there Louis intended to stay with his family, until the Land Leaguers either called off their boycott or else slaughtered him and his family.

The Stevenson biographer is fortunate to have a lengthy apologia from Louis on this hair-brained scheme, which he confided to Anne Jenkin; as a result of writing her husband's biography, Louis was once again on terms of the old intimacy with her and indeed at this stage of his life she was far more of a confidante to him than the hypochondriacal and often absent Fanny.

My work can be done anywhere; hence I can take up without loss a backgoing Irish farm; ... writers are so much in the public eye, that a writer being murdered would ... throw a bull's eye light upon this cowardly business ... I am not unknown in the States, from which come the funds that pay for these brutalities ... *Nobody else is taking up this obvious and crying duty* ... You will not even be murdered, the climate will miserably kill you ... Well, what then? ... the purpose is to brave crime ... I am married. 'I have married a wife.' I seem to have heard it before ... My wife has had a mean life[1] loves me[2] could not bear to lose me[3]. . . But what does she love me for? ... she must lose me soon or late. And after all, because we run this risk, it does not follow we should fail ... and I not taken with the hope of excitement? I was at first. I am not much now. I see what a dreary, friendless, miserable, God-forsaken business it will be ... am I not taken with a notion of glory? I daresay I am. Yet I see quite clearly how all points to nothing coming, to a quite inglorious death by disease and from the lack of attendance; or even if I should be knocked on the head as these poor Irish promise, how little anyone will care ... I do not love this health-tending, house-keeping life of mine ... The cause of England in Ireland is not worth supporting ... I am not supporting that. Home Rule, if you like ... populations should not be taught to gain public end by private crime ... for all men to bow before a threat of crime is to loosen and degrade beyond redemption the whole fabric of men's decency.[29]

There is no reason to think that Stevenson was anything other than in deadly earnest about this scheme. It was now mid-April 1887. Despite all their scheming, Fanny and Lloyd seemed bound for the burning fiery furnace. Desperately Fanny improvised, urging first that honour (that quality unknown to the Osbournes) demanded the completion of the Fleeming Jenkin book. RLS tore through that, but just as the hour of doom seemed about to strike, Fortune came to Fanny's aid. Thomas Stevenson, who had decamped to his beloved Edinburgh in April when he sensed his imminent death, suddenly grew much worse, so that it was obvious his end could not be long delayed. Louis and Fanny sped up to Edinburgh to be with him.

The telegram summoning them to the deathbed arrived on 7 May. By that evening they were in Edinburgh, but Thomas Stevenson died next day without being lucid enough to recognise his son. Louis was too ill to attend the funeral at New Carlton Burial Ground – in the spring of 1887 he was suffering from jaundice as well as attacks of 'bluidy Jack' – and was reduced to welcoming the mourners at Heriot Row, but he wrote a poem, 'The Last Sight', which has sometimes been cited as definitive evidence of egocentricity. He relates that at the deathbed someone asked his father to look up as his son was present; in a Poe-like cadence he tells the result:

And the dread changeling gazed on me in vain.

How much guilt Louis felt about his father's death is uncertain, though he told Mrs Sitwell that the loss of Thomas affected him deeply: 'I feel it more than I can say: every day more.' His most considered response was in a letter to Colvin in June:

About the death, I have long hesitated, I was long before I could tell my mind; and now I know it, and can but say that I am glad. If we could have had my father, that would have been a different thing. But to keep that changeling – suffering changeling – any longer, could better none and nothing. Now he rests; it is more significant, it is more like himself. He will begin to return to us in the course of time, as he was and as we loved him.

My favourite words in literature, my favourite scene – 'O let him pass,' Kent and Lear – was played for me here in the first moment of my return. I believe Shakespeare saw it with his own father. I had no words; but it was shocking to see. He died on his feet, you know; was on his feet the last day, knowing nobody – still he would be up. This was his constant wish; also that he might smoke a pipe on his last day.

RLS's ambivalence about his father persisted. He claimed to want to write more about him, but when a firm of Edinburgh publishers approached him in May 1888 about writing an official biography, he declined. But he was right about his father 'returning' to him. In the last year of his life he wrote to Adelaide Boodle: 'He now haunts me, strangely enough, in two guises: as a man of fifty, lying on a hillside and carving mottoes on a stick, strong and well; and as a younger man, running down the sands into the sea near North Berwick, myself – aetat 11 – somewhat horrified at finding him so beautiful when stripped.'[30]

There followed the predictable family wranglings before Thomas's will could be probated. It now transpired that the lawyer who drew up the will had mismanaged things so that at first it looked as though the Church of Scotland might walk off with the whole estate, in accordance with Thomas's wishes in an earlier will, until a codicil was discovered. It took a year for all arrangements to be finalised, but the immediate effect of the legacy was that Louis received £3,000, as promised in his mother's marriage settlement. The codicil allowed Maggie to have a further £2,000 outright and income for life from an estate of £26,000; thereafter the inheritance was to pass to Louis, then Fanny, then Lloyd. Thomas also enjoined his son to give financial help to Bob and to Katharine de Mattos, if ever they were in financial need.[31]

Louis now had the financial freedom he wanted and the ability to go anywhere in the world. It is more than a little suspicious that, immediately after Thomas's death, Louis's physicians ordered him to a hot, dry climate – Colorado or New Mexico was suggested – and there is circumstantial evidence that Louis 'set up' the medical report. Lloyd Osbourne reported his stepfather's jubilation when he announced the 'necessity' of quitting England: he was 'cheerful, even jubilant . . . He was plainly glad to be off, and the sooner the better.' His first step was to escape from Skerryvore: it was suggested that Maggie should sell the house at Heriot Row and move down to live in Skerryvore, while Louis and Fanny went globetrotting. Fanny realised that she had temporarily lost the struggle for power, but doubtless consoled herself with the thought that at last she had effectively secured the Stevenson fortune and that Louis would at least be far from the grip of Henley, Gosse, Bob or Baxter. One obvious ploy – to claim that she was too ill to travel – had been preempted by Maggie's brother, Dr Balfour, during the three weeks in May she and Louis stayed in Edinburgh to console the grieving widow. Balfour informed her that all the medical advice she had received to date was wrong, with the single exception of the physician who recommended the waters at Aix. Fanny was unaware of the ironical subtext, for the hidden meaning of Balfour's advice was that all her maladies were psychosomatic – as evinced by the harmless prescription of the baths at Aix as the only 'right' treatment. Fanny had little room in which to manoeuvre, so had to acquiesce in Louis's plans. Nevertheless, some pique is evident in her correspondence with friends: 'Louis is wild to start for America at once, which seems madness to me.' John Addington Symonds confirmed that Fanny prepared to pack for a further trip in her native land with a heavy heart: 'Mrs Stevenson wrote to me on their last day in London with really heavy accents of discouragement about their journeys, and my heart has often throbbed in imitation of the screw which was propelling them across the Atlantic.'[32]

Last-minute preparations now proceeded for the transatlantic crossing; passages were booked on the SS *Ludgate Hill*, London to New York. Sensing his mother's loneliness, Louis persuaded a reluctant Maggie to accompany them as far as Colorado, after which she could return to Skerryvore; this then involved tedious arrangements for the interim rental of the Bournemouth house. It seems that Fanny was not at her best during these last weeks in England, for on the very last evening in Bournemouth (19 August) she had a row with Colvin, who was helping them. Louis wrote hurriedly to Colvin to apologise for Fanny's 'meddling; wherein I cannot excuse her . . . I wish we could have left with a godspeed; but if that may not be, I know you will forgive us before long.' Another old Fanny enemy met them in London on the 20th. Gosse, who never saw RLS again, was surprised to find him stylishly dressed 'instead of looking like a Lascar out of employment, as he generally does'. From his lodgings in Finsbury Louis sent his last instructions to Baxter, who would act as his legal agent: these included an allowance of £40 a year payable quarterly to Bob who, according to Will Low, was starting to sink into middle age and was no longer the flamboyant character of even a few years earlier. Then, on 21 August, the Stevenson party – Louis, Fanny, Maggie, Lloyd and Valentine – made its way to the Royal Albert Docks for the short crossing to Le Havre, where the *Ludgate Hill* would take on extra passengers and freight before clearing for New York. In their cabin they found a crate of champagne sent as a farewell present by Henry James: 'they are a romantic lot – and I delight in them', the Master told Colvin. It was a symbolic gift, for Louis was now about to abandon the polite society of England for the rough life of the frontier and the ocean. It was not just in literature that he consistently moved in the opposite direction from his greatest admirer.[33]

The Closing of the Door 1887–88

The crossing of the Atlantic was not short on drama. First, at Le Havre, the Stevensons learned that the *Ludgate Hill* was very far from a cruise liner: the ship took on a consignment of apes for North American zoos and a large number of horses. Then, the normally easy August ocean crossing to New York turned into something like the dreaded North Atlantic passage in winter, with gales, squalls and high seas all the way, to the point where the captain altered course northward to the Newfoundland banks in an effort to avoid the track of the storm.

The Stevenson ménage reacted to all this along classically schizoid lines, so that the eleven-day voyage became almost a metaphor for the changing balance of the power between husband and wife. Fanny, at last given a valid reason for her illnesses, was, predictably, stricken with sea sickness, as were Valentine and Lloyd; Fanny found it particularly intolerable that while she writhed in her sickbed, the vessel pitching, rolling and yawing in forty-foot waves, she could see the melancholy faces of the French horses bobbing up and down past her stateroom window. Maggie, though, proved an outstanding sailor, while Louis was like a greedy boy let into a tuck shop: he developed an astonishing pair of sea legs and could be seen daily making his rounds, joking with the apes, dosing fellow passengers with his anti-seasickness 'remedy' – the case of champagne Henry James had sent him – and swapping naval lore with the officers. Of course he was pushing his luck too far, and went down with a heavy cold off Newfoundland, but his mind was already teeming with exotic plans. He and Fanny had planned to go to Algiers when they returned from America in 1880, yet never made the trip; the omens this time seemed better, and Louis was already pencilling in Japan as a possible destination; it was a country that had interested him ever since Taiso Masaki told him about Yoshida-Torajiro in 1878. Most of all, Louis exulted in the sheer, unwonted sensation of physical well-being. He wrote to Bob later: 'I was so happy on board that ship, I could not have believed it possible . . . I had literally forgotten what happiness was, and the full mind – full of external and physical things, not of cares and labours and not about a fellow's behaviour. My heart literally sang.' His mind turned to the prospect of further ocean cruising and to the restoration of long-forgotten physical skills for, as he told Walter Simpson: 'I have forgotten how to ride and how to skate; and I should not be the least surprised if I had forgotten how to swim.'[1]

Louis was unprepared for the warmth of his welcome in New York, where *Jekyll and Hyde* had made him famous, and for the pace of life in the New World. 'Nearly died of interviewers and visitors during twenty four hours in New York' was his cryptic comment later, as he reflected on the invasion by journalists of the suite at the Victoria Hotel reserved for him by his Boston admirers, the Fairchilds. The hectic pace had begun as soon as the *Ludgate Hill* anchored. Up the gangplank sprang his old friend, Will Low, with news that an eagerly awaited stage version of *Jekyll* was to open in Manhattan next week; Low was closely followed by E.L.Burlingame, editor of *Scribner's*, eager to close a deal before his rivals got to the famous author.

'America is . . : a fine place to eat in, and a great place for kindness; but, Lord, what a silly thing is popularity!' Louis wrote to Henry James. After twenty-four hours of reporters and editors, he could take no more and left hurriedly for Newport, Rhode Island, with Lloyd and Valentine, where they were to be the guests of the Fairchilds. He spent twelve days entranced by the 'fairyland' of Newport with 'one little rocky and pine-shaded cove after another, each with a house and boat at anchor'. The Fairchilds were easy-going hosts and did not mind that their distinguished visitor spent much of the time convalescent in bed.[2]

Back in New York, he heard from Fanny about the (successful) première of the T.R.Sullivan stage production of *Jekyll*, met the American artist J.W.Alexander, socialised with the Fairchilds, caroused with Will Low and posed for the celebrated sculptor Augustus Saint-Gaudens, who produced a medallion showing RLS in bed with his books. Bed was where he met most of his visitors from the world of publishing, including Richard Watson Gilder, whom Louis accused of being the selfsame man who had ignominiously kicked him out of the *Scribner's* office in an abortive visit during his first twenty-four hours in New York in August 1879. Most of Louis's time was spent trying to decide between the rival offers from Sam McClure of the *New York World*, who offered $10,000 a year for a weekly column from RLS, and E.L.Burlingame of *Scribner's*, who offered $3,500 for a series of twelve monthly essays on any subject of his choice. Though he did not make a final decision until he was domiciled at Saranac in the Adirondack Mountains, Louis opted for the nominally lower *Scribner's* offer, largely because Burlingame voluntarily offered back royalties on U.S. sales

of previous books – there was no international copyright agreement until
1890. Louis jokingly remarked that if things went on like this, he would
soon be a millionaire. It is certainly the case that in the U.S.A. he started
to earn sums undreamed of in Britain, even though the 'princely' amounts
paid to him were regarded as 'peanuts' by established American authors.[3]

Meanwhile Fanny and Lloyd were reconnoitring a suitable place to put
down semi-permanent roots. The original idea of going to Colorado had
been abandoned almost as soon as the Stevensons set foot on American
soil, ostensibly because of the high cost of living in the American West, but
really because Fanny feared that, at 5,000 feet, the Colorado resorts would
simply be the hated Davos writ large. At the beginning of October she and
Lloyd headed north, by river boat and train, to Loon Lake, then the northern
terminus of the New York state railway line. They pressed on another twenty
miles by buggy and team to Saranac Lake, 600 feet up in the Adirondack
wilderness, near the Canadian border. Here, at an isolated logging and
trapping village, Dr Edward Livingstone Trudeau, himself a consumptive,
had founded a sanatorium for tubercular patients in 1882. Fanny set about
looking for quarters and soon came to an agreement with a local guide,
huntsman and trapper named Baker to rent part of his house as separate
living quarters. Usually known as 'Baker's' the house was a crudely built
trapper's cottage largely on one floor, painted white, with green shutters,
red tiled roof and a large verandah. The section rented to the Stevensons was
separated from the Bakers' accommodation by firmly bolted double doors, so
that the entrance to the Stevenson quarters was through the kitchen; beyond
was a large sitting room with an open fireplace for log fires, a bedroom used
by Louis and Fanny, a small room used by RLS as a study, and another
small bedroom for Maggie, with two small 'servants' rooms' (occupied by
Lloyd and Valentine) upstairs in the one part of the house where it became
two-storied. Perched high on a forested ridge above the river, 'Baker's' was
only ten minutes walk away from the backwoods village of log cabins and
frame houses.

Fanny cabled for Louis and the others to join them, and they all
proceeded to camp out. It was Silverado on a larger scale: drinking water
had to be fetched from a spring and water for washing brought up from
the river by their landlord. The kitchen lacked teapots and coffee pots,
since the locals brewed both in saucepans, and egg-cups were unknown.
The Stevenson ménage settled into a spartan daily round. Louis and his
literary protégé, Lloyd, worked all morning, then the whole family lunched
at 12.30; afterwards they would take turns to drive out in the buckboard
which held just two people – and that with difficulty. Louis liked to take
long solitary walks in the woods, savouring the fall colours, but hated meeting
any of the locals; they sensed this, and it made him an unpopular figure in
Saranac.[4]

Dr Ruedi of Davos could have told his colleague at Saranac that RLS would not make an easy patient. Stevenson refused to follow the rigid regime laid down by Trudeau and at a personal level there was little rapport: Trudeau deplored his patient's smoking, while Louis, who had a lifelong horror of cruelty to animals, detested Trudeau's laboratory experiments with guinea pigs, when he would infect them with tubercular bacilli. Neither man appreciated just how big a figure the other was in his chosen field; the absence of personal chemistry was compounded by a prima donna-ish attitude on both sides; soon they were arguing about such trivia as the relative merits of American and European railway systems. People either loved or loathed RLS and he worked in much the same way: consummately charming when he took to someone, almost boorishly insulting if he did not. So it was with Trudeau, and Stevenson made plain his contempt in words that a century before would have resulted in an invitation to pistols at dawn: 'Your light may be very bright to you, but to me it smells of oil like the devil,' However, Trudeau's diagnosis – that RLS was a genuine consumptive whose tuberculosis was in remission – is particularly valuable in view of the still unfinished controversy about the exact nature of his pulmonary ailments, while RLS's refusal to fish or hunt, on grounds of cruelty to animals, gives us an important clue to why he was not popular with the locals.[5]

After the differential response to the sea crossing, it was almost predictable that Maggie would make a much better fist of adjusting to the rough conditions of life at Saranac than Fanny. The myth of Fanny as indefatigable nurse and sturdy pioneer woman is bolstered by those uncritical readers of the evidence who take the scene of Louis's arrival in Saranac – when he and Maggie found Fanny in the kitchen in petticoat and apron cooking dinner – as typical. In fact, the real pioneer woman in the Adirondacks was the hitherto protected and cosseted Margaret Balfour Stevenson. Will Low marvelled at her unfailing courage and cheerfulness, her omnipresent starched widow's cap, the way she was pleased with everything American: 'She had a keen sense of humour, and her conversation, without any pretension of brilliancy, for one of her most charming traits was a modest assumption of surprise that she should be the mother of so brilliant a son, was always interesting.' Maggie took it well when she complained of the draughts in the cottage and asked for a footstool, only to hear her son say that in his house there would be no fripperies and she could make do with a log. She would have Valentine light her fire at half past six in the morning, then stay in the warm, reading and writing letters; rather than disturb Louis and the other 'worker', Lloyd, she used to squeeze out of the house by one of its tiny windows.

Fanny, however, quickly found conditions at Saranac intolerable, became 'ill' and was absent for long periods. Those who still foster the myth of

Fanny as devoted nurse and lover need to explain why, in the American period of 1887–88, she was almost never at her husband's side. While Louis was in Newport in September, she was in New York; when he was in New York in October, she was in Saranac. After the briefest of settling-in periods, she departed for New York, to consult doctors, or so she said; but in reality she spent time in Philadelphia interviewing Walt Whitman and then in New York with Burlingame arranging for the appearance of her ill-fated short story, 'The Nixie', in the winter edition of *Scribner's*. When she returned to Saranac, she at once took to her bed, leaving the workers of the house, RLS and Lloyd, to do the household chores. Once on her feet again, she departed to visit her family in Indiana – Maggie meanwhile headed for the border to view the Niagara Falls – once again leaving Louis virtually alone. By the time Fanny returned to Saranac, it was the dead centre of a bitterly cold winter, so she departed at once for Montreal to purchase warm winter clothing for the family. There followed another period of absence in New York and then, as soon as conditions again made travel practicable, she was off again, California-bound, with lengthy and leisurely stops to visit her relations in Indianapolis and Danville, Indiana.[6]

From his correspondence, especially that part later ignored or censored by Colvin, emerge clear signs of frustration and impatience with his wife's behaviour on Louis's part. 'My wife again suffers in high and cold places; I again profit,' he wrote, significantly to Symonds, for Symonds knew perfectly well that if Stevenson had persisted with Davos he would never have suffered the dreadful haemorrhages of Hyères and Bournemouth; he also knew that the main objection to Davos had come from Fanny. To Adelaide Boodle he wrote two months later (in December): 'My wife is no great shakes; the place does not suit her – it is my private opinion that no place does – and she is now away down to New York for a change, which (as Lloyd is in Boston) leaves my mother and me and Valentine alone in our wind-beleaguered hill-top hat-box of a house.' In his letters to Fanny during her frequent absences, Louis's tone is that of resigned compassion, though one senses an undercurrent of irritation: 'Poor creature, this is to let you know that we have taken the bull by the horns and ordered from New York, all out of our own heads, the following articles: coffee, bacco box marked with my name, beer, list for windows, cheese, crackers, wine, coffee-pot and coffee-mill'; 'My dearest little man, I am just in bed, not quite A, and the lad is playing the devil in the next appartment [sic] which confuses me.' But sometimes the neglect of traditional wifely duties towards an invalid breadwinner, while she postured in New York with Whitman and Burlingame, led Louis to express more overt irritation, as when he explained to his patrons the Fairchilds that Fanny had not found the time to write them basic thank-you letters: 'My wife is incapable of the slightest exercise of any human art'; 'My wife cannot sleep at night, nor yet can she pluck up courage to write to you herself.'[7]

Even visitors were normally possible at Saranac only when Cerberus had been given the sop of travel. The Fairchilds came on a private visit but Fanny suspected them of having colds; after all the money and hospitality she had received from them, Fanny actually insisted they show their clean handkerchiefs through the window before she would admit them. Selectively read, all this concern for colds squares with the legend of Fanny as devoted nurse, but it is clear that it was herself, not her husband she was concerned for; otherwise why would she decamp for such long periods and then take to her bed on her return, leaving 'the patient on whom she lavished so much care' to do the washing up?

For the most part Louis had to make do with new friends by correspondence. One he liked was Owen Wister, later the author of *The Virginian*, to whom he had been introduced by Henry James. In 1887–88 Louis was much preoccupied with dreams – first in October when he wrote 'The Lantern Bearers' and 'A Chapter on Dreams', and in the New Year when he was hard at work on *The Master of Ballantrae* – and he liked to confide his oneiric theories to Wister, as when he wrote on the sensation of time: 'I never knew time really to elapse in dreams ... dreams are merely novels, they are made with every sort of literary trick; and a word stands for a year, if it is the right year.'[8]

On the rare occasions when Fanny was at home and healthy, she pestered RLS for help with revisions to *The Hanging Judge* – a continuing obsession – and browbeat him into insisting on publication of the dreadful *The Wrong Box*, supposedly a collaboration between Louis and Lloyd but really the Osbourne lad's virtually solo production. This attempt to make a comedy of errors out of a Victorian tontine and a misidentified corpse should never have seen the light of day – it is a truly calamitous apology for a novel – and it is worth asking why RLS was so insistent that it be published. It has been suggested that he wanted Lloyd as collaborator, as the young man was an American citizen and thus their joint works could not be pirated, but this hardly seems convincing, since Scribners had already more than reassured him on the pirating issue. The real reason for the publication of this wretched work, which could have done Stevenson's reputation lasting harm, was his fatherly concern for Lloyd and pressure from Fanny to make sure her beloved son succeeded in his chosen field. The Osbournes, both Fanny and Lloyd, and Belle, too, later, suffered from a well-known syndrome, whereby frequent contact with a genuine writer induces the feeling that 'anyone can do it', though the later careers of these self-styled authors adequately exposed the fallacy in their thinking.

The development of *The Wrong Box* was reported by Louis in a number of letters. To Henley he wrote that the tale was 'quite incredibly silly, and in parts (it seems to me) pretty humorous'. To Fanny he wrote: 'I quite chortle over some of it. Some of it, of course, is incredibly bad.' It was read aloud to the family at night and the proud but myopic mother thought it a creditable achievement for someone of nineteen. The professionals did not share her confidence. On one of his business trips to Saranac, Burlingame read it and rejected it out of hand for *Scribner's*. Sam McClure, however, touched RLS on the raw by giving sage advice. 'I read it and thought it a good story for a young man to have written; but I told Stevenson that I doubted the wisdom of his putting his name to it as a joint author. This annoyed him and he afterwards wrote me that he couldn't take advice about such matters.'

All true Stevenson lovers must agree with McClure that it was a great pity he ever saw fit to put his name on the title page – which was assuredly the only reason the work was ever published. Internal evidence shows no more than a page or so of RLS: there is the occasional striking phrase which clearly comes from him rather than Lloyd – 'That seat of Toryism, that cradle of Puseyism, that home of the inexact and the effete – Oxford'; 'nothing like a little judicious levity' – but most of the book gives comfort to the RLS-baiters who claim that he was always at heart a dilettante, and that beneath the concern for economy and fine style was an indifferent technician and a mediocre craftsman of story structure. The self-immolating Stevenson was usually reserved for intimate letters or private life but here it is on display in novel form.[9]

However, *The Wrong Box* formed a very small part of the complex business relationships RLS had with his American publishers – never so intense again as he was never again so accessible. Stevenson never had much of a head for business and, having accepted $8,000 from McClure for the serial rights to his next novel, found himself having to write a grovelling letter of apology to him, explaining that *Scribner's* already had the rights. McClure also bought *The Black Arrow* for American syndication but had to wait for Fanny's return from a jaunt before Louis could close the deal. Fanny notoriously disliked *The Black Arrow* and in dedicating the American edition to her Louis used an ironical tone which hints at his resentment of her self-assigned role as censor and critic on the hearth – a role in which she had been encouraged by Thomas Stevenson, whose populist tastes she shared:

> No one knows but myself what I have suffered, nor what my books have gained, by your unsleeping watchfulness and admirable pertinacity. And now here is a volume that goes into the world and lacks your *imprimatur*; a strange thing in our joint lives; and the reason of it stranger still! I have watched with interest, with pain, and at length with amusement, your unavailing attempts to peruse *The Black Arrow*; I think I should lack humour indeed if I let the occasion slip and did not place your name in the fly-leaf of the only book of mine that you have never read – and never will read.[10]

Occasionally Louis, as well as his wife, felt the need to escape the isolation of Saranac. In December 1887 he was briefly back in New York City again, and it was then that Saint-Gaudens introduced him to his hero, General Sherman. Three years from his death, the victor of Atlanta was already failing fast and at first took Stevenson for 'one of my boys'; when the mistake was rectified, a stimulating discussion on military tactics ensued, in which the well-read Louis more than held his own. Both men took away pleasant memories. RLS, who had always hero-worshipped soldiers, from Wellington to Gordon, thrilled to the experience of meeting a real-life hero of the Civil War, and told Will Low: 'It was the next thing to seeing Wellington, and I dare say that the Iron Duke would not have been half so human.' Sherman told Saint-Gaudens with a smile: 'He [RLS] is a fine old dog with enough of the Old Adam in him to suit even your Scotch taste.'[11]

As the New Year approached at Saranac, there were few occasions for travel, for the Stevensons were snowed in. Inspired by the similarity of the scenery to the Highlands, Louis began a tale of the 1745 rising that eventually became *The Master of Ballantrae*. There was much that was Scottish about the Adirondacks, from the venison and salmon trout the Stevensons cooked for dinner to the roaming cows that woke Louis in the morning by butting the wooden walls of the cottage; it was true that Saranac did not have the charm of Davos but Louis's health held up amazingly well – after leaving Bournemouth he chalked up a stretch of fifteen months without haemorrhage – and he fell ravenously on his food whenever he came in from the cold. Winter in the Adirondacks was beyond anything he had experienced yet, even in Davos. By December the thermometer was at twenty-five below zero; the walls of the cottage snapped and cracked as they expanded and contracted with the ice; Louis had frostbite on his ears; Valentine found one morning that the handkerchief under her pillow had frozen into a ball of ice; the kitchen floor, when washed with hot water, immediately became a skating-rink. Fanny came down from Montreal with the winter equipment, not a moment too soon, and Louis donned his thick buffalo-skin coat, Indian boots and astrakhan hat that made him look like an early Polar explorer. By the end of January 1888 the temperature had plummeted to forty below zero; whenever they ventured out in the buckboard they drove with three pairs of gloves and with hot soapstones to warm the feet and hands. It was so cold that if you touched metal your flesh stuck; one morning Louis's buffalo coat was stuck frozen to the kitchen floor while Valentine got her dress wet from the kitchen floor and walked around all day with a hem as heavy as chainmail. Louis arranged his routine around the winter conditions: he worked in the morning, drove, walked or skated after lunch and then rested until dinner at six, after which there was a short period of reading aloud or cards around the fire before the entire household retired early to bed with their soap-stones.

Most of the winter Louis worked away on what would be his finest complete work, *The Master of Ballantrae*. There was talk of another collaboration with Lloyd, on a novel about the Indian Mutiny, but this came to nothing. He corresponded at length with Henry James on the novel and on James's own work, read widely, and was among the first to spot George Bernard Shaw as a talent to note. Commenting to William Archer, who had sent him Shaw's novel *Cashel Byron's Profession*, he said how greatly he was impressed: 'It is *horrid fun*. All I ask is more of it . . . Tell Shaw to hurry up: I want another . . . (I say, Archer, my God, what women!)' And since it was now clear that mountain air would never suit Fanny, he persuaded her to try another ocean cruise. Together they pored over maps and considered various possibilities: Bermuda and the eastern seaboard, the Aegean, the Azores, the Indian Ocean, the Pacific. Fanny always loathed the sea, but by her constant 'altitude sickness' in mountain country she had effectively painted herself into a corner, since Louis, with his newfound financial independence, would never again consent to a Bournemouth-like existence.

During the coldest weeks at Saranac Fanny sought refuge in her overheated imagination. She always claimed to be psychic and in the snows she saw a 'fetch' or double of Charles Baxter in a towering rage. Impressed, Louis made a note of the exact time and later checked with Baxter. He confirmed that he had been reading a Stevenson book and suddenly came on a character which he thought was an offensive caricature of himself, whereat he threw the book out of the window in a rage. The story would be more convincing if Richard Le Gallienne, who told it, had not added that the book was *The Wrong Box*, thus destroying the point of the story, since that misbegotten novel was not published until the Stevensons were in the Pacific.[12]

Having spent two weeks away in Boston from 27 February–11 March, at the earliest possible moment Fanny escaped from Saranac west to California (she departed 31 March), calling first to see her mother again in Indianapolis. Louis confided to Coggie Ferrier: 'It is rather an anxiety to let her go alone; but the doctor simply forbids it in my case, and she is better anywhere than here – a bleak, blackguard, beggarly climate, of which I can say no good except that it suits me and some others of the same or similar persuasions whom (by all rights) it ought to kill.' He confessed himself in reasonable spirits: he was making more money than ever and looking forward to hiring a yacht for a cruise, but there was still an undertow of depression, though he was 'compared with last year in Bournemouth an angel of joy'. His immediate anxiety was one he had confessed to one of his correspondents, Miss Monroe, in December:

I myself dread, worse than almost any other imaginable peril, that miraculous and really insane invention, the American railroad car. Heaven help the man – may I add the woman – that sets foot in one. Ah, if it were only an ocean to cross, it would be a matter of small thought to me – and great pleasure. But the railroad car – every man has his weak point; and I fear the railroad car as abjectly as I do an earwig, and, on the whole, on better grounds.[13]

By mid-April Fanny was in California where she met her daughter Belle for the first time in nearly eight years. Belle was still crying poverty even though she and Joe Strong had insinuated themselves into the royal set at Honolulu, and to reinforce her 'penury' took Fanny to lodge with her in a suite of dingy rooms in a broken down lodging house. With her was her seven-year old son Austin, whom Fanny found shy, delicate and very ugly. An early visitor was Sam Osbourne's wife, Paulie, who arrived in a distraught state and, according to Fanny, fell on her knees in tears and exclaimed: 'You were right about that man and I was wrong.' The realisation of her own privilege led Fanny to one of her rare overt tributes to her husband: 'Imagine how humble I felt in my good fortune when I sat side by side with that poor woman whose case might have been mine – but for you.'

The Saranac household, meanwhile, finally moved out of winter quarters on 13 April. They went first to New York city, where Louis took a great liking to Washington Square – ironically the scene of a Henry James novel he particularly disliked. He liked to sit on a bench under the trees and once spent an entire afternoon there with Mark Twain, whose *Huckleberry Finn* he so much admired. Another favourite haunt was the Century Association near Union Square, a club much like the Garrick, where RLS added the American landscape and ecclesiastical painter, John La Farge, to the long list of artists and sculptors of his acquaintance. When Louis got bored with New York – which was soon – Will Low arranged transport for the Stevenson party over the Hudson to new lodgings at a little white-painted colonial inn on the Manasquan river in New Jersey.[14]

It was there that Louis sank to his lowest level since 1875, when he had contemplated suicide over Fanny Sitwell. The cause this time was, of course, the second Fanny. First came news from California that she was ill with a growth in her throat – suspected cancer – which might have to be operated on; needless to say, this was yet another episode in the career of the *malade imaginaire*. Far more seriously, came an irreparable quarrel with Henley, again about his wife. In retrospect, it is surprising that the breach over Fanny took eight years to develop, for there had been bad blood since the very first meeting. But by early 1888, Henley was severely depressed and he made the mistake of letting his guard drop and thus showing the depth of his hatred of 'that woman'.

Of the many straws in the wind, two stand out as of especial significance. First, dramatic irony – that continuing motif in RLS's life, arising from his peculiar taste for playing roles like the 'Thomson and Johnston' one. In 1882, Louis wrote to Katharine de Mattos, and at the end of a letter in which he complained about Fanny's being permanently and mysteriously ill, he wound up thus: 'I hope you know that we both loathe, deprecate, detest and sicken at the thought of you. Never lose sight of that. Again assuring you of my uncontrollable disgust. Believe me, Yours abhorrently.' Second is an indication of Henley's subterranean jealousy of RLS, and his feeling that Louis was selfish – he had not put his back into their joint playwriting ventures – unjustly lucky in his commercial success, and generally overrated. In a letter to Baxter in April 1886 he wrote about his friend: 'He looks well, I think; but he's more God-Almightified than I quite like. I suppose it's all right if you're a man of genius; but I can't stomach it all the same.'[15]

Depressed by many aspects of his family life and the continuing shortage of money, Henley opened the March 1888 issue of *Scribner's* to find a short story, 'The Nixie' by Fanny Vandegrift Stevenson. Now, in 1887, Fanny and Louis had been present at Henley's house in Shepherd's Bush when Katharine de Mattos spoke of a story she had been working on, in which a poetic young man meets a young girl on a train and eventually discovers she has escaped from a lunatic asylum. Fanny, used to making suggestions when no one wanted them, ventured the notion of making the young woman a nixie or water sprite and offered to collaborate with Katharine, who politely declined the offer. Since the idea did not seem immediately saleable, Fanny asked if she could take over the idea and rewrite it in her own way. Katharine reluctantly acquiesced, but in such a way that anyone used to reading the English cultural runes would immediately have construed her 'consent' as refusal. The rougher-hewn Fanny set to work to refashion the tale, despite her husband's warning to take the matter no further. Whatever possessed her to act in this way? Her sole reputable biographer sums up judiciously: 'Her feeble little tale had been accepted only because she was Mrs R.L.S ... Fanny's impulse was most probably sheer greed for recognition. She could never give up her hankering to be a literary lady in her own right.'[16]

All the subsequent trouble would have been avoided if Fanny had shared the 'by-line' with Katharine de Mattos and, preferably, given her the fee, as she was now rich while Katharine was poor. Seeing a fairly blatant act of plagiarism, Henley swooped. At last he had the pretext he needed for putting in her place this 'semi-educated woman' with her 'presumption and arrogance', her overweening conceit that forced RLS to defer to her literary judgement while he ignored that of his intellectual and creative peers, her neurotic behaviour that resulted in her invalid husband having to do household chores while she lolled in bed. He wrote to Louis as follows:

Dear Boy, If you will wash dishes and haunt back-kitchens in the lovely climate of the Eastern States, you must put up with the consequences ... I am out of key today. The Spring, sir, is not what it used to be ... *Enfin!* Life is uncommon like rot. *C'est convenu.* If it weren't that I am a sort of centre of strength for a number of feebler folk, I think I'd be shut of it dam soon ...

I read *The Nixie* with considerable amazement. It's Katharine's; surely it's Katharine's? There are even reminiscences of phrasery and imagery, parallel incidents – *que sais-je?* It is also better focused, no doubt; but I don't think it has lost as much (at least) as it has gained; and why there wasn't a double signature is what I've not been able to understand ...

Louis, dear lad, I am dam tired. The Chatelaine's away. The Spring is spring no more. I am thirty-nine this year. I am dam, dam tired. What I want is the wings of a dove – a soiled dove even! – that I might flee away and be at rest.

Don't show this to *anybody*, and when you write, don't do more than note it in a general way – By the time you *do* write, you will have forgotten all about it, no doubt. But if you haven't, deal vaguely with my malady. Why the devil do you go and bury yourself in that country of dollars and spew? ... However, I suppose you must be forgiven, for you have loved me much. Let us go on so to the end ... We have lived, we have loved, we have suffered; and the end is the best of all ... Forgive this babble, and take care of yourself and burn this letter. Your friend, W.E.H.[17]

Since this letter was the *casus belli*, it needs careful study. It is clear that the subtext, with its reference to washing dishes as well as to 'The Nixie', is an attack on the domineering Fanny. On the other hand, it is by no means so clear that the injunction to show no one the letter and to burn it relates to Fanny. Henley was well aware of the damage to one's reputation and earnings any suspicion of depressive illness might be, and it is unlikely, if his heart searchings had been about *Fanny alone*, that he would have provided her with such ammunition for a counterattack ('Henley wrote this while the balance of his mind was disturbed' etc.); nor would he have confided so deeply in RLS in the same letter, with his references to the Musketeers (with RLS as d'Artagnan, Baxter as Aramis and himself as Porthos). As Richard Aldington pointed out, the attack on Fanny takes up just six lines of a very long letter, and the mention of 'The Nixie' was as tactful as it well could be if the matter was to be mentioned at all. The most careful student of this entire incident, Edward H. Cohen, concludes that Henley's *accidie* constituted the main point of the letter.

A particular trigger for Henley's depression was the behaviour of his younger brother Edward, an actor who had toured with a recent financially disastrous 'road show' of *Deacon Brodie* in which Henley had invested money. Teddy gained notoriety through a bar-room brawl in Philadelphia, then came scrounging money off the Stevensons in New York while having the effrontery to stay in a more expensive hotel than any they could afford. RLS made very clear his distaste for Teddy: 'I have long groaned under this slavery to Teddy, a young man in whom I do not believe, and whom I much dislike . . . He let out to my wife he has been letting W.E. support his wife even during this campaign; and the drunken whoreson bugger and bully living himself in the best hotels, and smashing inoffensive strangers in the bar! It is all too sickening.' 1887–88 produced a litany of disasters for those close to RLS: Lloyd had his disappearing Sam, and Henley his dissolute Teddy, while even the staid Colvin had to report that his brother had gambled away the family funds, left his mother destitute and decamped in disgrace to Australia.[18]

Most of all, in the light of RLS's immediate overreaction, it needs to be pointed out that he was an early exponent of that besetting sin of the twentieth century: 'shoot the messenger'. The British political culture is overwhelmingly disposed to assign blame to the person who points out that wrongdoing has taken place, not to the initial wrongdoer; the mania for secrecy prevails over morality and whoever breaches this code is tagged with descriptions like 'troublemaker', 'malcontent', 'whistleblower'. One is tempted to observe that RLS would have been better served if he had bent his energies to vetoing the publication of 'The Nixie' rather than dashing off hysterical screeds to the man who pointed out the fact of its plagiarism.

On the other hand, anyone who knew Stevenson's moral code, with its emphasis on honour, chivalry and loyalty – the code, indeed, of a pre-1745 Highland chieftain – could have predicted the outcome:

My dear Henley,

I write with indescribable difficulty; and if not with perfect temper, you are to remember how very rarely a husband is expected to receive such accusations against his wife. I can only direct you to apply to Katharine and ask her to remind you of that part of the business which took place in your presence and which you seem to have forgotten; she will doubtless add the particulars which you may not have heard . . .

I am sorry I must ask you to take these steps; I might take them for myself had you not tied my hands by the strange step of marking your letter 'private and confidential'. . . . I wish I could stop here. I cannot. When you have refreshed your mind as to the facts, you will, I know, withdraw what you said to me; but I must go farther and remind you, if you have spoken of this to others, a proper explanation and retraction of what you shall have said or implied to any person so addressed, will be necessary.

From the bottom of my soul I believe what you wrote to have been merely reckless words . . . but it is hard to think that anyone – and least of all my friend – should have been so careless of dealing agony . . . This is the sixth or seventh attempt that I make to write to you; . . . You will pardon me if I can find no form of signature; I pray God such a blank will not be of long endurance.　　　　　　　　　　　　　ROBERT LOUIS STEVENSON[19]

Uncertain how to deal with this intemperate ultimatum, Henley did not reply immediately, possibly wishing first to talk the matter over with Baxter and Katharine de Mattos. When Louis received from Henley's assistant editor an enquiry about an article on Rodin he was to write for the *Art Journal*, RLS concluded that Henley was refusing to reply to him and that the gloves were off for a bare-knuckle fight. Ascertaining the full facts in a case was never Stevenson's strong suit: he liked to shoot from the hip and work through the fine detail later. So he dashed off a letter to Henley:

I am sorry you took so strong a step, and that you cannot write to me yourself upon a point of business.' Having dealt with the business of the article, he concluded: 'I will say no more on any other matter; indeed I now somewhat regret my last; for if you feel so much disinclined to write, it is perhaps better for you to leave it alone. On all this, judge for the best; and believe me still and always, if I never saw your face again, – Yours affectionately, Robert Louis Stevenson.

This was a clear gesture of reconciliation and appeared to intimate that his previous high tone had been adopted to soothe Fanny's ruffled feathers and that the apology was needed simply to appease her. But why put her in the picture in the first place? From all that followed it was obvious that Louis, while obeying the letter of Henley's instruction not to show his epistle to anyone, had nonetheless conveyed its gist to Fanny; nor, for all his high-minded declarations, did he burn it, as he had burned Fanny Sitwell's in the mid-70s when under a similar injunction. There is some evidence, therefore, that Louis himself was looking for an opportunity to settle accounts with Henley for the many real and imagined slights he had taken from him over the years.

Meanwhile Louis wrote to Baxter a long screed of self-pity and self-justification. 'I fear I have come to an end with Henley' was the key phrase. He pointed out that he had always tried to be a good friend to Henley, but that 'Burly' kept finding fresh excuses for enmity. He claimed he would have gone on making excuses for Henley if he had not attacked Fanny, and poured scorn on the 'private and confidential' marking which he, illogically, described as 'the baseness of his special form of the anonymous letter'. His aim now was to get an acknowledgement of the truth about the conversation in Henley's house at Shepherd's Bush. He conceded that he always thought the playwriting project futile and did it only to buoy Henley up; Henley meanwhile had no idea of the sacrifice of time and energy his collaborator had devoted to those hopeless plays. 'It will probably come to a smash', he concluded, when he would have to pay the penurious Henley an allowance and pretend it came from a rich benefactor. Expressing bafflement as to why people disliked him so much – referring to Eve Simpson, Anne Simpson, Louisa Purland and now Henley – he wound up by attributing his illness

during the last year at Bournemouth to Henley's persistent unkindness –
a charge which, however, he withdrew in another letter to Baxter the next
day. The mixture of self-justification in this letter found expression in a
fear, overtly declared, that Baxter might side with Henley.[20]

The next bombshell was a letter from Katharine, to whom Henley
had passed on the news of Louis's displeasure:

> As Mr Henley's very natural but unfortunate letter was written without my
> will or knowledge, I have refused to let him go further in the matter. He had a
> perfect right to be astonished, but his having said so has nothing to do with me.
> If Fanny thinks she had a right to the idea of the story, I am far from wishing
> to reclaim or to criticise her in any way. At any rate I cannot be said to have
> done any wrong or gained anything by the matter, and I therefore refuse to be
> questioned about it or to let anyone else be troubled any further; I am sick to
> death of the matter and the notion of any quarrel has made me quite ill. It is
> of course very unfortunate that my story was written first and read by people,
> and if they express their natural astonishment, it is a natural consequence and
> no fault of mine or anyone else ... I trust this matter is not making you feel
> as ill as all of us.

This marked a serious escalation of the conflict, since Louis could
no longer pass the matter off as a piece of spite by Henley; Fanny was
now in the dock for plagiarism. Louis's comment on this was a classic
of self-reflexive irony: 'Now that I suspect there was a petticoat behind,
Henley's conduct is more explicable, but the hope of any good result is
much less. For if Katharine wishes, she can keep him to any mark.'
His letter (to Baxter) is best described as hysterical. He claimed that
Katharine was Henley's protégée, that Henley had tried to sell Katharine's
original story but failed, and that Katharine had handed over the rights
to Fanny and even asked that a copy of Fanny's version of the story be
forwarded to her. It is worth pointing out that this is fantasy. Unless we
posit a conspiracy at once unrivalled for its spite and boneheaded in its
execution, it is inconceivable that Katharine 'made over' her interest in
the story to Fanny; for one thing, Henley would have written a 'j'accuse'
style of letter to Fanny, not RLS. Moreover, in no sense was Katharine
Henley's protégée, nor does any evidence exist that Henley ever tried to
place Katharine's story with a publisher. The remainder of Louis's letter
is of a piece with such wild fantasy:

> I need not remark how very small a degree of kindness it had required –
> supposing me ever in the wrong – to have said nothing of so small a matter;
> nor how very little an amount of tact would have enabled them to understand
> how much pain they would give ... I feel this business with a keenness that
> I cannot describe; I get on during the day well enough; only that whenever I
> think of it, I have palpitations. But at night! sleep is quite out of the question;

and I have been obliged to take opiates. God knows I would rather have died than have this happen. I am going to write of it no more; if I get a satisfactory answer – how can it be one? – good and well. If not, I will simply communicate no more with either . . . Pray pardon my pouring out to you. As I have said already you are the only one to whom I can unbosom . . . Events keep me quite apart from Simpson; of all my friends you and Colvin are the only ones that remain.[21]

Baxter, alarmed as much by the tone as the contents of the letter he had received from RLS, did his best to pour oil on troubled waters: he argued that Henley was a blunderer, a bull in a china shop and notorious for his gaffes and indiscretions, but was not malicious and did not intend to hurt Louis or Fanny. In his opinion, the abortive plays were at the bottom of the affair, since the only complaints about RLS he had ever had from Henley always centred on that business. Naturally too there was some jealousy: 'You have earned great success and fame and money, while he remains not only hard up but hampered by the misdeeds of the wretched Teddy.' Baxter sagely pointed out that charity from the rich to the poor always exacerbated envy instead of palliating it and urged Louis to make allowances and be grateful that Henley, though no gentleman, had conquered many congenital faults, given that he came from the same stock as the unspeakable Teddy. 'You must see that you would break the man's heart if you split with him. He loves you, snarls at you, envies you – if you were his wife he'd beat you; but he cannot get on without you.' To illustrate how easily misunderstandings could arise between friends, Baxter confided that there was a time in the early 1880s when he thought he was losing Louis's friendship, but that Henley had sworn up and down that Louis was not the kind to abandon old friends.

By now Louis had spotted a new angle to the quarrel, which awakened fresh fears. He suddenly remembered that his 'Skulduggery Songs' – a collection of bawdy and scatological verses – were in Henley's possession and might see the light of day if the quarrel was not composed. Concerned for Fanny's reputation, he suddenly realised that his own was not safe. His concern was heightened by what appeared to be a continuing silence from Henley and in a letter to Baxter on 12 April he hit rock-bottom: 'I wish I were dead and have no mind to die. The bottom wish of my heart is that I had died at Hyères; the happy part of my life ended there.'[22]

On 11 April Henley finally penned his reply to Louis's accusations. He chided him for overreacting but retracted nothing and struck the wrong note by a slightly patronising tone: he declared that when he got RLS's letter, he did not know 'whether to laugh or cry over it'. Meanwhile Louis was having the 'classical' second thoughts after his initial 'romantic' outburst. In a letter to Baxter on 16 April he appeared disposed to pardon Henley provided that in future his old friend wrote to him in a genuinely friendly way:

It is of course quite true that Katharine's attitude absolves him of three parts of what I had against him, but the fourth part that remains – that willingness to seethe up against me and mine in my absence and that heartless willingness to wound me – was, it seems the part that I most keenly felt . . . Friendship has surely some obligation of ordinary kindness; it is not a covert from behind which a man is to fill you with injuries and reproaches and escape himself.

He confessed that he had tried to dissuade Fanny from publishing the story, but did not mention that he had used his influence with Burlingame at *Scribner's* to get 'The Nixie' published. It is clear that he was by now increasingly uncertain of his moral position and wished to absolve himself of complicity in an act of plagiarism. One of the sentences in this letter to Baxter is particularly revealing: 'Suppose that I am insane and have dreamed all that I seemed to remember, and that my wife has shamefully stolen a story from my cousin, was this the class of matter that a friend should write to me?' There is further self-reflexive irony when Louis speaks of Henley as Katharine's knight-errant: 'it was all packed into him by an angry woman whom he admires – and what an angry woman is, we all know; and what a man is when he admires'.[23]

All this sounds like mote and beam stuff, but there is evidence that RLS was putting on a brave face to the world while being secretly angry with Fanny, whose overweening and ludicrous ambition had landed him in this imbroglio. There are distinct signs of disharmony in the correspondence between New York and San Francisco in April 1888. In one letter Louis said pointedly:

I envy you flimsy people who rage up so easily into hate . . . Excuse my little bitterness with "flimsy"; it is a tap in return for my thousands, and I don't believe it, dearest . . . the days go, and this is the more dreadful to me . . . I find it hard to think or write of anything else; and my work is at a stand . . . I have not had time to miss you; when I am alone I think of nothing but the one affair. Say nothing of it to anyone, please. If things go to the worst, we must bear this in mere silence.

Stevenson may not have believed 'flimsy' but Colvin certainly saw its implication, and in his 'edition' of the letters he changed 'flimsy' to 'flaming'; the implication of 'flimsy' is that it was Fanny's fragile ego that forced Louis to write the chilly letter of reproof to Henley that escalated the affair in the first place.[24]

The quarrel might now have petered out, had not the well-intentioned Baxter unwittingly stirred the pot by going down to London to try to get a retraction from Henley. Henley confirmed he had no wish or intention to hurt Louis and said he wished he had never put pen to paper on the subject. Convinced that the real villain was Katharine, Baxter secured an agreement with Henley that all correspondence between him and RLS should cease for six months. Henley, however, either could not resist having the last word or made a hamfisted attempt to mend the breach which merely served to open it wider. On 7 May Henley wrote to Louis to try to shift the blame for all their difficulties over to him, and to suggest that if he himself had not mentioned the 'Nixie' affair, others in literary London would have done so, far less charitably.

> Your letter is heart-breaking, and I do not know how to reply to it, for it convicts me (I now see) of a piece of real unkindness, unworthy of myself and our old true friendship. You may blame me in the bitterest terms you will for the cruel blunder I made in opening my mind to you, and I shall not complain, for I deserve them all. I should, I know now, have said nothing; and I shall never cease from regretting that I gave you this useless, this unnecessary pain.
>
> You must not believe, though, that I struck to hurt. I did not. I thought the matter one of little consequence. It seemed right that you should know how it looked to myself, and that there might well be the end of it. I was elbows deep in the business from the first, and I had (I thought) a right to make remarks. It was surely as well (I reasoned) that you should hear of certain coincidences from me as from another quarter. That I had any feeling of unfriendliness is what I want now explicitly to deny.

On paper that was a reasonable enough reply, but there was still no formal retraction of the implicit charge of plagiarism, and Louis by now had dug himself into a gambler's hole whereby he had to double or quit. The cold fury of the note he jotted at the top of Henley's letter is eloquent. 'His original position carefully saved throughout;[1] and yet I gave him my word as to certain matters of fact;[2] and yet the letter (in consequence of this) can never be shown to my wife;[3] and yet, even if he still thinks as he did, I think a kind spirit would have lied.'[25] Here Louis overlooked two things: the white lie or 'expedient exaggeration' was contrary to his own ethical code and he had not been prepared to lie in 1873 when his father's peace of mind and the general tranquillity of the family milieu at Heriot Row would have been guaranteed by venial mendacity; moreover, if Henley made a 'chivalrous' retraction, he would thereby brand Katharine as a liar for her refusal to confirm Fanny's story. All this was quite apart from the 'truth' about what transpired at Henley's house and the morality of Fanny's position, on both of which RLS was increasingly uncertain.

No such considerations weighed with him as he wrote angrily to Baxter on 22 May: 'You will observe that my delicacy in never referring to my wife's miserable position is construed (I must suppose) as a tacit condemnation; but to me, a married man, he writes a letter of reconciliation which I could never dare to show my wife.' In retaliation he informed Baxter that in future, if Katharine and Henley wanted to make their peace, they would have to do so directly to Fanny. 'To my wife, I shall (God forgive me) pretend that your plan has held all the time, and that I have not communicated with Henley.

So here you see I am still tricking and lying for him, and he cannot think once of my position.'[26]

By now Louis's rage was increasingly directed towards Katharine. In the Stevenson literature, Katharine consistently gets a bad press for her role in the 'Nixie' affair, and Baxter agreed with RLS that she was the evil genius: 'As for Katharine, she is really too steep. If there has been bad behaviour, hers has certainly been not the least, and I regard her as the wicked mainspring of all this distress.' Fanny's biographer tends to agree: 'Of the four parties to the quarrel – Henley vindictive, Fanny greedy, Katharine weak and Louis unreasonable – his behaviour was the least ungenerous and it was he who suffered most and longest.'[27] However, it is far from certain that this judgement can be sustained in the light of all the evidence; Colvin, for one, saw that the full story shed little credit on RLS and suppressed the details for that reason. In particular, Louis's rancour against Katharine is strikingly different from his complaisance towards Henley; where he allows him the benefit of every doubt, he allows her none, and this despite the fact that it was Henley who entertained the real animus against Fanny.

The question of money is especially relevant. Stevenson was the sort of man who encouraged his friends to speak their minds without fear or favour, and certainly with no fear of possible financial consequences if they did not say what he wanted to hear. For Fanny, by contrast, money was always a central concern, and she probably calculated that since Henley and Katharine were both Louis's 'pensioners' their mouths would effectively be stopped and they would be unable to comment on the 'Nixie' affair. One of RLS's first actions after he had sent off the initial stiff letter to Henley was to act quickly to safeguard Henley's financial position. He was not named in Louis's will, but hitherto Louis had felt confident that his heirs (the Osbourne family) would honour his wishes informally and keep up the subventions to Henley. Immediately after sending the first letter, he instructed Baxter to find some mechanism to make sure Henley received money after his death, as if from an anonymous benefactor, so as to stymie the expected counterattack from Fanny. He thus demonstrated as clearly as it was possible to do so that he thought Fanny far from blameless and had indited the stiff letter purely as window dressing to appease her. Yet towards Katharine he showed no such magnanimity. Despite the fact that Thomas Stevenson, though uninterested in Henley's fate, had expressly requested him to oversee Katharine's financial well-being, Louis, his heir, went out of his way to safeguard Henley's financial position while being vindictive towards his cousin. He instructed Baxter to secure an annuity for her twelve-year old daughter but to take the capital for the purpose out of the portion in his will he had earmarked for Katharine, in accordance with his father's wishes; before the quarrel, the situation was that the annuity and Katharine's legacy were to be separate charges on his estate.

The new beneficiary from Katharine's diminished fortunes was to be Lloyd, who now gained, in addition to the existing legacy, a further endowment made up by the capital previously set aside for the annuity. It was not therefore surprising that, in Louis's words, 'Lloyd approves of the letter to Katharine.' This letter was a minor masterpiece of mystification and obfuscation. First, Louis informed Katharine that he would not tell Fanny about the letter in which she refused to acknowledge having given permission for the use of the story. Then he enclosed a mysterious message from Fanny saying that there were always perils in epistolary communication and that letters could easily be misunderstood. What possible meaning this message could have had if Louis had not, after all, communicated to Fanny the contents of Katharine's letter is unclear. Not surprisingly, Katharine replied in equally cryptic vein: 'That was best. I am afraid to speak or breathe. There is devilry in the air.' It would not have been surprising if Katharine concluded that Louis was playing a double game and lying through his teeth.[28]

Incensed by this perfectly judicious rejoinder, Louis exploded with rage and produced an epistle which can only be adjudged a *tour de force* of Pecksniffery. He began by claiming that Katharine's cryptic notes were an attempt at apology (they clearly weren't) and upbraided her for not replying to Fanny. He could not appreciate that Katharine might have been genuinely baffled: on the one hand there was Louis saying he had not informed Fanny about the offending letter, and on the other there was Fanny talking in sibylline fashion about 'letters being misunderstood.' But as RLS hit his epistolary stride, he went more and more over the top in humbug. He referred to Katharine's original letter as 'a letter which, if I know anything of life, there is no other human being but myself who would have even tried to pardon'. More cant followed: 'There is always a door open: it is never too late to say, I have sinned – if not for others, at least for oneself.'

Katharine's reply is a convincing rebuttal of Louis's intemperate charges:

> I know this can never get better, but perhaps nothing can make it worse. So do listen when I once more assure you of my entire ignorance that Mr Henley was writing. If I had wished to write or to speak to anyone on the subject, I could have done it myself, but I never had any wish to do so. How well Mr Henley knows this he has perhaps told you. The letter in which I tried to do so was returned to Mr Baxter. I don't think I exaggerate when I say I was maddened with despair when I read your letter which taxed me with a dreadful preconceived plot. I can only myself know how impossible it would have been to me to do such a thing. How deeply sorry I am it is useless to try to say, and impossible not to remember all your past kindness, which has now turned into life-long distrust of me. If I have failed to understand anything said to me at Bournemouth or put a wrong construction on things, I am more grieved than ever, but I cannot say it has been intentional. KATHARINE DE MATTOS.[29]

A brief summary of the likely course of events and the motivations of the actors may be in order. Fanny, misunderstanding or ignoring English cultural nuances, got a story published through her husband's good offices that was really Katharine's intellectual property. Katharine was piqued by the plagiarism but realised that her own financial position depended on Louis, so prudently said nothing. Henley, in despair about his own financial and reputational position and plagued by family worries, especially his ne'er-do-well brother Teddy, and consumed also by jealousy of RLS and loathing of Fanny, allowed himself the luxury of a sideswipe on the subject of the plagiarism; he may have calculated that Louis's affection for him was such that *he* himself would never be cast adrift financially, or he may simply have determined to say his piece, regardless of consequences. Instead of dealing with the matter by giving his old friend a stern ticking-off, Stevenson made every mistake in the book: first he informed Fanny, thus opening Pandora's box; then he overreacted himself in a frankly hysterical manner; finally, he victimised Katharine simply because, when put on the spot, she was not prepared to lie and say that she had given Fanny permission. Indeed, there is in Louis's letters to Katharine such an irrational 'overplus' of rage that one begins to suspect that she was being made the butt for a more deep-seated psychic conflict and that in attacking Katharine Louis was really by transference expressing his anger at the one person he could not consciously condemn: Fanny.

It must be remembered that every time the quarrel showed signs of dying a natural death, it was the Stevensons who rekindled the embers and escalated the conflict. All Baxter's efforts to conciliate the parties were brutally jettisoned, and finally in May the kraken awoke and from her sickbed Fanny came bounding madly into the fray. In a letter to Baxter at the beginning of May, all her worst traits – posturing, hyperbole, fantasy, self-pity and paranoia – are on display. She began by claiming that she could never return to England now because the 'Nixie' affair was the talk of the London clubs and salons (it was not – it remained a closely guarded secret within the Stevenson inner circles) and because of 'the disgrace that has been put on me by Louis's friends'. She then claimed that Henley had virtually murdered Louis and announced her intention of taking a witch-like revenge: 'It is very hard for me to keep on living! I may not be able to, but must try for my dear Louis's sake. If I cannot, then I leave my curse upon the murderers and slanderers.' There followed an anglophobe rant, in which Fanny claimed to have given up her own country to live with RLS in Britain, in return for which the limeys were now treating her as a pariah. It cannot be too much emphasised that no one was treating her as anything, for almost nobody in Britain knew the story. The self-pity and paranoia continued:

I think it is almost better that we were both out of such a world. I never go to bed now but I am tempted sorely by the morphia and the arsenic that stand by my bed. I have always had courage before, but I feel beaten now. They say that one is supported by the consciousness of innocence. That is not true. Were I guilty – though of such a thing I could not be – I should brazen it out. It's the injustice – the injustice that eats at my soul . . . If it so happens that I must go back to perfidious Albion, I shall learn to be false for Louis's sake. I shall pretend to be their friend still – while he lives; but . . . in my heart I can never forgive those who have borne false witness against me – ! While they eat their bread from my hand – and oh, they will do that – I shall smile and wish it were poison that might wither their bodies as they have my heart. Please burn this letter lest it be said that I was mad when I made my will. Those who falsely (knowing it to be false) accuse me of theft, I cannot trust to be honest. They may try to rob my boy after they have murdered us.

Fanny wound up with a diatribe against the wickedness of her enemies: 'Are you like that? No, how could I have forgotten in my bitterness the one true man I believe in, Sidney Colvin – no thank God, *he* will not fail me.' The letter in its entirety provides an almost textbook illustration of her mental illness. Louis scarcely features in it except as a pretext and her real concern, as she lets slip eventually, is for Lloyd. The epistle is packed with absurdity. 'While they eat bread from my hand.' Such sentiments might have been acceptable from a self-made entrepreneur, but what are we to make of them in the mouth of a woman who inherited her money after manipulating the father of a man whom she had long hesitated about marrying? At the end of the letter she even manages to appeal for support from Baxter while accusing him of being false. Baxter's reply was dignified. 'I think you might have included me in the same category as Colvin.' He pointed out gently that no one in Britain except himself, Katharine and Henley knew about the matter 'so for heaven's sake don't imagine that England is ringing with it'.

But the tigress had the scent of blood and soon returned to the hunt. On 15 May she wrote again to Baxter to try to prevent the annuity being paid to Katharine's daughter. This time her machiavellianism was just a bit transparent. 'I have very little faith in these new-fangled annuity affairs, and it would be foolish to run the risk of losing a large sum of money, only to save Katharine any embarrassment she might feel after what she has done.' Money was the weapon she ached to use to compass her revenge: 'Already the hands that dealt me the cruellest blows are held out to be filled . . . Every penny that goes to them, any of them, goes with my bitterest ill-will.' She hinted that Baxter was culpable merely because he tried to mediate and continued her anglophobe ranting, this time declaring that she never wanted to see England again. In the stark madness into which she had temporarily slipped, she felt that the entire nation should be condemned because a single Englishman had caught her out in plagiarism; by the same logic Henley would have been entitled to claim that all Americans were psychotic.[30]

The irony of the entire 'Nixie' affair was that the most blameless person, Katharine, whose only fault was not to have been assertive enough in denying Fanny's right to her story during the original conversation in Shepherd's Bush, eventually suffered most. RLS appears in a bad light, and Fanny in a truly appalling one. Henley, whose mischievous stirrings made him the 'onlie begetter' of the fiasco, was partially readmitted into the Stevensonian fold, and Louis later sent him messages of condolence on the loss of his daughter and congratulation on the appearance of his verses; he sent these messages as if from Fanny also, though this was of course a polite fiction. Fanny admitted to Colvin in 1890 that she was glad to have slain the dragon of 'Burly' as she had never liked his influence on Louis. In return for Louis's magnanimity, in 1901, seven years after Stevenson's death, Henley launched a bitter attack on his old friend when Balfour's 'official biography' appeared. In a long article in *The Pall Mall Magazine*, he savaged RLS's reputation.

Henley's main point was that by 1901, with the Balfour biography, RLS had become encrusted with the barnacles of legend, and that the real Stevenson bore little relation to this 'RLS' of legend. 'For me there were two Stevensons: the Stevenson who went to America in '87; and the Stevenson who never came back. The first I knew and loved; the other I lost touch with, and, though I admired him, did not greatly esteem.' But as he progressed further into the article, Henley revealed that the true watershed between old and new Stevensons was 1879 – the year he went to America in pursuit of Fanny – for, as a Silverado squatter, 'in this last avatar the Stevenson of Mr Balfour's dream had begun, however faintly, to adumbrate himself.' In other words, the rot set in when Fanny became a fixture. A particular target for Henley was the 'preachiness' of *Lay Morals*, where Louis as 'Shorter Catechist' was most clearly on display.

> I will say at once that I do not love the Shorter Catechist, in anybody, and that I loved him less in Stevenson than anywhere that I have ever found him. He is too selfish and too self-righteous a beast for me. He makes ideals for himself with a resolute regard for his own salvation; but he is all too apt to damn the rest of the world for declining to live up to them, and he is all too ready to make a lapse of his own the occasion for a rule of conduct for himself and the lasting pretext for a highly moral deliverance to such backsliding Erastians as, having memories and a certain concern for facts, would like him to wear his rue with a difference.

Henley concluded that the Shorter Catechist reflected a potential that RLS had always had within him and which was encouraged by Fanny; there were two Stevensons and the young, riotous, intrepid, scornful one could have gone on to greater things if he had not been gelded by his wife. It was true that Stevenson did good in secret to those with whom he quarrelled, but this was a function of guilt: 'salving his conscience for a possible injustice, done in heat and apprehended too late for anything but a frank avowal and a complete apology; which in the circumstances the Shorter Catechist finds abhorrent and therefore immoral.' Moreover, Stevenson was not the hypersensitive, shrinking violet he pretended to be but a tough, ruthless streetfighter: 'to try a fall with him was to get badly handled, if not utterly suppressed.'[31]

Henley's bitter disappointment at the road not taken by RLS is every-where apparent. It was the young man's toughness and obstinacy, matching his own, that had initially attracted Henley, but when Louis became 'wom-anish', deferred to Fanny and let her play the man's role, as Henley saw it, he became disillusioned. It is tempting to see the Henley/RLS clash as the inevitable ultimate collision of a virile, Falstaffian temperament with a more exquisite and refined 'feminine' sensibility, but many observers thought that Stevenson was actually the tougher and more ruthless of the two. The distinguished academic, Sir Walter Raleigh, thought that Henley's was a richer, greater and more generous nature than Louis's, and that this fact was disguised by image-making: Louis consistently displayed his best face to the world while Henley showed his worst. 'You couldn't quarrel with Henley – not to last – because the minute you showed a touch of magnanimity or affection, he ran at you, and gave you everything and abased himself like a child. But RLS kept aloof . . . and chose his ground with all the Pharisee's skill in selecting sites. He had not a good heart.'[32] This, though, implies that Louis was insouciant about the loss of Henley, which is not true. The reason he wished he had died at Hyères was that he still lived an integrated life there, where he was not forced to choose between his wife and his best friend. He felt the defection of Henley keenly, and if he had mourned Ferrier as David mourned Jonathan, he lamented the separation from Henley as though part of his being had been truncated, as though he were Hal without Falstaff or Jim Hawkins without Silver.

Echoes of the famous quarrel are discernible in what is surely Stevenson's greatest complete full-length work, *The Master of Ballantrae*. Since the trigger for the conflict between the Durie brothers is a woman, it is tempting to see the guilt-ridden, Calvinistic, duty-driven Henry as a portrait of the new 'bourgeois' RLS aiming at commercial success, with James, the 'Master', the custodian of the life-enhancing Jacobite values, as a transmogrified version of Bob, who still clung to the values of the pre-Fanny RLS. That Alison Graeme represents Katharine de Mattos can be inferred not just from her 'treachery' but from her childhood memories of the times she, Henry and James played happily together – recalling the pony rides at North Berwick by the juvenile trio of Louis, Bob and Katharine. The theme of the decay of honour – so central to the pre-1745 Highland society – would have fed in both from the Henley quarrel and RLS's own stumblings, having promised to write for McClure when he already had a contract with Scribner's. Louis felt the contract fiasco deeply, as he told J.A.Symonds: 'It is hard work to sleep; it is hard to be told you are a liar, and have to hold your peace and think, "Yes, by God, and a thief too!"'33

Louis began writing *The Master of Ballantrae* in December 1887. By Christmas he had drafted ninety-two pages but shortly afterwards, as usual when he was working fast and at white heat, he ran out of steam. The quarrel with Henley supervened, and then the Pacific voyage, so that a year later, at Tahiti, he was no further than chapter six. In mid-February 1889, in Hawaii, he took it up again and finally completed it in May. Yet the Scottish sections of the book, which itself covers as wide a section of the globe as its peripatetic author, clearly derive much of their sensuous quality from the ice and snow of the Adirondacks. This is the darkest of all Stevenson's books – blacker even than *The Ebb-Tide*, which does at least offer some specious hope of redemption – and the only one of his works to which he was prepared unequivocally to grant the accolade of tragedy.

The Master of Ballantrae has been called Stevenson's tragic epic of the Jacobite rising of 1745, with *Kidnapped* as the comic version, but the '45 is used mainly as a point of departure. When Prince Charlie lands in Scotland in August that year, the Durrisdeer family do what many actual Scottish families did: they hedged their bets, sending one son out to fight for the Stuart pretender and another to enlist under the banner of the Hanoverian King George. Since James, the elder son, fights for Prince Charlie and the losing cause, he is attainted and loses both estate and lady (Alison), triggering in him an undying hatred for the younger brother Henry, who is the beneficiary of the Hanoverian victory. Such at least is the superficial situation, but Stevenson uses the context of fratricidal conflict to examine the theme of ambiguity at every level, from the psychological to the metaphysical.

The deep motif that runs through all Stevenson's Scottish novels is the struggle for the national soul between the contending traditions of Jacobitism and Calvinism. James is the Jacobite half of the Scottish psyche and is an affront to the Covenanting tradition at every level. He is good-looking – in Calvinistic thought physical beauty is mistrusted as the work of the devil – and he affronts notions of determinism and predestination by being the most existential of men. His life is literally aleatory: he tosses a coin to decide whether he or Henry should go 'out' for Prince Charlie, whether he should be friend or foe to the Chevalier Burke, which route he and Burke should take in the North American wilderness; James and Henry are the two sides of RLS: James the adventurer, as perfectly free as Byron's corsair, uninhibited by sexual fastidiousness; Henry the monogamous, dutiful drudge – the kind of man Stevenson despised but secretly feared he was himself. Henry's guilt and self-hatred reflect one aspect of the multiple ambivalences in RLS himself. On the one hand he wanted to jettison all the cultural lumber from his childhood, but on the other he feared that there might be something in the Calvinistic world view; he never got over the feeling that creative work was in some sense a way of cheating life or avoiding moral responsibility.

RLS himself was quite clear that the Master was an evil incubus. He told Colvin in December 1887: 'The Master is all I know of evil.' To Will Low he wrote in May 1889: 'I have at length finished *The Master*; it has been a sore cross to me; but now he is buried . . . his soul, if there is any hell to go to, gone to hell.'[34] But we should remember D.H.Lawrence's advice to trust the tale, not the teller: the treatment of evil in *Ballantrae*, as in *Jekyll* is far more complex than simple polarity between evil James and good Henry. The real incubus is the narrator and factor, Mackellar, and the Calvinism he represents. The story is presented almost entirely from Mackellar's viewpoint, yet Stevenson gives us many pointers that alert us that Mackellar is an unreliable witness. There are other signs that there is another side to James than the diabolical one we get from Mackellar: the biblical references to Esau and Jacob hint to the reader that it is Jacob (Henry) who is deceiving Esau (James), and if Secundra Dass is James's familiar, Mackellar surely stands in the same relationship to Henry. Most of all, knowing what we know of Stevenson's attitude to women, we can place his real attitude to Mackellar from the factor's revealing utterances: 'I had never natural sympathy for the passion of love; I have never had much toleration for the female sex, possibly not much understanding; and being far from a bold man, I have ever shunned their company.'

The most deep-running ambiguity in the novel is that it is far from certain where evil is to be located and who the truly malevolent brother is. Superficially, Henry is Jekyll to James's Hyde – his brother is the part of himself he cannot acknowledge – but Stevenson again points up the folly either of thinking that evil is something 'other', something 'out there', or of considering as evil everything a man may dislike or find inconvenient. Henry can neither discern the darkness in himself nor make any distinction between the lawlessness of smugglers – which he simultaneously deplores and is attracted to – and the genuinely diabolical qualities of his brother. Like Dr Jekyll, Henry tries to decant all the evil in the world, to make it a thing apart; he aims at perfection (an illusory goal) rather than integration (an attainable one). This is why the apparent victory after he has 'killed' his brother in the shrubbery duel is hollow; the satisfaction of his hate in this 'triumph' merely releases the true demons within himself; from a pillar of respectability he becomes a beater of servants. The duel is Henry's attempt to cut biology and id out of his life, leaving culture and superego, but when he thinks he has killed James, the sole result is that he grows listless and morbid, as though his very identity could only be asserted in contradistinction to James.

Yet the texture of *The Master* is even darker and more convoluted than in *Jekyll*. Henry's struggle is both with James as alter ego and within himself as he comes to terms with the James-like elements in his own nature. The side that is drawn to the freedom of the smugglers resents the determinism of the bookkeeper he is, under Mackellar's tutelage, but the bourgeois laird also resents the smugglers' contempt. The greater complexity is evident. In *Jekyll and Hyde*, Hyde resented Jekyll's disapproval of him and therefore moved towards the extremes of evil; but in *The Master of Ballantrae*, the apparently good man responds to the contempt of the bad by descending into the darkness. In a curious way the smugglers act as Henry's conscience, almost as though id had usurped the functions of superego, and Henry then projects his inner conflict into an external battle with James.

Further doubt is thrown on the nature of evil in *The Master* by the consideration that James, for all his global adventures, is essentially the same person at the end of the book as at the beginning. An old-fashioned hero, James, like Manfred, Melmoth, Rochester, Heathcliff and Henchard, often seems less the sinner than one sinned against by an ugly, alien society. He is no mere demon or incubus but is himself a divided self. On the one hand he is cunning, malignant, mocking, cruel, egotistical, insidious, false, murderous, vain, insolent, greedy, an artist in deceit, able to play at ingratiating hypocrisy or ingenuous insult with equal aplomb. But he is also witty, courageous, resourceful, handsome in figure, graceful in gesture, brilliant in talk, gallant and generous, a master diplomat well versed in the ways of court and camp in both East and West. Although he would stoop to any depths to attain his ends and has the tenacity of a tiger, he boasts that he never failed to charm any person when he so wanted and Mackellar refers to this aspect of the fallen Lucifer when he says: 'You could not have been so bad a man if you had not all the machinery of a good one.'

As a Jacobite survivor, James jettisons 'honour' in favour of personal gratification, thus symbolising the way capitalism overcame patriarchalism and feudalism in Scotland, turning clan chieftains into economic landlords rather than patriarchs and protectors of the clansmen. But a clan chieftain turned landlord was no match for the 'new men' in London. Henry, by contrast, is a constantly evolving dynamic character and he illustrates an old Stevensonian theme – that the civilised savage will always beat the unreconstructed variety, the dog the wolf, money the sword, the cunning Lowlander the ingenuous Highlander. In a contest of wills between the flamboyant, martial, flashy Alan Breck and the dour, inert, passive David Balfour, it is the Lowlander who will ultimately win every time. Just as the Hanoverians were superior in savagery to the Jacobites, and in Stevenson's day, the colonial powers with Maxim guns to the 'savages' they slaughtered, so in any long drawn out struggle it is the Lowlander (symbolised by Henry) who will win over the Highlander (James), even though for Stevenson this is the victory of the worse over the better. Henry, having at first been the hapless dupe of his diabolical brother, learns his lesson too well, jettisons his positive aspects (as James never does) and in the end becomes more demonic than his brother, with hellish acolytes at his bidding even more fearsome than the rogues James employs. This is the beginning of that motif of scepticism about civilisation and its supposed superiority to primitive values that would be so marked a feature of Stevenson's later work.

The multiple layers of ambiguity in *Ballantrae* can be seen also from its Janus-face: looking forward to the Conradian ideas of the later Stevenson fiction and back, in recapitulation, to his earlier work. RLS was much censured at the time, by Symonds especially, and has been by critics since, for working in motifs from his previous novels that seemed to have no place in the dark world of the Master and his brother: the two hurricanes (in the Minch and on the *Nonesuch*), the treasure buried in upstate New York and, most of all, the pirates. Of the latter Chesterton remarked: 'It is almost as if pirates were really a private mania with the author; and he could not keep them out of the tale if he tried; though pirates have really no more business in this tale than pirates in *The Wrong Box*.'[35] This is a misunderstanding. Stevenson needed the episode of the pirates to convince us of the awesome, almost inhuman, power of the Master, who subdues the pirate captain Teach with ease, pointing up the contrast between the banality of the pirates' evil and the more fearsome variety represented by James Durrisdeer. The effect is heightened since the pirates are themselves a much more terrifying breed than the tatterdemalion ruffians who sailed with Long John Silver on the *Hispaniola*. Stevenson makes the point with some brilliant economical effects, as when rape is hinted at: 'Twice we found women on board: and though we have seen towns sacked, and of late years, some very horrid public tumults, there was something in the smallness of the numbers, and the bleak, dangerous sea surroundings, that made these acts of piracy far more revolting.' Teach is an epigone to Silver but his dramatic function is to provide the missing half of Henry's personality: Teach, all animal energy, is a partial creature, the other side of the coin from Henry, who at this stage is all cerebration. Both are unintegrated beings, and Teach indeed has not the tenth of the brain and ambition of Silver; but once again we are alerted to the diabolical power of the Master by the reflection that Silver in turn is a mere remora fish swimming in the shadow of the great white shark that is James Durrisdeer.

If *Treasure Island* and *Jekyll and Hyde* form the obvious points of comparison touching pirates and the divided self respectively, *Kidnapped* is the obvious signpost for the Scottish themes both literal and symbolic.

The difference in tone between *Kidnapped* and *The Master* becomes clear from an examination of the great action scenes in each. The fight in the roundhouse in the former book, as has been well said, is all brilliance and ringing steel and pulsates with the love of battle; but the duel in the shrubbery in the latter is as sinister, black and ghastly as a scene in Webster. And it is surely significant that the master scene of conflict in *Kidnapped* is the famous *verbal* joust between David Balfour and Alan Breck, whereas in *The Master* the corresponding scene is Stevenson's unforgettable account of the duel between Henry and James:

> There was no breath stirring; a windless stricture of frost had bound the air; and as we went forth in the shine of the candles, the blackness was like a roof over our heads. Never a word was said, there was never a sound but the creaking of our steps along the frozen path. The cold of the night fell about me like a bucket of water; I shook as I went with more than terror; but my companions, bare-headed like myself, and fresh from the warm hall, appeared not even conscious of the change.

Moreover, just as the Master overcomes Teach, the symbol of the simple world of pirate evil, so does he overcome Alan Breck Stewart in the short post-Culloden scene. The triumph of the Master's duplicity over the ingenuous martial valour of Alan Breck symbolises the triumph of the new individualism of post-1745 Scotland over the collectivist clan system before that date, the advent of the clan chief as landlord and his demise as patriarch.

If *The Master of Ballantrae* is in some ways a masterly summation of all previous Stevenson themes, but raised to a new height and taken to a new depth, some of the influence may perhaps be attributed to a writer who was to be RLS's guide and mentor during the coming peregrinations of the Pacific; Herman Melville. It was Charles Warren Stoddard who first introduced RLS to Melville, in 1879; Louis devoured his works and called him 'a howling cheese' – a term of compliment. The influence of the great New Englander is visible in 'The Merry Men' but is overwhelming in *The Master of Ballantrae* – a point curiously unnoticed by Stevenson biographers hitherto. Most of them have fastened on the more superficial resemblances to Poe – the themes of a doomed house ('The Fall of the House of Usher'), the antagonism between brothers ('William Wilson'), being buried alive ('The Premature Burial') etc. Shrewdest and most perceptive of Stevensonians, Chesterton saw through the deficiencies of this critical approach; he pointed out that in the duel scene it was not the darkness of the night but its coldness and the light from the star-like candleflames that Stevenson dwelt on; this was the difference between the house of Durrisdeer and the House of Usher. 'Poe's ideal detective prefers to think in the dark', Chesterton points out, 'and therefore puts up the shutters even during the day. Dupin brings the outer darkness into the parlour, while Durie carries the candlelight into the forest.'[36]

By contrast the influence of Melville is pervasive. Superficially, *The Master of Ballantrae* is clearly in the category of the pursuit romance; the immediate trigger for its writing was Marryat's *The Phantom Ship* but the masterwork in this genre is *Moby-Dick*. Moreover, Stevenson's themes of ambivalence and ambiguity find their most sustained expression in Melville: the very title of Melville's most problematical work, *Pierre or the Ambiguities*, makes the point. Both writers shared the idea that good and evil were inextricably intertwined – 'good and evil braided be', as Melville put it in *Benito Cereno* – and that madness lay in wait for the human who would try to disentangle them. Henry's descent into madness recalls the increasing monomania of Ahab, and very similar imagery is used in both cases: Ahab talks of waxing fat on Moby Dick's blood and of being fuelled by hatred; Henry says, 'I grow fat upon it (hatred)' and Mackellar says of him: 'it was hatred and not love that gage him healfhful colours.' Part of the madness of both is the conviction that their enemies are immortal. 'Hast killed him?' 'The harpoon is not yet forged that will ever do that,' is a typical exchange in *Moby-Dick*, while in *The Master*, the imagery, with its talk of 'transfiguration', suggests that James is, if not god, then at least a fallen Lucifer. Henry says of his brother: 'He's not of this world . . . I have struck my sword through his vitals . . . I have felt the hirt dirk on his breastbone, and the hot blood spurt in my very face, time and again, time and again! . . . But he was never dead for that.'

Even more striking is the exact correspondence of certain key passages. When Ahab explains the deep meaning of his quest to Starbuck, he says:

All visible objects, man, are but as pasteboard masks. But in each event – in the living act, the undoubted deed – there, some unknown but still reasoning thing puts forth the mouldings of its features from behind the unreasoning mask. If man will strike, strike through the mask! How can the prisoner reach outside except by thrusting through the wall? To me, the white whale is that wall, shoved near to me. Sometimes I think there's naught beyond. But 'tis enough. He tasks me; he heaps me; I see in him outrageous strength, with an inscrutable malice sinewing it. That inscrutable thing is chiefly what I hate; and be the white whale agent, or be the white whale principal, I will wreak that hate upon him. Talk not to me of blasphemy, man; I'd strike the sun if it insulted me.

When Henry strikes James, precipitating the midnight duel, he cries: 'A blow! I would not take a blow from God Almighty!' Later, on the *Nonesuch*, Mackellar explains his fear of the Master: 'I had moments when I thought of him as a man of pasteboard – as though, if one should strike smartly through the buckram of his countenance, there would be found a mere vacuity within. This horror (not merely fanciful, I think), vastly increased my detestation of his neighbourhood.' Even the respective theories of the interpenetration of opposites are similar. In his later appearance in the fragmentary *The Young Chevalier*, James expresses his credo: 'The height of beauty is in the touch that's wrong; that's the modulation in the tune. 'Tis the devil we all love; I owe many a conquest to my mole . . . We are all hunchbacks, and beauty is only that kind of deformity that I happen to admire.' The sensibility is that of Claggart in Melville's *Billy Budd* when he cautions Billy for his admiration of the beauty of the night sky: 'Remember, Billy, beneath those stars is a universe of gliding monsters.'[37]

RLS himself considered that *The Master of Ballantrae* 'contains more human work than anything of mine but *Kidnapped*' though he thought it flawed because devoid of humour; it was a Stevensonian axiom that even the greatest tragedy had to contain some humour. However, it plumbed greater depths than *Kidnapped* while ascending to greater novelistic heights than *Jekyll and Hyde*, in which some of the same metaphysical themes are dealt with. The supremacy of *The Master* in the Stevenson *oeuvre* is attributable to what D.H.Lawrence called 'the most subtle form of interrelatedness'. Multiple ambivalences are contained within multiple ambiguities but all is carried forward on a near-perfect story structure; history and fiction, character and event correspond, and narrative structure matches narrative action; the familiar Stevensonian dilemma of values is resolved, albeit indirectly, while avoiding Flaubertian nihilism; and the philosophical and allegorical themes do not overwhelm the adventure, as they tend to in *Jekyll and Hyde*.

The ending has been much criticised, on the grounds that it resolves the plot by *deus ex machina* means, and that the melodrama of the Hindu live burial sits uneasily with the genuine drama that has gone before. Stevenson himself tended to agree on this point, and he wrote with an apology to Henry James:

'My novel is a tragedy; five parts of it are sound, human tragedy; the last one or two, I regret to say, not so soundly designed; I almost hesitate to write them; they are very picturesque, but they are fantastic; they shame, perhaps degrade, the beginning . . . the third supposed death and the manner of the third reappearance is steep, steep, sir. It is even very steep, and I feel it shames the honest stuff so far.'

We may allow that the ending does not match the first two-thirds of the novel, but this is a perennial problem with all Stevenson's fiction. Otherwise, his self-imposed strictures seem harsh: the failure to rise again the third time exposes Henry's madness in thinking his brother to be demi-god or devil, and the resurrection theme has an obvious symbolic resonance: the clearest way to show one's human, not divine, status is to fail to rise from the dead. Professor Eigner's comment is pertinent: 'There is no shrugging off of the tragic vision here. The story ends in the only way it could end:

with Henry's murder of his brother and the death which that murder brings
to Henry himself; a simultaneous death like those in "The Merry Men" and
in *Dr Jekyll and Mr Hyde*.'38

In this novel RLS also worked through the turbulent emotions of
separation from his 'brother' Bob, now lost to him because of the breach
with Katharine de Mattos. The devious-circling Henley was quick to play
up the rift and circulated literary London with his theory that Bob was
more talented than Louis but lacked his cousin's application and ambition:
'Confound him, if the beggar would only work,' Henley cried, in despair
that his thesis would never be verified. The year 1887–88 was a catastrophe
for Louis at an emotional level, and he later confessed that the quarrel with
Henley provided the third of his great 'to be or not to be' crises. The loss
of his actual father could be palliated by money and his own ambivalence,
but what could palliate the loss of both 'father figure' (Henley) and 'brother'
(Bob)? Increasingly he turned for solace to Lloyd, who in the same year had
also lost his natural father and the surrogate (Henley) he so revered, but
there was not much altruism in Louis's *cri de coeur* when he wished himself
and his family at the bottom of the Pacific. Writing to Baxter in May 1888 he
exclaimed: 'O, I go on my journey with a bitter heart. It will be best for all,
I daresay, if the *Casco* goes down with me. For there's devilish little left to
live for.'39

The *Casco* was the name of the yacht Fanny managed to hire in San
Francisco. In May RLS received the following excited cable: 'Can secure
splendid seagoing schooner-yacht *Casco* for $750 a month with the most
comfortable accommodation for six aft and six forward. Can be ready for
sea in ten days. Reply immediately, Fanny.' Louis cabled back: 'Blessed
girl, take the yacht and expect us in ten days.' Louis at once sent word
to Baxter to send him £1,000 of his £3,000 legacy (Maggie split the cost
of the seven-month cruise by putting up £1,000 of her money), explaining
that if he survived the voyage he could recoup the expense from the $10,000
offered by McClure for a series of letters from the Pacific.

At this stage the plan was for the Stevensons to sail first to the Hawaiian
islands, then on to the Society Islands, returning via the Galapagos and
Guayaquil, ready for a cruise among the Greek islands, when RLS would
work on a travel book to be illustrated by Will Low. To Lady Taylor Louis
wrote excitedly: 'From Skerryvore to the Galapagos is a far cry!' Outlining
his plans to come eastabout from Polynesia to Ecuador, Louis told Henry
James: 'and – I hope *not* the bottom of the Pacific . . . It seems too good to
be true.' He said to Will Low: 'I loved the Pacific in the days when I was at
Monterey, and perhaps now it will love me a little.' Actually the ambition to
rove among the coral atolls of that turbulent ocean had taken root earlier.
In 1875, just before his examinations for the bar, Louis talked animatedly
to a New Zealander visitor to Heriot Row, J.Seed, who urged on him the

desirability of the Navigator Islands, and specifically Samoa, as the perfect haven for those with respiratory complaints. Louis never forgot this early inspiration and built on it when in San Francisco in 1879–80; meeting Kanaka sailors and Queequeg-like harpooneers in waterfront bars; debating Melville with the Williamses; discussing his Pacific wanderings with Charles Warren Stoddard.

Accordingly, the quartet of Louis, Maggie, Lloyd and Valentine made haste to join Fanny on the western seaboard. From Manasquan they proceeded to New York and boarded the train for Chicago, travelling at first in luxurious carriages. In the windy city, however, there was an eight hour wait, followed by another encounter with the dreaded 'cars'. It took several days to reach Salt Lake City, and then the journey over the high sierras to Sacramento was accompanied by nose bleeds triggered by the high altitude. Fanny met the weary travellers in Sacramento on 7 June and accompanied them on the last stage to San Francisco, where an exhausted RLS took to his bed in the Occidental Hotel. Yet he was consoled by glimpses of the limpid waters of the Pacific and thought back to his dreams of paradise at Colinton Manse:

> I should like to rise and go
> Where the golden apples grow;
> Where below another sky
> Parrot islands anchored lie.[40]

He was now about to measure his dreams against reality.

13

Pacific Wanderer

In San Francisco it turned out that the hire of the *Casco* was not such a simple matter as had appeared from Fanny's cable. Before he committed himself finally, the schooner's owner, Dr Merritt, wanted to interview its would-be charterers. Earlier he had told Fanny: 'The yacht is the apple of my eye. You may think your husband loves you, but I can assure you that I love my yacht a great deal better.' He had seen material in the newspapers that hinted that Stevenson might be a crank or worse; and what was all this about taking his aged mother with him? At the interview Louis and Maggie carried all before them: Merritt told the *Casco*'s captain that Stevenson was no 'literary cove' but a down-to-earth man as sensible as anyone in the maritime business. He did, however, have his doubts about Louis's health and gave Captain Otis secret instructions to take with him all that was needful for a burial at sea. Otis himself was initially far from disposed to make a trip in the Pacific with raw tiros enthusiastic for 'fashionable yacht-sailing' and talked of looking for another berth; Merritt, on the other hand, was adamant that he would not entrust the *Casco* to any other master. Grumpily, Otis in turn interviewed RLS. Stevenson drew from him the admission that he had always wanted to revisit Polynesia and with his knowledge of nautical lore talked Otis round. A deal was struck, whereby RLS would charter the *Casco* at $500 a month plus all expenses and repairs for seven months, with the option of renewing for a further one, two or three months with the captain's approval; all landfalls were to be at the master's discretion.[1]

For the $2,000 lavished on the *Casco* trip RLS has been much criticised. Some claim that Belle Strong's sudden intimation of the wealth and prosperity of her stepfather aroused both cupidity and unreal expectations which were to have disastrous results later. Others contrast the Pacific roving of *this* writer, who was able to proceed in the *Casco* on the basis of inherited wealth, not his own earnings from writing, with those of Jack London in the *Snark* in 1907; at the age of thirty-one, six years Louis's junior, London was able not just to hire a schooner but to design and build one and then voyage through Polynesia *entirely* on the proceeds of his books. Professor Kiely thinks that the homiletic advice in 'Pulvis et Umbra', written a few months before the extravagant *Casco* trip, looks dangerously like bourgeois humbug: 'to earn a little and to spend a little less . . . to renounce when that shall be necessary.' This sounds especially steep when one considers that RLS had also been commissioned by McClure to write a series of fifty letters (2-3,000 words each) from the Pacific on subjects of his own choice, for which he would receive a fee of £20 per letter in England and a further $200 each in the U.S.A.[2] RLS, though, always thought his own peculiar situation was not one from which universal principles could be extrapolated, and it is true that not many writers have had to contend with two such incubuses as consumption (or whatever the exact pulmonary disease was) and the Osbourne family.

Louis went over to Oakland Creek to see the ship being fitted out. The *Casco* was a seventy-ton topsail schooner, ninety-five feet long, kept in immaculate condition with white sails and decks and polished brasswork. Originally designed for offshore racing in Californian waters, it was a veteran of Pacific cruises. In the cockpit, designed as a drawing room with cushioned seats all round, were the compass and the wheel. From the level of the deck and cockpit a companionway led down to the captain's cabin and the aftercabin, brightly lit from a skylight and four portholes, containing a fixed table and four sofas, above and behind which were three bunks for Fanny, Maggie and Valentine. There was a large mirror set in the wall flanked by two doors, one of which led to a small cabin occupied by Lloyd and beyond that to the dining room, from which in turn doors led to the pantry, galley and crew's quarters. The door on the other side of the mirror led to the large cabin occupied by Louis.

Fanny busied herself with preparations for the voyage, ordering the stores in meticulous detail, everything from flour and saltpork to whisky and tobacco. Belle Strong, with her knowledge of Hawaii, advised the women to jettison their 'civilised' clothes and instead adopt the *holaku* or 'Mother Hubbard' dress introduced by missionaries in the South Seas to the native women – a long loose gown flowing waistless from a yoke. These were as cool and comfortable as an Arab's robe and were worn without corsets, which made them seem 'daring' in the America of the 1880s. Worn underneath the 'Mother Hubbard' was a *muumu*, a straight full chemise or nightdress with a flounce around the hem. The three women went for fittings with a Chinese tailor and laid in supplies of the *holaku*. Fanny took to the dress and wore it for the rest of her life; so attired, chain-smoking and with closely cropped hair, she looked like the classical 'emancipated woman' of the times.

Fanny's state of mind as she prepared for a traverse of the Pacific was decidedly odd. She was always a poor sailor and was terrified of the sea, but by her constant discontent with any and every domicile except the ones

Louis himself hated she had backed herself into a geographical cul-de-sac. Perhaps it was fear of the unknown Pacific that made her cling to Belle, in a new and unexpected efflorescence of the maternal emotions she had felt for her daughter twenty years before, for there is something of the *cri de coeur* in her parting message to her, perhaps hinting at difficulties in the marriage with Joe Strong. 'My poor little soul ... I feel sick at heart when I think of you. Get away as soon as you can, my dear. There is nothing else you can do, and the sooner you go the better.'

It is possible that Fanny made an eleventh-hour bid to avoid the Pacific, for there are mysterious and cryptic hints about a growth in her throat (which Fanny claimed was cancer) said to have been operated on in the period between mid-April and meeting the rest of the family at Sacramento in early June. The day before leaving in the *Casco* she wrote to Baxter as follows:

> 'Dr Chismore, Louis's old doctor, and a very clever man, found it necessary to operate on a tumour in my throat. He had partly removed the thing when he discovered that a large artery was involved and any further use of the knife would be followed by the gravest consequences. So there was nothing to be done but an attempt at absorption. I was very skeptical at first, but I now believe that it is going to be successful. At any rate I can see him again when we come back this way, and then if it must come out whether or no, he is the only man I care to have touch me with knives.'[3]

This account sounds like either self-delusion or the naïve acceptance of a consoling story told her by Dr Chismore. If Fanny had cancer in the throat which was found to be inoperable, she would surely have died in the Pacific, for she did not come back 'this way' for seven years. Moreover, the calendar is against Fanny, for she could not have had such a serious operation and then not just been on her feet again but bustling around organising the *Casco* trip, all within six weeks. Sober medical opinion inclines to the view that she did not have a tumour but a cyst, that it was not in her 'throat' but in the back of her mouth, and that Chismore provided her with this involved story either to satisfy her taste for hypochondriacal melodrama or to justify a much larger than usual fee.

Meanwhile Louis learned from his conversations with Captain Otis that his plan to voyage Hawaii–Tahiti–Marquesas and then eastabout to the Galapagos and Guayaquil did not square with practical navigation. Such a route meant sailing in the teeth of the south-east trade winds and the south equatorial current. Patiently Otis talked him through the great Pacific voyages of the past from Magellan to Cook: all of them had gone westabout in the southern latitudes. Since Louis insisted on including the Marquesas in his itinerary, they ought to head for these islands first; even to sail from Hawaii to the Marquesas was problematical because of the need to make easting against the elements – and it was a superb feat of navigation nineteen years later when Jack London made that trip in the *Snark*.

Accordingly, when the Stevenson party embarked on 26 June on the *Casco*, which lay at anchor under the sea wall beneath Telegraph Hill, it was agreed that their first destination would be the Marquesas group of islands, 3,000 miles south-south-west of San Francisco, the most easterly islands in Polynesia. The departure was upbeat and dramatic. Louis's cabin was thronged with friends and reporters, Fanny's inundated with fruit and flowers. The Stevensons gave a party that evening, expecting to be under way next day, but there were various delays, so that it was 5.00 a.m. on 28 June before the waving figures of Belle and Dora Williams watched a tug finally tow the ship outside the Golden Gate into the big ground swell of the open Pacific.

RLS had often written about the sea, but at this stage he seriously underrated the perils he would face on the inaptly named Pacific Ocean. He did not yet know how dangerous were the hurricanes and typhoons (the nomenclature varied at different points of the ocean, and what was termed a typhoon in Micronesia was called a hurricane in Polynesia). In the vast 'fetches' of the unimpeded Pacific a storm could raise a wave fully one hundred feet from trough to crest; the highest recorded wave (112 feet) was observed by U.S.S. *Ramapo* in 1932, but Alain Gerbault, the great lone yachtsman and Stevenson admirer, who sailed from the Galapagos to Managareva and then followed RLS's track from the Marquesas in the 1920s, was caught in an enormous sea whose waves he estimated to be 120 feet high. How terrifying such an experience was is conveyed in the memoirs of one of RLS's great friends in Samoa, Marjorie Ide (later Mrs Shane Leslie), who tells of being in a typhoon: 'Never shall I forget what I saw. Not waves – for I had been in many heavy gales – but sheer grey walls of water, solid, towering mountains, at least ninety feet high, with white spume tearing, screaming off the tops of them far over the tops of our masts as we lay in the troughs between them.'[4]

The greatest danger on this voyage was not so much from calamitous seas themselves as from the undermanning of the *Casco*. There were only four crew members but no one else with a knowledge of seamanship or navigation, so in rough weather Otis's watch would last as long as the bad weather lasted, which could be seventy-two hours or longer. Had Otis been swept overboard during a squall, that would have been the end of the *Casco* and everyone in her. As it happened, for the first nine days of the voyage conditions were good. Maggie recorded in her diary that the swells were heavy, but the reality was that the *Casco* cut through the water so rapidly that it frequently put its rail under the surface in what seemed an alarming way. This sent the three women into panic, confirming all Otis's prejudices

about 'rich landlubbers', but Louis merely smiled and reacted with exhilaration. Otis began with an amused contempt for the writer – 'to say that
I was favourably impressed with the great author would be stretching the
truth' – but he soon learned to respect his utter fearlessness and testified
that RLS had two salient qualities: he had an instinctive sympathy for the
underdog and he did not know what fear was. For Fanny he had less time,
and had to admonish her sternly not to come up into the cockpit and talk
to the helmsman.

The *Casco* clocked up 256 miles in the first twenty-four hours and
continued to make good progress for the first nine days, even though on the
fifth day out from San Francisco they were passed at speed by a full-rigged
British ship bound round the Horn. Louis alternated his reading – Hardy's
The Woodlanders and Gibbon's *Decline and Fall* – with birdwatching. To the
limit of the north-east trades they had pilot birds in attendance, and when
they dropped away, their place was taken by boatswains – birds of ungainly
shape but beautiful in their white plumage when thrown into relief by the
waves. Louis preferred the pilot birds: 'it strikes one with surprise to see
the pilot bird squatten down upon the swells and greedily drink brine, and
almost with pain to see him wing stalwartly day after day with no more
considerable hope than now and then a piece of orange peel and now and
then a pot of floating grease.'

On the tenth day the barometer began to fall and Otis realised
he was on the edge of a cyclonic storm. Knowing how difficult such
storms are to escape if a ship is drawn within the outer rim, and
unable to calculate on which side of the hurricane the *Casco* stood,
Otis made a lucky guess and altered course westward. Even so, it
took thirty hours before they were clear of high seas, and for three
and a half days Otis had barely slept because of the potential danger.
Others were not so lucky. The fully-manned *Tropic Bird*, which left San
Francisco two days later, had encountered the outer rim, altered course,
and found itself in the eye of the revolving storm. If this had happened to
the singlehanded *Casco*, it would almost certainly have gone to the bottom
of the ocean.[5]

The *Casco* had acquitted itself well in the giant swells. The supreme
test of a sailing ship's 'sea-kindliness' is the length of time it can run
before the wind without 'pooping' a sea or taking such heavy water over
her sides that serious damage is done. Problems arise if the sea is running
faster than the ship, for in such a situation the helmsman, looking back
at the wall of water gaining on him, is apt to lose his nerve or, even if
he keeps it, to be badly hurt by the impact as the thundering avalanche
comes crashing down on the deck. If the helmsman leaves his post, for
whatever reason, it is likely that the ship will 'broach to' – swing round
broadside on to the next great wave – in which case it is most probable

that the helpless and vulnerable craft will be smashed and founder; it is a staple of marine insurance that the sudden disappearance of ships with all hands is caused by such 'broaching to' in the face of a giant wave.

Louis later used the experience of the coming of heavy weather in *The Wrecker*, where Otis appears lightly disguised as Owen Nares:

> We lay our course; we had been doing over eight knots since nine the night before; and I drew a heavy breath of satisfaction. And then I know not what odd and wintry appearance of the sea and sky knocked suddenly at my heart. I observed the schooner to look more than usually small, the men silent and studious of the weather. Nares, in one of his rusty humours, afforded me no shadow of a morning salutation. He, too, seemed to observe the behaviour of the ship with an intent and anxious scrutiny. What I liked still less, Johnson himself was at the wheel, which he span busily, often with a visible effort; and as the seas ranged up behind us, black and imminent, he kept casting behind him eyes of animal swiftness, and drawing in his neck between his shoulders, like a man dodging a blow. From these signs I gathered that all was not exactly for the best; and I would have given a good handful of dollars for a plain answer to the questions which I dared not put.

After narrowly avoiding the storm, Otis was in a particularly curmudgeonly mood, as he pondered the caprices of the Pacific, so unlike other oceans, an awesome cauldron of power where sudden atmospheric changes strike fear into the mariner's heart. The Stevenson ladies tended to find the laconic, pensive Otis boorish and to regard his clipped admonitions as the nagging of a man deprived of the comforts of hearth and home. Louis knew there was more to Otis than this and shared his concern when, on 19 July, as they neared the Marquesas, he spotted a cloud which 'had been visible for some time, a continental isle of sun and shadow, moving innocuously on the skyline far to windward; when upon a sudden this harmless-looking monster, seeming to smell a quarry, paused, hung awhile as if in stays, and breaking off five points, fell like an armed man upon the *Casco*.'

Otis's account is less literary but in some ways even more impressive in its workmanlike way, especially for those who prefer the prose of a Caesar to a Cicero.

> The squall, which was as black as a black cat, first passed the yacht to leeward; when well off the quarter, it suddenly turned and came down upon us, like the dropping of a cloak. All whips were let go, and the wheel was brought hard down; but before the *Casco* could be brought to the wind, she was struck and knocked down until the wind spilled out her sails, and the edge of the house was under water with the sea pouring over the cockpit like a torrent.'

Now was revealed the true reason for Otis's sergeant-majorly 'nagging' of the Stevenson women. He had repeatedly stressed the importance of keeping the lee-side deadlights closed and as repeatedly been ignored. When the squall struck they were open, despite his orders. The edge of the house went under water, and the deadlights were eighteen inches below the surface. The force with which the water poured into the cabin convinced Fanny, Maggie and Valentine that there was a high price to pay for fresh air below and that there was more to Otis's prescription than the petty manias of a cranky seaman.[6]

As the long stretch to the Marquesas neared its end, Louis and Otis were learning grudging respect for each other. Otis admired Louis's willpower, his courage and unflappability; Louis the captain's seamanship and complete lack of cant. Louis once overheard a conversation through the skylight in which Maggie asked Otis whether he had read any of her son's books. He replied bluntly that he had read *Treasure Island* and this had made him disinclined to continue with others. Maggie was perceptibly offended, but Louis at once went up on deck and engaged Otis in conversation. 'Captain, you have raised yourself in my estimation by your frank statement to my mother that you had only read one of my books through and that you did not care for the others; if you had told her that you had read them all and liked them, as most people tell me whether or not, I will be as frank and tell you that I would have thought you lied.'

In *The Wrecker* RLS again employs his favourite method of ambivalence within ambiguity, for at one level Loudon Dodd and Owen Nares (based on Otis) are two aspects of the divided self and at another level Nares is a composite of Otis and Louis himself. Nares as RLS alter ego comes through in the following exchange between Dodd and Nares. '"He was a pig of a father, and I was a pig of a son; but it sort of came over me I would like that fiddle and squeak again. Natural," he added; "I guess we're all beasts." "All sons are, I guess," said I. "I have the same trouble on my conscience; we can shake hands on that." But sometimes the characterisation of Nares is pure Otis as in this phlegmatic slice of scepticism: 'I can't see what anyone wants to live for, anyway. If I could get into someone else's apple-tree and be about twelve years old, and just stick the way I was, eating stolen apples, I won't say. But there's no sense to this grown-up business – sailorising, politics, the piety mill, and all the rest of it. Good clean drowning is good enough for me.'[7]

On 22 July 1888 Stevenson got his first sight of Polynesia. As he wrote: 'The first experience can never be repeated. The first love, the first sunrise, the first South Sea Island, are memories apart and touched by the virginity of sense.' Although day was supposed to follow night almost instantaneously in the tropics, here at just 8°S it took one and a half hours for the day to dawn: it was 4.00 a.m. when the first saffron streaks of dawn showed, but

5.30 a.m. before he could distinguish the clouds from the islands. The first island to appear, on the starboard bow, was Va-huna, with its truncated summit; almost abeam was their destination, Nuku-Hiva, still wreathed in clouds, and between the two, to the southwards, the first rays of the sun displayed the needles of Ha-pu.

The Marquesas islands - or at least their south-easterly fringe - were first discovered by the Mendaña expedition out of Callao in 1595, and named for his haughty wife, the Marquesa de Mendaña who accompanied her husband and the great pilot Quiros in the hunt for the 'isles of wisdom' (the Solomons). The twelve volcanic and mountainous islands, totalling 498 square miles, had been visited by Captain Cook in 1774; as the last islands between Polynesia and the South American coast 3,000 miles away they were a favourite revictualling stop for whalers but were finally occupied and brought under French administration in 1843. The fatal impact of the Europeans on the Pacific had had its usual effects: smallpox had reduced the population of Nuku-Hiva, the Stevensons' destination, from a precolonial 2,000 to a few hundred in 1864–65, and although the population had recovered to between 3–4,000 by 1888, the Stevensons had acted on the warnings in San Francisco, been vaccinated, and taken a further store of vaccine with them. Nuku-Hiva was fourteen miles long and ten miles wide, with mountains that rose steeply from the sea, producing the effect of medieval fortifications: there was one peak of 3905' and another over 3,000', and the only beaches were the mouths of narrow valleys which slipped into the sea to great depths.

As the *Casco* neared its anchorage in Anaho Bay, RLS noticed the razor's edge of the cliffs, the greenness of the dales, the birdsong, and the cleanness and lightness of the air; also: 'the bleating of the thousand sheep which are now being driven along a shoreside hill, thick as an army of marching ants.' As was customary in the Pacific, scores of small canoes manned by excited Polynesians, some in loin cloths, some in shirts, some tattooed from head to toe in patterns, came out to meet them, but Stevenson's debut as an island diplomat was scarcely auspicious. He became alarmed when 'cannibals' swarmed over the side of the *Casco* and gazed in wonderment at the three white women. 'I even questioned if my travels should be much prolonged; perhaps they were destined to a speedy end; perhaps Kauanui (the chief), whom I remarked there, sitting silently with the rest, for a man of some authority, might leap from his hams with an ear-splitting signal, the ship be carried at a rush, and the ship's company butchered for the table.'[8]

At this stage RLS knew nothing about Polynesian etiquette, which required a host to sit as a gesture of reconciliation; to remain standing was an insult. Stevenson unwittingly gave offence by continuing to write instead of sitting on the floor with his guests, and did not, as expected, clap his hands as a signal for the Marquesans to initiate a welcoming ceremony in song and dance. He was tactful enough to give presents, but once again alienated the islanders by not presenting them formally to the ranking chief – a breach of 'manners' that a few generations earlier would have spelled death to the donor.

The Stevensons spent fifteen days on Anaho beach, and in this time RLS made an intense study of the Marquesans and their islands. Nuku-Hiva, he later realised, was one of the most beautiful Pacific islands, second in his opinion only to Moorea in the Tahitian group. The Marquesas were fortunate as regards insect-borne diseases: mosquitoes and hence malaria were unknown and the hateful day-fly found only on Nuku-Hiva. As the months went on he learned to differentiate Marquesans' salient characteristics from those of other Polynesians. As they watched him writing up his journal, he in turn took note: 'The eyes of all Polynesians are large, luminous and melting; they are like the eyes of animals and some Italians.' The apparently menacing reception the *Casco* met with turned out to be largely a failure to communicate, since even the Marquesans, 'so recently and so imperfectly released from a blood-boltered barbarism' shared the general friendliness of the Polynesians. Louis noticed that the Polynesian languages were easy to smatter, but hard to speak properly, and that Polynesians had no trouble with English but found great difficulty with the structures of the French language.

RLS found the Marquesans more touchy than other Polynesians. They never forgot a slight or an insult – a propensity made more tiresome by the number of things they regarded as insults. When the Stevensons left Anaho Bay they found the presents they had given left untouched on the beach because they had not gone through the proper protocol, and there were other examples: when Louis offered biscuits and chocolate, when he asked to *buy* some coconuts, when a chance remark offended someone's idea of status. On the other hand he admired their reserve and dignity and thought them the handsomest race in the Pacific: six feet was the *average* height of the males, and they were strongly muscled, free from fat, swift in action and graceful in repose.

The near-extinction of the race from smallpox had bred a kind of national neurosis, wherein the thought of death was uppermost in their minds. Allied to this was a more keenly developed fear of ghosts than elsewhere in Polynesia, possibly because within a lifetime's memory the dead far outnumbered the living. The general depression was such that the entire body of Marquesan literature was being allowed to die out, in contrast to Samoa where every trifling incident inspired a new epic. The Marquesans were apathetic and listless and bothered to dress up only when a Western ship called; the rest of the time they sought solace in opium. 'The coral waxes, the palm grows, and man departs' was a favourite maxim of the Marquesan, usually delivered as the speaker folded his hands in resignation.

Economic life had declined even more proportionately than the death-rate, and suicide by hanging or poison was widespread.

> The Marquesan beholds with dismay the approaching extinction of his race. The thought of death sits down with him to meat and rises with him from his bed ... Praise not any man till he is dead, said the ancients; envy not any man till you hear the mourners, might be the Marquesan parody ... Fond as it may appear, we labour and refrain, not for the rewards of any single life, but with a timid eye upon the lives and memories of our successors; and where no one is to succeed, of his own family, or his own tongue, I doubt whether Rothschilds would make money or Cato practise virtue.

These reflections, and comparisons with conditions elsewhere in Polynesia, led RLS to propound a general law: 'Where there have been fewest changes, important or unimportant, salutary or hurtful, there the race survives. Where there have been most, important or unimportant, salutary or hurtful, there it perishes.' This 'law' receives support from the findings of modern sociology, for it has been discovered that national *angst* or psychosis is most usually associated with the *rate of change* rather than change itself.

Perhaps because of the fears of total extinction, the Marquesans were besotted with children, would never punish their offspring, and reacted to strangers either favourably or unfavourably entirely according to the reactions of the children. This prompted a further apothegm from RLS: early Polynesia, he declared, exhibited the spectacle of 'maneating among kindly men, child-murder among child-lovers, industry in a race the most idle, invention in a race the least progressive.' Levels of crime were high on the islands, but punishment by the French was effective since detection was easy, especially since most thefts did not involve the local currency, and deterrence cast-iron, as solitary confinement – the penalty prescribed for theft – was torture for a Marquesan. It also suited the French, who liked to use convict labour for essential public works.

According to RLS, the Marquesans had just two subjects of abiding interest. For the women it was the arrival of foreign whale boats: whalers used to call at the Marquesas to carry off a complement for a cruise, and although the abduction no longer obtained, the 'congress' did: 'the other day the whole school-children of Nuku-Hiva and Ka-pu escaped in a body to the woods and lived there for a fortnight in promiscuous liberty.' For the men the interest was to restrain the women by hundreds of meaningless taboos (properly *tapus*), which made Stevenson the feminist curl his lip.

Regard for female chastity is the usual excuse for the disabilities that men
delight to lay upon their wives and mothers. Here the regard is absent; and
behold the women still bound hand and foot with meaningless proprieties ...
How exactly parallel is this with European practice, when princesses were suffered
to penetrate the strictest cloister and women could rule over a land in which they
were denied the control of their own children.

Yet RLS recognised that *tapu* was a primitive form of property law
– here women were overtly recognised as property – so that if you ate
fruit from the orchard of another you incurred a curse which made you
fall down and die.[9]

After fifteen days in Anaho Bay, Otis took on a local beachcomber called
Regler to pilot the *Casco* round to Tai-o-hae on the south side of the island,
where they stayed ten days. Situated on the beach of a precipitous green
bay, this was the commercial, religious and civil capital of the Marquesas
but, more importantly, it was the locale of Melville's *Typee* – a book which
had fascinated Louis ever since Stoddard lent it to him in 1879, and he at
once set out on an expedition into the valley of the Typee. But the sight
of cannibal feasting places always sickened him and he was open about
this.

There are certain sentiments which we call emphatically human – denying the
honour of that name to those who lack them. In such feasts – particularly where
the victim had been slain at home, and man banqueted on ... a comrade with
whom he had played in infancy, or a woman whose favours they had shared –
the whole body of these sentiments is outraged. To consider it too closely is to
understand, if not to excuse, these fervours of self-righteous old ship-captains,
who would man their guns, and open fire in passing, on a cannibal island.

The trip caused RLS to have a dig at Melville, on the basis of
having called the valley of Hapaa 'Hapar': 'At the christening [of Melville]
... some influential fairy must have been neglected. "He shall be able
to see." "He shall be able to tell", "He shall be able to charm", said
the friendly godmother. "But he shall not be able to hear", exclaimed
the last.' This sally has provoked an answer from those who assert
Melville's claim to be a superior observer of the Pacific. Melville, it is
said, learned about savages from life, not from books; he lived among
cannibals, as Stevenson did not, and his superiority to RLS shows in his
total absorption in the Marquesas. RLS, by contrast, is accused of taking
to the Pacific an *a priori* Rousseauesque notion of the noble savage which
he hoped to find confirmed; in a word, he was taking his European mental
and cultural baggage to Polynesia. Professor Kiely argues that Melville's
description of Nuku-Hiva is far superior to Stevenson's because the
dialectic between home and abroad is absent; RLS, by contrast, was
at pains to explain what Nuku-Hiva was *not* in European terms. Kiely

continues: 'With the analogies to a church, a signboard, buttresses, a canopy and statuary, as well as a negative mention of smoky towns, the picture of a virgin land is confused, almost blurred.' Yet this is to ignore the powerful feeling for Scotland that made *Catriona* and *Weir of Hermiston* possible; if Stevenson had immersed himself totally in the Pacific, he would have produced only works like *The Beach of Falesá* and *Ebb-Tide*.[10]

On Nuku-Hiva RLS saw as little of the European population as possible; after all, he had not come 3,000 miles over stormy oceans, far from the main sea-lanes, to converse with the kind of people he would have crossed the street to avoid in London. Some of them, however, knew who he was and remembered him. When Jack and Charmian London came to Tai-o-hae in 1907 they found many traces of RLS. In the first place, the cottage they rented turned out to be the old clubhouse where Stevenson liked to drop in of an afternoon. Then they met a Mrs Fisher, who had met him in Anaho in August 1888 and who recalled: 'He used to go about barefoot, with his trousers and shirt-sleeves turned up, and never wore a hat; and 'most everyone thought he was a little crazy.' Nevertheless, RLS was frequently ashore as the guest of the French commandant (this was the administrative centre of Nuku-Hiva) and struck up a friendship with a French lay missionary, Michel Blanc, to whom he offered passage on the *Casco* for the run to Hiva-Oa, ninety miles to windward. Captain Otis, meanwhile, had used his time well. He dismissed the original steward and instead hired Ah Fu, who was to become a great favourite with the Stevensons. Additionally he signed on an ex-trading captain named Goltz, who shipped out as pilot and first mate, with special responsibility for taking the *Casco* through the perilous Low Archipelago.[11]

It was as well that Otis had found someone to relieve him on the bridge, for on the run to Hiva-Oa he experienced the worst seas of his life. Everyone on board except RLS was seasick (though Maggie's account claims she was the sole survivor and that even Louis succumbed), even Otis – for the first time ever. One of the squalls that hit them was so ferocious that it washed overboard the entire complement of pigs and sheep that Louis had bought at Tai-o-hae as gifts. RLS describes thus the experience of being in continuous high seas:

> the most miserable forty hours that any of us had ever passed. We were swung and tossed together all that time like shot in a stage thunderbox. The mate was thrown down and had his head cut open. The captain was sick on deck; the cook sick in the galley. Of all our party only two sat down to dinner. I was one. I own that I felt wretchedly; and I can only say of the other, who professed to feel quite well, that she fled at an early moment from the table.

Next day the ship beat through the Bordelais straits between Hiva-Oa and Tauata and came to anchor in Taahauku Bay on the south-western coast of the island in the late afternoon. There the *Casco* lay in a narrow, uncomfortable anchorage where it was tossed incessantly by the choppy swell caused by the funnelling of the sea through a narrow entrance between two promontories. Hiva-Oa was in the news at the time as a man named McCallum had made a fortune there from cotton and copra, thus luring out from the waterfront dives of San Francisco the low-life that was known in every Pacific community as 'the beach'. Hiva-Oa, twenty-two miles long and five miles wide, was not so beautiful as Nuku-Hiva but had a far more attractive climate, being exposed to the south-east Trades. In particular it boasted the long fertile Atuona valley, later to be made famous when Paul Gauguin came here in 1901 for the last two years of his life. Louis at once suggested to Brother Michel that they should go riding there, even though it was now the rainy season.

The ride into the interior on 26–27 August left Louis with conflicting impressions. 'I thought it the loveliest and by far the most ominous and gloomy spot on earth.' The ambiguity seemed to extend to the sexuality of the islanders. In the interior he met a beautiful Marquesan woman, reminiscent of Melville's Fayaway, who had had a whaling man as a lover. This set Louis thinking: 'Nor could I refrain from wondering what had befallen her lover; in the rain and mire of what sea-ports he had trampled since then; in what close and garish drinking-dens had found his pleasure; and in the ward of what infirmary dreamed his last of the Marquesas.' On the other hand, he encountered a Marquesan maiden who seemed to be no spirit but one imbued with the Christian sense of sexual shame. 'Nearby in the stream a grown girl was bathing naked in a goyle between the two stepping-stones; and it amused me to see with what alacrity and real alarm she bounded on her many-coloured underclothes. Even in these daughters of cannibals shame was eloquent.' Old Pacific hands were later to say that RLS had misinterpreted the gestures and was mistaken, or else had encountered the one true missionary girl in the entire islands.

Exhausted by his long ride in the Atuona valley, alternately overheated by the rays of the sun and chilled in the cool of the ravines, Louis developed a fever and hacking cough – only his second illness since leaving Bournemouth a year before. As he convalesced, he was irritated by the irruption of the local chiefs Paaaeua and Moipu, the Esau and Jacob of the island, representing respectively the past and the present, who vied for his attention – an irritation increased by the fact that Moipu was the universal cynosure of European eyes on Hiva-Oa yet Louis could not stand him. The two chiefs were forever upstaging each other in an attempt to get kudos from the reflected glory of the visitors. 'It was found impossible . . .

to get a photograph of Moipu alone; for whenever he stood up before the camera his successor placed himself unbidden by his side, and gently but firmly held to his position.'[12]

There was also a visit on the yacht from Mapiao, the local witchdoctor. Mapiao would not lift a finger for himself, even to stretch out and get a glass of water. He imperiously signed to Fanny to perform the chore for him. The sequel is disputed. Louis claims that Fanny misunderstood and hurled their guests' dinner overboard, but there is a suspicion that Fanny, never a woman to take a direct order lying down, made a 'deliberate mistake' to put the witchdoctor in his place. This time the strange actions of the Europeans were not construed as an insult: 'I must do Mapiao justice,' wrote Louis; 'all laughed, but his laughter rang the loudest.'

It was not often that Hiva-Oa played host to a foreign ship, but while the *Casco* was at anchor there also arrived the yacht *Nyanza*, captain Cumming Dewar, 'a man', reported Louis, 'of the same country and the same county with myself and one whom I had seen walking as a boy on the shores of the Alpes Maritimes'. Dewar and his party spent the evening and the next morning with the Stevensons, swapping lore about the Tuamotu archipelago, the next hazard to be faced by the *Casco*. Louis summed up his Marquesan experiences in the light of his many visits to old cannibal sites and his meetings with the native luminaries. He remembered the young chief Taipi-Kikino who had been so welcoming on Nuku-Hiva and the 'Polynesian Rob Roy' Kooamua, who now lived respectably in a European house but within living memory had dined on 'Long Pig'. The most impressive Marquesan he had met was Queen Vaekehu at Tai-o-hae. She was another ex-cannibal, tattooed from head to foot, who before her conversion to Christianity had been a great beauty over whom island warriors fought like Greeks and Trojans over Helen of Troy; like Helen she had been passed from victor husband to victor husband, entirely dependent on the fortunes of battle. As for cannibalism, Louis was learning tolerance; anthropophagy was disgusting to Europeans, but so was meat eating to vegetarians or Buddhists. Moreover, the alleged superiority of the European to the Polynesian seemed to him to consist in 'comparing Polynesians with an ideal person, compact of generosity and gratitude, whom I never had the pleasure of encountering; and forgetting that what is almost poverty to us is wealth almost unthinkable to them'.[13]

On 4 September the *Casco* was towed from its anchorage by a whaleboat, ran through the Bordelais Straits and set sail for the Tuamotu archipelago, alias the Paumotus, aka the Low Archipelago and the Dangerous Islands. In the nineteenth century this group was usually referred to as the Paumotus ('Submissive Islands'), so-called after their conquest by the Tahitians, but their true name, readopted in modern times, is the Tuamotus ('Distant Islands'). In electing to take the *Casco* into these dangerous waters, RLS was deliberately going in harm's way, and it is a measure of Otis's growing respect for him that he agreed to go. The Tuamotu archipelago, because of its treacherous currents and inhospitable shores, making accurate navigation all but impossible, has been responsible for more shipwrecks in the Pacific than all the hurricanes and typhoons put together. As RLS explained it:

> The huge system of the trades is, for some reason, quite confounded by this multiplicity of reefs; the wind intermits, squalls are frequent from west and south-west, hurricanes are known, The currents are, besides, inextricably intermixed; dead reckoning becomes a farce; the charts are not to be trusted; and such is the number and similarity of these islands that, even when you have picked one up, you may be none the wiser. The reputation of the place is consequently infamous; insurance offices exclude it from their field, and it was not without misgiving that my captain risked the *Casco* in such waters.

During the five-day passage from the Marquesas RLS claimed to have had a moment of truth, similar in some ways to the great scene in the try-works in *Moby-Dick*. He told Baxter:

> There was nothing visible but the southern stars and the steersman out there by the binnacle lamp . . . the night was as warm as milk; and all of a sudden I had a vision of – Drummond Street. It came to me like a flash of lightning; I simply returned thither and into the past. And when I remembered all that I had hoped and feared as I picked about Rutherford's in the rain and the east wind: how I feared I would make a mere shipwreck, and yet timidly hoped not, how I feared I should never have a friend, far less a wife, and yet passionately hoped I might; how I hoped (if I did not take to drink) I should possibly write one little book, etc, etc, etc. And then, wow – what a change! I feel somehow as if I should like the incident set upon a brass plate at the corner of that dreary thoroughfare, for all students to read, poor devils, when their hearts are down.[14]

All such dreamy nostalgia was an impossible luxury once the *Casco* reached the latitude of the Tuamotus. They picked up the classic weather of the dangerous archipelago: a big blow from the south-west and, much worse, an overcast sky, which made it impossible to take chronometer sightings. They were supposed to fetch Takaroa on their track but found themselves thirty miles off course. Now did Louis at last fully appreciate the words of his friend Charles Warren Stoddard: 'If you would have adventure, the real article and plenty of it, make your will, bid farewell to home and friends, and embark for the Paumotus.' On the morning of the fifth day, the *Casco* passed the uninhabited island of Tikei but soon afterwards, because of the swiftness of the currents and the impossibility of taking observations from the sun in a cloudy sky, Otis lost his way between Raraka and Kauehi, the latter an isle of singular eeriness from which came no sound but the cry of seabirds. Louis was incredulous and unsympathetic.

We were scarce doing three and a half; and they asked me to believe that (in five minutes) we had dropped an island, passed eight miles of open water and run almost high and dry among the next. But my captain was more sorry for himself to be afloat in such a labyrinth, laid the *Casco* to, with the dog line up and down, and sat on the stern rail and watched it till morning. He had enough of night in the Paumotus.

All of this rests on a misunderstanding of the technicalities of navigation. What happened was that Otis was sailing by dead reckoning, since he was unable to take observations, and because of the extreme swiftness of the currents missed the expected landfall. It was not until next day that the anxious Otis picked up Taiaro. At sunset he sighted Raraka but in the night, because of heavy squalls, the vessel's position again became uncertain. Tired of dodging between Raraka and Kauehi he decided to improvise a 'laying to' strategy. The problem was that the tactic of heaving to or allowing a ship to float like a log in a storm was too dangerous to employ in such a maze of reefs and lagoons unless there was an auxiliary motor on board. What happened was that Otis spent the night watching the log line, continually checking the charted course and praying that his passengers did not realise the danger they were in. The helmsman was constantly responding to Otis's orders as he gauged the tug and jerk of the helm and issued commands accordingly: 'Bow to port!' 'Bow to starboard!' 'Reduce sail!' 'Add sail!', and so on. Much of the navigation was by ear, as Otis seemed to pick up surf dead ahead every ten minutes; the islands, at right angles to each other, formed a channel through which the variable currents ran. Fortunately, at daybreak Otis found himself in the middle of the channel. Since the French navigation charts of the islands were utterly unreliable, Otis and his mate had to thread their way through the maze by sight. By mid-morning the *Casco*, on a rising tide, entered the narrow south-east opening of the great Fakarava lagoon. The ship ran through the north-eastern pass, among razor-sharp coral-heads that studded the lagoon for five miles on the approach to the harbour.

It seems likely that RLS, though appreciating that the Tuamotus were the trickiest islands in the Pacific to negotiate, never fully understood the feat of navigation that Captain Otis had achieved. In December 1907 Jack London, himself a skilled navigator, and his captain on the *Snark* found themselves completely unable to fetch Rangiroa, their destination in the Dangerous Archipelago, and in the end put about for Tahiti in despair. The classic Jack London short story 'The Seed of McCoy' vividly illustrates the nightmare of trying to navigate in the Tuamotus; unable to make landfall in the islands because of the treachery of the currents, a burning ship drifts all the way from Pitcairn Island (where Fletcher Christian and the *Bounty* mutineers sought refuge in 1789) to Tahiti. 'Are they not enticing, these names?' asked Charmian London. 'Listen – Mangareva, Oeno, Mururea, Athunui, Vahitahi, Negno-Nengo – and Fakarava.' Enticing perhaps, pretty poison, certainly. Jack London has one of his characters in 'The Seed of McCoy' refer to the cruise of the *Casco* in these waters thus: 'The currents are always changing. There was a man who wrote books. I forget his name, in the yacht *Casco*. He missed Takaroa by thirty miles and fetched Tikei, all because of the shifting currents.'[15]

Inside the Fakarava lagoon, the *Casco* found the most secure anchorage and the smoothest water since leaving San Francisco. The inner sea of the lagoon was 35 miles long and 13 miles wide, circled by a rim of palm-fringed coral only a quarter to half a mile in width. The waters of the lagoon, clear to a depth of many fathoms, surged with the ebb and flow of the tides that raced through the narrow openings. Louis at once grasped the difference between volcanic islands and coral atolls or the Marquesas and the Tuamotus: 'the Himalayas are not more different from the Sahara.' He was delighted with the 'ghost town' nature of Rotoava, the port of Fakarava and capital of the Tuamotus, but felt insecure about sleeping aboard the *Casco* in the lagoon, since both tidal waves and hurricanes were known to batter the island. He therefore rented a three-room shack with a verandah front and back; usually the arrangement was that Louis and Fanny took the front verandah and Lloyd the back, while Maggie and Valentine sat in opposite corners of the sitting room.

After breakfast at 6.00 a.m., cooked on a paraffin stove and usually consisting of coffee, soup, bread, butter and marmalade – they all returned to the *Casco* for lunch and dinner – Louis liked to sally forth and collect data for the letters he had contracted to write for McClure. In contrast to the Marquesans, he found the Tuamotans happy, healthy and peaceloving; they had never been cannibals, were not wealthy enough to attract the attention of European traders, were not riven by sectional rivalries and subsisted on a primitive economy of pearl shells, copra and a diet of fish, shellfish, breadfruit, bananas, taro and coconut. RLS noted the idiosyncrasies of the people: indifferent to leprosy but exaggeratedly fearful of elephantiasis, they reminded him in their mixture of superstition and rationality of his fellow Scots; where in Edinburgh the odd juxtaposition was that of Calvinism and drunkenness, here the syncretism was that of a belief in ghosts and the old deities with a devotion to Jesus Christ. 'So in Europe the gods of Olympus slowly dwindled into village bogies, so today, the theological Highlander sneaks from under the eye of the Free Church divine to lay an offering by a sacred well.' Officially, religious belief in the archipelago was divided between Catholicism and Mormonism, but there was a huge crossover rate and the islanders tended to opt for Catholicism when well and Mormonism when sick. A further complication was that the brand of Mormonism practised here was not the polygamous belief fostered by the

St Paul of the dispensation, Brigham Young, but the early pure doctrine of Joseph Smith. Naturally, behind the swapping between the Mormon and Catholic faiths lay paganism: the sister of one chief known to Stevenson 'was very religious, a great churchgoer, one that used to reprove me if I stayed away; I found afterwards that she privately worshipped a shark.'[16]

Louis repeatedly stressed the contrast between Marquesans and Tua-motans. As against the inertia and depression of the people of Nuku-Hiva and Hiva-Oa he found the Fakaravans flourishing, forward-looking, concerned with hygiene and interested in money; in the period 1830–50 when the danger to shipwrecked crews elsewhere in the Pacific was cannibalism, the Tuamotans liked to seize the crews and ransom them. The Marquesans had the palm for physical beauty and the Paumotan people were their inferior in looks and height – fully an inch shorter on the average; 'the Marquesan open-handed, inert, insensible to religion, childishly self-indulgent – the Paumotan greedy, hardy, enterprising, a religious disputant, and with a trace of the ascetic character.'

Increasingly Louis marvelled at the stamina of Polynesian women. In Fakarava he had personal experience of a woman who swam for nine hours in the ocean, helping her husband who would otherwise have given up; in Hawaii, later, he came across a woman who had breasted the flood for twelve hours in a high sea and come ashore with her dead husband in her arms. He found this sort of information fascinating and it deepened his resolve to be a serious chronicler of the Pacific. The conflict between his serious intentions and the colourful traveller's tales eventually led to the cancellation of the series of letters commissioned by McClure after thirty-four of them had appeared in print. McClure observed, somewhat unfairly and certainly inaccurately: 'There were two men in Stevenson – the romantic adventurer of the eighteenth century and the Scotch covenanter of the nineteenth century. Contrary to our expectation, it was the moralist and not the romancer which his observations in the South Seas awoke in him, and the public found the moralist less interesting than the romancer.'

The Stevensons always had problems wherever they put down roots, however temporary, but the farce that took place in Fakarava over the rented shack was egregious even by their standards. The pastor of Rotoava, Brother Taniera, who took the roving travellers under his wing, and arranged the rental, turned out to be a Polynesian convict sentenced to internal exile – showing that the combination of being a criminal and being a 'reverend' is by no means a feature unique to the twentieth-century U.S.A. He had been banished from Tahiti to Fakarava for spending tax money on his own pleasures, and in Rotoava he continued to take the same cavalier line with the property of others. He loftily rented the shack to the Stevensons but neglected to tell them that it was not his to rent, but belonged to a French

Tahitian named François, who was away with his family on a trading trip. One day the François family suddenly appeared after narrowly escaping drowning at sea. Disconcerted to find cuckoos in their nest, they nevertheless waited patiently until Taniera retrieved their clothes from their home. When Louis heard that François had lost his cutter, half a ton of copra and all his tools in a storm, he offered to advance him the rent. To Stevenson's amazement François refused on the grounds that Taniera was his friend. A puzzled RLS takes up the story:

> His friend, you observe; not his creditor. I inquired into that and was assured that Taniera, an exile in a strange isle, might possibly be in debt himself, but was certainly no man's creditor ... when the time came for me to leave ... I duly made my rent out to Taniera. He was satisfied and so was I. But what had he to do with it? Mr Donat, acting magistrate and a man of kindred blood, could throw no light on my story; a plain person, with a taste for letters, cannot be expected to do more.[17]

Old Pacific hands later opined that the correct course was for RLS to have sent back gifts later to François, since money was not then a common medium of exchange in Polynesia.

After two weeks in Fakarava, Fanny suddenly decided they should clear for Tahiti at once. The reason was that Louis could not shake off the cold he had caught in the Atuona valley on Hiva-Oa; even on the open verandah his breathing was laboured. Her peremptory instructions to Otis to take the *Casco* out on to the open sea at night led to a blazing row with the captain, who had never liked the way Louis allowed his wife to 'meddle'. Having got into the Fakarava lagoon by the skin of his teeth, Otis knew the conditions that awaited him outside its protective girdle and was in no mood to start until wind and waves were favourable. He pointed out to Fanny that the wind was against them, and even if it wasn't, in the prevailing conditions and at night they would be sure to run on to the knife-edged coral-heads. A compromise was reached. Next morning the *Casco* set sail and forty-eight hours later, after a 250 mile crossing the ship docked at Papeete. All the way, Louis had been burning up with fever. Lodged at first in the Hôtel de France, he was examined by a local physician who pronounced his condition grave, and predicted that the next haemorrhage would be fatal. Having faced death so many times, Louis was stoical. He called Otis in to instruct him on how to settle the affairs of the yacht, and the captain was amazed to find him smoking a cigarette and preparing to face the reaper with a smile and a jest.

Every time death was predicted for Louis, he confounded the critics. This time was no exception. Next morning he was much better and was removed to a cottage opposite the main entrance to the harbour. Here he rested for three weeks until he had regained his strength. His reputation for eccentricity lost nothing in the telling when, on the mend, he wandered absentmindedly from the garden, where he sat wearing pyjamas, with legs and arms rolled up, into the street, where he collided with Otis and the U.S. consul.

Papeete, the capital of Tahiti, disconcerted the Stevenson party, used so far to a more primitive way of life. With a population of 4,000 – half of them French, the others Tahitians and half-breeds with a sprinkling of other races – Papeete hovered disconcertingly between naïveté and sophistication. Maggie agreed with Cumming Dewar of the *Nyanza* that the splendour of Papeete harbour was let down by the squalor of the town and hit the nail on the head: 'I don't much like Tahiti. It seems to me a sort of halfway house between savage life and civilisation, with the drawbacks of both and the advantages of neither.' Social stratification in Papeete was very clear: there was the French official and administrative class at the apex, then the Cantonese who were the bankers, money changers and principal property owners; finally came the luckless native Tahitians, who lived in little villages along the shore from which came such a din that RLS, used to the absolute quiet of Fakarava, found it difficult to sleep. He got his revenge by setting the opening of his 'diabolical' novel *The Ebb-Tide* in the 'hell' of Papeete.

In his efforts to find a more congenial place to stay, Louis suggested to Otis the possibility of landfall on Huahine, the easternmost island of the Leeward Group of the Society Islands. Otis got out his charts and conferred with local mariners. His conclusions were mixed: on the one hand the reefs surrounding Huahine were dangerous and night sailing out of the question; on the other, there was excellent anchorage and a good pier inside the barrier. But when he mentioned the excessive rainfall, Louis, knowing the likely consequences for his lungs, decided against the idea; instead he suggested the village of Taravao, on the windward side of the island, on the tiny isthmus that almost bisects Tahiti – with the smaller and southern section being called Taiarapu.

On 28 October the *Casco* set sail once more. Once again they ran into foul weather and took thirty hours to beat up the sixty miles to Taravao, in the teeth of a gale the whole way. Caught in a cross sea in the turbulent Moorea channel, Otis at one moment thought they might have to abandon ship and ordered a boat lowered. Fanny scarcely improved her image in Otis's eyes by remarking as she saw the boat: 'Isn't that nice? We shall soon be ashore!' Louis was scathing about his wife's fatuousness: 'Thus does the female mind unconsciously skirt along the edge of eternity.' Even before this experience Louis was writing to Baxter and Colvin that the ever-present threat of shipwreck meant he sent all his 'copy' to England by separate routes, and about his general disillusionment with the inappropriately named ('Pacific, aw-haw-haw') ocean: 'the sea is a terrible place, stupefying to the mind and poisonous to the temper, the sea, the motion, the lack of space, the cruel publicity, the villainous tinned goods, the sailors, the captain, the passengers – but you are amply repaid when you sight an island, and drop anchor in a new world.' As Otis brought the *Casco* in to anchorage through heavy surf, Louis asked him with a ghost of a smile on his face 'if Captain Otis did not think such yachting gymnastics were rather risky sports for invalid authors to indulge in'.[18]

Taravao proved another disappointment. Wedged between two 7000′ mountains, it was spectacularly beautiful but not fit for European habitation. Surrounded by a dense forest of enormous trees and tangled undergrowth, it was hot, humid and mosquito-ridden, with never enough breeze to keep the insects away. Fanny, not convinced that Louis's convalescence was complete, insisted that they press on to a more airy spot and opted for Tautira on the far opposite end of the island from Papeete. Fanny persuaded a reluctant local trader to part with his waggon and team, and next day the party set out to cover the twenty miles overland to Tautira. They jolted uncomfortably over twenty-one streams, sustained by frequent cups of cocoa, but Louis was exhausted when he reached Tautira.

Tautira Louis described as 'mere heaven'. Set among fern forests beside the lagoon, sheltered from the north-west and east winds and allegedly with the best climate in the Pacific, it was a cluster of 'bird-cage' houses with neat lawns laid out under coconut palms and it satisfied the 'primitive' criteria, since just two white men lived there: a French gendarme and a Dutch priest. Tahitian houses, unlike others in the Pacific, had walls of split bamboo, affording privacy yet still allowing the circulation of air; in these latitudes wooden-walled European houses were unbearably stuffy. Fanny immediately rented one of the 'bird-cages'; Maggie thought the rent exorbitant, but it was more likely that the locals had no idea of what might constitute a fair rent and would have been content with a parting gift at the end of the tenancy. There for a week Louis tossed feverishly, his lungs congested, his mind oscillating between hallucination and dull torpor.

He was convinced it was Princess Moe who saved his life. Already celebrated after appearing in books by George Pembroke and Pierre Loti, Moe hurried home from Papeete once she heard of the foreigners' arrival and acted as hostess: she visited RLS daily, bringing him fresh white mullet, *miti* sauce, coconut milk, lime juice and wild red pepper. Of the royal house of Fa'a'a, she held the hereditary title of Matea of Tautira, and had diplomatically papered over a breach of Tahitian etiquette, since the Stevensons had arrived uninvited 'quite as if a Polynesian invaded one of Britain's royal estates, for these villages are on the same basis of royal domain'.[19]

After a week of this diet, Louis recovered and was able to appreciate fully both his 'Fairy Princess' (Moe) and the 'Fairyland' of Tautira. Moe, to show her authority, moved RLS into the *fare* (house) of the sub-chief Ori, leaving him just one room in which to store his belongings, and then moved Ori and his family into another *fare*. Despite this awkwardness, Louis made close friends with Ori, who had acted as host, without authority, before Moe arrived. Ori, 6'4" tall, was a Christian sub-chief who spoke good French and fair English; Louis described him as 'the very finest specimen of native we have yet seen . . . more like a Roman emperor in bronze'. In his imposing physicality Ori reminded RLS of Henley; explained the likeness to the chief and impersonated Henley's gestures and body-language; Ori, however, felt quite cast down at the thought that he could not match the flamboyance of the original. However, there was a touch of Henley in his attitude to Fanny: he did what even 'Burly' himself and RLS dared not do – he rebuked her for her extravagance. But Ori adored Louis, adopted him as his 'brother', insisted he stay in his house indefinitely and fed him when the Stevensons' food supplies ran out. Louis adjusted well to the local fare and never tired of fish, pig and *poi* – a sort of porridge of pounded taro with coconut cream, though his family did and longed for release from the predictable board.[20]

In this 'heaven' of Tautira, which Louis experienced as a kind of wonderful dream of fairyland – he dubbed the place Hans Christian Andersenville – he regained his health, played his flageolet, read Virgil and continued to work on the final stages of *The Master of Ballantrae*. He composed the first of his long poems inspired by Pacific legends – 'The Song of Rahero', a classic tale of revenge and dedicated it to Ori:

> Ori, my brother in the island mode,
> In every tongue and meaning much my friend.

Meanwhile, the Tautirans showered him and his family with kindness. Every morning the villagers would bring baskets of mangoes and papayas, whole stems of white mountain *fei*, bananas, fresh fish and their special delicacy – a calabash of fresh raw mullet with baked taro and breadfruit. Whenever Louis or one of his party went strolling by the river in the shade of the forest, they would be importuned with invitations to eat; to refuse these was a serious affront. The greatest cultural adjustment required was from Maggie who, after seeing a performance of overtly sexual dances, wrote: 'the more one sees and hears of what goes on here, the more one can understand the Indian system of early marriages!'[21]

Maggie was also the principal in the drama that kept the Stevensons in their paradise for so long. The *Casco* had lain at Taravao a few days before coming on to Tautira, thus increasing the prestige of the visitors. Maggie entertained thirty of the local women on board the yacht and in the course of the party offered a prayer that God should reveal to them any defects in the vessel. The blunt-spoken, no-nonsense Otis, in his contempt for 'psalm-singing females' who dared to cast aspersions on his beloved *Casco*, tested its seaworthiness by removing the copper sheeting from the masthead of the mainmast. He found it far gone with dry rot. It seemed that in their rush to get RLS out of San Francisco, on Fanny's urgent promptings, the eccentric millionaire Dr Merritt, and Otis himself, had both relied too much on assurances from the former sailing master that the masts were sound. It now transpired that the *Casco* had left California with a weakness in the mast, and this had been exacerbated by the hard strain of surf-riding and high seas, perhaps especially on the run from Papeete to Taravao.

Otis then took the ship back to Papeete by gentle stages but found that it would take five weeks to replace the mainmast. It was normally a one-week job but the only carpenter in the port with the skill to do the job was a beachcomber who first quoted an exorbitant fee and then refused to be rushed and took days off whenever he felt like it. The consequence was that by the end of November, Louis, without word from Otis, began to grow concerned. In expectation of an imminent departure he and Fanny spent £17 on 22 November on a great feast in thanksgiving to the people of Tautira: they laid on four large pigs, breadfruit, taro, bananas, pineapples, papayas, coconuts. Now it seemed there would be further delays. Louis confided his worries to Ori, who at once volunteered to make the journey to Papeete in a whaleboat, both to fetch provisions and to get word from Otis. He departed on 3 December and five days later was back with news of the *Casco*'s tardy progress. Among the provisions ordered from Papeete which Ori brought back was a bottle of champagne, which Louis opened for him at a celebratory dinner. Ori liked the sparkling wine so much that he announced his intention of imbibing the 'drink of kings' every day thenceforth – until he asked the price, whereat his handsome face fell and he mournfully poured back his refilled glass into the bottle.

It was 22 December before Otis finally brought the vessel round to Tautira for the next leg of the voyage, and then the hospitality mania of the Tautirans ensured that another three days were spent in joyous and sorrowful farewells, so that the travellers did not clear for the northward journey to Hawaii until Christmas Day. Although RLS was by now bored with the attractions of his paradise, he left with regret and later told Henry James that he would rather have received the eloquent letter of farewell Ori wrote for him than to have composed *Redgauntlet* or the sixth book of the *Aeneid*.[22]

The northward run to the Hawaiian islands completed the round of close encounters with the hazards of the Pacific that had plagued the travellers ever since leaving San Francisco. The only land they sighted for a month was on 27 December, forty-eight hours after clearing from Tautira, when they caught a distant glimpse of the most outlying island of the Tuamotu group. Then came a succession of calms which added to the difficulties of tacking against the north-west trades and against which the *Casco* made slight headway – just one degree of latitude a day, or sixty-five to seventy miles. This was exasperating, and passengers and crew alike grew despondent, with the single exception of RLS, whose very cheerfulness increased the tensions. Louis was still not entirely happy with Otis, whose dour 'Yankee' sensibility often grated; a letter to Baxter dated 6 October 1888 from Tahiti is full of complaints in broad Scots about the Bligh of the *Casco*. Fanny made things worse by an idiotic suggestion that everyone on board take it in turns to write and then read a short sketch of the cruise. They drew lots to decide turns: Louis got the 'pole position' while Otis was scheduled to appear last. Predictably, the offering of the professional author was praised, as was Fanny's effort, but Otis was the sort of man who did not compete where he could not be top dog; when his turn came round, a sudden 'illness' prevented the recital of his literary efforts.

It was 13 January 1889 before the *Casco* crossed the equator. About fifty miles north of the line the ship picked up a leading wind which gradually increased to a gale; the storm soon worked round abaft the beam, with the sea following the wind. As Otis pondered the strategy of heaving to, it suddenly came to his attention that the vessel was running short of food; the causes, it later transpired, were the seventeen days of calms, extra consumption over Christmas and the New Year and overliberality to the crew. Reduced to a diet of bully beef and hard tack, the travellers listened as Otis explained that they would starve before reaching Hawaii at their present rate of progress. The wind and the waves were making up all the time, and the captain's preferred strategy would be to reduce the risk to the ship by riding out the storm and living on short commons. But even the option of short commons was gone now, and there was no option but to crowd on sail and run before the wind, risking the well-known dangers of speed on a rising sea. When he explained what he intended to do, all but Louis were filled with trepidation.

The *Casco* was soon under double-reefed fore and main sails, with the bonnet off the jib, running before the gale that swept her along like a log on the surge. None of the passengers dared venture on deck, and only the best-lashed crew members could avoid being swept overboard. The hatches were made fast, the deck swept by on-crowding seas, and the cut of spray on the exposed face of the mariners was sharp and unpleasant. Waves broke across the bow and occasionally over the superstructure but the *Casco* was so well designed for Pacific venturing that water got into the cockpit only once. The Stevensons were hurled about in their cabins like eggs in a tin; Ah Fu was knocked headlong whenever he appeared with a platter; thunder and lightning added to the misery; Otis revised his opinion and said these were the worst seas he had ever experienced in his life. RLS, who later used the experience in *The Wrecker*, annoyed Otis by saying that he was enjoying the experience and once came into the captain's stateroom with eyes sparkling with enthusiasm, full of the new and desirable joust with the ocean. Otis, aware of the danger, could not be so sanguine; as the daily log of miles chalked up by the *Casco* increased – 170, 190, 230, 250 – so did the peril. The final two days of the storm were the most unpleasant as the ship endured the full weight of a North Pacific winter; the yacht was forced to lie in a frightening sea to clear the southern point of the isle of Hawaii safely. Hunger drove them on but, Otis later recorded: 'I am not sure that even the prospect of a good meal to a hungry stomach would have been a temptation to endure another twenty-four hours like the last experienced before we reached the lee of Hawaii.'[23]

After ten days of running before the wind they tucked under the protective cover of Hawaii and then experienced 200 miles of comparative smoothness as they glided past Maui, Lanai and Molokai and lay off Diamond Head on the southern tip of Oahu. Even then the ordeal was not over, for they were becalmed for twelve hours off Honolulu, eating bully beef and dreaming of the 'real' food ashore. Finally, at 9.00 a.m. one morning at the end of January the *Casco* picked up a stiff breeze and came roaring past Waikiki like a train.

It had been a sobering experience and Fanny declared that she would never go to sea again, apparently forgetting that such a resolution would condemn her to a lifetime on Oahu; in any case, Fanny regularly issued 'never again' threats and as regularly broke her own promises. Louis's idea all along had been that only at Hawaii could he see his way forward. If there was no money waiting for him, he and his family would have to bite the bullet and endure the long run to San Francisco 'one long dead beat in foul and at last in cold weather', and thence by sea to Panama to pick up a steamer for Southampton. If there was a substantial sum awaiting him in Honolulu from royalties and advances, he intended to pay off the *Casco* and return to San Francisco by more comfortable steamer, and then proceed across the United States in leisurely stages by train before taking the luxury German liner from New York to Southampton. His preferred option was to be rid of the *Casco* – not just so as to be free of Otis but to avoid any further possibility of incurring extra charges. As he explained to Bob: 'Second (what I own I never considered till too late) there was the danger of collisions, of damages, and heavy repairs, of disablement, towing and salvage; indeed, the cruise might have turned round and cost me double. Nor will this danger be quite over till I hear the yacht is in San Francisco.'[24]

There was money waiting for him in Honolulu, he did pay off the *Casco* and send it back to Dr Merritt in San Francisco, but there was no return by luxury liner. Stevenson's wanderings in the Pacific, it turned out, had only just begun.

14

Cruising on the Line

First to meet the *Casco* in Honolulu was Belle Strong, and it was with the Strongs that the Stevenson party dined, *aloha*-style, at the Royal Hawaiian Hotel, gorging themselves on the delicacies of which they had been starved in the past storm-tossed, short-commonsed week. In every important city there was now a Stevenson admirer, and here it was Mrs Caroline Bush who, after entertaining the writer and his family at her home for four days, gave RLS the use of her bungalow on Waikiki beach, which was then no more than twenty to thirty summer houses among the coconut palms along the beach. It was an hour's drive from town to the end of the mule-car line, after which one crossed a causeway and walked through a garden with pink oleander, scarlet hibiscus and tall algaroba trees 'whose fallen thorns drew yells of pain from the barefooted tenants'. Here, on 28 January Louis and Fanny set up yet another temporary home – this time for four months' duration.

All the Stevensons were taken aback by the pace of technological advance in Hawaii. Telephones and electric light came as a culture shock in reverse after the primitive Eden of Tautira. The house, originally described by Mrs Bush as a 'cottage', turned out to possess a large communal room with verandahs and a number of smaller rooms; in the garden, some distance from the house, was a hut which RLS used as a writer's 'den'. Here he put the finishing touches to *The Master of Ballantrae* and *The Wrong Box*, while anxiously writing to Baxter to learn his financial situation.[1]

Louis's first letter to Baxter from Honolulu is full of significant detail, and his attitude was divided between euphoria at what he had achieved on the dangerous cruise and guilt that he had acted irresponsibly as head of the family: 'if I have but nine months of life and any kind of health, I shall have both eaten my cake and got it back again with usury.' In the first place he rejoiced in the news of the birth of a daughter to Henley – unfortunately the girl died five years later – and revealed that it was Katharine de Mattos not Henley whom he considered the real enemy.

He little understands the harm he did me; but I am sure, upon all our cruise, the number of times we – all of us – longed for his presence would show it was no change of liking for him that we feel. For all that, time has not diminished my fear of him, and I doubt if I ever desire to correspond again. As for Katharine, I had an answer to my appeal, which settled that matter; I do not wish to see her.

In revealing that he had paid off the *Casco* and sent it back to San Francisco, he revealed a rapprochement with another father figure:

This reminds me, I believe I poured forth my sorrows over my captain in your ear. Patience and time have quite healed these conflicts; we do what we want now, and the captain is a trusted friend. It *did* require patience in the beginning, but the seed has borne a most plentiful crop, and we feel quite proud of our tame captain, and (as I say) really like the man.

Inevitably, there was news that Fanny was ill – the virtually guaranteed conditioned reflex if her husband was well. Later, in a letter to Bob, Louis let his exasperation with her invalidism show with two separate depreciatory references, but to Baxter he contrasted her malady with the health of the rest of the party: 'My wife is no great shakes: she is the one who has suffered most. My mother has had a Huge Old Time. Lloyd is first chop. I so well that I do not know myself – sea bathing, if you please.' A good index to RLS's sceptical attitude to his wife comes in the explanation as to why Valentine Roch had now left his service – she quit when the *Casco* docked. For many years after RLS's death the Osbournes encouraged the rumour that there had been some kind of dishonesty, and that Valentine had attracted the amorous attentions of the *Casco* crew members. Louis himself allowed this version to become credible by his infuriating habit of talking in abstract riddles – doubtless a habit he had picked up from Henry James – as in his remark on the break with Valentine: 'it has been the usual tale of the maid on board the yacht.' But the real reason for Valentine's departure was that Fanny finally threw one neurotic fit too many. That RLS sympathised with Valentine's plight is clear from his words to Baxter: 'Valentine leaves us here, to mutual glee. Stop her private wages and be ready (when she applies) to give her her little stock.' Valentine took a job as housekeeper in a San Francisco hotel, married, had a son whom she named Louis, and lived on into the 1940s.[2]

To the bungalow in Waikiki came a stream of visitors; in Hawaii people ignored the usual etiquette and called on the struggling author at any time of the day. One of the visitors described RLS as having 'burning eyes, such as I've never seen in a human being, as if they looked out from a fiery inside that was consuming him'. Another was a 35-year old Frenchman, who having had to leave France after a duel, had come out to the islands and married a Hawaiian girl; what was said between him and RLS was not known but to Louis's consternation the day after the talk he read a report in the newspaper that the man had blown his brains out. Another friend was Alan Herbert, a botanist, who saw a lot of RLS in the Kalihi botanical gardens near Honolulu, where the writer, fascinated by plant life, liked to come to relax. Invited to dinner to Waikiki, Herbert went there in full evening dress, expecting a formal affair, to be greeted by RLS in pyjamas – a juxtaposition that caused much mirth in the Stevenson household.

More usually the visitors came uninvited, lacked any perceptiveness and merely came to gawp at fame. On one occasion one of the female leaders of *haole* society, married to a man of influence in the islands, called unannounced and seemed to feel she was doing the author a favour, but was shown the door by Louis, who explained brusquely that he had work to finish; next day the woman's sister called, adopted a much more polite and deferential demeanour, and succeeded in getting on marvellously with the 'difficult prima donna'. Fanny, when not bedridden, either denied such people entrance at the door or, if admitted, soon motioned to them with signs to leave. As at Bournemouth, however, she extended her draconian policies beyond pests and applied them to genuine friends. One evening RLS was enjoying a hearty conversation about the sea when Fanny, from behind his chair, signalled to the visitor that he should leave. At the first hint he rose, but Louis implored him to stay as he was enjoying the talk so much. At this Fanny lost her temper and burst out: 'Oh, I know he wants you to stay and talk but I want him to go to bed.'[3]

Such solicitude for her husband was never in evidence whenever Belle and her ne'er-do-well husband appeared, which was every weekend; the excuse was painting but the reality was scrounging. By now Louis had in effect taken the feckless Joe Strong under his financial wing to join his many other 'clients'. The sole (and dubious) contribution Joe and Belle Strong made to the Stevensons' sojourn in Honolulu was to introduce Louis to the 'royal set' – the entourage of sycophants and hangers-on who battened off King Kalakaua, leader of the traditionalist, anti-capitalist faction. On their first full day in Honolulu the Stevensons had an audience at Iolani palace, to which they responded by inviting Kalakaua to a party on board the *Casco*. The party was notable for displaying the king's bibulous prowess. Louis watched open-mouthed as the monarch consumed five bottles of champagne and two of brandy, before going on to dinner on a visiting warship where he repeated his drinking marathon. 'A bottle of fizz is like a glass of sherry to him,' Louis wrote to Baxter in amazement. 'He thinks nothing of five or six in the afternoon as a whet for dinner . . . what a crop for the drink! He carries it, too, like a mountain with a sparrow on its shoulders.'

A few days later Kalakaua gave a *luau* at which Louis was the guest of honour; thereafter he became a favourite at the court, and this served to diminish the flow of visitors to the Waikiki bungalow, since the white population largely ostracised and despised the king. Unaware of all the nuances of island politics, Colvin unwittingly weighed in on their side when he wrote disgustedly to Baxter of the disadvantages of their old friend's existence in the Pacific: 'drinking with dusky majesties . . . isolation from anything like equals.' Yet the more RLS learned of the king's battle against the pro-U.S.A. whites, who eventually ended Polynesian rule in 1893 and procured the annexation of Hawaii by the States in 1898, the more he sided with the monarch and distanced himself from the *haoles* (foreign residents). He wrote to Baxter: 'the care of my family keeps me in Honolulu, where I am always out of sorts, amidst heat and cold and cesspools and beastly *haoles*.' In 1887 there had been a rising which imposed on the king the so-called '1889 constitution' by which he was shorn of real power. Naturally, like all supporters of traditional societies against the inroads of capitalism, RLS was accused of romantic daydreaming, gullibility and political naïveté, but he took comfort from his own conviction of rightness and the support of another Edinburgh Scot, the Hon. A.S.Cleghorn, who was likewise a ferocious royalist, having married a relation of Kalakaua. Stevenson's ambitions for a restored monarchy had a personal angle, too, in his warm feeling for the heiress presumptive, young princess Kaiulani, Cleghorn's daughter, who was on the point of being sent to England for her education and for whom he composed the following verses:

Forth from her land to mine she goes
The island maid, the island rose
Light of heart and bright of face:
The daughter of a double race.

Her islands here, in Southern sun,
Shall mourn their Kaiulani gone,
And I, in her dear banyan shade,
Look vainly for my little maid.

But our Scots islands far away
Shall glitter with unwonted day
And cast for once their tempests by
To smile in Kaiulani's eye.

Many critics, however, consider that the prose dedication to the poem is actually more affecting than the verse:

Written in April to Kaiulani, in the April of her age, and at Waikiki, within easy walk of Kaiulani's banyan. When she comes to my land and her father's, and the rain beats upon the window (as I fear it will), let her look at this page; it will be like a weed gathered and pressed at home, and she will remember her own islands, and the shadow of the mighty tree, and she will hear the peacocks screaming in the dusk and the wind blowing in the palms, and she will think of her father sitting there alone.

In August that year Kaiulani wrote RLS a touching letter from Wales, expressing the hope that by the time she finished school she would be able to take up the job as Stevenson's secretary that he offered her. Alas, the girl was to die young of consumption.[4]

With Kaiulani and Cleghorne on the steamer for San Francisco, Maggie departed, returning to Scotland to see her elder sister who was reported terminally ill and also to be on hand to assist Baxter sort out the problems from her husband's estate that still persisted. At this stage Louis fully intended to be back in Britain by the late summer – at least so he told Colvin, though a letter written at the same time to Henry James speaks of not coming home until 1890. He told Baxter that Hawaii was too cold for him, even at 75°F, and, since Tahiti was too far from Europe, he was thinking of settling in Madeira, which was only a week's sailing from England and would enable him to come to Britain every summer. But first he wanted to squeeze in one final Pacific cruise, since the effects of oceaneering had been so beneficial. Fanny was not quite so enthusiastic: she resented being seasick, having to decide about meals and having to act as Florence Nightingale when sailors came to her with cracked heads during heavy weather. However, as she told Mrs Sitwell:

> It seems a pity to return to England until his [RLS] health is firmly re-established, and also a pity not to see all that we can quite easily from this place; and which will be our only opportunity in life. Of course there is the usual risk from hostile natives and the horrible sea, but a positive risk is so much more wholesome than a negative one, and it is all such a joy to Louis and Lloyd. As for me, I hate the sea, and am afraid of it (though no one will believe that because in time of danger I do not make an outcry – nevertheless I am afraid of it, and it is not kind to me) but I love the tropic weather, and the wild people, and to see my two boys so happy.[5]

Louis originally intended to make his final Pacific cruise in the barquentine auxiliary steamer, *Morning Star*, a missionary ship that plied through the islands of Micronesia; when this proved impossible he switched his affections to the *Equator*, on the strength of its having breasted so well the recent great hurricane in Samoa. But before he could head westwards, he had urgent family problems to settle. As always the trinity of Fanny, Lloyd and Belle proved a major thorn in his side.

Belle Strong continued awkward, suspicious and resentful in her stepfather's company, even as she soaked up his subventions. In the nine years since Louis had last dealt with her, she had improved not at all. Most of this time she spent spongeing at Kalakaua's court or importuning RLS for money while her improvident spendthrift of a husband neglected his painting commissions and tried to match the monarch drink for drink. The Strongs' first child Austin was delicate and sickly but a veritable Hercules next to the second son, Hervey, born in the mid-1880s. When he was eleven months old, the Strongs went on one of their scrounging expeditions to the McKee sugar plantation on Maui; while there the baby fell dangerously ill with dysentery. A servant was dispatched on a forty-mile ride round the island to fetch a doctor; there arrived a forlorn quack, worn out with attending to a local dysentery case and himself destined to die a few days later. This hapless Aesculapius examined the child perfunctorily and advised the distraught Belle to let him sleep; Belle did so, and described the sequel laconically: 'My baby slept, but he never woke again.'

So far, having married a ne'er-do-well young man and lost her second male child, Belle seemed to be walking uncannily in her mother's footsteps, but no second RLS appeared as her saviour. Instead, Joe Strong's behaviour deteriorated. On top of drunken binges and philandering at wild parties, Strong managed to get his body badly sunburnt on a fishing trip to Waikiki beach and then developed blood poisoning. The loss of weight and later of livelihood, since he could no longer paint, precipitated him into a nervous breakdown. Or so Belle claimed. She went on to say that while Joe was in a sanatorium, she happened to be sorting through his effects and came on a pile of unpaid bills. In despair she then applied to Louis to liquidate the debt and, of course, he paid up. Then, after a long period in which Belle allegedly feared for Joe's sanity, she was sent for by the director of the sanatorium: 'And there stood Joe, completely recovered in body and his mind at peace.' This sounds like the tallest of tall stories; evidently Belle was not Sam Osbourne's daughter for nothing. The entire episode has a suspicious flavour, and the elaborately staged 'breakdown' and 'recovery' look like transparent devices for wringing money out of the ingenuous RLS; for all his scepticism about meaning in the universe, he always found it hard to believe how cynical people could be, especially people he knew.

When Louis arrived in Honolulu at the end of January 1889, the Strongs sensed the advent of a meal ticket. Louis and Fanny were both driven to the edge of patience by Joe's utter unreliability, self-indulgence, drunkenness and drug-taking (opium obtained from the Chinese community). Belle, meanwhile, still nursing obscure grudges against Louis, whose provenance depends on which story we choose to believe about the events of 1879–80, made it clear that she was always prepared to accept RLS's money, but never his advice. Louis's friends in England became increasingly exasperated by his tolerance for this grasping pair. Colvin referred to Belle as 'a really degrading connection' and a year later wrote to Baxter: 'If there are to be hurricanes, I wish Belle and Joe Strong and all that lot may be at sea in a leaky ship.'[6]

Joe Strong was originally included in the *Equator* party, but shortly before sailing, there was a major row; Fanny finally became exasperated that Louis went everywhere on foot to save money while the man he was maintaining drove around the island in carriages. She forced Louis's hand and there was a showdown: 'He explained to poor Joe with brutal frankness that I advised that he was to spend no money without permission, that abject obedience . . . was to be expected from him.' Thrown off the cruise, Strong made a dramatic comeback by presenting himself at the Waikiki bungalow the same evening and making a dignified, sorrowful and affectionate apology; he acknowledged that RLS had given him an opportunity to amend his life and that he had thrown it all away; the last three months had been the happiest of his life, he said; then he kissed them both and walked away.

It was a consummate piece of acting: Strong did not overplay his hand, become maudlin or burst into tears. He played brilliantly on RLS, knowing that the stance of heroic acceptance of fate would most appeal to him, and he threw in just a hint of possible suicide as well. Louis was so affected that he ran after Joe and offered him another chance. Either Joe Strong was a brilliant showman – for, having been forgiven, he thereafter showed not the slightest sign of rehabilitation or redemption – or he was the sort of self-deceiving charlatan who really believed in his own special effects. At any rate he signed a paper putting himself entirely in Stevenson's hands and was then taken back on the *Equator*.

Thinking that her marriage was effectively ended and glad to see the back of Joe on the *Equator*, Belle fully expected to be allowed to stay in Honolulu with Austin, with RLS paying all the bills. But one afternoon, about a fortnight before the *Equator* was due to leave, she was summoned to the bungalow for a stiff interview with Louis and Fanny. They told her she must take a steamship to Sydney with Austin and wait there till called for; she would be paid a certain allowance per month and her future would be decided on at the end of the *Equator* cruise. Belle was angry and pleaded desperately to be permitted to remain in Honolulu, where she had many friends: 'it was a stormy interview,' she recalled, . . . 'but nothing I said made any impression on either my mother or Louis.'[7]

RLS's conflict with Fanny was a very different affair. His ambition was to write a definitive, scholarly book about the Pacific, hanging historical and anthropological insights on a narrative line ostensibly about travel – a more comprehensive, polished and wide-ranging volume than the inchoate essays that made up the book published as *In the South Seas*. In Fanny's eyes this academic ambition took RLS farther away from the crock of gold she yearned for. She put the issue vividly (if disingenuously) in a letter to Colvin:

Louis has the most enchanting material that any one ever had in the whole world for his book, and I am afraid he is going to spoil it all. He has taken it in to his Scotch Stevenson head ... that his book must be a sort of scientific and historical impersonal thing comparing the different languages (of which he knows nothing, really) and the different peoples ... Suppose Herman Melville had given us his theories as to the Polynesian language and the probable good or evil results of the missionary influence instead of *Omoo* and *Typee* ... and the whole thing to be impersonal, leaving out all he knows of the people themselves. And I believe there is no one living who has got so near them or who understands them as he does ... Louis says it is a stern sense of duty that it is at the bottom of it, which is more alarming than anything else ... I am going to ask you to throw the weight of your influence as heavily as possible in the scales with me ... otherwise Louis will spend a good deal of time in Sydney actually reading other people's books on the Islands. What a thing it is to have a 'man of genius' to deal with. It is like managing an overbred horse. Why with my own feeble hand I could write a book that the whole world would jump at ... Even if I thought it a desirable thing to write what he proposes, I should still think it impossible unless after we had lived and studied here for some twenty years or more.[8]

This was a direct attack on the imaginative project RLS had laid before Colvin, who was in a slightly difficult position as he had just assured Baxter that the collection of essays to be published as *In the South Seas* would make more money than *The Master of Ballantrae*. However, Colvin had his own agenda, which was to encourage Louis to return from the Pacific as soon as possible; twenty years' research would banish him from Britain forever, and already Stevenson's friends in London were growing tired of his encomia on life under the Southern Cross. He therefore endorsed Fanny's criticisms, not noting their essential absurdity and destructiveness, as shrewdly underlined by J.C.Furnas:

Her bill of particulars shows a curious fear of objectivity. 'Impersonal' is twice used as a reproach ... her sense of outrage over his intention actually to consult previous writers who might throw further light on what he had been seeing. That objective sense demanded twenty years in the islands is absurd exaggeration and contradicts her assertion that, after ten months in the Pacific, Louis understands Islanders better than anybody else alive ... This [sc. *In the South Seas*] might have been indeed a magnificent book if Fanny had not been snapping at his heels and Colvin baying at him from a frustratingly long distance. As it was, these two bakers pulling at a very sinewy devil skewed the work into a huddle of ill-assorted elements that, individually, are very well handled and invaluably immediate.[9]

Why was Fanny so determined to stifle RLS's planned master history of the Pacific, when she had been complaisant ten years before about a similar project to write the history of the Highlands? Almost certainly the answer is that in the European days Fanny felt she had the upper hand in the dynamic relationship, that the bohemian who had fallen for her charms in Barbizon was still in evidence. Once launched on the Pacific rovings, however, Louis seemed to grow and mature with leaps and bounds and to be evolving beyond her reach. At an unconscious level she may have feared that she was 'losing' him, not in the sense that he was looking for another woman, but that he had accelerated while she stood still; the revised, expanded and polished version of *In the South Seas* might therefore have been perceived by this 'psychic' with the famous sixth sense as the reification of her inarticulate fears.

At least Stevenson perceived the conflicts with his wife and with Joe Strong. He failed to see the manifold ways in which Lloyd Osbourne was a threat to his objective interests, because of the peculiar myopia with which he regarded the young man until the very last year of his life. Someone not afflicted with Lloyd-blindness might have picked up the hint from Lloyd's statement of support for his mother in the wrangle over how the Pacific book should be written; such was the lad's confidence that he could do no wrong in RLS's eyes that he vouchsafed his opinion to his stepfather's closest friend, Baxter, and inveighed against his mentor's plan to write 'something very serious and solid, cutting away by the board the most of our charming and strange adventures which he denounces as "egoistical"'. Scant gratitude, this, to a man who had spoiled him, indulged his whims, allowed him to cling to his mother's apron strings and encouraged his absurd fantasy of becoming a great writer. 'Lloyd is quite the literary man,' purred the proud but foolish Fanny in a postscript to one of Louis's letters to Baxter. The reality of the disastrous collaborations with Lloyd, when Louis tried to give him an unjustified entrée into professional authorship, without any of the hard work, discipline and training the calling requires, is best expressed by Arthur Johnstone, who observed the duo in tandem in the Pacific years: 'This collaboration throughout will seem to be one of those uncalled-for literary happenings that defies explanation, unless it be attributed to an influence arising out of familiar associations.' That elaborate euphemism for Fanny's pushing relentless ambition on behalf of her offspring is matched by Johnstone's blunt assessment of *The Wrong Box*: 'the volume remains as thoroughly an amateur's effort as was ever placed before the public under the protection of a popular name.'[10]

Stevenson's inability to see through Lloyd until the very end is a classic example of what William James called the 'will to believe'. There is something touchingly naïve about the way he assesses the young man's motives in a letter to Baxter in February 1890: 'Lloyd was to have gone to Cambridge; now, seeing me saddled with this mule-load of struggling cormorants [i.e. the Strongs], he seems to be about refusing to go. I respect the impulse, yet I feel I shall, and should, oppose the decision.' Needless to say, Louis did *not* oppose Lloyd's refusal to go to Cambridge; a more clear-sighted man would have seen there was never the remotest chance that Lloyd Osbourne would give himself up to three years of disciplined study. He had not done so in Edinburgh, once he realised there was no royal road to riches, nor would he at any time in the future. He hated to be away from his mother for any length of time, and he was determined to win fame as an author; in both these ambitions Fanny abetted him at all points. He *was* prepared to go on long travelling jaunts, especially to escape boredom or hard work. He waited until 1890, when the period of cruising the Pacific was over and the likelihood of sustained and committed effort loomed during the construction of the Vailima house in Samoa, to plead the necessity of his being sent to England to 'sell Skerryvore and settle business matters there' even though that task was already being performed efficiently by Maggie and Baxter.

As with the West Indies trip earlier, RLS swallowed the bait and paid for an extravagant round-the-world visit to Britain, commencing in Australia. His shameful indulgence of Lloyd emerges clearly in a note written in Honolulu in June 1889 when he set pen to paper as follows: 'I, Robert Louis Stevenson acknowledge having received as a loan from Lloyd Osbourne the sum of $1,000.' Now, since the Osbournes were penniless in 1880 when Louis married Fanny, and Lloyd had never done a day's work nor inherited from his father, how could he possibly have acquired $1,000 for RLS to borrow? The inference must be that Lloyd had gulled Louis into writing him a bogus IOU so that, in the event of his stepfather's sudden death, he would have an undisputed claim against the estate for a *personal* legacy.

While in Britain in the autumn of 1890, Lloyd revealed himself in his true colours for anyone with eyes to see. On 4 December he wrote to Baxter: 'Tomorrow I leave for foreign parts – I am pretty dead sick of the world – a common lodging house having broken my spirit and inflamed my temper.' While in England he wrote just one letter to his benefactor – typically, RLS explained this deficiency on the ground that the others Lloyd 'must have' sent had been 'lost', though mysteriously there is no record of a loss of letters from any other correspondent at this time. In this one letter Lloyd managed to stir up Louis against Henley once more; he sent word that Henley had not called on Maggie while in Scotland and this, predictably, whipped Louis up into a lather: 'I have taken a good deal from Henley for myself and my wife, for a wife counts on the same plane as her husband; this treatment of an old lady, recently bereaved and very lonely, I refuse to pass over – the supplies are stopped. He may go and beg from whom he pleases: no threepenny piece of mine goes near him.' At last Fanny had the complete vengeance she had been thirsting for since early 1888, but it is typical of the absurdly naïve trust Louis had in Lloyd that he should have been prepared to condemn his friend on the boy's uncorroborated say-so.[11]

Partly to escape from the pressures of extended family, on 26 April RLS set out on the steamer *W.G.Hall* to visit the islands of Maui and Hawaii. He went ashore at Hawaii and spent a week at Kona on the lee shore as the only white man in a Polynesian village. The Kona coast is one of the most beautiful areas in the Pacific with a shoreline full of bays, shrubberies of wild fruit and flowers, and with the peaks of Mauna Loa and Mauna Kea jutting 13,000' into the clouds. Fanny gave a jaunty account of the trip: 'Louis went to one of the other islands a couple of weeks ago, quite alone, got drenched with rain and surf, rode over mountain paths – five and a half hours one day – and came back home none the worse for it.' But Louis confided to Baxter the real subtext of the trip: 'If only I could stay there the time that remains, I could get my work done and be happy; but the care of my family keeps me in vile Honolulu, where I am always out of sorts, amidst heat and cold and cesspools and beastly *haoles*.'[12]

After two weeks back in Honolulu, RLS embarked on the *Mokolii*, bound for the leper colony of Molokai. The 'leper problem' in the Hawaiian islands became notorious when it was revealed to the wider world that those suffering from the disease were systematically rounded up and sent to the northern coast of Molokai, accessible only by sea or by hair-raising and hairpin bridle-tracks; however this should not have occasioned so much surprise since isolation of lepers, as on South Africa's Robben Island, was common in the nineteenth century when the disease was thought highly contagious. The island of Molokai, forty miles across the Kaiwi channel from Honolulu, is thirty-five miles long and about seven wide; open to the Trades, it enjoys a cool breeze except when stormwinds whirl in from the ocean. On the northern shore the Makanalua peninsula juts two and a half miles outward from the precipitous cliffs, hundreds of feet high, and it was here that the leper colony was situated; visiting ships stood off the village of Kalaupapa, to which rowboats took visitors the last quarter mile ashore. Of the twelve days Louis spent on Molokai seven of them were in the leper colony and he confessed to Fanny that he derived much strength from Mother Maryanne and the Belgian nuns who went ashore with him and whose mission was to live, and probably die, among the lepers. He told Fanny: 'I do not know how it would have been with me had the sisters not been there. My horror of the horrible is about my weakest point; but the moral loveliness at my elbow blotted all else out.' Shamed by their example, he declined to wear gloves when playing with the leper children and tried to convert horror into pity in his deeply-felt poem 'To Mother Maryanne':

> To see the infinite pity of this place,
> The mangled limb, the devastated face,
> The innocent sufferer smiling at the rod –
> A fool were tempted to deny his God.
> He sees, he shrinks. But if he gaze again,
> Lo, beauty, springing from the beast of pain!
> He marks the sisters on the mournful shores;
> And even a fool is silent and adores.[13]

Having neglected the formalities about obtaining an exit permission as well as an entry permit, Louis experienced some difficulty in being allowed back on board the *Mokolii* when his stay on Molokai was over; some fast and persuasive talking was necessary to browbeat the captain. Perhaps in some ways he would have welcomed a period of enforced confinement on the island while Fanny took the government offices of Honolulu by storm, for his thoughts were now much on martyrdom. While among the lepers, RLS heard much of Father Damien, 'the hero of Molokai', a simple man who had died earlier the same year aged forty-nine after spending the last sixteen years of his life in the settlement, and he wrote at length about him to his mother, to Colvin, and to James Payn. He summed up his findings:

> Of old Damien, whose weaknesses and worse perhaps I heard fully, I think only the more. He was a European peasant, dirty, bigoted, untruthful, unwise, tricky, but superb with generosity, residual candour and fundamental good humour; convince him that he had done wrong (it might take hours of insult) and he would undo what he had done and like his corrector better. A man, with all the grime and paltriness of mankind, but a saint and hero all the more for that.[14]

Louis's visit to Molokai had a dramatic sequel eight months later. After Damien's death, his cult and the volume of his admirers grew, there were suggestions that the Catholic process of beatification be instituted prior to full canonisation, and as an immediate step it was proposed that a monument be erected to commemorate his martyrdom. This drew the wrath of Protestant missionaries in the Pacific, between whom and the Catholics there had always been ferocious rivalry. In Sydney early in 1890 RLS learned of a letter written to the Revd H.B.Gage by (incredibly) a Revd Dr. C.M.Hyde of Honolulu, assuring him that Damien's reputation was absurdly overblown, that he was in fact a stupid and dirty peasant who had caught leprosy by sleeping with one of the women in the colony. Louis immediately sprang to Damien's defence with an open letter to Dr Hyde that became almost as famous as Zola's '*J'accuse*' during the Dreyfus affair.

Louis began by acknowledging that he knew Dr Hyde socially – he had met him in Honolulu and found him obliging – but declared that there were higher duties than gratitude and this would be so even if Hyde had saved him from starvation. He then laid into Hyde, accusing him of envy, malice, hypocrisy and the breach of all unspoken moral rules; the only effect of Hyde's outburst, he was sure, would be to make the canonisation of Damien more likely. Louis then went on to describe the scene on his arrival at Molokai, the weeping nuns bidding farewell to the outside world, the stairs at the landing place crowded with 'the horror of a nightmare', the ordeal of the lazaretto – an ordeal from which a normal man would shrink not from fear of infection but because of the atmosphere of pain, pity and disgust. 'I do not think I am a man more than usually timid; but I never recall the days and nights I spent upon that island promontory (eight days and seven nights) without heartfelt thankfulness that I am somewhere else.' He wrote in his diary of a 'grinding experience' and jotted in the margin: 'harrowing is the word'; when he left the shores of Molokai behind him, he kept repeating: "Tis the most distressful country that ever yet was seen.'

RLS conceded that on Molokai Damien was unpopular, and was considered officious, and to have fallen into the indigenous ways of the Kanaka. He also noted in his diary that Damien was shrewd, ignorant and bigoted. Having conceded all this, he then moved over on to the attack.

> 'Damien was coarse.' It is very possible. You make us sorry for the lepers who had only a coarse old peasant for their friend and father. But you, who were so refined, why were you not there, to cheer them with the lights of culture . . . 'Damien was dirty.' He was. Think of the poor lepers annoyed with this dirty comrade! But the clean Dr Hyde was at his food in a fine house . . . 'Damien was bigoted' . . . his bigotry, his intense and narrow faith, wrought potently for good, and strengthened him to be one of the world's heroes and exemplars.

As for the accusation that Damien was impure in his relations with women, this was a pure canard; how could Hyde possibly know this was true? In any case,

> If the story were a thousand times true, can't you see you are a million times lower for daring to repeat it? . . . I fear you scarce appreciate how you appear to your fellow-men; and to bring it home to you, I will suppose your story to be true. I will suppose – and God forgive me for supposing it – that Damien faltered and stumbled in his narrow path of duty; I will suppose that, in the horror of his isolation, perhaps in the fever of incipient disease, he, who was doing so much more than he had sworn, failed in the letter of his priestly oath . . . The least tender should be moved to tears. And all that you could do was to pen your letter to the Reverend H.B.Gage.

Many facets of Stevenson's personality are revealed in this letter. The guilt and self-reproach he felt after leaving Molokai; his perennial hatred of the 'unco' guid' – for Hyde's strictures seemed uncomfortably like his father's Calvinism; his quixotry and desire for martyrdom, so clearly evinced in his support of the Boers, his championship of Gordon, his desire to defend the Curtins against the Irish boycotters, and much else. He was quite clear in his own mind that he had written a libel, that in any ensuing legal case he would be bound to lose, and that he would be ruined. There can scarcely be any doubt of the defamatory intent of the following passage, in which he accuses Hyde of hypocrisy:

> When we have failed, and another has succeeded; when we have stood by and another has stepped in; when we sit and grow bulky in our charming mansions, and a plain uncouth peasant steps into the battle, under the eyes of God, and succours the afflicted, and consoles the dying, and is himself afflicted in his turn, and dies upon the field of honour – the battle cannot be retrieved as your unhappy irritation has suggested. One thing remained to you in your defeat – some rags of common honour; and these you have made haste to cast away.

Stark ruin faced the Stevenson family and one can imagine the mixture of horror and frustration with which the three mercenary Osbournes contemplated their likely future. To save face with Louis, however, they had no choice but to support him in his quixotry.[15]

The Hyde affair prompts many reflections. In the first place it is clear that in his overt anger over the Damien letter RLS also tapped into a deeper core of rage, that the Revd Hyde was in some ways the object of a freefloating 'overkill' of anger connected with a whole host of other things: his childhood, his father, the world as he saw it in all its evil. Some have even suspected him of using the Damien affair to open fire on the missionaries and white supremacists he so disliked in Honolulu and who were the principal obstacles to Kalakaua's ultimate dream of a confederation of Pacific islands. Secondly, the letter produced some of his finest writing, and indeed it is a masterpiece of satire whose components Arthur Johnstone analysed as follows.

> Stevenson's work may be properly called an example of composite satire . . . in comparing the Damien letter with the ancient satirists, Stevenson's effort will be found to include all the scorn and invective of Archiolochus, the permeating ethic element of Simonides of Amorgus; the rhetorical finish of Juvenal, together with several of the minor excellencies drawn from the Greek and Roman authors. If modern writers are considered, it will be seen that, while he wrote letters with the haste and disingenuousness of Erasmus, it contains as well the pungency of Byron's invective – but without his descriptive wanderings – together with the sharp, incisive thrustings of Carlyle; on the other hand, it lacks the staid playfulness of Thackeray and the overflowing wit and exaggeration of Butler, just as it cleverly escapes the brutalities of Swift.

Thirdly, RLS has been criticised for conceding too much to Dr Hyde; on this view he and Hyde were at one in accepting that Damien was a man of lax morality, and indeed Stevenson admits as much in a letter to Colvin in June 1889. The Executive Officer of the Hawaiian Board of Health investigated the various stories about the priest's alleged lechery with leper women and found them to be wholly without foundation. The only charge sustained was that Damien was dirty, and from his unsalubrious personal habits he was thought to have contracted the disease. There was in fact no good evidence at all for Damien's alleged sexual peccadilloes, but it is almost as though Stevenson wanted the priest to have erred so that he could sustain his thesis of the sinner who is closer to God than the 'unco' guid' divine. Fourthly, although part of us feels that Hyde deserved what he got for his dishonest tittle-tattle, another part admires the Christian spirit in which the clergyman took RLS's diatribe. When he had it in his power to ruin the author, he brushed aside the attack as a fleabite and described his assailant as 'a bohemian crank, a negligible person whose opinion signified nothing . . . his invective may be brilliant, but it is like a glass coin, not golden, shivered into fragments of worthless glitter when brought to the test of truthfulness.'[16]

Initially, Louis was unrepentant and quite prepared to take the consequences of his libel: 'I have struck as hard as I knew how,' he told Maggie. Six months later his ardour had cooled and he wrote to Mrs Fairchild:

On the whole it was virtuous to defend Damien; but it was harsh to strike so hard at Dr Hyde. When I wrote the letter I believed he would bring an action, in which case I knew I could be beggared. As yet there has come no action. The injured Doctor has contented himself up to now with the (truly innocuous) vengeance of calling me 'a Bohemian Crank' and I have deeply wounded one of his colleagues whom I esteemed and like.[17]

All this lay in the future when Louis returned to Honolulu from Molokai in June 1889. Awaiting him was news of Colvin's serious financial embarrassment after his brother's peculations. In contrast to his vindictive attitude towards Henley, RLS was sweetness and light itself when dealing with Colvin. To Baxter he wrote:

I have at last definite news of Colvin, which alarms and distresses me. If I had had it in time, I would have given up this cruise and come home. Pray remember, if ever he should be in need of help, *you are to strain my credit to bursting, and mortgage all I possess or can expect*, to help him. I hope this is strong enough; if I return to find myself deep in debt, I shall be only pleased if it was done for Colvin.

Preparations now proceeded rapidly for embarkation on the *Equator*, bound for the Gilberts. When he first decided on another cruise, RLS had in mind a complete sweep of the major islands of Micronesia (the Gilberts, Marshalls and Carolines) and then either direct passage to Sydney in a trader or a return to Tahiti via Fiji, Tonga and the Friendly Isles; from Tahiti or Sydney he would take fast steamer to San Francisco and then home. But the *Equator*'s itinerary was less certain as it depended on trade, whereas the *Morning Star* had been a missionary steamer with a fixed schedule, so beyond the Gilberts uncertainty loomed. When Louis agreed the terms of the charter with the liberal and obliging owner, a Mr Wightman of San Francisco, it was agreed that in return for a lower fee, the schooner would do some business while taking the Stevensons through Micronesia, that they would certainly visit the Kingsmills, Ponape and Manila, and would land the travellers in China, whence they could take ship to England. A fixed sum was agreed for the trip from Honolulu to Butaritari and the Kingsmills, with the proviso that whenever the ship anchored in the islands, even for five minutes, Stevenson would have the right to call for a three-day stopover without extra charge.

Fanny's superstitious influence can be seen in two deeply rooted beliefs Louis continued to entertain: one went back to the prophecies of a High-land sibyl, when he was seventeen, to the effect that he would visit America and be much on the sea; the other was his profound conviction that he would die by drowning. Yet unlike those figures of myth who tried vainly to prevent prophecies from being fulfilled by avoiding any possible context in which they could come to pass, Louis went out fearlessly to confront the element that, he thought, contained his doom: 'I cannot say why I like the sea; no man is more cynically and constantly alive to its perils; I regard it as the highest form of gambling; and yet I love the sea as much as I hate gambling.'

However, the idea of 'good luck' did have some validity on this voyage. Just before the *Equator* sailed, two Belgians approached RLS and begged to be allowed to accompany the Stevensons. Louis refused. Years later he learned that these Belgians were notorious pirates, who made a practice of taking passage on schooners between the isles, poisoning all others on board, selling the schooner when they reached port and then repeating the process. A cook had survived one poisoning attempt and informed against them, as a result of which the Belgians had been sentenced to death in Manila, but the duo somehow escaped execution and ended up in a French prison from which they were paroled. Their eventual fate is not known.[18]

On 24 June 1889, six months to the day after the arrival of the *Casco* in Honolulu harbour, the schooner *Equator* cleared for the Gilberts. The *Honolulu Advertiser* remarked drily as the ship departed – and perhaps this is an indication of RLS's unpopularity among the *haoles* for his support of Kalakaua: 'It is to be hoped that Mr Stevenson will not fall victim to native spears; but in his present state of bodily health, perhaps the temptation to kill him may not be very strong.'

The sixty-four-ton *Equator* was a spanking new ship, built in San Francisco in 1888, but destined for an inglorious later life as a Pacific tugboat. In 1955 she was sunk to become a breakwater at the mouth of the Snohomish river in Washington state, but was raised to the surface and towed to the Seattle docks in 1967.[19] Her captain, Denis Reid, was a small fiery Scotch-Irishman, an expert draughts player; more Scots than RLS in his Caledonian chauvinism, he wore a Highland bonnet in the Pacific isles and kept up unremittingly the singing of a music-hall repertoire that contained just two items: 'Annie Laurie' and 'In the Gloaming'. Among the other crew was a Norwegian mate, a Finnish second mate, a Russian ex-sea captain, the runaway son of a New Zealand parson who had been taken on as cook, and Ah Fu, who since his engagement in the Marquesas had gradually made himself indispensable to Fanny and declared that he would cut off his right arm to help 'Misee Stevens'. Ah Fu's English afforded the ship's company much amusement. The subject of Bullu Hayes, the famous Pacific desperado came up, and Ah Fu interjected: 'I know that fella plenty.' 'I'm afraid he was a very bad man,' said Louis.' 'Him sonofabitch,' replied Ah Fu.

Reid, despite his youth – he was still in his twenties – was a great seaman and had carried the *Equator* safely through the great hurricane of 16 March 1889 which devastated Samoa, arriving at Apia with all sails and spars intact – the only ship within a 200-mile radius to remain afloat except the British warship HMS *Calliope*. Sadly, Reid was later imprisoned in Levuka for fraudulent sale of a vessel; his mate Anderson and several of the crew died of flu on the return voyage to San Francisco, and one of the crew was swept overboard in a gale; all in all, Stevenson's comrades on the *Equator* turned out to be ill-starred.

On the run to Butaritari they at first experienced perfect weather – fine days and glorious nights – and Louis in particular thrilled to the intimacy the low-lying schooner could achieve with the sea. Joe Strong soon showed the hollowness of his 'repentance' at Waikiki by becoming difficult and temperamental and achieving universal unpopularity. He set up his easel on deck and then claimed that one of his canvases had sustained damages to the extent of $500. He was picky and fastidious about his food and annoyed the assembled company by declaring that he would rather die than eat shark meat. Lloyd Osbourne and the young cook Thomson Murray MacCallum colluded to teach Joe a lesson and prepared a dish of shark disguised as curried minced beef. Over coffee Lloyd revealed all; Louis and Fanny laughed heartily but Strong rushed from the room, threw up over the rail, and never forgave MacCallum.

The cook, though, became friendly with Lloyd and thus a great favourite of Fanny and Louis. On one occasion they were struck by a squall, and the Stevensons in their starboard stateroom were rolled against the wall instead of being thrown out on the floor. Louis sent for MacCallum and gave him a message: 'Oh, Murray, I wish you would present my compliments to Captain Reid and tell him how much we appreciate his thoughtfulness in having the squall strike us while the schooner was on the starboard tack, and thus saving Fanny and myself the inconvenience of being thrown out of bed.' When Reid heard this, he laughed and said: 'All right, Murray, give him my love and tell him to go to the devil.'[20]

So close did relations between Reid and the Stevensons become that Louis first began to toy with the idea that would later take a firm hold: making a permanent home in the Pacific. He discussed with Reid the possibility of going into business together as copra traders under the legend 'Jekyll, Hyde & Co.' They projected the purchase of a schooner, *The Northern Light*, which Reid said could be bought for $15,000, the craft to be half yacht and half trader but wholly self-supporting; they would not live on it permanently but would pick it up at intervals and enjoy it as a floating home.

On 14 July 1889 they arrived in the Gilberts. Butaritari, which enjoyed a superb ocean climate, alternating days of blinding sun and bracing wind with nights of heavenly brightness, was similar in size to Fakarava, though somewhat wider, measuring perhaps a quarter of a mile from beach to beach; Louis found the restricted life on such islands not much of an advance on life on shipboard. The island was ruled by a 'constitutional' monarch, Tebureimoa, who was the hereditary king but had been shorn of all his power by a committee of nobles known as 'the Old Men'. RLS was not impressed by the king:

> he wore pyjamas which sorrowfully misbecame his bulk; his nose was crooked and cruel, his body overcome with sodden corpulence, his eye timorous and dull; he seemed at once oppressed with drowsiness and held awake by apprehension ... first and last I always had the same impression; he seemed always drowsy, yet always to hearken and start; and whether from remorse or fear, there is no doubt he seeks a refuge in the abuse of drugs.

Though not administered by the U.S.A., Butaritari was firmly within the U.S. sphere of influence, since most of the traders and missionaries were American. Ten days before the *Equator* docked, King Tebureioma had lifted the taboo on alcohol to celebrate the Fourth of July, so that when the Stevensons arrived they found the entire population roaring drunk and Tebureioma unwilling to restore the taboo. The chaos Louis and his family thus stumbled into disturbed them for Louis pointed out:

> the conduct of drunkards even at home is always matter for anxiety; and at home our populations are not armed from the highest to the lowest with revolvers and repeating rifles, neither do we go on a debauch by the whole townful – and I might rather say by the whole polity – king, magistrates, police and army joining in one common scene of drunkenness. It must be thought besides that we were here in barbarous islands, rarely visited, lately and partly civilised. First and last, a really considerable number of whites have perished in the Gilberts, chiefly through their own misconduct; and the natives have displayed in at least one instance a disposition to conceal an accident under a butchery, and leave nothing but dumb bones.

The Stevensons debated sleeping on board while the revelry went on but finally decided this would mean running away from the very adventures they were supposed to be seeking. Instead they sent for their revolvers and began to practise target shooting at bottles, ostentatiously so that the locals would get the point; apparently they were particularly impressed by Fanny's marksmanship. They then rented a house next door to one of the bars but could get no work done because of the noise. Scenes of barbarous degradation were commonplace: one that particularly upset Louis was a fight between two of the local women, one clothed, the other unclad, the couple gouging and punching while a drunken mob cheered them on. Already the myth of the noble savage was taking a knock and perhaps as early as 1889 RLS realised with a heavy heart that the Pacific would not provide him the Eden he sought.

> The harm done was probably not much, yet I could have looked on death and massacre with less revolt. The return to these primeval weapons, the vision of man's beastliness, of his ferality, shocked in me a deeper sense than that with which we count the cost of battles. There are elements in our state and history which it is a pleasure to forget, which it is perhaps better wisdom not to dwell on. Crime, pestilence and death are in the day's work; the imagination readily accepts them. It instinctively rejects, on the contrary, whatever shall call up the image of our race upon its lowest terms, as the partner of beasts, beastly itself, dwelling pell-mell and hugger-mugger, hairy man with hairy woman in the caves of old. And yet to be just to the barbarous islanders we must not forget the slums and dens of our own cities; I must not forget that I have passed dinnerward through Soho and seen that which cured me of my dinner.

At first, the house where the Stevensons lodged and the surrounding neighbourhood were left alone after it had been explained to the king that RLS was an intimate friend of Queen Victoria, and that if any damage were done the queen would send a warship to chastise the Gilbertese. But a few days later two stones were hurled into the house, narrowly missing Louis's ear; enquiries revealed that the king had broken his promise and that the bacchanalia threatened to get out of hand. The perennial problem was that South Sea Islanders could only be stopped from drinking if the *tapu* was reintroduced and in the meantime any trader refusing to sell drink would be killed. Louis persuaded the two American traders, Rick and Tom, to stop the flow of liquor but the German trader, Mueller, kept up the supply. Louis bearded Mueller in his lair and a stormy interview ensued, at the end of which Mueller reluctantly agreed to stop the sale of alcohol provided the Stevenson party guaranteed to defend him with their guns. On the first night when he shut up shop, Louis, Fanny and Lloyd took up station to defend Mueller; their feelings are described by Louis:

Scott talks moderately of looking forward to a time of fighting 'with a feeling that resembled pleasure'. The resemblance seems rather an identity. In modern life, contact is ended; man grows impatient of endless manoeuvres; and to approach the fact, to find ourselves where we can push our advantage home, and stand a fair risk and see at last what we are made of, stirs the blood. It was so at least with all my family, who bubbled with delight at the approach of trouble; and we sat deep into the night like a pack of schoolboys, preparing the revolvers and arranging plans against the morrow.

The moment of truth never came. Suddenly the crisis was over and the taboo reintroduced. RLS could never work out whether Mueller's action had forced a recognition of necessity, whether the king had finally seen the light, or whether the 'Old Men', fearful that their authority too might be swept away in the gale of the world that was beginning to blow on the island, had made an eleventh hour intervention. However, certain it was that on 24 July the nightmare was over and in an ensuing five-day festival the Gilbertese performed brilliant music, complete with conductor, to which Louis responded by giving a magic lantern show. While the *Equator* was away on its commercial errands, the Stevensons spent a further month on Butaritari, enabling Louis to pinpoint the differences between Micronesians and Polynesians. Where the Polynesians were unchaste and hag-ridden with bogies, the Micronesians deplored sexual promiscuity and showed little terror of the dark; the race could not compare with the Tahitians or Marquesans in point of female beauty, though there were some individual girls of great prettiness; all in all, it was the 'virility of sense and sentiment' that most distinguished the Gilbertese from the eastern Polynesians.[21]

When the *Equator* returned, the cruise through the Gilberts continued. There were brief calls at Abaiang, Marakei and Tarawa, then Reid put the schooner on a southerly track, bound for Nonuti and Tapiteuea. When the wind suddenly came fair for Apemama, he changed tack and headed there instead, arriving at the north passage of the island on 1 September 1889. This caused consternation with some Gilbertese passengers from the island of Peru, who were terrified at the reputation of Apemama's ruler and feared they would all be slaughtered; as Louis explained, Tembinok of Apemama was 'the last tyrant, the erect vestige of a dead society . . . Tembinok figures in the patriotic war-songs of the Gilberts like Napoleon in those of our grandfathers.' The king, however, seemed at first to belie his ferocious reputation and paid for the onward fares of the Micronesian passengers on the regular island-hopping service provided by the *Janet Nicholl*.

The Stevenson party was keen to go ashore, but the necessary permission could not be obtained until Tembinok came on board to dine. The Napoleon of the Gilberts, who had been prevented only by American warships from conquering the entire group, resembled an Italian princeling of the Renaissance, not just with the strongly aquiline nose and expression of remarkable cunning familiar to students of Florentine painting, and in his complexion – no darker than a Sicilian's – but in the Machiavellian role he played in Gilbertine politics. Like many Pacific potentates, he was immensely fat and had declined into virtual immobility before he took up walking. He had a long black mane of hair, an imperious eye, a shrill voice as powerful and uncanny as a sea-bird's, and his beaked profile reminded Louis of the mask of Dante. His apparel was eccentric, as he wore anything from jacket and trousers to a woman's frock. Sole master of the islands of Apemama, Aranuka and Kuria, Tembinok had once made a disastrous foray into business on his own, lost heavily, and thereafter resigned himself to taking percentages from the traders, aware that he was being cheated but content merely to keep a 'hitlist' of those who drove too hard a bargain. It was well known that house after house and chest after chest in the palace precinct was crammed with antiques and memorabilia: clocks, musical boxes, blue spectacles, umbrellas, knitted waistcoats, bolts of stuff, tools, rifles, fowling-pieces, medicines, sewing machines, stoves, European foods, but he was never satisfied with his haul. 'He is possessed by the seven devils of the collector. He hears a thing spoken of, and a shadow comes on his face. "I think I no got him," he will say; and the treasures he has seem worthless in comparison.'

Apemama was by now the only place in the Pacific where a white man might not simply land at will, and RLS was anxious about whether permission would be granted. Everyone knew the story of how Tembinok had at first seemed to welcome a missionary, but kept him on the island just long enough to learn English, then dismissed him with a warning never to return on pain of death. When Captain Reid made the formal request, Tembinok made no answer, as if he had not heard, but thereafter scrutinised the party constantly, as if he were a portrait painter sizing up a subject. After two days of frustrating waiting, Tembinok sent Louis a message that he had passed muster: 'I look your eye. You good man. You no lie.' Having decided to bestow his favour, Tembinok ordered his labourers to transport four huts from the other side of the island for the Stevensons (they called the quartet 'Equator City') which he then at once tabooed, so that his guests would not be bothered by interlopers; Louis later discovered that they had been billeted hard by the islanders' favourite water-hole, were therefore deeply unpopular, and would probably have been slaughtered out of hand if someone had assassinated Tembinok and they were deprived of the royal protection. The much-prized water-hole was in fact a turbid pool which rose and fell with the tides and was full of brackish water that filtered through the coral of the beach; since Tembinok sent them a supply of fresh coconuts every evening, they used the pool only for washing and bathing.

The only Apemamans allowed to breach the taboo were the slaves made over by the king for their use, including three buxom girls who spent most of their time frolicking in the pool.

'Equator City' was unfortunately plagued with flies, who seemed to be present in their millions; when they retired for the night, the mosquitoes took over. In desperation Fanny constructed a kind of house of mesh which was hung over the hut used as a communal dining room and study. Here for three weeks they lived in total peace of mind in their charming little basket-work houses, resembling the 'bird-cages' of Tautira; clean and airy, the huts stood on stilts about four feet from the ground, with hanging lids for doors and windows. Here Ah Fu baked bread, cakes and pies in a Dutch oven – a shallow iron pot with a flat cover on which live coals could be piled; he also roasted wild chickens which he shot with a gun borrowed from the king, but they were rubbery and tasteless, with a vague seagull flavour. The spartan diet on Apemama was the greatest problem, especially as this seemed to be the only island in the Pacific where there was a scarcity of fish. The Stevensons became tired of alternating tinned food with salt beef and pork and of baking weevily flour so infested that, even after careful sifting, there were always dozens of little black threads in their bread; their rice was similarly speckled and the butter invariably rancid and the only fresh vegetable was an enormous edible root like a yam, which could be boiled and pounded into a paste ... On rare occasions there was a treat of turtle steaks and soup, washed down with lashings of the Californian claret they had brought with them. Yet it was mainly the fresh coconuts and their milk that kept them healthy.

They seldom walked anywhere except to the seaward side of the island, half a mile away, which was also tabooed, possibly because it was always cool and free from flies and mosquitoes and therefore kept as the king's private preserve. On these walks their slave-girls would trail behind them like puppies, possibly having been instructed to report on their 'masters'' every movement. The girls' favourite diversion was to strip off all their clothes and plunge into pools of fresh water.

They saw almost nothing of the islanders, and when they did it was to experience dour hostility and glowering eyes if they so much as petted a child, but the few hints they picked up convinced Louis the locals were slaves in all but name. Later, when he saw Tembinok at close quarters, he learned to his disgust that the king also doubled as soothsayer, witchdoctor and thaumaturge: he liked to predict which ships would be arriving at the island but always had a plausible excuse if his predictions turned out wrong. Louis cynically concluded that the sources of authority in all societies, whether 'civilised' or 'barbarian', were always the same and rested on trickery: 'I used to regard the king with veneration as he thus publicly deceived himself. I saw behind him all the fathers of the Church, all the philosophers and men of science of the past before him, all those that are to come; himself in the midst; the whole visionary series bowed over the same task of welding incongruities.' As an experiment, when he caught cold he submitted to being treated by the king's sorcerers and recorded cynically:

> A reader of the Arabian nights felt quite at home. Here was the suffumigation; here was the muttering wizard; here was the desert place to which Aladdin was decoyed by the false uncle. But they manage these things better in fiction. The effect was marred by the levity of the magician, entertaining his patient with small talk like an affable dentist, and by the incongruous presence of Mr Osbourne with a camera. As for my cold, it was neither better nor worse.[22]

During his time on Apemama, Louis took three important decisions. The first, and most important, was that he would not return to Britain but spend more time in the Pacific, which so agreed with him. This meant that, as a working writer, he had to be near a fast mailship service. There were only four such places in the entire Pacific: Suva in Fiji, Apia in Samoa, Papeete and Honolulu. RLS had already ruled out Papeete and Honolulu as places in which to settle semi-permanently, both because they were too polluted by civilisation and because he disliked the respective influence of the Americans and the French. Since Louis liked Polynesians and was not attracted by what he had read of the Melanesians, Samoa seemed to him the only conspicuous island group on a main transport and communications grid which still boasted an uncontaminated people.

The second was to abandon the idea of going into partnership with Reid. The weeks of trading on the *Equator* had pointed up the seamy side of such a life, the deceit, trickery, false scales, bamboozling and chicanery involved in dealing with the natives who were themselves systematically dishonest. The irony of this decision was that he had originally started to write a new novel on the *Equator* to raise the $15,000 he needed as capital to go into business with Reid but, once launched, the novel acquired a momentum of its own which made Louis want to go to Samoa so as to be able to dispatch the manuscript to his London publishers.[23]

The third decision was to write the new novel in collaboration with Lloyd and to base it on a bizarre story they had heard just before leaving Honolulu, when a handful of shipwrecked sailors from the *Wandering Minstrel* staggered into the port with a mysterious and unfathomable story about a rogue cargo. *The Wrecker*, begun in Apemama and worked at for the next two years before publication in 1892, is in some ways the oddest and most intriguing of all RLS's productions. It is a valuable work to quarry for Stevenson's life, containing as it does a kind of recapitulation of his career, with scenes set in Scotland, in Paris, Fontainebleau, the eastern seaboard of the U.S.A., San Francisco, the Marquesas, Hawaii and Midway Island.

Moreover, the characters are all based on identifiable figures who were important in RLS's life: Nares on Otis, Pinkerton on McClure, and Dodd on Will Low. There are important clues to Stevenson's attitude to fathers and to women. A would-be artist, Dodd seeks a new life in France, but his lack of success makes him more dependent than ever on his millionaire father – a clear echo of Stevenson's own experience. Nares describes his filial experience thus: '"He was a pig of father, and I was a pig of a son; but it sort of came over me I would like that fiddle to squeak again. Natural," he added, "I guess we're all beasts."

"All sons are, I guess," said I. "I have the same trouble on my conscience; we can shake hands on that."'

And on women Pinkerton says: 'Every man is bound to marry above him; if the woman's not the man's superior, I brand it as mere sensuality.'24

The complex relationship of *The Wrecker* to the rest of the Stevensonian *oeuvre* derives additional depth from the interaction of themes within the novel and the possible new meanings they set up when applied externally to the rest of the canon. *The Wrecker* can be viewed as *Treasure Island* rendered naturalistically – Loudon, for instance, is Jim Hawkins grown up but still a pawn in other men's games –, with all the banality and trivia of actual commercial treasure-hunting. Recent critics have seized on its 'modernist' aspects: the open-ended mystery story which, as RLS conceded, 'consists in beginning the yarn anywhere but the beginning and finishing it anywhere but the end'; and the 'deconstruction' of the myth of buried treasure.

Familiar Stevensonian themes appear which shed light on other works in the canon. The outlaw-artist motif, for example, made its debut in 'The Story of a Lie' where 'Admiral' Van Tromp pretended to be a talented artist but in fact lived a parasitic existence in the bohemian quarter of Paris. Loudon Dodd is a kind of halfway house between Van Tromp and James More MacGregor, the villain of *Catriona*: both Tromp and MacGregor are rejected violently by their daughters when they learn the truth. Superficially, no doubt, this can be read as a reference to Belle Strong's vehement rejection of her father Sam Osbourne, but it is possible that some deeper projection is at work here, perhaps to do with Stevenson's own feelings of guilt and worthlessness: by transference the young woman rejecting the untrustworthy older man could be the older woman (Fanny) rejecting the younger man – which would be a not untypical fantasia of the RLS unconscious.

The relationship between Dodd and Pinkerton also irresistibly recalls that between David Balfour and Alan Breck and is thus yet another twist in the tale of Stevenson the divided self. The *Treasure Island* motif also continues in that Pinkerton is a naturalistic Silver: he is a buccaneer or pirate to whom business is high adventure.

Reality was his romance. Suppose a man to dig up a galleon on the Coromandel coast, his rakish schooner keeping the while an offing under easy sail, and he, by the blaze of wreckwood, to measure ingots by the bucketful on the uproarious beach: such an one might realise a greater material spoil; he should have no more profit of romance than Pinkerton when he cast up his weekly balance-sheet in a bald office.

Eventually, Dodd supports Pinkerton, but can only do so on inherited money; until then, hopeless at business himself, he has been carried by the other man. Once again Stevenson illustrates his preference for honest evil over hypocrisy, James Durrisdeer over Henry; Dodd is a humbug who, after fulminating against opium smugglers, sets out to be one himself.

Yet if Pinkerton and Dodd are, once again, respectively the man RLS would like to have been and the one he feared he actually was, these two aspects of the self in turn have their *döppelgangers*. Tommy Haddon is Pinkerton's *alter ego*, as Norris Carthew is of Dodd. The resemblance between Carthew and Dodd is particularly close: both went to college and both were rescued from penury in almost identical ways, Carthew by Haddon as Loudon was by Pinkerton. *The Wrecker*, then, fuses both the David Balfour/Alan Breck pairings (as well as Jim/Silver) with a quite separate Jekyll and Hyde mirroring, producing the archetypal Stevensonian theme of ambivalence within ambiguity.

The Wrecker is a classic example of a novel where the sum of the parts do not knit up into a whole. Individual passages – on San Francisco, Pacific navigation, storms at sea – are among RLS's very best writings and the separate episodes in a sprawling worldwide canvas – including a Hardyesque view of Dorset – are absorbing and highly enjoyable. But there is no proper story structure and there are far too many diversions and irrelevancies that clog the action. Some critics have suggested that Stevenson was trying to ape the later Dickens in employing such a convoluted approach to narrative, but a better comparison would be with the multiple viewpoint of a work like Conrad's *Chance* which wraps the most technically elaborate coating around a simple adventure story. Others have detected the influence of Henry James, especially in RLS's statement that he wanted to fuse the traditional adventure story with 'some picture of the manners of today in the greater world.' The problem is that this ensnares the author (or authors, depending on what view we take of Lloyd's collaboration) into the trap of devoting the first eight chapters to the story of Loudon Dodd before the main matter of the book, the mystery surrounding the wreck of the *Flying Scud*, is even broached.

The character of Loudon Dodd also means that Stevenson dealt himself a poor hand at the outset. As Eigner has noted: 'Dodd is perhaps the extreme example in Stevenson of the essentially unromantic man placed in the inherently romantic situation.' Dodd is presented as the greatest of life's failures in an *oeuvre* not notably short on inert non-achievers, and in some ways the ending of *The Wrecker* is even more hopeless and pessimistic than *The Master of Ballantrae*, resembling nothing so much as the nihilistic conclusion of Flaubert's *L'Education Sentimentale*. The wreck foundering in the fathomless Pacific is a metaphor for the meaning of the life of Everyman (Loudon Dodd).

There are, moreover, technical weaknesses in *The Wrecker*, and not just 'naturalistic' errors like the implausibility of bribing the Customs officials at Oahu in the manner described, or the inaccuracies in the nuances of the behaviour of the American (as opposed to British) characters. The main plot strains credibility, for the wreckers destroy $10,000 of rice that could have been transferred to the *Norah Creina* and sold in Honolulu, to get at $5,000 worth of opium. Yet, most of all, what stood between *The Wrecker* and success was its elaborate, discursive approach, which was not suited to Stevenson's talents. His great strength as a writer was his dedication to economy, yet here he seemed to break his own rules and play deliberately to his weaknesses.

The most plausible explanation is that he did not approach *The Wrecker* in the mood of high seriousness that animated his commitment to his best work. In such a *jeu d'esprit* he could write an 'entertainment' rather than a novel (to use the Graham Greene term) and thus let Lloyd Osbourne have his head. The terms in which Louis and Lloyd recalled their collaboration supports this thesis. Here is Lloyd: 'It was exhilarating to work with Stevenson; he was appreciative, so humorous – brought such gaiety, *cameraderie*, and goodwill to our joint task. We never had a single disagreement as the book ran its course; it was a pastime, not a task ... Am I wrong in thinking that some of that zest is to be found in *The Wrecker*?' And here is Louis: 'It's glorious to have the ground ploughed, and to sit back in luxury for the real fun of writing, which is rewriting.' In other words, Louis did not approach the task in full seriousness, and paid the price in loss of critical esteem – a critical failure made more unbearable to him by the reflection that in commercial terms *The Wrecker* sold better than *The Master of Ballantrae*. This was yet another instance of Louis's being the net loser by his indulgence towards the Osbourne family. There is something disquieting about the way an incontestably great writer dangerously encouraged the adolescent writing fantasies of a callow, semi-educated twenty-one-year old, and James Pope-Hennessy is deadly accurate when he says: 'In effect, he was prostituting himself to give Fanny's son the illusion of something valuable to do.'[25]

Towards the end of the three weeks initially agreed with Tembinok as stopover time, the Stevensons saw more and more of the king. Louis bought the local totem shell set in a wooden box – 'the devil-box of Apemama' – as a gift for Andrew Lang who delighted in such artefacts, but a later measles epidemic on the island was later blamed on the sale of the fetish. Tembinok liked Fanny – 'she good; look pretty; plenty chench (sense)' – offered her a sewing machine and was so intrigued by European cooking that he sent his own chef to learn about it. The man proved to be an idle and incorrigible rogue. When they reported his misdeeds to the palace, Tembinok got out his Winchester and drove the man out; the Stevensons arrived at the thatched palace to see the royal cook running off in a zigzag manner as bullets pinged around him. The disgraced chef then took to hanging around Equator City in the darkness, frightening Fanny and worrying Louis with the thought that he might suddenly go berserk; they hesitated to report his prowlings for fear of what Tembinok might do to him. One night Louis caught the man and gave him a good kicking, after which there was no further trouble, though they later heard that the cook had learned nothing from his mistakes and had eventually been shot dead by Tembinok in a drunken rage.

The end of the third week arrived, and then the end of the fourth week, but there was still no sign of the *Equator*. Fearful that the ship had foundered in a hurricane, and seriously concerned by their rapidly diminishing food stocks, Louis went to the king as a suppliant, petitioning for further provisions. Tembinok purred with delight at the request and threw open his storehouses, putting at the white man's disposal beef, pork, flour, rice, sugar, tea and coffee. While Louis and Lloyd were in the warehouses taking their pick, they marvelled at the cornucopia of trade goods stored there: mirrors, a large rocking horse, prams, French clocks, cut-glass vases, silver candelabra, silk parasols, toy steam engines, surgical instruments, sewing machines – anything, in fact, that had ever caught the royal fancy. Tembinok also ordered his fishermen to deliver a supply of fresh turtle meat to his guests.

Even as they finished their turtle steaks, the king sent word that a sail had been sighted on the horizon. This, however, turned out to be not the *Equator* but the copra-bearing schooner *H.L.Tiernan* bound for Samoa. After a drunken dance Tembinok gave in the *Tiernan*'s honour, Louis purchased stores from the captain and even debated whether or not to take passage with her to Samoa, since by now, with the *Equator* three weeks overdue, general opinion was that she had been lost in the vastness of the Pacific. It is disputed why Louis did not, after all, take up the option to ship out with the *Tiernan*; he claimed the money asked for the passage was too steep, but Lloyd's story was that his mother had one of her famous forebodings. All that is certain is that, after two days, in which RLS bought liberally from the ship's stores, including several barrels of prime-quality corned beef and a dozen cases of a superb Pontet-Canet, and two nights of riotous dining when the champagne corks flew, the *Tiernan* left without the Stevenson party. It was fortunate that they did not sail with the ship, for shortly afterwards it capsized in a squall; six people died and the mate and survivors reached land close to death from hunger, thirst and exposure after days in an open boat. As Lloyd wrote: 'We often congratulated ourselves afterwards that Captain Sachs' terms had been too high; had they been more moderate we might all have perished.'

Shortly afterwards, at the beginning of the seventh week, the *Equator* arrived, having been becalmed while returning from Azorae island to the south. The Stevensons were glad to greet their 'home' again, even in the shape of the familiar stuffy little cabins against which they had so often inveighed. There followed an emotional parting with Tembinok. The king had tears in his eyes as he grasped Louis's hands in his own and told him how much he had learned about the world from the white men, whom he called his 'books'; he would never forget Stevenson and would think of his visit until he died. 'I think you never saw a king cry before,' Tembinok said. 'You are a ver' good man. I think you are the best man I ever know.'

For the first two days as they sailed south, the heat was unbearable. The floor of the cabins was so hot that no one was able to stand on it with bare feet and sleep was all but impossible. The sun warped the decks so that when the rains came, there were leaks in the cracks and berths became flooded. Lice abounded, and cockroaches the size of toads. Above all was the stench of copra and the acrid 'steam' made by fermented copra. The devoted Ah Fu moved Fanny's bedding into a small galley-way, where she tried to sleep fully dressed, under an umbrella. Then storms struck and followed them all the way to Samoa. There was a serious emergency when the vessel nearly hit a reef in heavy weather, and Reid ordered the lifeboats made ready with food and water for an imminent 'abandon ship' call; the subsequent boat voyage of 400–500 miles would have been a grim affair. On another occasion, a violent squall sprang up out of a dead calm and was nearly the end of them, as it caught the ship with all sails set. The foremast snapped across and the foresail downhaul fouled in the wreckage. The crew panicked but Ah Fu climbed to the top of the galley with a knife and cut the rope which freed the rigging. However, Ah Fu's exploits, it turned out, were actuated more by folly than heroism. Next morning it was found that the signal halyard was missing; only several weeks later did Louis discover that Ah Fu had coiled it into a rope and presented it to Fanny, as he had heard her admiring it.

On the morning of 7 December 1889, after twenty-six days at sea, the *Equator* fetched the coast of Samoa. The party was in poor shape after all the buffetings from the waves. Lloyd's legs were ulcerated, Joe Strong in disgrace again after he had failed to carry out his tasks as voyage photographer on Apemama, and increasingly Louis felt that he could not subject the unstable Fanny to more such cruises, as he candidly admitted to his mother, and so reversed the decision he had taken on Apemama. To

Colvin he wrote: 'I am minded to stay not very long in Samoa' and estimated his date of arrival in Britain as June 1890, having visited Fiji and Tonga and then returned homewards via Sydney, Ceylon, Suez and Marseilles. He talked excitedly of the sights and sounds of London: 'I can hear the rattle of the hansom up Endell Street and see the gates swing back, and feel myself out upon the Monument steps – Hosanna! home again.'[26] He had no inkling that he had already reached the only real home he would ever know in his short life.

Samoa: First Year

The Samoan islands, known to the early Pacific explorers as the Navigators, lie just to the east of the International Date Line, at 14 S′ 170–172′W and form an archipelago of volcanic islands. The largest of them, Savaii, was in 1890 inhabited only along its coastal fringe, but eight miles across the Apolima strait is the island of Upolu, 580 miles square, with its capital and port Apia, approached through coral reefs by a dangerous fresh-water channel. Forty miles to the east is Tutuila, which possesses by far the best harbour of the group in the form of Pago-Pago, actually a flooded crater. What gave Upolu its precedence among Samoan islands was that it had the most cultivable land, the greatest population and was the customary headquarters of the Samoan 'kings'.

The *Equator* entered the bottle-shaped harbour and anchored in the neck of the bottle. The view from shipboard afforded a perfect vision of the forest and jungle-strewn hill slopes, and the green conical Mount Vaea, though the first impression was bound to be disappointing; if an improvement on Fakarava, Upolu could scarcely compete with the dramatic prospects of the Marquesas, the high mountains of Hawaii or the all-round beauty of Tahiti. Along the shore lay the many victims of the great hurricane of January 1889: U.S.S. *Trenton Nipsic* and *Vandalia* and the German warships *Adler* and *Olga*; of the warships at anchor in Apia bay on that fateful day, only H.M.S. *Calliope* successfully defied wind and wave and got out of the harbour to the comparative security of the open ocean.[1]

Among those who came out to meet the *Equator* was Harry J. Moors, an American trader from Michigan, a friend of Joe Strong's from previous Pacific meetings, who offered to put them up and make all necessary introductions in Apia. After making their farewells to Captain Reid, Louis and his family went ashore in the Moors's boat. Then they sauntered down Apia's main street, gazing in wonderment at the extent of German 'occupation' of the island. Alongside the expected and now familiar basket-shaped houses of the Samoans, and the churches white-plastered with coral blocks, were the many signs of the white man's presence in dominant force; the tawdry bars, the long pier and warehouse of the so-called 'German firm' (*Deutsche Handels und Plantagen Gesellschaft fur Sud-See Inseln zu Hamburg* – the so-called 'Long Handle' firm which, backed by Bismarck and the German government, aimed at a monopoly of Samoan trade), the trading companies and the low white wooden houses of the European and American traders. The Apia waterfront has always appalled travellers by its dingy, rusty, broken-down quality and the human flotsam matched the squalid physical surroundings; there was a large 'beach' population of drifters and no-goods and the town was popularly known as 'the Hell of the Pacific'. Yet Louis had already seen enough of the Pacific not to let considerations like this bother him. Instead, he concentrated on the sense-impressions; the smell of copra, wood smoke, baking breadfruit, fruit and tropical flowers, especially the scarlet frangipani; the sight of *lavalava* tunics – a skirt worn from the waist by men and from the breast by women – brown skin burnished with perfumed coconut oil, and tattoos from waist to knee on the men which looked at first sight like underdrawers.

The appearance of the Stevenson party made it look at first as though the circus had come to town to add a dash of colour to the tawdry surroundings. When the Revd W.E.Clarke of the London Missionary Society caught sight of them, he assumed that a troupe of strolling players from San Francisco had landed. Fanny, in her Mother Hubbard, wore a straw hat and carried a guitar – because all musical instruments left aboard the *Equator* would have been stolen; Lloyd, who had had his ears pierced before leaving San Francisco and wore large gold earrings and dark blue glasses, clutched his ukelele; the long-haired Louis was barefoot, dressed in calico shirt, cotton trousers and a yachting cap; the moustachioed Joe Strong, often seen with a parrot on his shoulder, looked like a pirate at the best of times, and the presence of Ah Fu added an Oriental flavour to the motley.[2]

They went first to Moors's house. The American trader recalled that Louis had disembarked seeming to be weak and listless, but on sampling Apia soon acquired a spring in his step, declared it 'grand' and was so excited that he could not sit still in the Moors house but prowled around the room, throwing dozens of questions at his host. Moors was a wealthy and influential man and was to play a major role in the Stevensons' life. Married to a Samoan and with a daughter at school in the U.S.A., he owned a chain of outlying trading posts and was the leader of the English-speaking business community's commercial struggle against German dominance. Moors was also import-export supremo, banker, factor and, since in Samoa business and politics were always interlinked, leader of the anti-German political faction. However, there was a dark side to the man, as he made use of 'blackbirded' labour. Since Samoan tradition and culture were antipathetic to agricultural labour, the local cocoa and pineapple plantations depended on the labour of Melanesians abducted in the Solomon islands and elsewhere; the anti-German propaganda sheets advertised this practice as a purely Teutonic activity, but the Anglo-Saxons never disdained 'blackbirding', and among them was Moors. When in Sydney in March 1890, RLS explained his friendship with Moors:

> The man himself is a curious being, not of the best character; has been in the labour trade as supercargo; has been partner with Grossmuhl, the most infamous trader in these waters, the man who is accused of paying natives with whist counters; has settled down at last in Apia, where everyone owes him money on mortgage, where his business is both large and growing, and where he took a great though secret part in the late war. I was forced to be his guest, rather against my will, for his looks, his round blue eyes etc. went against me, and the repulsion was mutual. However, we both got over it, and grew to like each other; and it's my belief he won't cheat me. He is highly intelligent; tells a story well and from a veracious understanding: of all the scores of witnesses I examined about the war, H.J.M. was the only one whom documents invariably corroborated and also (although the most open enemy of the Germans at the time) appeared to suffer from no bias in the retrospect.[3]

Moors took Stevenson on a tour of the whole island of Upolu. Louis found it far less beautiful than Tahiti or the Marquesas and did not entirely relish the 'nature tamed' aspect of the island – largely a function of the German plantations with their myriad regular avenues of palm. He was not particularly attracted by the Samoans themselves: they were courteous and chaste, true, but also thieves and beggars. Most of all, he had reservations about the pervasive German influence in the islands. Linguistically this presented no problem, and he took pleasure in brushing up the language he had not used since 1872, but politically it made him uneasy, especially when it became very clear that the Germans operated an unofficial policy of Teutonic supremacy in every sphere; this point was borne in on him when he was arrested and fined for riding fast in the street, which he had done only after being almost ridden down by the manager of 'the German firm', leading him to conclude that speed limits were not enforced.

How Louis reached his final decision is not clear, but within a very short time Moors had persuaded an already half-convinced RLS that he should make his home in the Pacific. He urged on him the convenience of Samoa, just as well served by transport systems as Tahiti but without the hateful French colonial presence. There were monthly ships from San Francisco to Sydney and back, which called at Apia with the mail; the German steamer *Lübeck* of the Norddeutscher Lloyd from Bremen plied between Apia and Sydney, and the New Zealand vessel, the *Richmond*, picked up passengers in Samoa on its circular run from Auckland to Tahiti and back; and a cable sent from Upolu would reach London within a week. 'Barkis is willin',' said Louis cryptically, indicating Fanny's consent to their experimental residence in Upolu. But Moors also persuaded Louis to become a landowner and planter in Samoa, and for this he has been widely criticised on grounds of irresponsibility – plantation ownership was a precarious high-capital, low-profit enterprise whose benefits, if any, would pay off only in the long-term – and machiavellianism: he hoped to broker all the RLS investments. There are even those who accuse Moors of using RLS as a pawn in an elaborate anti-German political game, hoping to use his fame to draw further Anglo-Saxon funds and settlers to the island to overturn German hegemony.

However, Stevenson was not quite the naïve innocent abroad that this formulation requires. When he made his decision to become a man of property in Samoa, he told Baxter:

The price of the house will be considerable; my expenses will have to be faced before we have cattle, feed, and vegetables. On the other hand, once faced, there is my livelihood, all but books and wine, ready in a nutshell; and it ought to be more easy, and it would be certainly (by all the laws of arithmetic) less expensive, to save and to repay afterward. Excellent, say you, but will you save? and will you repay? I do not know, said the Bell of Old Bow. But, on the other hand, will you tell me how much I shall lose, if I delay building my house and mounting my plantation, and must live at heck and manger, paying three prices for one, after I have paid back the money, and while I economise, under this drain, the fresh capital necessary for the installation? It seems clear to me.[4]

He did, however, take Moors's advice about a site for his property. Apia itself was too hot and humid, but on the slopes of Mount Vaea, about two and a half miles from the town, amid fresh mountain air where the nights were cool, was an estate known as Vailima – 'the place of the five waters' – for sale at ten Chile dollars (the universal currency of the Pacific) an acre; since ten Chilean dollars was then the equivalent of £1–8s–4d, it is clear that Louis spent over £400 on the land alone. Moors explained that the real estate was peculiarly suited to Stevenson's needs, as the locality had the reputation of being a haunt of *aitus* (ghosts), so that he would be free from the incursions of inquisitive Samoans. The deal was quickly struck. Louis bought 314½ acres of land, ranging in altitude from 600 to 1,500 feet, containing waterfalls, precipices, ravines, tablelands and the fabled five streams (which turned out to be four). There was an amazing variety of prospect and scenery; forest, sea, mountains and the warships in Apia harbour. It was agreed that the Stevensons would return to England and wind up their affairs there while Moors set to work as their factor, clearing the land and building a temporary cottage in which they would live while the main house was under construction.

At almost every stage in Stevenson's life after 1879 he was beset by problems arising from his wife or her family, and the period around New Year 1890 was no exception. Almost Louis's first task when he set foot on Samoan soil was to decide what to do about Joe Strong who claimed (and appeared) to be suffering acute heart problems. Louis solved the problem by packing him off at once to his wife in Australia, but not without misgivings, as his letters to Baxter show. 'This of Joe Strong's illness and probable death is a serious consideration: it means a certain addition to my cares, no doubt of that; and suppose him to die, what the mischief am I to do with The Widow? Poor Joe, he was a great annoyance, even to the last. On Apemama, after some miserable misconduct, I had to take all the photographic business out of his hands. And yet he was so pleasant that I never felt my affection shaken, even in our rows; I could far better have parted from his wife.' Similar sentiments were expressed by Fanny:

> As to poor Joe Strong it was to be sooner or later, and the sooner the better for him and all connected with him. It sounds hard to say this, but I do not mean it that way. There are few people towards whom I feel more tenderly than towards Joe, but we know, as he knows himself, that he is better out of it. All I ask is that the crossing may be made without pain or fear; and that I believe may happen. If he faints, there can be no return, and I trust that may be the way of it. It seemed almost cruel to ask the doctor, as we have just done, what we should do if he appeared to be on the point of fainting. He is a sweet, engaging, aggravating creature, refined, artistic, affectionate, as weak as water, living in vague dreams. One needs to be a millionaire to support him and a philosopher to love him. We're not the one, but I think something of the other, and we do love him.[5]

However, Joe Strong, as it later transpired, was manipulating Louis just as much at this juncture as in the earlier histrionic episode at Waikiki; like many first-rate charlatans, he had the capacity for temporary belief even in the illusions he spun himself and clearly convinced a doctor or two of the imminence of cardiac arrest. The irony, of course, was that he took in the greatest *malade imaginaire* herself: Fanny. It almost goes without saying that when Fanny landed in Samoa, she took to her bed with another mysterious ailment. Undoubtedly part of the reason this time was dismay at her husband's enthusiasm for a permanent life in the Pacific and distaste for Moors, between whom and Fanny a state of undeclared war always existed. This accounts both for Fanny's pressure for rapid departure from the island – she was originally to have left for Australia on New Year's Day with Lloyd on the *Lübeck* – and for the peculiar domestic arrangement whereby Fanny, Lloyd and Ah Fu lived in a cottage out in the bush while Louis stayed in Moors's house. RLS provided no explanation for this other than the irritatingly cryptic remark: 'I live in Apia for history's sake with Moors', but it is already noticeable that Fanny and he were spending less and less time together and that their main experience of a shared bedroom was in the cramped conditions of a stateroom on board a Pacific vessel. The American year 1887–88 was noteworthy for the long months Fanny spent apart from Louis and, Pacific voyages apart, the pattern would hold good thereafter. If, as Louis told Baxter, he had never been happy since Hyères, Fanny, it seems, was never happy after Bournemouth. Although permanent settlement in the Pacific meant the permanent overthrow of all his friends in London she so detested, Fanny knew that the price she was paying was steep and in a remarkably confused letter she confided to Mrs Sitwell her severe reservations about Louis's plan to be a Samoan landowner:

> Because I make my sacrifice with flowers on my head and point out the fine views on the way, do not think that it is no sacrifice and only for my own pleasure. The Samoan people are picturesque, but I do not like them ... My time must be so arranged as not to clash with them. I shall be able to get no servants but cannibal black boys ... A great part of the housework I shall have to do myself, and most of the cooking. The land *must* produce food enough for us all, or we shall have nothing to eat. I must also manage that. Oh, it makes me tired to speak of it; and I never feel well, then. I don't want to complain. I am not complaining, really, only telling you ... I do want Louis, and I do want everybody to think I like going to Samoa – and in some ways I do like it; I don't want people to think I am making a sacrifice for Louis. In fact I *can't* make a sacrifice for him; the very fact that I can do the thing in a way makes a pleasure to do it, and it is no longer a sacrifice, though if I did it for another person it would be.[6]

During his initial two months in Samoa, 1889–90, RLS wrote up a legend he had heard on the 'big island' of Hawaii as a short story, 'The Bottle Imp', about a demon who would give the owner of the bottle anything he desired in return for the loss of his soul; the only way to avoid the consequences of the Faustian pact was to sell the bottle on at a loss. This story was first published in the *New York Herald* early in 1891, but made its greatest impact after being translated by a Samoan missionary for reproduction in a comic-style paper produced for the natives. At once the Samoans were able to solve a riddle that had long puzzled them: how could a mere teller of tales be wealthy? Knowing nothing of the simultaneity of world-wide communication made possible by books, and regarding stories and, especially, visual representations of the magic-lantern type as the expression of naturalistic truth, the Samoans naturally assumed that the source of RLS's riches was this exact imp that he kept in a bottle. The seeds of his later reputation as the thaumaturge 'Tusitala' were already being sown.[7]

In February 1890, Louis and Fanny boarded the *Lübeck* for Australia. The plan was that after meeting Joe and Belle Strong in Sydney and deciding on their future, they would proceed to England on the Orient or P & O line. The passage on the *Lübeck* provided the Stevensons with one of their few incident-free sea voyages. They were the only passengers on a large ship, the captain was charming, the weather delightful, and there was excellent table wine available at a shilling a bottle. Louis was not surprised to learn that the Norddeutscher Lloyd line was losing 20,000 marks a trip with the *Lübeck*, but he rejoiced that the loss was taken 'like a gentleman'; it was the first pleasing aspect of German civilisation he had encountered in the South Pacific. Yet even in such halcyon conditions, Louis, a born worrier, found something to fret over. This time it was Joe Strong, and he confided to Baxter:

> The magic lantern job is given up. Impossible to make Joe Strong work, however little; and now his health is gone, and it would be cruel to try. With all that, he is so extravagant that I despair of supporting him. Yet the fool is thoroughly loveable; he has every good quality that I don't possess, and none that I do; and it's scarce too much to say that I despair of being able either to desert or to support, either to leave or tolerate the man.[8]

Thoughts of his friends also troubled him, and he often wondered why it was that he seemed to attract so much ill-luck in human relationship. Fanny had offended Baxter by some of her remarks, and Louis's first task in Samoa had been to smoothe Baxter's ruffled feathers, scarcely to be assuaged by the absurd stories RLS sent on to Scotland about Fanny's having twice seen Baxter's 'fetch'. But Baxter would have been consoled by Louis's frank admission that, of all his old friends, only he and Colvin remained. Fearing that Colvin was laid low by stress and financial anxiety, Louis implored Baxter not to succumb to mental or physical illness:

> You do not know what you become to me, how big you bulk; you must not measure it by my mean letters, nor by anything that I shall ever say; you remain alone of my early past, truer now than ever, and I cling to the thought of you. Hard thoughts I sometimes have of others, God forgive me; I cannot get farther yet than that ugly half word of pardon, and even so, said with a grimace; I prefer to think of two that have stood by me, you and Colvin, with a warmth that grows ever greater. When we talk you shall tell me, and I will try to learn, where I have been in fault with the others; I will take hard words from you and believe hard judgements, but not by letter, please, only when we meet.

The former friends whose defection caused Louis the greatest grief were Bob and Henley, and in the correspondence with Baxter there is much cryptic worrying away at this theme. From Sydney, in March, he wrote: 'I need not say, my dear Charles, that all you have done for Bob and Henley exactly pleases me. You have nothing to do with either; you acted according to my instructions in making both the loans, whereof no more, and you love me.' Yet sometimes the sense of loss led to explicit laments, as in a letter to Baxter in August 1890: 'Even Bob writes to me with an embarrassment which communicates itself to my answers. Our relation is too old and close to be destroyed; I have forgiven him too much – and he me – to leave a rupture possible; but there it is – the shadow.'9

The sense of loss was so great that on the *Lübeck* Louis actually resumed temporarily his 'dear lad' routine with Henley (this was before Lloyd managed to inject his poison and kill off the relationship) and wrote in friendly fashion about his daughter. It is significant that the *coup de grâce* was eventually given to the Henley relationship not by the quarrel over Fanny's plagiarism but because of a slight allegedly offered by Henley to *Maggie*. Suspicions that Louis and Fanny were subtly growing apart – suspicions fed by their many separations – receive clear confirmation in a letter from RLS to Colvin in August 1890, making clear that the 'either me or them' choice which his wife had forced on him was really too high a price for him to pay: Louis told Colvin: 'Since my dear wild noble father died, no head on earth, *and not my wife's* [italics mine] is more precious to my thought than yours.'10 The spectacle thus arises of both partners to the marriage trapped by circumstances in the South Seas – once again a scenario light years away from that of the match made in heaven in which some biographers would have us believe.

Anxiously awaiting the Stevensons in Sydney were the Strongs. Belle had had a tough six months of it, as the £200 Louis remitted to cover her expenses had not arrived on time and she had been reduced to borrowing from King Kalakaua's agent in Australia, living in a theatrical boarding house betimes. The arrival of the feckless Joe at the beginning of January scarcely helped matters. Now came word that her mother and stepfather were due to check in at the prestigious Victoria Hotel. Here was Belle's chance to demonstrate that she and Joe were rehabilitated and to ingratiate herself. She sped over to the Victoria to catch the tail-end of an *opéra bouffe*. Two things were entirely predictable about Victorian travellers: one was that Richard Burton would fall out with the captain of whichever ship he travelled on; the other was that Robert Louis Stevenson would be involved in rows with hotel-keepers. Louis had arrived at the Victoria and asked for a suite on the first floor. To his fury, he was taken up to a dingy room on the fourth floor and given no assistance with his luggage. He stormed back down to the desk to demand an explanation. To the casual onlooker the explanation was clear enough: there amongst the elegant clientèle of Sydney's *haute-bourgeoisie* was a woman in a flowing *holoku* with a complexion as dark as any Polynesian, and a cadaverous long-haired man in a creased ill-fitting suit with a wide, floppy straw hat on his head; to make matters worse, their effects consisted of three cedarwood chests tied with rope, several Tokelau buckets made from tree-trunks, rolls of *tapa* cloth, bulging palm-leaf baskets, matting, and burnished calabashes and coconut shells tied up with fish netting. No one is more snobbish than a hotel clerk, and the man had obviously weighed them up as the flotsam and jetsam of 'the beach', doubtless in Australia to scrounge passage in the steerage on some tub.

Into this scene of low farce burst Belle. She suggested they go across the road to the less fashionable Oxford Hotel. Here they were courteously received and given the best suite in the establishment – a whole floor of rooms – without cavil. Next morning Sydney's newspaper headlines were full of the arrival of the famous author of *Jekyll and Hyde*. Realising his disastrous gaffe, the Victoria's clerk contacted the manager, who came to apologise and beg Louis to return at half-rate, little realising that the Victoria had succeeded in breaching the magma of a volcanic latent Stevensonian rage about the behaviour of hotels. Louis refused the offer curtly, but took grim satisfaction in obliging the Victoria to bring over in baskets every day the letters addressed to him care of the Victoria. It is apparent that he was already in an ugly mood when he saw the Revd Dr Hyde's letter about Damien which provoked him to the famous 'libel'.[11]

Sydney was never a lucky place for RLS, even though he liked it and Fanny did not; snobbish about the 'criminal stamp' of the faces of Australians, who, she could not forget, were descended from convicts, she had long since failed to endear herself to the land of the Southern Cross by ingenuously asking an Australian what 'Sydney ducks' (convicts) were. No sooner had Louis begun to make friends with local artists and writers, haunting Circular Quay, and prowling through the bookshops in search of detective novels and cheap thrillers – his favourite relaxation fare – than he went down with the old litany of ailments, not experienced since Papeete: coughing, headaches, fever, pleurisy, loss of appetite and, finally, 'bluidy jack' itself. His friends suggested he move into the Union Club, where admirers and gawpers could not reach him as they could at the Oxford. There was one snag – or perhaps if the construction we have put on the Stevensons' private life is correct it was not such a snag: the Union was a gentleman's club, women were not admitted, so Fanny could not nurse him. Although Fanny usually did little more than fuss and fume before taking to her bed herself whenever Louis was ill, she had an irrational belief in the curative effect of her presence. Jeremiahs warned of the unsalubrious nature of Sydney, and she began to fear that Louis might never emerge from the club alive. Knowing how he always took a turn for the better once at sea, she set about finding a berth, in *any* vessel, going *anywhere*.

As bad luck would have it, they had no sooner arrived in Sydney than a seamen's strike broke out and the waterfront was littered with idle vessels going nowhere. If Fanny knew her Melville, she would have remembered the description of Jonah 'prowling among the shipping like a vile burglar' and considered how apt it was for her as she traipsed around the shipping offices in the harbour. At last she found what she was looking for. A minor trading firm named Henderson and Macfarlane had a small fore-and-aft rigged steamer – a kind of maritime turboprop – called the *Janet Nicholl*, bound out for the Gilberts and crewed by Kanakas, and thus unaffected by the strike. At first the owners turned down flat the idea of an eccentric white woman and her dying husband shipping out under their ensign, but they had reckoned without Fanny's determination once her blood was up. It was not just Colvin and Henley who had noted that jutting jaw with trepidation, and soon the Scottish owners of the *Janet Nichol* came under her sway and agreed terms.

Louis's health picked up as soon as he heard the news of another joust with the Pacific, especially as his family worries were temporarily in abeyance. As he wrote to Baxter: 'I must tell you that the Strongs have been behaving excellently. Joe still lives, but in great and unceasing danger. Belle has been a kind nurse to him; both have lived all this while on their allowance and not made one penny of debt. I cannot tell you how encouraging this is, and how it reconciles me with life.' Fanny, however, did not agree with this analysis, though her version of events was no doubt coloured by the consideration that her beloved Lloyd had had to undergo 'hardship' while lodging with the Strongs; nor could she decide exactly why this arrangement had been entered into, at one time claiming that it was an economy measure, at another alleging that Louis had posted him in the Strong household as spy-cum-policeman. At all events, Lloyd, whose indisposition always increased in direct proportion to the amount of routine work he was asked to do, soon cracked under the regime. 'When I go to the house,' reported Fanny, 'he clings to me as he did when he was a baby in arms. Though the table at their boarding house is better than ours, the bread is as dust in his mouth, and the meat and vegetables are no more than shadows to him.'[12]

Leaving the Strongs on a tight leash under the watchful eye of his bank, Louis embarked on the *Janet Nicholl* with Lloyd and Fanny on 11 April 1890, expecting to be away from Australia for four months on a cruise to theoretically unknown destinations, though in fact Louis knew the Gilberts loomed large in the itinerary. Ah Fu left them to see his widowed mother in China, promising Fanny faithfully that he would return and work for her at Vailima. He took with him his accumulated wages plus a gift of £50 from RLS, but never returned and was never seen or heard from again.

The embarkation was made via an open rowing boat and in a cold drizzle. The Strongs waved as Louis went aboard, still an invalid, laid out like a board and rolled like a mummy in a blanket. There were to be three other passengers: one of the owners (Henderson), a veteran trader named Ben Hird and Jack Buckland, destined to be the model for Tommy

Hadden in *The Wrecker*. Buckland distinguished himself by reeling off the gangway drunk as he boarded and had to be fished out of the sea. Known as 'Tin Jack' in the islands, where he spent most of the year as a penurious trader, Buckland liked to come to Sydney each year to receive his income as a 'remittance man' and then spend it all in one long drunken binge. He also fancied himself as an actor, but his Shakespearean declamations always had Louis in fits of laughter – though he always concealed his mirth so as not to hurt Jack, of whom he was very fond.

The *Janet Nicholl*, a combined steamer and sailing ship of 600 tons, with its screw propellers, spacious deck and two bathrooms, was in some ways like an Atlantic liner in comparison to the *Equator*. Her worst fault was that in rough weather she was 'the worst roller I have ever been aboard of'. The first port of call was Auckland in New Zealand, but the crossing of the Tasman Sea in heavy weather took a week. As usual, the stoical RLS played down the ordeal: 'The lively Jane as she is called by those who know her is just illustrating her skittishness,' he wrote to his mother, 'and my hand of write suffers in consequence.' The reality was grimmer. Confined to his cabin, with the ports closed and at first on a permanent diet of egg-nogg, he was later revolted by the ship's food, insofar as he was able to eat it, for in squalls he was forced to hang on to his bunk with one hand and hold the plate with the other; the knife and fork, as he told Colvin, had to be manipulated with his eyelid.[13]

In Auckland Fanny went shopping but so did Buckland, and therein nearly lay disaster. A lover of practical jokes, 'Tin Jack' bought a consignment of fireworks to amuse the islanders and some cartridges; included in his haul was ten pounds of 'calcium fire, safe as a packet of sugar' according to the chemist. All this was stowed in the cabin Buckland shared with Lloyd. The *Janet Nicholl* sailed in the evening of 19 April but had not got beyond Auckland light when, about 10.30 p.m., there was a terrific explosion in the Lloyd/Buckland cabin; red, blue and green rockets whizzed into the saloon and soared high above the deck. The helmsman deserted his post in a panic and it took the captain, who had known nothing of this dangerous cargo, several minutes to appreciate the situation and order pump and hose. Covering himself with a blanket, he took the hose into the middle of the inferno and extinguished the flames just in time to save the ship. He took days to recover from the effect of the fumes. Had the wind been in a different quarter or had the cartridges exploded, the vessel would have been lost. In the confusion Fanny managed to stop two black boys from throwing a blazing trunk overboard, inside which were all RLS's manuscripts. But most of the Stevensons' personal effects were lost, all Lloyd's photographs, and husband, wife and stepson were left with just the clothes they were wearing; almost predictably, the culprit 'Tin Jack' lost nothing at all.

21. Lloyd Osbourne, aged 20, in 1888

22. The schooner *Casco* off Vancouver

23. The Stevensons being entertained by King Kalakaua and his sister, Princess Liliuokalani, in Honolulu

24. RLS with Fanny and a missionary priest. A photograph
taken by Lloyd Osbourne
25. At 'Sans Souci', Butaritari

26. The SS *Janet Nicholl*
27. RLS with Kalakaua (*right*), Fanny (*left*), his mother and
Lloyd on board the *Casco*

28. The house at Vailima, Samoa
29. Family and servants, Vailima, 31 July 1892: with RLS are
Joe Strong (with parrot); Mary, the Australian maid; Margaret
Stevenson; Lloyd Osbourne; Fanny; Belle Strong and her son,
Austin

30. RLS in Samoa

31. RLS dictating to Belle at Vailima, 1892
32. RLS with Fanny, Belle and members of his household on
the verandah at Vailima

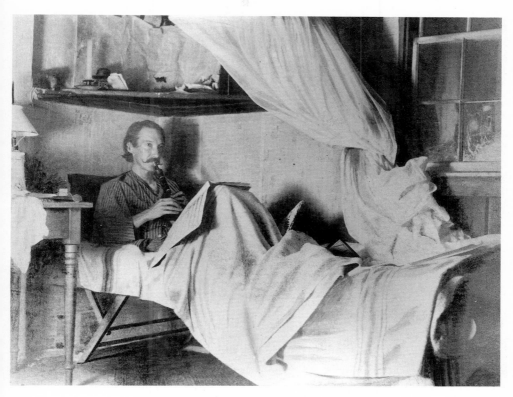

33. RLS playing his flageolet in bed at Vailima
34. RLS lying in state

35. Bas relief medallion by Augustus St Gaudens
36. RLS's tomb on Mt Vaea, Samoa

Three days of fine weather were followed by a gale, but RLS, by now indifferent to the fury of the Pacific, worked right through it. Passing by Curtis and Sunday Islands, the ship anchored at Savage Island in the Bermadec group on 27 April. Louis, now recovered in health, went ashore, and found further evidence of the idiosyncratic ways of Polynesians.

> The path up the cliffs was crowded with gay islandresses (I like that feminine plural) who wrapped me in their embraces, and picked my pockets of all my tobacco, with a manner which a touch would have made revolting, but as it was, was simply charming like the Golden Age. One pretty little stalwart minx, with a red flower behind her ear, had searched me with extraordinary zeal; and when, soon after, I missed my matches, I accused her (she still following us) of being a thief. After some delay, and with a subtle smile, she produced the box, gave me *one match*, and put the rest away.14

On 30 April the *Nicholl* reached Apia, and the Stevensons spent Mayday riding out to Vailima to inspect the progress of the work. Good progress had been made, just as Moors had assured them, and Louis felt his faith in the man amply vindicated.15 They rejoined the ship for its north-easterly cruise through the Tokelaus and Line Islands (past Swayn's Island to Penrhyn). At Penrhyn the ship turned due west and sailed through the Tokelaus to the Ellice Islands; everywhere they went, they found the islands full of leprosy and elephantiasis. From the Ellice islands the track lay north towards the Gilberts, the first of which, Arorai, was reached on 9 June. Threading through the islands, a week later they came to their old haunts at Apemama. Tembinok was away on another island, but the Stevensons followed him there with gifts. As they were rowed along the beach they heard the cry of 'Pani! Pani' ['Fanny'] go up from the king's harem. Minutes later they were ushered into Tembinok's presence. He seemed unsurprised to see them, but showed he was still friendly by steering the royal boat when they all returned for a celebration on the *Janet Nicholl*.

Tembinok's rather dour mien was explained by an epidemic of measles ravaging the islands, clearly a 'present' from the white man but attributed by the superstitious islanders to the loss of the 'devil box' to the Stevensons in 1889. Only when he was alone with the Stevensons in their cabin did the old Tembinok return. He embraced his old friends with tears of joy and, over champagne, revealed that his apparent lack of emotion when they suddenly reappeared in his life was the result of a dream which told him he was about to meet Louis and Fanny again.

On 17 June the *Janet Nicholl* proceeded to Marakei and Tarawa in the northern Gilberts, where another fellow Scot, Captain John Cameron, supercargo on the *Lizzie Derby* out of San Francisco, made Louis's acquaintance over a game of chess. Two days later the ship was at Jaluit, the seat of government for the German-controlled Marshall Islands, and on

20 June Louis recorded his farthest point north in Micronesia with a visit to Majuro, 'a pearl of atolls'. The *Janet Nicholl* then returned to Apemama via Abaiang, but it was here, on 1 July, that Louis's health, which had held up wonderfully for two months, broke down again and he began to spit blood. He attributed this to overwork 'in a wild cabin heated like the Babylonian furnace'. He wrote to Burlingame: 'I find the heat of a steamer decidedly wearing and trying in these latitudes, and I am inclined to think the superior expedition rather dearly paid for. Still, the fact that one does not even remark the coming of a squall, nor feel relief at its departure, is a mercy not to be acknowledged without gratitude.'[16]

On 3 July the ship was at Aranuka, one of Tembinok's islands, where the Stevensons again met the king. Henderson agreed to give a lift to the entire royal court – boat, harem, bodyguard and full entourage – back to Apemama, which meant twenty-four hours of gross overcrowding, with two hundred extra passengers crowding into every foot of the ship's decks. After a final emotional farewell with the monarch, now (rightly) convinced he would never see the Stevensons again, the *Janet* headed for New Caledonia. They had already called at thirty-three islands in three and a half months, though seldom for more than a few hours at a time, and Louis was beginning to grow bored; speaking of the 'low islands' he remarked: 'hackney cabs have more variety than atolls.' On 26 July the ship reached Noumea in New Caledonia. As this was to be the only glimpse of Melanesia on the trip, Louis requested Fanny and Lloyd to continue on to Sydney while he stayed behind to observe life in this French penal colony.

For once Fanny's health seemed tolerable – much better than on the *Equator* – and she later described the cruise on the *Janet Nicholl* as the happiest time of her life. Certainly she and Louis resumed full marital relations on this voyage, for she later told Will Low she had been pregnant and miscarried (she was now fifty). Low, who knew her well, dismissed this as another of Fanny's fantasies, and the best critics agree with him. However, parting from Louis brought bad luck, for on the last lap from Noumea to Sydney the *Janet Nicholl* ran into a cyclonic storm and was very nearly lost on the Australian coast.[17]

Louis stayed a week in Noumea, constantly attended by a doctor; it seems that the desire to investigate the convict system was a fairly transparent excuse to get some proper nursing and recover from his illness. He read a book appropriate to the French criminal ambience – Zola's *La Bête Humaine* – but, as could have been predicted, strongly disliked it: '"Nervous maladies: the homicidal ward" would be a better name. O, this game gets very tedious.' Low in spirits, he claimed that his only wish now was to see the house in Samoa built before he died, so that he would have something to leave Fanny and Lloyd. He took ship for Sydney early in August but again caught a cold as soon as he set foot

in Australia and was once more holed up in the Union Club while Fanny
and Lloyd stayed with the Strongs in their boarding house.

Louis had expressed great cynicism about human beings in a letter to
Baxter from Noumea; he had apparently not realised that success breeds
envy and enmity *ipso facto*: 'My dear Charles, it is a very poor affair to
(what is called) succeed. My faults whatever they were, were taken very
easily by my friends till I had (what is called) succeeded; then the measure
was changed.' He was even (unwontedly) cynical about his beloved Lloyd,
whom he dispatched from Sydney to Europe to expedite the winding up of
business there and accompany Maggie back from Scotland: 'Please guide
Lloyd all you can ... He is not – well – not a man of business.' What he
found waiting for him in Sydney increased his cynicism. There was the
abiding hostility of all his British friends towards Fanny; and there was the
incorrigible Joe Strong.

After lying low for a while, Strong had resumed his old habits. He continued to take dole from Louis, even as the provider refrained from buying
new clothes as part of an economy drive, but seemed to take the line that
Louis 'owed' him his basic subsistence and that anything he earned thereafter was personal spending money. To his consternation, Louis learned that
Strong had secretly sold some paintings and had re-equipped his wardrobe,
complete with silk handkerchiefs. The information came from Belle, who
was beginning to soften in her hostility to her stepfather and actually felt
guilty about Joe's behaviour. Even worse was the realisation that money
RLS loaned Strong earlier in the year for a family holiday – and which
he had sent for to Scotland against Baxter's express advice – had not been
spent on a holiday at all; Belle and Austin had seen nothing of it, but Joe
had spent it in Sydney's bars and brothels. Now Louis wrote to Baxter in
angry frustration:

It is this which has filled me with an angry bitterness intolerable to endure.
And the money for having his child's tooth stopped – O Christ Jesus! it is
sometimes too much to have to support this creature ... this money which was
stolen from me – for he owes me his body, his soul and his boots, and the soup
that he wipes on his moustache ... And yet withal he's kind of innocent ... He
is the place where an innocent child has made a mess on the hearth-rug, and I
wish somebody would mop it up ... Belle has behaved really well this time; if
I took notice of anything it would only make him think that Belle has peached;
he would only take it out of her worse than he is doing; and the person who
would suffer would be the one who has dealt (I must say – and never thought
to be able to say it of her –) honestly and kindly to me. So there's nothing to
do but grin and bear, and keep the money to a fixed sum ... Hard is the lot
of him who has dependants. But I should not say that. For nearly six months
Belle has been a hitherto unheard-of model of gratitude; by which I mean that

she has never said a word of thanks; but gone ahead, and managed the money the way I wished her to, and met my views in every way in her power, against all obstacles. This sort of thing more than repays a man for a little money, which I do not feel, and a great deal of money, which I own I feel like hell . . . It ain't charity; I never was guilty of that. Only a person hates to see a pensioner cocking snooks at him, and putting himself up on the top of a monument of mean, greedy-child selfishness . . . And you can't strike the insane, let alone the dying . . . who (and whose wife and child) is – are – your dependants.

Louis decided to solve the problem by bringing Belle and Joe out to Samoa so that he could keep an eye on them and curb their excesses. Though not blind to Belle's faults, he felt that she had at least been trying to accommodate herself to the regime he prescribed for her. It was typical of Louis, though, to wrap up *realpolitik* with sentiment. He took Belle aside for a long talk and told her that, lacking a family of his own, he wanted her and Lloyd to be his children and heirs. It was presumably in response to this magnanimity that Fanny offered to sell Skerryvore to help with the expenses of Samoa. At first Louis demurred, on the grounds that the house had been a personal gift to her from Thomas Stevenson, but he soon allowed himself to be persuaded. Among the other tasks Lloyd was now to perform in England was to oversee the sale of the Bournemouth house.[18]

Meanwhile RLS's British friends became increasingly dismayed as it became clearer and clearer that the only way they would ever see him again was by making the long trip to the Pacific. At first, the proposition was that the Stevensons would settle in Samoa but still come back to Britain on visits. Even this alarmed Colvin and, on learning of the purchase of Vailima, he wrote to Baxter as follows: 'I have a long letter from Fanny – bringing the fulfilment of an old fear . . . the fear that it would end in their settling for good in the South Seas.' He gave it as his opinion that if RLS remained in the Pacific, he would be 'lost so far as keeping the powers of his mind and doing work goes'. But by August 1890 the drama had moved on a couple of episodes and it was now likely that Louis would *never* return. From the Union Club in August Louis wrote to Henry James, the one person he thought might understand and not put *his* interests first:

> I must tell you plainly – I can't tell Colvin – I do not think I shall come to England more than once, and then it'll be to die. Health I enjoy in the tropics; even here, which they call sub-or semi-tropics, I come only to catch cold . . . How should I do in England? . . . Am I very sorry? I am sorry about seven or eight people in England, and one or two in the States. And outside of that, I simply prefer Samoa . . . The sea, islands, the islanders, the island life and climate, make and keep me truly happier. These last two years I have been much at sea, and I have *never wearied*.

When this news leaked out, Fanny was universally pilloried as an ogress keeping her husband in a gloomy Pacific island. This time even Colvin broke his usual vow of silence and criticised Fanny openly. Louis reported back to Colvin that when Fanny read these charges set down in a letter she cried all night at the thought that she had lost the good opinion of the only one of her husband's intimates she had counted on as a friend. Fanny wrote reproachfully to Mrs Sitwell to say she was merely doing what Colvin had long urged her to do: settle in the place that was best for Louis's health. To Colvin she made the same point, underlining the fact that she personally contemplated life in Samoa without enthusiasm; on the Samoans themselves she added: 'I do not like them. I do not trust them.' Louis completed the quartet of letters to the Colvins by writing to Colvin's future wife, also his own lost love: 'Remember that, though I take my sicknesses with a decent face, they do represent suffering, and weakness, and painful disability ... Try and get Colvin, without giving him an idea that he has hurt us, to write a kindlier letter to Fanny.'[19]

In September 1890 Louis and Fanny left Sydney for Apia in the *Lübeck*. Louis was in sombre and thoughtful mood, by now regretful that he had plunged so intemperately into the fray on Damien's behalf, risking ruin, and remorseful about his rudeness to William Dean Howells in 1887. Perhaps to show that, Damien notwithstanding, there was no bad blood between him and the Protestant missionaries in the Pacific, he used the one-day stopover at Tonga to give a lecture at a missionary college. The gesture seemed to cheer him, and he spoke of making further cruises, to Fiji and back to Tahiti. The onward trip to Samoa was notable only because a young German pantryman named Paul Einfurer became obsessed with their tales of Vailima, followed them ashore at Samoa and plagued them for a job until Louis consented, with misgivings, for Einfurer spoke little English and had already given evidence of his bibulous tendencies.[20]

On landing in Samoa they found that Moors had cleared about a dozen acres and erected the temporary cottage. With almost no furniture except the beds they had brought from Sydney, they were at first obliged to rough it. Moors was pleased with himself for having made good his promise, but Fanny found fault with everything: with the kitchen, which was in a separate building eight yards from the house, posing logistical problems in the rainy season; and with the lack of pigpens or chicken-runs to house the animals she had brought with her. The 'little two-storied wooden box of a cottage' provided cramped accommodation in the 'master's quarters' upstairs: a sitting/dining room fourteen feet by sixteen, with no ceiling and open to the iron roof; a much smaller bedroom and a tiny storeroom. Downstairs slept 'Ben' the head ganger with his Samoan wife and child, and three Kanakas. Moors had had the inside painted a lugubrious black and white, so Fanny tried to improve the appearance of the upstairs by unpacking some rich tawny *tapa* cloth and nailing it to the walls.

According to local lore, Vailima had once belonged to a blind Scottish blacksmith, and had been cultivated in the past, but the jungle had reclaimed its own until Moors's gang began work. The cleared area was still only partially recovered, as the labour gangs had worked round the biggest obstacles. Still standing were a number of giant trees, mainly banyans, up to one hundred and fifty feet in height and thirty feet in girth: these provided a nature garden in miniature, for their trunks were festooned with creepers, orchids grew in the forks of their branches, fruit-eating bats roosted in the high places until dusk, and the foliage played host to hundreds of rich-throated birds. On each side of the clearing was a stream and one of them, constantly fed by a waterfall and fringed by wild orange trees, converted naturally into a deep clear swimming pool. The house and clearing faced the sea, and the surge and thunder of the booming surf were clearly though distantly audible. On one side of them the forested slopes rose to Mount Vaea, 1,300' feet high, and on the other they could see clear to the distant blue mountains of Atua.

Fanny set to work to convert the clearing into a kitchen garden. The cleared area was not quite virgin, for here and there she and her Samoan helpers came on ancient groves still producing: bananas, taros, frangipani, papaya, lemons. Among these she spread the seeds she had brought from Sydney: melons, tomatoes, lima beans, mangoes, pineapples, as well as buffalo grass for the planned paddock. Then the weeding commenced, and RLS threw himself into manual labour with gusto. 'Nothing is so interesting as weeding,' he wrote to Colvin with momentary hyperbole. 'I went crazy over the outdoor work, and had at last to confine myself to the house, or literature must have gone by the board.'

Gradually the Stevensons began to assemble the nucleus of a staff. Henry Simile, a young man recommended to them by the Reverend Mr Clarke of the London Missionary Society on the basis of his ability at missionary English, and who claimed to come from a long line of chiefs on the other big Western Samoan island of Savaii, soon proved his worth after a shaky start. He was good at overseeing the labourers and was unfailingly courteous and helpful to Fanny. Louis confided to Colvin: 'I once loathed, I now like and – pending fresh discoveries – have a kind of respect for Henry.' As he laboured over his South Seas letters, Louis's work was chequered by Fanny's cries and exclamations, and he passed on some of the dialogue to Colvin:

'Paul, you take a spade to do that – dig a hole first. If you do that, you'll cut off your foot!'
'Here, you boy, what do you do there? You no got work? You go find Simile; he give you work. Peni, you tell this boy he go find Simile, suppose Simile no give him work, you tell him go'way. I no want him here. That boy no good.'
PENI (from the distance in reassuring tones): 'All right, sir!'
FANNY (after a long pause): 'Peni, you tell that boy go find Simile! I no want

him stand here all day. I no pay that boy. I see him all day. He do nothing.

Through this cacophony Louis worked away, completing the South Seas letters, polishing up *The Wrecker* and drafting sketches for the new novel that would eventually appear as *The Ebb-Tide*. He would break for lunch at midday – typically beef, soda-scones, fried banana, pineapple in claret, and coffee. At night dinner might be stewed beef and potatoes, baked bananas, new loaf-bread hot from the oven, pineapple in claret. In the afternoon he would walk in the forests and ponder the silent malice of nature; in his view the Samoan jungle was certainly not neutral and he reflected on this to Colvin in one of many passages in his *oeuvre* that point forward towards Conrad:

> My long silent contests in the forest have had a strange effect on me. The unconcealed vitality of these vegetables, their exuberant number and strength, the attempts – I can use no other word – of the lianas to enwrap and capture the intruder, the awful silence, the knowledge that all my efforts are only like the performance of an actor, the thing of a moment, and the wood will silently and swiftly heal them up with fresh effervescence ... the whole silent battle, murder, and slow death, of the contending forest; weigh upon the imagination.[21]

The combination of weeding and the sense of being engaged in a gigantic and unavailing struggle against natural forces found expression in one of RLS's *Songs of Travel*:

> Thick round me in the teeming mud
> Briar and fern strove to the blood:
> The hooked liana in his gin
> Noosed his reluctant neighbours in:
> There the green murderer throve and spread,
> Upon his smothering victims fed.[22]

Even as they struggled against mud and grime, the Stevensons received some unexpected visitors. The American painter John La Farge, whom Louis already knew slightly, was travelling in the Pacific with his friend Henry Brooks Adams, Harvard historian and scion of the great Boston Adams family that had given the United States its second and sixth presidents. Grandson and great-grandson of presidents, Adams it was who first advocated that the United States take on the British empire in a struggle for global hegemony. Since the first stirrings of American expansionism took place in Samoa, and Adams regarded the British as deadly rivals, there was more than mere Bostonian patrician hauteur at play in the lofty and dismissive way he described his first meeting with RLS. Omitting to mention that Fanny and Louis had been struggling to erect a greasy black cooking stove on the day he dropped by (17 October), Adams laid about him:

> Our European rival, Robert Louis Stevenson, lives in the hills and forest,

where he cannot rival us in social gaiety. We have been to see him and found him, as he declared, very well. I should need to be extremely well to live the life he has led and is still leading, but a Scotchman with consumption can defy every fatigue and danger. His place is, as he says, 'full of Rousseaus', meaning picturesque landscapes. I saw no Rousseaus, the day being unfavourable, but I saw a very dirty board cabin, with a still dirtier man and woman in it, in the middle of several hundred burned tree-stumps. Both the man and the woman were lively, and in their respective ways amusing, but they did not seem passionately eager for constant association with us, and poor Stevenson can't talk and write too. He naturally prefers writing.

But as he hit his stride, Adams became more acidulous.

A two-storey Irish shanty ... squalor like a railroad navvy's board hut ... a man so thin and emaciated that he looked like a bundle of sticks in a bag, with ... dirty striped pyjamas, the baggy legs tucked into coarse woollen stockings, one of which was bright brown in colour, the other a purplish dark tone ... a woman ... (in) the usual missionary nightgown which was no cleaner than her husband's shirt and drawers, but she omitted the stockings ... her complexion and eyes were dark and strong, like a half-breed Mexican ... Though I could not forget the dirt and squalor, I found Stevenson extremely entertaining.

The Americans noted, as their compatriot Moors had, that RLS in conversation could not be still but sat down, jumped up, darted off and flew back, with a different physical movement for each sentence he uttered, his eyes and features gleaming with a hectic glow. They discussed Samoans, about whom Stevenson was indifferent: he said that the most beautiful place he had seen in the Pacific was Nuku-Hiva and the Tahitians the finest race; compared with them Samoa and the Samoans were nothing much; but for all that, he declared he would never leave the island to make a home elsewhere and expressed his incomprehension as to why anyone who had the choice of living in the Pacific would choose to live elsewhere. Adams, who was making the trip as therapy after the recent death of his wife, thought that Samoa was very little changed from pagan times, with Christianity a thin veneer, but was struck by the absence of the fabled easy sexuality. As respectable *haoles*, not the scum of the 'beach', he and La Farge had to sustain their rank and could not have casual liaisons with Samoan women; a relationship with a 'respectable' Samoan woman, on the other hand, meant a long courtship through third parties, a payment of 300 dollars to the girl's family as compensation, and formalities like divorce and marriage just as in the United States, but with the added lifetime burden of having to support an extended family.

Early in November Louis returned the Americans' call. The supercilious Adams found him cleaner this time, was impressed by his wide knowledge, but still found his conversation 'inconsequential', doubtless because it was not the ponderous excursus into modern and medieval history Adams was used to at Harvard. 'We like him, but he would be, I think, an impossible companion,' he wrote patronisingly. 'His face has a certain beauty, especially the eyes, but it is the beauty of disease. He is a strange compound of callousness and susceptibility, and his susceptibility is sometimes more amusing than his callousness.'[22]

The brush with Adams was not the only clash of British and American sensibilities in October 1890, but the other collision was overt. In a passage so revealing of the latent tensions in the marriage that Lloyd and Belle later crossed it out (it was restored by scholars using magnifying glasses and ray techniques), Fanny noted in her diary on 23 October, just after Adams's visit: 'Louis says that I have the soul of a peasant, not so much that I love working in the earth and with the earth, but because I like to know that it is my own earth that I am delving in. Had I the soul of an artist, the stupidity of possessions would have no power over me. He may be right.'

It is difficult to know how to take this. Probably Louis simply got tired of the bawled orders to the labourers while he was trying to work and came out with an irritable aside. Or perhaps the visit from Adams and La Farge had irked him and he took out his bad feeling on Fanny. Whatever the case, she was unable to shrug it off as a momentary expression of pique but worried away at it, analysing the possible meanings of 'peasant' and writing pages of self-justification. On 5 November, a full two weeks after the offending remark, she was still turning it over and over in her mind. Her never very deeply submerged paranoia joined forces with the old fantasy about being secretly 'creative'; to her perfervid mind, Louis had delivered the ultimate insult, for instead of regarding her as *homo faber* ('the artist') – to use Hannah Arendt's phrase – he placed her as *animal laborans* ('a worker'). The fact that Louis had backtracked and said she should take the remark as a compliment did not assuage her, for she clung to her abiding fantasy about being 'creative'. Evidently Louis got tired of her endless harping and accused her of self-indulgence, pointing meanwhile to the burden he was bearing. There is something deeply unbalanced about the 5 November diary entry, where she almost suggests the domestic animals are in league with Louis against her, and the mixture of guilt, self-assertion and self-contradiction makes this outburst almost a model case study for psychiatrists to chew on:

> I am feeling very depressed, for my vanity, like a newly felled tree, lies prone and bleeding. Louis tells me that I am not an artist but a born, natural peasant. I have often thought *that* the happiest life and not one for criticism. I feel most embittered when I am assured that I am really what I had wished to be. Of course, I meant a peasant without aspirations. Perhaps if I had known in time, I should have had none of it! I have been brooding on my feelings and holding my head before the glass and now I am ashamed. Louis assures me that the peasant class is a most interesting

one and he admires it hugely. I have just read the notice of the death of an Englishwoman. 'She,' says the journal, 'though possessing neither personal charm nor beauty, was a most interesting woman.' I wonder how she would like that description could she know of it? Louis says that no one can mind having it said of him that he is not an artist unless he is supporting his family by his work as an artist, in which case it is an insult. Well, I could not support a fly by my sort of work, artistic or otherwise. I am reminded of a friend of Louis, a poet I think who, when asked why he looked so gloomy, broke out with, 'I want praise and I don't get enough of it!' I am afraid I want no praise for what I do not possess. I so hate being a peasant that I feel a positive pleasure when I fail in peasant occupations.

My fowls won't lay eggs, and if they do, the cocks ... eat them. The pigs, whom I loathe and fear, are continually climbing out of their sty and doing all sorts of mischief ... I love the growing things but the domestic beasts are not to my taste. I have, too, such a guilty feeling towards them, for I know if their murder is not contemplated that at least they will be robbed of their young at my instigation.[23]

Those who had studied Fanny closely would have been able to predict the next stage: psychosomatic illness. After working with gusto throughout October, almost immediately after her 5 November diary entry she began to complain of blinding headaches and took to her bed; by Christmas 1890 the headaches had become earache. Louis went back to supervising the labour gang. He set himself the task of making a path up the gorge of stream above the house and to widening the track that led down to Apia; even when completed, it was never practicable for wheeled vehicles in the rainy season. Stables were built for riding horses and the pack animals, pens for cows and fenced and wired runs for ducks, chickens and hogs. He was delighted to find that for the first time in his life he could exert himself, break sweat and breathe deep without falling victim to haemorrhage or weeks of exhaustion. The toil resulted in one of Louis's best poems, 'The Woodman':

> Mid vegetable king and priest
> And stripling, I (the only beast)
> Was at the beast's work, killing; hewed
> The stubborn roots across, bestrewed
> The glebe with the dislustred leaves;
>
> I spied and plucked by the green hair
> A foe more resolute to live
> The toothed and killing sensitive ...
> I saw him crouch, I felt him bite
> And straight my eyes were touched with sight.
> I saw the wood for what it was:

The lost and the victorious cause,
The deadly battle pitched in line,
Saw silent weapons cross and shine:
Silent defeat, silent assault,
A battle and a burial vault.
Thick round me in the teeming mud
Briar and fern strove to the blood . . .

Green conquerors from overhead
Bestrode the bodies of their dead;
The Caesars of the silvan field,
Unused to fail, foredoomed to yield:
For in the groins of branches, lo!
The cancers of the orchid grow . . .[24]

When Fanny sank into her cycle of indisposition, Louis liked to mount a horse one day a week and gallop down to Apia to enjoy the social life. Mornings at the mission house might be followed by lunch at the German or U.S. consulates and a visit to one of the German warships in the afternoon, rounded off by a Samoan feast with one of the chiefs in the evening. On quieter visits he would spend much time conversing with Moors, who was never at ease with RLS if Fanny was present; even when she was not, there was always the fear that she would come storming in in the middle of an animated conversation and terminate proceedings with her perennial excuse, impervious to logic and argument alike: 'too much talk is not good for Louis'. Louis liked to tell ghost stories and though he admitted he had never seen one, he persisted in believing in them, in the face of sceptics like Moors. His American host found him a strange mixture of the spiritual and the bohemian and, like all who met him, commented on how apt it was that he was the author of *Jekyll and Hyde*: 'the truth is that there were two Stevensons . . . this strange dual personality'. RLS often rhapsodised on the charms of island life, and claimed to pity his benighted friends in Europe who knew nothing of the splendours of the Pacific: 'Half the ills of mankind might be shaken off without doctor or medicine by mere residence in this lovely portion of the world.'

Moors also found Louis's idiosyncratic morality hard to adjust to. A clerk in his employment was having an affair with the Samoan wife of a lawyer named Carruthers. RLS learned that the adultery had been condoned once, and he thought that right and proper, adding that in such a case there could be no second chances. When he heard from Moors that the affair had been resumed and rediscovered, he was so angry that he told Moors he could no longer dine with him, lest he run into the offending clerk. Moors, who had had various 'wives' and a string of casual paramours, tried to make light of Louis's 'unbalanced' protests but when he saw that Stevenson was in deadly earnest, dismissed the clerk even though he had previously declared him to be indispensable to his business.

It may have been Louis's outbursts on this occasion that led Moors to record:

> When in a rage he was a study. Once excite him, and you had another Stevenson. I have seen him in all moods. I have seen him sitting on my table, dangling his bony legs in the air, chatting away in the calmest manner possible; and I have seen him become suddenly agitated, jump from that table and stalk to and fro across the floor like some wild forest animal . . . His face would glow and his eyes would flash, darkening, lighting, scintillating, hypnotising you with their brilliance and the burning fires within. In calm they were eyes of strange beauty, with an expression that is almost beyond the power of pen to describe.[25]

On his trips to Apia RLS often saw Adams and La Farge, who did not leave Samoa until early 1891. Like many visitors – and here Stevenson's special talent for empathy and acclimatisation, so unlike that of other *haoles*, needs emphasising – Adams found Samoans inscrutable and vaguely menacing. He was irritated by the way they would invariably parry questions about their traditional culture and became convinced that under the superficial structure of Christianity was a secret pagan priesthood more powerful than the official chiefs, complete with supernatural powers, invocations, prophecies, charms and the whole paraphernalia of primitivism. He learned that the chiefs despised native missionaries as lower-class opportunists and that old women and young chiefs disliked the white man because all the young Samoan girls wanted to marry one; the older chiefs, however, were sympathetic to this aspiration. He also noted the breach between liberal white missionaries and the fanatical indigenous variety, who struggled to hold on to their precarious power with ultramontane anti-pagan doctrines.

In general Adams displayed the unease and vague paranoia familiar to us in the twentieth century under the umbrella term 'culture shock'. In this, as in so many ways, he and Stevenson were chalk and cheese, and it is not surprising that their half-dozen or so sustained encounters were always uneasy affairs. On 26 November Louis and Fanny went to dine with Adams and La Farge, and the occasion brought Adams out in a further bout of concealed antagonism, later divulged to his American correspondents:

> Last evening [Stevenson] came at five o'clock and brought his wife to dine with us. Their arrival was characteristic. He appeared first, looking like an insane stork, very warm and restless . . . Presently Mrs Stevenson, in a reddish cotton nightgown, staggered up the steps, and sank into a chair, gasping and unable to speak. Stevenson hurried to explain that she was overcome by the heat and the walk. Might she lie down? . . . Stevenson says his wife has some disease, I know not what, of a paralytic nature, and suffers greatly from its attacks. I know only that when I arrived soon afterwards, I found her on the piazza chatting with

Mrs Parker, and apparently as well and stalwart as any other Apache squaw . . .

It was then the Stevensons' turn to entertain, but when Adams went to Vailima a second time he was annoyed to find the cuisine defective.

Stevenson himself seems to eat little or nothing, and lives on cheap French vin ordinaire when he can get it. I do not know how this regime affects his complaint, for I do not know what his complaint is. I supposed it to be phthisis or tubercular consumption; but I am assured here that his lungs are not affected. The German physician here says that the complaint is asthma; but I am too weak in knowledge to explain how asthma should get relief from a saturated climate like this, when constant exposure leads also to severe colds, not easily thrown off. Asthma or whatever you please, he and his wife, according to their account, rarely have enough to eat in the house.

Louis anticipated (or intuited) his complaint in a letter to Adams's fellow East coast patrician, Henry James, doubtless smarting under the implied rebuke when Adams and La Farge sent their breakfast ahead of them in a basket: 'I would go oftener to see them, but I had to swim my horse the last time I went to dinner, and have not yet returned the clothes I had to borrow . . . They I believe would come oftener to see me; but . . . we have almost nothing to eat; a guest would simply break the bank . . . What would you do with a guest at such narrow seasons? eat him? or serve up a labour boy fricasseed?' Adams's insensitivity was truly astonishing. He knew that the Stevensons were pioneering in the wilderness, and must have heard from Moors the stories of their privation, such as the day they lunched on an avocado and a tin of sardines and had a single breadfruit for supper. And yet he seemed to expect to dine as if he were in New York or Boston and attacked RLS in his letters for 'gloating' over discomfort; Stevenson, he alleged, seemed to think that all travellers should sail for months in small cutters rancid with coconut oil and mouldy with rain, and should live on coral atolls with nothing but coconuts and poisonous fish to eat. Perhaps it was some obscure sense that RLS's example exposed his own inadequacy that led Adams to make his most vicious epistolary attack yet in December:

We found Stevenson and his wife just as they had appeared at our first call, except that Mrs Stevenson did not think herself obliged to put on slippers, and her night-gown costume had apparently not been washed since our visit . . . both Stevenson and his wife were very friendly, and gave us a good breakfast – or got it themselves, and kept up a rapid talk for four hours . . . Both La Farge and I came round to a sort of liking for Mrs Stevenson, who is more human than her husband. Stevenson is an *a-itu* – uncanny. Their travels have broken his wife up; she is a victim to rheumatism which is becoming paralysis, and I suspect, to dyspepsia; she says that his voyages have caused it . . . Compared with their shanty a native house is a palace; but this squalor must be somehow due to his education . . .. His early associates were all second-rate . . . He does not know the difference between people . . . he mixes them up in a fashion so grotesque as if they were characters in his *New Arabian Nights*.

Adams followed with an acknowledgement of his own snobbery, as if that were somehow a palliative, but then capped the concession with an even more egregious manifestation of snobbery, contrasting RLS unfavourably with La Farge:

> He [La Farge] sees all around a character like Stevenson and comments on it as if it were a painting, while Stevenson could never get within reach of him if they were alone on an atoll. The two characters in contact are rather amusing as contrast; the oriental delicacy of La Farge seems to be doubled by the Scotch eccentricities and barbarisms of Stevenson who is as one-sided as a crab, and flies off at angles, no matter what rocks stand in his way.

Adams appears to have been one of those people with a visceral antipathy for Stevenson, like Leslie Stephen, but without Stephen's appreciation of his myriad talents. Perhaps the dislike was grounded in incompatibility of temperaments, as the dour Bostonian is seldom congenial to the Celt, nor vice versa, and it is significant that Henry James, whose response was so different, was both a lover of the old world and had Scottish and Irish blood; Adams, by contrast, disliked the British and, as his remarks show, had little sympathy for the Caledonian sensibility. Certainly his assessments are passing fatuous. One can shrug off the fastidious Bostonian snobbery, and the snidery of his comment that the Stevensons would have been better employed buying a bar of soap than purchasing Vailima. But his unfavourable comparison of an authentic genius with a minor landscape painter whose name is known only to a handful of art critics is breathtaking and compounded as an asinine judgement by the further prophecy that La Farge would be better known in 1990. Adams's use of the give-away phrase 'first-rater' – the kind of judgement invariably offered by people who are themselves second-raters – makes nineteenth-century Harvard sound like another purveyor of the odious Balliol cult of 'effortless superiority' – another phrase habitually used by people whose only superiority is in their arrogance. Unlike John Addington Symonds, who had used similar arguments when he first met Louis, Adams did not recant, nor did he have the moral or intellectual capacity to do so.

The preference for Fanny expressed by Adams would be more convincing if not vitiated by his ludicrous medical diagnosis, but here he had a vested interest, for he wanted to prove to his own satisfaction that only neurotics or malcontents liked the Pacific and was thus prepared temporarily to yoke the 'half-breed Mexican Apache' to his intellectual chariot. That Adams feared and loathed the Pacific as much as Fanny did is clear from other correspondence:

This is what seamen call Paradise. To me the South Seas are vile. Three days out of four we have head-seas, or cross-seas that knock us all about, and feel like the British channel. The trade-wind never blows steadily; but, like any other wind, hauls round a head after a day or two; a heavy swell is always coming in from the south or somewhere to roll one out of one's meals; and the sea is dull in color; the sky is grey and almost cold; even the sunsets and sunrises are spiritless. I have now sailed over this ocean in pretty much all seasons, and ought to know it from end to end; so I look forward with abject horror to twelve or fourteen thousand more miles.

Despite his protestations that RLS knew no first-class people – as if Adams's cronies like John Hay could be put in the same class as Meredith, Henry James or even Henley and Fleeming Jenkin – Adams continued to be haunted by the memory of the 'scarecrow' he met in Samoa and, long after Stevenson's death, entered some judgements that make the analysis offered above more than surmise:

I used to feel a sympathy – naturally repressed as far as expression went – with poor old Louis Stevenson when he came down for a chat with La Farge. Stevenson's mind was as Scotch as mine was Yankee. Instinctively we each felt that the other could give him nothing he wanted. Stevenson's view of the South Seas was that of a serious-minded Scotchman who is consumed with desire to understand his wayward and fanciful and immoral children. So Stevenson communed with La Farge, and I have often wondered whether he ever got far enough to ask himself whether La Farge and he were looking at the same thing. La Farge, I know, never was in the least perplexed, though often amused, by the way Stevenson saw things, and the pathetic desire he had to feel them differently.

Three years later he confessed that reading his brother Charles Adams's life of their father made him feel he had sinned by reading such stuff, and the same impression was made on his mind by a perusal of RLS's letters: 'I am reading Robert Louis Stevenson's letters, which make me crawl with creepy horror, as he did alive.'[26]

As 1890 drew to a close, Louis's letters displayed a rare optimism, tempered only by concern about Fanny's incessant illnesses. He found a new hero to admire in the shape of James Chalmers, author of *Pioneering in New Guinea*, whom he described as 'the most attractive, simple, brave and interesting man in the whole Pacific' and whom he rated second only to Gordon as a moral example. He kept track of the rising literary stars in Britain and found a kindred spirit, as he told Henry James: 'Kipling is by far the most promising young man who has appeared since – ahem – I appeared. He amazes me by his precocity and various endowments. But he alarms me by his copiousness and haste . . . at this rate his works will soon fill the habitable globe.' Soon Louis was writing letters of congratulation to the new literary Young Lochinvar. Kipling replied in the character of his

Irish soldier Terence Mulvaney, to which RLS responded with a letter
written as if from Alan Breck Stewart. As he rode around Upolu on his
favourite horse Jack (who later fell out of favour through recalcitrance), he
made plans for a meeting with Colvin in the winter of 1891 but showed that
it was, at least unconsciously, a fantasy by the unreality of the arrangements
he proposed: at one time the rendezvous was to be Ceylon, then it was
Shepheard's hotel in Cairo, which he planned to reach after a long winter
tour of India and Persia.

At one time he planned to go to Auckland to meet a missionary friend
before proceeding to Sydney to meet Maggie and Lloyd on their return from
England but Fanny, ill with earache, refused to accompany him, 'hating the
sea at this wild season; I don't like to leave her; so it drones on, steamer
after steamer, and I guess it'll end by no one going at all.' Christmas Eve
found RLS in dampened spirits: 'my wife near crazy with ear-ache; the
rain descending in white crystal rods and playing hell's tattoo, like a *tutti* of
battering rams, on our sheet-iron roof.'[27] There was a slight improvement
next day, for the Christmas dinner was held at Moors's house. Apart from
the Stevensons and some of Moors's pet Samoans, there were two other
local white residents present (one of them the lawyer Carruthers who had
the adulterous wife) and as guests of honour the Bakers of Tonga. Baker
was exactly the sort of person to appeal to Louis, as rumour made him
guilty of rape, judicial murder, poisoning, abortion and misappropriation
of public money. It is significant, too, that when Louis and Moors wanted
to enjoy themselves they did not invite Adams and La Farge.

16

Samoa: Second Year

Early in January 1891 Louis set off for Sydney to meet his mother and Lloyd, leaving behind a stricken Fanny, too ill to face the wind and waves. It was not without misgivings that he parted from his wife, for he sensed that her troubles were mainly mental and, in addition, local lore said that another great hurricane was overdue like the one two years before that sank the German navy. Both fears were warranted, and the fearsome precipitation so well described in another of RLS's best Pacific poems, 'Tropic Rain', duly made its appearance while he was away; Fanny and the household were forced to shelter in the stables as the worst of the hurricane tore a swathe across Upolu. Cyclonic storms always touched a chord in what one might call Stevenson's 'collective unconscious', for even before he had experienced them directly, he intuited their awesome power. For Melville the principle of evil was represented in nature by the shark, and even Adams's letters betray a deep fear of man's ancient pelagic enemy; sharks never appear at all significantly in Stevenson's Pacific writings, but hurricanes are a constant motif: 'I have always feared the sound of the wind beyond everything. In my hell it would always blow a gale.'[1]

'I have been very ill since Louis went,' Fanny confided to Mrs Sitwell, 'though of course he doesn't know that, and it has been a little alarming to find my head going wrong in the middle of the night, and no one on the premises but an imbecile drunken German man.' Fanny's neurotic illnesses were always exacerbated by stress, and this time the stress came from the drunken antics of Paul Einfurer. When the *Lübeck* came back to Samoa from Sydney on its scheduled run, the bibulous German got together with his old cronies among the crew. After a mammoth drinking session in Apia, Einfurer brought his tipsy companions back to Vailima together with a white woman of the sort Somerset Maugham would later celebrate. Fanny does not give all the details, but it appears that the sailors became threatening when she ordered them off the premises and swore foul abuse at her. In retaliation Henry Simile laid about Einfurer's woman with a horsewhip, one of the sailors tried to run him down with his horse, and at length the tardy constabulary were summoned from Apia. The upshot was the dismissal of Einfurer and the determination by the faithful Simile never to let his mistress out of his sight while the master was away.[2]

Meanwhile Louis was once again tasting the perils of the Pacific. Close to Fiji the *Lübeck* broke its shaft; the chief engineer mended it twice but twice more it broke down. The situation was potentially hazardous: in hurricane waters and in the hurricane season they dared not stop, had to switch to canvas and then crowd on sail to make significant progress. There was no hope of help for, as Louis told Colvin: 'the Pacific is absolutely desert. I have sailed there now some years; and scarce ever seen a ship except in port or close by; I think twice.'

The *Lübeck* limped into Sydney harbour, just too late to meet his mother and Lloyd off the SS *Lusitania* on 18 January. He joined up with them according to the pre-arranged contingency plans but immediately fell ill. Instead of trundling her son on to the first Samoa-bound steamer, Maggie insisted that he recuperate in Australia; she moved them out of the downtown hotel into a cheaper boarding house where she nursed Louis, allowing him to go down to the Union Club for lunch occasionally. Louis tried to work at routine matters and wrote to Baxter about the family wrangles over the estate – David Stevenson was still claiming a portion of Thomas's assets – but Sydney never agreed with him and at last, on 22 February, Maggie gave up and had him carried from his bed on board the *Lübeck*.

Louis was despondent, as he told Colvin.

> It is vastly annoying that I cannot go even to Sydney without an attack; and heaven knows my life was anodyne. I only once dined with anybody; at the club with Wise; worked all morning . . . lunched in the boarding-house, played on my pipe; went out and did some of my messages; dined at a French restaurant, and returned to play draughts, whist or Van John with my family.

He could not write, for two days found his mind wandering and was particularly irritated that his chess playing was poor and erratic when normally he could beat anyone. Maggie tried to ease his mind on the score of money worries by drawing £500 on the open letter of credit with which Baxter had provided her. Before he left, Louis had another long talk with Belle. He told her that as it was clear to him now that his health would never permit him to return to Britain, he wanted a proper family circle in Samoa, and had therefore decided that Belle and Lloyd would be his adopted daughter and son in all but name. It was Honolulu all over again. By now Belle had put down roots and made friends and pleaded to be allowed to stay in Australia. Louis, however, was firm: the Strongs' residence in Samoa was the condition for his continued financial subventions. It was settled that the Strongs would have three months' grace to wind up their affairs and make their farewells and would then travel to their new home at Vailima.[3]

The 'adopted son', never happy when away from his mother, had pressed on to Samoa immediately and arrived on 5 February 1891. Unwittingly Lloyd was bringing his mother a fresh source of stress in the form of a companion he had picked up in the Line Islands called King. Bearded and with flame-coloured hair that reminded Moors of a Titian painting, King held himself out as a prospective overseer but almost immediately fell foul of Fanny. He tried to persuade her to provide passage money and an 'outfit' allowance for his fiancée, who would be a companion for Maggie on her arrival, but struck the wrong note by insisting that she should not be asked to do manual work. Fanny told him coldly that the bush was no place for 'fine lady companions', that she herself would act as Maggie's companion, and that she could not have in her household someone not prepared to do what she herself did, instancing the fact that she had blacked her own shoes that very morning. King further alienated Fanny by his taste for drink. When the hurricane struck, Fanny moved bedding, mosquito nets and candles into the stables, which were sturdier and more weatherly than the cottage. There ensued a comedy of errors. First she trod on a nail so that Lloyd had to carry her to the stables in the dark and dropped her in a puddle when he paused to rest. Then, when they reached the stables, they found the door locked. Simile informed them that King had taken the key away with him when he went off drinking with Einfurer, who was on notice pending Louis's return. When entrance was at last obtained, there followed several days of life in a manger, lying in wet beds, bailing out flood water and being devoured by mosquitoes all the while. When the hurricane blew itself out, they inspected the damage to the cottage: it had a port list like a stormbound liner and inside damp and mildew were everywhere.

Like most people who swam into Fanny's ken, King did not last long. He survived at Vailima until mid-1891 then quit, telling Moors he could no longer bear Lloyd's arrogance and conceit and complaining that 'the women were too much for any man.' When he made his decision to leave, he burst into RLS's study to pour out his bitterness about Fanny and Belle. Louis put his pen down, yawned, sat back in his chair, clasped his hands behind his head and said: 'Well, King, you know what women are! You understand their ways!' He then paused a moment and said: 'By Jove, no! How can you? Show me the man who does!'[4]

Louis arrived back in Samoa, still ill, on 4 March. Maggie, whose first excited glimpse of the green island of Upolu – 'the Ireland of the Pacific', she called it – soon gave way to dismay when she saw the primitive conditions in which her son and daughter-in-law were living, decided to return to Sydney and then take a trip to New Zealand, where her youngest brother was Marine Engineer to the Colony. It was agreed that she would return in mid-May, by which time Louis and Fanny hoped that the new house at Vailima would be completed. Once again Moors was architect, builder and entrepreneur for the entire operation and he began by instilling some realism into his clients. Louis had come back from Sydney with an ambitious plan for a great house that would cost $20,000; Moors beat him back to $7,500, arguing that his current income would not permit such an expenditure, on top of the original $4,000 for the land and $1,000 for the cottage. More to the point, it was Moors's money Louis was speculating with, for the American advanced him the cash as an unsecured loan, to be repaid from future earnings. The total spent on Vailima did in the end amount to $20,000, for in addition to the initial outlay of $12,500 an extension was built, with a magnificent reception hall for parties, at a cost of a further $7,500. When Fanny sold the property at the turn of the century, the most she could get for it was $10,000.

Vailima was a further source of stress for RLS. The annual cost of its upkeep was $6,500 (roughly £1,300), yet even when he was banking a regular £4,000 a year in the last five years of his life he worried continually about being able to earn enough money. According to the terms of his father's will, Fanny, Lloyd and Belle would be taken care of after his death, but what a Scots Calvinist thought an adequate sum to sustain life and limb did not meet the aspirations of the Osbournes. Everyone who has put the Vailima accounts under the microscope has come away appalled. 'A couple of infantile spendthrifts' was Aldington's comment after seeing the way Louis and Fanny frittered their money away. Louis, it is true, was careless with money and could not be bothered with the boring chore of sifting through household accounts item by item. But the other members of his household were out-and-out extravagant; 'Mrs Stevenson and Mrs Strong were not the most economical women in the world', Moors commented drily. All kinds of nonsensical expenditures went through on RLS's nod. The pleasure-loving Lloyd brought back an ice machine from Scotland, which was an unnecessary luxury and anyway never worked properly, having been carelessly selected by the boy genius. Fanny insisted on installing a fireplace and brick chimney which failed to draw – at Latitude 13° S of the Equator! Her 'justification' was palpable nonsense. She claimed that Louis did not feel at home without a hearth even though he did not work in the room where it was situated. And she claimed that she needed the fire to warm the sheets, though no sheets were ever taken into that room.[5]

In addition to all these unnecessary expenses, RLS had to pay for a whole raft of hangers on: Joe Strong, King, later Graham Balfour and Austin Strong, as well as entertaining native chiefs and throwing parties for visiting British warships like HMS *Curaçao*. He also maintained three or four saddle horses and two large cart horses imported from New Zealand and a farm of cows, pigs and poultry which always ran at a loss. Apart from raids by rats and chicken-thieves, RLS took further losses from a 'scam' worked by Joe Strong who, when he arrived and was assigned farmyard duties, fed lime to the fowls instead of seed and pocketed the difference.

For all that, when the new two-storied Vailima residence neared completion in March 1891 it was an imposing sight and justified Moors's boast that 'the house is the best one for money that has ever been erected in Samoa', though one wag referred to it as 'an Irish castle of 1820 minus the dirt'. Painted peacock-blue, with a red-iron roof, Vailima was equipped with shutters against gales and gauze-screened windows to keep out mosquitoes, cockchafers, moths, beetles and other insects. There were no doors, only hanging mats or curtains, but a verandah ran along the whole north side of the house, both upstairs and downstairs. In the bathroom and kitchen the water was piped from storage tanks filled when the rain poured down the corrugated roof. The dining room was temporarily the main room, papered with yellowish *tapa*, the woodwork a dull blue, the window hung with curious Indian fabrics of yellow silk and silver, a fireplace in the corner and an American stove. The large downstairs room, the last to be completed, was 60 feet long and 40 feet wide, ceiled with varnished Californian redwood. Furniture included leather armchairs, a Chippendale sideboard and a corner cupboard containing precious old china; the walls were hung with paintings by Bob and a portrait of RLS by Sargent. Louis's study was a small room off the library – actually an enclosed bit of the north-west corner of the upper verandah. Two windows opened seaward at the front, from which ships approaching the port, though not Apia itself, could be descried; another at the end gave a view of Mount Vaea. Shelves laden with books ran round the room on all sides, and the only furniture was a large deal-table, a couple of chairs and a locked stand of six Colt's repeating rifles; also a narrow bed where RLS sometimes reclined and a patent table that could be swung over the bed and raised or lowered at will.[6]

Such was the original Vailima house, around whose supposed opulence legends later grew. When *The Wrecker* proved a financial success, a second two-storey block was added to the original house. Meanwhile the original cottage was used sometimes as guest quarters and sometimes as a bachelor den for Lloyd; it was also the Strongs' 'apartment' when Joe and Belle first came to Samoa. Fanny set to work to turn the main house into the cynosure of the islands. From the households of Heriot Row and Skerryvore came mahogany and rosewood furniture, chests of silver and linen, mirrors, a piano, a Rodin sculpture, wine glasses, decanters and, above all, books. An invitation to dinner at Vailima became one of the most sought-after social occasions in the South Pacific.

By the middle of the year the household began to take shape. On 15

May, Maggie returned from her trip to New Zealand with her new maid, Mary Carter, to find her room ready in the new house. She was delighted with the large sliding doors, more than half glass, which opened on to the verandah, and loved her room, with its view of the sea, its floor covered with white, soft and thick Samoan mats and its walls painted green and hung with *tapa* and flags and other memorabilia from the *Casco*. Then, in late May, Belle and Joe Strong arrived with their son Austin, three cats and 'Cocky', Belle's white cockatoo, who liked to perch on her shoulder. The three cats were a useful addition to the anti-rodent force, as there were now twelve cats at Vailima to deal with the menace from bush rats. It was agreed that the Strongs would help in the work of the estate and take their meals in the main house while lodging in the original cottage, but Joe Strong soon showed that he was as hopeless as ever. Put in charge of the fowls, he was so incompetent that most of them died, though he secured a reprieve when Maggie, alarmed at the disappearance of seventy out of ninety-five chickens, turned detective and discovered that the culprit was a cannibal drake. There were frequent rows between Fanny and Joe on the grounds of his uselessness, which Belle and RLS, now moving closer to a new entente, helped to patch up. Joe also annoyed Fanny by his appearance. She had aspirations to head the Upolu expatriate social set, yet here was Strong, habitually dressed in a brightly flowered *lavalava* instead of trousers, with a bandanna knotted over his shirt, a visored cap and Cocky riding on his shoulders, looking for all the world like one of the pirate characters from *Treasure Island*.

The key to the smooth running of Vailima was the commitment of Stevenson's Samoan servants. Very soon Louis and Fanny decided that white labour always brought a legion of problems so they dispensed with it. Paul Einfurer got his marching orders, as did the white carter whom RLS had always disliked for his habit of calling Polynesians 'niggers'. When Louis returned from Sydney, he discovered that the carter had been riding his horses while he was away, contrary to express instructions, so sacked him on the spot. Moors noticed a tendency in RLS to take massive blows of fortune on the chin but to explode with rage over relatively trivial matters. The carter was a case in point, but this time RLS, who nicknamed himself 'the old man virulent' because of his quick temper, took a leaf out of Moors's book and sacked the man with a jeering smile. When Fanny was away in Fiji in August, Belle and Lloyd prevailed on Louis to get rid of the rest of his white staff, including an overseer who had to be compensated as he was on a contract.

By the end of 1891 the staff at Vailima was Samoan only, with the exception of a Tongan refugee from the Bakers' dictatorial regime, a Wallis Islander, a Fijian and a 'blackbirded' labourer from the Solomons. The Solomon islander had run away from a German plantation after being brutalised and fetched up at Vailima one day, starved and with long whip-welts scarred into his back; Louis bought his indentures from the Germans and took him on at Vailima, despite the Samoans' prejudice against Melanesians. However, the mainstay of the hired help were Henry Simile and Lafaele, 'a huge mutton-headed Hercules' who became the chief gardener. He and Fanny invented a sort of pidgin dialect, impenetrable and incomprehensible to all others, in which, to the stupefaction both of the whites at Vailima and the Samoans, they used to jabber away contentedly. There was a momentary scare in late 1891 when it looked as though Henry Simile would be leaving them to get married on Savaii, but his romance did not prosper and he returned soon afterwards, delighted to resume his favourite pastime of sitting around the hearth, watching the fire.[7]

Soon there were as many as nineteen servants inside and out, many of them acquired in circumstances of serendipity. One morning a young, handsome Samoan, with limed hair and a red flower behind his ear, was discovered sitting on the ice-chest in the back verandah. He explained that Henry Simile owed him two Chile dollars and he was prepared to wait all day until Simile returned from the fields to get them. Some instinct made Lloyd, who had been appointed major-domo to the household, offer him a job as cook, but the young man, whose name was Talolo, declined on the grounds of his ignorance of cookery yet was eventually persuaded. He became the most dependable of all the Samoans at Vailima and Lloyd, never one to sell his own real or imaginary achievements short, dated the turning point at Vailima from the coming of Talolo. Other fixtures were Sina, Talolo's wife, Taullo his mother, and Mitaele and Sosimo, his brothers.

Samoans had a reputation among whites in the Pacific for being lazy, shiftless, surly, hostile and uncooperative, and it never ceased to amaze the many old Pacific hands who came up to Vailima that none of these characteristics was in evidence among RLS's servants: 'you never see a Samoan run except at Vailima', was the received opinion among the 'beach'. The explanation is threefold. In the first place, RLS was devoid of racial prejudice, and had a natural sympathy for the underdog; these were rare traits among whites in the colonial era, and Samoans intuited them and responded accordingly. He won their hearts by deferring to Samoan folkways, customs and etiquette, even in contexts where he found them irrational, mysterious or inexplicable. The fact that he was a landowner, with a stake in the country and a Samoan 'family', not a temporary government official living in a rented house, also bound the local people to him. His generosity was also legendary, and 'once Tusitala's friend, always Tusitala's friend' became proverbial.

Secondly, Stevenson's nostalgic feeling for the ethos of the Scottish clans stood him in good stead in Samoa, since he regarded himself as an old-style patriarch, like Cameron of Lochiel or Cluny MacPherson, with quasi-familial duties towards his extended family of retainers. Used to being regarded as units of labour by thrusting South Seas capitalists, the Samoans responded enthusiastically to the idea of being valued and trusted members of a clan, and accepted readily that in return absolute and unquestioning obedience would be required. Once the feelings of organic solidarity took root, RLS's Samoans gave him the kind of devoted service no amount of mere wages could procure. They responded well to his strict but just system of discipline, which took account of the Samoan love of system. Every man had his work outlined in advance, and some even had typewritten lists of their duties. Fines were imposed for minor offences, though always with the consent of the culprit, who was given the option of receiving his pay to date and being dismissed. These fines went into the coffers of the missionary society representing the delinquent's denomination, though in fact almost all the servants at Vailima were Catholics; for serious offences a formal court-martial would be convened.

Thirdly, RLS had a reputation both as man of wealth and warlock. Louis's retainers glowed with pride as successive steamers brought further evidence of their master's riches from Europe. Samoans could not conceive how 'book-making' could produce wealth, so were inclined to settle for the explanation that it was the bottle imp of the Stevenson story that provided the money. Even important chieftains, on being shown around Vailima, sometimes asked in a whisper if they could be granted the great favour of gazing on the bottle; naturally the more Louis denied that there was such a bottle, the more they became convinced that he guarded it jealously.

Louis rehearsed the Samoans' fascination with the rich man of Vailima in his Pacific poems, where he imagines them pondering the enigma:

> What ails the boss, they ask,
> Him, richest of rich, an endless task
> Before the earliest birds or servants stir
> Calls and detains him daylong prisoner . . .
>
> How can he live that does not keep a shop?
> And why does he, being acclaimed so rich,
> Not dwell with other gentry on the beach?
> But harbour, impiously brave,
> In the cold, uncanny wood, haunt of the fleeting brave?

Fanny's reputation also fed into and enhanced Louis's. Samoans liked the fact that RLS had an older wife, since traditionally they gave an exalted place in council to any man presumed to have the wise advice of an older woman. Fanny soon became known in local lore as an *aitu* because of her myriad skills. She had a seemingly magical touch with plants and made them grow where no one else could; she had all manner of remedies and nostrums at her command for sickness; she played elementary conjuring tricks on her retainers to reinforce her claims as a sorceress; and her domineering personality, piercing eyes and abrupt mood changes all contributed to the image of a witch. 'I am glad to say', she wrote, 'that the gossip among the natives is that I have eyes all around my head and am in fifty places at once, and that I am a person to be feared and obeyed.'

Since it was a common perception among traditional peoples in Africa, Asia and Oceania in the nineteenth century that the white man was a spirit and came from the land of the dead, RLS's status as magus and thaumaturge had three main components: he was an *aitu* himself, he commanded a spirit in a bottle and he had as a wife a woman who was an important witch in her own right.

Of the many examples that could be provided of the special affection felt for RLS by his Vailima retainers, three may be allowed to speak for themselves. In the first place, Samoans requited his sensitivity towards their mores by waiving their customary etiquette in the 'big house' and accepting the puzzling new arrangements that obtained there. In a royal Samoan household the wife ranked third behind the daughter and the eldest sister; at Vailima, by contrast, Fanny ranked second only to Louis himself in power while deference was paid by all to Maggie as matriarch and 'constitutional monarch'.

Secondly, the Vailima Samoans gained status both directly as RLS's 'clansmen' and indirectly from his charisma and influence. One of them, Elina, had a wen on his neck and was thus considered virtually an 'untouchable' in the local culture, for Samoans feared and despised physical deformity. For a long time Elina resisted the importunities of the Stevenson household to undergo the simple operation that would remove the unsightly excrescence on his neck. At last Louis wore him down, took him to the operating theatre of a German doctor, and personally gave him the chloroform. As he lapsed into unconsciousness, Elina repeated the mantra: 'I belong Tusitala ... I belong Tusitala.' The operation was a complete success, Elina sped to his native island of Savaii, and was not only received as the prodigal son but came back to Vailima having been honoured with the title of minor chieftain.

If Elina's example seems too pragmatic to convince of genuine affection, there can be no doubting the feelings of Sosimo. One morning Sosimo, who was not on duty, appeared with Louis's first coffee of the day, accompanied by an exquisitely cooked omelette. Louis complimented him on his culinary skills: 'Great is your wisdom,' he said, using the formulaic phrase. 'Great is my love,' came the answer.[8]

It would be wrong, however, to suggest that RLS and the Samoans lived together in some smug and cosy utopia. He was well aware of their faults and refused to sentimentalise them: 'like other folk,' was his description, 'false enough, lazy enough, not heroes, not saints, ordinary

men, damnably misused.' Fanny, though she overcame her initial dislike
and suspicion of Samoans, always found them more or less a trial when it
came to carrying out simple orders. She once told a new employee to take a
bucket of water upstairs; he promptly took the pail in his teeth and shinned
up the verandah post. On another occasion she reproached the groom with
not watering a horse and he claimed that, although the others needed water,
this particular specimen came from a breed that could survive without it.
Maggie's white starched widow's caps, which she wore unceasingly in the
Victorian manner, were a continual bone of contention. Samoan males had
no compunction about doing laundry and a huge Samoan took pride in his
crisp handiwork with the iron, but the trade-off was that he liked to take
some of them home as keepsakes and parade round the village looking like
a Victorian dowager empress. The fashion for widow's caps caught on. The
houseboys liked to don the caps and parade round the kitchen with primly set
mouth, in imitation of Maggie. Eventually more and more servants decamped
to their villages on their days off wearing the fashionable headdress, while
Maggie wondered why her large supply of caps dwindled daily.[9]

One mark of the affectionate regard in which the Samoans held the
Stevenson family was the variety of names they gave them. Louis was
known as 'Tusitala' – 'teller of tales', 'writer of books' or, as RLS
translated it, 'Chief White Information'; his reputation was preserved in
Samoan songs and boatmen have been known to keep time to 'Tusitala
ma Aolele'. Fanny was known variously as 'Aolele' – 'flying cloud' –
because of her restless bustling about and also 'Tamaiti' – 'madame'.
On her frequent off days, when the crossgrained characteristics were to
the fore, another nickname made its appearance: 'O le Fafine Mamana
o i le Mauga' – 'the Witch Woman of the Mountain'. Belle was 'Teuila' –
'adorner of the ugly' for her habit of treating the staff as dress-up dolls.
Significantly, Lloyds, who was at once a hard-driving taskmaster and an
idler, was known only as 'Loya' – the Samoan phonetic approximation
of Lloyd. His unpopularity with the Samoans is not surprising given his
attitudes, and he seems to have had almost as many problems when
dealing with servants as his mother. In a letter to Baxter, in which he
complains about the financial and administrative laxity of his benefactor
and stepfather, occurs this supercilious sentence: 'I am trying to run the
whole establishment with natives, who are cheap, willing and haven't yet
learned the cast-iron character of servants' departments.' Even Louis, who
had a blind spot for this singularly unpleasant young man, allows some of
his less charming characteristics to be seen in his verse portrait of Lloyd
as overseer:

> He in the midst, perched on a fallen tree,
> Eyes them at labour, and, guitar on knee,

Now ministers alarm, now scatters joy,
Now twangs a halting chord – now tweaks a boy.
Thorough in all, my resolute vizier,
Plays both the despot and the volunteer,
Exacts with fines obedience to my laws
– And for his music too exacts applause![10]

Gradually Louis settled into a routine in the new house. A typical day would be as follows. At 5.45 in the morning his servant Paul would come to the lower room where he slept – for by this stage in the marriage he and Fanny had separate bedrooms – with tea, bread and a couple of eggs. Rousing himself from his primitive cot of mats, pillows and a blanket – incidentally no sheets were used in the house, so the 'justification' for the fireplace at once falls down – he would work sitting up in the bed for three hours, then at nine o'clock would go weeding by the side of his favourite stream until about 10.30. He liked weeding so much that he sometimes had to drag himself away to get his daily quota of writing done. Lunch would take place at 11.00 a.m. and at 12.30 or thereabouts he would start to write in earnest; if inspiration failed, he would go back to his weeding for a couple of hours and then read until dinner at 5.30 p.m. After dinner there would be a further spell of writing.

Towards the end of 1891 RLS actually recorded his movements during a single day. He woke early and worked on the verandah until 5.55 a.m. when the enormous Wallis Islander brought him an orange as an aperitif. A quick breakfast was followed by a solid stint of work from 6.05 a.m. until 10.30, when it was time for him to play schoolmaster: at this juncture he was teaching Austin Strong about Carthage and the Punic wars. After lunch at 11.00 a.m. he reread Chapter 23 of *The Wrecker*, then he, Lloyd and Belle made music (Louis on the flageolet) until 2.00 p.m. There followed two more hours of work, half an hour's loafing, a bath at 4.30 and a mango as aperitif prior to dinner at 5.00 p.m. Afterwards there was a smoke – all the whites at Vailima except Maggie were heavy smokers and liked to roll their own; additionally RLS himself liked 'Three Castles' and 'Capstan', generally preferring the products of W.D. & H.O. Wills to American brands – and a few hands of cards until 8 p.m., when Louis retired to his room with a pint of beer and a hard biscuit; shortly afterwards he turned in.

Life at Vailima was even more pleasant for those of its residents (i.e. everyone but RLS) who did not have the burden of writing and earning on their shoulders. Food at their disposal included *taro* – the best local substitute for the potato – bananas, breadfruit, coconuts, oranges, gavas, mangoes, limes, citrons, pineapples, pawpaw, granadillas, avocado pears, lemons, plums, egg-plant and sweet potato. Protein was provided in the form of prawns and sea-fish, pigeons, mallards and *manume'a* – a kind of Samoan moorhen. Every afternoon a bowl of refreshing *kava* was left on the sideboard at 2 p.m., to be consumed on a help-yourself basis. During the dry season from April to October, the average temperature was 85°–90° at noon and 70° at dusk, but the thermometer never dipped below 62° or higher than 95° in the shade. There were no snakes on Samoa and no anopheline mosquitoes to spread malaria, though filariasis and elephantiasis were beginning to make inroads; indeed RLS had noticed them, as well as leprosy, at Penrhyn during the *Janet Nicholl* cruise and feared they might become pandemic in the Pacific.

That apart, life in Samoa was an idyll for moneyed Europeans. The swimming pool in the ferny shade under the waterfall was a popular gathering place for the family in the late afternoon. Sometimes a half-hearted attempt would be made to play cricket on the lawn which Louis had had laid out for croquet, the players using the unripe fruit from overhanging orange trees as cricket balls. If there was a formal dinner with guests, the household would dress in its best, with the mandatory tropical white shoes and the men in cummerbunds. A meal at Vailima was a treat, for RLS was a fine judge of cuisine, a lover of fine wines, a connoisseur of soups, and liked to experiment with cocktails; often there would be a tray of the newest craze from the bars of the U.S.A. on the verandah. All the whites at Vailima consumed vast amounts of coffee and the very best roasts were broken out when guests came; they were habitually treated to a 'Stevenson special' – coffee served with sugar that had been soaked in burnt brandy.

Stevenson was always a voracious and omnivorous reader, and although Moors states that the Vailima library contained no more than five hundred volumes, mainly works on Scottish history and folklore, there is ample evidence that RLS kept up with all the latest publications in Europe as well as returning over and over again to his old favourites. Among books mentioned as present and future reading in 1891 are Flaubert's letters, Plato's *Phaedo*, Montaigne, William James's *Principles of Psychology*, Meredith's *One of Our Conquerors*, Henry James's *The Tragic Muse*, Gosse's *Father and Son*, Huysman's *Là-Bas*, Taine's *Origines de la France Contemporaine* and Kipling's *Life's Handicap*. The hardy perennials were also well represented; from Sydney in January he wrote to Marcel Schwob that although Dumas in general could not be mentioned in the same breath as Shakespeare, he preferred *Viscomte de Bragelonne* to *Richard III*: 'Richard III's a big black gross sprawling melodrama, writ with infinite spirit, but with no refinement or philosophy by a man who had the world, himself, mankind and his trade still to learn.'[11]

If ever he suffered from writer's block, he would mount up and ride 'Jack' at great speed into Apia in search of inspiration; he was an excellent rider, aided by his jockey's weight – he never got above eight stone. 'The orange is squeezed out,' would be a typical remark as he burst into Moors's house in search of excitement. If he could not find it there, he would seek out some of the characters from the 'beach' in the waterfront bars and dives or collar a newly-arrived sea-captain to hear more amazing tales of the Pacific.

Such recharging of the imaginative engines was necessary since, with one exception, RLS did not leave Upolu in the year 1891 after his return from Sydney. The exception was, in its way, important, for in April he accompanied Harold Sewall, U.S. Consul-General, on a visit to Tutuila in Eastern Samoa. He spent three weeks in what would later be American Samoa, partly in Pago-Pago, partly circumnavigating Tutuila by easy stages in a whaleboat, and partly in a vain attempt to reach the islands of Manu'a in a small schooner – an ambition later fulfilled when he was a guest on board HMS *Curaçao*. Louis found the eastern Samoans a more lubricious lot than their western brethren and even his broadmindedness in matters sexual was strained by the open lewdness and obscenity of the Tutuila dances. 'No sense of shame in this race is the word of the superficial, but the point of the indecent dance is to trifle with the sense of shame; and that ... the chief actor should be a maid further discloses the corrupt element which has created and so much loves this diversion; for it is useless to speak, the Samoan loves the business like pie.'[12]

While circumnavigating Tutuila in the whaleboat, Louis was reading Virgil and when he reached Aoa Bay, he thought the place exactly like the haven described in the *Aeneid*. The interpenetration of past and present, so potent a theme in all his best fiction, again found expression in his reverie as he spent a morning entirely alone in the bay:

I had Virgil's bay all morning to myself, and feasted on solitude, and overhanging woods, and the retiring sea. The quiet was only broken by the hoarse cooing of wild pigeons up the valley, and certain inroads of capricious winds that found a way hence and thence down the hillside and set the palms clattering; my enjoyment only disturbed by clouds of dull, voracious, spotted and not particularly envenomed mosquitoes. When I was still, I kept Buhac powder burning by me on a stone under the shed, and read Livy, and confused today and two thousand years ago, and wondered in which of these epochs I was flourishing at that moment; and then I would stroll out, and see the rocks and woods, and the arcs of beaches, curved like a whorl in a fair woman's ear, and huge ancient trees, jutting high overhead out of the hanging forest, and feel the place at least belonged to the age of fable, and awaited Aeneas and his battered fleets.

From the calm of Aoa bay to the turbulence of the short, sixty-mile stretch of sea between Pago-Pago and Apia was an unpleasant jolt. Because of a peculiar confluence of north and south currents this short

strait can sometimes resemble a boiling rapid, and on this occasion Louis
and his companions spent a worrying twenty-eight hours in an open boat,
averaging two miles an hour. To cap all, when they finally reached Apia,
Sewall had lost his keys and had to break into his own storeroom, so that
it was past midnight when they got to bed. Next morning it transpired that
Sewall had forgotten the horse he had promised to have ready for Louis
for the return journey to Vailima. Impatiently Louis set off on foot. It was
three miles on an uphill gradient to Vailima. The road was good for the
first stretch as far as the village of Tangungamnono, and was shaded by
palms and banana trees. Beyond the village Stevenson forked right, at a
point where Mount Vaea first comes into sight. The track then led into
the forest and was entirely enclosed by a canopy from the jungle. Louis
fancied himself as an expert in the byways in the Vailima environs, decided
to take a short cut and soon got lost. By the time he had extricated himself
from the jungle, retraced his steps and staggered into Vailima, it was dinner
time, and the next day he went down with a fever from which he took a
week to recover.[13]

In terms of RLS's literary output, 1891 was the one year when his
productions were entirely on Pacific themes. Nothing more clearly shows
his courage, integrity and strenuousness than his decision to persist in this
vein after all the brickbats thrown at him. The disappointment over the *In
the South Seas* letters had been egregious. He had made just £1,000, about
a third of the money McClure promised him, after the cancellation of the
series, and Fanny had nagged at him mercilessly to make the essays more
commercial, even threatening at one time that if he persisted in his scholarly mode she would gather together her own letters and publish them as
a rival attraction. The 'peasant' row that caused so much unpleasantness
– and temporary breakdown in Fanny – in 1890 had as its subtext the
simmering row between Fanny, the representative of Mammon, and Louis,
the representative of art. As she recorded plaintively: 'he says I do not take
the broad view of an artist but hold the cheap opinion of the general public
that a book must be interesting.' Moreover, Louis was annoyed that the
letters were published in book form before he had a chance to polish them
and he always regretted that he never had the time to rework the material
into the truly great book on the Pacific he knew he was capable of writing.

To confront the public with a book of Pacific ballads after such 'malice domestic, foreign levy' took courage, yet Louis was defiant and told
H.B.Baildon with reference to his long ballad on Rahero: 'If the historian,
not to say the politician, could get that yarn into his head, he would have
learned some of his ABC. But the average man at home cannot understand
antiquity; he is sunk over the ears in Roman civilisation; and a tale like that
of Rahero falls on his ears inarticulate.'[14]

Stevenson's Pacific ballads are uneven in quality but scarcely deserve the critical roasting they received from critics in Britain. 'Tropic Rain' and 'The Home of Tembinoka' are particularly good, as in the following economical rendering of a Polynesian dance:

> Night after night in the open hall of dance,
> Shall thirty matted men, to the clapped hand,
> Intone and bray and bark.

The 'Song of Rahero' contains, in Part Two, a memorable evocation of the coming of a tropical storm:

> But as when the weather changes at sea, in dangerous parts,
> And sudden the hurricane wrack unrolls up the front of the sky,
> At once the ship lies idle, the sails hang silent on high,
> The breath of the wind that blew is blown out like the flame of a lamp,
> And the silent armies of death draw near with inaudible tramp.

On the other hand, it has to be conceded that some of the lines are clumsy and unlyrical, redolent perhaps of the banal Tennyson of *Mecanophilus*, as in the following:

> Soon as the oven was open, the fish smelt excellent good.
> In the shade, by the house of Rahero, down they sat to their food,
> And cleared the leaves in silence, or uttered a jest and laughed,
> And raising the cocoa-nut bowls, buried their faces and quaffed.

Interestingly, one of the most nuanced responses to 'Rahero' came from Henry Adams, for when the ballad appeared, he and La Farge were with Princess Moe on Tahiti, and it was from her that RLS had first heard this archetypal tale of bloody revenge; indeed he wrote half of the verses at Tautira and polished them off on the *Casco* on the stormy run to Hawaii over New Year 1890. Adams was led to revise his opinion of RLS somewhat when he discovered his high reputation at Tautira – where he was known as Teriitera – met Ori, to whom he bore letters of introduction from Stevenson, and generally took notice of the primitive conditions in which RLS had lived and worked in Moe's village. When Ori read the letters from Louis, he adopted Adams too as his 'brother', thus compounding the confusion and ill-feeling in the village among the chiefly hierarchy – for it was felt that Ori, by handing out such distinctions without going through the feudal hierarchy and seeking permission of the paramount chiefs, was guilty of a form of *lèse-majesté*. Adams tried to pooh-pooh the whole business and in the process belittle RLS:

> Apparently we are destined to play second to Stevenson. For myself I don't care, and am willing to play second to anyone who goes first – Stevenson or Goward or even James G.Blaine or Benjamin Harrison – but it is hard on the immortal Scotchman. If you have read his ballad of Rahero just out, you will

see it is dedicated to Ori, and the dedication is rather the prettiest part of it. Ori exchanged names 'in the island mode' with Stevenson, giving him the name Teriitera, and Stevenson takes it *au sérieux*, as the ballads show. Much was said on the subject, and Stevenson's name here is always Teriitera. I dreaded a repetition of this baptism, and tried to show total indifference to the native custom, but last evening when we were talking over absinthe before dinner, Ori informed me that I was to take his name, Ori, and then and there I became – and had to become – Ori, and he Atamu. La Farge also had to go through the same process. Although Ori is, I think, only a nickname, and probably not an island title like Teriitera, it happens to be the name used by Stevenson in dedicating his poem. I presume that Stevenson – and Teriitera –, and I are brothers of the Teva class, and that his poem bears my name. The situation is just a half-tone too yellow-green. I fear that Stevenson will fail to enjoy the jest.

Yet after this supercilious effusion, Adams allowed himself to assess the work rather than the man.

His Legend of Rahero is extremely well done, and has only the fault of being done with more care than the importance of the legend deserves. In reading it, one is constantly worried by wondering that he should have worked too hard on so slight a subject. Rahero was a very subordinate figure in history, and connects with nothing. The legends and poetry of the island can be made interesting only by stringing them on a narrative, and Stevenson could have done it better than anyone else, for he has a light hand, when he likes, and can write verse as well as prose.[15]

Despite the caveat, this appreciation was light-years ahead of the sardonic and sneering reception of the ballads in Britain. While RLS had been in Europe, his work had been badly underrated; as soon as he went to the Pacific, it became the fashion to praise his early work and deprecate that inspired by the Pacific. Typical was Gosse's reaction:

What do you think of Stevenson's *Ballads*? I confess we are all disappointed here. The effort to become a Polynesian Walter Scott is a little too obvious, the inspiration a little too mechanical. And – between you and me and Lake Michigan – the versification is atrocious. Nor is his prose above reproach. There has been a good deal of disappointment among the few who have read the approaching South Sea letters. The fact seems to me that it is very nice to *live* in Samoa, but not healthy to write there. Within a three-mile radius of Charing Cross is the literary atmosphere, I suspect.

Some of the attempts to denigrate 'Rahero' were too clever by half. Sidney Dark cited the couplet:

So the sound of the feast gallantly trampled at night,
So it staggered and drooped, and droned in the morning light.

Then he asked: 'How on earth can a feast either gallantly trample, or stagger or droop or drone?' This is pedantry: it is quite clear that it is the *sound* that is supposed to be doing all these things.

McClure, who was visiting England at this time, commented on the almost universally hostile reception of RLS's work. He found his friends, Henley especially, sneering and depreciatory, and envious and resentful of his success in the United States. Even Colvin was lukewarm, and McClure noted his well-known tendency to criticise everything Louis sent him in manuscript and to advise him to withdraw it from publication; Colvin's 'justification' for this severity – that RLS, as a genius, had to be judged by harsher standards than ordinary writers, never convinced McClure. Only Henry James stood firm and proved himself a true friend: 'His interest in Stevenson's health, his work, his plans for the future, was wholly affectionate, wholly disinterested . . . his loyal generous feeling I have never forgotten.'[16]

Despite all the negative feedback from London, and the lack of enthusiasm within his own home, the dauntless Stevenson pressed on. At the end of 1891 he told Burlingame that he had just finished his historical and political survey of Samoa, *A Footnote to History*, Hand declared:

> Here is, for the first time, a tale of Greeks – Homeric Greeks – mingled with moderns, and all true; Odysseus alongside of Rajah Brooke, *proportion gardée*; and all true. Here is for the first time since the Greeks (that I remember) the history of a handful of men, where all know each other in the eyes and live close in a few acres, narrated at length, and with the seriousness of history.[17]

However, the truly great literary event of 1891 was the completion of the novella *The Beach of Falesá*, apparently sparked by a letter from a trader named Francisco Valleiro who wrote to him in May 1891 with news that he had been 'taboed [sic] for nine months . . . it is the longest Taboe ever ben heard of throo the whole grupe of islands.' From the germ of this idea – what would cause a white trader to be tabooed – came a thrilling tale of the struggle for island mastery between the acceptable and unacceptable faces of European commerce. Begun in November 1890, chiefly written in September 1891 and published in 1892, *Falesá* indicated a new bearing in the Stevenson fictional *oeuvre*. RLS was justifiably proud of it, and sent detailed instructions about its publication to Baxter in October. The themes are complex: imperialism, the fatal impact of Europeans on the Pacific, miscegenation, colonial mentalities, the corruption of 'civilisation' by 'barbarism' – which is why both this book and *The Ebb-Tide* were such potent influences on early Conrad, especially, *Heart of Darkness*, and beyond that on other literary studies of colonialism, Orwell's *Burmese Days*, for example. The book is a disguised attack on European imperialism but links organically with *The Master of Ballantrae* in that it too contains a devil – this time Captain John Randall – and the demon is loose in the Eden of the South Seas. The allegorical motif links the battle against the islanders' superstition with RLS's own battle against the superstitions of his Calvinistic upbringing. As a deep subtext is the characteristic Stevenson concern with morality and the notion of a categorical imperative guiding human beings even in contexts where they are ostensibly free from the constraints of civilisation and the moral law: the hero, Wiltshire, moves from initial self-interest to other values.[18]

Wiltshire is the most autobiographical of all Stevenson's heroes. Both he and Case are selfish and cynical traders, but it is commitment to Uma that gives Wiltshire the moral palm and, in story terms, enables him to defeat Case. Where Case has violated the white man's code by using the islanders' superstitions against them, embraces what is worst about the Pacific and uses it for evil ends, Wiltshire embraces what is best in the islands and uses his European 'superiority' for good ends. Although there is a clear Conradian flavour to much of *Falesá* (Uma as Aissa, for example), the analogy ultimately breaks down in that RLS's evil in this book is banal rather than metaphysical. Here again we can discern the attempt to throw off the Scottish baggage of his youth, for RLS breaks clear away from the treatment of evil as the manifestation of the devil, so evident in his Scottish fiction, to present a more 'modern' notion. Actually, it is possible to disentangle a number of levels at which evil operates in *Falesá*: as hocus-pocus (the business with the Aeolian harps); the 'hell is heaven' inversion of Case, with his contempt for the stupidity of man-made laws; and as the admixture found in all sane human beings. RLS admits the evil in his own nature by dwelling on the cruelty and even sadism with which his alter ego Wiltshire dispatches Case in the climax of the story.

As with many Stevenson novels, *Falesá* opens brilliantly. No writer knew better than RLS how to apply to literature the techniques of mental association and suggestion he had learned from dreams. In his outstanding description of the Pacific at daybreak in midsummer he begins with the painterly qualities of a Bob or a Sargent then, by use of the single word 'sneezing', switches to association or suggestion, all the time maintaining a perfect balance, not overdoing or omitting anything essential:

> I saw that island first when it was neither night nor morning. The moon was to the west, setting, but still broad and bright. To the east, and right amidships of the dawn, which was all pink, the day-star sparkled like a diamond. The land breeze blew in our faces, and smelt strong of wild lime and vanilla; other things besides, but these were most plain; and the chill of it set me sneezing. I should say I had been for years on a low island near the line, living for the most part solitary among natives. Here was a fresh experience; even the tongue would be quite strange to me; and the look of these woods and mountains, and the rare smell of them renewed my blood.

Given the problem RLS had with his endings, and the number of unfinished projects that bore his name, it is much more surprising to find that the ending is also masterly, so that *Falesá* has strong claims to be considered Stevenson's most formally perfect work of fiction. When Wiltshire has defeated Randall and insisted on marrying the Polynesian girl who has been his mistress (here we see the RLS ethic, as applied to Fanny, transferred to his fiction), he muses that all life is a compromise and he will have to abandon his ambitions to be an affluent English innkeeper:

> My public house? Not a bit of it, nor ever likely. I'm stuck here, I fancy. I don't like to leave the kids, you see: and – there's no use talking – they're better here than what they would be in a white man's country though Bess took the oldest up to Auckland, where he's being schooled with the best. But what bothers me is the girls. They're only half-castes of course; I know that as well as you do, and there's nobody thinks less of half-castes than I do; but they're mine, and about all I've got. I can't reconcile my mind to their taking up with Kanakas, and I'd like to know where I'm to find the whites?

In his ambivalence, disliking their personal qualities while protecting them because they are 'his', we surely get a clue to Louis's attitude to his own 'half-castes', Belle and Lloyd.

Falesá displays all the Stevenson virtues: economy, brevity, beauty, the simultaneous engagement of conscious and unconscious. It also adds some features new to his work: the sacrifice of incident to psychology – also anticipating Conrad – and a linguistic originality which works in sailor's argot, American slang, Samoan, colloquialism and obsolete diction. Louis told Henry James – the one man he could trust to understand and sympathise with his intentions – that he wanted to create a style that would be a cross between a ledger-book and an old ballad. James thought RLS had been completely successful: 'The art of *The Beach of Falesá* seems to be an art brought to perfection and I delight in the observed truth, the modesty of nature of the narrator ... primitive man doesn't interest me, I confess, as much as civilized – and yet he *does*, when you write about him'.[19]

James's was an important opinion to sound on this particular book, since for the first time RLS tackled the subject of sex head-on, but without any of the 'master's' obfuscation. As has been well said: 'The deception that Henry James could manage in his writing about sex, and that was indeed his way with language, was foreign to Stevenson. Stevenson could no more hide what was going on in his fiction than James could express it plainly.' RLS, like Hardy, suffered from being blatant in his criticisms of religion and open in his discussion of sexuality; indeed, it is hard to imagine a book more calculated to offend Victorian sensibilities than *Falesá*, with its concentration on the trinity of taboo subjects – sex, religion and politics – and its stirring up the depths of the murky Victorian collective unconscious in the treatment of racism, colonial exploitation and miscegenation. After three years in the Pacific, RLS, it seems, was beginning to forget how repressed Victorian England was, for in the Pacific the later censure of *Falesá* for 'immorality' was greeted with roars of laughter. The perennial Stevensonian duality found a new focus in Samoa: not only did RLS delve searchingly into Scotland's past while confronting the political problems of Samoa's present, but, immersed as he was in the more open and liberal Pacific culture, he tried to communicate with an Anglo-Saxon culture in many ways antithetical to it.

There were two aspects of *Falesá* European editors particularly objected to. One was the open and unapologetic expression of sexuality, as when Wiltshire, seeing Uma, says: 'The want of her took and shook all through me, like the wind in the luff of a sail.' Stevenson's editors solved this problem by excising all the original erotic references to Uma. The other was the farcical 'one night marriage' Wiltshire contracted with Uma, a meaningless ceremony 'legitimating' sexual intercourse with her, which Wiltshire blamed on the missionaries: 'If they had let the natives be, I had never needed this deception, but taken all the wives I wished, and left them when I pleased, with a clear conscience.'

The 'marriage certificate' was a copy of such documents routinely drawn up in the Pacific, and appears in *In the South Seas*, in the chapter describing liaisons between white traders and Polynesian wives; that it caused not a ripple when that book was published shows that RLS's non-fiction attracted few readers. The document read as follows: 'This is to certify that Uma, daughter of Favao of Falesá island of – is illegally married to Mr John Wiltshire for one night, and Mr John Wiltshire is at liberty to send her to hell next morning.' In all the early editions of *Falesá*, this certificate was cut out or inaccurately worded – a favourite ploy was to substitute 'week' for 'night', as RLS tetchily explained to Colvin, then acting as his agent: 'Yesterday came yours. Well, well, if the dears prefer a week, I'll give them ten days, but the real document, from which I have scarcely varied, ran for one night.'[20]

In the 1890s Victorian sexual *angst* came to a head in a number of coexistent manifestations: the Vizetelly prosecutions for publishing Zola's 'obscene' work, the Oscar Wilde trial, the uproar over the Jack the Ripper murders, and much else. 1891, the year of *Falesá*, was also the year when Hardy's *Tess of the D'Urbervilles* was published, and the frank avowal of sexuality in that novel caused its author problems similar to those of RLS with *Falesá*, though Louis scarcely helped the cause of greater freedom in sexual matters by joining in the chorus of disapproval of *Tess*. The remarkable thing about these two cases is the way the editors wielded the scissors and blue pencil with gusto, even when they had no reason to fear prosecution, suggesting that Grundyism was by no means restricted to the benighted 'God-fearing' classes. Beneath the fuss and froth about the marriage ceremony was a deep anxiety that the very roots of marriage, the chief symbol of social order, were being subtly subverted; the fear became overtly expressed in 1895 with the publication of Hardy's *Jude the Obscure*. In despair at the attitude of editors, RLS concluded that *any* discussion of sex in fiction, whatever the context, would mean trouble; this was especially the case with periodical and magazine editors, and he was prepared to forego serialisation if he could thereby attain freedom of expression. Yet even that hope was vain. The most recent in-depth study of *Falesá* concludes glumly: 'For Stevenson, *Falesá* reduced itself to a simple lesson; no sex.' This was a hard blow to take. The backlash from the 'moral majority' occurred at the exact time he approached maturity in his art and felt confident enough to deal with man-woman relations in an adult way.

Yet the controversy over sex was only part of the ordeal by publisher that *Falesá* unleashed: his editors wanted to shortchange him and hoodwink him financially even as they gelded and bowdlerised his text, and in this ambition they were helped by the supposedly devoted Colvin, who should have known better. As Barry Menikoff has said: 'We must recognise that from start to finish there was nothing in *Falesá* that could truly please the people who were responsible for the production of Stevenson's books and for the promotion of his reputation. They could not do anything explicit about his chosen story, his *donnée*, but they would, and they did, eviscerate it.'

In the last five years of his life, RLS was increasingly worried about money and took on as many projects as possible, trying to maximise revenue. He would demand higher royalty rates and, when that proved inadequate for his purposes, renounced royalties for an outright sale of copyrights. To Baxter he complained about the mangling of his texts by editors but made no public protest to his publishers. The alternation between rage and charm, which Moors had noticed, was part of a personality that had no middle range and therefore found toughness in business difficult. As part of the tenderness he displayed to others and needed from them, Louis liked to have close personal relations with publishers and editors, rather than holding them aloof at a normal business level. He would joke with Burlingame and then switch into another gear and suddenly assert his artistic integrity. This oscillation was disastrous for, instead of reading it as lack of integration, Burlingame simply interpreted it as the 'temperamental' antics of an author who blew hot and cold; in the end Burlingame and Scribners simply dealt with the serious bits of Stevenson's letters by disregarding them.

The one publisher to whom RLS displayed overt anger was McClure, significantly the one to whom he was personally closest; as Menikoff says: 'In McClure Stevenson must have seen the commercial side of himself that he pursued with passion and alternatively loathed.' Baxter tended to encourage him in this and wrote, concerning McClure's commission: 'Scratch a Yankee and out comes a Jew.' Those who believe, with Jung, in 'synchronicity' will be interested to learn that in the very month Baxter indited those remarks, Louis himself was protesting his pro-Semitic credentials to Adelaide Boodle: 'What a strange idea to think me a Jew-hater! Isaiah and David and Heine are good enough for me; and I leave more unsaid. Were I of Jew blood, I do not think I could ever forgive the Christians.'[21]

Worst of all crosses for Louis to bear was the treacherous, venal and unscholarly attitude of Colvin. Having been loaded with academic honours, Colvin betrayed his own calling by being quite prepared to put out a corrupt text of Stevenson's work to satisfy the susceptibilities of the late-Victorian reading public. In effect though not name RLS's London editor, he acted in a singularly high-handed way and never consulted the author on many major decisions. RLS had no confidence in Colvin's abilities as a 'line editor' but did not actually forbid him to play that role; as with Burlingame, Louis occasionally put his foot down, but so halfheartedly that Colvin learned to ignore his protestations. Too far from London adequately to supervise his productions, he allowed Colvin to become the final decision-maker by default.

Colvin was the very last person to whom this role should have been devolved. He suffered from the delusion, common to academics, that a critic is as 'creative' as a writer of fiction, and therefore failed to recognise that it was the opinion of the creator, not some self-appointed editor-in-chief, which was important. He hated the fact that RLS had settled in Samoa, was bored by and resentful of the Pacific's role in Louis's creative life, and thought it impaired and vitiated his art – though Colvin always had a ludicrous Platonic ideal of an RLS book, in terms of which whatever the novelist was doing or wherever he was, it was always somehow destroying his art. As Louis passed out of his sphere of influence and he decisively lost the battle for the right to guide the genius to Fanny, Colvin appears to have manifested more and more unconscious hostility towards his one-time protégé. He nagged him for 'overproduction', drawing from Louis in September 1891 the following *cri de coeur*: 'What ails you, miserable man, to talk of saving material? I have a whole world in my head.' His criticism of Louis's work was ungenerous, unhelpful and wrongheaded, but his constant carping depressed the Samoan exile. Colvin wrote once to Cassell's with arrogant disdain for Louis's opinion: 'May the publication proceed under the circumstances, or must we wait till the great man's views after seeing a proof copy of the book can reach us?'

Menikoff, who has made a minute study of Colvin's behaviour over *The Beach of Falesá*, concludes thus:

> Colvin exhibited the curious attitude of the man whose best friend is virtually his sinecure, and who on occasion vents his anger and hostility towards the source of his support. Colvin's superior tone exasperated and demoralised him . . . Colvin's relationship with Stevenson was marked by 'secrecy and indiscretion' to use the novelist's terms, or by calculation and manipulation, to use more contemporary ones.[22]

Louis was particularly angered by the arrangements Colvin made for publication of *Falesa*. Burlingame and Scribner's at first tried to persuade RLS to postpone publication on the grounds that the novella was both too short (30,000 words) and 'too strong'. Louis agreed to postponement on the strict condition that, when finally published, the story should not appear in the same volume as 'The Bottle Imp' – a totally different story in mood and intention. Yet Cassells in London, for their own commercial reasons, were determined to do precisely that, and were aided and abetted by Colvin. In the end Louis was presented with a *fait accompli*.

He was so angry that he could not write to Colvin direct, but informed Baxter that from now on he was his literary agent. This was a wise decision. Baxter was the one friend who never disappointed him in personal terms and never tried to thwart his artistic intentions. He proved remarkably efficient as a literary agent, and his meticulous fidelity to Louis's instructions contrasted strikingly with Colvin's cavalier insouciance. Baxter was contemptuous of Colvin's abilities as a businessman and negotiator, thought him (rightly) a mere belle-lettrist, and was especially scathing about the botch Colvin had made of the serialisation rights for another RLS Pacific short story 'The Isle of Voices'. With virtual plenipotentiary powers from the end of 1892, Baxter made an immediate commercial success and was almost singlehandedly responsible for selling Louis's books at auction. At last McClure met his match, as soon became evident in the complex financial wranglings over American rights for *Falesá* and, later, *Catriona*. By 1893 Louis and Baxter had had enough of Burlingame and Scribner's. Louis flatly refused to work to their schedules and time limits, expressed stupefaction at the poor sales of *The Wrecker* in the U.S.A. and said of the royalty Burlingame offered him: 'I should not think it fair to myself to sacrifice any more of my books upon such terms as Scribners offered.' He and Baxter agreed that the best strategy in future was to demand lump sum payments for books instead of royalties, so as to shift the financial burden on to the publishers.[23]

It was a sign of the essential weakness of Louis where his friends were concerned that he could never cut them dead, no matter how atrociously they had behaved. No sooner had he snubbed Colvin by making Baxter his literary agent than he began mending fences with the culprit. In granting Baxter plenipotentiary business powers in December 1892, he suggested that Colvin still be allowed some editorial input – a decision of consummate folly in the light of the way Colvin had gelded and bowdlerised *Falesá*. He resumed correspondence with Colvin in January 1893 but instead of putting him 'on a warning' he tried to carry off the new arrangements with Baxter with a joke: 'if you please I would have you two arrange grounds and responsibilities between the twae o'ye.'[24]

Louis's desperate reluctance to sever ties irrevocably with old friends emerges clearly in his agonising over Henley, as confided in great detail to Baxter. Gradually his fury over Henley's supposed discourtesy to his mother and 'Burly's' treachery in traducing him to McClure subsided. When returning from Sydney in the *Lübeck* in March 1891 his emotions were still red-hot, if not now at white heat:

> As for Henley, what a miss I have of him. The charm, the wit, the vigour of the man haunt my memory; my past is all full of his big presence and his welcome, wooden footstep. Let it be a past henceforward: a beloved past without continuation. I had a letter from him the other day in which he signed himself "my old friend." I accept the phrase; I am his old friend; I was, not am, his friend. The affair is ended, the record closed, without ill will on my side and without irritation. I believe I see him without prejudice; I believe I know what arguments he can bring forward in his own defence. They leave me very cold, for this reason: that I do not think he should have argued. But I grant them valid, a fair set off. He may win the cause then; I am quite satisfied if I lose the half friend. The only pity is it was not earlier.

Baxter made no comment and later in the year, when Louis was discussing with him the disposal of the rights in the four plays he and Henley had written together, he gave Baxter a nudge: 'You say nothing of the Henley affair, from which I gather you disapprove. Well, you are very likely right; it makes a damned hole in my life. I am always thinking of things I want to say to him, but *que voulez-vous*? he wore me out. I have no ill feeling, plenty of kind ones, but no desire to go back into that doubtful medium.'

Baxter had long since given up trying to pour oil on troubled waters. He was irritated by Henley's combative manner and his desire always to reopen old wounds. When he reacted coolly to 'Lacrimae Rerum', Henley's poetic version of the estrangement from RLS, Henley declared: 'CB has gone over to the enemy.' This was paranoia: Baxter was genuinely fond of both men and he never really forgave Fanny for bringing about an irreparable breach. But Henley's attitude of 'who is not for me is against me' nettled him enough to elicit a complaint to Samoa, at which Louis pounced: 'I was relieved to find you did not too severely blame me re Henley; vexed to find he had got in trouble with you also. I do find his arrogance surprising, and being (I am told) a somewhat arrogant bird myself, I should be a judge. I cannot but think there must be much whiskey in that head.' He would have been interested to learn that Colvin concurred; in a letter to Baxter in which he wondered how Louis's earnings could possibly meet the outgoings on Vailima, he remarked of Henley: 'he seems born to leave himself unfriended in the long run.'

At the end of 1891 Louis replied affectionately to a letter from Baxter, in which his old friend informed him that he was now a dedicated freemason and a leading light of the Edinburgh lodge. But he found himself unable to shake loose of Henley; as the white whale had done with Ahab, so Henley continued to 'task' him:

> All you say of Henley I feel; I cannot describe the sense of relief and sorrow with which I feel I am done with him. No better company in God's earth, and in some ways a fine fellow, a very fine one. But there has been too much hole-and-cornering, and cliquing and sweltering; too much of the fizz and cackle of the low actor lot; and of late days, with all sorts of pleasant and affecting returns of friendship when we met, too much and a too visibly growing jealousy of me. It made my life hard; now it leaves it a good bit empty. *Et puis après?* So they both died and went out of the story; and I daresay young fellows short of a magazine article in the twentieth century (if our civilisation endures) will expose the horrid R.L.S. and defend and at last do justice to the misused W.E.H. For he is of that big, round, human, faulty stamp of man that makes lovers after death. I bet he has drunk more, and smoked more, and talked more sense, and quarrelled with more friends than any of God's creatures; and he has written some A-1 verses.

There is ambivalence and some uncertainty and unease there, and gradually Louis softened still further in his attitude to Henley. As he was growing away from Fanny in the last years of his life, and disillusioned with Colvin for his cynical inability to defend his interests, it is more than likely that he often conducted an interior dialogue on the origins and causes of the famous quarrel, for in Henley he might have found a proper editor and a doughty defender against niggardly and pusillanimous publishers; Baxter could play the latter role but not the former. However, there is evidence that Baxter was as careless in the disposal of personal correspondence as he was punctilious in the transaction of business. Somehow Henley got hold of some of the RLS letters to Baxter and snorted with contempt at what he read: 'A curious letter from RLS', he wrote in August 1891, 'whose fatuousness in regard to me is something prodigious'.[25]

Certainly by the autumn of 1891 Louis needed *some* trusted friend to lean on, for Fanny was beginning the eighteen-month descent that would take her into total insanity (albeit temporary) by 1893. A deeply intuitive woman, Fanny sensed that Louis no longer needed her so much at any level. She had forfeited his confidence by siding with the philistines over both *In the South Seas* and *A Footnote to History*, and sexually their relationship seems to have all but petered out. When to the long periods the couple spent apart is added the quota of Pacific cruising without privacy, the frequent rows and the separate bedrooms, and the fact that at Vailima one or other of them was always ill, we can reasonably infer that physical intimacy occurred but rarely in the Pacific period. Colvin later claimed in extenuation of his 'blue-pencilling' conduct over *The Beach of Falesá* that he tried to suppress the evidence of RLS's growing preoccupation with sex, evinced in the letters by his frank appraisal of the maid Faauma's physical charms, to protect Fanny and thus paper over the cracks in the marriage. There is also evidence that Fanny was jealous of the increasing role of Belle in Louis's life, and maybe she had heard the rumours of her daughter's sensational approach to RLS in San Francisco in 1879.

Fanny's attempts to sublimate both libido and would-be creativity via gardening led to increasing monomania as she corresponded obsessively with the Botanical Gardens at Kew and Colombo, yet most of her sowing and planting operations ended in failure. On one occasion she sent Lafaele to Apia to fetch the latest seed specimens from Europe and told him to be very careful about the labels, so she would know which one corresponded to the correct packet; Lafaele returned with a packet carefully wrapped in a banana leaf; it contained all the labels. On another occasion she tried to make beer out of bananas, but the brew exploded and the odour of fermentation pervaded the Vailima estate for weeks. Everything seemed to conspire against her; she fell into melancholia after reading a newspaper report that Adams and La Farge had been snubbed at Vailima. Her state of mind became increasingly worrying to the other inhabitants of Vailima, and it was agreed that she should go to Fiji on her own for a two-month convalescence. She departed at the beginning of August, but in her troubled state of mind found the hotels in both Suva and Levuka inadequate and noisy and returned at the end of the month.[26]

Her mental deterioration soon became evident. She suffered from the alternating delusions of grandeur and feelings of persecution typically found in paranoid neurosis; she loved scheming and planning secret stratagems. On one occasion she summoned a startled gardener and told him to cut a low door into the kitchen from Maggie's room, but added that she required him to cut through the wooden boards just as they were as she could not match the paint. Her biographer comments: 'More than ever Fanny was a prey to fears and fancies. Her bizarre imagination was frequently used to win cooperation from her helpers.' She approached all the issues that vexed her in a roundabout way. Angered by Joe Strong's drinking and shiftlessness, she took it out on Louis: 'Sometimes everything he did was wrong. She had lectured Belle on the merits of a low voice, but now her own echoed shrill and strident. Every conversation turned into an argument, then a quarrel.' The words are those of her best biographer, Margaret Mackay.

Increasingly, too, she confided her reservations about RLS to her diary. In November there was an argument about patriotism, recorded by Fanny as follows:

It is the only subject on which Louis, ordinarily so brilliant a talker, babbles like poor Poll . . . the moment that grace was said and before dinner had commenced, Louis *declared* a toast in the voice of one doubtful of being obeyed. We supposed that we were to drink to Miss Ide, but no, it was 'her blessed majesty the Queen'. Then in an aggressive manner he turned to Lloyd, saying, 'You can drink to the president *afterwards* if you like'. I am writing this down hoping that Louis may see it and realize how foolish and childish and in bad taste the whole thing is. Henley, I see, is about to publish a book containing everything he can find in praise of England. I need not say that Lloyd smiled and did not offer any but a social toast.[27]

This is singularly revealing on the interpersonal dynamics at Vailima. Louis was the exact opposite of a chauvinist, but a sentimental love of one's country is a healthy emotion and it is hard to see why it is 'foolish and childish and in bad taste'. Much more so was the churlish and boorish attitude of her beloved Lloyd, who repaid all the kindness, consideration and financial largesse of his stepfather in this self-regarding way. The reference to Henley, too, is significant, showing that this scar itched all the more as she and Louis drew apart. Then, too, there is the inevitable association of ideas between Henley and Britons in general, and the consequent anglophobia, as in her famous outburst in 1888.

When Fanny was angry with Joe Strong, she allowed herself to pitch into Louis, presumably because he was not the primary focus of her rage and could therefore prevent the row from becoming volcanic through chain reaction. When she felt directly angry with Louis, she usually made Maggie the butt. Given her record with servants, it was perhaps inevitable that she should soon have quarrelled with her mother-in-law's maid, Mary, a spirited girl who quite correctly stood her ground and would not be used as a general fetcher and carrier, stating calmly that she took orders from 'Aunt Maggie' and no one else. Mary, however, found the strain of being in the same house as 'the bedlamite' as taxing as Valentine Roch had in earlier years, and went back to Australia as soon as her contracted year of service was up.

Incensed by Mary's 'impertinence', Fanny sought a pretext for a quarrel with Maggie, and found it on the issue of religious observance. Maggie protested that the household was atheistic, that at prayer time she was left alone to pray with the servants, most of whom were 'idolatrous' papists; her particular target of complaint was the Strong family, who decamped in haste whenever mention was made of prayers – evidently Maggie knew it was useless to protest about the beloved Lloyd so did not include him in her delation. Instead of humouring the old lady from whom she had received so many kindnesses in the past, Fanny chose to take the high moral ground and confided to her diary:

I see again she dislikes the life here which we find so enchanting and is

disappointed and soured that she is not able to persuade us to throw it all up
and go to the colonies. We have given colonies a fair trial and they mean death
to Louis, whereas this is life and reasonable health.

I think she could be happier if she had some occupation, but I can't think
of anything she would like. All the rest of us have every moment accounted for
and are all enthusiastic in our different departments. It is very difficult for me
to understand that anyone can prefer a life of calls, leaving and receiving cards,
with a proper church and inverted meals and a nap on Sundays, to this open air
paradise where one feels so near to heaven that to believe ill is almost impossible.

Fanny put Maggie in her place by setting Lloyd on to her and forcing her
by relentless nagging and cross-questioning to read boring books about life
in the Pacific with titles like *Tropical Industries*. There is a clear undercurrent
of bullying perceptible in Fanny's diary entry: 'Lloyd . . . keeps a sharp eye
upon her to see that she reads it. He fears her enthusiasm is not at proper
temperature. She seems to work away at it most gallantly.'

Just occasionally, Fanny allowed the outer world to see the true state
of affairs at Vailima. On one occasion at Moors's house in Apia, Louis
was discussing his ill-starred collaborations, explaining to Moors that *The
Wrong Box* was almost wholly Lloyd's work but that his contribution to *The
Wrecker* was virtually nil – which certainly explains the differential quality
of the two books. They proceeded to talk about *The Dynamiter* and Louis
was just explaining that he had allowed many of the weak passages in that
book to stand out of deference to Fanny when the lady herself burst in
on the scene. Moors takes up the story: 'I am sadly afraid that the lady
overheard some of the uncharitable remarks I had been making . . . At all
events she lectured me for exciting her husband, and insisted on his going
to bed forthwith.'[28]

In the middle of all this stress with Fanny, Lloyd, the Strongs, Henley,
Colvin, Burlingame, McClure, when RLS might well have felt himself a
perfect Ishmael, with every man's (and woman's) hand against him, it is
remarkable how stoically and courageously he endured all. He rejoiced in
his new-found health. At the end of 1891 there was a severe flu epidemic
in Samoa which resulted in many deaths: 'my first visit to Apia was a shock
to me; every second person the ghost of himself, and the place reeking with
infection.' But he was now so much stronger physically that he could pass
through a town full of influenza patients and emerge unscathed. It was
therefore on a defiantly upbeat note that he ended the year, writing to Henry
James of his plans to come to Royat in France in 1892, where he hoped his
friends would visit him. Of course, all depended on Fanny's being well: 'She
will over to England, but not I, or possibly incognito to Southampton, and
then to Boscombe to see poor Lady Shelley.'[29] But whether Fanny would
ever be easy enough in her mind to do anything but act the 'witch-woman
of Vailima' (as the Samoans called her) was a moot question.

17

Samoa: Third Year

In 1892 Stevenson was sucked deep into the maelstrom of Samoan politics, and responded to the challenge enthusiastically. 'I never saw so good a place,' an Irishman said to RLS, 'you can be in a new conspiracy every day!' All *haoles* who came to the islands tended to catch the bug.

'If you want a lecture on Samoan politics,' wrote Henry Adams to Elizabeth Cameron, 'I am in a fair way to be able to give you one; for though I loathe the word, and of all kinds of politics most detest those of islands, I am just soaked with the stuff here, where the natives are children, full of little jealousies and intrigues, and the foreigners are rather worse than the natives. The three foreign powers have made a mess, and the natives are in it.'[1]

The three powers – Germany, Britain and the United States – had indeed made a mess. Of the three, Britain had the most marginal interests in the Pacific as an area of influence. Germany and the United States, on the other hand, had such intense geopolitical aspirations that the great naval historian and theorist of sea power, Alfred Mahan, later such an influence on Theodore Roosevelt and other advocates of American expansionism, predicted as early as the 1880s that war between these two powers was inevitable some day. Germany's interest in Samoa was overwhelmingly determined by *Deutsche Handels und Plantagen Gesellschaft fur Sud-See Inseln zu Hamburg* – the 'German firm' which, with the backing of Bismarck and his successors, aimed at a monopoly of Samoan trade, though the Imperial government was also mindful of the possible strategic implications for a forward policy in China and Melanesia.

U.S. interest in Samoa began with the desire to provide an 'infrastructure' for its Pacific whaling fleets, and the Americans staked a claim to the fine harbour of Pago-Pago in Tutuila as early as 1839. Gradually the American and German sectors (roughly eastern and western Samoa) interpenetrated with the British as third horse in a troika. Following the abortive 1878 Washington conference, called to iron out differences in the region, Great Power tensions intensified, especially when the 'door-slamming' panic of 1884 (the fear that Germany without colonies would lose its place in the sun) impelled Bismarck to colonial expansion. Meanwhile different imperatives were directing the gaze of Americans across the Pacific; with the imminent closing of the frontier in the West (usually dated around 1890), both republican 'virtue' and American surplus capital needed new outlets. Although it was only in 1898 that a conscious American decision was made to go for economic empire, Mahan and those who thought like him were, already in the 1880s, urging that the U.S.A. regard the Pacific as *mare nostrum*. Men like Adams and La Farge agreed with him: as La Farge wrote after his visit: 'I am impressed by the force that Americans could have for good, and by careful calculation on the part of those who know us best, the Germans and English, upon our weakness of action and irresponsibility and our not knowing our enormous power. The Pacific should be ours and it must be.'[2]

However, a certain puzzle still attaches to the determination of the U.S.A., long before the acquisition of the Philippines, to go to almost any lengths to have a say in the affairs of Samoa, where her commercial interests were negligible. In December 1893, when the U.S.A. was already inextricably embroiled in the affairs of the island, President Grover Cleveland, in his first annual message to Congress, spoke of the unwisdom of his country's having departed from its traditional policies so far as to become entangled in an international dispute with Germany and Britain.[3]

Yet in Western Samoa it was the Germans who were the principal actors. 'The true centre of trouble, the head of the boil of which Samoa languishes, is the German firm,' wrote RLS. The German firm had vaulted past the small-scale entrepreneurship of foreign adventurers lusting after copra, employed 800 imported (blackbirded) men and women as a kind of slave labour on its plantations and exported vast amounts of coffee, cacao and pineapples at huge profits. The German consul was the mere creature of the firm which, with its ability to call on Berlin for troops and warships, resembled nothing so much as the East India Company in the heyday of 'John Company'. Inevitably, tensions arose between this aggressive, thrusting brand of capitalism and the traditional society of Samoa. As RLS pointed out:

> They are Christians, church-goers, singers of hymns at family worship, hardy cricketers; their books are printed in London by Spottiswoode, Tribner, or the Tract Society; but in most other points they are the contemporaries of our tat-tooed ancestors who drove their chariots on the wrong side of the Roman wall. We have passed the feudal system; they are not yet clear of the patriarchal. We are in the thick of the age of finance; they are in a period of communism.

Complementing, and sometimes parallelling, the Great Power rivalry were complexities deriving from Samoa's internal politics. The 'king' or Malietoa of Apia was simply the chief recognised as supremo by the other chiefs on the basis of prestige and the acquisition of titles or 'names', much as Agamemnon was recognised as high king by the other Achaean chiefs for the venture against Troy (The title of Malietoa means 'highest name'). However, in a situation where two or more highly prestigious chiefs arose simultaneously, the result was a lack of settled charismatic authority. In the 1880s there was tripartite rivalry between Laupepa, who arrogated the title of Malietoa, and the two 'pretenders', Tamasese and Mataafa, chiefs, respectively, of the provinces of Aana and Atua. Of the three rivals, by far the most impressive was Mataafa, who was immortalised by Stevenson.

Mataafa, born about 1832, was a tall, powerful, white-haired man with white moustache with an underhung jaw that gave him the appearance of a benevolent mastiff. A devout Catholic, he appeared to RLS to have the dignified but insinuating bearing of a priest, and was rigid in the observances of his faith. Never married, but with a natural daughter who acted as hostess for his guests, by the time of Stevenson's arrival in Apia he had long since taken a strict vow of chastity – 'to live as Our Lord lived on this earth' – and to the stupefaction of other Polynesians kept his vow. Though a Catholic, Mataafa was not the kind of Christian who believed in turning the other cheek: when a Wesleyan missionary remonstrated with him for cutting off the heads of the men he killed in battle, Mataafa, with his biblical knowledge, shot back: 'Is it not so that when David killed Goliath, he cut off his head and carried it before the king?'[4]

RLS was sometimes accused of over-romanticising Mataafa, but Henry Adams concurred in his high estimate: 'I think he would be a marked man anywhere, but he is a long way the most distinguished chief in these islands, and the only one we have met who carries his superiority about him so decidedly as to set him at once apart.' Margaret Villiers, Countess of Jersey, who met both Laupepa and Mataafa in 1892, had this to say of them: 'Laupepa ... a gentle amiable being who seemed rather oppressed by the position into which he had been thrust by the Powers. His rival Mataafa was undoubtedly the stronger of the two.'[5]

To make the plantation system work, the German firm had to combine exploitation with brutality. Although the use of the whip was commonplace against Melanesian blackboys, such summary justice was not so easily applied against Samoans who, lacking western notions of private property not obviously in the fiefdom of some chief, raided the German plantations for easy pickings. To deter such marauders, the Germans insisted on a system of punishment by imprisonment, but then found that such a desire collided with traditional Samoan customs in more ways than one. In the first place,

Polynesians did not understand the notion of incarceration: RLS recalled with amusement the time the French resident in the Marquesas asked where the prisoners were, and the jailer replied that he believed they were all away making family visits. In addition, Samoans regarded the idea of impartial justice as a joke, put kinship before the law and, as judges, were prepared to condemn only men from other clans. Infuriated, the Germans insisted on the right to mete out punishment in the Samoan islands and duped the chiefs into handing over their prerogatives to a 'council' consisting of two Germans and two tame Samoan stooges. Once they saw how they had been gulled, Laupepa and the other forty-eight high chiefs approached the British to offer them suzerainty of the islands (November 1885).

When the Germans learned of this 'perfidy' they deposed Laupepa as Malietoa and instated Tamesese, who played a shadowy role in these events, as the new king. Britain and the U.S.A. at first responded supinely to this overt German bid for hegemony and restricted themselves to sending out Commissioners to investigate. Until 1887 there was an uneasy interlude, in which Laupepa grew weaker and Tamasese stronger. Using the German military adventurer Brandeis as its front man, Berlin humiliated an embassy sent from Hawaii to negotiate and forced it to retire before it could present credentials, then declared war on Laupepa, who quickly surrendered, and was sent into exile, first to Germany and then to the island of Jaluit in the Marshalls. But Mataafa, who had backed Laupepa against Tamasese, continued to resist. He watched angrily as the Germans successively transferred to Tamasese first his own title of Tuiatua and then Laupepa's name of Malietoa. Then, in September 1888, he raised the standard of revolt, bolstered by secret assurances from Britain and the U.S.A. At first he swept all before him and killed or wounded fifty-six German troops in a famous victory at Fangalii. Berlin prepared to send out reinforcements, and the Americans and British to resist this; war was imminent when the terrible hurricane of March 1889, which devastated the German Samoan squadron, brought a breathing space. The would-be combatants came to their senses and agreed to meet in conclave in Berlin.[6]

At the Berlin Conference in 1889 Bismarck decided, sensibly, not to go to war with the Anglo-Saxon powers over Samoa. He disowned the bullying tactics of the German firm and gave assurances that he would not seek revenge for the defeat at Fangalii. Tamasese's government fell, devastating the ruler, who died of frustrated hopes a few years later. But if the Germans had pledged themselves not to avenge Fangalii, they had not forgotten nor forgiven the author of their humiliation. Just when it seemed that Mataafa must at last become Malietoa, the Germans brought back Laupepa from the Marshalls to spite him. On the respective positions of Laupepa and Mataafa, RLS had this to say: 'The one returned from the dead of exile to find himself replaced and excelled. The other, at the end of a long, anxious and successful struggle, beheld his only possible competitor resuscitated from the grave.'

At first Mataafa and Laupepa coexisted peacefully, with Mataafa as, to use Bagehot's terminology, the 'efficient' head of Samoa, and Laupepa the 'dignified' aspect, or, to use RLS's language, kingmaker and creature: 'I repeat the words king-maker and creature; it is so that Mataafa himself conceives of their relation; surely not without justice; for, had he not contended and prevailed, and been helped by the folly of consuls and the fury of the storm, Laupepa must have died in exile.' But by the time RLS was saying goodbye to Adams and La Farge at the end of 1890, strong rumours were already spreading that the two rulers were at loggerheads.

It was at this juncture that the unwieldy administrative process agreed by the powers at Berlin in 1889 made its mark. The agreement postulated a theoretically autonomous native government, a President to advise (but really to control) it, and a chief justice to recommend legislation to the native government and to be the final legislator in the municipality of Apia, as well as a court of last resort, with the three consuls in the wings with ill-defined powers. As one wag remarked, instead of one king, there were now six.

The idea was to appoint neutral personnel to the key offices of head of the Supreme Court and president of the municipal council of Apia. Because the three nations had failed to agree a candidate, according to the arbitration procedures enshrined in the Berlin Act, the choice fell to Norway and Sweden; the Swedes accordingly sent out as chief justice Baron Conrad Cedarcrantz, who arrived in Apia to take up his duties on 2 January 1891. The municipal council consisted of six local members and a president who had to be a foreigner; Baron Senff von Pilsach was appointed to the post and disembarked in the islands on 21 May 1891. To ensure neutrality, the work of the council had to be ratified by the three consuls, British, German and American; there were also to be three land commissioners, one from each of the three powers, to investigate Samoan claims that land titles granted to foreigners had been alienated fraudulently. As one jaundiced observer of this complicated Ruritanian administrative structure remarked:

> One of the most fatuous schemes ever devised for governing a country ... the natives were to be governed by a king whom the majority did not obey; the whites by a German president of Municipality, who was also to act as adviser to a king that did not want his advice. The consuls were to sit still and watch; and over all was set a Swedish Chief-Justice, to intervene in the disputes that were certain to ensue.[7]

Cedarcrantz and von Pilsach, ironically named 'the twins', got off to a bad start and soon alienated all the whites in Samoa except the bought-and-paid-for creatures of the German firm. Von Pilsach, within days of arriving, got embroiled in a long-running dispute about which currencies and which coins should be legal tender. Cedarcrantz, a young Swedish lawyer with a squint, soon found himself out of his depth. Apart from knowing no English – which made negotiations with the British and U.S. consuls difficult – he at once fell out with the Land Commission over the scope of its surveys and alienated the Samoans by his slow, ponderous methods: temperamentally, he was the kind of person who needed all the time in the world to come to the simplest decision, whereas the Samoan chiefs wanted swift action. Beyond this, he was widely considered as a German dupe; he had to implement the three-power decision to recognise Laupepa as Malietoa, when the majority of Samoans wanted Mataafa as their king. Tamasese's death on 17 April 1891 strengthened Mataafa's hand, since his rabidly anti-German followers switched their allegiance to the 'pretender', thus quickening tensions in the islands.[8]

The Mataafa/Laupepa rivalry added a religious flavour to the turbid stew of Samoan politics, since Mataafa was a Catholic and the Protestant missionaries (Wesleyan and London Missionary Society, as divided in their aims as they were hostile to the Catholic missionaries) tried to promote Laupepa as the champion of Protestantism; this tactic backfired, however, for xenophobia actuated the majority of Samoans far more than religious factionalism. In May 1891 Mataafa made a kind of unilateral declaration of independence and thenceforth regarded himself as king; the three consuls responded by warning that they would resist by force any attempt to set him up as Malietoa. In Samoan terms political legitimacy *required* a Mataafa kingship, but the Powers regarded his defiance of their authority as rebellion and instructed the 'twins' to take all necessary measures up to and including confiscation of the estates of the pro-Mataafa chiefs and their followers.

Stevenson always tended to overstress the analogy between Samoa in the 1890s and the Highlands of Scotland before the 1745 rising but, given his sentimental Jacobitism and his preference for traditional societies over those annexed as appanages to the international economic system, he became a fervent supporter of Mataafa. To him Mataafa was 'Charlie over the water', Laupepa and his minions the Campbells, and the Germans in Samoa the equivalent of the Hanoverians in London one hundred and fifty years earlier. Sometimes, however, he found more exact parallels: 'the tale of David and Saul would infallibly be re-enacted; once more we shall have two kings in the land – the patent and the latent . . . Against such odds it is my fear that Mataafa might contend in vain; it is beyond the bounds of my imagination that Mataafa might not contend at all.' He had little time for Laupepa: 'Capable both of virtuous resolutions and of fits of apathetic obstinacy, his Majesty is usually the whip-top of competitive advisers; and his conduct is so unstable as to wear at times an appearance of treachery which would surprise himself if he could see it.'9

RLS saw himself in the role of honest broker between Mataafa and Laupepa but, as an amateur politician, he needed supporters. Moors was on his side, as was Bazett Haggard, brother of the famous novelist, the British Land Commissioner and the only one in post right from the beginning of the new arrangements. The Americans were firm allies, especially Henry C.Ide who came to take up the position as U.S. Land Commissioner; the third post was filled by Carl Eggert for Germany. Louis could depend on U.S. Consul Sewall up to a point, but he was a career bureaucrat who took his orders from Washington, where Samoan policy could change overnight; for all that, Sewall vetoed a German proposal to disarm Mataafa by force. Louis should have been on firmer ground with the British consul, but the two individuals who occupied the post in his time did not get on with him. The first was the blimpish martinet Colonel de Coetlogon, who exploded angrily when RLS paid a call on him on Sunday; such was the Stevenson code, however, that Louis overlooked the snub in consideration of the relief work Coetlogon did for Samoans wounded in the fighting that raged sporadically through Upolu. Coetlogon's successor, Cusack-Smith, whose principal distinction seems to have been that he had an attractive wife, described by Adams as a 'young blonde of the modern British type, rather pretty and painted-silky in costume', behaved in a way that suggested profound jealousy and resentment of the famous novelist.10

Stevenson's ultimately successful battle to defeat the 'twins' and get the 1889 Berlin Act amended occupied much of his time between the two trips to Australia (April 1891-January 1893). At first Louis's relations with Cedarcrantz were cordial: while RLS was recovering from the fever he caught after his exertions in Eastern Samoa in April 1891, the young Swede came up to Vailima to see the invalid and complimented him on the building of part of a new road down to Apia. But once recovered, Louis was soon deep in conclave with Father Didier, Mataafa's confessor. When Mataafa broke with the Powers in May 1891, uncertainty enveloped Vailima, not least because all the male servants and labourers were Mataafa men, thought likely to desert en masse once Mataafa raised his clan. Wild rumours of a war to the knife in which all whites would be massacred ran through the island. Louis wrote to Colvin: 'I have no belief in this, and should be infinitely sorry if it came to pass – I do not mean for *us*, that were otiose – but for the poor deluded schoolboys who should hope to gain by such a step.' However, despite his scepticism, he laid plans for defending Vailima – reminiscent of the tactics employed in the stockade in *Treasure Island* or the roundhouse in *Kidnapped* – shrewdly observing to

Colvin: 'as in all massacres, the one you don't prepare for is the one that comes off.'[11]

It did not take Louis long to become disgusted with the new 'government' of Samoa. Cedarcrantz and von Pilsach and their underlings spent all the revenues collected in the islands on official salaries and lavish housing while providing no funds for much-needed roads and services. When this was pointed out by the local newspaper, the government secretly bought up the organ as its own mouthpiece, but the clandestine purchase became public knowledge when the gold paid out was discovered in government wrappings, and it was revealed that the Chief Justice and the President had exhausted the treasury just to stifle criticism.

RLS was personally plunged into the maelstrom when he again crossed swords with a Protestant missionary. The Revd Arthur E. Claxton of the London Missionary Society held the post as Native Advocate to the new Land Commission, and in a conversation with U.S. consul Sewall in July 1891, soon after Mataafa announced he would no longer be bound by the Berlin agreement, Claxton suggested to Sewall that Mataafa be lured to Apia by a safe-conduct issued by Sewall and then kidnapped. Sewall indignantly turned down the idea of such treachery and told Louis about the overture; justifiably incensed, Louis included the story in his book *A Footnote to History*. Claxton was forced to resign and return to London to answer for his conduct to the L.M.S., but before he went he considered sueing RLS for libel. Moors and Carruthers got together to stymie this: Carruthers refused to take the case for the prosecution, and Moors retained for RLS the only other lawyer in the island – in some versions of the story, he retained Louis himself, who was after all a qualified advocate – thus making an action technically impracticable. It may or may not be relevant to note that both Claxton and Cusack-Smith, two Britons who might in the normal course of things have been expected to support their fellow-countryman, were also, according to Adams, the only Britons on the island who had pretty, attractive wives – Mrs Claxton being 'pretty and not over-missionaried'. Since Louis was always susceptible to personable women, and they were usually attracted to him, is it too far-fetched to suggest that in both cases of enmity there might have been a 'hidden agenda'?[12]

By September 1891 Louis's disillusionment with the administration in Samoa was total, and he now openly spoke of the 'twins' being a mere smokescreen to maintain German hegemony. Although he liked Cedarcrantz personally – 'intelligent, pleasant, even witty, a gentleman' – he thought that by deferring to the Germans on all important issues he had betrayed the meaning of his office. Cedarcrantz alienated native Samoans by his announcement that there would be no election for king – which Mataafa was sure to win – until after Laupepa's death. The Samoans replied with the slogan 'no election, no taxation', depriving the

Chief Justice of revenues and forcing him into desperate measures in the effort to raise funds. Moreover, every decision taken by the Chief Justice since his arrival smacked of incompetence or insensitivity: the climax was reached in September when the Swede suddenly decamped to Fiji without warning – actually to put himself through a crash course of English so that he could cope professionally with the tripartite administration – and, without any consultation with consuls or council, left effective power in Samoa in the hands of von Pilsach.

Von Pilsach had all of Cedercrantz's intellectual failings without any of his personal charm and his stewardship soon erupted in a scandal exposed to the world by Stevenson. Some pro-Mataafa chieftains had been rounded up and sentenced to six months in jail under a dubious 'prevention of terrorism' provision, from which incarceration, however, it was feared the enraged locals would free them. Lacking the manpower to defend his prisoners adequately, the Swedish commandant of the jail appealed for help to von Pilsach; the egregious president of the council 'solved' the problem by placing charges of dynamite around the prison, threatening to detonate them if any attempt was made to rescue the prisoners. To try to cover his tracks, von Pilsach compounded his idiocy with illegality; he sentenced the six chieftains to exile in the Tokelaus, without legal justification and in the knowledge that to a Polynesian exile was worse than death. Louis at once took up the cudgels for the men and wrote to von Pilsach to demand an explanation for his conduct; the President replied, but waffled and flannelled instead of answering the specific questions Louis had put to him.[13]

Dismayed by the loss of his reputation over the dynamite affair, von Pilsach handed in his resignation (October 1891); unwilling to admit publicly that the Berlin agreement was a fiasco, the powers refused to accept it; von Pilsach responded by tendering it again. With one of his opponents fatally wounded, Louis's confidence rose; despite accusations of 'meddling in politics' he headed a deputation to see Laupepa, to urge an accommodation with Mataafa. Although Laupepa's reception of him was surly and grudging, Louis sensed his own growing power: 'a few days ago this intervention would have been a deportable offence,' he told Colvin; 'not now, I bet, I would like them to try.' Yet his enemies tried to clip his wings: Cusack-Smith colluded with Cedarcrantz to issue a new proclamation, whereby no one could interview the Malietoa without the permission of the consuls, two days' notice and an approved 'interpreter' (i.e. spy). Still, Louis remained jubilant and told Colvin he much preferred being in Samoa with its rumours of war than in 'decrepit peace' in Middlesex.

By his open support for Mataafa and campaign against the Berlin Act, Louis put himself in a position where his enemies could brand him anti-German. Even established German friends now refused to make the trip to Vailima, and ostracism was all but complete; soon the manager of the German plantation at Vailele was the only Teuton who would speak to him. By the end of December, the first of his letters in the London *Times*, exposing German misdeeds and the fatuousness of the Berlin Act, reached Samoa. Louis was delighted and unrepentant: 'I am still taboo; the blessed Germans will have none of me; and I only hope they may enjoy the *Times* article. 'Tis my revenge.' After further public revelations of Cedarcrantz's incompetence and ignorance of Samoan life and culture, the chief justice could not but regard RLS as his prime enemy. In December 1891 Fanny wrote in her diary: 'When we were in Apia the other day Louis came face to face with the baron and baroness. If a glance could kill, he said, he must have fallen before the baroness's eyes.'[14]

When Cedarcrantz returned from Fiji, he made another mistake by trying to solve the revenue problem: he decreed that import and export duties should be paid to the Samoan government, not the municipality of Samoa. When no import duties were paid at all by Samoans in protest against the postponed election for Malietoa, Cedarcrantz next illegally seized the municipal rates levied on whites. Even worse than this error was his asinine way of implementing it. Von Pilsach sued the municipality for the funds, and 'represented' both sides to the dispute himself in a case heard *in camera* by Cedarcrantz! Louis expressed his contempt for this comic opera corruption by stating openly: 'Such an official I never remember to have heard of, though I have seen the like, from across the footlights and the orchestra, evolving in similar figures to the strains of Offenbach.' When this became known, the Council held a special meeting and moved a vote of no confidence in von Pilsach. This passed unanimously and von Pilsach adjourned the meeting; the municipality then appealed to the three powers, who overruled the Chief Justice.[15]

Any hope of a quick campaign to take out Mataafa and present the powers with a *fait accompli* was dashed when a violent cyclonic storm in the middle of the hurricane season wrecked houses, a schooner, warehouses and plantations; so much breadfruit and bananas were lost that famine threatened the islands, so that thoughts of war became chimerical. By the spring of 1892 events seemed to be moving decisively in RLS's direction. The foreign residents of Apia voted unanimously that the Berlin Act should be modified and at a public meeting on 29 February, under Stevenson's chairmanship, resolved to send recommendations to the British consul for transmission to the three powers. Louis and Moors pressed for a resolution that von Pilsach and Cedarcrantz be dismissed forthwith, but at this the hotheads on the Council who had been speaking up vociferously for the most extreme measures developed cold feet. RLS learned a bitter political lesson from this. As Moors reported: 'He was very disappointed; but it afforded him another opportunity of noting what a strange and complex thing is man. Here we had a number of prominent people whose braggadocio was enough to have conquered the world, if talk and threats could do it, but who, when it came to acting, shrank ignominiously out of sight.' However, there was compensation for Louis. A German trader at the beginning of the meeting demanded to have minuted his objection to the chairing of the meeting by a 'frivolous novelist'; but at the end of the marathon session he stopped the person proposing the thanks to the chairman and insisted on doing it himself.[16]

Throughout 1892 the pace of Louis's political activity quickened. His principal object was to get Mataafa to go along with the interim arrangements whereby Laupepa was Malietoa, in the confidence that he would win handsomely the election for king when it finally came; meanwhile he had to convince Laupepa of his sincerity as mediator and go-between. On 16 April Laupepa was a lunch guest at Vailima, and on 1 May the Stevenson household paid a return visit to the Malietoa, where they were royally feasted: Maggie noted down that whole roast pigs, duck, chicken, pigeon, shell-fish, baked yams and *taro* pudding were on the menu. Louis told Laupepa that he was shortly to visit Mataafa and arranged a business meeting with the Malietoa at which they would discuss all the difficult matters separating the two claimants for royal office. However, Laupepa failed to appear at the rendezvous; another meeting was arranged, and again Laupepa failed to show, leading to the clear inference that Cedarcrantz and Cusack-Smith had advised him to have nothing to do with Stevenson.

On 7 May Louis visited Mataafa as planned, in company with Fanny and Belle, whom the Samoans thought were Tusitala's two wives. Mataafa showed the affection and consideration he always felt for RLS, even timing a strike by his followers – to insist on payment in future being made in U.S. dollars instead of the Chilean currency which the Germans could manipulate – for a time when the cacao planting was over and Stevenson was away from Vailima. Louis reciprocated the feeling: 'He is a beautiful, sweet old fellow, and he and I grew quite fulsome on Saturday night about our sentiments.' A week later Louis took his mother to see Mataafa and thereafter he was in regular contact. On one occasion he rode twenty miles on 'Jack' in the morning chill and without breaking his fast, ten of them in drenching rain, taking sixteen fences on the way; there followed six hours of political discussions using an interpreter and fitful sleep in a rude hut. Dr Ruedi of Davos would not have recognised him.[17]

The highspot of Louis's regular visits to Mataafa was the meeting he arranged between the Pretender and Margaret Villiers, Countess of Jersey. In August 1892 the Countess, wife of the governor of New South Wales, arrived in Samoa as the guest of Bazett Haggard, Louis's best friend among the British on Upolu. The Countess, who was accompanied by her daughter and brother, Captain Rupert Leigh, commented: 'Our host Barrett [sic] Haggard, brother to Rider Haggard and to William Haggard whom we had known in Athens, was a great character. When he visited Sydney he was known as "Samoa", for he never talked of anything else, which was perhaps not surprising under the circumstances.' The Countess was regarded as a valuable political ally, so on 23 August Laupepa gave a dinner in her honour; she, however, was not overly impressed by him. Hearing from Louis of the much greater charisma and gravitas of Mataafa, she determined to pay him a visit and, together with Louis and Haggard, plotted how she could avoid the restrictions of protocol which forbade such a visit.

It was decided that she and Leigh would visit Mataafa incognito, in the guise of Stevenson's relatives. She took the name of 'Amelia Balfour' and rode with Belle to confuse government spies; Fanny declined to go with her. On the journey, Belle revealed an eccentric side that fuelled the persistent gossip that she was 'no lady'. Margaret Villiers fancied herself an emancipated woman, but within strict limits, and she was taken aback by the following incident: 'Mrs Strong, be it understood, regarded any kind of fitting garment as a foolish superfluity. On this occasion she had donned corsets for the convenience of a long ride, but when, in twilight, we neared our destination, she slipped them off and gave them to an attendant, bidding him be a good boy and carry them for her.'

At Mataafa's village a feast had been prepared, complete with the usual *kava* cocktail, made from the roots of a pepper-tree, chewed up and then soaked in water: it was said to have no effect on the head but to numb the lower limbs if too much was imbibed; the Countess found it merely 'rather like soapy water'. Mataafa made it clear he knew very well who she was by handing her the loving-cup, which was always given in strict order of precedence. If she had really been 'Amelia Balfour', a relative of RLS, it would have been an unpardonable insult to pass by Tusitala, the male head of the household; but Mataafa shrewdly demonstrated that he was no 'noble savage' but someone who understood the nuances of the European class system very well. Louis, who had prepared for the visit by sending the Countess a whole system of quasi-Jacobite codes and cant names – satisfying the 'Mr Libbel' taste for involved practical jokes – reproved her laughingly: 'Oh, Amelia, you're a very bad conspirator.'

After an overnight stop in a large hut, with Mataafa and his warriors on one side of a *tapa* curtain and Belle and the Countess on the other, the party returned in triumph to Apia. Louis wrote excitedly: 'It is all nonsense that it can be concealed; Miss Amelia Balfour will be at once identified with the Queen of Sydney, as they call her; I would not in the least wonder if the visit proved the signal of war . . . the thing wholly suits my book and fits my predilection for Samoa.'[18]

All of this political activity provoked the authorities as it was meant to. One of the first signs of trouble was a visit to Vailima by Cedarcrantz in May 1892, surprising in itself as for the previous five months Louis had refused to speak to him and all communication had been by means of a painful exchange of blunt letters. Moors told Louis that the Chief Justice had been cock-a-hoop since the last batch of mail arrived by steamer and surmised that he had been promised warships so that he could move decisively against Mataafa; Louis, however, wondered whether the visit was not more to do with some personal restraining order on him, or even deportation, whose possibility was currently the subject of 'Chinese whispers' on the Apia waterfront. Louis, still angry that all this military activity might have been sanctioned to cover 'the salaries of two white failures', refused to receive the Swede in person and left it to Fanny to make excuses. Fanny found Cedarcrantz making small talk with Maggie and apologised that her husband was too ill to come down to see him, at which transparent nonsense Maggie visibly blanched. However, the jesuitical Fanny later found a way to justify her white lie: 'So far as the chief justice was concerned my statement was quite true, as Louis declared to meet the man would cause him a serious illness.' Louis's account of the mysterious visit was suspiciously bland: 'My three ladies received him ... he was very agreeable as usual, but refused wine, beer, water, lemonade, chocolate, and at last a cigarette. Then my wife asked him, "So you refuse to break bread?" and he waved his hands amiably in reply.'[19]

Deportation was Cedarcrantz's trump card and he was encouraged by Cusack-Smith to believe that the British government would make no objection. First, however, the Chief Justice tried a number of other stratagems to bring Stevenson to heel. At first he gave him the nod to continue his work of conciliation, which led Fanny to exclaim in puzzlement: 'I don't understand the affair. Last week they were openly talking of deporting Louis because he had been to see Malietoa. Now it is proposed that he communicate with Mataafa to exactly the same effect as he did on his own volition, and this from the government.' Then there was financial chicanery involving the Apia bank of Aspinall and Hayhurst. Moors warned RLS, who had deposited money in the bank, that a plan was afoot to freeze his assets, pleading the inability of the bank to honour his cheques. Louis stormed down to Apia, presented a cheque for the full amount he had on deposit and gave the partners until next morning to think about the consequences of non-payment: they paid up.

Other attempts to silence RLS involved a plan for Laupepa's warriors to attack Vailima, but since Stevenson's retainers were all Mataafa men, such an attempt would have triggered outright civil war, and was therefore abandoned as too risky. There was also a hair-brained scheme to bribe a sea-captain to shanghai RLS – which would have been a bizarre example of life imitating the art of *Kidnapped*; this too was discarded as likely to have international repercussions. Finally, Cedarcrantz concluded that the only option left was to play the trump card of deportation. He began by trying to deport a half-caste British subject, Charles Taylor, who had helped Louis in his dealings with Mataafa but refused to play informer. Louis struck back vigorously but warned Colvin: 'There is great talk in town of my deportation; it is thought they have written home to Downing Street, requesting my removal, which leaves me not much alarmed; what I do rather expect is that H.J.Moors and I may be haled up before the Chief Justice to stand a trial for *lèse-majesté*. Well, we'll try and live it through.' For all his bravado, the 'smart money' of the 'beach' bet that the arrival of HMS *Ringarooma* in November with sealed orders meant that Stevenson's fate was also sealed.[20]

Cedarcrantz meanwhile worked hand in glove with Cusack-Smith to secure deportation, but Louis hit back with another spate of letters to *The Times* and alerted Colvin, who began pulling strings in Whitehall. It was not a moment too soon. The combination of the unwelcome light shed on British policy in Samoa – or rather the fact that there was no policy – by Louis's *Times* letters, and Cusack-Smith's hostile minutes, had led to a climate in the Foreign and Colonial Offices where the deportation of Robert Louis Stevenson was being seriously considered. Colvin went to the very highest levels, learned of Cusack-Smith's enmity, which he passed on to Louis, and counterattacked by suggesting to the Foreign Office mandarins that they might like to withdraw Cusack-Smith and appoint Louis consul instead.[21]

Louis closed the range on Cusack-Smith by trying to pin him down to an identification with Cedarcrantz's policies, which he could then use as ammunition in London. He asked 'whether the Samoan government being bound to account to the ratepayers, any legal duty to pay taxes can be held to survive for British subjects'. Alarmed that he was now being personally targeted by the scalding pen of RLS, Cusack-Smith appealed to Sir John Thurston, High Commissioner of the Western Pacific, to back him up. Thurston responded in December 1892 with a *Regulation for the Maintenance of Peace and Good Order in Samoa*, which prescribed fines and imprisonment for any British subject guilty of sedition against the properly constituted authorities of Samoa; sedition was defined as 'all practices, whether by word, deed or writing, having for their object to bring about in Samoa, discontent or dissatisfaction, public disturbance, civil war, hatred or contempt towards the King or Government of Samoa or the laws or constitution of the country, and generally to promote public disorder in Samoa.'

It was in effect a gagging act, but it was always a mistake for the 'big battalions' to try to shut RLS up. He at once escalated the conflict by enlisting the support of the Jersey family and Sir George Grey, as ex-governor and ex-premier of New Zealand, doyen of Pacific statesmen. Finally he wrote to Lord Rosebery, Gladstone's Foreign Secretary, to make a formal complaint about Cusack-Smith and Thurston: 'As a British subject

I refuse entirely to be gagged.' The result of all these representations and Colvin's discreet lobbying in the corridors of power was that Cusack-Smith and Thurston were put firmly in their place: Thurston was coldly informed to take no steps regarding Stevenson without first consulting London, and Rosebery wrote in person that the Pacific dispatches he had read gave no cause for anxiety on the score of the novelist's 'meddling'.[22]

By mid-1893 Louis had routed his political enemies among the British. An even more spectacular victory came his way at the end of the long campaign against Cedarcrantz and von Pilsach. It had been predicted that the publication of *A Footnote to History* would be the final nail in Stevenson's coffin but, although it ruffled feathers in Berlin, Germans in Samoa thought it a not entirely unfair picture of the recent history of the troubled islands. World opinion had meanwhile swung against the unmodified Berlin Act and particularly against the Tweedledum and Tweedledee of the piece. Cedarcrantz and von Pilsach were recalled in disgrace; a new German, E.Schmidt, was appointed as president of the council while Henry Ide, who had resigned in disgust at Cedarcrantz's interference after just one year as U.S. Land Commissioner, was invited back as the new Chief Justice; he arrived in Apia on 3 November 1893 and Cedarcrantz departed by the same steamer. The Land Commission then got down to serious work and wound up its business by December 1894, having confirmed fifty-six per cent of land claims by German subjects, seven per cent by U.S. citizens and just three per cent by Britons.[23]

The sacking of his old enemies did not occasion any joy in the Stevenson breast; it was typical of him to fight hard to gain a moral point but then to feel sorry for the vanquished foe. He referred to 'the two dwindling stars. Poor devils! I like the one, and the other had a little wife, now lying in! . . . When I heard that the C.J. was in low spirits and never left his house, I could scarce refrain from going to him.' What might have sounded like humbug in other men was the literal truth in Louis's case, for on 12 September, when Cedarcrantz still intended to deport him, and all the rumours said that Louis's departure was imminent, Louis went to a public ball in Apia, bumped into Cedarcrantz in the press and shook his hands. RLS's rare ability to distinguish the man from the office comes through clearly in his account of the meeting and its sequel during the quadrille:

> The deuce of it is that personally I love this man; his eye speaks to me, I am
> pleased in his society. We exchanged a glance, and then a grin; the man took me
> in his confidence; and through the remainder of that prance, we pranced for each
> other. Hard to imagine any position more ridiculous; a week before he had been
> trying to rake evidence against me by browbeating and threatening a half-white
> interpreter; that very morning I had been writing most villainous attacks upon
> him for *The Times*; and we meet and smile, and – damn it! like each other. I
> do my best to damn the man and drive him from these islands; but weakness

endures – I love him. This is a thing I would despise in anyone else; but he
is so jolly insidious and ingratiating! No, sir, I can't dislike him; but if I don't
make hay of him, it shall not be for want of trying.[24]

In his love of the man but detestation of the despotic authority he
wielded, RLS was replaying with Cedarcrantz the psychic drama he had
acted out with his father.

Henry James expressed the fear that Stevenson's 'apparent plenitude of
physical life' in Samoa would be bound to affect adversely his literary
output, but in 1892, as his immersion in local politics increased, so too did
his productivity as a writer. On 17 May he finished *A Footnote to History*,
then after a brief 'holiday' began work on *The Young Chevalier*, whose design
he had sketched in the first months of the year. This was to be *the* RLS
Jacobite novel, based on the limbo period of Prince Charles Edward Stuart
in 1749–50, and featuring reappearances by both Alan Breck and the Master
of Ballantrae. Only one chapter survives, with a portion of another, but what
remains is a fragment of brilliant promise, making all lovers of Stevenson and
Jacobite lore regret that he did not see fit to press on with it. As so often with
RLS, he laid it aside when he encountered a 'block' and never returned to it.
Instead, he switched to another work in the Jacobite vein and, writing at great
speed between the end of May and the end of September, produced one of
his finest works, *Catriona* (known in the U.S.A. as *David Balfour*). This was
the fulfilment of an old promise to take the story of *Kidnapped* to a satisfying
conclusion; many critics complained that the first David Balfour novel had
been wrapped up with too great haste. To produce a novel of this quality
at such speed and in the midst of such political turmoil argues that RLS
was now at the height of his powers and fully justifies Fanny's judgement:
'Never was a novel written in more distracting circumstances.'[25]
   On 30 September he wrote to Colvin: 'David Balfour done, and its
author along with it, or nearly so.' He reported that the *Beach of Falesá*
and *Catriona* 'seem to me nearer what I mean than anything I have
ever done; nearer what I mean by fiction; the nearest thing before was
Kidnapped ... I am not forgetting *The Master of Ballantrae*, but that
lacked all pleasurableness, and hence was imperfect in essence.' He
later told Meredith he was convinced it was his best book and wrote to
Mrs Sitwell in the last year of his life: 'I shall never do a better book.'
His admirers largely agreed: J.M.Barrie wrote in December 1892 while
it was being serialised to say: 'I think the first four chapters of *David
Balfour* the finest beginning you have ever done.' Meredith agreed: 'As
for the writing, I say nothing more than that it may be the emulation
of young authors to equal it.' It was a commercial success too: after
serialisation in Britain and the U.S.A. in the winter of 1892–93 it was

published in book form in 1893; McClure paid him an advance of $8,000
(£1,600).

Although Alan Breck Stewart reappears in *Catriona*, in this sequel to
Kidnapped the Highland/Lowland conflict has a sexual dimension, with the
fiery Catriona taking on David Balfour this time. *Catriona* is a world away
from *Kidnapped* in tone and sensibility, which is why the youthful aficionados
of the boys' adventure features of the first book could not follow the author
into the jungle of sexual politics. This posed problems for the author too.
He wrote to Colvin in May: 'With all my romance I am a realist and a prosaist,
and a most fanatical lover of plain physical sensations plainly and expressly
rendered; hence my perils. To do love in the same spirit as I did (for instance)
D.Balfour's fatigue on the heather; my dear sir, there were grossness – ready
made!'[26] But in many ways the novel does recapitulate *Kidnapped*: the trek
of the lovers from Rotterdam to Leyden parallels the flight in the heather,
and the superb quarrel between David and Alan in the earlier book has as
its analogue the 'cold war' between David and Catriona.

This time around no one could doubt the similarities between RLS
and David Balfour. All his life Stevenson fought against the conviction
that he was a moral coward, and that his upbringing had made him so,
since his scepticism was cowardice (he thought), cowardice the mark of
the bourgeoisie, and Calvinism the legitimating ideology of the Lowland
bourgeois coward. At some level he always felt guilty that he had not gone
to Ireland in 1887, and that he had used illness and his father's death as
an alibi. This self-disgust is reflected in David's ambivalence: he wants to
give evidence at the trial of James Stewart of the Glen, wrongly accused
of compassing the murder of 'Red Colin' Campbell, but is afraid of the
consequences, so welcomes his imprisonment on the Bass Rock; his jailer
sees through his halfheartedness: 'Ye see, I was never entirely sure which
way of it ye really want it.' The contrast to Valjean in Hugo's *Les Misérables* is
plain: Valjean insists on testifying and seeing justice done though the heavens
fall – which they do – and it is clear why RLS admired him so much. Beyond
that, there is a clear parallel between David Balfour on Bass Rock and RLS
on Samoa: 'It seemed to me a safe place, as though I was escaped there out
of my troubles. No harm was to be offered me; a material impossibility, rock
and the deep sea, prevented me from fresh attempts.'[27]

However, it would be a mistake to push the parallel between RLS and
David Balfour too far. The 'Lowland inertia' which was such a feature of
Kidnapped reappears as a key Balfour trait, to the point where Professor
Kiely and others are prepared to argue that David is either impotent or
sexually inadequate, as evinced symbolically by his inability to use a sword.
Yet this reading, which leans heavily on an interpretation of Catriona as
harridan or 'ballbreaker', is surely overheated; Balfour may be the inept
and inactive post-Romantic Victorian hero but he is not as feckless as this.

RLS had always expressed the view that all perfect art must contain some humour, but hitherto he had not been able to integrate it satisfactorily into his dramatic or tragic work. As has been well said, many of the characters in *New Arabian Nights* – like the young man with the cream tarts, or the man who wants to be murdered as he has read Darwin and can't bear the idea of being descended from an ape – fit more easily into the universe of the theatre of the absurd. And even in *The Master of Ballantrae*, Mackellar and Burke, the court jesters to Henry and James respectively, do not really work at this level. In *Catriona*, for the first time RLS pulls off a kind of Shakespearean integration of comedy and drama, so that the 'signing off' reflections do not jar and seem organic to what has gone before: 'For the life of man upon this world of ours is a funny business. They talk of angels weeping; but I think they must more often be holding their sides, as they look on.'

Yet the real success of *Catriona* is in its treatment of women. It has been argued that Catriona herself is colourless and insipid, but this view can scarcely survive a close scrutiny of the chapters where David and Catriona cohabit chastely, and where the sexual electricity is palpable. What has prejudiced readers against Catriona is that Stevenson made her representative of sexuality while giving the wit and strong personality to Miss Grant, almost as though Catriona was a kind of refined version of Hardy's Arabella in *Jude the Obscure*, and Miss Grant was Sue Bridehead. It was symptomatic of Stevensonian duality that even when he at last presented women convincingly in one of his novels, he could not decide which of his heroines he preferred. 'I am very anxious to see what you will think of my two girls,' he wrote to Colvin in June. 'My own opinion is quite clear; I am in love with both. I foresee a few years of spiritual flirtations . . . For the duration of the two chapters in which I dealt with Miss Grant, I totally forgot my heroine, and even – but this is a flat secret – tried to win away David. I think I must try some day to marry Miss Grant.' Fanny later revealed that Barbara Grant was modelled on Coggie Ferrier, who combined beauty with a caustic tongue, and confirmed Louis's transfer of affections: 'From Catriona, who was meant to be the conventional heroine of the book, my husband gradually transferred his attention to Miss Grant, and it was with great difficulty that he was able to keep her in the secondary position in the story.'

Critics have always preferred Prestongrange's daughter to Catriona, and J.A.Hamerton thought that, paradoxically, the character of Miss Grant revealed more about the essential RLS than David Balfour did: 'His was just that quality of wit, that fine manner and great gentleness under a surface of polished raillery. For there was about him an extraordinary kindness and tenderness. No man was so deferential, so encouraging, so much interested in the homely affairs of another.'[28] There is just one slight problem about David Balfour's amatory tensions: at eighteen he seems a trifle on the young side. RLS had given hostages to fortune by making David seventeen at the beginning of *Kidnapped* – almost certainly a decision influenced by the consideration that his favourite fictional character, d'Artagnan, was seventeen at the start of *The Three Musketeers*.

RLS's growing confidence, much in evidence in *Catriona*, accounts for the excellence of his two female characters. He wrote to Colvin exuberantly:

> As for women, I am no more in fear of them: I can do a sort all right, age makes me less afraid of a petticoat, but I am a little in fear of grossness ... This has kept me off the sentiment hitherto, and now I am to try: Lord! Of course Meredith can do it, and so could Shakespeare ... And hence how to sugar. Of course I mean something different from the false fire of Hardy – as false a thing as ever I perused, unworthy of Hardy and untrue to all I know of life. If ever I do a rape, which may the almighty God forfend! you would hear a noise about my rape, and it should be a man that did it!

The reason Louis had hitherto kept off significant women in his novels was twofold: he refused to write about them if he had to submit to the whims of Grundyism; and Fanny disliked his female characters. She claimed to find them wooden, but a more likely explanation is that, rendered truthfully, they both got in the way of sales to the conventional Victorian bookbuying public and revealed more about her husband and herself than she cared to have known. The greater freedom Louis enjoyed in *Catriona* is further evidence that he was breaking free of her gravitational pull; but he still had to suffer censorship from Colvin and his editors. The most notorious example is the following change from manuscript to printed page: in his manuscript Louis had David Balfour say: 'I am thanking the good God that he has let me see you naked'; the published version reads: 'I am thanking the good God that he has let me see you so.' Sometimes Louis grew weary with the struggle to be truthful about sex. He told Lloyd:

> How the French misuse their freedom; see nothing worth writing about save the eternal triangle; while we, who are muzzled like dogs, but who are infinitely wider in our outlook, are condemned to avoid half the life that passes us by. What books Dickens could have written had he been permitted! Think of Thackeray as unfettered as Flaubert or Balzac! What books I might have written myself!

RLS was twenty years too early to be a D.H.Lawrence, and he could never employ the circumlocutions of Henry James, but he still managed to slip a remarkable amount of sexuality past the unsleeping censors, as in this description of Marie-Madeleine in *The Young Chevalier*:

She was of a grave countenance, rarely smiling; yet it seemed 'to be written upon every part of her that she rejoiced in life. Her husband loved the heels of her feet and the knuckles of her fingers; he loved her like a glutton and a brute; his love hung about her like an atmosphere; one that came by chance into the wine-shop was aware of the passion; and it might be said that by the strength of it the woman had been drugged or spellbound. She knew not if she loved or loathed him; he was always in her eyes like something monstrous – monstrous in his love, monstrous in his person, horrific but imposing in his violence; and her sentiment swung back and forward from desire to sickness. But the mean, where it dwelt chiefly, was an apathetic fascination, partly of horror: as of Europa in mid-ocean with her bull.[29]

It was no wonder that J.M.Barrie wrote to Stevenson in 1894: 'I think there can be no question that the love story of Catriona and David is the best thing you have ever done. And it is just about the only thing I thought you could never do.' Brimful of confidence, RLS decided to face the greatest challenge: a novel where the protagonist was a woman and all the leading characters were female. He planned a story of a doomed love affair between a South Seas planter and a woman, to be entitled *Sophia Scarlett* – 'a kind of love affair between the heroine and a dying planter who is a poet! large orders for RLS.' Sadly, this made even less progress than the novel about Prince Charles Edward Stuart, and was laid aside in favour of the planned 'Scottish trilogy' – *Catriona*, *The Young Chevalier* and *Weir of Hermiston*.[30]

In addition to the two major projects completed in 1892, and the two started and laid aside, Louis also began jotting down ideas for a boy's book to be called *The Go-Between*. His pace of work was nothing short of remarkable, not only in view of the turbulence of Samoan politics, in which he was deeply inveigled, but because of the stress engendered by his family. First, there was Lloyd. Almost to the end of his life RLS continued to idolise the young man, though this 1893 pen portrait provided for J.M.Barrie is surprisingly clearheaded for one who was always prepared to make excuses for him and give him the benefit of every doubt:

Six foot, blond, eye-glasses – British eye-glasses too. Address ranging from an elaborate civility to a freezing haughtiness. Decidedly witty. Has seen an enormous amount of the world; keeps nothing of youth, but some of its intolerance. Unexpected soft streak for the forlorn. When he is good, he is very, very good, but when he is cross he is horrid ... Rather stiff with his equals, but apt to be very kindly with his inferiors – the only undemonstrative member of the family, which otherwise wears its heart on both sleeves.

'Whatever Lloyd may have contributed to the general good at Vailima – and it does not seem to have been much – he clearly took out a great deal more.' This, from Jenni Calder, is the most charitable possible interpretation that squares with the facts. RLS was still blind to his stepson's utter ruthlessness. Lloyd returned from a long trip to Scotland in February 1891, yet within ten months of not very arduous duties as an overseer at Vailima, he felt himself under the absolute necessity of getting away for another extended holiday, this time to San Francisco. Heedless of or indifferent to Louis's financial problems, he wheedled the money out of him for a lengthy sojourn in California. Well might RLS comment that Lloyd had seen an enormous part of the world; he had seen most of it with his stepfather's funds. As for RLS's political ambitions, Lloyd had only contempt as he made clear later in a remarkable example of patronising *de haut en bas* superciliousness: 'Samoa filled his need for the dramatic and the grandiose; he expanded on its teeming stage, where he could hold warriors in leash and play Richelieu to half-naked kings.'

After RLS's death, Lloyd realised that any biographer examining the Vailima years would soon spot the negligible contribution he had made to the household and his leech-like battening on Stevenson. Panicking at the thought that Colvin would be writing the authorised biography, in August 1899 he addressed him in his favoured peremptory style: 'You would very greatly oblige me by getting in the introductory to the Samoan life, the fact that in 1891 I was offered the secretaryship of the Samoan Land Commission, and in 1892 was invited by S.S.McClure to enter his publishing business and refused in both instances owing to Louis's very strongly expressed desire for me to remain with him until his death.'[31] Every single one of these statements is mendacious: there is no documentary record of either of these offers, and the idea of such a politically sensitive post as secretary to the Land Commission being offered to the stepson of a man who was, in the eyes of the Powers, a 'troublemaker' is consummately risible, even if we could overcome our *a priori* stupefaction at the idea of Cedarcrantz and von Pilsach seeking out a *flâneur*, armed only with riding whip and guitar, for a position of responsibility. Moreover, Lloyd's own words tell against him. RLS did not think he was on the point of death in Samoa, and in any event had already exhorted Lloyd to depart for Cambridge on a three-year course of study.

1892 also saw the end of Joe Strong, whose lazy and incompetent contributions to life at Vailima had by this time taxed RLS's patience to the utmost. Noting a mysterious 'inventory shrinkage', Louis set a trap for the pilferer and discovered Strong at work during the night, robbing the cellar and storeroom with the use of a duplicate key. In fury at being discovered, Joe maligned Belle and Fanny all over Apia. The crisis came in the summer. For a long time the Vailima household had wondered about his frequent visits 'to the dentist' in Apia which somehow always necessitated his walking back in the moonlight late at night. Then it was discovered that Strong had been leading a double life, cohabiting with a Samoan 'wife' – a mistress from his pre-1889 days in Upolu – in the day and returning for subsistence to Vailima at night; at Vailima he was also carrying on an affair with the maid, Faauma, whose beauty Louis often commented on. Since Joe's bigamy was an open secret among the 'beach' there was no lack of witnesses and Belle was able to obtain a swift divorce; Louis was made sole guardian of the child.

In despair at the loss of his meal-ticket, Strong went up to Vailima to petition Louis for another chance, but he had played the role of meek penitent once too often and Louis gave him short shrift. His visit occurred late one night, and he came unannounced; Fanny saw him emerging from Louis's room like an apparition, and the shock brought on an attack of angina. In fury at being rebuffed, Strong stormed into the home of his old friend Moors, where he found a willing audience; as Fanny put it: 'for some reason, only explainable by Joe Strong, he is our bitter enemy; more particularly Lloyd's and mine; we two being Joe's pet aversion.' Here Fanny was being disingenuous: she must have known that it was her rudeness and brusqueness that had alienated Moors; as for the enmity between Lloyd and Strong, this is surely a case of two idlers competing for the same space.[32]

Louis's anger towards the man to whom he had given so many chances can be gauged from one simple fact which, on paper, sounds like the action of an unbalanced man. A cache of goods arrived from New South Wales for Vailima in 1892, and a photograph was taken of the happy event, featuring RLS, Lloyd, two Samoans and Joe Strong in the centre of the composition; when collecting together snapshots for his album later, Louis cut Strong out of the picture and carefully matched the foliage of the trees so that the omission would not be noticed. Doubtless Louis's anger was enhanced by the consideration that the fallout from the crisis with Joe Strong had largely descended on him, for Fanny's depression, plainly noticeable in 1891, had by 1892 taken such a hold that Louis feared for her sanity.

There were many factors at play in Fanny's breakdown. One was the stress of Vailima, both objective, in that running the estate was an ordeal, and subjective, in that Fanny invested so much of her identity in the struggle against the wilderness and took it as a personal insult when the jungle would not stay tamed. She found the jealousy of the white community hard to bear and resented the canards directed by the 'beach' against the 'folks on the hill'. She did not have Louis's sense of the absurd and gift for puncturing scurrility with humour; when he heard the rumour that Belle was his daughter by a black woman, he entered into the spirit by weaving fantasies around this woman, whom he imagined as a Moroccan. Sometimes when Fanny's caustic tongue ran away with her, Louis would say in tones of injured innocence: 'Moroccy never spoke to me like that!'

As supervisor of all additions and improvements to the house, director of agriculture and sole correspondent with the Botanical Gardens at Kew, Brisbane, Honolulu and Florida, Fanny had the most difficult job at Vailima and worked hard at it; it was a mortification to her that her golden dream of making Vailima self-sufficient – through the sale of coffee, cacao and vanilla on the market – never came true. In comparison to her labours, Lloyd's tasks as bookkeeper, general manager and overseer of the gang of outside boys were a mere part-time job, and Belle's role as châtelaine – in charge of the house, its staff and their training – was a bagatelle. All the real discipline on the estate had to come from her. Using her reputation as witch, when she suspected Lafaele of being the culprit after the theft of three piglets, she put her 'magic' into operation. First she engaged him in conversation, then advanced the two forefingers of her right hand towards his eyes; when he closed them, she substituted two left forefingers, touched him on the eyes and meanwhile tapped him on the back with her right hand. When Lafaele opened his eyes, he saw the right forefingers being withdrawn; Fanny then told him she had raised her devil and that from now on the man who had stolen her piglets would not be able to sleep properly.

In her agriculture Fanny was unlucky, and a much more balanced person would have become exasperated by the recurring comedy of errors that beset her enterprises. On one occasion she asked Lafaele to plant vanilla seedlings; he proceeded to plant them upside down. Fanny then sent him into Apia on an errand while she and Belle replanted them right side up. Down in Apia, Lafaele had been brooding about his mistress's displeasure and decided to return at night while the family was asleep and give Fanny a surprise by planting the seedlings properly. He returned, replanted them and next morning showed his handiwork to Fanny in triumph: the seedlings were now upside down once more and did not survive. That was not the worst of it: every now and then Fanny was pulled up short by the vast chasm that separated her from the mental world of the Samoans, as when Lafaele asked permission to poison the family of a man he disliked, and another servant, Arak, requested leave to take a gun and kill Melanesian 'blackboys' who were skulking in the bush as refugees from the German plantations.

Beyond the alien inefficiency of her helpers, Fanny had Nature to contend with, and she gradually became convinced that the jungle was involved in a personal conspiracy against her. She later told Gosse that she had been driven almost mad by the monstrous rapidity of the growth of vegetation in Samoa, and her attitudes influenced RLS in his essay 'Pulvis et Umbra' of which the critic Edward Marsh said in 1892: 'the weird and beautiful "Pulvis et Umbra" strips the idea of man to an abhorrent nakedness only to show how wonderful and consoling are his imperfect virtues.' There is a case for saying that in their superstitious view of Nature and refusal to believe that the elements were neutral, Louis and Fanny were too alike in

sensibility and therefore bad for each other. Fanny's sense of a hostile and
malevolent nature fed into RLS's abiding sense of Calvinistic evil, and he
wrote:

> I wonder if anyone had ever the same attitude to Nature as I hold, and have held
> for so long? This business fascinates me like a tune or a passion; yet all the while
> I thrill with a strong distaste. The horror of the thing, objective and subjective, is
> always present to my mind; the horror of creeping things, a superstitious horror of
> the void and the powers about me, the horror of my own devastation and continual
> murders. The life of the plants comes through my finger-tips, their struggles go
> to my heart like supplications. I feel myself blood-boltered; then I look back on
> my cleared grass, and count myself an ally in fair quarrel, and make stout my
> heart.

All this has struck some observers as over-ripe in more senses than one.
Professor Kiely sees a sexual aetiology and remarks: 'In its combination of
disgust and fascination, it is a response comparable to that of an adolescent
to the first signs of his own puberty.'[33]

However, there were elements in Fanny's increasingly severe mental illness that had no rational basis whatsoever. Her hysteria over Joe
Strong's final disgrace was followed by an even steeper overreaction on
the subject of Countess Jersey. Fanny took an instant dislike to her titled
visitor, finding her too much like Kipling's Mrs Hawksbee and part of a
'selfish champagne Charlie set', as she wrote to Mrs Sitwell. She resented
the fact that the Countess was every bit as emancipated, unconventional and
adventurous as she was herself, and even more that Louis liked her and
made a fuss of her. Fanny pointedly refused to join the 'Amelia Balfour'
expedition to Mataafa's village in August 1892, and a year later was still
fuming about the female type she imagined Lady Jersey to represent. 'What
sort of a devil from hell is the British matron, and why should I, of all
people in the world, take her for my pattern in conduct? It is like being
a sham paralytic. I fear I shall carry away something yet. I always despised
Mary Shelley, and here I am no whit better. I despise myself and that's the
fair truth.'

Louis admitted later that Fanny's jealousy over Countess Jersey turned
the time of her visit into a 'wretched period' at home. Her biographer,
Margaret Mackay, comments:

> She kept on nagging with such wild unreason as never before. It was almost
> more than he could bear. Any woman must be going out of her mind to make
> such a mountain out of a molehill . . . It may have struck him with a shock in
> those early months of her 'neurasthenia' that his own wife was the embodiment
> of a female Jekyll and Hyde. His success emphasised her own failure as a creative
> artist. Her coin of love/hate had admiration on one side, subconscious envy on
> the other.[34]

Why did she break down after years of struggle just when she seemed to have attained what she wanted? It is a well-observed phenomenon that people often crack from delayed stress, so that the usual chain of cause and effect seems unduly attenuated; the example of those who die young after surviving the savage sea for months in an open boat is sometimes cited. It may be that the impetus for Fanny's breakdown came from the accumulated stresses of the past; but it is also possible that it came from her fears of the future. In all kinds of ways Louis seemed to be growing away from her and making it clear that she was no longer indispensable. He did not depend on her nursing in Samoa, as his health was excellent; and as he had the wider expatriate community of Apia to draw on, he was not in thrall to her as in the cocoon of Hyères or the icy cage of Davos. Perhaps, most of all, with his new-found confidence that was enabling him to produce masterpieces like *Falesá* and *Catriona*, he had outgrown her artistically and no longer relied on her advice. The planned Scottish trilogy seemed especially threatening, for there he was returning to themes and roots where she was an alien. It was true that he still needed her help at Vailima, but to a woman of Fanny's temperament that was not enough; her vanity required that she be all in all to him, and if this was not possible, she would (albeit unconsciously) strike back at him.

It is also possible that she found his new freedom in treating sexual themes an obscure threat. Louis was a faithful husband and had a rigid moral code, but to a mentally disturbed woman such considerations mean little. It was clear to her that he had a roving eye and a rare appreciation of female beauty: his description of the beautiful body of Faauma, Lafaele's mistress (and sometime Joe Strong's) – as also his observation of the contours of Java as she bent over the fireplace – made that plain. This could be one of the reasons for her many sudden and unannounced irruptions into Moors's house. Mrs Maryland Allen, who in the first decade of the 1900s met many Samoans with strong memories of RLS, reported that Fanny was deeply unpopular with them for this practice. 'Wife?' said one. 'She was not his wife, she was his policeman.'[35]

Louis's public loyalty to his wife was striking. In a letter to Miss Taylor in October 1892, at the height of Fanny's psychic hurricane, he wrote:

Ill or well, rain or shine, a little blue indefatigable figure is to be observed howking about certain patches of garden. She comes in heated and bemired up to the eyebrows, late for every meal. She has reached a sort of tragic placidity. Whenever she plants anything new, the boys weed it up. Whenever she tries to keep anything for seed, the house boys throw it away. And she has reached that pitch of a kind of noble dejection that she would almost say, she did not mind.

In his poems there is further praise: in 'My Family' he describes

Fanny and Belle as 'My pair of fairies plump and dark' and says he has no need of fame or wealth as long as he has these two by his side. Yet there are more ambivalent strains in the verses: the duo are distinguished from European women by 'the naked foot, the indiscreeter petticoat' and of the two:

> One apes the shrew, one the coquette.

In a judgement that looks forward to Katharine Osbourne's dithyramb about Fanny's 'primitive' qualities, he says she is:

> More like what Eve in Eden was.

The lynx-eyed Lloyd, who, even Belle admitted, was in the habit of rewriting 'verbatim' conversations so that he (Lloyd) always appeared in the best possible light, spotted that not all RLS's poetic references to his mother would stand critical scrutiny if he was successfully to promote the legend of Louis and Fanny as latter-day Romeo and Juliet, so, with Belle's help, he doctored the published version of the poem 'To the Stormy Petrel'. And it was left to Moors to point out that the 'shrew' and the 'coquette' were often at each other's throats, that yet another occasion for Fanny's unbalanced outbursts in the years 1891–93 was her resentment of the growing understanding between Belle and her husband, to the point where it was Belle, not she, who became the principal literary confidante.[36]

Most of the time Louis used soft words to turn away wifely wrath, so that Moors and others concluded that he was dominated by Fanny and that in his eyes she could do no wrong: 'I make bold to say,' declared Moors, 'that neither was his character bettered by it [his marriage], nor his art benefited her ... Mrs Strong, too, was headstrong and talkative, and generally got her way.' It is true that Louis was extremely indulgent to his two women (and his three when Maggie was there), but he was no hen-pecked inadequate, and was quite capable of putting his foot down when the invisible line was crossed; his basic position was that he would give women under his protection anything so long as they did not transgress his personal moral code. Louis admitted he quite liked disputes but hated it if people were angry with him as a result of rows or disagreements. When he claimed he was of a forgiving nature, Fanny denied it and said that Louis merely thought he forgave but, like a true Celt, 'lays the bundle on the shelf and long after takes it down and quarrels with it'. Louis protested at this injustice: 'No, it is on the shelf, I admit, and I would let it stay there. But if anyone else pulled it down, I would tear it with fury. In fact I am made up of contradictory elements, and have a clearing house inside me where I dishonour cheques of bitterness.'

A spendthrift himself, he indulged Fanny and Belle in their love of luxury. A letter from Fanny to Mrs Sitwell in September 1892, requesting her to purchase and send out a blue lace mantle lined with Surah silk, shows the mistress of Vailima on typical form. The entertainments, displays, parties and balls given at Vailima – and that made it the social magnet of Samoa – were partly Louis displaying his lust for life, and partly also his indulgence of Fanny's social ambitions and a way of warding off her depressions. Later, of course, when Fanny and her family began to be criticised for their extravagance and the way they had turned RLS into a workhorse, Fanny subtly tried to deflect criticism by alleging that most of the 'unnecessary' expenditures at Vailima were incurred when Louis tried to help Mataafa; she instanced the expenses involved in his plan to build a mill for manufacturing fibre, whose object was raising the living standard of Mataafa's men and which came to nothing because of the outbreak of the 1893 civil war.[37] Those who had scrutinised the accounts closely, like Baxter, knew better.

Even though she was losing her literary influence, Fanny still intervened whenever she suspected her husband of wanting to tell the truth about his marriage by winks and nods in his work. One of the short stories that was to comprise the farrago published as *Island Nights Entertainments* – principally notorious because it achieved the juxtaposition of the 'Island Voices' and 'The Bottle Imp' with *Falesá* against which Stevenson had struggled so long – was 'The Waif Woman'. Based on a Norse saga, this was a tale of a possessive wife whose sexual allure gave her mastery over her husband and whose greed was punished by fate. Fanny was adamant that this story should not see the light of day; she saw clearly enough that the woman was herself. She prevailed, but to preserve the Fanny and Louis of legend pretended that the story had been 'rejected' by the publishers – an impossibility at this stage in RLS's career, as she knew well – and encouraged Belle to promote a report to this effect. Those, like J.C.Furnas, who claim that this story's non-appearance was due to reasons other than Fanny's intense opposition, do their credibility no good by attempting to deny the obvious.[38]

Even more telling circumstantial evidence that RLS intended 'The Waif Woman' as a hint to his public of the true state of affairs at Vailima is that he originally intended it to be juxtaposed to 'The Bottle Imp'. Now the subtext of the 'Bottle Imp' was the moral of a woman who would do anything for her husband. In the 1920s Hellman seized on this piece of evidence and declared: 'It becomes manifest that in the final period of his life he decided he has been too much the chivalrous husband, and, under the guise of fiction, he had at last decided to give the world a chance to guess the truth.' For this he had been much pilloried, especially by J.C.Furnas. Yet there is still more circumstantial evidence backing Hellman, for those who are prepared to investigate minutely. It is clear that, despite his public avowals of loyalty to Fanny, Louis sometimes let his irritation with her slip out. He told Colvin that he was beginning to have a suspicion of the true scope and extent of his wife's mental illness; for weeks on end she was a stranger, and the moods, tantrums and illusions made him aware something was badly wrong. For this reason he preferred to stay in his room working or decamp to Apia, and he confessed to Colvin that he felt annoyed when he had to break off work on 19 May, to celebrate his twelfth wedding anniversary.[39]

Then there is the continuing riddle about the provisions of his will. The original will, dated 14 June 1889 in Honolulu, bequeathed his property in life rent to Fanny and in fee to Lloyd. The other beneficiaries were Nellie Sanchez, Belle, Austin, Joe Strong, Colvin, Bob and Katharine de Mattos. Against Fanny's frequently reiterated pleas Louis refused to cut Katharine de Mattos out of the will. The suggestion thereby planted – that he did not regard Fanny as blameless in the affair – is reinforced by his even more bizarre refusal to drop Joe Strong when a new, and final, will was drawn up in September 1893. The inference must be that his initial anger towards Joe had cooled and, on due reflection and in the light of Fanny's crazed behaviour during 1891–93, he decided there was something to be said for Strong's version of events, as assiduously peddled by Moors.[40]

The other clue lies in RLS's attitude to Henley. Because of the inevitable association of ideas in his mind between Fanny on the rampage and the dreadful quarrel of 1888, an oscillation in his sentiments towards Henley can almost be taken as a barometric reading of the stage of his relationship with his wife. In Honolulu in 1889, when the dust had settled from the heat of battle, RLS revolved in his mind what he really thought about the quarrel and who was really culpable. The result was his poem 'In Memoriam E.H.' – a paean to Henley's mother who had so heroically brought up six children after her husband died penniless. This was an obvious olive-branch to Henley and a tacit admission that he thought Fanny had been in the wrong.

Now, in 1892, he wrote to Henley to compliment him on his latest volume of verse. And to Baxter he was even more fulsome in his praise: 'His new volume is the work of a real poet . . . How poorly Kipling compares! K. is all smart journalism and cleverness: it is all bright and shallow and limpid, like a business paper – a good one, *s'entend*; but there is no blot of heart's blood and the Old Night; there are no harmonics; there is scarce harmony, to his music; and in Henley – all of these.'[41]

There is sourness, too, in Louis's asides to Baxter in August and September about the new wing to Vailima that Fanny, in alliance with Maggie, was insisting on having built; the reason is also of passing interest:

Now I seem to be let in for the addition to my house. It is no choice of mine – and I dislike it. But Lloyd has no room . . . I wished to build him a cottage ad interim; and my mother, who saw it would postpone, perhaps prevent, the rest of the house, objected . . . To tell you the truth I am most unhappy that I have got embarked in the building of this new house, and I know there is going to be the deuce to pay to get to the year's end.

The three women entered into the Vailima extension project with gusto – Fanny perhaps less so because of her depression. It was a consummate piece of extravagance, designed to make Vailima a glittering venue for balls and parties, so that the initial expense contained a multiplier entailing further expense. Far from feeling guilty about the extra strain imposed on Louis through having to earn another $7,500, Belle later brazened it out and claimed that most of the expense at Vailima was due to RLS's unpredictability: she and the other women never knew how many of his cronies he would bring back from Apia for dinner!

The new wing consisted of two blocks of equal size, the second slightly behind the front level of the original house. Downstairs there were three rooms, bathroom, storeroom and cellars, while upstairs were five bedrooms and a library. On the ground floor a verandah, twelve feet deep, ran in front of the whole house and along one side of it. A large hall, about 60′ long by 40′ wide, lined and ceiled with varnished redwood, occupied the whole of the ground floor; here were the busts of the Stevenson ancestors, two Burmese gods flanking the great staircase, the piano, some carved heirloom cabinets dated 1642, the Sargent portrait of RLS with Fanny in the background, the St Gaudens medallion, and other family pictures and treasures, especially the big built-in safe believed to contain the bottle imp from the story.

The completion of this wing was the signal for a frenzied burst of entertainment at Vailima. There were dinner parties whenever a British or American warship came to port, for in Louis the Anglo-Saxon navies had a great champion: he used to have a printed list of all warships that visited Apia fixed like a shingle on his front door, to which the names of each succeeding ship would be added. A particular favourite was HMS *Curaçao*, in which Louis finally succeeded in his ambition – thwarted in 1891 when with Sewall – of visiting the more remote islands of eastern Samoa; he liked to invite the ship's band up to Vailima for an evening of music-making, good food and good wine. Maggie left a record of the fare for one evening's reception of the *Curaçao*: roast pig with *miti* sauce, fricasséed chicken, baked *taro*, coconut cream baked in leaves, Cape gooseberry tart, fine wines. Louis also loved entertaining on a more intimate scale: Sewall, the U.S. consul, was a frequent visitor, and Henry Ide and his daughter, and Bazett Haggard. Additionally, he gave a weekly party for the Samoans and half-castes he liked, and whom he could not invite to his grander receptions because of the snobbery and prejudice of the time; this was usually an informal affair with cakes and lemonade on the front verandah, at which the family would be the only whites present. Small wonder that he described his rate of expenditure as 'hellish' and claimed that he grew grey when he pored over the monthly accounts with Lloyd. Baxter warned him that he was overextending himself: 'My trouble is that there will require to be a very large production to keep up present expenditure, and that is of course a matter of health. It cannot be imprudent to overhaul all unnecessary expense and get the place as soon as possible into a source of profit. This is not Preaching. It is only the Prudent Forelook of the painful Doer.'[42]

Part of the trouble was Louis's exuberant, expansive, Celtic hospitality and his gregarious spirit. Some of the tension with Fanny came from their differential perceptions: Fanny liked hardly anybody, but Louis was intensely interested in people and had catholic tastes; high society or waterfront bar, it mattered not to him so long as he could meet larger-than-life characters or people with fascinating stories to tell. He had been severely prejudiced against the steamship captain Morse by his reputation, but when they met Louis liked him immensely: 'he has a wonderful charm of strength, loyalty and simplicity.' But the initial meeting with Morse was vitiated by a scourge just beginning to appear in the Pacific: tourism. Louis spent an uncomfortable hour on board Morse's ship being photographed as the local celebrity by female tourists and was 'dogged about the deck by a diminutive Hebrew with a Kodak, the click of which kept time to my progress like a pair of castanets . . . the whole celebrity business was particularly characteristic. The captain has certainly never read a word of mine; and as for the Jew with the Kodak, he had never heard of me till he came on board.'

His love of people extended to the 'natives'. When Vailima's new wing was being built, a hundred Melanesian 'boys' were employed, with twenty-four oxen, under the direction of two German overseers. Louis loved to listen to their chatter: he noted how they referred to cattle as 'bullamacow' and tried to engage them in conversation with a cheery 'good morning'. Having only ever received a grunt in reply, if that, he was almost resolved to give up but tried one last time. As he reached the end of a line of workers, one of the blacks called out, in perfect English, 'You good man – always say "good morning".' Louis commented in amazement: 'It was good to think that these poor creatures should think so much of so small a piece of civility and strange that (thinking so) they should be so dull as not to return it.'

As a kindly man, he did not find it easy to impose draconian measures on his work force, so that when the harsh Lloyd was away in San Francisco on his mandatory annual jaunt, staff discipline suffered. A twelve-year old boy, Mitaiele, went berserk in June and had to be manacled prior to 'therapy'; in what Louis describes as 'pure Rider Haggard', a local remedy was applied to his eyes, ears and nose to chase away evil spirits. The dementia vanished as though by magic, but the other Samoans backed the boy's story to the hilt and swore up and down that they had seen the lad's family ghosts appear and call on him to vanish into the forest.[43]

When Lloyd returned from San Francisco in August he came accompanied by a Stevenson relative named Graham Balfour, later destined to be RLS's first biographer. This time the Osbournes finally found someone they liked. Lloyd's enthusiasm did not wear off after the first flush, as it had with King, and, *mirabile dictu*, Fanny took to him also. Balfour filled the vacuum left at Vailima by Joe Strong, and the flighty Belle was soon wishing he would fill it in another sense. Fanny encouraged the fantasy that Balfour might be persuaded to marry Belle and wrote to Mrs Sitwell: 'It will be a wrench when he goes. He says he will come back, but I know what will happen; he will marry somebody, and we'll hate his wife, and there'll be the end of it; for of course, if we hate his wife, he must hate us.'

However, the displaced Joe Strong was still not quite out of the picture, for he continued to 'decorate the beach', as Louis put it; he sometimes bumped into Strong in Apia and Joe carried the encounter off with bluff geniality as though nothing had happened. It irritated Louis that such an irresponsible and feckless parent as Joe still had access to his son, and he determined to whisk the boy away out of his reach. A pretext was afforded by the sudden death of Nellie Sanchez's husband in California (ironically from the disease, consumption, that was supposed to be going to carry Louis off). Louis decided that Austin Strong should be educated in California; if he boarded with Nellie, this would provide him with the pretext for sending her generous sums for his maintenance without appearing to be doling out charity. The upshot was that Louis assumed the rent and other expenses for a cottage near Stanford University, where Austin would attend a preparatory school with the intention of attending the university later. In September Austin waved goodbye to his mother; Louis put him in the charge of Captain Morse for the journey, and sealed the deal in the captain's stateroom with a river of iced champagne.[44]

1892 undoubtedly saw RLS at his peak, miraculously when one considers the financial problems and threats of deportation he was labouring under, to say nothing of the anguish caused by Fanny's continued mental illness. Seemingly like Buddha, able to meditate while tigers roared around him, Louis not only achieved his best ever literary productivity, both in terms of absolute output and earnings, but found time for an amazing amount of reading – and all this while maintaining a hectic social life. He wrote to William Morris to congratulate him on *Sigurd the Volsung*; waded through a mass of historical material Andrew Lang had sent him as research notes for *The Young Chevalier*; wrote a lengthy (hostile) critique of Hardy's *Tess of the D'Urbervilles*; wrote to Barrie with detailed criticism of the plot and structure of Meredith's *Richard Feverel*; and devoured masses of Henry James, Kipling and Barrie, his 'Muses Three'. A letter to Colvin in September provides a characteristic snapshot of RLS the reader:

I am now well on with the third part of *La Débâcle* (by Zola). The two first I liked very much; the second completely knocking me; so far as it has gone, this third part appears the ramblings of a dull man who has forgotten what he has to say – he reminds me of an MP. But Sedan was really great, and I will pick no holes. The batteries under fire, the red-cross folk, the county charge – perhaps, above all, Major Bouroche and the operations, all beyond discussion; and every word about the Emperor splendid.

Such was RLS's energy at the time that he chided Henry James for under-production: 'With Kipling, as you know, there are reservations to be made. And you and Barrie don't write enough.'

In his euphoria at his new-found health and energy, Louis began to reconsider all his projects for visiting Europe; the farthest he now felt inclined to venture was Ceylon. But, after all, why should his friends not come out to visit him? Two weeks would bring them to San Francisco and another two to Samoa. He urged the trip particularly on Barrie, telling him that the Pacific did wonders for the health and everyone foreign on Samoa except his wife had Scots blood in their veins; besides, 'the natives are the next thing conceivable to the Highlanders before the '45.'[45] Louis forgot, however, that the key to 1892 was that he had not strayed beyond Samoa. Failure to appreciate that lesson was to bring him low the following year.

18

Samoa: Fourth Year

1893 opened inauspiciously with an influenza epidemic in Samoa, brought to Apia by a passing ship. First to succumb at Vailima was Maggie, who panicked and took the first steamer to Sydney. Fanny and Lloyd suffered from mild doses, whose main symptoms were ulcerated throats, but soon after his mother's departure Louis was stricken, sustained a couple of haemorrhages and for most of January was seriously ill. He had begun the year with a flourish, switching impulsively to a new novel, *St Ives*, at which he worked from 8 am. to 4 p.m.; it was the combination of flu and overwork that brought him low.

Unable to work or even to lean forward for fear of triggering another bloody flux, Louis was reduced to writing on a slate at his side. As always when ill, he pretended to be another person – this time the imaginary character was a Mr Dumbey – showing clearly his need to detach himself from this tubercular alien 'thing' that occupied his body, and pointing once again to the conclusion that the deep springs of Jekyll and Hyde came from his illness.

And now, for the first time, the extravagant spendthrift Belle finally earned her keep at Vailima. Towards the end of 1892, seeing RLS struggling with a mountain of correspondence, Belle offered her services as secretary; thereafter Louis always referred to her as 'the amanuensis'. When she saw the agonised frustration of this creative artist, now unable to speak because of illness, who a few days before had been dictating *St Ives* to her while he acted out all the characters, with gestures and voices to match, she hit on the idea of communicating in deaf-and-dumb language. The first experiment was a success and together they completed five pages; when he became too exhausted to continue, Fanny would entertain him by playing patience and he would point to the cards she should play.

Gradually Belle and Louis increased the daily output to seven pages;

Louis felt his strength returning and tears stood in his eyes at the thought that he would be able to continue his work. He was also deeply moved by the loyalty of his favourite Samoans. Although Polynesians were as contemptuous of emptying slops as Europeans would be of cheating at cards, when the entire household was ill in the last week of January Henry went round with a slop-bucket and encouraged the sick by entering their mosquito nets, Catholic and Protestant alike, to pray with them. The result was predictable: Henry himself then went down with the flu.[1]

By mid-February Louis had recovered and ate a whole chicken and a tower of hot cakes at breakfast to celebrate. It was decided that the family would go down to Sydney to convalesce; Maggie had by this time decided that she needed a break from life under the Southern Cross and had sailed for Scotland, where she remained for the next twelve months. The sacking of von Pilsach and Cedarcrantz had perceptibly altered German attitudes to RLS and they now apparently considered him a man worth conciliating: 'the manager of the German firm (O strange, changed days) danced attendance upon us all morning; his boat conveyed us to and from the steamer.'

The SS *Mariposa* called first at Auckland, where Louis had a long talk with Sir George Grey on Samoan affairs: Grey agreed with him on every point, declared that Providence had brought him to Samoa, and even committed himself in writing to the proposition that the forcible disarming of Mataafa and his warriors by the Powers would be a grave error. Louis was also interviewed by W.H.Triggs, reporter on the *Christchurch Press*, and gave him a scoop by divulging his true feelings about Samoa, which were that he lived there partly for his health and partly for romantic reasons; he had no particular sentiment for Upolu *per se*. When Triggs later sent him a proof of his intended article, stating that Stevenson lived on the island *purely* for his health, Louis sent back the following correction: 'Certainly if this were all I would prefer to go to hell ... Honolulu suited me equally well, the high Alps probably better. I chose Samoa instead of Honolulu, for instance, for the simple and eminently satisfactory reason that it was less civilized.'[2]

Another interview when he docked in Sydney, with what Fanny sardonically referred to as a 'lady journalist' from London, conducted in a draughty part of the ship, was allegedly the cause of a heavy cold which caused the family to beat a rapid retreat from Sydney after a few days, instead of the planned three weeks. The sojourn in Sydney comprised little more than a dinner at the Cosmopolitan Club, a visit to a physician, and a prowl through the bookshops. Dr Fairfax Ross, who gave him a thorough medical examination, gave his opinion that his patient was suffering from 'exposure, malaria, worry and over-work'; the theme of worry and overwork was to be stressed by many observers during the last two years of his life. Louis always tended to disappoint his more superficial admirers, who had stereotypical ideas on how a celebrity should behave, and he notably disabused a bookish, would-be cerebral assistant in a bookshop, who proudly brought out the latest Barrie, Meredith and Anstey for his perusal; RLS, however, with his fondness for reading pulp fiction to relax with, bought *The Sin of a Countess, Miriam the Avenger* and *The Lady Detective.*

Wherever he went in Sydney, Louis was lionised, but celebrity status merely made him keener than ever to return to the obscurity of Samoa:

> I found my fame much grown on this return to civilisation. *Digito mostrari* is a new experience; people all looked at me in the streets of Sydney; and it was very queer. Here (Samoa) of course, I am only the white chief in the Great House to the natives; and to the whites either an ally or a foe. It is a much healthier state of affairs. If I lived in an atmosphere of adulation, I should end by kicking against the pricks. O my beautiful forest, O my beautiful shining, windy house, what a joy it was to behold them again! No chance to take myself too seriously here.[3]

The other thing he was finding increasingly hard to bear about 'civilisation' was the noise: 'I am like my grandfather in that, and so many years in these still islands have ingrained the sentiment perhaps.' Whether stress, chill or virus was the dominant factor, he fell ill again in Sydney and made a miserable return to Samoa; once again there was an invalid household at Vailima for by April Fools' Day, 1893, the entire extended family of whites (including Graham Balfour who had been along on the trip) was ill.

Suddenly an old acquaintance, who had dropped RLS because he thought him a spent force and an embarrassment to his own would-be glittering career, resumed correspondence. Edmund Gosse now realised that Stevenson was anything but a spent force and broke the ice by dedicating a book to him. 'Since Byron was in Greece, nothing has appealed to the ordinary literary man as so picturesque as that you should be in the South Seas,' he wrote, and in successive letters proceeded to lay it on with a trowel. He confessed that he had at first been put off the *Island Nights* collection, but now realised that *The Beach of Falesá* was Louis's best work. He praised *Catriona* but revealed his own inadequacy as a critic by saying he missed RLS's personal voice – exactly what he should have missed if Stevenson was a first-rate novelist, at least when we understand what Gosse meant by 'voice', which he revealed in a characteristically mean-spirited twist in the tail: 'To me you always seem an essayist writing stories rather than a born novelist.'

Gosse also had news of Hardy, whom he compared unfavourably with Louis as a practitioner of fiction. There were also the sad tidings of the death of John Addington Symonds in Rome, on one of his rare trips away from Switzerland – for by now Symonds had become institutionalised at Davos in the way experienced by Hans Castorp in Mann's *The Magic Mountain.*

'Poor dear Symonds', Gosse reported,

> used to be so indignant with you for being so respectable. Fancy, he used to say, having the chance to lounge about in palmy coves with a few hibiscus flowers on, with the most beautiful people in the world, and then building oneself a sort of Scottish manse in a wilderness. What would Symonds have been in Samoa? I think he fancied the joys of becoming a kind of aesthetic beachcomber. I expect he would soon have pined for the Scottish manse.

For once the gossipy, malicious Gosse was not stirring the pot; his characterisation of Symonds's opinion of RLS really was the truth. Symonds spotted the similarities between Kipling and RLS and in February 1892 wrote to Gosse as follows:

> Your gossip concerning the Kiplings gave me great amusement. I wish I had known him as well as I knew Louis Stevenson. They are two of the most typical eccentricities of genius – so idiosyncratic and yet so impossible to conceive of except in the second half of the nineteenth century. Stevenson has long been lost to me. I cannot keep in touch with a man in the South Seas who does not live like a native and with the natives.

Here was irony indeed. Of the two men whose initial reaction to RLS was that he had not been in contact with enough first-class minds, Henry Adams criticised him for living in excessively primitive conditions, while Symonds censured him for the exactly opposite fault.[4]

Louis was glad to have news of the outer world to distract him, for in early 1893 the gale blowing in Fanny's mind finally built up into a Force Twelve hurricane. Close observers of RLS might have spotted the illogicality whereby he went to Sydney in February 1893 to convalesce, when he knew very well that Sydney did not agree with him, and was likely to precipitate a fresh outbreak of illness. There was in fact a secret reason for the trip: the hope that a change of scene might jolt Fanny into normality; for by now she was in the grip of temporary insanity. As her biographer puts it: 'For a while she was wildly wandering, despite the helpless efforts of her husband, aided by Belle and Lloyd. There was a dreadful scene which went on all night. For the first time she was physically obstreperous. She wanted to run away and for two hours Louis and Belle held onto her bodily to keep her from rushing from the house.'[5]

In Sydney, where they stayed at the Oxford Hotel, Fanny was largely confined to her room and went through a calm and quiet phase; Louis, also ill, was in bed in the adjoining room. He once agreed to receive a reporter, but while he was explaining that, though he liked *Kidnapped* best of his novels, his single best piece was 'Thrawn Janet', Fanny wandered into the room and began to harangue the interviewer; all that was nonsense, she said; her favourite was the biography of Fleeming Jenkin, which was the only one of her husband's books that had brought tears to her eyes.

Knowing of his wife's love of extravagance and finery, Louis tried to 'buy off' her psychosis by purchasing entire new wardrobes of clothes, but this ploy did not work; Fanny started having all her old fixations again and began hallucinating. 'Fanny saw you twice today,' was one of RLS's asides to Baxter. Dr Fairfax Ross, who was treating Louis for his physical health, took Fanny under his wing but confessed himself out of his depth; as he told Colvin in London later: 'of her condition he thinks ill – both as to body and mind.' Louis meanwhile was unable to bring himself to admit the true state of affairs to Colvin and hid the truth in a blanket of obfuscation, covering her mental illness with general valetudinarian tales: 'Fanny quite sick, but I think slowly and steadily mending: Belle in a terrific state of dentistry troubles ... and myself ... a fine pleurisy.'[6]

Back in Vailima the household spent many anxious weeks waiting for her to run amok and making contingency plans for how to restrain her. At last, in April, Louis broke down and admitted to Colvin what he had been living through:

> Well there's no disguise possible. Fanny is not well – we are miserably anxious. I may as well say now that for nearly 18 months there has been something wrong; I could not write of it; but it was very trying and painful – and mostly fell on me. Now we are face to face with the question: what next? The doctor has given her a medicine; we think it too strong, yet dare not stop it; and she passes from death-bed scenes to states of stupor. Rosse, Dr in Sydney, warned me to expect trouble so I'm not surprised; and happily Lloyd and Belle and I work together very smoothly and none of us gets excited. But it's anxious ... I am stupid and tired and have done little even to my proofs. It is awful good those children are so good to me; or I'd be in a horrid pickle.

He went on to say that for eighteen months he had

> felt so dreadfully alone ... You know about F., there is nothing you can say is *wrong*, only it ain't right, it ain't *she*; at first she annoyed me dreadfully; now of course that one understands, it is more anxious and pitiful. The dr. has been. 'There is no danger to life,' he said twice – 'Is there any danger to mind?' I asked – 'That is not excluded' said he. Since then I have had a scene with which I need not harrow you; and now again she is quiet and seems without illusions. 'Tis a beastly business.

Louis explained that at first all her rage was directed against him: 'She made every talk an argument, then a quarrel; till I fled her and lived in a kind of isolation in my own room ... I am broken on the wheel or I feel like it ... Belle has her faults and plenty of them; but she has been a blessed friend to me.'

The local physician Dr Funk gave her strong sedatives, as a result of which she alternated between hypermania and catalepsy. She had her most insane fit of all, but this time it was gentle, full of wistful hallucinations; Dr Funk again thought her life was not in danger but would not vouch for her mind. On one occasion he was just getting into his carriage to drive back to Apia when he was called back upstairs to witness his patient's relapse into a frightening scene; finally she calmed down and this time seemed to be free of delusions.

Colvin apart, Louis was still doing his best to pretend to the world that all was normal. There is, however, a hint of what was going on in a pen-portrait of his family he sent to J.M.Barrie, who was by this time so obsessed with RLS that he wrote letters full of imaginary conversations between his hero and his wife. Urging Barrie to come out to Samoa to see for himself, he explained what he would find when he set eyes on Fanny:

> Infinitely little, extraordinary wig of grey curls, handsome waxen face like Napoleon's, *insane black eyes*, boy's hands, tiny bare feet, a cigarette, wild blue native dress usually spotted with garden mould. In company manners presents the appearance of a little timid and precise old maid of the days of prunes and prisms – you look for the reticule. *Hellish energy, relieved by fortnights of entire hibernation. Can make anything from a house to a row, all fine and large of their kind ... Doctors everybody, will doctor you, cannot be doctored herself ... A violent enemy, a brimstone friend ... Is always either loathed or slavishly adored; indifference impossible. The natives think her uncanny and that devils serve her. Dreams dreams and sees visions* (italics mine).[7]

However, just at that moment the strategy of concealment was in danger, for Isla Sitwell, a relative of Fanny Sitwell's, was due at the island, having been invited to stay at Vailima. Desperate remedies were considered; perhaps Fanny would have to be shut up in a wing of the house like Mrs Rochester and the story given out that she was away on a trip; but in the end it was decided that Lloyd would have to entertain their guest at Apia's best hotel and politely send him on his way by the next steamer.

Just at the right moment Fanny turned the corner. 'You can't conceive what a relief this is,' Louis wrote to Colvin; 'it seems a new world. She has such extraordinary recuperative power that I do hope for the best. I am as tired as a man can be.' On 17 April Louis wrote to his mother that the new medicine from Funk seemed to be working, and that they had successfully entertained Isla Sitwell without embarrassment. Only now, when his wife was on the mend, did he admit to his mother what he had gone through. 'Fanny was devilish ill ... No doubt but [she] had an alarming illness ... Now we are all recovered or recovering – Belle protests against this and says to tell the truth that Fanny is not recovering. But though it is true she seems to have taken a cast back, she is far indeed from being so dreadfully ill as she was before.' Belle added a pessimistic postscript: 'She lies in bed, does not smoke, doesn't want to eat, or speak; Louis does not want to alarm you, but I think you should know what a really anxious time we are going through ... I would like to see her take an interest in something.'

Louis and Belle took turns to sleep in her room so that she was never left unattended. On 22 April Louis wrote to Colvin: 'Well, Fanny *is* really better, nothing to the contrary, and I shall get Belle to sign the same and show this to be neither deception nor self-illusion.' The amanuensis duly added: 'She is really, Belle.' Louis reported a further strong sign of recovery: 'Last night the cats woke her and me about ten, Belle was not yet in bed; so we all three sat in my room and had some grog and a cigarette, and were as jolly as sand boys. It was delightful: Fanny as nice as possible, and did not seem ill one particle. Yesterday, too, she went all round her garden with an umbrella, and quite tired me out following her.'[8]

What was the cause of Fanny's spectacular breakdown in 1893? The evidence suggests it was overdetermined in a number of different ways. As Louis grew apart from and beyond her, her jealousy of his success as a writer – a jealousy she could not consciously acknowledge – became an overpowering anger that had to be directed inward; it had always been her dearest wish to be 'creative' and now finally she had to concede that the wish was a fantasy. But this Rio Negro, as it were, fed into a mighty Amazon of guilt and confusion about her identity as a woman. The normal travails, miseries and anxieties of the menopause were her lot; additionally she would have brooded on the fact that she and Louis had had no children, which would almost certainly, by association of ideas, have triggered memories of the loss of her son Hervey in 1875. It is not surprising that the guilt and depression precipitated by all this would have caused a kind of psychic overload.

Louis had often lost patience with his wife when her behaviour was merely neurotic and hypochondriacal; but when he saw her in danger of being overwhelmed by madness, his behaviour was exemplary and faultless. Love of children and compassion for the underdog were almost the strongest emotions he had, and both would have been energised by the pathetic, raving specimen in the body of the erstwhile pioneer woman. Additionally, Louis was no ingrate: he remembered all the times Fanny had nursed him, even though their number was far less than later legend would make them out to be, and he was grateful and wanted to reciprocate. To help his wife through the worst of her mental 'white out', he even seems to have made promises to her that went against his own code. It is likely that in her fits Fanny blurted out her feelings of anger that Louis had not always supported her wholeheartedly in conflicts with his friends, for at the very time of her recovery we find him writing to Baxter as follows:

The only thing I want is to be sure that codicil in favour of Mrs Strong is in order. I wish you would send me also an abstract of my will. I am beginning to think twice about sending so much of my money – I mean my father's money – to Bob and Katharine. My own people are going to be poor enough; and really R and K are the most indifferent and unfriendly people in the world ... Bob never answers my letters, Katharine does not correspond, and I mean distinctly to use a pruning knife upon that side; of course my father's expressed wish binds me to do something, and something I must do. But I am far more bound and far more concerned to do well by Lloyd and something for Belle and the child.

Louis had the support of the few friends in England to whom he could confide the secrets of his marriage. Henry James was one, but his letter of sympathy reads as stiltedly as Edith Wharton's Jamesian parodies: 'I know what you all magnificently eat and what dear Mrs Louis splendidly (but not somewhat transparently – no?) wears. Please assure that intensely remembered lady of my dumb fidelity.'[9]

Fanny's return to sanity was attended by a subtle alteration in the way she viewed the world. It is likely that, as she wrestled with her demons, she concluded, to her own satisfaction at least, that she had in the past been too much Louis's 'creature'; if he now wanted to go in a new direction without her, very well, she would do likewise. Such an interpretation would explain two emergent facets of Fanny after mid-1893; a kind of proto-feminism and a fanatical – the word is not too strong – involvement in Samoan politics. The feminism corresponds, on this view, to her perception that her old relationship with Louis was no more; the political participation to an attempt to outreach Louis in one of his chosen spheres of involvement.

On 20 July she confided to her diary a regret that she was Louis's chattel and could not earn her own money:

I wonder what would become of a man, and to what he would degenerate, if his life was that of a woman's; to get 'the run of her teeth' and presents of her clothes, and supposed to be always under bonds of deepest gratitude for any further sums. I would work very hard to earn a couple of pounds a month, and I could easily earn much more, but there is my position as Louis's wife, therefore I cannot.

This is largely self-delusion: 'easily earn much more' at what? She had not been notably successful as an earner before she teamed up with Louis, and it is likely that, used by now to a steady income from his writing, she fell into the delusion, common to intimates of writers, that 'anyone can do it'; alternatively, the fiction that her services were in demand had it not been for the prior and peremptory claims of RLS may have been rationalisation along the lines practised by Lloyd.

There are also new signs of assertiveness in her refusal to play the role

Louis thought best for her, which was to keep her head down if civil war came; Fanny interpreted this as a prescription to ape the British female and in the event of trouble 'retire to a back apartment with some crochet work and not ask what is going on'. She hit back by insisting on going to a 'ball' in Apia which Louis claimed was merely an excuse for the 'beach' to have a legitimised orgy; Fanny and Belle insisted on going nonetheless, and Fanny claimed that Louis was furious and 'still in the sulks' days later.[10]

Even more striking is the way she became a fervent devotee of Mataafa. The decision of the Powers to proceed with the compulsory disarming of Mataafa and his followers struck Louis as a combination of folly, danger, expense and treachery: 'Politics is a vile and bungling business. I used to think meanly of the plumber, but now he shines beside the politician . . . I always held (upon no evidence whatever, from a mere sentiment or intuition) that politics was the dirtiest, the most foolish, and the most random of human employments. I always held, but now I know it.' On the other hand, he took to heart the advice from Sir George Grey that change in Samoa could come about only gradually; if he was really sincere in his desire to see Mataafa as Malietoa, Grey argued, he should lobby patiently through the channels. There are clear signs in the correspondence from Lord Rosebery in 1893 that Louis took the advice; Rosebery became friendly and intimate, confessed his admiration for *Catriona*, but counselled that, for reasons of *haute politique*, Her Majesty's Government could not at present work for radical change in the constitutional arrangements of Samoa. Louis contented himself with offering his services as mediator between Laupepa and Mataafa, but this was curtly turned down. He was despondent at the drift to war between the two chiefs. 'It is dreadful to think that I must sit apart here and do nothing. I do not know if I can stand it out. But you see, I may be of use to these poor people, if I keep quiet, and if I threw myself in, I should have a bad job of it to save myself.'

After the dismissal of Cedarcrantz and von Pilsach, and in the interim before the new Chief Justice, Henry Ide, arrived, the Powers appointed a British official, Thomas Maben, as 'Secretary of State for Samoa'. Louis had many passages of arms with Maben, and his frustration led him to fantasise in his letters to Colvin about the desirability of the 'man on horseback': 'If we could only have MacGregor here with his schooner, you would hear of no more troubles in Samoa. That is what we want, a person who knows and likes the natives, *qui paye de sa personne*, and is not afraid of hanging when necessary. We don't want bland Swedish humbugs, and fussy footering German barons. That way the maelstrom lies, and we shall soon be in it.'[11]

Fanny, however, acted like a wild-eyed revolutionary and would not hear of compromise; reports of the taking of heads in the preliminary skirmishes of the civil war brought her to boiling point:

Louis commands that we keep the peace with Maben; not only that, but
to be friendly with him. Until the blood of women is washed from Maben's
hand I cannot touch it. I do not myself feel innocent. Thinking we did right
both for Mataafa and for Samoa, and for the fear of bloodshed, we counselled
peace. But the fact is that remotely, because of our advice, these women's heads
were brought in to the representatives of the three great powers, and like cowards
they sit silent . . . I wonder at the forbearance of these Samoans. Were I Samoan
I would, and I feel successfully, agitate for a massacre of the whites.

Fanny taunted Louis with a circumspection amounting to cowardice;
knowing that he regarded quietism in all forms as the refuge of the coward,
we can imagine how the taunt must have stung. She upbraided him with
reneging on his perennial support for the underdog and reminded him how
often he had broken bread with Mataafa and pledged him loyalty:

I intend to do everything in my power to save Mataafa; doubtless very little,
but it shall be my utmost. And if Louis turns his face from him by the fraction
of an inch, I shall wear black in public; if they murder him, or if he is brought
into Apia as a prisoner I shall go down alone and kiss his hand as my king. Louis
says this is arrant mad quixotism. I suppose it is; but when I look at the white
men at the head of the government, and cannot make up my mind which is the
greater coward, my woman's heart burns with shame and fury and I am ready
for any madness.

The French have an expression: '*Les absents ont toujours tort*'; on one
notable occasion Fanny declared that it was the absent one who was in
the right, for her old adversary H.J.Moors was away from Samoa for much
of 1893, attending the World's Fair at Chicago (where he met McClure). At
a lunch at Haggard's in July while the civil war between Laupepa and
Mataafa raged, Fanny worked herself into a fury about Maben, who was
trying to put the entire blame for the hostilities on Mataafa. 'Suddenly I
rose up, said vehemently that all the white men in Samoa were cowards,
and left the party. I am afraid I behaved very badly. At luncheon healths
were being drunk, and I drank the health of H.J.Moors, my worst enemy,
and the only white man clinging to Samoa who is not a coward.'[12]
At the end of June the long-threatened war between Mataafa and Laupepa
at last broke out. The Stevensons were unable to keep out of the conflict.
Louis, stopped at a ford by a picket with Winchesters, talked his way across
the no-man's land into Mataafa's lines, and was both amazed and depressed
at the extent of warlike preparations he found. Another visit to Mataafa, this
time with Fanny, seemed for a moment likely to end in disaster. On their way
back from Mataafa's outposts they passed through a Laupepa village, whose
inhabitants knew all about the Vailima whites and their political sympathies.
Fanny failed to keep up with Louis and Lloyd; they looked back to see her
surrounded by armed men; in alarm they rode back only to discover that her

horse had baulked and the warriors had come to her assistance. Although Mataafa and Laupepa had both placed a taboo on Vailima, which lay between their territories, Louis did not know this and took seriously the rumours that the Samoans would use the pretext of civil war to massacre all whites on the island. He therefore tried to import an extra cache of guns and ammunition; when forbidden to do so by British regulations, he obtained them through Lloyd who, as a U.S. citizen, was able to plead the Second Amendment of the Constitution, allowing all Americans to bear arms.

Fanny's vociferous support for Mataafa made it difficult for Louis to stifle his own inclinations and assume a mask of neutrality. Soon rumours about the role of Vailima in the war were flying thick and fast – that he was smuggling in weapons for Mataafa, who had no shortage of arms and ammunition despite the official embargo; that a secret tunnel had been built between Vailima and Mataafa's village. But the sober truth was that Louis and Fanny restricted their activities to strengthening the defences at Vailima and visiting the hospital in Apia where wounded men were being tended and where they witnessed many men bleeding to death from gunshot wounds before they could be operated on.

'All seems to indicate a long and bloody war,' Louis wrote, as Mataafa, outnumbered and outgunned, nonetheless gave ground stubbornly as he retreated from Vaitele; the fact that resistance to Laupepa was far sterner than expected was a blow to the Malietoa and his German puppetmasters. Yet it was soon apparent that Mataafa 'who might have swept the islands a few months ago' had lost ground considerably. Louis thought that after his initial reverses Mataafa should have switched operations to the island of Savaii, where he could have carried on a protracted Fabian campaign, but by choosing to dig in he had become 'only the stick of a rocket'. When Mataafa did at last try to take his forces across to Savaii, he found that Laupepa's men were present in strength at all the potential beachheads, so had to retreat disconsolately to Upolu. The last straw was when the British warship HMS *Katoomba* arrived, with heavy guns and orders from London to blast Mataafa into surrender. RLS, who seemed never to dislike a sea-dog, took to its captain Bickford in a big way, and lamented he had not arrived ten days earlier when he could have parted the combatants.

On 18 July, after a bloody three-week war, Mataafa surrendered. A warship brought the old king and his chieftains round to Apia as prisoners. Louis and Lloyd sped down to the harbour and were the first aboard and the only friendly faces the prisoners had seen; Mataafa looked old and broken and made a rambling speech to Louis. From his own enquiries among the wardroom officers, Louis learned that the hawkish captain had given Mataafa just three hours to surrender, which even the officers thought was draconian; and their sympathies had increased when the warriors spent their first night aboard in weeping and lamentation.[13]

Mataafa and his higher chiefs were exiled to the German-controlled Marshalls. There they were kept for five years and released in 1898 on condition that Mataafa signed a protocol, pledging complete loyalty to Laupepa; even so his return was delayed, for Laupepa died just as the articles of release were signed, and the Powers did not want Mataafa back in Samoa until a new king was elected. While he was in exile on the Marshalls, he received from RLS via Graham Balfour a supply of *kava* and some trade cloth for shirts and *lavalavas*, indicating Stevenson's continuing commitment to him. Mataafa's defeat was a source of mortification to Louis, not only because he had backed the losing side but because the 'beach' spread the rumour that RLS had been Mataafa's military adviser, and it had been because of the Scot's disastrous strategy and tactics that Mataafa had been defeated. Nothing was more calculated to incense Louis: he had always said that, if his health had permitted it, he would have been a Burton or a Gordon; he had made an intense study of the '45, Wellington's Peninsular wars and Garnett Wolseley's worldwide campaigns, and, like many scholars interested in military history, he prided himself on the fantasy that, once given high command, he could have been a great captain.

Fanny, however, saw in Mataafa's defeat an example of Albion's perfidy and reverted to the anti-British sentiments last overtly expressed at the time of the quarrel with Henley. Speaking of her *bête noire* Maben and other Great Power officials in Samoa, she declared: 'We have seen two instances, one of English honour, the other of American chivalry; only thank God the American is only a sham article, being of English colonial birth and bearing all the marks of Jewish extraction.'[14] Let us grant Fanny the benefit of every doubt, and concede that her remark might not have been so anti-semitic as it sounds; let us grant also that Louis, for his part, sometimes wrote in ways that could be construed as anti-American – and McClure notably objected to some of the passages in *The Wrecker* on these grounds; even so, surely she was not so obtuse as to be unaware that the driving force in Samoan politics came from Berlin, not London.

That RLS did any literary work in the first six months of 1893, while war and rumours of war pervaded the island and a different kind of civil conflict was fought out in Fanny's mind, is surprising; that he finished his last complete work is astonishing. In Sydney, though ill and anxious about Fanny, he wrote the essay 'Rosa quo locorum'; he also sketched an outline for a short story, 'Death in the Pot', about California and began work on a story to be called 'The Owl' – about the Chouans in 1793. But his greatest achievement was the writing of *The Ebb-Tide*, which occupied him from February to June. Based on an idea that he had first jotted down in the winter of 1889–90, this dealt with the nemesis of three Pacific beachcombers, who are gulled into a scheme to make their fortune but end up defeated by the white ruler of a remote island. The task of writing it was nearly as grim as the tale itself; Louis wrote to Colvin on 25 April: 'O, it has been such a grind! I break down at every paragraph ... and lie here and sweat, till I can get one sentence wrung out after another.' When RLS finally laid down his pen on 5 June 1893, he wrote to Colvin: 'I ... have spent thirteen days about as nearly in Hell as a man could expect to live through ... about as grim a tale as was ever written, and as grimy, and as hateful.' Colvin, initially disappointed, sat up and took notice at the last two chapters, but thought them too grim to be published in book form, unless RLS was prepared to see his reputation harmed.[15]

Although this was theoretically another collaboration with Lloyd Osbourne, Lloyd's work was limited to some impressionistic writing in the first four chapters – significantly, he contributed nothing to the best part of the book. As ever, Louis made excuses for his 'collaborator': 'I think it rather unfair on the young man to couple his name with so infamous a work.' Moreover, despite Colvin's fears, *The Ebb-Tide* did well commercially; it was serialised and then published as a book in 1894 and netted RLS about £950.[16]

At root yet another of RLS's tales probing the nature of evil, *The Ebb-Tide* was certainly the most pessimistic so far. Of the accuracy of its portrait of the 'beach' there can be no doubts; as Arthur Johnstone commented: 'It is typical of a class of cosmopolitan characters still extant in the Pacific Ocean.' On the exact significance of the tawdry trio of treasure-hunters there is less agreement. The three men, Davis, Huish and Herrick, can be seen as three aspects of a single sensibility – the triad marking an advance on the duo in *Jekyll and Hyde* and seeming to fulfil Stevenson's prophecy that the human personality would one day come to seem multitudinous. Ever since Plato divided mankind into guardians, auxiliaries and workers, supposedly representing the tripartite nature of the human personality, the triadic approach has been influential in Western civilisation, all the way from the Christian Trinity to Freud's ego, id and superego. Naturally, fanciful readings of *The Ebb-Tide* abound: in one, Davis as captain represents superego, Huish id and Herrick ego (it has even been pointed out that the way Huish refers to Herrick – 'Errick' – is germane, since in Liverpool demotic argot the proper name 'Eric' is always rendered as 'Ego'). This human trilogy confronts Attwater, the Lord of the island, who may be God or the Devil. Alternatively, and more persuasively, one can see Herrick aiming for integration by rejecting the claims of both Attwater (superego) and Huish (id).

Certainly, Herrick, who is a kind of transmogrified RLS – we can infer this from his love of Virgil – attempts in his own limited way to solve the Tolstoyan question of what Man should do. RLS rejects the solutions of orthodox religion or a world without morality: Davis chooses the former at the cost of becoming a cipher or less than human; Huish chooses the second, which is the way of death; only Herrick achieves some kind of perilous equilibrium. Herrick had already faced the Davis option: 'there were men who could commit suicide; there were men who could not; and he was one who could not.'

In *The Ebb-Tide* RLS decisively breaks with his early notion of evil as diabolical in favour of evil as banality or, at best, braided with good in the Melvillean way. For Stevenson human degeneracy, or the spectacle of mankind in the lower depths, was more terrifying than any visitation from a demon. There is a clear echo of Melville in the symbol of hope – a ship's figurehead whose whiteness turns out on closer inspection to be 'leprous' – recalling the multiple ambiguities in Melville's famous chapter on the whiteness of the whale in *Moby-Dick*. This is why it is a mistake to claim, as some have done, that Huish is Stevenson's only wholly evil character. He is a contemptible and loathsome whiner, it is true, and his Cockney twistedness was undoubtedly in Jack London's mind when he portrayed Muggeridge in *The Sea Wolf*; but he is recognisably human in his weakness. Even Davis is allowed some lines that express the RLS viewpoint: 'No man's got a family till he's got children. It's only the kids count.'

The trio of Huish, Davis and Herrick achieve a spectacular come-uppance when confronted by the terrifying figure of Attwater. A monster who conflates the 'business' of profiteering with fundamentalist Christianity in the typical manner of the Victorians, Attwater is also the Yahweh of the Old Testament, a cruel, jealous God who points forward to the fascist dictators of the twentieth century, almost as though the pessimistic Stevenson sensed the direction in which mankind was heading. His Old Testament sense of justice has no place in it for compassion or the law of love; as Eigner pointed out, the pitifully inadequate trio who scheme to despoil this island Prospero of his treasure 'have about as much chance as Chaucer's reprobates have of killing death in *The Pardoner's Tale*'. RLS did not make the mistake of caricaturing types of human beings he disliked: he conceded Attwater his fearsome power and charisma while making his own distaste clear; Attwater's status as ogre is evinced by his attitude to women – for RLS misogynism was always a sign of a warped human being. Attwater mistrusts women as the source of temptation and regards sex as a trap for the unwary; to put sexuality in its place he marries off the one pretty girl on the island to a servant, against her will. Many critics have resented the ease with which RLS gave Attwater his victory. Chesterton made the point with his usual elegance: 'I do not object to the author creating such a loathsome person as Mr Attwater; but I do rather object to his creating him and not loathing him ... there would be no objection if he loathed and admired Attwater exactly as he loathed and admired Huish.'[17]

The Ebb-Tide is full of autobiographical hints, making it an outstanding source for the life in the work. Superficially, the character of Attwater was based on Colvin's friend A.G.Dew-Smith, the Cambridge don RLS met while staying in Colvin's rooms in Trinity in the late 1870s. At a deeper level Attwater is a barely disguised portrait of Thomas Stevenson and represents in hyperbolic form all that Louis most feared and despised in his father. The fanatical Attwater looks forward to the even more fully-blown portrait of the tyrannical patriarch in *Weir of Hermiston*; Herrick is to Attwater as Archie is to Adam Weir in the later novel.

The abandonment of the hope implicit in *The Beach of Falesá* is symbolised by Attwater's destruction of the figurehead; in terms of RLS's life it is possible to read this as the destruction of the utopian dreams he took to Samoa, the end of innocence, the impossibility of believing in 'noble savages' or the possibility of a better world. And since the destruction of these hopes is carried out by Attwater (Thomas), we can also interpret this as Stevenson's gloss on the final triumph of determinism over free will. Yet it is not only in the treatment of his Scottish legacy that Stevenson reveals his pessimism; one can also clearly discern the disillusionment with life in Samoa, and especially the nightmare period of Fanny's psychosis, in the notion of the island heaven as in reality a hell. The impossibility of escaping moral dilemmas or indeed any of the pressing problems of the human condition by going to live on an island is a theme only just under the surface. Like so many would-be refugees from reality, RLS discovered that, in the words of the cliché, he could not run away from himself. He still had fevers and haemorrhages, he still had his ailing wife on his hands, he still wished he could move on to fresh locations, and he still suffered from Calvinistic guilt about the justifiability of making a living from writing. As he wrote to Colvin: 'A sailor, a shepherd, a schoolmaster – to a lesser degree, a soldier and (I don't know why, upon my soul, except as a schoolmaster's unofficial assistant, a kind of acrobat in tights) an artist, almost exhaust the category of the few possible and dignified ways of life.'[18]

Louis was well aware of white exploitation in the Pacific – how could he be unaware when runaway 'blackboys' from the German firm fetched up at Vailima? – but he no longer believed that the Pacific was a prelapsarian Eden destroyed by the coming of the white man; he had seen too many heads taken by Mataafa's warriors, too much casual brutality of the kind meted out by Tembinok in his palace, and too many cannibal feasting places for that. Yet the realisation that new skies do not change human nature led him into the near-nihilism of *The Ebb-Tide*. If *The Beach of Falesá* showed the optimism of RLS in 1891, *The Ebb-Tide* showed how far he had fallen in eighteen months, and the period is almost exactly that of Fanny's illness and the destruction of his hopes for a Samoa ruled by Mataafa.

The critic Walter Allen suggested that RLS's distinctive contribution to the novel was to marry Flaubert with Dumas. *The Ebb-Tide* shows the nihilism of Flaubert virtually overwhelming the extrovert Porthos-like qualities always perceptible in the early novels (with the exception of *The Master of Ballantrae*) and indeed Louis explicitly stated that he wanted to make his second Pacific novel an extended *Monte-Cristo*-like tale, but changed his mind and cut it down to novella length. The decision did not please his English critics. Leslie Stephen hated the three anti-heroes, possibly precisely because RLS dispensed with most of the external Dumas-like trappings of the adventure story, but, soberly considered, there is something unintentionally hilarious about a critical sensibility that could swallow Long John Silver yet strain at Huish and Davis. In Stephen's antipathy it is hard not to see a quasi-Jamesian fastidiousness at work, a conviction that true literature could not be about *canaille* like these people.

In completing this book in the midst of external strife and domestic turmoil, Louis pushed himself to the limit of his stamina. In August after a game of tennis with Graham Balfour he suffered his most serious haemorrhage yet on Samoa. Medical investigation revealed that it had been triggered by the swinging of the raquet; the resultant deep breathing caused a rupture of the inelastic supporting tissue of the lungs, probably a break in the tender area of a former lesion. The immediate sequel was four days lying flat on his back, with absolute peace and quiet. But when a measles epidemic began to sweep over the island, it was thought best that Louis seek a safer haven for convalescence; Sydney was out as being too obviously disagreeable, so this time Louis elected to travel north, to Hawaii, where he had enjoyed good health in 1889.

He arrived in Oahu on 20 September, accompanied by Graham Balfour and his valet Ta'alolo, by heredity a minor chief in Samoa. Stevenson's regard for Ta'alolo was such that on one occasion, invited to take a drink in a saloon, he insisted that his valet come in too and refused to drink in the establishment when the barman insisted it was 'whites only'. Ta'alolo fell ill with measles on the trip north and at first it was doubtful that he would be permitted to land at Honolulu; eventually the Hawaiian Board of Health relented and allowed him ashore on condition he was placed in quarantine in a hut on the beach.

Louis was looking forward to plunging into politics as avidly in Hawaii as on Samoa, but he found that much had changed since his visit four years before. His old friend, the great toper Kalakaua, had died in January 1891, and then his sister Lilioukulani had reigned for two years until the political faction controlled by U.S. planters overthrew her (January 1893). In Hawaii the voices of American expansionists like Mahan and Adams were heard even more loudly than on Samoa; 'as regards the Hawaiian problem, take the islands first and solve the problem afterwards', said Mahan, anticipating Theodore Roosevelt's 'bully' tactics. In 1893 the self-appointed Hawaiian president and leader of the putschists, Sanford Dole, petitioned Washington to annex the islands, but incoming president

Grover Cleveland, an anti-imperialist, quashed the bill in Congress; not until the high-tide of U.S. imperialism in 1898 would Hawaii finally be annexed. Lilioukulani appealed to Cleveland to restore her, and there was at one time a presidential scheme to land marines on the islands, but the planters mobilised their lobby on Capitol Hill to thwart the plan. For seven years Dole's 'revolutionary' government was prepared to sit it out, knowing that annexation by the U.S.A. was sooner or later inevitable.

Louis at once unfurled his colours by visiting the deposed Lilioukulani and spending most of his time with A.S.Cleghorn; Kaiulani was still absent in England. But any hope of influencing politics in Hawaii was vain. In Samoa there was at least a genuine power vacuum into which the three powers poured; in Hawaii all military and political power was in the hands of the annexationists, who in turn represented the interests of hundreds of millions of invested domestic and foreign capital. Any fully-fledged royalist campaign in Hawaii would have been crushed utterly. In Samoa RLS had the British government in London to appeal to, but in the Hawaiian case he had no Colvins and Roseberys to lobby in Washington.

Looking around for a focus for his ardent royalism, Louis found it by attacking William T.Stead, editor of the *Review of Reviews* which frequently attacked the British royal family. A favourite RLS ploy was to order a light-red Californian burgundy in his club just before dinner, and then launch into a tirade against Stead. When he had worked himself up into a rare fury, he would finish his peroration and then glare around the room, waiting for anyone to answer him. Nobody ever did, and RLS was reduced to gulping down his burgundy and storming out of the room.

During his visit Louis stayed outside Honolulu in the Sans Souci Inn and ventured into the city just eight times, never for more than a few hours at a time; most of his trips out were to see Cleghorn at Ainah Au. Even the Sans Souci Inn contained more of the trappings of civilisation than he cared for. He developed a particular aversion to the telephone, by this time widely in use in Hawaii, and declared that he had gone to Samoa to escape such abominations; the declaration would have been more telling had he actually been able to operate the phone, but on the few occasions when he used it, he got friends to dial the number for him.

Elected honorary chieftain of the Thistle Club of Honolulu – a club for expatriate Scots – he delivered a memorable lecture on Scottish history there to a sell-out audience and later described the evening spent there as his happiest in the entire Pacific period. Arrangements were made for a second lecture, but fate was dogging him. If RLS took a fancy to a hackman, he always insisted on employing the same man over and over again. This time the beneficiary of his favours was an Irishman named Quinn. On the morning of 28 September Louis asked Quinn to take him for a drive around the park, but Quinn's horse promptly bolted. There followed a hair-raising and highly dangerous eight minutes, with the horse at full gallop, before Quinn regained control. Louis sat white-faced throughout the ordeal, but when order was restored and the horse was trotting, he said with a smile:

> Oh Quinn, brave and witty jehu, I don't like this new animal of yours; I have an idea that he is a bit of a politician, like yourself, and is apt to take his bit in the teeth; and Quinn, I don't altogether think he is safe. Now, you held him beautifully, and the ride was all that could be desired, *under the circumstances*; but don't you think, as a politician, Quinn, that we had better drive him to the stable and exchange him for an author's horse before we return to Sans Souci?[19]

Suffering from the shock of the near-fatal accident, Louis took to his bed in the Sans Souci. For the next fifteen days he lay ill in bed, rousing himself on just two occasions, for a consultation with a detective, and to write to the *Pacific Commercial Advertiser*, whose editor he had granted a long interview on first arrival, to speak in support of the Sans Souci Inn, which had been unfairly maligned in the press. Louis always relished detective stories and newspaper accounts of murders and liked to weigh the evidence and work out the likely innocence or guilt; he once questioned an expert for three hours on the Lizzie Borden case. The opportunity to play Sherlock Holmes came when one of the government detectives, a man of American parentage who had been born and raised in Japan, consulted him about a difficult case, the solution of which would bring the detective a large fee. After he had explained his theory, Stevenson lapsed into a reverie, from which he emerged after half an hour to point out the deficiencies in the detective's theory and to substitute one of his own; the detective then applied Louis's ideas, solved the case and won a $1,000 fee.

After two weeks of fever, and with no significant improvement in sight, Louis cabled Fanny to take ship up to Hawaii to nurse him. She arrived on 19 October, by which time he was just able to walk around the verandah. Powerful draughts which kept him asleep for fourteen out of every twenty-four hours did the trick, so that by 23 October he was well enough to lunch on board an American warship. Next day he and Fanny took the steamer back to Samoa. This was his last view of the world outside Samoa and Louis, with an intuition that he would die young, felt in his bones that he would never see Hawaii again.[20]

News of the trip energised Gosse into some forced levity and he wrote to ask whether RLS had really been to Hawaii, since the newspapers were always full of reputed exploits by him – all fantasy:

> 'All our readers will rejoice to learn that the aged fictionist Louis Robert Stevenson has ascended the throne of Tahiti of which he is now a native'; 'We regret to announce the death, in Cairo, of the well-known author, Mr Stevenson'; 'Mr Stevenson is now in Paris'; 'The vineyards which are cultivated in the island of Samoa by Mr Stevenson have been visited by desolating storms; the gifted romance writer fears that he will, this season, export none but elderberry wine';

'Mr R.L.Stevenson, who is now 31 years of age, is still partial to periwinkles, which he eats with a silver pin, presented to him by the German population of Samoa.'[21]

Once back in Samoa and recovered from his illness, Louis threw himself into humanitarian work on behalf of the imprisoned Mataafa chiefs. He was not well enough to celebrate his birthday properly on 13 November – the festivities were put back a week – but on 15 November he hired a carriage and drove ostentatiously to Apia jail to take *kava* and tobacco to the twenty-three chieftains incarcerated there. Louis was expecting trouble with the authorities, but the warden turned out to be a man with whom he got on supremely well. Baron von Wurmbrand was an Austrian soldier of fortune, currently occupying the rank of captain, who had seen service in Turkey and Serbia before coming out to the Pacific: 'a charming, clever, kindly creature, who is adored by *his* chiefs (as he calls them) meaning *our* political prisoners.'

On Boxing Day 1893 the chiefs responded by inviting the Stevensons to a Samoan feast inside the jail courtyard and making them a present of *ulas* – valuable necklaces of scarlet beads. Louis wrote proudly to Colvin: 'No such feast was ever made for a single family and no such present was ever given to a single white man.' He also claimed that their visit was risky, since in theory the Samoans could have seized them as hostages and bartered their way to freedom, and this was why the normally affable Wurmbrand was glad to see them go. However Wurmbrand was soon glad of the good offices of the Stevensons. There has always been in the German tradition the absurd custom that prisoners should pay for the expenses of those who guard or punish them – a tradition which reached its *reductio ad absurdum* under the Nazis when the families of prisoners executed for political offences were billed for the full cost of the executions. When the resources of the Samoan chiefs gave out, the tables were turned with a vengeance, for Wurmbrand either had to let them starve or pay for their subsistence out of his own salary. He wrote to Louis with a plea for help, to which the master of Vailima responded with predictable magnanimity. Fanny, however, took advantage of the debt of gratitude Wurmbrand was under to smuggle out one of her favourite chiefs who was sick, so that she could nurse him at home. When this leaked out, Wurmbrand was summarily dismissed from his post. Louis showed his contempt for the Powers by inviting the baron to stay free of charge at Vailima and making him guest of honour at the party he gave for Washington's birthday in February 1894; shortly afterwards Wurmbrand took service as the chief of the King of Tonga's bodyguard.[22]

The conclusion of Louis's last full year on earth provides motive and opportunity for a close-up view of everyday life at Vailima. RLS was both a precisian and an immensely hard worker, which is why his prodigious output – particularly impressive from a semi-invalid – was never produced at the expense of quality. Rising with the sun, he always did his best work in the mornings, but sometimes did an eight-hour writing day though he considered that 'about three hours too many'. He was always an omnivorous reader, although a visiting journalist from the *Spectator* expressed himself disappointed at the narrow range of his interests after inspecting the library at Vailima. The shelves were full of every conceivable book on Pacific travel and exploration, but otherwise, with the exception of military treatises and monographs on Wellington's campaigns, consisted of well-thumbed classics. The *Spectator*'s critic expressed snobbish fastidiousness at finding Sophocles and the *Odyssey* present only in translation, but conceded the presence of a Latin Horace. As might have been expected, French literature was well represented: Balzac, Hugo, Mérimée, Daudet, Maupassant were there in force, and indeed the fiction of France loomed large in Stevenson's reading during 1893. He sampled Anatole France, whom he did not like, but partially revised his opinion of Zola on the basis of the incandescent first two-thirds of *La Débâcle* and suggested that Zola admirers ought to like *The Ebb-Tide*. Apart from Henry James, Meredith, Kipling and Barrie, the British author who most intrigued him this year was Conan Doyle. On 30 May Doyle wrote to say that he considered 'The Pavilion on the Links' 'the first short story in the world' and thanked RLS for 'all the pleasure which you have given me during my lifetime – more than any other living man has done'. Louis wrote back with glowing praise for Sherlock Holmes and *The Refugees* – lauded as a Dumas-like historical novel – invited Doyle to visit him in Samoa and waited with whetted appetite for *The White Company*, which its author characterised as far better than his Holmes stories. In other letters about writing in 1893 he debated the role of the visual sense in *Catriona* with Henry James, jousted with Meredith, asked for Jerome K.Jerome's latest to be sent out to him, and expressed interest in Lady Charlotte Guest's translation of the *Mabinogion*.[23]

Doubtless he would have been content if all his correspondence could have been about literary matters. But every post also brought mail from Baxter or McClure or Burlingame about the inevitable quadrille of British serialisation, U.S. serialisation, British book publication, American book publication. Additionally there was a huge shoal of miscellaneous mail, which arrived in a great waterproof bag; Louis always emptied it personally while his family sat in an expectant circle on the floor. He began by tearing up any letter where his name was spelled as 'Stephenson'. Then he sorted through the remainder, putting it in three separate piles; there were begging letters; admiring epistles – which he always answered if he thought the writer sincere or if they came from children or sick people; and complimentary copies of books from first-time authors or manuscripts from aspiring ones

– in this case he tended to write a few words of encouragement to the good and ignore the bad.

Apart from writing and reading, Louis's greatest love was to go riding in the solitude of the forests on 'Jack': 'I get my horse up sometimes in the afternoon and have a ride in the woods; and I sit here and smoke and write, and rewrite, and destroy, and rage at my own impotence from six in the morning till eight at night, with trifling and not always agreeable intervals for meals.' On one occasion Jack bolted and Louis had another close brush with death; when he told the story of his narrow escape back at home, Fanny queried why he had not simply jumped off. 'It was ten miles from home,' replied Louis. 'Well,' said she, 'isn't it better to be ten miles from home than in heaven or hell?'

It would be a mistake to think of life at Vailima as the rugged experience of the frontier or even as the austerity of an Indian hill-post. The fortnightly steamer service both kept Louis in touch with 'civilisation' and brought in its luxury goods – ice, fresh oysters, French wines. From New Zealand he and Fanny could import horses or cows for milk and butter; there was an excellent butcher and a first-class baker in Apia, fresh fish could be bought on the beach, eels and fresh-water prawns were plentiful in the streams, wild pigeons could be shot from Vailima's back door, while by 1893 Fanny had mastered poultry farming, so that first-rate chickens and eggs were being raised on the estate.

One result of this embarrassment of riches was a steadily increasing round of social life: afternoon teas, picnics, evening receptions, dinner parties, private and public balls, paperchases on horseback, polo and tennis parties. RLS had never learned to dance but did so at the age of 40 to take part in the Apia balls, since not to do so would have been regarded as the mark of a superior 'standoffish' person; however, he never danced anything in public but a quadrille. Some of the public engagements had their farcical side as Fanny recalled: 'I have known Apia to be convulsed by a question of precedence between two officials from the same country, who each claimed the place of honour at public functions; burning despatches on the subject were written, and their respective governments appealed to. Well has Apia been called "the kindergarten of diplomacy".'

The amount of food and drink consumed was often prodigious, so that if RLS had not had his peculiar malady, he would certainly have ballooned up into a portly expatriate. On *ava* drinking he commented: 'This is a thing in which I consider myself a past master, and there are perhaps not twenty whites in the world who could say as much.' A dinner at the Haggards' consisted of soup, tomato and crayfish salad, Indian curry, a tender joint of beef, a dish of pigeons, plus pudding, cheese, coffee and fine wines. In September, when Louis had fourteen bluejackets from the band of HMS *Katoomba* up to Vailima to give a concert, he laid on chicken, ham, cake, fruit, coffee, lemonade and copious rounds of claret negus, flavoured with rum and limes. Always a friend of the Royal Navy, he was delighted at their good behaviour in the midst of plenty: 'This education of boys for the navy is making a class wholly apart – how shall I call them? – a kind of lower-class public schoolboy, well-mannered, fairly intelligent, sentimental as a sailor.'

However, the many interruptions due to the tiresome requirements of Samoan etiquette were not so welcome. A Samoan *malanga* (visiting party) expected the chief of Vailima to be instantly visible with his interpreter at his elbow to make the oration, and his maids to be at hand with the *ava* bowl for refreshment. Sometimes Louis had to leave his writing in mid-sentence, thus losing his thread, to attend to the 'honour' of receiving local dignitaries.

Occasionally he would give up smoking and drinking after a warning from some local quack, but always resumed soon afterwards. He reported one experiment at teetotalism to Henry James in June 1893:

> I am so made, or so twisted, that I do not like to think of a life without red wine on the table and tobacco with its lovely little coal of fire . . . Suppose somebody said to you, you are to leave your home and your books, and your clubs, and go out and camp in mid-Africa, and command an expedition, you would howl and kick and flee. I think the same of a life without wine and tobacco.

A few days later he told Colvin that after a day of absolute temperance he woke up to the very same headache whose occurrence had led the local doctor to advise him to become teetotal; quinine was at once used and a decision taken to abandon temperance.[24]

Stevenson has often had the tag 'aesthete' attached to his name, but there is no particular sign in his daily life of the glorification of the arts. The Italian painter, Count Nerli, visited Samoa in 1892 and was a frequent visitor to Vailima while he painted RLS's portrait, but Louis, doubtless influenced by Fanny, who said Nerli had tried too hard to capture the Hyde-in-Jekyll, did not buy it; it is, however, the most penetrating study ever done of him. In Sydney in March 1893 he sat for a sculptor but the resultant bust, he informed St Gaudens, looked more like Mark Twain than Robert Louis Stevenson. His contacts with Rodin, Will Low, Sargent and others had left him interested in painting and sculpture, but he had no patience with the sensibility of a Gauguin or with the idea of sacrificing everything else in life to one's art. Once, during a discussion on Jean-François Millet, founder of the Barbizon school, he derided the idea of sacrificing one's family for art and declared forthrightly to Belle and Lloyd: 'You know well enough I would save my family, if it carried me to the gallows' foot.' He also believed that writers were more interesting than painters: 'The study of painting or music does not expand the mind in any direction save one. Literature, with its study of human nature, events and history, is a constant education, and in that career a man cannot stick at one place as the painter and musician almost invariably does.'

He did, however, unlike all his close friends, have an extraordinary love of music, and would often play so dolefully on his flageolet as to constitute a social menace; his friend and solicitor Carruthers once threatened to take legal action to stop the noise of the crazed flute. Lloyd Osbourne recalled this aspect of his stepfather:

> Looking back, I can recall how constantly he spoke of music. He would recur (sic) again and again to dozens or so of operas he had heard in his youth, repeating the names of the singers – all of them German mediocrities . . . and he would talk with the same warmth and eagerness of the few great instrumentalists he had heard in London concerts. And it was always, of course, with an air of finality, as of a man speaking of past and gone experiences that could never be repeated. He bought an extraordinary amount of printed music – Chopin, Grieg, Bach, Beethoven, Mozart – and would pore over it for hours at a time, trying here and there, and with endless repetitions, to elucidate it with his flageolet.[25]

The sayings and *obiter dicta* of RLS were eagerly scribbled down for posterity by Lloyd, Belle and visitors to Vailima. Moors remembered his favourite expression of qualified approval: 'It's better than a dig in the eye with a sharp stick.' Belle noted his secretiveness: when he was going out and did not want the family to know where he was going, he would announce that he was going to call on Gray and MacFarlane (the name of a well-known Edinburgh store). But it was Lloyd who was most of all his Boswell, and his verbatim jottings powerfully suggest the flavour of the man:

> I am the last of Scotland's three Robbies, Robbie Burns, Robbie Fergusson, and Robbie Stevenson – and how hardly life treated them all, poor devils . . . I am not a man of any unusual talent, Lloyd. What genius I had was for work! . . . The bourgeoisie's weapon is starvation. If as a writer or an artist you run counter to their narrow notions they simply and silently withdraw your means of subsistence. I wonder how many people of talent are executed in this way every year . . . We don't live for the necessities of life; in reality no one cares a damn for them; what we live for are its superfluities . . . The saddest object in civilisation, and in my mind the greatest confession of its failure, is the man who can work, who wants to work and is not allowed to work.[26]

By the standards of the day he counted as a feminist, would never allow jokes on the subject of 'wallflowers' or 'old maids', and declared that he would never forgive Thackeray for the old age of Beatrix nor W.S.Gilbert for the humiliating personage of Lady Jane. Once, when he heard censorious gossip about a 'fallen woman', he cut through the humbug by declaring: 'Poor thing, perhaps we could do something for her.' For all that, RLS acted as a clan patriarch. Belle remembered: 'Louis was truly British in one respect, he was the head of his house, his word was law, and the whole family, ourselves included, revolved round him.' He had a code according to which everything said in his house was confidential and not to be repeated outside, and that at mealtimes nothing irritating or controversial was to be said; it was to be agreeable talk or nothing; small talk was frowned on; and instead he encouraged the art of general conversation in the French style.[27]

To Moors and other friends in Apia he would tend to expand more on his theories of writing than he did to his family. He particularly detested the philistinism, so prevalent now one hundred years after his death, whereby editors cut out Latin tags and foreign words on the ground that the most ignorant reader might be made to feel inadequate by confronting them; this he regarded as truckling to the lowest common denominator. And he loathed the allied populist prejudice against the use of unusual words, arguing that if the words existed and were in the dictionary, they should be given regular exercise so as not to perish from atrophy and desuetude.

Yet there were some matters he could divulge only to his closest friends in Britain. His letters to Baxter contained frequent nostalgic lamentations for the far away and long ago Scotland of his student days. On 6 June 1893 he wrote to Colvin:

> I am exulting to do nothing. It pours with rain from the westward, very unusual kind of weather. I was standing out on the little verandah in front of my room this morning, and there went through me or over me a wave of extraordinary and apparently baseless emotion. I literally staggered. And then the explanation came, and I knew I had found a frame of mind and body that belonged to Scotland, and particularly to the neighbourhood of Callander. Very odd these identities of sensation, and the world of connotations implied; Highland huts, and peat smoke, and brown swirling rivers, and wet clothes, and whisky, and the romance of the past, and that indescribable bite of the whole thing at a man's heart, which is – or rather lies at the bottom of – a story.[28]

Contemporary observers on Samoa were remarkably convergent in their assessment of Stevenson's character and attributes. All found him to be intolerant of evil, absurdly chivalrous, resentful of injustice, headstrong, impulsive and contemptuous of conventions when they were in collision with what he considered right and good. His love of children was evident, as well as his warm feeling for people of mixed race, who were usually held at arm's length in both white and Samoan communities; from one of them, Charles Taylor, whom RLS described as a 'sesquipedalian half-caste', he learned the modicum of Samoan he knew.

Moors was the RLS-watcher who most clearly conveyed his charisma. He found that there was a magnetic quality about Stevenson that made you want to open up to him and reveal all the innermost secrets. Although a poor public speaker, Louis had the eloquence of an actor: 'His face carried absolute conviction; and when he was burning with indignation, the fire in his eye showed it more clearly than any words could do.' As to whether he was a religious man, opinions differed, with some 'placing' him as a deist, though Moors thought the episode that so upset Henley, when Louis taught Sunday school for a month to please his mother, was undertaken purely as a role-playing experiment. He did not believe in hell – 'not in a lake of fire, anyway, nor in a remorseless, unappeasable God' – and had a most ambivalent attitude to Christianity; if anything he inclined towards Catholicism for its emotional appeal, and most of the 'boys' at Vailima were Catholics. There was also some dispute as to whether he was a real or bogus bohemian. An anonymous critic wrote in 1901: 'the truth is that Stevenson was not a Bohemian of the true breed. He was essentially the burgess masquerading as the Bohemian; that was just the difference between him and his no less brilliant though less celebrated cousin Bob.' But Moors thought this a hopelessly simplistic view: he pointed to the celebrated RLS carelessness about appearance – he usually wore a soft shirt and white flannel trousers with a red sash round the waist, so that he looked like an eccentric or misfit. 'Stevenson, though he was more or less a dual personality, was mostly Bohemian . . . the truth is there were two Stevensons . . . this strange dual personality.'

Since the two points in dispute are his religiosity and his eccentricity, perhaps we will leave the last word on RLS in 1893 with the missionary S.J.Whitnee, another of his tutors in the Samoan language, who provided this end-of-year snapshot:

> He was as active and restless as if his veins had been filled with quicksilver. He had a cigarette between his fingers and occasionally between his lips; but it was constantly going out after a few puffs. There was a strong rail running along the front of the balcony for safety. He, like the rest of us, had a chair, but he occupied it only a few minutes at a time. Then he strode along the balcony and poised himself upon the rail. Anon, he slid off, took a few steps, and dropped into his chair.[29]

19

Samoa: Final Year

'I am tired out and intend to work no more for six months at least,' Louis wrote to his mother on New Year's Day, 1894. Needless to say he did not keep this resolution, but 1894 was remarkable for the number of *taedium vitae* or *memento mori* remarks RLS let slip. To Baxter, in September, he wrote: 'I have been so long waiting for death, I have unwrapped my thoughts from about life so long, that I have not a filament left to hold by; I have done my fiddling so long under Vesuvius, that I have almost forgotten to play, and can only wait for the eruption, and I think it long of coming. Literally, no man has more wholly outlived life than I.' To Mrs Sitwell he said, in ironical rebuttal of the old adage: 'I was meant to die young and the gods do not love me.' And to Marjorie Ide, daughter of the new chief justice, he confided:

> I do not want to live to be old. I am ready to go at any time. I consider that a man who dies at forty-five years of age is to be envied. I can imagine nothing worse than to grow to be a helpless old man, a burden to one's friends, seeing one's powers gradually weaken, one's ideas exhausted and pleasure in life gone. Far better is it to pass away in the prime of life, at the height of popularity, when one's fame has reached its summit, and then be mourned by everybody.

Similar sentiments were expressed in a letter to Henry Baildon at the end of January: Louis said that long life might mean living to be impotent or forgotten; if, on the other hand, he died now or in six months time, he could fairly conclude that he had had a splendid life on the whole.

For most of his life Stevenson had held his physical debility responsible for the moods of 'black dog' that occasionally overcame him; now, in his last year of life, he began to doubt that this was so. A close student of RLS's Vailima years has concluded as follows:

> The long self-exile of Robert Louis Stevenson provided a romantic glow to

his career, and the partial restoration of health and consequent mobility which he found in Samoa may well have added a few years to his life. But the costs in spirit were heavy. Isolated from his literary and artistic friends, nagged by a sense of creeping estrangement, nervous over the collapse of his wife, and wearied by the misbehaviour of his numerous dependants, Stevenson did not find Vailima a haven of rest and peace.[1]

Some RLS students have speculated that Louis's creative juices were drying up and link this in turn to the source of his imagination as the child's ability to disregard reality. It is true that in his five years in Samoa Louis lost all his remaining illusions and that he did not have his mother's safety valve, memorably described by Colvin when he spoke to Lloyd Osbourne of Maggie 'whose peculiar gifts of disguising all facts at all unpleasant, whether from others or from herself, you must have known by your own experience'. Yet Louis was adamant that he became *more* a child, not less, as he grew older: 'As I go on in life, day by day, I become more of a bewildered child. I cannot get used to this world, to procreation, to heredity, to sight, to hearing; the commonest things are a burthen.' However, it is more likely that as he became more realistic and cynical (in the best sense of seeing how things really are rather than how one would like them to be), his fantasies of perfect freedom receded and the weight of determinism returned him in effect to some of the Calvinistic gloom of his early years, and particularly the idea of death as the wages of sin, and the realisation of mortality as each individual's Calvary. The frequent intimations of mortality in the last year at Vailima can perhaps be read, together with the evidence from his last two incomplete novels, as a coming to terms with Calvinism, and an appreciation that true mental health consisted in welcoming death much as his own Will o' the Mill did.

Such an interpretation might explain the puzzling institution of formal prayers at Vailima in the last period, which so greatly provoked Henley's fulminations against the 'Shorter Catechist'. Fanny maintained that the prayers, composed by Louis and later published, were a form of social control inculcating organic solidarity among the extended 'family', and necessary because 'the average Samoan is but a larger child in most things.' But it is much more likely that they represented Louis's attempts at realism and integration – an attempt to salvage all that was most valuable from the past and from religion and to fuse it into a new synthesis; the institution of the Vailima prayers certainly did *not* indicate a return by Louis to the faith of his fathers in any traditional sense.[2]

There were many sources of disillusionment for RLS in his last year. Even though he was now earning around £5,000 a year, outgoings constantly outstripped income. Money was needed for Lloyd's holidays, Belle's fripperies, Austin's education, Fanny's medical bills, Graham Balfour's trips to Mataafa in the Marshalls, and for the constant round of socialising and parties which satisfied Fanny's social aspirations and helped to keep her sane. Louis was not helped, either, by Colvin's cavalier attitude towards money; even as he criticised Louis's productions and colluded with publishers in the bowdlerising of his work, he consistently drew too much money from the account left with Baxter, to the point where Louis had to write a tactful letter on the subject, drawing attention to the manifold expenses of Vailima. Appalled, either genuinely or feignedly, by the financial situation thus revealed, Colvin wrote to Baxter to shift the blame on to the spendthrift Osbournes and the absurd literary aspirations of Lloyd: 'that . . . his next non-collaboration book will determine his holding or losing his place is to my mind certain . . . Work done under the kind of brain-pressure which he has been suffering of late cannot be of the best.'

This was clever, for by drawing attention to the prodigality and extravagance of the Osbournes, Colvin distracted attention from his own (admittedly lesser) propensity to live off immoral earnings. Colvin was on firm ground too in underscoring the 'spend, spend, spend' mentality of Fanny and Belle. Moors reported disgustedly that Stevenson, 'a sick man, was indeed the Work Horse supporting with difficulty, and in a trembling way, the whole expense of a large household of idling adults'. So alarmed was he was by the baneful influence of the Vailima women, and the deleterious impact of the collaborations with Lloyd, that he suggested to Louis that he retire for long periods of serious writing to an eyrie on Nassau Island, which Moors had purchased in 1892. At first Louis demurred, but by 1894 was at last ready to undertake the experiment; unfortunately death intervened.[3]

Another possible source for the weariness and depression Louis manifested in 1894 was his growing conviction that Germany was winning the political and diplomatic battle for Samoa, and that the western islands of the group, at least, would soon become German colonies. This is exactly what happened in 1899 when Samoa was partitioned: all the islands east of longitude 171 were given to the U.S.A. while Germany received Western Samoa in return for substantial German concessions to Britain elsewhere in the world, especially in Africa. The only aspect of this absorption that would have pleased RLS was the final vindication of Mataafa. After Laupepa's death in 1898 and Mataafa's return to Samoa, an election for king was held in which Mataafa secured an overwhelming majority; the then Chief Justice (Chambers) ruled in favour of the minority candidate Tanu, thus triggering another civil war, which ended in U.S. intervention and the treaty of partition.

1894 saw more wars and rumours of war, which disturbed Louis, and indeed much of his writing of St Ives was done to the distant booming of guns. There was, however, one significant difference between this situation and that obtaining in 1892–93; instead of an enemy as Chief Justice Louis now had his good friend Henry Ide, the former Land Commissioner, who had been in Upolu since the beginning of the previous November. As for the new Council President, Emil Schmidt, Marjorie Ide was adamant that RLS disliked him, but she may have been confusing him with the German consul Becker, whom (unlike Cedarcrantz) he detested at both an official and personal level; certainly there is no trace of animosity to Schmidt in Louis's own correspondence, and he described him to Colvin as 'rather a dreamy man, whom I like'.[4]

Consequently, Louis's role in island politics, already considerable, actually increased. When Chief Tui told him in January he would raise his clan against the authorities, no matter how hopeless the cause, Louis acted as intermediary and there was no war. But in April in the Atua district the partisans of young Tamasese — whom Lady Jersey had described in 1892 as the only Samoan with the square head and broad limbs of a Roman emperor — rose and were bloodily suppressed after a long campaign brought to a close by a naval bombardment in which British warships took part. This time Louis did not support the rebels, as he had the previous year when Mataafa was their leader, but bent his energies in two directions: he lobbied Cusack-Smith and the consuls to provide better conditions for the Mataafa chieftains in Mulinu'u jail; and he wrote a further series of letters to *The Times* in London to publicise the continued deadlock in Samoa. Nearer home he had to make a Solomonic judgement. It was an abiding fear at Vailima that in the event of civil war the Stevenson retainers would be called out by their respective chiefs. One of the Vailima favourites was a man named Talolo, who had a weak heart. One day the man's father arrived bearing a mobilisation order from the clan chief. Louis took the father aside and lectured him: 'Who is the father of this boy, you who wish to send him where he may be killed by the sword or die of exposure in the woods, or I, who wish to save his life by keeping him safe at home?' The father confessed himself defeated by this parable and departed empty-handed.[5]

By mid-1894 RLS was restored to favour with Laupepa. Louis stood surety to free one of Mataafa's chiefs, Poe, from jail and posted a bail-bond of one hundred dollars to guarantee that he would not join the Tamasese rebels. Laupepa construed this as a friendly act and came up to Vailima to repair the breach caused by Stevenson's open partisanship for Mataafa the year before. The visit got off to a shaky start when Louis, as was his custom when white visitors arrived, blew the *pu* or war-conch to summon the plantation workers. Some men might have feared an assassination attempt, but Laupepa did not quail; he simply stood his ground and looked at Louis with an enquiring smile. Yet worse was to come. Laupepa noticed a pistol mounted in mother-of-pearl, a gift to Louis from the Shelleys in the Bournemouth days, and, with the lack of embarrassment common to Polynesians, asked if he could have it. Since this was a visit of reconciliation, Louis could scarcely say no, and handed the gun to Fanny to load.

She discovered something wrong with the trigger and clicked it four times, while Laupepa stood in front of her to watch. At this point some instinct made her open up the pistol and, to her horror, in the fifth chamber was a cartridge; if she had clicked it just once more she would probably have killed Laupepa. The extent of international repercussions, the certainty of deportation, and the likelihood of much worse – possibly a murder trial – can only be imagined. Even more farcical was the sequel. Learning that Louis had presented Laupepa with a pistol, the egregious Cusack-Smith wrote to demand that he get it back, as such a gift infringed the disarming Act.[6]

The friendship of Chief Justice Ide and his daughter was important to Louis. Marjorie Ide, who was a teenager at the time, but noted down all she saw for later use, is a particularly good source for RLS at this phase of his life. She had intrigued Louis on her very first visit to Vailima as a child in 1890 when he gave her a non-functioning Swiss music box to keep her amused while the adults talked and promised she could keep it if she managed to mend it, which she did. Four years later, she was a close observer of his foibles. He liked coconut juice so much that one day, when the company was discussing what they would do if cast away on a desert island and condemned to die of thirst, Louis sprang up and exclaimed: 'I wouldn't die of thirst; I'd die of rage!' Marjorie also testified to his impulsive and melodramatic nature: during the Atua rebellion he would come riding up to Vailima in a great lather to announce that Tamasese's men intended to slaughter all whites; when Henry Ide cautioned him not to listen to hearsay, Louis replied gravely: 'Chief Justice, you are not to expose yourself and your daughters.' Ide merely laughed for, as his daughter said, 'there was probably no more danger than there would be in a quiet New England town.'

Another female observer of his last year noted Louis's tendency to 'shoot from the hip'. Marie Fraser mentioned an expatriate woman on Samoa on whom Louis called one day. He noticed that the Samoan girls employed in the house were wearing European dresses, and one of his particular horrors was the thought that the traditional culture of Samoa would be broken down by Europeanisation, including the wearing of Western clothes. He at once expostulated on this to the woman, who replied: 'Yes, they are all clothed; no woman shall come into my presence who shows any part of her body.' At this Louis lost his temper and blazed at her. 'Woman,' he thundered, 'is your mind so base that you cannot see and admire what is beautiful in the form God Almighty has created? Do you not understand that their own dress is right for the climate and their simple way of living? And do you not see that the first thing you do on landing on this beautiful island is to pollute their minds and sully their modest thoughts?'

Marjorie Ide was prepared to forgive Louis his spontaneous outbursts, as she knew they proceeded from a good heart. She was less enamoured of Fanny's gaffes, seeing in them merely the impatience and bad temper of a martinet. Once a newspaper reporter came to Vailima and found Louis out. Fanny agreed to talk to him instead, but then irritated the man by her 'clever-clever' smart-aleck answers. 'What are Mr Stevenson's intentions?' he asked. 'Strictly honourable, I assure you,' said Fanny. Infuriated by her mockery, the journalist returned to Australia and wrote a story that RLS kept a pet crab at Vailima that ate the grass and saved him having to mow the lawn; when Louis read the story and learned the genesis of its composition, he was furious with Fanny for her lack of tact.[7]

Apart from Ide and Haggard, Louis's favourite guest in 1894 was General James Mulligan, who arrived to replace Sewall as U.S. consul in August. Mulligan's personal charm and witty conversation enlivened what would otherwise have been many a dull evening for Louis at Vailima. According to Moors, Mulligan worshipped the ground RLS trod on and became a fanatical collector of Stevenson memorabilia, to the point where he once stole one of the author's autographed copies: 'To him RLS were sacred initials, the words Robert Louis Stevenson a magic spell. Any scrap of paper he could get hold of bearing either initials or name was planted away in Mulligan's "holy of holies".' It is both a tribute to the Americans and a reproach to the British that their respective consular officials should have been so respectively sympathetic and antipathetic to genius.[8]

Two other sympathetic souls got close-up views of Stevenson in 1894. One was A. Safroni-Middleton, who shipped out from England as an apprentice before the mast on an Australia-bound clipper and later made his way to Samoa. He reported:

There were *two* Robert Louis Stevensons, one a sobersided prematurely ageing man writing books, the other a lank-haired, boyish, haggard being who seemed to be forever wandering by night like a lost soul seeking to find its real self . . . RLS at home and subjected to the domestic restraint of his faithful guardian wife, and surrounded by Samoan servants, seemed a strangely humbled man. His expressive eyes seemed to hold the light of tragedy. Notwithstanding the spacious comfort of his apartments, well furnished, good wine and assiduous comfort of those he loved, an atmosphere of gloom prevailed.

The other observer was Sydney Lysaght, an emissary from Meredith, who stayed at Vailima at the end of March. He wrote of RLS as follows:

He was so slender that he looked taller than he actually was; he was barefooted and walked with a long and curiously marked step, light but almost metrical, in accord, it seemed, with some movement of his mind. It was his constant habit to pace to and fro as he conversed, and his step and his speech seemed in harmony . . . [of his eyes] you may see them in his many photographs, wide apart, alert as at times when he was listening attentively, but not as when they brightened at a memory nor as when they flashed with indignation, nor as when the smile forerunning a humorous thought was dawning in them . . . His appearance on horseback was amusing – dressed in white, with riding boots and a French peaked cap, chivalrous in his bearing, but mounted on a horse which would not have been owned by any self-respecting English costermonger, he would almost suggest a South Sea Don Quixote. But in spite of appearances his horse was not an unserviceable beast, and perhaps few better can be found on the island.

Lysaght brought a letter from Meredith, and this was perhaps the one occasion where political differences – Stevenson a Tory, Meredith a radical – got in the way of their immense mutual admiration. Lysaght seconded the opinions in Meredith's letter – that RLS was cut off from important stimuli in Samoa – and Louis replied with some heat, which made Lysaght think a nerve had been touched. Developing his theme that it was better to be removed from the influences of the London literary milieu, Louis declared: 'Human nature is always the same, and you see and understand it better when you are standing outside the crowd.' When this was reported to Meredith, he struck back vigorously: 'Human nature is not always the same. The same forces may be always at work but they find different expressions in every generation, and it is the expression that chiefly concerns the writer of fiction.'[9]

It is interesting that the great figures of late Victorian literature – Henry James, Meredith, Kipling, Barrie, Conan Doyle – all treated RLS with great respect and sensitivity. Not so the venal second-rater and academic drudge Colvin, who did little to help his friend and sometime protégé during his last year of life. The six-month period from October 1893 to March 1894 is full of constant carping complaints from Colvin: he complained of Louis's allegedly waning talent, warned that his work would suffer if he remained in Samoa, poured out vitriol about Samoan affairs which he detested, and urged him to return home when he knew that Louis could not do so; to Louis's frequently reiterated plea that Colvin should travel to meet him in Hawaii, or at least in San Francisco, Colvin consistently turned a deaf ear. Stung by all this, Louis replied sharply:

> Please remember that my life passes among my 'blacks or chocolates'. If I were to do as you propose, in a bit of a tiff, it would cut you off entirely from my life. You must try to exercise a trifle of imagination, and put yourself, perhaps with an effort, into some sort of sympathy with these people, or how am I to write to you? I think you are truly a little too Cockney with me.

Louis's outburst was largely waste of ink. Smarting under his demotion as literary agent and Baxter's elevation, and resentful at being rapped over the knuckles for treating Louis's money as his personal cornucopia, Colvin began a whispering campaign against Baxter, while remaining on superficially cordial terms with the Scottish lawyer and complaining to *him* about

RLS. Baxter was going through a crisis in his life, since his beloved wife Grace died in 1893 – and there are some who think that news of this was the crucial element that snapped Fanny back out of her madness, since she wrote Baxter a deeply sympathetic letter of condolence in May 1893. A further blow came in 1894 when his father died. None of this affected Colvin: in his letters to Louis he sniped away about Baxter's alleged drunkenness, claimed he had gone to pieces after the death of his father, and wrote spiteful innuendoes about the power of attorney Baxter had in Stevenson's affairs. Eventually Baxter learned what Colvin had been saying about him behind his back and he refused for a time to answer his letters, emboldened no doubt by a jaundiced remark from Louis in March 1894: 'Colvin (between ourselves) is a bit of an old wife, and has so often predicted that a book would be my ruin in January, and by July defied me to do anything as good, that I have ceased to pay very much regard.' Yet it was typical of RLS that when his two oldest remaining British friends started to become seriously alienated, he tried to pour oil on troubled waters: 'Grzz – you pair of mongrels, keep the peace!' he wrote to Baxter in September.

How great a contrast all this was to the attitude of the faithful Henry James can perhaps be gauged from the remark of Graham Balfour – who had met the 'master' in London – that James could have taken a First on any Samoan subject. As Colvin continued to nag, Louis wrote to him no more about his Samoan experiences but substituted James as his confidant on Polynesian matters. In July he wrote excitedly to him about a cruise to eastern Samoa he had just taken as guest of HMS *Curaçao*. This time he had managed to reach the island of Manu'a that had evaded his efforts in 1891: unaccountably overlooked in the tripartite carve-up, it was an independent island ruled by a 20-year old half-caste girl. After a two-day stay Louis wrote to James: 'I tasted on that occasion what it is to be great. My name was called next after the captain's, and several chiefs (a thing quite new to me, and not at all Samoan practice) drank to me by name.' As a result RLS was an honorary member of the *Curaçao* wardroom, and Vailima was thrown open to its officers: the road to Vailima was now known as the *Curaçao* track and his verandah as the *Curaçao* club. It was to James too, rather than Colvin, that Louis confided his literary interests: having completed his investigation of Renan, he was newly converted to Anatole France on the strength of *Abbé Loignard* – 'I don't think a better book was ever written.'[10]

The faithful Baxter also came up with a brilliant money-making wheeze, seized on with avidity by Louis and even more so by Fanny and Lloyd. This was nothing less than an 'Edinburgh Edition' of RLS's complete works, and some of Louis's happiest moments in 1894 were spent planning its layout and deciding which short stories should be grouped with which. Another literary correspondence this year was with Yeats, whose 'Lake Isle of Innisfree' Louis so admired. The two men had corresponded before, in 1891, but now Louis wrote to say that the perusal of 'Innisfree' was one of the three great moments of verse reading in his life, when he was most transfixed by the awe and mystery of poetry; the other two were when he read Swinburne's *Ballads* and Meredith's 'Love in a Valley'.[11]

Louis kept up the pace of his own productions and by the end of November 1894 had written what amounted in printed terms to more than 700,000 words in four years – and there were many incomplete fragments besides. At the end of 1893 he planned a book on seventeenth-century Scotland, to be called *The Heathercat*, but soon laid it aside.[12] He then took up the novel on which he had been labouring off and on throughout 1893 – *St Ives* – but by autumn 1894 was sick of it again and never completed it; the nearly complete work is perhaps three chapters away from its conclusion, and two very different Stevenson lovers, Arthur Quiller-Couch and Jenni Calder, separated by almost a century, have written endings that tie together the threads based on Stevenson's intentions.

St Ives is another of the RLS novels in which the autobiographical elements are manifest, rather than latent, as in *The Ebb-Tide, The Beach of Falesá and The Master of Ballantrae*. The hero is a Frenchman, imprisoned in Edinburgh Castle, who makes good his escape prior to a number of picaresque adventures. As a Frenchman in Scotland, he symbolises the alienation of RLS from the Calvinism of 'Auld Reekie'; as a prisoner he symbolises the 'prisoner' of Heriot Row in thrall to an oppressive father. His escape south of the border is a wonderful example of dream or fantasy as wish, for St Ives absconds without having to destroy a father; nor did RLS manage to win the girl who had led to the first serious breach with his father.

Important as it is as a psychological document, showing RLS trying to come to terms with his dead father and with Scotland – and possibly unconsciously also with an intimation of his own approaching death – *St Ives* is minor Stevenson, recapitulating themes better done elsewhere: the heroine Flora is ersatz Catriona, the escape from the castle echoes the escape in *The Black Arrow*, the pursuit through Scotland reflects the flight in the heather in *Kidnapped*, and the attempt to return to Edinburgh to testify recalls the situation in *Catriona*. There is even a warming over of the old theme of doubles, for much play is made of the physical similarity between the 'good' Anne St Ives and his evil cousin Alain; the valet tells him: 'Indeed, Mr Anne, you two be very much of a shape.'[13]

More interesting to the biographer is the complex four-way wrangling between RLS, Baxter, Burlingame and McClure about the American publication of the book, and the way Louis involved them as researchers in finding authentic materials for his rather bizarre finale, involving hot-air balloons and American privateers – which he never got round to writing.

The Americans were severely buffeted in the process, as two letters, respectively dealing with Burlingame and McClure, make clear: 'We shall have no more royalties from the States. A sum down will have to be agreed upon for every book you shall publish in future' . . . 'McClure has sent the MS here, or what was left of it, accompanied by an hysterical letter about the death, suicide, madness and starvation of all his employees. As if that mattered! 'Tis a whimsical creature.'[14]

In 1894 RLS also failed to complete a second, much more important, novel, also set in the year 1814, but perhaps taken by Louis no farther than its halfway mark. *Weir of Hermiston* has as its theme the anti-capital punishment son of a hanging judge who is condemned to death by his own father after killing the man (his friend) who has seduced his girlfriend; in the section left uncompleted the hero escapes from jail with the aid of a sept of Highland brothers and departs for the U.S.A., reunited with his wronged sweetheart. Louis wrote the first words of the novel in October 1892, having set *The Young Chevalier* aside to concentrate on it, but then got sucked into *The Ebb-Tide* and the early chapters of *St Ives*; finally, in September 1894, when he became bored with *St Ives* he returned to *Weir*.

Louis had high hopes for *Weir*, which he felt had to be 'either something different or I have failed', for this was a time when he was plagued by self-doubts and in some moods wondering whether he ought not to go back to the start, serve another literary apprenticeship, and turn himself into a different kind of writer. Lloyd Osbourne later wrote of his stepfather: 'His half-finished book, *Hermiston*, he judged the best he had ever written, and the sense of successful effort made him buoyant and happy as nothing else could.'[15]

Weir of Hermiston has some claims to be the most textured of Stevenson's novels. At the basic level it is a tale of heroic adventure; it is also in allegorical terms an epic of Scotland's story; it develops the themes of power and ambition from his previous novels; and it deals, albeit tangentially, with the savage repression of the Gael. One of *Weir*'s claims to greatness is that it is not, as *St Ives* largely is, a paean of nostalgia for Scotland, but adumbrates themes also relevant to the Pacific experience – the repression of 'old' Scotland by the new 'civilisation' from England being analogous to the destruction of ancient Samoan modalities by the great Powers. A lawyer himself, RLS habitually showed a contemptuous attitude for the law as the locus of civilisation – this was inherent in his dangerous skirmishing with libel actions involving two different missionaries. Some critics have seen RLS as closer in spirit to nineteenth-century U.S.A. than to British culture, and there is certainly a frontier panache about the way the struggle is resolved in *The Beach of Falesá*; and Louis's three courtroom scenes (in *Hermiston, Catriona* and the play, *The Hanging Judge*) scarcely show the majesty of the law in a good light. However, the

'American' view of RLS should not be pushed too far, and Eigner has elegantly summed up its limitations: 'Stevenson does not, like Twain, see the savage as one whom society has not yet spoiled and who is therefore less evil. He sees him merely as one whom society has not yet armed and who is consequently less dangerous.' This highlights the difference between the youthful radicalism of Twain and the conservatism of his friend RLS, but it also shows that one common critical view, emphasising a bifurcation between the 'Scottish' Stevenson of the late period (*Catriona, St Ives, Weir of Hermiston*) and the Pacific RLS (*The Beach of Falesá, The Ebb-Tide* and the ballads) rests on a misunderstanding; his psyche may have been fragmented but his work was synoptic.

However, what there is in *Weir of Hermiston* is a new pessimism born of the cynical realism of his last years. After all his denunciations of Zola and the Hardy of *Tess of the d'Urbervilles*, it is ironical to see him coming to rest at a position very close to theirs. The emphasis on ancestry and atavism recalls Zola's treatment of heredity in the *Rougon–Macquart* cycle. And Stevenson's handling of Fate irresistibly brings Hardy to mind. 'Fate played his game artfully with his poor pair of children' is like an unconscious echo of the famous conclusion to *Tess*: 'The President of the Immortals had finished his sport with Tess.' Indeed, if finished, *Weir of Hermiston* would certainly have provoked a direct comparison with *Tess*, since both works are based on the themes of ancestry, seduction and murder; perhaps Louis had some inkling of the direction in which he was headed, and the awkwardness of his position in the light of his denunciations of *Tess*, for he wrote to Barrie describing his heroine as 'what Hardy calls (and others in their plain way don't) a Pure Woman'.

The heavy hand of Fate is everywhere apparent in *Weir*, thinly disguised under the veneer of romance. Scots are shown as peculiarly marked down by destiny: 'For that is the mark of the Scot of all classes: that he stands in an attitude towards the past unthinkable to Englishmen, and remembers and cherishes the memory of his forebears, good or bad; and there burns alive in him a sense of identity with the dead even to the twentieth generation.' This emphasis on history has led the critic Irving Saposnik to declare: 'Throughout the novel there is an inescapable feeling that all has happened before, that his participants are acting out a repetition of what legend has determined as inevitable action.' In *Weir* RLS reaches the end of a rebellious career that had taken him from the psychological through the moral to the metaphysical: starting with the revolt against his parents and their Puritanism, he went on to lock horns with the Victorian bourgeoisie for its Grundyism and philistine attitude to art; by the end of his life he was ready to echo Lear:

Like flies to wanton boys are we to the gods, they kill us for their sport.[16]

There is some dispute in critical circles as to whether the Old Testament or Greek tragedy is the correct paradigm for the assessment of *Weir*, but if we accept Eric Auerbach's argument that Homer is rich in visual detail and imagery where the Old Testament is virtually barren of it – and then remember that RLS conceded Henry James's criticism that there was nothing for the eye in *Catriona* ('death to the optic nerve!' Louis cried defiantly), then the Old Testament would seem the better exemplar. Even so, such a categorisation engenders its own problems, for the last page Louis ever wrote contains an image as powerful as the pity of Achilles for Priam in Book 24 of the *Iliad*. When Archie took the sobbing Kirstie in his arms, 'he felt her whole body shaken by the throes of distress, and had pity upon her beyond speech.'

The Biblical reading of *Weir of Hermiston* would place Adam the patriarch and old Kirstie as figures from the Old Testament with Archie and Mrs Weir as representatives of the New and the law of love. But across that duality Stevenson has layered others; in particular he develops the themes of *Jekyll and Hyde* in that Archie represents the conscious and the other characters represent the unconscious. Superficially, Frank Innes is the Hyde shadow figure ('Enter Mephistopheles' is the title of the chapter where he first appears), extroverted, sociable and disloyal where Archie is introverted, eremitic and steadfast, or perhaps a better comparison would be with Utterson and Enfield in *Jekyll and Hyde* or even the brothers Durie in *The Master of Ballantrae*. Frank Innes is a double in a complex sense, since Archie's crime against his father – defamation – is the same as Frank's against him. But *all* the characters in this novel appear to be aspects of Stevenson, illustrating both the motif of role confusion noted in RLS's early life – Mrs Weir, for example, is much younger than Adam and belongs to her son's generation – and the fulfilment of the prophecy in *Jekyll and Hyde*: 'Man is not truly one, but truly two. I say two, because the state of my own knowledge does not pass beyond that point. Others will follow, others will outstrip me on the same lines; and I hazard the guess that man will ultimately be known for a mere polity of multifarious, incongruous, and independent denizens.'

One of the reasons *Weir* is so highly regarded in some Stevensonian circles is that it is the only one of RLS's novels that attempts to solve the problems of the father figure *and* the mother figure; it is not surprising that Jungians like Barbara Hannah regard it as a key text. That RLS in the last year of his life was coming to terms with his father and reinterpreting some of their old conflicts becomes clear from his letter to Adelaide Boodle in July 1894, assuring her that she was right: the last painful memories of

Thomas had faded away, to be replaced by more positive images from his prime: 'He now haunts me, strangely enough, in two guises: as a man of fifty, lying on a hillside and carving mottoes on a stick, strong and well; and as a younger man, running down the sands into the sea near North Berwick – myself, *aetat* 11 – somewhat horrified at finding him so beautiful when stripped.' Maggie had helped in the process of acceptance and reconciliation: doubtless beginning to be apprehensive as to how posterity would view her husband's treatment of her famous son, she was at pains to explain that it was not the literary career Thomas objected to but Louis's religious apostasy. That was not enough to silence the voices of criticism and Colvin wrote to her in 1896 to rebuke her for understating her son's ordeal: 'I think his cousin Bob, Baxter, Mrs Sitwell and myself were the only people in the world who knew what Louis was inwardly suffering.'[17]

RLS takes a more complaisant view of Adam Weir than of Attwater, showing the softening of his attitude towards his father, and indicating that the powerful paternal archetype in his psyche was ceasing to paralyse him. While Adam Weir is a hanging judge, his relish in passing draconian sentences, RLS seems to suggest, means he has embraced the savagery in his own nature and thus faced up to reality, rather as he himself now took a balanced view of the savage aspects of life in Polynesia. He portrays in Archie a man who, by not understanding his father, does not understand himself, and the implicit reproach is directed as much at himself as at his fictional creation. Politically, too, *Weir* underlines Louis's conservatism in political and social matters. Stevenson was like Dickens in that he could pluck at the heartstrings over an *individual* injustice, but drew back at any political prescription that tried to deal with injustice *in general*; and he was like Hardy in that he could see the pity, terror and tragedy endemic in capital punishment while defending the institution itself. Louis's short shrift with *bien-pensant* liberals was manifest in a letter to J.A.Symonds in the spring of 1886: 'As for those crockery, chimney-piece ornaments, the bourgeois (*quorum pars*), and their cowardly dislike of dying and killing, it is merely one symptom of a thousand how utterly they have got out of touch of life. Their dislike of capital punishment and their treatment of their domestic servants are for me the two flaunting emblems of their hollowness.'

However, a balanced view of life did not mean substituting father figure as benevolent despot for father figure as black tyrant; Louis did not swing by reaction into a sentimental view of patriarchs. In the part of the book he never wrote he intended Adam to pronounce the death sentence on his own son and then die from the shock of what he had done. Although assured that naturalistically such a scenario could never take place, Louis (unlike Hardy) preferred dramatic plausibility to documentary truth and insisted that such an outcome was psychologically necessary: Archie's new life in the U.S.A. could begin only if the father died instead of the son, just as it was Thomas's death in 1887 that enabled *him* to take ship for America.

If Adam Weir represented Louis's most successful attempt to come to terms with the dread patriarch of Heriot Row, the female characters in the novel represent his *only* fictional attempt to solve the oedipal confusion over his mother and the long line of older women or surrogate mothers that ended with Fanny. The perception of female sexuality is split as between older and younger Kirsties. If we accept that 'Cummie' both formed and distorted young Louis's image of woman, then the elder Kirstie emerges as much more than a naturalistic portrait of Cummie transfigured by imagination; she is also what Jungians would call 'a highly positive anima figure'. There are further confusions, too, in that there are elements of Maggie alongside the Cummie elements in the elder Kirstie; if Adam's biblical passion is anger, Kirstie's is lust. Her apparently caring and protective attitude to Archie masks a sexual passion:

> Her passion, for it was nothing less, entirely filled her. It was a rich, physical pleasure to make his bed or light his lamp when he was absent, to pull off his wet boots or wait on him at dinner when he returned. A young man who should have so doted on the idea, moral and physical, of any woman, might be properly described as being in love ... This perpetual hunger and thirst of his presence kept her all day on the alert. When he went forth at morning, she would stand and follow him with admiring looks. As it grew late and drew to the time of his return, she would steal forth to a corner of the policy wall and be seen standing there sometimes by the hour altogether, gazing with shaded eyes, waiting the exquisite and barren pleasure of his view a mile off on the mountains.

The elder Kirstie becomes jealous of her younger namesake, a jealousy increased by the realisation that the young girl that Archie loves is no youthful copy of herself, with golden locks, but a dark-haired beauty. There is a Lawrentian feel to the passage where she lies tossing in bed, beset by an insane sexual jealousy. Both Kirsties present aspects of the desired RLS female – one nubile and desirable, the other a matron but significantly childless; the wish for the ideal female to be both sex-object and mother is clearly on view here, and we begin to understand how the puzzling marriage to Fanny relates at a deep level to Stevenson's oedipal confusion. Barbara Hannah has made much of the fact that RLS died on the very day he wrote the scene between Archie and the younger Kirstie when 'he saw for the first time the face of woman as she is.' Hannah argues that at the very point Louis had to deal head-on with women, as opposed to refracting the feminine through maternal images, the shock to him as an artist was so great that he expired. Her idea is that the oscillation between elder and younger Kirstie showed RLS in a fool's paradise of sexuality; in Jungian terms his integration could only have come about if he had approached the ambiguous face of woman via Frank Innes (evil) as well, thus providing the classical four-sided dimension so beloved of Jung.

Many RLS lovers have claimed that *Weir of Hermiston* is his greatest work; even his inveterate critic and belittler, E.F.Benson, claimed that with this book Stevenson finally became a writer to take seriously. Lysaght, who discussed the novel at length with the author, reported: 'He expressed to me, as I believe he wrote to Sir Sidney Colvin, his opinion that in this story he had touched his high-water mark ... the strongest scene in the book was to be the one where Kirstie comes to her lover when he's in prison and confesses she's with child by the man he's murdered.' Others point to Louis's notorious difficulties with endings and are sceptical. Despite its impressive architecture and the profundity of its ideas, in terms of direct reader response *Weir of Hermiston* does not grab by the throat as *The Master of Ballantrae, The Beach of Falesá.* and *Kidnapped* do, and there has always been a minority viewpoint that the work is overrated simply because it is unfinished, so making it possible for each reader to imagine the master-piece that might have been; it thus joins the canon featuring Schubert's Unfinished Symphony, Mahler's Tenth, 'Kubla Khan' and *Edwin Drood*. Echoing Tacitus's *capax imperii nisi imperasset*, the minority view holds that an estimation of *Weir* as a work in the highest class is attributable more to this fantasy element than to the possibilities endemic in the text, and that at the very best its ending would have been as unsatisfactory as the conclusion to *The Master of Ballantrae*, if only because the moral dilemmas Stevenson posed were *in principle* incapable of satisfactory solution.[18]

One thing can be said with certainty: in his last years Louis's thoughts increasingly turned to Scotland. This was partly a natural consequence of working on the Scottish trilogy which, especially in the case of *The Young Chevalier*, brought an avalanche of mail from the Jacobite-obsessed Andrew Lang in the form of rare historical documents and copies of manuscripts. But it was partly also the result of the prompting of his dreams, which so often now took him back to the land of his childhood; those psychoanalysts who believe in 'death drive' would regard this as the sign of the unconscious preparing ignorantly for its own extinction. Yet it would be a mistake to think of Stevenson's many reflections on Scotland in his last months simply as nostalgia: he *did* love his native land, but was not blind to the defects of its inhabitants, and in a letter to J.M.Barrie on 13 July 1894 he told how Scottish culture had led him to abandon fishing and throttle back on levity when he was twenty. In 1871 he was in Kirriemuir, he wrote, on his way to Glenorgil to fish a real trout-stream, when he took shelter from the rain and found baskets of trout still kicking in agony, which cured him of angling for good. A little later at Balnamoon, he entertained the dinner table with tales of his mock fear of geese; one of two gorgons present put on a pair of eyeglasses, fixed him with a basilisk stare and said in a clangorous voice: 'You give me very much the effect of a coward, Mr Stevenson.' Moreover,

Louis never forgot that it was Scotland and its Calvinism that had made his childhood a nightmare: reading Renan's *Origines* reminded him of the unacceptable face of religion, and he wrote to Colvin: 'I remember when I was a child, and we came to the Four Beasts that were all over eyes, the sickening terror with which I was filled. If that was Heaven, what, in the name of Davy Jones and the aboriginal nightmare, could Hell be?'[19]

Nor did RLS necessarily turn to thoughts of Scotland because of *conscious* dissatisfaction with his life in the Pacific; it was more complex than that. The Pacific satisfied his aspirations at many levels: at Vailima he could be the new laird of Abbotsford and thus emulate the 'father figure' Sir Walter Scott in more ways than one; his health was near-perfect as long as he did not stray too far south or north (to Australia or Hawaii); and he came as close to perfect freedom as anyone could, never having to indulge the quotidian prejudices of London's Victorians or Edinburgh's 'unco' guid' burghers who, as Colvin reported, still harboured a grudge over Louis's bruising treatment of them in *Edinburgh: Picturesque Notes*. It is true that over the years Louis had become disillusioned with the barbarism, indolence, depravity and superstition of Polynesians and found it harder and harder to sustain the idea of the 'noble savage', but to admit that his Eden was an illusory one would rob his life of all meaning. This is why he felt compelled to blame Europeans for *everything* that was wrong with the Pacific; the only time he criticises his beloved Samoans is for firing first during Mataafa's defeat of the Germans at Fanagalii and even then he makes excuses: 'Conceive this people steadily as schoolboys, and conceive the elation of any school if the head boy should suddenly arise and drive the rector from the school-house.'

For this stance Stevenson has been much criticised, and from two sides. On the one hand he is accused of taking a patronising 'natives as children' attitude, familiar from the Victorian explorers of Africa. On the other, he is indicted for a bookish *a priori* view of Polynesia, whereby the noble savage is always good and the European interloper always bad; he drew particular criticism down on his head for writing his first letter on Samoan affairs to *The Times* before he had visited the islands and purely on the basis of hearsay fed to him in Hawaii. Perhaps the optimistic *The Beach of Falesá* has some of the 'noble savage' quality in it, but Louis soon disowned his more ingenuous perceptions, telling Colvin that the story was 'a hallucination I have outlived'.

RLS's ambivalence towards the Pacific is actually his greatest strength as an artist. Those who criticise him for having taken his European intellectual baggage to Polynesia ignore the ways in which the dialectic between Scotland and the South Seas was so fruitful: he was able to write such powerful work on Scotland at the crossroads between tradition and modernity (as in *Catriona* and *Weir of Hermiston*) precisely because he lived in a society that was (in his mind at least) identical to that of Scotland before the '45. Yet for Louis the association of ideas between the Pacific and Scotland went deeper than politics; it extended to the perception of nature itself, as Lysaght discovered:

> Out over the great plain of the Pacific was a sky of such starlight as we do not see at home; the tropical forest all about us was invariably silent, and from far away came the unvarying sound of the waters breaking on the coral reefs. He revelled in the beauty of the scene but he admitted that he would gladly have exchanged it for the mist-enfolded coasts of the little islands he had left far away in the wintry seas.

Often it was the very beauty of Polynesia that, paradoxically (or perhaps we should attribute it to Calvinistic guilt?) triggered genuine attacks of homesickness and nostalgia for the old familiar faces and places; while living in Moe's village at Tautira in Tahiti in November 1888 he composed a poem which may stand for the many occasions he regretted that the sailor could never return from the sea nor the hunter come home from the hill:

> Home no more home to me, whither shall I wander?
> Hunger my driver, I go where I must.
> Cold blows the winter wind over hill and heather;
> Thick drives the rain, and my roof is in the dust.
> Loved of wise men was the shade of my roof-tree,
> The true word of welcome was spoken in the door.
> Dead days of old, with the faces in the firelight,
> Kind folks of old, you come again no more.
>
> Home was home then, my dear, full of kindly faces;
> Home was home then, my dear, happy for the child.
> Fire and the windows bright glittered on the moorland,
> Song, tuneful song, built a palace on the wild.
> Now when day dawns on the brow of the moorland,
> Lone stands the house and the chimney stone is cold.
> Lone let it stand, now the folks are all departed,
> The kind hearts, the true hearts, that loved the house of old.[20]

The complexity of Stevenson's nostalgia for Scotland deepens when we realise that it was not the actual present Scotland he yearned for but the imagined Scotland of the past. RLS's writings are suffused with a sense of the past-in-the-present, of such a definitive style that Jungians have cited his work as evidence for the 'collective unconscious'. This notion of a transcendent Scotland in an immanent Pacific is a powerful motif in the late Stevenson *oeuvre* and also informed his feelings about travel in other parts of the world. He hoped one day to visit India, but what interested him there was not Delhi or Agra but the old Danish settlements in the Bay of Bengal. Moreover, RLS preferred the Scotland of his memory and imagination to the reality, and it is unlikely that, after his Polynesian experiences, he would have gone back there to live permanently even if he had miraculously come into full health. After the first memorable occasion when Louis and Fanny visited Mataafa and drank *ava* with him and his chiefs, he said to Fanny: 'Could we ever stand Europe again? Do you appreciate that if we were in London, we should be *actually jostled* in the street? And there is nobody in the whole of Britain who knows how to take *ava* like a gentleman.'

Thoughts of Scotland led by association of ideas to the friends he had known there in the old pre-Fanny days, and in the last six months of his life RLS made a real attempt to build bridges to the two whose loss he felt most keenly: Henley and Bob. He told James Payn in August that he often thought of his visits on a winter's afternoon to Henley in the Edinburgh Infirmary. Earlier that year terrible news had come in: Henley's only child, the adored golden-haired, six-year old Margaret, Barrie's model for Wendy in *Peter Pan*, died, making Henley the third of those close to RLS (the others were the two Fannies) who had lost a child. Louis wrote Henley a touching letter of condolence. 'There is one thing I have always envied you, *and envy you still*.' But to Baxter he wrote: 'Of Henley I cannot speak. It is too sad. I never envied anyone more than I did him when he had child, and it proved – or seemed to prove – healthy. Alas! I might have spared my envy. After all, the doom is common to us: we shall leave none to come after us, and I have been spared the pain – and the pleasure. But I still sometimes wish I had been more bold.' This is eloquent on Louis's attitude to his own childlessness, and shows that it was not just Fanny who regretted that she had not borne children in her second marriage.

Yet Fanny was completely unable to make common cause with someone out of shared grief; the hurt of 1888 still rankled. The upshot is clear in a letter from Louis to Baxter in August:

> I have had a letter from Henley, which I thought in very good taste and rather touching. My wife, with that appalling instinct of the injured female to see mischief, thought it was a letter preparatory to the asking of money; and truly, when I read it again, it will bear this construction. This leads us direct to the consideration of what is to be done if H. does ask for money. I may say at once that I give it with a great deal of distaste. He has had bad luck of course; but he has had good luck too and has never known how to behave under it. On the other hand I feel as if I were near the end of my production. If it were nothing else, the growing effort and time that it takes me to produce anything forms a very broad hint. Now I want all the money I can make for my family and, alas, for my possible old age, which is on the cards and will never be a lively affair for me, money or no money, but which would be a hideous humiliation to me if I had squandered all this money in the meanwhile and had to come forward as a beggar at last. All which premised, I hereby authorise you to pay (when necessary) five pounds a month to Henley. He can't starve at that; it's enough – more than he had when I first knew him,

and if I gave him more it would only lead to his starting a gig and a Pomeranian dog.

Those were fateful words. When Graham Balfour published his biography of RLS in 1901 he quoted this phrase from this letter, omitting Henley's name and leaving it as 'Z'; but he overlooked the fact that 'Pomeranian dog' was obviously an in-joke shared by Louis and Henley in their palmier days, for Henley knew at once who was being referred to. White with fury, he penned his famous demolition job on RLS, 'the Seraph in Chocolate' for the *Pall Mall Magazine*, adding as a Parthian shot that the attitude evinced by the phrase 'scarce becomes the lips of a man who had several kennels of Pomeranians and gigs innumerable'.[21]

Louis's other attempt at conciliation was more successful – and it must be said that to give charity with such bad grace to Henley was almost worse than giving nothing at all. With Bob he fared better. When he was laying plans for the Edinburgh edition of his works in May, he planned six sets, each dedicated to a particular person. One of the dedications was to read as follows: 'To Robert Alan Mowbray Stevenson. *Olim Arcades ambo*' ('Once we were Arcadians together' – a quotation from Virgil's *Eclogues*). The 'once' sounded pointed, rather like when Louis referred to Henley as 'my *old* friend', but he must have started thinking about Bob, for in mid-June he wrote him a very long letter, ostensibly about the genealogy of the Stevenson family but really with copious detail about everyday life in Samoa, of the kind Colvin found boring. This time Bob, who had so irked Louis by not replying to his letters, wrote back affably, so Louis dug down a layer to reveal to Bob some of his deeper thoughts on life. In the last letter exchanged between the cousins, written on 18 September, Louis uttered his valedictory thoughts on the subject of sexuality:

> If I had to begin again – I know not – *si jeunesse savait, si vieillesse pouvait* . . . I know not at all – I believe I should try to honour sex more religiously. The worst of our education is that Christianity does not recognise and hallow sex. It looks askance at it, over its shoulder, oppressed as it is by reminiscences of hermits and Asiatic self-torture. It is a terrible hiatus in our modern religions that they cannot see and make venerable that which they ought to see first and hallow most. Well, it is so; I cannot be wiser than my generation.[22]

RLS's thoughts in 1894 were full of regret; regret that he had not fathered a child; regret that he had not been bolder in his treatment of sexuality; regret that he had not been a different sort of novelist; even regret that he had been a writer at all. For it was in this final period that his feelings of guilt about the 'confidence trick' involved in being a writer combined with his fading energies to slow down his work-rate, and this is surely the true explanation for his failure to complete *St Ives* and *Weir of Hermiston*. To Henry James he wrote in July: 'I am in one of those humours when a man wonders how anyone can be such an ass to embrace the profession of letters and not get apprenticed to a barber or keep a baked potato stall.' To Colvin he expressed the feeling that his work hitherto had not been entirely genuine:

> I know I am at a climacteric for all men who live by their wits, so I do not despair. But the truth is I am pretty near useless in literature . . . Were it not for my health which made it impossible, I could not find it in my heart to forgive myself that I did not stick to an honest commonplace trade when I was young, which might now have supported me during these ill years. But do not suppose me to be down in anything else; only, for the nonce, my skill deserts me, such as it is or was. It was a very little dose of inspiration and pretty little trick of style, long lost, improved by the most heroic industry . . . I am a fictitious article and have long known it. I am read by journalists, by my fellow-novelists and by boys . . . And I look forward confidently to an aftermath; I do not think my health can be so hugely improved without some subsequent improvement in my brains . . . I cannot take myself seriously as an artist, the limitations are so obvious. I did take myself seriously as a workman of old, but my practice has fallen off, I am now an idler and cumberer of the ground.

Strongest of all 'guilty' statements is this:

> 'Why the artist can *do nothing else* . . . continually exercises myself . . . *David Balfour* is a nice little book, and very artistic and just the thing to occupy the leisure of a busy man; but for the top flower of a man's life it seems to be inadequate. Small is the word; it is a small age, and I am of it. I could have wished to be otherwise busy in this world. I ought to have been able to build lighthouses and write *David Balfour* too.'[23]

Superficially life at Vailima continued as before. There was the usual crop of visitors – this year brought French and Austrian noblemen, Albert de Lautreppe and Count de Silva, a friend of Wurmbrand's, an Austrian officer married to the daughter of an American millionaire. Louis was sad to see Wurmbrand go to take up his post in Tonga, for his position as chief cowherd at Vailima had afforded both RLS and Wurmbrand much amusement. Louis was always won over by amateur theatricals at their most ludicrous and he often laughed heartily at the memory of Wurmbrand singing 'Cruiskeen Lawn', which he had learned in broken Irish, to a tune of his own. But he was not one of those who enjoy a joke only if it is at someone else's expense. One of his favourite stories concerned the time he spent as an experimental Sunday School teacher. Finding his class of Samoans terminally bored by Bible stories, he bribed them by offering sixpence to the first questioner; nobody spoke, so Louis advanced the bidding by sixpences up to two shillings and sixpence, at which point someone called out: 'Who made God?' Louis admitted this ended his career as a missionary but that it was worth the half crown.

By now the Germans on the island had learned to tolerate Stevenson, though there was still one die-hard editor who attacked him once a week in a German publication. Generally, though, he was as welcome on board German warships as on his beloved *Curaçao*, and he joined in equestrian paper-chases with the clerks of the German firm; on one occasion he scandalised the island's missionaries by riding fifteen miles on 'Jack' on the sabbath to carry off the third prize. Yet it was always HMS *Curaçao* that was the real social magnet. Feeling itself embarrassed by the constant lavish hospitality at Vailima, the wardroom organised a sumptuous officers' ball on the ship. Next day two of the 'below decks' men appeared at Vailima: 'Me and my messmates invites Mr and Mrs Stevenson, Mrs Strong, Mr Osbourne and Mr Balfour to a sailors' ball in the same' all as last night, not forgetting young Boskin.'

'Young Boskin' (Austin Strong) returned from California in April; the educational experiment there had not proved a success. Like all the Osbourne sept, Austin could never settle to anything, and when he sent him off to school in New Zealand at the end of October, in the care of the Stevenson cousin Lewis Henry Balfour Wilson, Louis explained that the boy was 'not very forward in his schooling and not very brilliant at understanding'.[24]

For the first six months of 1894 the only other white adults at Vailima were Belle and Fanny, whose more and more frequent quarrelling led Louis to retreat increasingly to his eyrie at the top of the house; Fanny still resented Belle's role as amanuensis and (in her terms) literary usurper, for she still felt that if she could not give Louis children, she should at least be able to play midwife to his brainchildren. Louis was therefore glad when Vailima's full white complement was brought up to strength at the end of June: first Graham Balfour returned from his wanderings in Europe and the Pacific, and then Lloyd returned from an extended holiday in New Zealand, where he met Maggie off the ship; Louis's mother had finally decided to sell up in Scotland and make a permanent home in the South Seas.

When he could play patriarch, reasonably confident that in an extended gathering there would be no scenes from Fanny, Louis was at his most relaxed. He liked to hold forth on his theories as a 'cynical epicurean', would often display a feminine vanity and wear his favourite trio of topaz (his birth stone) rings, inside two of which were his initials, and once even tried to learn to sew, sitting on a sofa by the window in a long blue and white Japanese kimono, his bare feet on the tiger rug. Louis liked having Graham Balfour around, for he was the rare bird who actually got on with all the Osbournes: Lloyd shared with him as bachelor quarters the original shack, now refurbished and known as 'Pineapple Cottage'; Belle secretly wished the young man would propose to her; while Fanny made him her confidant. Balfour amused them by announcing that he was taking Will o' the Mill as his guide and mentor in life, but he once carried the role of stoic philosopher too far by trying to compose the parties when Louis and Fanny were quarrelling: at this 'impertinence' they predictably turned and rended him together.

Balfour left a memoir from which the flavour of these family conversations can be inferred. They usually took the form of some *ex cathedra* pronouncement from RLS, wittingly or unwittingly controversial, that had the immediate effect of setting the cat among the pigeons. One RLS observation which seemed too close to home was as follows: 'The spice of life is battle; the friendliest relations are still a kind of contest; and if we would not forgo all that is valuable in our lot, we must continually face some other person, eye to eye, and wrestle a fall whether in love or enmity.' It might have been expected, from his contempt for the taste of the mass reading public, that RLS would not be particularly enamoured of 'common sense', and so it proved when Balfour ventured a defence of that bulkwark of British empiricism. 'I was assailed with a denunciation of its meanness, its lack of imagination and its poverty of spirit which, even through twenty years of an official career, have ever since caused me to distrust that bourgeois rule of life.'25

One of the great talking points among the six white adults was the impending Edinburgh edition of Stevenson's works. Three of the proposed marked copies were reserved for Bob, Colvin and Baxter, but Lloyd and Belle were to be rewarded with their own commemorative set, complete with Latin tags: the dedication to Lloyd would read *'Quorum pars magna fuit'* ('Of which he had a large share', from Virgil's *Aeneid*); to Belle the inscription would be *'Filiae amicae gratae'* ('To a fond and beloved daughter'). Pride of place, though, went to Fanny, the dedicatee of the entire edition, for whom Louis composed the following verses:

> I see rain falling and the rainbow drawn
> On Lammermuir: hearkening, I hear again
> In my precipitous city beaten bells
> Winnow the keen sea wind; and looking back
> Upon so much already endured and done
> From then to now – reverent, I bow the head!
>
> Take thou the writing; thine it is. For who
> Burnished the sword, blew on the drowsy coal,
> Held still the target higher, chary of praise
> And prodigal of counsel (censure?) – who but thou?
> So now, in the end, if this the least be good,
> If any deed be done, if any fire
> Burn in the imperfect page, the praise be thine!

However, for reasons unexplained, Fanny did not like the poem and the verses were omitted from the dedication; by now Fanny was consciously preparing to propagate the legend of RLS, with herself as devoted nurse and carer, and there may have been something here – perhaps the word 'censure' – that struck the wrong note from her point of view.

Still sleeping in separate rooms, the Stevensons may have been drifting even further apart in the final months; one good reason will appear shortly. There is something naïe about the way Maggie reports that Fanny has gone to stay in a hotel in Apia, because she has a cold and fears to give it to Louis (August). Vailima was easily big enough for them not to come into contact with each other if that was the object, and Fanny could have had her meals brought to her room; moreover Fanny had a very bad attack of bronchitis in July, did not move out, and was quite content to have Louis breakfast with her in her room; let us remember also how much Fanny detested hotels.[26]

While Fanny was in Apia, Louis received his greatest tribute yet from the Samoans he had so assiduously befriended. Mataafa's chieftains were at last released from Mulinu'u jail and, led by Poe, came up to Vailima with a proposal: in return for all Tusitala's kindness, they wanted to build a road between Vailima and Apia, to be called *Mea-Alofa* ('the gift of love'). The mask of reserve Samoans usually donned in the presence of *haoles* was torn away, and Louis felt almost embarrassed by the heartfelt way the chiefs referred to their great friend Tusitala. Even more astonishing was the Samoans' voluntary assumption of this *corvée*-like task for, as Louis explained to Colvin, this was the least conceivable thing for them to undertake: 'Think of it! It is road-making – the most fruitful cause (after taxes) of all rebellion in Samoa, a thing to which they could not be wiled with money nor driven back by punishment. It does give me a sense of having something in Samoa after all.'

By early October the 'Road of the Loving Heart' was finished. On the seventh of the month Louis gave a feast to celebrate, and among the novelties he produced for his guests' delectation was tinned salmon; one of the chiefs put an opened tin to his mouth and swallowed the contents, juice and all, down to the dregs. The twenty-two chiefs then added their name to the legend pasted up on a billboard at the beginning of the turn-off to Vailima from the cross-island road, and the message to posterity was of simple eloquence: 'We bear in mind the surpassing kindness of Mr R.L.Stevenson and his loving care during our tribulations while in prison. We have therefore prepared a type of gift that will endure without decay forever – the road we have constructed.'[27]

After his death, some of Stevenson's admirers, in a burst of hyperbolic imagination, tried to turn him into a mythical being – running at a tangent to the more banal legend constructed by Fanny and her coterie – and some went so far as to portray him as a Christ-like figure. He certainly qualified in one sense; he nursed a Judas among his disciples. In the last three months of his life Louis's eyes were finally opened to the true moral nature of Lloyd Osbourne. He suddenly discovered that Lloyd had taken a Samoan girl as his mistress but had no intention of marrying her; what was worse, when Louis taxed him with this, he said he refused to be the parent of half-caste children. This was an offence against the RLS code twice over: the refusal to marry a woman you had slept with if she wanted matrimony was beyond the pale in Louis's eyes, and indeed this fixed point of his moral compass was the chief reason he had married Lloyd's mother; and the refusal to accept paternity of the offspring of a liaison with a Samoan woman was a denial of the moral position expressly taken up by RLS in *The Beach of Falesá*, as Lloyd knew very well.

The resultant explosion when Louis turned on his treacherous ingrate of a stepson is probably the true reason Fanny decamped to the Apia hotel at the end of August. All her life Fanny had been able to avoid choosing between her son and her husband simply because Lloyd had always been Louis's cynosure; now she had to choose and, as anyone who knew the intense relationship between her and her beloved son could have predicted, she chose Lloyd. But as she brooded in Apia, Fanny, knowing how unbending Louis could be when his moral blood was up, came to realise that this wrangle might spell the end of all her dreams; what instructions might not an enraged Louis send to Baxter, who held the purse-strings? Maybe even the hated Henley and Katharine de Mattos might triumph after all and emerge as beneficiaries in his will. She therefore decided to cut the Gordian knot. She summoned the luckless recipient of Lloyd's favours and threatened her with all the retribution imaginable, insinuating that she had Tusitala's full backing. The ingenuous Samoan girl was out of her depth: she knew the reputation of the Witch Woman of the Mountain, and she knew too the Samoan legend that Tusitala was all-powerful: had he not ridden out the hurricane when all the powerful representatives of Germany and Britain wanted him deported? She fled in despair and was said to have died of grief and shame not long afterwards; many years later, after her marriage to Lloyd, Katharine Osbourne wormed the story out of him, having been ignorant of it when she accepted his suit.[28]

Louis was aghast that, after all the favours and privileges he had showered on Lloyd, the young man could requite him thus. It is worth pausing a minute to establish just how generous Louis had been to him in that very year, to say nothing of all the money he had lavished on him in the previous fourteen years. For two months Lloyd had been on a skating holiday near Mount Cook in the Southern Alps in New Zealand (South Island), and Louis requisitioned funds from Baxter to pay for it. The cost for the two months was £120: projected on a per annum scale this is *twelve times* the amount Louis thought was quite adequate for Henley to live on or, to put it another way, Lloyd spent in two months what Henley would have had to live on for two years. One can well imagine Louis's fury when, backed by Fanny, Lloyd refused to 'take orders' from Louis, or to accept that he had any moral responsibility to him. He argued that Louis had had amatory dalliances as a youth that had not committed him to marriage, forgetting the all-important difference that Thomas Stevenson had forbidden his son to 'save' any of the fallen women he consorted with. Many years later Lloyd obliquely tried to have the last word in this argument by writing of Louis: 'He was no saint . . . His early life had been tempestuously intermixed with those of many women, and I have never heard him express a wish that it might have been otherwise.'

However, Lloyd implicitly accepted one of Louis's dicta, which is that the best way to tell a lie is to tell the truth. He provided graphic and convincing details of a harrowing scene when RLS broke down in tears after an emotional attempt at rapport, but clearly changed the circumstances of the outburst. According to Lloyd, Stevenson had read parts of *Weir of Hermiston* aloud to the extended family, and all had commented but Lloyd. When Lloyd made as though to go to bed, Louis grabbed his arm and accused him of insulting behaviour. Lloyd claimed he had said nothing because he had been awestruck by the story's brilliance and that the pair of them sat up all night like lovers, their arms clasped around each other, while Louis poured out his woes. Lloyd continues: 'Until then I had never conceived the degree of his daily sufferings; the petty, miserable dragging ailments that kept him in a "perpetual torment"'. He spoke of the "physical dishonor"; of the "degradation" of it; of moments when he had longed for death.'

Most of the story rings true. We can readily accept that Louis accused Lloyd of insulting behaviour, that he wept and poured out his grief in the way described. What is incredible is that Louis should have behaved like this over *Weir*, for any opinion he once had of Lloyd as collaborator had long since vanished, as his letter to Bob in September makes clear. When we remember Belle's comment that Lloyd habitually rewrote history to show himself in the best light, we can infer that this scene, or something very like it, almost certainly took place – hence the circumstantial authenticity of the tale – but that its genesis was not a literary dispute but the much more important moral matter of the Samoan mistress.[29]

As he approached his forty-fourth birthday, Louis felt weary. He was oppressed by the terrible heat which seemed to presage a fearful hurricane season, depressed by the wrangling with Lloyd, gloomy about the coming of genuine middle age, anxious that his stamina for writing seemed to be fading, intermittently ill to the point where he was suffering dry throat and swollen legs as side effects of the laudanum he took to ward off fever and, above all, deeply worried about money. His very last letter to Gosse was on the subject, and on 4 November he wrote to Baxter to ask his advice on how soon it would be before he could live on the income from his capital and royalties; he calculated he needed £1,200 a year to live, provided economies were practised. 'This would practically bring us to a bearing: a circumstance extremely desirable in my present condition of health and mind. Not that I am ill, only that my digestion has quite taken leave of me in the meantime, and that for work I am literally and totally unfit.'

There were two great social occasions at Vailima in November. The very last public celebration was the Thanksgiving Dinner but before that came the 13th, when Louis's forty-fourth birthday was celebrated in style: for the great feast given that day a whole heifer was roasted in a Samoan oven, along with twenty pigs, fifty chickens and seventeen pigeons; fruit and vegetables were represented by twelve large yams, 430 *taro* roots, eighty arrowroot puddings, 804 pineapples and twenty bunches of bananas – Maggie made the precise count. 'Dear Lou,' she wrote in her diary, 'what cause for thankfulness it is that he has been spared to see his 44th birthday in so much health and comfort.' Perhaps in compensation for Lloyd's treachery, Louis invited more and more young men from HMS *Curaçao* and *Wallaroo* up to the house. Two young lieutenants in particular, Eeles and Meiklejohn, became special protégés, but Louis did not limit his favour to the officer class. At the end of November, three Scots sailors from HMS *Wallaroo* made the pilgrimage up to Vailima and were rewarded with a tour of the house conducted by Louis in person; he showed them memorabilia, including a specimen of Gordon's handwriting from Khartoum, in Arabic letters on a cigarette paper, framed for safety between two pieces of glass, and gave one of the sailors, an Edinburgh man, a signed copy of *Underwoods*, his book of verse.[30]

Monday 3 December 1894 was Louis's last day on earth. For a day or two Fanny had been feeling that something dreadful was about to happen to someone dear to them. It has been also alleged that Louis had a premonition of approaching death, reflected in one of the 'Vailima prayers' ('For Strength'), but Fanny claimed that Louis had a bad feeling about Graham Balfour, then visiting Mataafa in the Marshalls, and became convinced he would be shipwrecked. Certainly when Fanny voiced her fears, Louis made light of them, and tried to cheer her up at elevenses by reading a section from the latest chapter of *Weir of Hermiston* and playing a hand or two of patience with her; the two of them concluded that it could not be to either of *them* that the dreadful thing was about to happen. In the morning he worked on *Weir*, then in the afternoon dictated some letters, rode to Apia and back and went for a swim. The row with Fanny about a lecture tour of the U.S.A. – which he was reluctant to undertake but which she urged on him because of the generous fee – and which, according to some biographers, happened on this last afternoon, must have taken place on some earlier occasion.

After a swim and a change of clothes Louis came downstairs and, finding Fanny still gloomy, suggested they make a 'Vailima salad' complete with mayonnaise dressing. He went down to the cellar and brought up a bottle of burgundy, and then stood chatting happily to Fanny on the verandah, helping her to mix the oil and lime juice. Suddenly he put his hand to his head and cried: 'What's that? Oh, what a pain! Do I look strange?' Masking her concern, Fanny lied and said no, but seconds afterwards Louis fell to his knees. With the help of the butler, Sosimo, she guided him through the door of the great hall into his grandfather's armchair, where he at once lost consciousness. Fanny tried to revive him with brandy and by calling his name, but there was no response. She called out for Maggie and Belle, the alarm was raised, and Lloyd ran over from Pineapple Cottage. He found Louis lying back, breathing harshly, eyes wide open. The women called for a bed to be brought in, and Lloyd and the servants lifted him into it. Against Lloyd's protests – for he remembered Louis had said he wanted to die with his boots on – the three women took off his boots. Lloyd then mounted his horse and rode down to Apia at a gallop to get Dr Funk; word was also sent to Dr Anderson on *HMS Wallaroo*. Funk's initial diagnosis was that Louis had had an apoplectic fit from a blood clot on the brain and Dr Anderson, when he arrived, concurred that a cerebral haemorrhage had occurred. Seeing Fanny rubbing brandy into her husband's skeletal arms, Anderson in an unguarded moment said: 'How can anybody write books with arms like that?' The distraught Fanny rounded on him: 'He has written all his books with arms like these.' Louis never regained consciousness and after two hours in coma died at 8.10 p.m.

Louis's sudden death shocked his wife and mother so much that the reality took some time to sink in. Next day Maggie wrote to her sister Jane Whyte Balfour: 'How am I to tell you the terrible news that my beloved son was suddenly called home last evening.' As the truth sank in, Maggie went over and over past events, seeking consolation. 'I don't think I was ever before so terribly impressed with the greatness of the struggle that my beloved child had made against his bad health,' she wrote to her sister on 13 January 1895. She remembered how years before, someone had tried to comfort Louis by pointing out that the Balfours always got stronger as they grew older. Louis replied grimly: 'Yes, but just as I begin to outgrow the Balfour delicacy, the Nemesis of the short-lived Stevensons will come in and finish me off.'[31]

Since Louis had to be buried by 3 p.m. next day, according to the advice of the doctors on the decomposition of corpses in the tropics, Fanny enlisted the help of the Samoan chiefs who had built the Road of the Loving Heart to cut a path up to the summit of Mount Vaea, Louis's chosen resting place. By early afternoon on the 4th the toiling work party had completed the task. At 1 p.m. the Samoan pallbearers began the difficult ascent – made more difficult because they held the coffin shoulder-high. At the top, the service was read and the coffin lowered into place; later, a large tomb built of cement blocks was placed over the grave. In 1897 a plinth was added, flanked by two bronze plaques. One, in Samoan, bore the legend: 'The Tomb of Tusitala', followed by Ruth's speech to Naomi: ' . . . thy people shall be my people, and thy God my God; where thou diest, will I die . . .' On the other side was the 'Requiem' which Louis had written many years before:

> Under the wide and starry sky,
> Dig the grave and let me lie
> Glad did I live and gladly die,
> And I laid me down with a will.
>
> This be the verse you grave for me;
> Here he lies where he longed to be;
> Home is the sailor, home from sea,
> And the hunter home from the hill.

Epilogue

Death came to RLS from an unexpected direction: not from tuberculosis but from a stroke, brought on by stress and overwork, which in turn was caused by the demands of his extravagant family. Given all the self-doubts that plagued him while he strove to bear this burden, perhaps we might conclude judiciously that at some level he was glad to be quit of life. There was a sense in which, like Will o' the Mill, he had already made his peace with death, as one of his verses from the 1880s indicates:

> The look of Death is both severe and mild,
> And all the words of Death are grave and sweet,
> He holds ajar the door of his retreat;
> The hermitage of life, it may be styled;
> He pardons sinners, cleanses the defiled,
> And comfortably welcomes weary feet.
> The look of Death is both severe and mild,
> And all the words of Death are grave and sweet.

Quite apart from his fame in the wider world, and the imperishable achievement of his work, he left behind a great reputation in the Pacific. Samoans, missionaries, traders, officials, even his enemies in Polynesia, all concurred: 'this was a man.' One traditional Samoan song describes the search among the whites for a man as good and kind as Tusitala: the Samoan asks officials, ships' captains and consuls where such another man may be found among the *haoles*, and they all reply: 'There were none like him and he has gone.'

There are even grounds for suspecting that the Samoans mourned him more than his own family did, for, with the exception of Maggie, who departed to live with her sister in Scotland, unable to live in the house with so many memories of her son, evidence of genuine grief is hard to find. Lloyd Osbourne made his usual response to any crisis that impinged on the temple of his selfhood by departing on a long sea cruise. Fanny's case is even more curious for, now, surely, a woman with such a shaky hold on reality should have broken down. Fanny did not do so: if anything, she seemed to blossom; her biographer wrote: 'there seems to have been a certain lessening of her tension. Stationary in death, Louis was more wholly hers than he had been for the years in which he had been outgrowing her. She no longer had to keep up with him.'

The most poignant lament for Louis's death came, strangely enough, from Henry James, who has always appeared to the world as the most desiccated and etiolated of sensibilities, but now rose to great heights of eloquent sympathy:

> My dear Fanny Stevenson,
> What can I say to you that will not seem cruelly irrelevant or vain? . . . You are such a visible picture of desolation that I need to remind myself, that courage, and patience, and fortitude are also abundantly with you . . . To have lived in the light of that splendid life, that beautiful, bountiful being – only to see it, from one moment to the other converted into a fable as strange and romantic as one of his own, a thing that *has* been and has ended, is an anguish into which no one can enter with you fully and of which no one can drain the cup for you. You are nearest to the pain, because you were nearest the joy and the pride . . . He lighted up one whole side of the globe, and was in himself a whole province of one's imagination . . . He has gone in time not to be old, early enough to be generously young and late enough to have drunk deep of the cup . . . When I think of your own situation I fall into a mere confusion of pity and wonder, with the sole sense of your being as brave a spirit as he was (all of whose bravery you shared) to hold on by . . . More than I can say, I hope your first prostration and bewilderment are over, and that you are feeling your way in feeling all sorts of encompassing arms – all sorts of outstretched hands of friendship. Don't, my dear Fanny Stevenson, be unconscious of *mine*, and believe me more than ever faithfully yours,
>
> Henry James.[1]

Whenever a great man dies, one hears of wrangling over the succession or the legacy, whether moral or material. Robert Louis Stevenson was no exception, and battle was soon joined between his old friends and the Osbourne clique to decide who would be the keepers of the flame. Curiously, neither side in the dispute was committed to the truth. Colvin's edition of the RLS letters would have been a disgrace if produced by any scholar with a reputation; for a so-called friend to suppress, censor, distort, mangle and bowdlerise, as Colvin did with Stevenson's correspondence, was treachery of a high order. The net effect of his actions was to play into the hands of the opposition, for the Fanny-approved 'authorised biography' by Graham Balfour, which appeared in 1901, was hagiographic distortion that complemented perfectly Colvin's adulterated version of the letters.

Trouble was brewing even as Baxter arrived in Samoa, bearing the first two volumes of the Edinburgh edition; he had heard of Louis's death while passing through the Suez canal. Fanny received him coolly: now that her husband was dead she had no need to dissemble her true feelings about his old friends. Disconcerted by his reception, Baxter nonetheless acted in every way as an honourable man and a true friend of the deceased. Stevenson's will left personal estate in Britain of £15,525 and, as the relict of a member of the Scottish Bar, Fanny also received a pension of sixty pounds a year – in itself quite enough on which to live simply, at any rate according to Louis's own prescription for Henley. Half of the British estate was to be held by Maggie until her death, and a further third was bequeathed to Alan Stevenson's children – Bob, Katharine and Dora. The residue went to Lloyd after a life interest to Fanny and, in addition, Maggie's half reverted to the Osbournes after her death in 1897. All books, manuscripts, furniture, and other effects were Fanny's, as was the literary estate and its royalties. The one problem was Vailima itself, the title deeds of which Louis made over to Baxter in 1892, so that it could not be confiscated by the Germans in retaliation for his political 'meddling'. Clearly Baxter had a moral case to return the deed to Fanny, but there was no binding legal one, and a less scrupulous man might have refused to disgorge the document, defying Fanny to take legal action and maybe consume the entire worth of the property in costs. Baxter, however, made the deed over to Fanny on 3 March 1895; his immediate reward was to be the object of Fanny's complaints when he returned to Britain, on the grounds that the news he brought back from Samoa was an infringement of the Osbourne's 'intellectual property' (by which they meant that Baxter had made the sale of a 'Last Days of RLS' publication less plausible). This was also the reason for her ludicrous letter to Colvin in 1895 when she complained that Lloyd's health had suddenly broken down 'under, I really do believe – the strain that Charles (Baxter) has put upon him'.[2]

The strain that Lloyd was feeling was doubtless the stress of realising that the workhorse and milch-cow had gone, and that income from the royalty account was decreasing. The ultimate horror – that Lloyd might have to work for a living – was, however, averted when the full Edinburgh edition was published, bringing in an immediate £5,000 from brisk sales. At about the same time, too (1897), Maggie died, leaving further funds to the Osbournes in accordance with her son's will. As she lay terminally ill and delirious with pneumonia, Maggie 'saw' her son at the foot of the bed. 'There is Louis! I must go,' she exclaimed, fell back unconscious and died the next day.

Maggie's death was both motive and opportunity for a fresh period of peregrination by the Osbournes. They had spent a year in San Francisco between April 1895 and May 1896, during which Fanny managed to fall out with her old friend Dora Williams on the subject of spiritualism, but then returned to Vailima for another year, lacking the funds for the globetrotting so dear to Lloyd's heart. On Maggie's death, Fanny sold Vailima for the paltry sum of £1,750 to a German ex-timber merchant from Vladivostok, reserving for herself an acre of ground at the summit of Mount Vaea and the access road leading up the mountainside; she was never a business-woman but, with Louis as breadwinner, she had not needed to be. In 1911 the merchant sold it to the German government for £6,000, and after the First World War, it passed into the hands of the New Zealand Government who administered Samoa under a League of Nations mandate.

Fanny and Lloyd then set out on a journey to Britain, where they finally routed Louis's old friends. After a visit to Scotland, Fanny rented a house in Dorking, where she had a gall-bladder operation, emerging, according to Henry James, 'looking like an old grizzled lioness'. It was from the Dorking house that Lloyd directed operations for the downfall of Colvin as RLS's official biographer. It had been Louis's wish that Colvin should undertake the writing of his life, and he had even suggested the split of profits from the venture: one-third to Colvin and two-thirds to Fanny and Lloyd. The avaricious Lloyd did not like these terms and, as his son revealed to the *Times Literary Supplement* in March 1960, had all along been determined to wrest the project from Colvin's grasp. Colvin played into his hands by his slow, ponderous methods. Idiotically, he decided to concentrate on his bowdlerised edition of the RLS letters before writing the life, which gave Fanny and Lloyd the excuse they needed, first to pressurise and fluster him, and finally to force him to resign from the biography and hand it over to Graham Balfour, who was their creature. By 1899 it was more important than ever to have a 'safe' biography, since a waspish sketch of RLS's life which appeared in 1898, written by Louis's old adversary Eve Simpson, actually told the truth about the escapades of his youth and young manhood.[3]

As part of their scheme to deliver a knock-out punch to Louis's old friends, Lloyd tried to enlist Baxter on his side against Colvin, and actually boasted to him about the way he was wearing Colvin down in a war of attrition. Then in April 1899 Lloyd wrote exultantly to Baxter: 'Last mail I received a sad, smooth letter from Colvin, acquiescing in the inevitable, and resigning the *Life* . . . He seemed very crushed in his letter, and it would be well to keep him in that condition. There's no more fight in him. It's pleading now.' So far from colluding with Lloyd, Baxter wrote to Colvin to ask him to reconsider, and wrote a tough letter to Fanny, reminding her of Louis's wishes, which alarmed Colvin by its vehemence. Baxter was unconcerned: 'I don't care whether you like my onslaught on Fanny or not she deserves it!'

Having disposed of Colvin and after ruthlessly beating him down to a total fee of £100 for the edition of the letters, Fanny and Lloyd turned to settle accounts with Baxter. By this time he had remarried and was in severe financial difficulties with a failing business, but Fanny would not lift a finger to help him. Baxter had made over the deed to Vailima without demur, had taken no significant payment for the many lucrative deals he negotiated for Louis in the last three years of his life, and had thought up the idea of the Edinburgh edition which brought Fanny much-needed cash when she was in dire straits. His reward for all this was to be turned away from the Stevenson trough by the more powerful Osbourne snouts. Baxter's only crime, apart from a bluff forthrightness which Fanny regarded as her monopoly and therefore detested in others, was to have served RLS faithfully and loyally over the years, unlike Bob, Simpson or Henley. Colvin, too, had been faithless, and it is difficult to feel much sympathy for him in the hour of his defeat by the Osbournes; he was like them in that his main interest in Louis was as a source of money, and his rout was really no more than a case of biter bit.[4]

Nor was Fanny prepared to dip into her purse to help the needy Bob, who died in 1900, leaving an impoverished widow and two children. Henley was made of sterner stuff, for he neither asked nor expected favour, and when the absurd Lloyd, with his habitual sense of the realities, went down to Worthing by train in hopes of seeing his childhood hero, Henley refused to receive him. Henley was biding his time, and his chance came in 1901 with the publication of Balfour's two-volume life of RLS. Henley's 'review' of this book gave him the pretext for an onslaught on the post-Fanny Stevenson, which became the sensation of literary London in the Edwardian decade. His dismissive phrases: 'The Shorter Catechist', 'Seraph in Chocolate' and 'barley-sugar effigy' blasted the entirely mythical creature which Balfour, abetted by Fanny and Lloyd, had constructed. Henley lashed Louis as a vain and selfish egotist, narcissistic and egomaniacal: 'Withal, if he wanted a thing, he went after it with an entire contempt for consequences. For these, indeed, the Shorter Catechist was ever prepared to answer; so that, whether he did well or ill, he was sure to come out unabashed and cheerful.' Implicitly placing Fanny in the dock for her influence on Louis, he conceded that she would not have been able to influence where there was not already a pre-existing disposition and that 'the Shorter Catechist' was obviously the essential Stevenson, not the riotous, intrepid, scornful young man he had known. Henley wound up with an attack on the most sacrosanct part of the RLS legend: that he was a martyr to consumption who had struggled heroically against this affliction. He gave this argument short shrift: there were many people, in slums and elsewhere, who had struggled heroically against tuberculosis and other diseases, but they had not been able to devote their lives to what they most wanted to do (in Louis's case, writing), nor did they have money for champagne and global travel; morally, Henley argued, we ought to admire more the simple tubercular shirt-maker than the privileged novelist.[5]

Henley went to his grave in 1903 having said his piece and finally expressed the hatred he felt for Fanny – for it was obvious that his real target was the Vandegrifter – a woman who had ruined a young man of great promise. Baxter and Colvin, who survived Fanny, kept their heads down until her death and even after; at their deaths, respectively in 1919 and 1927, Baxter and Colvin had made no dents in the monolith erected by the Osbournes and Balfour to a totally fictitious RLS. Colvin, indeed, was content to rest quiet, for at the age of 56 he finally married Fanny Sitwell (they had had to wait until the deaths of spouses and mothers) and thus, in a sense, vanquished the genius who had always eclipsed him and who is the only reason we still remember the sometime Keeper of Prints and Drawings in the British Museum.

1901 was a bad year for Fanny, for the year of Henley's onslaught was also the time she and Lloyd's wife came to the parting of the ways. Five years earlier Lloyd had married Katharine Durham, from a Quaker family in Springfield, Illinois. At first Fanny approved of the match, for she saw in Katharine an aspiring bluestocking who reminded her of herself when young. But Katharine proved her match in willpower and obstinacy as well as in cerebral ambitions, and became increasingly unprepared to tolerate the intimate, almost incestuous relationship between her husband and mother-in-law. Lloyd was quite prepared to spend long periods away from Fanny if he was on a trip, a cruise or driving a car – for he became a life-imitating-art version of Mr Toad, with a mindless devotion to fast roadsters – but if he wanted intimate contact or consolation he went to her rather than his wife. Moreover, he resented the expenses of the two children Katharine had borne him. As Katharine said: 'Lloyd Osbourne did not like having children. They were an expense, they took care and attention he wanted the monopoly of. They entailed responsibility he refused.'

Once Fanny realised that Katharine was not prepared to toe her line, she forced the weak Lloyd to take her side against his own wife, and eventually to leave her. Katharine wrote of 'such terrible heartbreaking memories . . . the injustice, the cruelty'. Belle joined in eagerly on her mother's side and when Lloyd went to New York to oversee the staging of a play, she hinted to her brother that Katharine had been unfaithful in his absence. In the end Fanny gave Lloyd an ultimatum; he could have all the money he needed for his extravagant lifestyle provided he left Katharine; or he could stay with his wife and earn his own living. Fanny knew her son and knew the right card to play: the weak, lazy Lloyd deferred to her. There was a stormy interview with Katharine, during which Lloyd said to her: 'Her [Fanny's] hellish inquisition of you has left an ineffaceable impression on me and you will have to go.'

The battle raged on. Infuriated by his philandering, Katharine would not give him a full divorce, but in 1909 sued for legal separation and claimed $300 a month maintenance on the ground that Lloyd's monthly income was $500. Lloyd, who had advertised himself as the heir of RLS, claimed he had contributed some of the best parts to their 'co-authored' books, and held himself out as a professional writer, alleged he had earned nothing that year and had lived off his mother; either this was true, in which case he finally stands forth in clear light as the talentless nonentity he was, or it was false, in which case he stands indicted as a liar attempting to defraud his own children.

When Fanny died in 1914, she left an estate worth £120,500 to Belle, with instructions to pay Lloyd $300 a month for life; in addition he received the reversion of the estates of Thomas and Robert Louis Stevenson and all RLS's lucrative royalties. He had finally achieved his life's ambition of moneyed ease and idleness, and in 1916, when Katharine finally agreed to a divorce, he remarried, this time to a woman who accepted his stipulation that there must be no children. For the rest of his life he existed as *flâneur*, dilettante and drone, being well-known at the Lambs club in New York and the night-spots of Paris. He died in California in 1947.

By the second decade of the century, more and more informed people were coming to realise that Katharine Osbourne's apparently wild allegations about the Osbournes were the sober truth. Fanny made a bad public relations mistake by leaving a contemptuous bequest to Katharine:

> To Katharine Durham Osbourne, of incredible ferocity, who lived on my bounty for many years, at the same time pursuing me with malicious slander, I leave five dollars.

This action finally opened people's eyes to the reality of Fanny. Fanny Sitwell, now Mrs Colvin, professed herself disgusted, and the Princeton scholar of Stevensoniana, Helen Purdy, who had previously supported the Osbourne clique against Katharine, withdrew from the fray. It was a sadder and wiser woman who wrote about the sale of RLS manuscripts in 1919: 'How could Sidney Colvin sell those Stevenson letters? I did not expect much better of Isobel Strong Field and Lloyd Osbourne ... It seems as if those most closely connected with RLS hastened to make all they could from the connection.'[6]

After all her years of hypochondria, Fanny finally succumbed to a stroke at the age of 74 in Santa Barbara, California, following a peripatetic final fifteen years that had taken her from Madeira to San Francisco, back to Europe for numerous motoring holidays with Lloyd, and finally to southern California. Her ashes were taken back to Samoa and placed in an urn next to Louis's grave on Mount Vaea. During the last ten years of her life she had a close relationship with a secretary, Edward Salisbury Field, who was the same age as Austin Strong. It was always said that 'Ned' Field was

Fanny's lover, and Henry James, who met the couple, certainly believed so.

In the very year of Fanny's death (1914) Belle married Ned Field; she was 56 and he was in his mid-thirties. The Midsummer Night's Dream wheel of fortune, linking Fanny and Belle, had come full circle. Both Fanny and Belle were dark women, both extravagant and spendthrift, both lost young children, both had first husbands who were philanderers, and both had much younger second husbands. Fanny had wanted Bob and Bob had wanted Belle, but when Fanny accepted Louis, Belle tried to move in on him too. As the final and most important point of similarity, both had second husbands who died young leaving them a fortune. As a final twist, both Ned Field and Austin Strong, the educationally backward boy, became successful playwrights, so that Belle's husband and son actually had plays running on Broadway at the same time. Ned Field died in 1936, having made a small reputation as a playwright and a lot of money as a realtor. On some of the land he bought oil was struck, so that Belle ended her life as a millionairess. She died in 1953, in her ninety-fifth year, having survived both Lloyd and Austin.

The potentialities latent in Fanny and her children, which were later so dramatically actualised, really make it impossible to argue against the thesis that Robert Louis Stevenson was a martyr to the greedy, grasping Osbourne family. There is a school of thought that holds that criticism of Fanny, *any* criticism, is *ipso facto* 'misogynistic', and it is true that Fanny alienated all the males who swam into her ken: not just Henley, Bob, Simpson, Baxter, Colvin and the other 'old faithfuls' but also Gosse, Low, Lang, Moors, Carruthers and dozens of others. 'Except for Henry James, to be a friend of Fanny's was to quarrel with her, it seemed,' was Margaret Mackay's verdict. Even the 'master', it transpired, had no particularly high opinion of her; there is his 'poor, barbarous and merely *instinctive* lady' remark to Bruce Porter in 1907, and there is also this, five years earlier, when asked for a letter of introduction to Fanny: 'Only remember this – that *she* . . . was never the person to have seen, it was RLS himself.'[7] Yet it was not just men who found Fanny intolerable; the list of women who found her dislikable or antipathetic is almost as long: Mrs J.A.Symonds, Emma Hardy, Alice James, Fanny Sitwell, Valentine Roch, Eva Simpson, Anne Simpson, Louisa Purland, Countess Jersey, Marjorie Ide, Katharine Osbourne. Fanny even quarrelled with her close friend, Dora Williams, and had frequent rows with Belle.

Fanny's lack of success at being 'teacher, tender comrade, wife' produced the agonies of Louis's later years. His undoctored letters make it clear that he failed to find his paradise in Samoa where, relieved from the TB-inspired debility of Europe, he fell victim to cerebral haemorrhage brought on by overwork and anxiety caused by the Osbourne clan. His adopted family, having destroyed the old companionship he had with his friends, substituted nothing in its place except a demand for luxuries that required a writing pace that was beyond him. Fanny, Lloyd and Belle could do little to help him, but their waywardness and financial irresponsibility drained him, and after Fanny's breakdown in 1893 he was effectively on his own. As he struggled to survive his final year on willpower alone, he must often have reflected that his most pessimistic conclusions about the world were true. We shall leave the last words with him, both written in the 1880s, the first in verse, the second in prose, but surely expressing thoughts that were often with him as he boarded his ship of death in 1894:

> If that which should be is not; that which is
> Oh God, how greatly should not be; and all
> From dawn to sunset and from birth to grave
> Be, or appear, Oh God, evil alone;
> If that be so, then silence were best.

It is the history of our kindnesses that alone makes this world tolerable. If it were not for that, for the effect of kind words, kind looks, kind letters, multiplying, spreading, making one happy through another and bringing forth benefits, some fifty, some a thousandfold, I should be tempted to think our life a practical jest in the worst possible spirit.[8]

NOTES

References to Stevenson's works are mainly to the Tusitala Edition (35 vols 1924). Vols 31–35 comprise the letters, hereinafter referred to as *Letters* I-V. Manuscript source references are to the Beinecke Collection at Yale University (B), the National Library of Scotland (NLS), or to the Huntington Museum (HM).

Introduction

1. *The Letters of Gerard Manley Hopkins & Robert Bridges* ed. Claude Colleer Abbott (Oxford 1935) p.228
2. Arthur Quiller-Couch, *Adventures in Criticism* (1896) p.184
3. Frank Swinnerton, *Robert Louis Stevenson* (1924) p.163
4. Thomas Beer, *The Mauve Decade: American Life at the End of the Nineteenth Century* (Garden City 1926) pp.177–78
5. E. F. Benson, *As We Were* (1930) pp.319–21; 'The Myth of RLS', *London Mercury*, July–August 1925
6. *Daily Chronicle*, 24 April 1897; John Jay Chapman, *Emerson and Other Essays* (N.Y. 1901) p.221; F. R. Leavis, *The Great Tradition* (N.Y. 1963) p.6
7. G. K. Chesterton, *Robert Louis Stevenson* (1927) pp.49–51, 93, 251
8. Leslie Fiedler, *Cross the Border–Close the Gap* (N.Y. 1972) p.102
9. Andrew Noble, 'Highland History and Narrative Form in Scott and Stevenson', in Noble, ed. *Robert Louis Stevenson* (1983)
10. S. S. McClure in Rosalind Masson, ed. *I Can Remember Robert Louis Stevenson* (1923) p.305
11. J. M. Barrie, *An Edinburgh Eleven* (1889) pp.96–107; *Margaret Ogilvy* (1896) pp.129–47; John Hamerton, *Stevensoniana* (Edinburgh 1910) pp.232–38; Janet Dunbar, *J. M. Barrie, The Man behind the Image* (1970) esp. pp.146, 205; Dennis Mackail, *The Story of J. M. Barrie* (1941), esp. pp.7, 59, 258; cf. also R. D. S. Jack, *The Road to Never Land* (Aberdeen 1991); Andrew Noble, loc. cit. p.173; Susan Buchan, *John Buchan by his Wife and Friends* (1947) pp.138, 142, 178–79;

cf. also John Buchan, *Memory Hold the Door* (1940); William Buchan, *John Buchan: a memoir* (1982)

12. George Bernard Shaw, Preface to *Major Barbara* in *Works of Shaw*, 33 vols (1930), 11 p.208; Rhode Brooke Balfour to Mrs Austin Strong, 14 July 1937, B.8195

Chapter 1

1. Graham Balfour, *The Life of Robert Louis Stevenson*, 2 vols (1901), i. p.14; J. A. Steuart, *Robert Louis Stevenson, Man and Writer*, 2 vols (1924), i. pp. 11–35
2. 'Memoir of Himself', *Tusitala* 29 p.149
3. 'Records of a Family of Engineers', *Tusitala* 19 pp.163
4. J. C. Bay, *The Unpublished Manuscripts of Robert Louis Stevenson's Record of a Family of Engineers* (1929)
5. 'Records', *Tusitala* 19 pp.216–330
6. 'Thomas Stevenson', *Tusitala* 29 pp.65–70. See also Craig Mair, *A Star for Seamen* (1978)
7. *Travels with a Donkey*, *Tusitala* 17 p.197
8. 'Thomas Stevenson,' *Tusitala* 29 p.68
9. Bay, *Unpublished Manuscripts* p.52
10. Rev. Lewis Balfour to Thomas Stevenson, 10 December 1850, B.3948
11. Alexander H. Japp, *Robert Louis Stevenson* (1905) pp.219–20
12. RLS to Thomas Stevenson, 28 March 1854, 7 August 1856, B.3440–3441; Margaret Stevenson to Thomas Stevenson, 7 June 1852, 1 November 1854, B.5654–5655
13. *Weir of Hermiston*, *Tusitala* 16 pp.52–53
14. Janet Adam Smith, ed. *Collected Poems of Robert Louis Stevenson* (1950) p. 361
15. Robert T. Skinner ed. *Cummy's Diary* (1926) p.41
16. H. L. Rymor to Margaret Stevenson, 1895, B.5419; Eve B. Simpson, *Robert Louis Stevenson's Edinburgh Days* (1913) p.106; Rosalind Masson, ed. *I Can Remember Robert Louis Stevenson* (Edinburgh 1925) p.2
17. 'Memoir of Himself', *Tusitala* 29 p.154
18. Balfour, *Life*, i. p.32
19. RLS to Mrs Sitwell, autumn 1874, NLS
20. *Collected Poems*, op. cit. pp.86–87
21. 'Memoir of Himself', *Tusitala* 29 p.153; Richard Aldington, *Robert Louis Stevenson, Portrait of a Rebel* (1957) p.21
22. 'Memoir of Himself', *Tusitala* 29 p.151
23. RLS to parents, June 1884, B.3537; RLS to Cummy, July/August 1886, *Letters*, iii. pp.100, 103
24. RLS to William Archer, 20 March 1886, *Letters*, iii. p.45; Edmund Gosse, *Leaves and Fruit* (1924) p.330
25. 'Memoir of Himself', *Tusitala* 29 p.154

26. RLS to Cummy, 1871 n.d., *Letters*, i. pp.37–38
27. 'Nurses', *Tusitala* 30 pp.170–72
28. 'Memoir of Himself', *Tusitala* 29 pp.157–58
29. *Tusitala* 26 pp.1–49
30. Balfour, *Life*, i. p.37
31. Diary of Margaret Stevenson, B.8377
32. Thomas Stevenson to RLS, 13 May 1855; n.d. 1855, B.5953–5954
33. *Tusitala* 28 pp.79–90; 'Notes from his mother's diary', *Vailima* edn 26 p. 293; 25 pp.14–23; *Tusitala* 29 p.156
34. *Tusitala* 29 p.153; 'To Auntie', *Collected Poems* p.408
35. 'Memoir of Himself', *Tusitala* 29 p.152; 'An Old Scots Gardener', ibid. pp.39–43; Balfour i. p.38; Masson, *I Can Remember* p.8; *Collected Poems* pp.385–86, 407; 'The Manse', *Tusitala* 29 pp.52–58
36. 'Memoir of Himself', *Tusitala* 29 p.156; 'Child's Play', *Tusitala* 25 pp.106–16
37. Masson, *I Can Remember* pp.13–14; RLS to William Archer, 17 October 1880, B.2631; Margaret Stevenson to Baxter, 23 March 1896, B.5600; J. Balfour Paul to Margaret Stevenson, 9 January 1895, B.5366; Thomas Stevenson to RLS, 16 June 1860, B.5755
38. 'The Coast of Fife', *Tusitala* 30 pp.9–10; Masson, *The Life of Robert Louis Stevenson* (1923) p.39
39. Masson, *I Can Remember* pp.3, 5, 8; H. B. Baildon, *Robert Louis Stevenson* (1901); *Tusitala* 29 p.159; *Weir of Hermiston, Tusitala* 16
40. Masson, *I Can Remember* pp.17, 20, 22, 32; Balfour i. p.54; 'Child's Play', *Tusitala* 25 pp.106–16
41. Balfour, *Life*, i. pp.65–66; RLS to Thomas Stevenson, n.d. 1863, October 1863, B.3441–3442; RLS to Margaret Stevenson, October, 12 November, 19 December 1863, B.3311–13; cf. also *Letters* i. pp.3–4
42. Robert T. Skinner, ed. *Cummy's Diary*, op. cit. pp.139, 143, 75, 46
43. *Tusitala* 29 pp.29–30; RLS to Thomas Stevenson, Feb–March 1864, B.3444–3445
44. Masson, *I Can Remember* pp.5–6; B.3433; Baildon, op. cit. p.22
45. RLS to Thomas Stevenson, n.d. 1865, B.3448; 'Crabbed Age and Youth', *Tusitala* 25 pp.39–50
46. *Tusitala* 3. p.xxiii; 30 pp.14–15, 20; Balfour, *Life*, i. pp.59–60, 67–68; *Letters* v. p.128; De Lancey Ferguson & Marshall Waingrow, eds. *Robert Louis Stevenson's Letters to Charles Baxter* (hereinafter *Baxter Letters*) (Yale 1956) pp.354, 360; B.3449; Masson, *I Can Remember* p.34
47. 'Memoir of Himself', *Tusitala* 29 p.161
48. Japp, op. cit. p.245; Aldington op. cit. p.25; Jenni Calder, *RLS: A Life Study* (1980) pp.32–36
49. Pieter Penzoldt, *The Supernatural in Fiction* (1952); *Baxter Letters* p.254; Fanny Stevenson, *Our Samoan Adventure* (1956) p.36
50. 'A Humble Remonstrance', *Tusitala* 29 pp.137–38

Chapter 2

1. 'Some College Memories', *Tusitala* 29 pp.12–18
2. 'A Foreigner at Home', *Tusitala* 29 pp.1–11; J. A. Steuart, *Robert Louis Stevenson* p.75; Masson, *I Can Remember* pp.49–50; 'Lay Morals', *Tusitala* 26 pp.5–49; 'Crabbed Age and Youth', *Tusitala* 25 pp.39–50
3. 'Lay Morals', *Tusitala;a* 26 pp.5–49
4. Masson, *I Can Remember* pp.49, 77; James Pope-Hennessy, *Robert Louis Stevenson* (1974) pp.16–17
5. RLS to Margaret Stevenson, July 1868, *Letters*, i. p.14; B.3315–3318; Thomas Stevenson to RLS, 11 September, 2 October 1868, B.5755–5756; 'The Coast of Fife', *Tusitala* 30 pp.9–19
6. 'The Education of an Engineer', *Tusitala* 30 pp.20–28; RLS to Margaret Stevenson, 11 September 1868, *Letters*, i. pp.18–20, same to same, 3–26 September 1868, B.3319–3326; RLS to R. A. M. Stevenson, September 1868, B.3551; *The Portfolio* 5 (November 1874) pp.173–76; Balfour, *Life*, i. p.71
7. RLS to Margaret Stevenson, September–October 1868, *Letters*, i. pp.24, 26–29, *Tusitala* 30 pp.27–28; RLS to R. A. M. Stevenson, 17 November –10 December 1868, B.3553
8. RLS to Margaret Stevenson, 18, 20 June 1869, B.3327–3329; same to same, 5 August 1870, *Letters*, i. pp.30–35; Masson, *I Can Remember* p.74; Huntington, HM 2403; *Scribner's Magazine* 25 (January 1899) pp.41–48; 'Memoirs of an Islet', *Tusitala* 29 pp.59–64
9. Margaret Stevenson diary, *Vailima* 26 p.322; Balfour, *Life* i. p.85; *Collected Poems* pp.81, 101
10. *Memoir of Fleeming Jenkin*, *Tusitala* 19 passim, esp. pp.128–32; 'Talk and Talkers', *Tusitala* 29 pp.78–80
11. 'A Foreigner at Home', *Tusitala* 29 p.9; Masson, *I Can Remember* pp. 49–52; 'A College Magazine', *Tusitala* 29 pp.28–31; Edmund Gosse, *Biographical Notes on the Writings of Robert Louis Stevenson* (1908) p.97; RLS to Margaret Stevenson, *Letters*, i. pp.14–15; cf. also RLS to Margaret Stevenson, RLS to R. A. M. Stevenson, B.3314, 3318; 3350–3355
12. 'The Morality of the Profession of Letters', *Tusitala* 28 pp.51–61; 'Books which have influenced me', *Tusitala* 28 pp.62–68; 'A Gossip on a Novel of Dumas's', *Tusitala* 29 pp.110–118
13. Masson, *I Can Remember* pp.75–79, 95; *Baxter Letters* pp. 21, 360; Balfour, *Life*, i. pp.77–79; William Kirk Dickson, *The History of the Speculative Society* (1905); *Tusitala* 25 p.29, pp.31–36; Alexander Grant, *The Story of the University of Edinburgh*, 2 vols (1884), ii. pp.489–92
14. *Baxter Letters* pp.vii–xvi, 48, 95, 98, 239, 256; Masson, *I Can Remember* pp.100–101; Balfour, *Life*, i. pp.89–92
15. 'Edinburgh: Picturesque Notes', *Tusitala* 26 pp.135–97
16. 'Old Mortality', *Tusitala* 29 pp.19–27; RLS to R. A. M. Stevenson, 29 March 1870, B.3556; *Collected Poems* p.69
17. 'Edinburgh: Picturesque Notes', *Tusitala* 26 pp.135–97

18. 'Edinburgh: Picturesque Notes' ibid.; *Baxter Letters* pp.48, 95, 98, 239; *Tusitala* 1 pp.xx; David Daiches, 'Stevenson and Scotland', in Jenni Calder, ed. *Stevenson and Victorian Scotland* (Edinburgh 1981) pp.11–32

19. 'A Foreigner at Home', *Tusitala* 29 p.6; *St Ives, Tusitala* 15 p. 113

20. RLS to R. A. M. Stevenson, 2 October 1868, n.d. 1875, B. 3552; *Collected Poems* pp.113, 305

21. *Tusitala* 1 p.xv; 29 p.89; *Weir of Hermiston, Tusitala* 16 p. 5

22. *Tusitala* 29 p.35; *Collected Poems* p.63; RLS to R. A. M. Stevenson, 16 June 1870, B.3556; Compton Mackenzie, *Robert Louis Stevenson* (1968)

23. Masson, *I Can Remember* p.115; *Baxter Letters* pp.40–42, 86, 91; Jenni Calder, *RLS. A Life Study* (1980) p.54

24. *Collected Poems* pp.82, 338–40; 'Notebooks', *Tusitala* 29 pp.171–72

25. George S. Hellman, *The True Stevenson* p.72; Steuart, op. cit., i. pp.129–34; Masson, *Life* p.80; Aldington, op. cit. p.47; J. C. Furnas, *Voyage to Windward* (1952) pp.393–99

26. Jenni Calder, *RLS. A Life Study* op. cit. p.54

27. Colvin to Balfour, n.d. 1901, NLS; Colvin to Lloyd Osbourne, 13 July 1899. B.4346; RLS to Henley, 17 August 1979, *Baxter Letters* p.66; RLS to Trevor Haddon, 1880, *Letters*, ii. p.201; Graham Balfour to Colvin, 18 February 1923, B.3919

28. David Daiches, *Robert Louis Stevenson* (1947) pp.89–90

Chapter 3

1. Balfour, *Life*, i. p.106; M. M. Black, *Robert Louis Stevenson* (1898) pp. 72–74; B.6400; RLS to Maud Baington, n.d. 1871, *Letters*, i. pp.35–36

2. Vincent Starrett, *Bookman's Holiday* (1942) pp.212–33; J. W. Herries, *I Came, I Saw* (1937) pp.286–87; Margaret Stevenson's diary, *Vailima* ed. 26 p.324; 'Old Mortality', *Tusitala* 29 p.25; RLS to Margaret Stevenson, 23, 25 July, 1, 2 August 1872, B.3330–3331, 8073–8075; *Letters*, i. pp.45–52

3. W. E. Henley, *Essays* (1921) pp.117–18; W. B. Yeats, *The Trembling of the Veil* (1955) pp.132–33; Edmund Gosse, *Biographical Notes on the Writings of Robert Louis Stevenson* (1908) p.19; *Tusitala* 29 p.77

4. R. A. M. Stevenson to RLS, autumn 1873, B.5677; RLS to R. A. M. Stevenson, October 1872, B.3557; RLS to Margaret Stevenson, 25, 27 December 1872, B.3332–3333; RLS to Baxter, 16 January 1873, *Baxter Letters* pp.20–23

5. RLS to Baxter, 2 February 1873, *Baxter Letters* pp.23–25; Baxter to RLS, 23 September 1891, ibid. p.289

6. RLS to Colvin, 18 September 1873, B.7962; RLS to Mrs Sitwell, 6, 9 September 1873. NLS; cf. *Letters* i. p.70

7. RLS to Mrs Sitwell, 9, 10, 12, 13, 17 September, NLS MSS 99 ff. 3, 13–15, 41, 57, 63, 73; RLS to Colvin, 16, 23 September, B. 2976–2977

8. *Tusitala* 29 pp.69–70; Japp. op. cit. pp.21, 27

9. Masson, *I Can Remember* p.53–58; Aldington, op. cit. p.47

10. RLS to Mrs Sitwell, 16 September 1873, *Letters*, i. pp.74–77

11. 'The Story of a Lie', *Tusitala* 14 pp. 143–203; *Tusitala* 22; *The Wrecker*, *Tusitala* 12; *Weir of Hermiston*, *Tusitala* 16 p.22

12. 'A Chapter on Dreams', *Tusitala* 30 pp.41–54

13. RLS to Gosse, 1879–80, B.3153–54; *Tusitala* 29 p.180; 'Reflections and Remarks on Human Life', *Tusitala* 26 pp.76–90

14. RLS to Henley, July–August 1887, *Letters*, iii. pp.133–34; Japp, op cit. pp. 22–23

15. E. V. Lucas, *The Colvins and their friends* (1928) pp.338–41; RLS to Margaret Stevenson, 29, 31 July 1873, B.3335, 8076; Masson, *I Can Remember* pp.88–89; *Letters*, i. p.65

16. *Letters*, iii. p.237; Lucas, *The Colvins*, op. cit. pp.67–68

17. RLS to Mrs Sitwell, NLS Ms. 99 ff. 3–16

18. RLS to Mrs Sitwell, ibid. ff. 16–63

19. RLS to Mrs Sitwell, 8 October 1873, ibid. f. 74; RLS to Mrs Sitwell, 14 October 1873, *Letters*, i. pp.84–85

20. Steuart, *Robert Louis Stevenson* i p.90; RLS to Colvin, 15, 16 October 1873, *Letters*, i. pp.86–87; RLS to Margaret Stevenson, October 1873, B.3336–3338; RLS to his parents, 29 October 1873, B.3484; RLS to Colvin, October 1873, B.2978–2979; RLS to Mrs Sitwell, 4 November 1873, NLS Ms. 99 f. 78

21. 'Ordered South', *Tusitala* 25 pp.61–72; RLS to Margaret Stevenson, 9 November 1873, B.3338

22. RLS to Mrs Sitwell, 6 November 1873, NLS Ms. 99 ff. 82–91; *Letters*, i. pp.89–98

23. RLS to Mrs Sitwell, 13 January 1874, NLS Ms. 99 f. 128; *Letters*, i. pp.78–79, 99–101

24. RLS to Baxter, 15 November 1873, *Baxter Letters* p.31; *Letters*, i. pp. 106–09

25. RLS to Mrs Sitwell, January–February 1874, NLS Ms. 99 ff. 128–60; *Letters*, i. pp.113–47; *Collected Poems* pp102–4; RLS to his parents, January–March 1874, B.3491–3498; RLS to Colvin, January–February 1874, B.2988–2991; RLS to Margaret Stevenson, January–March 1874, B.3343–3356

26. Malcolm Elwin, *The Strange Case of Robert Louis Stevenson* (1950) p.76

27. R. A. M. Stevenson to RLS, March–April 1874, B.5659–5689; *Letters*, i. pp. 124–30; RLS to Margaret Stevenson, 6 April 1874; RLS to Mrs Sitwell, April 1874, *Letters*, i. pp.148–50

28. RLS to Colvin, Spring 1874, B.2992–2993; *Letters*, i. pp.157–65

29. *Letters*, i. pp.166–82; R. A. M. Stevenson to RLS, July 1874, B. 5692; RLS to Mrs Sitwell, NLS Ms. 99 ff. 194–220; 'An Autumn Effect', *Tusitala* 30 pp. 67–85

30. *Letters*, i. pp.165–208; RLS to Mrs Sitwell, September–November 1874, NLS Ms. 99 ff. 230–54

31. *Letters*, i. p.218; RLS to Mrs Sitwell, December 1874, NLS ibid.

Chapter 4

1. *Letters*, i. pp.185–212; RLS to Mrs Sitwell, November 1874, NLS Ms. 99 ff. 256–59

2. *Letters*, i. pp.222–26; Masson, *I Can Remember* pp.118–32

3. Henley to Colvin, 14, 21 March, 15 April 1876, B.4693–4695; *Letters*, i. pp. 185–86, 216–17, 226–27; Jerome H. Buckley, *William Ernest Henley* (Princeton 1945) pp.53–55; John Connell, *W. E. Henley* (1949); *Collected Poems* pp.126–7

4. Henley to Harry Nichols, HM 30928–30929; Henley to RLS, 15 April 1875, B.4695; RLS to Colvin, July 1875, B.3012, Henley to Margaret Stevenson, February 1876, B.4691, 5616; Margaret Stevenson to Henley, B.; Edward H. Cohen, *The Henley-Stevenson Quarrel* (Florida 1974) p.12; *Blackwood's Magazine* 254 (September 1943)

5. *Letters*, i. pp.204–06; Masson, *I Can Remember* p.68; Cohen, op. cit. p. 7

6. *Letters*, i. pp.216–17, ii. pp.338, 342–43; Calder, *RLS* op. cit. pp. 65, 95, 155, 164

7. Andrew Lang, *Adventures among Books* (1905) p.51; Will H. Low, *A Chronicle of Friendship 1873–1900* (1908) p.153

8. Low, *Chronicle* op. cit. pp.159–61; R. A. M. Stevenson to RLS, March–July 1874, B.5687–5692; same to same, March 1875, B.5694

9. 'Fontainebleau', *Tusitala* 30 pp.93–116; 'Forest Notes', ibid. pp.117–40; RLS to Margaret Stevenson, 7 April 1875, B.8078; *Letters*, i. p.236

10. *Tusitala* 1 p.xx; *Letters*, ii. p.254; *Tusitala* 17 p.xiii; Lang, *Adventures*, op. cit. p.49

11. *Letters*, i. pp.229–38; RLS to Colvin, July 1875, B.3010–3011; Masson, *I Can Remember*, pp.19, 65; RLS to Mrs Sitwell, NLS Ms. 2187/1; *Tusitala* 27 p.121

12. RLS to Mrs Sitwell, August 1875, B.3275; *Letters*, i. p.238, ii. pp. 6–8, 16–24; Masson, *I Can Remember* p.80; Edmund Gosse, *Critical Kitcats* pp.278–83; RLS to Margaret Stevenson, 7 August 1876, B.3361; R. A. M. Stevenson to RLS, 11 April 1876, B.5699

13. *Familiar Studies of Men and Books*, *Tusitala* 27 pp.1–79, 202–44; Masson, *I Can Remember* pp.90–93; Lucas, *Colvins* pp.84–85; Sidney Colvin, *Memories and Notes of Persons and Places 1852–1912* (1922) pp.112–13; *Letters*, i. pp.135–36, 149, 151, 158–59, 161–63; *Cornhill Magazine* 30 (August 1874) pp.179–94; Stephen to Colvin, 20 March, Stephen to RLS, 15 May 1874, B.5547, 5549; Balfour, *Life*, i. p.139

14. Margaret Stevenson diary, *Vailima* ed. 26 p.327; Masson, *I Can Remember* p.52; *Tusitala*, 5, 25, 26, 27, 28; *Letters*, i. pp.64, 173–75, 210–16, 233–38, ii. pp.14–19; RLS to R. A. M. Stevenson, autumn 1874, B. 3560, Stephen to RLS, 24 February 1876, B.5555; RLS to Colvin, February 1876, B.3018; *Academy*, 3 June 1876, p.532; 10 October 1874 p.406; 2 January 1875, pp. 1–2; *Cornhill Magazine* 33 (May 1876) pp.545–61; 34 (December 1876) pp. 695–717; Japp, *Robert Louis Stevenson*, op. cit. pp.166–69

15. *An Inland Voyage*, *Tusitala* pp.1–126; *Letters*, ii. pp.23–26; *Collected Poems* p.84; RLS to Colvin, August 1876, B.3021; RLS to Margaret Stevenson, 9 September 1876, B. 3362; Walter Simpson to RLS, 13 February 1877, B.5501

Chapter 5

1. For Fanny's early years see Margaret Mackay, *The Passionate Friend* (1969); Nellie Sanchez, *The Life of Mrs Robert Louis Stevenson* (1920)
2. Lloyd Osbourne, *An Intimate Portrait* (N.Y. 1924) pp.1–5; Isobel Field, *This Life I've Loved* (1937) pp.104–05; Fanny Osbourne to Timothy Rearden, 1875 B.8141
3. Sam Osbourne to Timothy Rearden, 5 April 1876, B.8269
4. Sanchez op. cit. p.48; Isobel Field, *This Life* pp.102–3
5. Elsie Noble Caldwell, *Last Witness for Robert Louis Stevenson* (Norman, Oklahoma, 1960) p.6
6. Fanny Osbourne to Timothy Rearden, n.d. 1876, B.8141
7. *Tusitala* 1 p.xxvii
8. Fanny Osbourne to Timothy Rearden, n.d. 1876; 13 December 1876; 11 April 1877, B.8141–8143
9. R. A. M. Stevenson to RLS, 11 January 1879; autumn 1879; January 1880, B.5702, 5707, 5708
10. Richard Le Gallienne, *The Romantic Nineties* (1951) pp.63–64; Roger Lancelyn Green, *Andrew Lang* (Leicester 1946) p.178
11. Thomas Stevenson to RLS, 18 January, 5 February 1877, B.5759–5760
12. RLS to Margaret Stevenson, January–February 1877, B.3363–3365; *Letters*, ii. p.27
13. *Cornhill Magazine* 34 (August 1876) pp.169–76; 'Virginibus Puerisque', *Tusitala* 25 pp.1–20
14. 'On Falling in Love', *Cornhill Magazine* 35 (February 1877) pp.214–20; *Tusitala* 25 pp.21–29
15. *Collected Poems* p.32; *Tusitala* 22
16. Sidney Colvin, *Memories and Notes of Persons and Places 1852–1912* (1921) pp.129–30
17. Birge Harrison, 'With Stevenson at Grez', *Century*, December 1916
18. Henry James to Bruce Porter, February 1907, in Leon Edel, *The Life of Henry James* (1987), ii. p.595; Edel, *Diary of Alice James* (1965) p.93
19. George S. Hellman, *The True Stevenson* (Boston 1925) pp.71, 82, 231; Katharine Osbourne, *Robert Louis Stevenson in California* (Chicago 1914); Katharine Osbourne to Gosse, 16 August 1922, B.8263
20. Pope-Hennessy, *Robert Louis Stevenson* op. cit. p.102; Furnas, *Voyage to Windward* op. cit. p.132
21. Fanny Osbourne to Timothy Rearden, 11 April 1877, B.8143
22. Steuart, *Robert Louis Stevenson*, op. cit. p.231
23. RLS to Colvin, 1 January 1878; RLS to Thomas Stevenson, 15 February 1878; RLS to Henley, February 1880; 'Familiar Studies', *Tusitala* 27 pp.34, 44
24. Furnas, *Voyage*, op. cit. p.400
25. RLS to Mrs Sitwell, August 1877, B.3276; *Letters*, ii. pp.28–33
26. Thomas Stevenson to RLS, 30 August, 5 September, 7 October 1877, B. 5761–5763; RLS to his parents, n.d. 1877, B.3366; *Letters*, ii. pp.33–34

27. Fanny Osbourne to Timothy Rearden, 27 November 1877, B.8144
28. *Letters*, ii. pp.35–40; Will Low, *Chronicle*, op. cit. pp.187–93
29. RLS to Henley, spring 1878, NLS
30. RLS to Margaret Stevenson, 17, 27 February 1878; B.3367–3369; *Letters*, ii. pp.41–48
31. RLS to Colvin, n.d. 1878, B.3028; *Letters*, ii. pp.40–44; *Baxter Letters* pp. 50–52
32. Furnas op. cit. p.136; RLS to Colvin, February 1878, B.3027
33. *Letters*, ii. pp.46–48
34. *Baxter Letters* pp.52–53; *Letters*, ii. p.44
35. Mackay, *Violent Friend* op. cit. pp.53–54

Chapter 6

1. RLS to Baxter, August–September 1878, *Baxter Letters* pp.53–54; RLS to Mrs Sitwell, August 1878, NLS.
2. *Letters*, ii. pp.48–53; *Baxter Letters* pp.55–57; 'A Mountain Town in France', *Tusitala* 17 pp.131–44
3. *Travels with a Donkey*, *Tusitala* 17 pp.127–51; Gordon Golding, ed. *The Cévennes Journal: Notes on a Journey through the French Highlands* (Edinburgh 1978)
4. Hamerton to RLS, 14 January 1879, B.4505; Lucas, *Colvins* pp.110–11
5. RLS to R. A. M. Stevenson, 6 August 1879, B.3561; Margaret Stevenson to RLS, July 1879, B.5630
6. Paul Maixner, ed. *Robert Louis Stevenson: The Critical Heritage* (1981) p.73
7. *Letters*, ii. p.54; *Baxter Letters* pp.58–61; RLS to Margaret Stevenson, 25 November 1879, B.3371; Margaret Stevenson diary B.7304
8. 'An Apology for Idlers', *Cornhill Magazine* (July 1877) pp.80–86; *Tusitala* 25 pp.51–60
9. Leslie Cope Cornford, *Robert Louis Stevenson* (1900), pp.89–90
10. *Cornhill Magazine* 37 (January 1878) pp.41–60; *Tusitala* 8 pp. 57–86
11. Balfour, *Life*, i. p.160
12. Caldwell, *Last Witness*, op. cit. p.278; Stephen to RLS, 29 September 1877, B.5561; Isobel Strong, *Memories of Vailima* (1902) pp.45–46
13. RLS to Trevor Haddon, 23 April 1884; RLS to Gosse, 1 December 1894, *Letters*, v. pp.182–84
14. 'The English Admirals', *Cornhill Magazine* 38 (July 1878) pp.36–43: *Tusitala* 25 pp.86–97; 'Crabbed Age and Youth', *Cornhill Magazine* 37 (March 1878); *Tusitala* 25 pp.39–50; 'Aes Triplex', *Cornhill Magazine* 37 (April 1878); *Tusitala* 25 pp.73–81 'El Dorado', *Tusitala* 25 pp.82–85; Henley to RLS, April/May 1878, B.4714; 'Lay Morals', *Tusitala* 26 pp.5–49
15. 'A Lodging for the Night', *Tusitala* 1 pp.219–40; 'The Sire de Maletroit's Door', *Temple Bar* 52 (January 1878) pp.53–69; *Tusitala* 1 pp.243–64; *Letters*, i. p.241
16. Leslie Stephen to RLS, 7 June 1878, B.5562; *New Arabian Nights*, *Tusitala* 1; Lloyd Osbourne, *An Intimate Portrait*, op. cit. pp.10–12; Balfour, *Life*, i.

p.152; Margaret Stevenson diary, *Vailima* 26 pp. 331–32; G. K. Chesterton, *Robert Louis Stevenson*, op. cit. p.171

17. *Letters*, ii. p.9; *Tusitala* 1 p.xxviii
18. 'Providence and the Guitar', *Tusitala* 1 pp.267–97; Balfour, *Life*, i. pp. 152–53; 'The Pavilion on the Links', *Cornhill Magazine* 42 (September 1890) pp. 307–27, 430–51; *Tusitala* 1 pp.159–216
19. Baildon, *Robert Louis Stevenson*, op. cit. p.22; Gosse, *Biographical Notes on the Writings of Robert Louis Stevenson*, op. cit. p.98; RLS to Colvin, spring 1879, B.3030–3031
20. Lucas, *Colvins* p.109; RLS to Henley, 23 January 1880, *Letters*, ii. p.98; Jenkin to RLS, 15 June 1880, B.4988; *Baxter Letters* pp.281–82, 291
21. *Baxter Letters* pp.62–63; *Letters*, ii. pp.58–59
22. Janet Adam Smith, *Henry James and Robert Louis Stevenson* (1948) p.152
23. RLS to Gosse, in Mattheison, Paul F., and Michael Millgate, *Transatlantic Dialogue: Selected American Correspondence of Edmund Gosse* (1965)
24. Caldwell, *Last Witness* op. cit. p.9
25. Lloyd Osbourne, *An Intimate Portrait* op. cit.; Mackay, *Violent Friend* p.58
26. RLS to Colvin, 1879, B.3032–3034
27. Colvin to Gosse, 6 February 1879 in Charteris, *Gosse* op. cit.; Pope-Hennessy, op. cit. p.120
28. RLS to Henley, spring 1879; RLS; *Baxter Letters* p.63
29. RLS to Margaret Stevenson, May, July 1879, B.3373, 3375; *Baxter Letters* pp. 64–65; *Letters*, ii. pp.60–62
30. Margaret Stevenson diary, op. cit; Charteris, *Life and Letters of Sir Edmund Gosse*, op. cit. p.120; *Baxter Letters* p.65
31. RLS to Colvin, August 1879, B.3035–3036; RLS to R. A. M. Stevenson, B 3560; *Letters*, ii. p.72
32. RLS to Mrs Sitwell, August 1877, B.3276; Thomas Stevenson to RLS, July 1879, B.5765; 'The Story of a Lie', *Tusitala* 14 pp.143–44
33. 'Lay Morals', *Tusitala* 26 pp.5–49

Chapter 7

1. *The Amateur Emigrant*, *Tusitala* 18 pp.1–73; cf. also the annotated edition by Roger G. Swearingen, 2 vols (Ashland 1977)
2. RLS to Henley, 17 August 1879, B.3162; *Baxter Letters* p.66
3. *The Amateur Emigrant*, *Tusitala* 18 pp.81–123
4. RLS to Henley, 23 August 1879, *Letters*, iii. pp.74–75
5. *The Amateur Emigrant*, *Tusitala* 18 pp.122–23
6. RLS to Gosse, 8 October 1879, *Letters*, ii. pp.77–78
7. Lloyd Osbourne, *An Intimate Portrait* p.16
8. Caldwell, *Last Witness* p.10; RLS to Baxter, 9 September 1879, *Baxter Letters* p.68
9. Fanny Osbourne to Timothy Rearden, 1879, B.8146–8147
10. RLS to Colvin, September 1879; RLS to Gosse, 8 October 1879, *Letters*,

ii. pp.75–78; RLS to Baxter, 24 September 1879, *Baxter Letters* pp.67–69

11. Fanny Osbourne to Timothy Rearden, 1879, B.8145, 8148

12. RLS to Colvin, 21 October 1879, B.3040

13. Anne B. Fisher, *No More a Stranger* (1946) pp.131–36; Anne R. Isler, 'Robert Louis Stevenson in Monterey', *Pacific Historical Review* 34 (1965) pp. 305–21; *Letters*, ii. pp.79–86; James D. Hart, *From Scotland to Silverado* (1966) pp.xxvii–xxviii

14. Nellie Sanchez, *The Life of Mrs Robert Louis Stevenson* p.56; Masson, *I Can Remember* p.189; *Tusitala* 18 pp.127–42

15. *Letters*, ii. pp.76–77; RLS to Henley, n.d. 1880, NLS; *Tusitala* 18 p. xv.; *Collected Poems* p.139

16. *Tusitala* 18 pp.127–42; *Collected Poems* p.410; Lloyd Osbourne, *An Intimate Portrait* p.18

17. *Baxter Letters* pp.70–76; *Letters*, ii. pp.88–91

18. RLS to Gosse, 15 November 1879, B.7986; *Letters*, ii. pp.79–84; Sanchez, *Life of Mrs Robert Louis Stevenson*, op. cit.

19. RLS to Baxter, 15 October 1879, *Baxter Letters* p.71; RLS to Colvin, 21 October 1879, B.3040

20. Calder, *Life Study*, op. cit.; Katharine Osbourne to Edmund Gosse, 16 August 1922, B.8263

21. Thomas Stevenson to Colvin, 10 November 1879, B.5747; Colvin to Baxter, November 1879, B.4178

22. *Letters*, ii. pp.90–91; Colvin to Baxter, November 1879, B.4178

23. *Letters*, ii. pp.164–70; 'Thoreau', *Cornhill Magazine* 41 (1880) pp.665–82; *Tusitala* 27 pp.80–105; Monterey State Historical Museum, Ms.1490; Sanchez, *Life*, op. cit. pp.60–70; Masson, *I Can Remember*, p.190

24. Colvin to Baxter, 22 December 1879, B.4179; Henley to Colvin, 2 January 1880, B.4670

25. Charteris, *Life and Letters of Edmund Gosse*, op. cit. pp.120–28; *Letters*, ii. pp.909–91, 98–100

26. RLS to Gosse, 8 December 1879, *Letters*, ii. pp.86–88

27. RLS to Colvin, 26 December 1879, B.3044; *Letters*, ii. pp.92–93

28. RLS to Colvin, spring 1880, B.3045; cf. also B.6062

29. RLS to Colvin, January 1880, B.3048; *Letters*, ii. pp.93–102

30. *Baxter Letters* pp.74–75

31. *Baxter Letters* pp.75–77; Thomas Stevenson to Baxter, October 1879, B.5746; Thomas Stevenson to RLS, 11 March 1880, B.5766

32. RLS to Gosse, 23 January 1880, B.7988; Thomas Stevenson to Colvin, 8 January 1880, B.5748; Colvin to Baxter, 12, 27 January 1880, B.4180–4181; Margaret Stevenson to RLS, 22 March, 21 April 1880, B.5631, 5633

33. Charles Warren Stoddard, *Exits and Entrances* (1903) p.16; Sanchez, *Life* p.72; *Letters*, ii. pp.107–08; RLS to Stoddard, May 1880, B.3569–3570

34. *Tusitala* 18 pp.143–52; 'The Old Pacific Capital', *Fraser's Magazine* 131 (November 1880) pp.647–57; cf. also Anne R. Isler, *Happier for his Presence, San Francisco and Robert Louis Stevenson* (1949)

35. *Baxter Letters* p.77; RLS to Colvin, March 1880, B. 3050; *Letters*, ii. p. 109

36. RLS to Colvin, spring 1880, B.3051; RLS to Ferrier, 8 April 1880; RLS to Gosse, 16 April 1880, *Letters*, ii. p.109–12
37. Colvin to Baxter, 23 November 1880, B.4185
38. Sanchez, *Life* p.64; *Letters*, ii. pp.105–06; RLS to Colvin, March 1879, B.3034
39. RLS to Colvin, April 1880, B.3052; *Letters* ii. p.113; *Baxter Letters* p. 78
40. RLS to Thomas Stevenson, n.d. 1880, B.8085; Thomas Stevenson to RLS, May 1880, B.8301, 5767
41. RLS to P. G. Hamerton, July 1881, *Letters*, ii. pp.156–58; Furnas, *Voyage to Windward* p.162
42. Sanchez, *Life* p.78
43. *The Silverado Squatters*, *Tusitala* 18 p.159
44. RLS to Colvin, May 1880, *Letters*, ii. pp.116–17
45. *The Silverado Squatters*, *Tusitala* 18 pp.155–247; cf. also John E. Jordan, ed. *Robert Louis Stevenson's Silverado Journal* (San Francisco 1954)
46. *The Silverado Squatters*, *Tusitala* 18 pp.205–08
47. RLS to his parents, June 1880, B.3502; RLS to Colvin, B.3054; Aldington op. cit. p.123; Elwin, *Strange Case*, op. cit. p.149
48. *The Silverado Squatters*, *Tusitala* 18 pp.241–42; Fanny Stevenson to Dora Williams, June 1880, B.3836; Anne R. Isler, *Stevenson at Silverado* (Idaho 1939)
49. Mackay, *Violent Friend* p.82
50. RLS to Margaret Stevenson, 30 June, 6 July 1880, B.3376; John E. Jordan, *Stevenson's Silverado Journal*, op. cit. p.xvii
51. Masson, *I Can Remember* p.190

Chapter 8

1. Fanny Stevenson to Margaret Stevenson, 16 July 1880, B.3745
2. Calder, *Life Study* p.112
3. Margaret Stevenson diary, B.7304
4. Sanchez, *Life* pp.83–84; Steuart, *Robert Louis Stevenson*, op. cit., i. p. 287
5. Masson, *I Can Remember* p.10; Thomas Stevenson to Dr W. Bamford, 10 June 1880, B.5741
6. Fanny Stevenson to Dora Williams, September 1880, B.3837; *Tusitala* 2 p. xx
7. Sanchez, *Life* p.85; Margaret Stevenson diary, September 1880, *Vailima* 26 pp.335–336; *Collected Poems* p.337; RLS to Colvin, September 1880, B.3055; *Letters*, ii. p.127
8. Sanchez, *Life* p.86
9. RLS to Henley, November 1881, *Letters*, ii. pp.177–78; Henley to Colvin, 24 May 1876, B.4706; Calder, *Life Study* p.122; Furnas, *Voyage to Windward* p.283
10. Lucas, *Colvins* op. cit. p.128; Colvin to Baxter, 15 June 1881, B.4186
11. Malcolm Elwin, *Old Gods Falling* (1939) p.143; R. A. M. Stevenson to RLS, September 1880, 23 April 1882, summer 1884, 9 January 1885, B.5709, 5710, 5715, 5716
12. Steuart, op. cit. i. pp.294–95; Elwin, *Old Gods*, op. cit. p.152

13. 'The Character of Dogs', *Tusitala* 29 pp.93–102; *Letters*, ii. p.122; Masson, *Life* p.73

14. RLS to his parents, 28 October 1880, B.3504; RLS to Baxter, 28 October 1880, *Baxter Letters* p.81

15. *Letters*, ii. pp.127–28; Steuart, ii. p.7

16. 'Davos in Winter', *Pall Mall Gazette* 499, 21 (February 1881); *Tusitala* 30 pp. 147–50; J. A. Hamerton & John Grant, *Stevensoniana* (1910) pp.64–65; Lloyd Osbourne, *Intimate Portrait* pp.26–27; *Tusitala* 2 pp.xii–xiii

17. J. A. Symonds to Horatio Brown, 27 February 1881 in Herbert M. Schueller & Robert L. Peters, eds *The Letters of John Addington Symonds*, 3 vols (Detroit 1969) (hereinafter *Symonds Letters*, ii. p.664; cf. also ibid., ii. pp.659, 668; Colvin, *Memories* pp.132–33; *Letters*, ii. pp.132–33

18. Phyllis Grosskurth, ed., *The Memoirs of John Addington Symonds* (1984) pp. 261–79; Llewellyn Powys, *Swiss Essays* (1947); Horatio F. Brown, *John Addington Symonds. Letters and Papers* (1923) p.111

19. Gosse, *Critical Kitcats*, op. cit. p.287; RLS to Colvin, 1880–81, *The Autobiography of Margot Asquith*, 2 vols (1920), i.p.202

20. RLS to his parents, 10, 18, 28 November 1880, B.3505–3508

21. RLS to Margaret Stevenson, 15 December 1880, B.3379; Lloyd Osbourne, *Intimate Portrait* pp.36–41; *Tusitala* 25 p.94; Gosse, *Critical Kitcats* p. 292; *Scribner's Magazine* 24 (December 1898) pp.709–19; *Tusitala* 30 pp.191–96

22. RLS to Baxter, 27 February 1881, *Baxter Letters* p.85

23. RLS to his parents, 27 January 1881, 3511; RLS to Margaret Stevenson, 5 February 1881, B.3380; Fanny Stevenson to Margaret Stevenson, autumn 1880, B.3748; Fanny Stevenson to Timothy Rearden, autumn 1880, B.8149

24. Mackay, *Violent Friend* p.100; *Letters*, ii. pp.134–42; RLS to Thomas Stevenson, December 1880, December 1880, B.3459–3460; RLS to Colvin, December 1880, B.3057

25. RLS to Colvin, spring 1881, B.3059; RLS to Margaret Stevenson, March, 4 April, B.3383–3384; *Letters*, ii. pp.143–44; *Collected Poems* p.137–38; RLS to his parents, 1 April 1881, B.3512

26. RLS to Margaret Stevenson, March 1881, B.3382; *Letters*, ii. p.147

27. RLS to Colvin, April–May 1881, B.3060–3061; RLS to his parents, 1, 5 May 1881, B.3513–3514; Sanchez, *Life* p.92; *Baxter Letters* p.88; *Letters*, ii. p.147

28. Masson, *I Can Remember* p.197; *Baxter Letters* p.90; Steuart, i. p.343; B.7056; *Letters*, ii. pp.162–63

29. 'The Body Snatchers', *Tusitala* 11 pp.183–203; Isobel Rae, *Knox the Anatomist* (1964); 'Thrawn Janet', *Cornhill Magazine* 44 (October 1881) pp.436–43; *Tusitala* 8 pp.107–120; 'The Merry Men', *Cornhill Magazine* 45–46 (June–July 1882) pp.679–95, 56–73; *Tusitala* 8 pp.1–56; 19 pp.191–92; Lucas, *Colvins* p.130; *Letters*, ii. pp.148–51. For discussion of the stories see Coleman O. Parsons, 'Stevenson's use of Witchcraft in "Thrawn Janet" ', *Studies in Philology* 43 (July 1946) pp.551–71; John Robert Moore, 'Stevenson's source for "The Merry Men" ', *Philological Quarterly* 23 (April 1944) pp.135–40; L. M. Buell, 'Eileen Earraid: Beloved Isle of Robert Louis Stevenson', *Scribner's Magazine* 71 (February 1922) pp.184–95

30. RLS to Colvin, December 1890, *Letters*, iv. pp.34–42; *Tusitala* 8 pp. 1–56
31. Masson, *I Can Remember* p.198
32. Hamerton, *Stevensoniana* pp.70–73; Balfour, *Life*, i. p.190; *Letters*, ii. pp. 151–59; Masson, *I Can Remember* p.202; Walter Simpson to RLS, 5 November 1881, B.5506; Fanny Stevenson to Dora Williams, September 1881, B.3842; Margaret Stevenson to RLS, 5 November 1882, B.5637; RLS to Colvin, June 1881, B.3062–3063
33. *Tusitala* 2 p.xix; RLS to Mrs Sitwell, August 1881, *Letters*, ii. p. 165; RLS to Gosse, 19 August 1881, ibid. p.167; RLS to Baxter, August 1881, *Baxter Letters* p.92
34. Thomas Stevenson to RLS, 31 October 1880, 7 September 1881, B.5768, 5770; RLS to Colvin, September 1881, Lucas, *Colvins* pp.152–53
35. *Tusitala* 2 pp.xviii–xx; Japp, *Robert Louis Stevenson*, op. cit. p.13; Thomas Stevenson to RLS, 26 February 1882, B.5771; Lloyd Osbourne, *Intimate Portrait* p. 30
36. Japp p.10; Gosse, *Critical Kitcats* pp.289–91; Hamerton, *Stevensoniana* pp. 55–61; *Letters*, ii. pp.164–65; Gosse to Clark, 19 October 1911 in Charteris, op. cit. pp.330–31
37. *Letters*, ii. pp.168–71
38. W. H. Bonner, *Pirate Laureate* (1947) p.197; Burton E. Stevenson, *Famous Poems and Controversies which have Raged Around Them* (1923) pp.321–40; John Robert Moore, 'Defoe, Stevenson and the Pirates', *Journal of English Literary History* 10 (1943) pp.35–60
39. David Barrett, *A Stevenson Study* (1924) p.10–16; G. A. England, 'The Real Treasure Island', *Travel* 52 (January 1929) pp.17–21, 41–45
40. Alexander Reid, 'Robert Louis Stevenson – a Psychological Novelist?' *Scotland's Magazine* (January 1960) pp.55–56
41. *Treasure Island, Tusitala* 12 pp.xi–xxxi; RLS to Henley, 25 August 1881, *Letters*, ii. pp.168–69
42. Leslie Fiedler, *No! In Thunder* (Boston 1960)
43. Kiely, *Robert Louis Stevenson and the Fiction of Adventure* (Harvard 1965); RLS to Henley, n.d. NLS; *Tusitala* 2 pp.xxix
44. W. B. Yeats to RLS, 24 October 1891, B.5912; Jack London, 'These Bones Shall Rise Again', in *Revolution* (1901); *Letters*, iii. p.27
45. Lloyd Osbourne, *Intimate Portrait*, p.30; 'The Stimulation of the Alps', *Tusitala* 30 pp.155–58; cf. also Balfour, *Life*, i. pp.180–83
46. RLS to Thomas Stevenson, 3 October, 9 December 1881, B.3462–3463; *Letters*, ii. pp.170–75, 179, 181–82, 189, 191; Lloyd Osbourne, *Intimate Portrait* p.26; Lucas, *Colvins* p.131–33; Charteris, *Life and Letters of Gosse*, op. cit. p. 149; 'Talk and Talkers', *Cornhill Magazine* 45 (April 1882) & 46 (August 1882) pp.410–18, 151–58; *Tusitala* 29 pp.71–92; 'Samuel Pepys', *Cornhill Magazine* 44 (July 1881) pp.31–46; *Tusitala* 27 pp.179–201; E. M. Clark, 'The Kinship of Hazlitt and Stevenson', *University of Texas Bulletin: Studies in English* 4 (1924) pp.97–114
47. *Collected Poems* pp.287–300; Balfour, *Life*, i. p.184
48. J. A. Symonds to H. F. Brown, 1, 10, 13 November 1881, *Symonds Letters*,

op. cit. ii. pp.701–03, 708; W. G. Lockett, *Robert Louis Stevenson at Davos* (n.d.) pp.244–45; Margaret Symonds (Mrs W. W. Vaughan), *Out of the Past* (n.d.) p.224

49. Symonds to Gosse, 13 December 1881, *Symonds Letters*, ii. pp.721–22; RLS to Gosse, December 1881, NLS Ms. 8760 f. 38
50. Hamerton, *Stevensoniana* pp.64–65; Louis L. Cornell, 'A Literary Joke by RLS: Interpretation and Commentary', *Columbia Library Column* 17 (February 1968) pp.17–26
51. Fanny Stevenson to Margaret Stevenson, October, 3 December 1881, B.3753, 3755; Elwin, *Strange Case* op. cit. p.171
52. RLS to Baxter, 14 November, 15 December 1881, *Baxter Letters* pp.94–95, 97–98; Fanny Stevenson to Margaret Stevenson, 9 December 1881, B.8158; Fanny Stevenson to Timothy Rearden, autumn 1881, B.8151; Fanny Stevenson to Dora Williams, November–December 1881, August 1882, B.3844–3845
53. Charles W. Garrard to RLS, 5 April 1882, B.4472; RLS to R. A. M. Stevenson, spring 1881, B.3562; same to same, April 1882, *Letters*, ii. p.200
54. RLS to Gosse, 26 December 1881, B.7998; cf. NLS Ms. 8790 f. 46; RLS to Colvin, 27 December 1881, B.3385; *Letters*, ii. pp.178–82; J. A. Symonds to Horatio F. Brown, 4 March 1882, *Symonds Letters*, ii. p. 732
55. RLS to Baxter, 19 October 1881, February 1882, 22 February 1882, *Baxter Letters* pp.94, 100–02; RLS to Colvin, 17 April 1882, B.3388
56. RLS to his parents, February 1882, B.3515–3516; RLS to Colvin, 3 January 1882, B.3386; *Letters*, ii. pp.182–97; Balfour, *Life*, i. p.200

Chapter 9

1. *Symonds Letters*, op. cit., ii. pp.745, 758–59; *Meredith Letters*, op. cit. II pp.692–93 *Letters*, ii. pp.201–05; *Baxter Letters* pp.103–04; RLS to Colvin, 30 July 1882, B.3389
2. John Cameron to RLS, 19 August 1982, B.4158; *Letters*, ii. pp.57, 181, 193, 202; *Baxter Letters* p.103; 'The Treasure of Franchard', *Longman's Magazine* 1 (April 1883) pp.672–94; 2 (May 1883) p.83–112; *Tusitala* 8 pp. 171–236
3. Fanny Stevenson to Dora Williams, October 1882, B.3847; Mackay, *Violent Friend* p.111
4. RLS to Fanny Stevenson, October 1882, *Letters*, ii. pp.213–16; RLS to Fanny Stevenson, October 1882, B.3278–3279
5. RLS to Margaret Stevenson, 21 October 1882, B.3390; RLS to Thomas Stevenson, 17 October 1882, B.3464; RLS to Colvin, October–November 1882, B.3390–3393; RLS to Colvin, October 1882, B.3069; Sanchez, *Life* p.99
6. *Baxter Letters* pp.100, 103–07; RLS to his parents, 9, 21 October 1982, B.3518–3519
7. *Letters*, ii. pp.219–23; RLS to Colvin, 23 December 1882, 23 January 1883, B.3395–3396; Aldington, p.149; Furnas p.191
8. Colvin to Baxter, December 1882–January 1883, B.4188; RLS to Thomas Stevenson, 11 January 1883, B.3465; RLS to his parents, 24 January 1883, B.3521; RLS to Colvin, January–February 1883, B.3070

9. RLS to his parents, January, 15 February 1883, B.8093, 3524; RLS to Colvin, February 1883, B.3071–3072; *Letters*, ii. pp.223–28

10. Mrs M. L. Ferrier to RLS, 4 February 1883, B.4469; RLS to Elizabeth Ferrier, 30 September 1883, B.7978; Margaret Stevenson to RLS, September 1883, B.5638; Steuart, ii. p.24; *Letters*, ii. pp.257–60, 274–75

11. RLS to Colvin, June–July 1884, B.3077–79; *Letters*, ii. pp.228–32; W. H. Garrod, 'The Poetry of Robert Louis Stevenson', in *The Profession of Poetry* (Oxford 1929) pp.179–93; cf. also 'The Poetry of R. L. Stevenson', in *Essays Mainly on the Nineteenth Century Presented to Sir Humphrey Milford* (Oxford 1949) pp.42–57

12. Fanny Stevenson to Margaret Stevenson, spring 1883, B.3769

13. Fanny Stevenson to Dora Williams, May–June 1883, B.3848

14. *Collected Poems* pp.332–33

15. RLS to Thomas Stevenson, 17 March 1883, *Letters*, ii. pp.233–34; Thomas Stevenson to RLS, 19 May 1884, B.5780; RLS to R. A. M. Stevenson, October 1883, *Letters*, ii. pp.270–72; Masson, *I Can Remember* p.71

16. Fanny Stevenson to Margaret Stevenson, July 1883, B.3733–3744

17. Masson, *I Can Remember* p.198; Colvin, *Memories and Notes* pp.110–11

18. *Baxter Letters* pp.119–20; *Letters*, ii. pp.251–52; Fanny Stevenson to Margaret Stevenson, December 1883, B.3406

19. RLS to Henley, April–May 1883, *Letters*, ii. pp.235, 243–46; RLS to his parents, 8 May 1883, B.3527; RLS to Margaret Stevenson, 1 March 1883, B.3399

20. RLS to his parents, 5 May 1883, B.3526; Fanny Stevenson to Margaret Stevenson, October 1883, B.3788; *Letters*, ii. p.238; Fanny Stevenson to Baxter, 15 December 1883, *Baxter Letters* pp.127–28

21. RLS to Gosse, 26 September 1883, B.8007; *Letters*, ii. pp.261–62, 276, 278, 290–91

22. RLS to his parents, 25 December 1883, B.3529; Thomas Stevenson to Fanny Stevenson, 26 September 1883, B.5794; RLS to Thomas Stevenson, 12 October 1883, *Letters*, ii. pp.287–89

23. RLS to Margaret Stevenson, late 1883, B.3409; Fanny Stevenson to Dora Williams, 1 July 1883, B.3489; *Letters*, ii. p.239; Sam Osbourne to Lloyd Osbourne, 5 February, 1 August, 13 August 1883, B.5358–5361; Aldington, *Portrait of a Rebel* p.180

24. RLS to Fanny Stevenson, 1883, B.3281; Fanny Stevenson to Margaret Stevenson, 24 October 1883, B.3799

25. Saposnik, op. cit. p.188; *Tusitala* 4 pp.vii–xi; RLS to Henley, April, May, June 1883, *Letters*, ii. pp.235, 245–46

26. *Tusitala* 4; Gosse, introduction to *New Arabian Nights* in 1906 edition of works, iv. pp.3–4

27. RLS to Miss Monroe, June 1886, *Letters*, iii. pp.92–93; RLS to Trevor Haddon, 23 April 1884, *Letters*, ii. pp.305–06

28. Eigner pp.54–55; Janet Adam Smith, *Henry James and Robert Louis Stevenson*, op. cit. p.150

29. *Tusitala* 9 p.156

30. *Letters*, ii. p.226, iii. p.308; Masson, *I Can Remember* pp.206–08; Balfour, *Life*, i. p.208

31. *The Times*, 25 May 1919; Ruth Marie Faurot, 'From Records to Romance. Stevenson's The Black Arrow and the Paston Letters', *Studies in English Literature 1500–1900* 5 (1965) pp.677–90; Hamerton, *Stevensoniana* pp. 113–14

32. *Baxter Letters* pp.129–35

33. Fanny Stevenson to Margaret Stevenson, January–February 1884, B.3787–3789; Fanny Stevenson to Mrs Sitwell, February 1884, B.3790–3794; Fanny Stevenson to Baxter, 4 February 1884, B.3621; *Baxter Letters* pp.136–39

34. *Letters*, ii. pp.293–304

35. Henley to Baxter, 3, 4 February 1884, B.4603–4604

36. Fanny Stevenson to Baxter, 4, 25 February 1884, *Baxter Letters* pp. 136–40; *Tusitala* 4. p.xvi

37. RLS to Simpson, B.3269; RLS to Margaret Stevenson, 19 April 1884, B.3411; Fanny Stevenson to Mrs Sitwell, spring 1884, B.3797

38. Balfour, *Life* i. p.215; RLS to Thomas Stevenson, 12 April 1884, B.3533; *Baxter Letters* p.147; Masson, *I Can Remember* p.198; *Tusitala* 3 p.xi; Fanny Stevenson to Mrs Sitwell, 27 March 1884, B.3795; Fanny Stevenson to the Stevenson parents, 25 March, April 1884, B.3823–3826; Fanny Stevenson to Mrs Sitwell, spring 1884, B.3797

39. Fanny Stevenson to Henley, 2–3 May 1884, B.3702; Fanny Stevenson to Mrs Sitwell, 18 May 1884, B.3801; *Letters*, ii. pp.302–11

40. Fanny to Henley, 3 May 1884, B.3703; Fanny Stevenson to the Stevenson parents, April 1884, B.3826; Fanny Stevenson to Mrs Sitwell, 18 May 1884, B.3801

41. RLS to Colvin, July 1884, B.3082; RLS to his parents, 27 June 1884, B.3538; Fanny Stevenson to Henley, June 1884, B.3538; Fanny Stevenson to Henley, June 1884, B.3705; *Letters*, ii. pp.313–17

Chapter 10

1. Fanny to Mrs Sitwell, October, 11 November 1884, B.3732, B.3803; Fanny Stevenson to Colvin, November 1884, B.3638–3639; RLS to Thomas Stevenson, 29 October 1884, B.3473; Thomas Stevenson to RLS, 14 October 1884, B.5783; *Letters*, iii. pp.7–17; *Baxter Letters* pp.151–55

2. Fanny Stevenson to Henley, August 1884, B.3710; R. A. M. Stevenson to RLS, 9 January 1885, B.5716; R. A. M. Stevenson to Fanny Stevenson, August 1884, B.5738; RLS to Thomas Stevenson, 5 November 1884, B.3474; *Tusitala* 5 p.xvi; *Letters*, iii. pp.16, 43

3. C. L. Cline, ed. *The Letters of George Meredith* (1970), ii. pp.750–51; M. W. Dilkes, *Blood and Thunder* (1949) p.167; Hesketh Pearson, *Beerbohm Tree, His Life and Laughter* (1956) pp.48–50; Coulson Hernahan, *Celebrities. Little Stories about Famous Folk* (1923) pp.21–23

4. RLS to Henley, March 1885, *Letters*, iii. p.44; Fanny Stevenson to Henley, August, autumn 1884, B.3707, 3710; Lloyd Osbourne, *Intimate Portrait* pp. 56–57

5. Henley to Baxter, 11 July 1884, B.4610; Henley to Fanny Stevenson, Fanny Stevenson to Mrs Sitwell, 11 November 1884, B.3803
6. Henley to RLS, 14 July 1883, B.4678; RLS to Henley, December 1884, *Letters*, iii. p.28
7. Mackay, *Violent Friend* p.134; *The Dynamiter, Tusitala* 3 p.190
8. Chesterton, *Robert Louis Stevenson*, op. cit. p.167; Thomas Stevenson to RLS, 7 January 1885, B.5788; RLS to Colvin, January–February 1885, B.3085–3087; *Letters*, iii. pp.33–37; Ian Onsby, *The Detective Story in English Fiction from Godwin to Doyle* (Harvard 1976) pp.145–46; John Cawelti, *Adventure, Mystery and Romance: Formula Stories as Art and Popular Culture* (Chicago 1976) pp. 100–01
9. Fanny Stevenson to Margaret Stevenson, November 1884, B.3803, 8160; 'Virginibus Puerisque', *Tusitala* 25 pp.1–38; *Letters*, iii. pp.8–9, 12, 14–15, 16–17, 20, 23, 26, 29–30, 36–37
10. Simpson to RLS, 18 November 1884, 7 January 1885, B.5515–5516; RLS to Baxter, 16 November 1884, 11 August 1892, *Baxter Letters* pp.155, 302
11. RLS to Simpson, November 1884, *Letters*, iii. pp.10–11; Thomas Stevenson to RLS, November 1884, B.5784–5787; RLS to Thomas Stevenson, November 1884, 20 March 1885, B.3475–3476; RLS to Coggie Ferrier, 12 November 1884, *Letters*, iii. p.18; *Athenaeum* 11 October 1884 p.465; 25 October 1884 p.529; *Tusitala* 19 pp.216–19
12. Fanny Stevenson to Colvin, November 1884, B.3638–3639; Henley to Colvin, Fanny Stevenson to Dora Williams, April–May, October 1885, B.3855–56
13. Fanny Stevenson to Dora Williams, April–May 1885, B.3855; *Letters*, ii. pp. 41–42
14. RLS to Fanny Stevenson, July 1885, April 1886, B.3282–3286; Henley to Baxter, 19 April 1884, B.4607; Masson, *I Can Remember* pp.210–12
15. Una Taylor, *Guests and Memories* (1924) pp.69, 362–67, 406; Adelaide Boodle, *RLS and his Sine Qua Non* (1926)
16. RLS to Margaret Stevenson, 15 December 1884, B.3413; RLS to Will Low, 22 October 1885, *Letters*, iii. pp.51–52; Fanny Stevenson to Colvin, 1885, Lucas, *Colvins* pp.161–65; Evan Charteris, *John Sargent* (1927) pp.69, 79–80
17. R. A. M. Stevenson to RLS, 1885, B.5717; R. A. M. Stevenson to Fanny, April 1886, B.5739; Fanny Stevenson to Henley, 13 November 1885, B.3715; *Letters*, iii. pp.62–63
18. RLS to Elizabeth Anne Ferrier, 30 September 1883, 27 January 1886, B.7978–7979
19. Fanny Stevenson to Henley, 1885, B.3714; *Baxter Letters* p.85; Fanny Stevenson to Baxter, September 1885, B.3627; Gosse, *Critical Kitcats* pp. 292–99
20. William Archer, 'RLS at Skerryvore', *Critic* 5 November 1887; 'RLS: His Style and Thought', *Time*, November 1895; 'In Memoriam RLS', *New Review*, January 1895; Hamerton, *Stevensoniana* pp.77; *Letters*, iii. pp.54–62
21. Leon Edel, *Henry James, The Middle Years* (1963) pp.61–62; Janet Adam Smith, *Henry James and Robert Louis Stevenson*, op. cit. pp.91–92; Henry James to RLS, 2 August 1887, B.4938; Lang to RLS, December 1874, 29 January 1880, December 1884, 25 July 1886, B.5026, 5035, 5056, 5083
22. *Collected Poems* p.476; *Letters*, iii. pp.24–25, 57–58

23. *Collected Poems* pp.128–29; Pope-Hennessy, op. cit. p.175
24. Fanny Stevenson to Colvin, summer 1885, B.3641–3642; Leon Edel, *The Diary of Alice James* (1965) p.93
25. Fanny Stevenson to Henley, 1885, B.3711–3712; Fanny Stevenson to Colvin, September–October 1885, B.3644–3646; Henry James to Colvin, autumn 1885 B.4904
26. Henley to RLS, November 1885, B.4846; RLS to J. A. Symonds, 3 March 1886, B.5829; *Symonds Letters*, iii. pp.120–21, 81; Edgar C. Knowlton, 'A Russian Influence on Stevenson', *Modern Philology* 14 (December 1916) pp. 449–54
27. Balfour, *Life*, ii. pp.15–16; *Letters*, iii. p.114; *Tusitala* 20 p. 310; Kenneth Graham, 'Stevenson and Henry James: A Crossing', in Andrew Noble ed. *Robert Louis Stevenson* (1983) pp.23–46
28. 'Wellington', *Tusitala* 28 pp.132–34; B.8400, 7128–31; Hamerton, *Stevensoniana* pp.113–14; Will Low, *Chronicle*, op. cit. p.335; *Letters*, iii. pp.2–3, 23, 30–36, 49; Frank Swinnerton, *Robert Louis Stevenson* (1924) pp.135–36
29. *Memoir of Fleeming Jenkin*, *Tusitala* 19 pp.1–152; Anne Jenkin to RLS, 28 December 1885, B.4978; Swinnerton, op. cit. p.79
30. Masson, *I Can Remember* pp.214–16; Fanny Stevenson to Margaret Stevenson, 10 September 1885, NLS 1898; Fanny Stevenson to Colvin, September 1885, B.3643
31. *The Life of Thomas Hardy* (1962) pp.179–80; Purdy & Millgate, *The Collected Letters of Thomas Hardy* (1978) pp.146–47; Michael Millgate, ed. *The Life and Work of Thomas Hardy* (1984) pp.187, 191, 259–60
32. Fanny Stevenson to Henley, August 1885, B.3713; *Letters*, iii. p.50; Fanny Stevenson to Baxter, September–October 1885, *Baxter Letters* p.164
33. *Letters*, iii. pp.37–39, 86–87, iv. p.180; Fanny Stevenson to Colvin, November 1886, B.3660; Jerrold E. Hogle, 'The Struggle for a Dichotomy: Abjection in Jekyll and His Interpreters', in William Heeder and Gordon Hirsch, *Dr Jekyll and Mr Hyde after One Hundred Years* (Chicago 1985) pp.161–207 (at p.207); Elwin, *Old Gods* p.181; Sanchez, *Life* op. cit.; *Tusitala* 1 p.xxii
34. Mackay, *Violent Friend* p.147; Boodle, *Sine Qua Non*, op. cit. p.11; *Baxter Letters* p.342; *Letters*, iii. p.115; RLS to Henley, summer 1885, B.8043; Lloyd Osbourne, *Intimate Portrait* pp.64–66

Chapter II

1. *Letters*, iii. p.83; Myron G. Schultz, 'The Strange Case of Robert Louis Stevenson', *Journal of the American Medical Association* 216 (April 1971) pp. 90–94; Sanchez, *Life* pp.118–19; *Tusitala* 30 pp.51–52; Elwin, *Strange Case* pp.201–02; Hellman op. cit. p.132
2. 'A Chapter on Dreams', *Tusitala* 30 pp.41–54
3. RLS to his parents, May 1885, B.3541
4. Karl Miller, *Doubles* (1985); Vladimir Nabokov, *Strong Opinions* (N.Y. 1973); Fredson Bowers, ed., *Vladimir Nabokov's Lectures on Literature* (1980); Richard

Ellmann, *Yeats, The Man and the Masks* (N.Y. 1948) p.73; Rosemary Jackson, *Fantasy: the Literature of Subversion* (1981) pp.114–16

5. See additionally Harry M. Gedulf, ed. *The Definitive Dr Jekyll and Mr Hyde Companion* (N.Y. 1983); Gordon Hirsch & William Veeder, eds *Dr Jekyll and Mr Hyde after One Hundred Years* (Chicago 1985)

6. RLS to Jenkin, April 1882, B.3177; Fanny to Colvin, December 1885, B.3651; *Collected Poems* pp.124–26

7. 'Crabbed Youth', *Tusitala* 25 pp.39–50; 'Pulvis et Umbra', *Tusitala* 26 pp.60–66

8. Kiely, op. cit. p.42; Fredric Jameson, *The Political Unconscious: Narrative as a Socially Symbolic Act* (Ithaca 1982) p.104

9. Chesterton, *Robert Louis Stevenson* pp.65–67

10. Hirsch & Veeder, *Dr Jekyll and Mr Hyde*, op. cit.

11. RLS to Gosse, 2 January 1886, *Letters*, iii. pp.69–71

12. Hirsch & Veeder, op. cit.; RLS to J. A. Symonds, spring 1886, *Letters*, pp 80–82

13. Barbara Hannah, *Striving towards Wholeness* (1971) p.54

14. Mark Kanzer, 'The Self-Analytic Literature of Robert Louis Stevenson', in George B. Wilbur & W. Muensterberger, *Psychoanalysis and Culture* (1951) pp.425–35 (at p.431)

15. Colleer Abbott, ed., *The Letters of Gerard Manley Hopkins & Robert Bridges* (Oxford 1935) p.228; Maixner, op. cit. p.229; RLS to Will Low, 2 January 1886, *Letters*, iii. pp.67–68; J. A. Symonds to RLS, 3 March 1886, *Symonds Letters*, iii. pp.120–21

16. Sidney Dark, *Robert Louis Stevenson* (1900) p.169; 'John Knox', *Tusitala* 27 pp.202–44

17. RLS to Gosse, 17 June 1886, B.8025; Gosse to RLS, 15 July 1886, Charteris, op. cit. pp.187–89; William Morris to George Bernard Shaw, 14 October 1886 in Norman Kelvin, ed. *The Collected Letters of William Morris*, 2 vols (Princeton 1987), ii. p.582

18. RLS to Thomas Stevenson, 18 January 1886, B.3478; Thomas Stevenson to RLS, January 1886, 17 May 1886, B.8302, 5793; RLS to Colvin, 10 June 1886, B.3092; RLS to Margaret Stevenson, 28 June 1886, B.3418; *Letters*, iii. pp.76–77, 88, 95–96, 104–05

19. *Baxter Letters* pp.164–66; RLS to Fanny Stevenson, April 1886, B.3287–3289; Fanny Stevenson to Mrs Sitwell, April 1886, B.3738; RLS to Margaret Stevenson, April 1886, *Letters*, iii. p.90; Fanny Stevenson to Colvin, spring 1886, B.3653–3657

20. *Collected Poems* pp.2, 354; Fanny Stevenson to Colvin, December 1885, B.3652; RLS to Colvin, April 1886, *Letters*, iii. p.88

21. Rosamund Gilder, ed., *Letters of Richard Watson Gilder* (1916) pp.121–22; Will Low, *Chronicle* pp.298, 319–21; Fanny Stevenson to Colvin, 1886 in Lucas, *Colvins* p.168; Fanny Stevenson to Colvin, July 1886, B.3658; *Letters*, iii. pp.100–06, 183–84; *The Times*, 6 September 1886; *Baxter Letters* p.199; Fredric Grunfeld, *Rodin* (1988) pp.260–65

22. RLS to his parents, 3 February, April 1886, B.3542–3543; RLS to Thomas Stevenson, 21 January 1886, B.3479; Fanny Stevenson to Colvin, September

1886, B.3659; Fanny Stevenson to Dora Williams, January, April 1887, B.3859, 3861; *Letters*, iii. pp.88, 116; *Baxter Letters* p.170

23. *Tusitala* 24 pp.221–94; *Tusitala* 6 pp.vii–x; John Carter, 'The Hanging Judge Acquitted', *Colophon* 3 (Spring 1938) pp.238–42; Michael Balfour, 'In Defense of the Hanging Judge', *New Colophon* 3 (1950) pp.75–77; F. B. Warner, 'The Hanging Judge Once More Before the "Bar" ', *Papers of the Bibliographical Society of America* 70 (1976) pp.89–96

24. Eigner p.119; Fanny Stevenson to Dora Williams, April 1886, B.3458; RLS to Margaret Stevenson, 8 October 1885, B.3415; *Letters*, iii. p.74

25. *Baxter Letters* p.170; Fanny Stevenson to Mrs Sitwell, 1 January 1886, B.3737; RLS to Henley, spring 1887, B.3170; RLS to Thomas Stevenson, 23 May 1886, B.3480; Fanny Stevenson to Dora Williams, October/November 1885, B.3857; April 1887, B.3860; *Tusitala* 1 p.xxiv

26. Lloyd Osbourne, *Intimate Portrait* pp.67–68; Fanny Stevenson to Colvin, 1 May 1887, B.3664; RLS to Baxter, 2 December 1887, *Baxter Letters* pp.177–78; Fanny Stevenson to Dora Williams, June 1887, B.3862

27. RLS to Fanny Stevenson, 1886, B.3296; Walter Simpson to RLS, 28 December 1886, B.5522; J. A. Symonds to H. F. Brown, 4 July 1887, *Symonds Letters*, iii. p.249; B.5824, 5830

28. *Baxter Letters* pp.172–73; *Letters*, iii. pp.98–99, 111–12; RLS to Colvin, spring 1887, B.3098–3099; Fanny Stevenson to Colvin, early 1887, B.3663

29. RLS to Anne Jenkin, 16 April 1887, *Letters*, iii. pp.125–28; Lloyd Osbourne, *Intimate Portrait* pp.69–70

30. RLS to Fanny Osbourne, April 1887, B.3298; *Baxter Letters* pp.173–74; *Collected Poems* pp.281–82; RLS to Colvin, June 1887, *Letters*, iii. p.132; B.4453; RLS to Adelaide Boodle, 14 July 1894

31. Colvin to Gosse, 1 February 1887, B.8214; John Thomson Mowbray to RLS, 27 May 1887, 18 February 1888, B.5255–5256; Fanny Stevenson to Colvin, summer 1887, B.3668

32. Lloyd Osbourne, *Intimate Portrait* pp.71–72; Fanny Stevenson to Henley, June–July 1887, B.3719; Fanny Stevenson to Colvin, June 1887, B.3666; J.A. Symonds to Horatio Brown, 9 September 1887, *Symonds Letters*, iii. pp. 267–68; Fanny Stevenson to Colvin, May/June 1887, in Lucas, *Colvins* pp.173–77

33. *Baxter Letters* pp.174–75, 178–80; *Letters*, iii. pp.135–36; RLS to Colvin, 19 August 1887, B.3101; Gosse to Armour, 21 September 1887 in Charteris op. cit. pp.216–17; Gosse, *Critical Kitcats*, op. cit. p.297; Will Low, *Chronicle* pp.358–61; Henry James to Colvin, 21 September 1887, B.4905

Chapter 12

1. Fanny to Dora Williams, September 1887, B.3865; RLS to Colvin, 22 August, September 1887, B.3102–3103; Fanny Stevenson to Colvin, 4 September 1887, Lucas, *Colvins* p.178; RLS to Henry James, *Letters*, iii. pp.141–44; Henry James to Colvin, 21 September 1887, B.4905; Fanny Stevenson to Nellie Sanchez,

September 1880, B.3730; RLS to R. A. M. Stevenson, October 1887, *Letters*, iii. pp.146–47; RLS to Simpson, July 87, *Letters*, iii. p.134

2. *Letters*, iii. pp.143–45; Will Low, *Chronicle* pp.371–86

3. S. McClure, *My Autobiography* (1914) pp.184–85; Masson, *I Can Remember* pp. 292–93; Rosamund Gilder, *Letters of Richard Watson Gilder* (1916) pp.145–48; Low, *Chronicle* pp.387–95

4. *Letters*, iii. pp.146–56; *Baxter Letters* pp.176–78; RLS to Burlingame, October–November 1887, B.2895–2898

5. E. L. Trudeau, *An Autobiography* (1916) p.228

6. Low, *Chronicle* pp.378–79; *Letters*, iii. pp.151, 160–61; Fanny to Dora Williams, April 1888, B.3865

7. RLS to J. A. Symonds, 21 November, 6 December 1887, *Letters*, iii. pp. 16–61; RLS to Adelaide Boodle, December 1887, ibid., iii. pp.164–65; RLS to Fanny Stevenson, autumn–winter 1887, B.3301–3305; RLS to Mr and Mrs Charles Fairchild, 21 September, October 1887, B.3128–3132

8. *Letters*, iii. p.190; *New York Herald*, 8 September 1887; Hamerton, *Stevensoniana* pp.83–84; *Tusitala* 30 pp.29–54, Henry James to Owen Wister, 1887; RLS to Owen Wister, spring 1888, B.8118

9. *Tusitala* 11 pp.1–82; *Letters*, iii. pp.155–56, 162–63, 235, 277; McClure, *My Autobiography*, op. cit. p.188; RLS to Colvin, 9 April 1888, B.3107; Lloyd Osbourne, *Intimate Portrait*, pp.79–81; Balfour, *Life*, ii. pp.32–34; RLS to Burlingame, 1888–89, B.2912–2922

10. McClure, *My Autobiography* pp.185, 189–90; Roger Burlingame, *Of Making Many Books* (1946) pp.18–19, 93, 96, 212–13, 231–33, 250–51, 260–61; RLS to Charles Scribner, October–December 1887, B.3233–3253; RLS to E. L. Burlingame, 1887–88, B.2895–2905

11. Low, *Chronicles* p.402; Augustus St. Gaudens, *Reminiscences* 2 vols i pp.373–83 (1913); St. Gaudens to RLS, 28 December 1887, B.5421

12. *Letters*, iii. pp.148–79; RLS to Colvin, March 1888, B.3105–3106; Richard Le Gallienne, *The Romantic Nineties* (1951) pp.64–65

13. *Letters*, iii. pp.175–79, 186–87, 167; Margaret Stevenson, *From Saranac to the Marquesas and beyond* (1903) pp.33–42

14. RLS to Mrs Vandegrift, 12 April 1888, B.3593; Fanny Stevenson to RLS, April 1888, B.3744; *Tusitala* 18 p.xvi; Low, *Chronicle* pp.400, 407–18; Margaret Stevenson, *From Saranac to the Marquesas* pp.10–39

15. RLS to Katharine de Mattos, 1882, B.3192; Henley to Colvin, 1 April 1886, B.4622

16. Mackay, *Violent Friend* p.170

17. John Connell, *William Ernest Henley*, op. cit. pp.113–14; Cohen, *The Henley-Stevenson quarrel*, op.cit.

18. Aldington op. cit. p.193; Cohen *The Henley-Stevenson quarrel* 22; RLS to Baxter, 20 December 1887, *Baxter Letters* pp.182–83; Colvin to RLS, 2 February 1888, B.4392; W. E. Henley, *A Book of Verses* (1888) pp.47–48

19. *Baxter Letters* pp.191–92

20. RLS to Henley, March 1888; RLS to Baxter, 23, 24 March 1888, *Baxter Letters* pp.192–99

21. ibid. pp.200–01, 213
22. B.4030; B.2786; *Baxter Letters* pp.202–06
23. *Baxter Letters* pp.207, 210–13
24. RLS to Fanny Stevenson, April 1888, B.3306, 3744; *Letters*, iii. pp. 191–92
25. *Baxter Letters* pp.216–17
26. ibid. pp.223–27
27. Baxter to RLS, 6 June 1888, B.4033; Mackay, *Violent Friend* p.174; Cohen, op. cit. pp.62–63; *Baxter Letters* pp.230–31
28. *Baxter Letters* pp.195, 209, 218, 225, 227
29. ibid. pp.227–28, 235
30. Fanny Stevenson to Baxter, May 1888; *Baxter Letters* pp.218–22; Baxter to Fanny Stevenson, 31 May 1888, B.4055
31. W. E. Henley, 'RLS', *Pall Mall Magazine* 25 (December 1901) pp.505–14
32. Connell, op. cit. p.292
33. RLS to J. A. Symonds, 21 November 1887, *Letters*, III pp.160–61
34. RLS to Colvin, 24 December 1887, *Letters*, iii. pp.170–71; RLS to Will Low, May 1889, *Letters*, iii. pp.160–62
35. Chesterton, *Robert Louis Stevenson*, op. cit. p.163
36. RLS to Baxter, 6 September 1888, *Baxter Letters* p.236; Chesterton op. cit. p. 47
37. *Tusitala* 10 pp.94, 163; 16 p.175; Herman Melville, *Moby-Dick*, Chapters 35, 130
38. RLS to Colvin, 14 January 1889, *Letters*, iii. pp.223–29; RLS to Henry James, March 1888, *Letters*, iii. pp.182–83; Eigner p.191
39. Low, *Chronicle* p.474; *Baxter Letters* p.223
40. RLS to Colvin, May 1888, B.3108, *Letters*, iii. pp.192–94; *Baxter Letters* pp. 222–25; Low, *Chronicle* p.428; *Letters*, i. p.235, ii. p.114; Stoddard, *Exits and Entrances* p.14; *The Wrecker*, *Tusitala* 12 pp.123–24; Margaret Stevenson, *From Saranac to the Marquesas* pp.47–53; *Collected Poems* pp.366–67

Chapter 13

1. Margaret Stevenson, *From Saranac to the Marquesas* op. cit. pp. 54–57; B.6071; B.1699; Alexander Findlay, *A Directory for the Navigation of the South Pacific Ocean* (1884); Joshua Slocum, *Sailing Alone Around the World* (1900) pp.155–56
2. McClure, *My Autobiography*, op. cit. p.191; cf. also Peter Lyon, *Success Story. The Life and Times of S. S. McClure* (1963)
3. Fanny Stevenson to Isobel Strong, 27 June 1888, B.8167; Fanny Stevenson to Baxter, 25 June 1888, *Baxter Letters* pp.233–34
4. *U.S. Naval Institute Proceedings* (1933); L. Draper, 'Freak Ocean Waves', *Weather* 21 (1966); Bernard Gorsky, *Trois tombes au soleil* (Paris 1976) p.305; Marjorie Ide (Mrs Shane Leslie), *Girlhood in the Pacific* (1942) p.93
5. Low Mss, Huntington; Arthur Johnstone, *Recollections of Robert Louis Stevenson in the Pacific* (1905) pp.13–21; Balfour, *Life*, ii. pp.43–44
6. *The Wrecker*, *Tusitala* 12 pp.187–88; Balfour, *Life*, ii. p.44; Johnstone, op. cit. p.21
7. Johnstone pp.24–25; *The Wrecker*, *Tusitala* 12 p.217
8. *In the South Seas*, *Tusitala* 20 pp.1–9; Low Mss, Huntington

9. *In the South Seas*, *Tusitala* 20 pp.1–119; Fanny Stevenson to Dora Williams, July 1888, B.3867; Margaret Stevenson, *From Saranac to the Marquesas* pp. 73–82; *Letters*, iii. p.202

10. *In the South Seas*, *Tusitala* 20 p.87; Kiely, op. cit. p.167

11. Charmian London, *The Log of the Snark* (1915) pp.100, 114; Lloyd Osbourne to Baxter, August 1888, B.5629; Fanny Stevenson to Dora Williams, 20 August 1888, B.3868; Margaret Stevenson, From Saranac, op. cit. pp.106–19

12. *In the South Seas*, *Tusitala* 20 pp.55–119; Margaret Stevenson, *From Saranac* pp.121–40; Fanny to Dora Williams, 1 August 1888, B.3369; *Scribner's Magazine* 75 No. 4 (April 1924) pp.408–10

13. *In the South Seas*, *Tusitala* 20 pp.93–104; J. Cumming Dewar, *Voyage of the Nyanza* (1892) pp.171–72; Margaret Stevenson, *From Saranac*, op. cit. pp. 140–42

14. *In the South Seas*, *Tusitala* 20 pp.123–29; *Letters*, iii. p.203–04; RLS to Baxter, 6 September 1888, *Baxter Letters* pp.235–36; Margaret Stevenson, *From Saranac* pp.143–47

15. *In the South Seas*, *Tusitala* 20 pp.126–29; Johnstone op. cit; Jack London, *The Seed of McCoy*; Charmian London, *The Log of the Snark*, op. cit. pp.163–70

16. *In the South Seas*, *Tusitala* 20 pp.139–56; Fanny Stevenson to Dora Williams, November 1888, B.3869; Margaret Stevenson, *From Saranac*, op. cit. pp. 147–63

17. *In the South Seas*, *Tusitala* 20 pp.156–75; McClure, *My Autobiography* p. 192

18. Margaret Stevenson, *From Saranac*, op. cit. p.170; Dewar, *Voyage of the Nyanza* pp.178–79; *Letters*, iii. pp.205–09; Caldwell, *Last Witness* p.68; Johnstone, op. cit. p.40

19. *Letters*, iii. pp.210–12; George Pembroke, *South Sea Bubbles* (1872); Pierre Loti, *Mariage de Loti* (Paris 1880); Leslie Blanch, *Pierre Loti: Portrait of an Escapist* (1983) pp.72–81 *Collected Poems* p.265

20. RLS to Colvin, 4 December 1888, *Letters*, iii. pp.216–23; RLS to Baxter, 10 November 1888, *Baxter Letters* pp.237–38; *Tusitala* 10 pp.xvi–xvii

21. *Letters*, iii. pp.210–16; 'Song of Rahero', *Collected Poems* pp.181–209; Margaret Stevenson, *From Saranac* p.193

22. Fanny Stevenson to Colvin, 4 December 1888, B.3670; Margaret Stevenson, *From Saranac* pp.226–44; *Letters*, iii. pp.211–23; John Hart to RLS, 12 August 1889, B.4350; Sanchez, *Life* p.143

23. *Letters*, iii. pp.224–33; Johnstone pp.47–48; Margaret Stevenson, *From Saranac* pp.253–55

24. RLS to Colvin, 14 January 1889, *Letters*, iii. pp.224–26; RLS to R.A.M. Stevenson, February 1889, *Letters*, iii. pp.231–33

Chapter 14

1. Isobel Field, *This Life* p.222; Martha May McGaw, *Stevenson in Hawaii* (Honolulu 1950)

2. RLS to Baxter, 8 February 1889, *Baxter Letters* pp.240–41; *Letters*, iii. pp.229–33; Margaret Stevenson to RLS, 12–14 May 1889, B.5645

3. Lloyd Osbourne, *Intimate Portrait* pp.196–98; Johnstone, op. cit. pp.57, 66
4. Lloyd Osbourne to Baxter, 4 March 1889, B.5270; RLS to Baxter, 8 February, 8 March, 10 May 1889, *Baxter Letters* pp.240–48; *Letters*, iii. p.235; *Tusitala* 10 pp.xvii–xviii; *Collected Poems* p.266; Kaiulani to RLS, 7 August 1889, B.5013; Colvin to Baxter, 12 March 1889, B.4191; Kalakaua to RLS, April 1889, B.5014
5. Fanny Stevenson to Mrs Sitwell, March 1889, *Letters*, iii. pp.238–41; cf. also *Letters*, iii. pp.235–37, 241–42
6. Isobel Field, *This Life* pp.202–207; Colvin to Baxter, 12 March 1889, 6 March 1890, B.4191, 4195
7. Field op. cit. p.221; Fanny Stevenson to Mrs Sitwell, 18 June 1889, B.3672; RLS to Baxter, 16 June 1889, *Baxter Letters* p.230; *Scribner's Magazine* (April 1924) pp.410–12
8. Fanny Stevenson to Colvin, 21 May 1889, B.3671; *Letters*, iii. pp. 253–55; Lucas, *Colvins* p.219
9. Colvin to Baxter, 28 April 1889, B.4193; *Letters*, iii. pp.260–61; Furnas, *Voyage*, op. cit.
10. Lloyd Osbourne to Baxter, 16 June 1889, B.5271; *Baxter Letters* p.243; Johnstone pp.195, 197
11. RLS to Baxter, February 1890, *Baxter Letters* pp.257–58; RLS to Lloyd Osbourne, 18 June 1889, B.3208; Lloyd Osbourne to Baxter, 4 December 1890, B.5280; *Letters*, iii. pp.305–13; RLS to Baxter, 6 December 1890, *Baxter Letters* p.274
12. McGaw, op. cit. pp.64–82; RLS to Baxter, 10 May 1889, *Baxter Letters* p.248; *Letters*, iii. pp.253–55
13. Masson, *I Can Remember*, pp.222–23; RLS to Fanny Stevenson, May 1889, *Letters*, iii. pp.255–59; *Collected Poems* p.266; RLS to Burlingame, June 1889, B.2921; RLS to Sister Maryanne, 22 May 1889, B.3189
14. RLS to Margaret Stevenson, June 1889, B.3424; *Letters*, iii. pp.259–64; Charles Warren Stoddard, *The Lepers of Molokai* (1885); Gavan Daws, *Holy Man: Father Damien of Molokai* (1973)
15. 'An Open Letter to the Rev Dr Hyde of Honolulu', *Tusitala* 21 pp.30–41; Isobel Field, *This Life* pp.270–71; George MacKaness, *Robert Louis Stevenson: His Association with Australia* (1935) pp.12–13
16. Johnstone pp.76–80, 84–85, 188; *Letters*, iii. pp.259–61; Daws, *Holy Man* pp.227–32; cf. also Harold Winfield Kent, *Dr Hyde and Mr Stevenson. The Life of the Rev Charles McEwen Hyde* (1973)
17. *Letters*, iii. pp.293, 314; *Baxter Letters* pp.264–65
18. RLS to Baxter, 7 June 1889, *Baxter Letters* p.249; RLS to Colvin, 2 April 1889, *Letters*, iii. pp.243–44; *Tusitala* 12 pp.xv–xvii
19. *Seattle Times*, 24 July 1966; *Seattle Post Intelligencer*, 24 July 1966; *Everett (Washington) Herald*, 17 July 1966, 23 August 1971; cf. also *Overland Tribune*, 14 July 1957; *The Sunday Oregonian*, 8 August 1982
20. Thomas Murray MacCallum, *Adrift in the South Seas* (Los Angeles 1934) pp.233–37; Field, *This Life* p.227; *Tusitala* 12 pp.xv–xvii
21. RLS to A. Rick, 7 August 1889, B.3221; *In the South Seas*, *Tusitala* 20 pp.213–71 *Letters*, iii. p.266

22. RLS to Margaret Stevenson, 30 September 1889, B.3425; *Letters*, iii. pp. 266–68; *Tusitala* 12 pp.viii–ix, xxi–xxiii
23. *Tusitala* 12 pp.xi, xxi; MacCallum, *Adrift*, op. cit. p.239
24. Andrew Farrell, ed., *John Cameron's Odyssey* (1928); *The Wrecker*, *Tusitala* 12 pp.42, 89, 217
25. *Tusitala* 12 pp.404–56; *Letters*, iii. p.268; iv. p.210; RLS to Burlingame, 1890–92, B.2926–2951; Balfour, *Life*, ii. pp.33–34, 75, 137–38; Lloyd Osbourne, *Intimate Portrait* pp.107–08; Eigner p.1–2; Saposnik p.129
26. *Tusitala* 12 pp.xi–xiv, xxii–xxiii; *Letters*, iii. pp.267–78; *In the South Seas*, *Tusitala* 20 pp.276–321; Lucas, *Colvins* pp.222–31; Fanny Stevenson to Dora Williams, December 1889, B.3872; Fanny Stevenson to Colvin, 20 January 1890, B.3673

Chapter 15

1. *A Footnote to History*, *Tusitala* 21 p.204
2. H. J. Moors, *With Stevenson in Samoa* (1910) pp.4–5
3. RLS to Baxter, 20 March 1890, *Baxter Letters* p.266
4. RLS to Baxter, December 1889, August 1890, *Baxter Letters* pp.252–55, 279–84; Moors op. cit. p.11
5. *Baxter Letters* pp.254, 262; Fanny Stevenson to Colvin, 20 January 1890, B.3673
6. *Baxter Letters* p.253; Fanny Stevenson to Mrs Sitwell, B.503–505
7. Basil F. Kirtley, 'The Devious Genealogy of the "Bottle Imp" Plot', *American Notes and Queries* 9 (January 1971) pp.67–70; Joseph Warren Beach, 'The Sources of Stevenson's "The Bottle Imp" ', *Modern Language Notes* 25 (January 1910) pp. 12–18
8. RLS to Burlingame, February 1890, B.2923; *Letters*, iii. pp.285–91; RLS to Baxter, 3 February 1890, *Baxter Letters* pp.257–59
9. *Baxter Letters* pp.259, 263–64, 270
10. RLS to Henley, February 1890, B.3171; RLS to Colvin, August 1890, B.3110
11. Isobel Field, *This Life* pp.266–67; RLS to Margaret Stevenson, 5, 20 March 1890, B.3426–3427; *Letters*, iii. pp.292–94
12. RLS to Baxter, 7 March 1890, *Baxter Letters* p.262; cf. p.262
13. Isobel Field, *This Life* p.295; Fanny Stevenson, *The Cruise of the Janet Nichol* (N.Y. 1914) pp.1–2; RLS to Margaret Stevenson, April 1890, B.8083; RLS to Burlingame, April 1890, B.2927
14. Fanny Stevenson, *Cruise* pp.7–15; *Letters*, iii. pp.294–97; *Baxter Letters* p. 267
15. H. J. Moors to RLS, 18 February 1890, B.5428; Fanny Stevenson, *Cruise* pp.28–32
16. Masson, *I Can Remember* pp.226–228; *Letters*, iii. pp.298–302; Fanny Stevenson, *Cruise* pp.33–160
17. Fanny Stevenson, *Cruise* pp.161 et seq.; *Letters*, iii. pp.303–06
18. RLS to Baxter, 1 September 1890, B.7939; Isobel Field, *This Life* p. 278
19. Colvin to Baxter, 13 March 1890, B.4196; Fanny Stevenson to Colvin, January, 12 April 1890, B.3674–3675; RLS to Henry James, August 1890,

Letters, iii. pp.306–07; RLS to Colvin, August 1890, B3110; Fanny Stevenson to Colvin, August 1890, B.3676; *Letters*, iii. pp.302–11

20. RLS to Margaret Stevenson, September 1890, B.3428–3429; RLS to Mr and Mrs Charles S. Fairchild, September 1890, B.3136
21. Adams to Anne Cabot Mills Lodge, 21 October 1890; Adams to Elizabeth Cameron, 17, 26 October, 8 November 1890 in *Letters of Henry Adams 1858–1891* (1930) pp.425–26, 429–30, 435, 440
22. Moors to RLS, 10 August 1890, B.5250; *Letters*, iv. pp.9–23; *Collected Poems* pp.245–86, esp. p.278
23. Fanny & Robert Louis Stevenson, *Our Samoan Adventure*, ed. Charles Neider (1956) pp.54, 61–62
24. *Letters*, iv. pp.16–39; *Collected Poems* pp.276–80
25. H. J. Moors, *With Stevenson in Samoa* (1910) pp.9–28; Adams to Elizabeth Cameron, 8 November 1890, *Letters of Henry Adams*, op. cit. p.440
26. Adams to Elizabeth Cameron, 8, 27 November, 15 December 1890 in *Letters of Henry Adams* pp.441–56, 451–53; RLS to Henry James, 29 December 1890, *Letters*, iv. pp.43–45; Adams to Elizabeth Cameron, 14 June 1891 in *Letters of Henry Adams* p.490; Adams to Elizabeth Cameron, 31 December 1897, 19 February 1900 in *Letters of Henry Adams 1892–1918*, ed. Worthington Chauncey Ford (Washington 1938) pp.139–40, 269
27. *Letters*, iv. pp.32–45; *Our Samoan Adventure* p.83

Chapter 16

1. Fanny Stevenson to Mrs Sitwell, January 1891, Mackay pp.238–39; *Collected Poems* pp.280–81; *Letters*, iv. pp.32–33; *Adams Letters*, op. cit. pp.463, 477
2. Fanny Stevenson to Mrs Sitwell, January 1891, Mackay pp.238–39; Fanny Stevenson to Dora Williams, January 1891, B.3874
3. *Letters*, iv. pp.47–54; Margaret Stevenson, *Letters from Samoa 1891–1895*, Marie Clothilde Balfour, ed. (1908) pp.22–31; Margaret Stevenson to Baxter, 1 February 1891, B.5590; Isobel Field, *This Life*, p.278; *Baxter Letters* p. 276
4. *Our Samoan Adventure*, op. cit. p.97; Fanny Stevenson to Dora Williams, March–April 1891, B.3875; Margaret Stevenson, *Letters from Samoa* p.33; Moors, *With Stevenson* p.46
5. Margaret Stevenson to Baxter, 1891, B.5591; *Our Samoan Adventure* p.104; Moors, *With Stevenson* pp.46–47, 64; Aldington p.215
6. Moors to Rev Merritt A. Farren, 1891, B.3251; *Letters*, iv. pp.65–72; *Tusitala* 15 pp.vii–ix; Moors, *With Stevenson* p.44; Lloyd Osbourne and Isobel Strong, *Memories of Vailima*, op. cit. p.89
7. *Our Samoan Adventure* p.110; Margaret Stevenson, *Letters from Samoa* pp. 52, 78; Moors, *With Stevenson* p.28; *Letters*, iv. pp.58–63, 65–67, 74–76, 101–05, 121–23
8. Margaret Stevenson, *From Saranac* p.247; *Letters from Samoa* p.111; *Collected Poems* pp.317–18; Sanchez, *Life* p.192; *Letters*, v. p.87; Caldwell, *Last Witness* pp.243–44; Osbourne & Strong, *Memories of Vailima* pp.90–95, 146

9. *Letters*, iv. p.97; *Collected Poems* p.400; Caldwell, *Last Witness* p.242

10. Margaret Stevenson, *Letters from Samoa* p.96; Lloyd Osbourne to Baxter, 15 October 1891, B.5283; Osbourne & Strong, *Memories of Vailima* p.142; *Collected Poems* pp.313–15

11. *Letters*, iv. pp.50–52, 108–112, 126–28; Moors, *With Stevenson*, pp. 49–52; B.6958; *Tusitala* 21 pp.307–16

12. *Letters*, iv. pp.34–39, 63–64; Moors, *With Stevenson* pp.49, 103; Balfour, *Life*, ii. pp.115–17; *Tusitala* 21 p.50; *Baxter Letters* pp.278–79

13. *Letters*, iv. pp.65–67; Balfour, *Life*, ii. pp.118–21; *Our Samoan Adventure* p.110

14. *Letters*, iii. p.309; iv. pp.55–57, 67, 77; B.7628

15. *Letters*, iv. pp.55–57; *Collected Poems* pp.181–209, 272–76, 280–81; Adams to Elizabeth Cameron, 23 February, 1 March, 8 March, 17 May 1891 in *Letters of Henry Adams*, op. cit. pp.467–68, 473–74, 480, 487

16. Gosse to Armour, 31 January 1891, Charteris, *Gosse*, op. cit. p.225; Dark, *Robert Louis Stevenson* p.280; McClure, *My Autobiography* pp.194–95; Masson, *I Can Remember* p.303

17. *Letters*, iv. pp.125–26; RLS to Burlingame, November 1891–February 1892, B.2942–2947

18. Francisco Valleiro to RLS, 4 May 1891, B.5889; RLS to Colvin, 6, 25 November 1890, April 1891, *Letters*, iv. pp.20, 25, 75, 99–101; *Baxter Letters* pp.286–87; Albert J. Guerard, *Conrad the Novelist* (Cambridge, Mass. 1958) p.43

19. *Tusitala* 13 pp.1, 75; Janet Adam Smith, *Henry James and Robert Louis Stevenson* (1948) pp.230, 233

20. *Tusitala* 13 pp.6–12; RLS to Colvin, 17 May 1892, *Letters*, iv. pp. 183–84; Barry Menikoff, *Robert Louis Stevenson and the Beach of Falesá* (Edinburgh 1984) p.89

21. Menikoff pp.25, 75, 93; Baxter to RLS, 15 May 1891, B. 4034; *Letters*, iv. pp.79–80

22. *Letters*, iv. pp.93–100; Menikoff pp.7, 23

23. *Baxter Letters* pp.303–18; Baxter to RLS, 7 June 1893, B.4043; RLS to Burlingame, 3 January, 16 April, May 1893, B.2955–2958

24. *Baxter Letters* p.318; *Letters*, v. pp.1–11

25. *Baxter Letters* pp.274–75, 277–78, 281–82, 283, 289–90, 294; Connell, *Henley* op. cit. pp.213–14; Colvin to Baxter, 4 February 1891, B.4207; Henley to Bruce, 8 August 1891, B.4660

26. Fanny Stevenson to Dora Williams, April 1891, B.3876; *Our Samoan Adventure* p.120

27. Mackay, *Violent Friend* p.250; *Our Samoan Adventure* p.140

28. *Our Samoan Adventure* pp.130, 142; Moors, *With Stevenson* pp.95–96

29. *Letters*, iv. pp.112–14, 118–19, 126–28; Margaret Stevenson, *Letters from Samoa* pp.98, 105

Chapter 17

1. *Tusitala* 21 p.84; Adams to Elizabeth Cameron, 9 October 1890, *Letters of Adams*, op. cit. p.421

2. George Turner, *Samoa a Hundred Years Ago and Long Before* (1884); Sylvia Masterman, *The Origins of International Rivalry in Samoa 1845–1884* (1934); Alfred Mahan, *The Interest of America in Sea Power, Present and Future* (1911) pp.35, 49; John La Farge, *Reminiscences of the South Seas* (N.Y. n.d) p.78

3. James D. Richardson, *A Compilation of the Messages and Papers of the Presidents 1789–1897* (Washington 1899), ix. p.439

4. *A Footnote to History, Tusitala* 21 pp.71–240

5. *Letters of Adams*, op. cit. p.421; Adams to Elizabeth Cameron in *Letters of Henry Adams 1892–1918* (1938) p.22; Margaret Villiers, *Fifty-One Years of Victorian Life* (1922) p.297

6. *A Footnote to History, Tusitala* 21 pp.92–198

7. *Letters*, iv. pp.47–50; Basil Thomson, 'The Samoan Agreement in Plain English', *Blackwoods Magazine* (December 1889)

8. *A Footnote to History, Tusitala* 21 pp.212–40; Villiers, *Fifty-One Years*, op.cit. p.292–93; *Letters of Adams 1838–1891* p.458; George K. Ryder, *The Foreign Policy of the United States in Relation to Samoa* (Yale 1933) pp.525–30

9. ibid.

10. Moors, *With Stevenson* pp.81–86, 148–49; *Letters of Adams 1838–1891* p.459; Fanny Stevenson to Colvin, December 1892, B.3677; Ryder pp.536–37

11. *Letters*, iv. pp.65–67, 81–84, 88–92

12. *A Footnote, Tusitala* 21 ibid.; Moors, *With Stevenson* pp.128–46; RLS to Arthur E. Claxton, 1 October 1892, B.2795; *Letters of Adams*, op. cit. p.459

13. *Foreign Relations of the United States 1894*, Appendix 1 pp.529–38; Moors, *With Stevenson* pp.148–49; RLS to Von Pilsach, 26 September 1891, October 1891, B.8061, B.3217; Von Pilsach to RLS, 2 October 1891, B.5384; *The Times*, 17 November 1891; *Letters*, iv. pp.93–100; *Our Samoan Adventure* p.127

14. *Letters*, iv. pp.101–05, 108–12, 117–19; *Our Samoan Adventure* p.150

15. *Foreign Relations of the United States 1894*, Appendix 1 pp.543–45; Moors, *With Stevenson* pp.155–69; *The Times*, 17 November 1891

16. Moors, *With Stevenson* p.170; *Letters*, iv. pp.134–35; Margaret Stevenson, *Letters from Samoa* p.138

17. Moors op. cit. pp.103–06, 155–60; *Letters*, iv. pp.171–72, 174–81, 188–95, 206–07; Margaret Stevenson, *Letters from Samoa* pp.157, 161, 165–68, 174–83

18. Villiers, *Fifty-One Years*, op. cit. pp.293–305; *Letters* iv. pp.216–17, 223–230, 235–36; Margaret Stevenson, *Letters from Samoa* p.226; Moors op. cit. p.66

19. *Letters*, iv. pp.183–84; *Our Samoan Adventure* pp.186–88

20. *Our Samoan Adventure* pp.143, 194; *Tusitala* 15 p.xv; RLS to Cedarcrantz, 13 September 1892, B.2970; Moors, op. cit. pp.160–70; Margaret Stevenson, *Letters from Samoa* pp.242–43

21. *The Times*, 4 June, 23 July, 19 August, 17 October 1892; Colvin to Baxter, 8, 11 November 1892, 17 January 1893, B.4225, 4226, 4232; Foreign Office Records 58/266 passim

22. F.O. 58/266; Masson, *I Can Remember* p.252; RLS to Cusack-Smith, 18 October 1892, 22 May 1893, B.3119, 3120; RLS to Earl of Jersey, 3 February 1893, B.8048; RLS to Lord Rosebery, May/June 1893, B.8066

23. Ryden, op. cit. pp.540–41; *Letters*, iv. pp.247–50, 265–67, 268–69, 271–73; v. pp.4–9

24. *Letters*, iv. pp.83, 230–34; *Our Samoan Adventure* p.204; Moors p.103

25. Henry James to Colvin, 1892, B.4908; *Letters*, iv. pp.105, 123, 137, 154, 162–63, 167–68, 184, 187, 195–96, 205, 218, 220, 244; *Our Samoan Adventure* p. 163; *Baxter Letters* p.301; Balfour, *Life*, ii. p.140; *Tusitala* 7 p.xv

26. *Letters*, iv. pp.184, 244; v. pp.75, 125; J. M. Barrie to RLS, 24 December 1892, B.3957; C. L. Cline, ed. *The Letters of George Meredith*, op. cit., iii. p.1153

27. *Tusitala* 7 pp.118–26

28. *Letters*, iv. p.196; *Tusitala* 7 p.xvi; Hamerton, *Stevensoniana* p.142

29. RLS to Colvin, 18 May 1892, *Letters*, iv. pp.184–87; Lloyd Osbourne, *Intimate Portrait* p.133; *Tusitala* 16 pp.171–72

30. J. M. Barrie to RLS, 4 February 1894, B.3960; *Letters*, iv. pp.149, 150, 168, 182; B.8311; *Tusitala* 15 pp.xi–xii

31. *Letters*, iv. pp.137–38; Calder, *Life Study* p.324; Lloyd Osbourne, *Intimate Portrait* p.129; Lloyd Osbourne to Colvin, 17 August 1899, 8 September 1899, B.5326, 5328

32. *Our Samoan Adventure* p.208; Belle Strong to Jane Whyte Balfour, 1893, B.5308; *Baxter Letters* p.302

33. Fanny Stevenson to Mrs Sitwell, September 1892, B.3740; 'Pulvis et Umbra', *Tusitala* 26 pp.60–66; Christopher Hassall, *Edward Marsh* (1959) pp.28–29, 85–86; Kiely, *Robert Louis Stevenson and the Fiction of Adventure* pp.53–54

34. Fanny Stevenson to Mrs Sitwell, September 1892, B.3740; RLS to Colvin, August 1892, *Letters*, iv. pp.218–32; *Scribner's Magazine* (April 1924) pp. 418–19; Mackay, *Violent Friend* pp.261–63

35. *Letters*, v. pp.4–101; Hellman, *The True Stevenson*, p.234

36. *Letters*, iv. pp.247–50; *Collected Poems* pp.311–12, 318; Caldwell, *Last Witness* p.284; Strong & Osbourne, *Memories of Vailima* pp.73–74; B.7044–7046

37. Moors, *With Stevenson* p.197; Fanny Stevenson to Mrs Sitwell, September 1892, B.3740; *Memories of Vailima* pp.37–38; *Tusitala* 15 p.xiii

38. RLS to Colvin, 4 December 1892, *Letters*, iv pp.268–69, v. p.5; B.3677; Hellman, op. cit. pp.217–29; Furnas, *Voyage* p.404

39. Hellman, op. cit. p.230; *Lanes of Memory* (N.Y. 1927) pp. 140–42; *Letters*, iv. pp.188–95

40. B.7162, 7164

41. *Collected Poems* p.267; RLS to Henley, 1 August 1892, B.3172; *Baxter Letters* p.301; *Letters*, iv. pp.209–10

42. *Baxter Letters* pp.303–05, 307; *Letters*, iv. pp.163–68, 196, 262–65, 268–69, 276–77; Margaret Stevenson, *Letters from Samoa* pp.220, 254

43. *Letters*, iv. pp.197–200, 205–06, 218–222, 251–56, 262–65

44. *Letters*, iv. pp.218–22, 242–46; Fanny Stevenson to Mrs Sitwell, September 1892, B.3740; Belle Strong to Charles Warren Stoddard, 3 February 1892,

B.8311; *Baxter Letters* p.305; Margaret Stevenson, *Letters from Samoa* pp.212, 227

45. *Letters*, iv. pp.159, 211–12, 242–46, 257–59, 271–75

Chapter 18

1. Margaret Stevenson, *Letters from Samoa* pp.251, 259–60; *Tusitala* 15 p. xii; Isobel Field, *This Life* pp.296–302; *Memories of Vailima* pp.11–12; *Letters*, v. pp.4–11
2. *Memories of Vailima* pp.18–19; *Letters*, v. pp.12–16; Sir George Grey to RLS, 30 March 1893, B.4491; Caldwell, *Last Witness* p.298
3. *Tusitala* 15 p.xii; *Memories of Vailima* pp.20–23; Colvin to Baxter, 22 July 1893, B.4256; *Letters*, v. pp.17–19; B.7924; Masson, *I Can Remember* p.234
4. *Letters*, v. pp.20, 39–41; Gosse to RLS, 7 July, 19 August, 13 November in Charteris, *Gosse*, op. cit. pp.229–31; J. A. Symonds to Gosse, *Symonds Letters*, iii. pp.664–65
5. Mackay, *Violent Friend* p.275
6. Colvin to Baxter, 22 July 1893, B.4256; RLS to Colvin, 1 March 1893, B.3430; RLS to Ethel K. Stoors, 26 February 1894, B.3572
7. RLS to Colvin, 17 April 1893, B.3431; Barrie to RLS, 29 January, 22 July 1893, B.3958–3959; RLS to Barrie, 2 April 1893, *Letters*
8. RLS to Colvin, April n.d., 21–22 April 1893, B.3112–3114; RLS to Margaret Stevenson, 17 April 1893, B.3431
9. *Baxter Letters* pp.333, 336; Henry James to RLS, 1893, RLS to Henry James, June 1893, *Adam Smith*, op. cit. *Letters V* pp.42–45
10. *Our Samoan Adventure* pp.243, 219, 221–23
11. *Letters*, v. pp.21, 23–28, 32–38, 42–45, 56–60; Cusack-Smith to RLS, 23 May 1893, B.4440; Earl of Jersey to RLS, 10 September 1893, B.5006; RLS to Cusack-Smith, 22 May 1893, B.3120; Thomas Maben to RLS, 28 April 1893, B.5171; Lord Rosebery to RLS, 15 March, 4 September 1893, B.5416–5417
12. *Our Samoan Adventure* pp.229, 232, 235–36
13. RLS to Mr & Mrs Fairchild, 1893, B.3139; *Letters*, v. pp.56–67; *Our Samoan Adventure* p.239; *Tusitala* 15 p.ix; *Memories of Vailima* p.45
14. *Our Samoan Adventure* pp.241–42, 244, 249–50
15. *Letters*, v. pp.13, 24–28, 32–38; Balfour, *Life*, ii. p.143; B.4251–4256, 4395–4397
16. *Letters*, v. pp.77–79; Balfour, *Life*, ii. pp.33–34; B.7268, 8251, 8270
17. Johnstone, *Recollections* p.218; *Tusitala* 14 pp.1–140;   ; Eigner, *Robert Louis Stevenson* op. cit. Chesterton, op. cit. p.133
18. Colvin, *Memories* pp.126–27; *Collected Poems* pp.341–43;
19. *Letters*, v. pp.76–77, 92–94; W. D. Puleston, *Mahan* (Yale 1939) p. 182; Johnstone, op. cit. pp.100–33, 266, 278; McGaw, op. cit.
20. RLS to Colvin, 15–17 October 1893, B.3435; *Letters*, v. pp.83–85; Johnstone, op. cit. pp.108–09, 280–81; Masson, *I Can Remember* p.274
21. Charteris, *Gosse* p.232

22. *Memories of Vailima* pp.49–50; *Letters*, v. pp.83–85, 97–101, 114–15; Wurmbrand to RLS, 9 June 1894, B.5911

23. Caldwell, *Last Witness* p.304; Hamerton, *Stevensoniana* p.113; Moors, *With Stevenson* pp.87–93; RLS to Gosse, 10–18 June 1893, B.8028; Conan Doyle to RLS, 30 May 1893, B.4455; RLS to Conan Doyle, 5 April, 12 July, 23 August, *Letters*, v. pp.22, 68, 71–72, 74–77, 96–101

24. *Memories of Vailima* pp.28, 34; *Tusitala* 15 pp.viii–ix; Caldwell, op.cit. p.305; *Letters*, v. pp.28–30, 42–45, 56–60, 78–82

25. Moors, *With Stevenson* pp.61, 72–73; *Letters*, v. pp.31–32; *Memories of Vailima* pp.26–27; Masson, *I Can Remember* p.245

26. Moors op. cit. p.80; *Memories of Vailima* p.42; Lloyd Osbourne, *Intimate Portrait* pp.131–34; Hamerton, *Stevensoniana* pp.157–62

27. *Memories of Vailima* p.33; Isobel Field, *This Life* p.239; Masson, *I Can Remember* p.266

28. *Baxter Letters* pp.300, 314, 330; *Letters*, v. pp.32–38, 89–90; Moors, op. cit. p.37; *Our Samoan Adventure* p.213

29. Moors, op. cit. pp.32–35, 49, 75–79, 102–03, 107; Hamerton, *Stevensoniana* p.153; Masson, *I Can Remember* pp.231–32

Chapter 19

1. RLS to Margaret Stevenson, 1 January 1894, B.3436; RLS to Mrs Sitwell, 1894, *Letters*, v. p.125; RLS to Baildon, 30 January 1894, B.2635; *Baxter Letters* p.367; Marjorie Ide, *Girlhood in the Pacific* p.36; Bradford Booth, 'The Vailima Letters of RLS', *Harvard Library Bulletin* 15 (1967) pp.117–28

2. Colvin to Lloyd Osbourne, 13 July 1899, B.4346; *Letters* v. pp.108–84; *Tusitala* 21 p.1

3. Katharine Osbourne to Gosse, 16 August 1922, B.8263; Colvin to Baxter, 18 October 1894, B.4314; Moors to Merritt A. Farren, 16 December 1916, B.5247; Moors pp.197 et seq

4. Masson, *I Can Remember* p.253; Marjorie Ide, *Girlhood in the Pacific* p.30; Margaret Villiers, *Fifty-One Years*, op. cit. p.304; Margaret Stevenson, *Letters from Samoa* pp.285–86, 291; *Letters*, v. pp.112–13, 118–21

5. Villiers, *Fifty-One Years* p.304; Margaret Stevenson, *Letters from Samoa* pp. 282, 285–86, 291; RLS to Cusack-Smith, 9 June 1894, B.3122; *The Times*, 2, 30 June 1894

6. Margaret Stevenson, *Letters from Samoa* p.279; *Tusitala* 15 p.xiv; Cusack-Smith to RLS, 14 May 1894, B.4441

7. Ide, *Girlhood*, op. cit. pp.29–30, 37, 39; Marie Fraser, *In Stevenson's Samoa* (1895) pp.70–83, 133–45, 162–69

8. *Tusitala* 15 p.xvi; Ryden, op. cit. pp.541–43; Moors, op. cit. p.59

9. A. Safroni-Middleton, 'With RLS in Old Samoa', loc. cit.; Masson, *I Can Remember* pp.258–65; *The Times*, 4 December 1919; *Letters*, v. pp.114–23

10. Colvin to RLS, 2 February 1888, 15 October, 2–3 November 1893, 20 February, 21 March, 13 July, 9 August 1894, B.4395–4403, *Letters*, v. pp.

118–21, 137–39; *Memories of Vailima* p.56; *Baxter Letters* pp.332, 348, 368, 370

11. *Baxter Letters* pp.342–47; *Letters*, v. p.121; Masson, *I Can Remember* p.263

12. *Letters*, v. pp.91, 134; Baxter to RLS, 22 January 1894, B.4049

13. *Letters*, v. pp.8–9, 112, 118, 123, 124, 160; B.2962–2965; *Baxter Letters* pp. 320–21, 334, 357, 359; Colvin to Baxter, 13 October 1894, B.4312

14. RLS to Burlingame, 12 June, 16 October 1893, B.2929, 2962; RLS to Baxter, 17 April, 12, 17 August 1894, *Baxter Letters* pp.351, 361, 365

15. *Letters*, iv. pp.253–54; v. pp.5, 16, 28–29, 70; B.4235–36, 4240, 4498–99; Lloyd Osbourne, *Intimate Portrait* pp.136–39

16. *Tusitala* 16 p.54; Eigner p.115; Saposnik p.126; RLS to Barrie, November 1892, *Letters*, iv. pp.257–59

17. *Tusitala* 16 pp.111–18; RLS to Henry James, December 1893, *Letters*, v. pp. 96–97; RLS to Adelaide Boodle, ibid. v. pp.141–43; Margaret Stevenson to Colvin, 3 May 1896, B.5602; Colvin to Margaret Stevenson, 21 March 1896, B.4386; Barbara Hannah, *Wholeness* p.68

18. RLS to J. A. Symonds 1886, *Letters*, iii. pp.80–82; *Tusitala* 16 p.52; Masson, *I Can Remember* pp.263–64; Benson, *As We Were* pp. 275–76; Furnas, *Voyage* pp.366–67; Daiches, *Robert Louis Stevenson* pp.99–140

19. Andrew Lang to RLS, 1892–94, B.5114–5127; *Baxter Letters* p.354; *Letters*, v. pp.27, 126–27, 146–52

20. *A Footnote to History, Tusitala* 21 p.185; *The Times*, 11 March, 1889; Colvin to Baxter, 2 July 1894, B.4302; Masson, *I Can Remember*, p.267; *Collected Poems* p.256

21. Masson, *I Can Remember* p.284; *Baxter Letters* pp.350, 362; *Pall Mall Magazine* (December 1901)

22. *Baxter Letters* p.356; *Letters*, v. pp.130–35, 164–69; RLS to R. A. M. Stevenson, September 1894, B.3567

23. *Letters*, v. pp.137–39, 171–72; *Our Samoan Adventure* p.255

24. *Letters*, v. pp.114–15, 118–21, 141–43, 152–54; Masson, *I Can Remember* pp. 266, 274; *Memories of Vailima* p.60; RLS to Lewis Balfour, 31 October 1894, B.8115

25. *Letters*, v. pp.130–35; Margaret Stevenson, *Letters from Samoa* pp.260–78; *Memories of Vailima* pp.24, 32, 38, 59; Masson, *I Can Remember* p.282–85

26. *Baxter Letters* p.356; Margaret Stevenson, *Letters from Samoa* p.287; *Letters*, v. pp.141–43

27. *Letters*, v. pp.160–62, 174–76; Margaret Stevenson, *Letters from Samoa* pp. 290–97; *Memories of Vailima* p.67

28. Alice Brown, *Robert Louis Stevenson. A Study* (Boston 1893) pp.45–46; Moors, op. cit. p.115; Mackay, *Violent Friend* p.299; Katharine Osbourne, *Stevenson in California*, op. cit.

29. *Baxter Letters* p.353; Lloyd Osbourne, *Intimate Portrait* pp.136–39; *Tusitala* 1 p.xxiv; *Letters*, v. pp.164–65; RLS to R. A. M. Stevenson, September 1894, B.3567

30. *Letters*, v. pp.16–62, 174–80, 182–84; *Baxter Letters* pp.369–79; Marie Fraser, *In Stevenson's Samoa* pp.22–37; *Memories of Vailima* pp.71–73

31. Margaret Stevenson, *Letters from Samoa* pp.314–27; Lloyd Osbourne, *Intimate Portrait* p.144; *Tusitala* 21 pp.3, 24; Fanny Stevenson to Mrs Sitwell, December 1894, B.3741

Epilogue

1. *Tusitala* 23 p.138; *Memories of Vailima* p.149; Mackay, *Violent Friend* p.312; Leon Edel, ed. *Henry James Letters IV 1895–1916* (1984) pp.212, 241
2. Henry James to Gosse, 27 August 1895, B.4918; Fanny Stevenson to Colvin, 30 October 1895, B.3684
3. Fanny Stevenson to Dora Williams, August 1896–March 1897, B.3880–3883; same to same, 16 September 1898, B.3889; Fanny Stevenson to Belle Strong, 23 November 1898, B.8169; Margaret Stevenson, *From Saranac* p.xix
4. Fanny Stevenson to Belle Strong, 1898, B.8168; Lloyd Osbourne to Baxter, 15 April, 28 April 1899, B.5291, 5294; B.5296–5300; Baxter to Colvin, 4 May 1899, B.3972; Baxter to Lloyd Osbourne, 31 May, 7 June 1899, B.3991–3992
5. Henley, 'RLS', *Pall Mall Magazine* 25 (December 1901) pp.505–14
6. Hellman, *True Stevenson*, passim; Katharine Osbourne, *Robert Louis Stevenson in California* (Chicago 1911), passim; Katharine Osbourne to Gosse, 16 August 1922, B.8263; Christopher Hassall, *Edward Marsh*, op. cit. p.86; Mackay, *Violent Friend* pp.315–60
7. Mackay, *Violent Friend* p.314
8. *Collected Poems* pp.94–95, 261–62; RLS to Gosse, 15 November 1879, *Letters*, ii. p. 84

BIBLIOGRAPHY

Works listed were first published in London unless otherwise indicated.

Abbott, Claude Colleer, ed. *The Letters of Gerard Manley Hopkins and Robert Bridges* (Oxford 1935)

Adcock, A. St J., ed. *Robert Louis Stevenson—His Work and His Personality* (1924)

Aldington, Richard, *Portrait of a Rebel: Robert Louis Stevenson* (1957)

Allen, Walter, *The English Novel* (1954)

Asquith, Margot, *Autobiography*, 2 vols (1920)

Baildon, H. B., *Robert Louis Stevenson* (1901)

Balderston, Daniel, *El precurso velado: R. L. Stevenson en la obra de Borges* (Buenos Aires 1985)

Balfour, Graham, *The Life of Robert Louis Stevenson*, 2 vols (1901)

Barrett, David, *A Stevenson Study: Treasure Island* (1924)

Barrie, J. M., *An Edinburgh Eleven* (1889)

Barrie, J. M., *Margaret Ogilvy* (1896)

Bay, J. C. B., *Echoes of Robert Louis Stevenson* (1920)

Bay, J. C. B., *Unpublished Manuscripts of Robert Louis Stevenson's Record of a Family of Engineers* (1929)

Beckson, Karl, *Arthur Symons. A Life* (Oxford 1987)

Beer, Thomas, *The Mauve Decade, American Life at the End of the Nineteenth Century* (N.Y. 1926)

Benson, E. F., *As We Were* (1930)

Blanch, Leslie, *Pierre Loti: Portrait of an Escapist* (1983)

Bonner, W. H., *Pirate Laureate* (1947)

Boodle, Adelaide, *R.L.S. and His Sine Qua Non* (1926)

Brown, Alice, *Robert Louis Stevenson: A Study* (Boston 1893)

Brown, George, *Pioneer Missionary and Explorer* (1908)

Brown, Horatio F., *John Addington Symonds* (1903)

Brown, Horatio F., *Letters and Papers of John Addington Symonds* (1923)

Buchan, John, *Memory Hold-the-Door* (1940)

Buchan, Susan, *John Buchan by his Wife and Friends* (1947)

Buchan, William, *John Buchan: a memoir* (1982)

Buckley, Jerome Hamilton, *William Ernest Henley* (Princeton N.J. 1945)

Burlingame, Roger, *Of Making Many Books* (N.Y. 1946)

Butcher, Lady Alice Mary, *Memories of George Meredith* (1919)

Calder, Jenni, ed. *The Robert Louis Stevenson Companion* (Edinburgh 1980)

Calder, Jenni, *R.L.S.: A Life Study* (1980)

Calder, Jenni, ed. *Stevenson and Victorian Scotland* (1981)

Caldwell, Elsie Noble, *Last Witness for Robert Louis Stevenson* (Norman, Oklahoma, 1960)

Carney, Seamus, *The Killing of the Red Fox* (Moffat, 1989)

Cawelti, John, *Adventure, Mystery and Romance: Formula Stories as Art and Popular Culture* (Chicago 1976)

Chapman, John Jay, *Emerson and Other Essays* (N.Y. 1909)

Charteris, Evan, *The Life and Letters of Sir Edmund Gosse* (1931)

Charteris, Evan, *John Singer Sargent* (1927)

Chesterton, G. K., *Robert Louis Stevenson* (1927)

Churchward, William B., *My Consulate in Samoa* (1887)

Cline, C. L., ed. *The Letters of George Meredith* (Oxford 1970)

Cohen, Edward H., *The Henley-Stevenson Quarrel* (Florida 1974)

Colvin, Sidney, *Memories and Notes of Persons and Places, 1852–1912* (1921)

Connell, John, *W. E. Henley* (1949)

Cunningham, Alison, *Cummy's Diary*, ed. Robert T. Skinner (1926)

Daiches, David, *Robert Louis Stevenson* (1947)

Daiches, David, *Robert Louis Stevenson and His World* (1973)

Dalglish, Doris N., *Presbyterian Pirate* (1937)

Dark, Sidney, *Robert Louis Stevenson* (1932)

Daws, Gavan, *Holy Man: Father Damien of Molokai* (1973)

Daws, Gavan, *A Dream of Islands* (1980)

Day, A. Grove, ed. *Travels in Hawaii* (Honolulu 1973)

Dewar, J. Cumming, *Voyage of the Nyanza* (Edinburgh 1892)

Disher, M. W., *Blood and Thunder* (1949)

Doyle, Sir Arthur Conan, *Through the Magic Door* (1907)

Dunbar, Janet, *J. M. Barrie: The Man behind the Image* (1970)

Edel, Leon, *Diary of Alice James* (1965)

Edel, Leon, *Henry James. The Middle Years* (1963)

Edel, Leon, *Selected Letters of Henry James* (1988)

Edel, Leon, *Complete Notebooks of Henry James* (1987)

Edel, Leon, *The Life of Henry James. Vol. 1. (1843–89)* (1977)

Edel, Leon, *The Life of Henry James. Vol. 2. 1890–1916* (1977)

Edel, Leon, ed. *Henry James Letters* III 1883–95 (1980)

Edel, Leon, ed. *Henry James Letters* IV 1895–1916 (1984)

Edel, Leon and Powers, Lyall H., *The Complete Notebooks of Henry James* (1987)

Edwards, Owen Dudley, *Burke and Hare* (Edinburgh 1980)

Eigner, Edwin M., *Robert Louis Stevenson and the Romantic Tradition* (Princeton 1966)

Ellmann, *Yeats: The Man and the Masks* (1948)

Elwin, Malcolm, *Old Gods Falling* (1939)

Elwin, Malcolm, *The Strange Case of Robert Louis Stevenson* (1950)

Farrell André, ed. *John Cameron's Odyssey* (1928)

Ferguson, De Lancey & Marshall Waingrow, eds, *Robert Louis Stevenson's Letters to Charles Baxter* (1956)

Fiedler, Leslie, *No! In Thunder* (Boston 1960)

Fiedler, Leslie, *Cross the Border – Close the Gap* (N.Y. 1972)

Field, Isobel Osbourne Strong, *This Life I've Loved* (1937)

Field, Isobel Osbourne Strong (with Lloyd Osbourne), *Memories of Vailima* (N.Y. 1902)

Findlay, Alexander G., *A Directory for the Navigation of the South Pacific Ocean* (1884)

Fletcher, C. Brunsdon, *Stevenson's Germany. The Case against Germany in the Pacific* (1920)

Ford, Worthington Chauncey, ed. *Letters of Henry Adams 1858–1891* (1930)

Ford, Worthington Chauncey, ed. *Letters of Henry Adams 1892–1918* (1938)

Fraser, Marie, *In Stevenson's Samoa* (1895)

Furnas, J. C., *Anatomy of Paradise* (1950)

Furnas, J. C., *Voyage to Windward* (1952)

Geduld, Harry M., *The Definitive Dr Jekyll and Mr Hyde Companion* (N.Y. 1983)

Gibson, John S., *Deacon Brodie: Father to Jekyll and Hyde* (Edinburgh 1977)

Gilder, Richard Watson, *Letters* (1916)

Golding, Gordon, ed. *The Cévennes Journal: Notes on a Journey through the French Highlands* (Edinburgh 1978)

Gorsky, Bernard, *Trois Tombes au Soleil* (Paris 1976)

Gosse, Edmund, *Critical Kitkats* (1896)

Gosse, Edmund, *Biographical Notes on the Writings of Robert Louis Stevenson* (1908)

Gosse, Edmund, *Silhouettes* (1925)

Gosse, Edmund, *Leaves and Fruit* (1927)

Grant, Alexander, *The Story of the University of Edinburgh*, 2 vols (1884)

Graves, Robert, *The Common Asphodel* (1949)

Green, Martin, *Dreams of Adventure, Dreams of Empire* (1980)

Green, Roger Lancelyn, *Essays and Studies* (1950)

Green, Roger Lancelyn, *Andrew Lang* (Leicester 1946)

Grierson, H. J. C., ed. *The Letters of Sir Walter Scott*, 12 vols (1932)

Gross, John, *The Rise and Fall of the Man of Letters* (1969)

Grosskurth, Phyllis, ed., *The Memoirs of John Addington Symonds* (1984)

Grunfeld, Frederic, *Rodin* (1988)

Guthrie, James, *Robert Louis Stevenson* (1920)

Gwynn, Stephen, *Robert Louis Stevenson* (1939)

Hamilton, Clayton, *On The Trail of Stevenson* (1915)

Hamilton-Paterson, James, *Seven-Tenths, The Sea and its Thresholds* (1992)

Hamerton, John, *Stevensoniana* (Edinburgh 1910)

Hannah, Barbara, *Striving towards Wholeness* (1971)

Hart, James D., ed. *From Scotland to Silverado* (Cambridge, Mass. 1966)

Hassall, Christopher, *Edward Marsh, A Biography* (1959)

Hellman, George, *The True Stevenson* (Boston 1925)

Hellman, George, *Lanes of Memory* (1927)

Henley, William Ernest, *Essays* (1921)

Henley, William Ernest, *A Book of Verses* (1888)

Herries, J. W., *I Came, I Saw* (1937)

Hernahan, Coulson, *Celebrities: Little Stories about Famous Folk* (1923)

Hillier, Robert Irwin, *The South Seas Fiction of Robert Louis Stevenson* (N.Y. 1989)

Hopkins, Gerard Manley, *Correspondence of, with Richard Watson Dixon* (1935)

Howells, Mildred, ed. *Life in Letters of William Dean Howells* (1928)

Isler, Anne Roller, *Stevenson at Silverado* (Idaho, 1939)

Isler, Anne Roller, *Happier for His Presence* (Stanford, Calif. 1949)

Jack, R. D. S., *The Road to Never Land* (Aberdeen 1991)

Jackson, Rosemary, *Fantasy: the Literature of Subversion* (1981)

Jameson, Fredric, *The Political Unconscious: Narrative as a Socially Symbolic Act* (Ithaca 1982)

Japp, Alexander H., *Robert Louis Stevenson* (1905)

Jersey, Countess of (M. E. Villiers), *Fifty-One Years of Victorian Life* (1922)

Johnstone, Arthur, *Recollections of Robert Louis Stevenson in the Pacific* (1905)

Jordan, John E., *Robert Louis Stevenson's Silverado Journal* (San Francisco 1954)

Kelman, John Jr, *The Faith of Robert Louis Stevenson* (Edinburgh 1903)

Kelvin, Norman, ed. *The Collected Letters of William Morris*, 2 vols (Princeton 1987)

Kent, Harold Winfield, *Dr Hyde and Mr Stevenson: the Life of the Rev. Charles McEwen Hyde* (1973)

Kiely, Robert, *Robert Louis Stevenson and the Fiction of Adventure* (Harvard 1965)

Knight, Alanna, *Robert Louis Stevenson Treasury* (1985)

Labor, Earle, Leitz, Robert & Shepard, Milo, *The Letters of Jack London*, 3 vols. (1989)

La Farge, John, *Reminiscences of the South Seas* (N.Y. n.d.)

Lang, Andrew, *Essays in Little* (1891)

Lang, Andrew, *Adventures Among Books* (1905)

Lawson, M. S., *On the Bat's Back* (1950)

Le Gallienne, Richard, *The Romantic Nineties* (1925)

Leavis, F. R., *The Great Tradition* (N.Y. 1963)

Leslie, Mrs Shane (Marjorie Ide), *Girlhood in the Pacific* (n.d.)

Lockett, W. G., *Robert Louis Stevenson at Davos* (n.d.)

London, Charmian, *The Log of the Snark* (1915)

London, Jack, *The Cruise of the Snark* (1913)

Loti, Pierre, *Mariage de Loti* (Paris 1880)

Lovett, Richard, *James Chalmers: His Autobiography and Letters* (1902)

Low, Will H., *A Chronicle of Friendships, 1873–1900* (1908)

Lucas, E. V., *The Colvins and Their Friends* (1928)

Lyon, Peter, *Success Story: the Life and Times of S. S. McClure* (1963)

MacCallum, Thomas Murray, *Adrift in the South Seas* (Los Angeles n.d.)

Mackail, Denis, *The Story of J. M. Barrie* (1941)

McKay, George L., *A Stevenson Library: Catalogue of the Edwin J. Beinecke Collection*, 6 vols (Yale 1961)

Mackay, Margaret, *Sharon* (N.Y. 1948)

Mackay, Margaret, *The Violent Friend* (1969)

McClure, S. S., *Autobiography* (1914)

MacCulloch, J. A., *R. L. Stevenson and the Bridge of Allan* (Glasgow 1927)

MacGaw, Sister Martha Mary, *Stevenson in Hawaii* (Honolulu 1950)

McLaren, Moray, *Stevenson and Edinburgh* (1950)

McLynn, Frank, *The Jacobites* (1985)

McLynn, Frank, *Charles Edward Stuart* (1988)

Mahan, Alfred Thayer, *The Interest of America in Sea Power, Present and Future* (N.Y. 1911)

Mair, Craig, *A Star for Seamen: the Stevenson Family of Engineers* (1978)

Maitland, Frederic William, *The Life and Letters of Leslie Stephen* (1906)

Maixner, Paul, ed., *Robert Louis Stevenson: The Critical Heritage* (1981)

Marcus, Steven, *The Other Victorians* (1966)

Masson, Flora, *Victorians All* (1931)

Masson, Rosaline, *A Life of Robert Louis Stevenson* (1923)

Masson, Rosaline, ed. *I Can Remember Robert Louis Stevenson* (Edinburgh 1922)

Masson, Rosaline, *Poets, Patriots and Lovers* (1933)

Masterman, Sylvia, *The Origins of International Rivalry in Samoa 1845–1884* (1934)

Mattheisen, Paul F., & Michael Millgate, *Transatlantic Dialogue; Selected American Correspondence of Edmund Gosse* (1965)

Menikoff, Barry, *Robert Louis Stevenson and the Beach of Falesá* (Edinburgh 1984)

Miller, Karl, *Doubles* (1985)

Millgate, Michael, *Thomas Hardy* (1982)

Millgate, Michael (& Purdy), *Collected Letters of Thomas Hardy*, 2 vols (1978)

Millgate, Michael, ed. *The Life and Work of Thomas Hardy* (1984)

Miyoshi, Masao, *The Divided Self* (N.Y. 1969)

Moore, George, *Confessions of a Young Man* (1888)

Moors, Harry J., *With Stevenson in Samoa* (1910)

Morris, David B., *Robert Louis Stevenson and the Scottish Highlander* (Stirling 1929)

Munby, F. A., *The House of Routledge* (1934)

Munro, Neil, *The Brave Days* (Edinburgh 1931)

Nabokov, Vladimir, *Strong Opinions* (N.Y. 1973)

Nabokov, Vladimir, *Lectures on Literature* (ed. Fredson Bowers) (N.Y. 1980)

Noble, Andrew, ed. *Robert Louis Stevenson* (1983)

Onsby, Ian, *The Detective Story in English Fiction from Godwin to Doyle* (Harvard 1976)

Osbourne, Katharine Durham, *Robert Louis Stevenson in California* (Chicago 1911)

Osbourne, Lloyd, *An Intimate Portrait of RLS* (N.Y. 1924)

Pearson, Hesketh, *Beerbohm Tree: His Life and Laughter* (1956)

Pembroke, George, *South Sea Bubbles* (1872)

Penzolt, Pieter, *The Supernatural in Fiction* (1952)

Pitt, David, *Tradition and Economic Progress in Samoa* (Oxford 1970)

Pope-Hennessy, James, *Robert Louis Stevenson* (1974)

Powys, Llewellyn, *Swiss Essays* (1947)

Puleston, W. D., *Mahan* (Yale 1939)

Quayle, Eric, *Ballantyne the Brave* (1967)

Quiller-Couch, Arthur, *Adventures in Criticism* (1896)

Rae, Isobel, *Knox the Anatomist* (1964)

Raleigh, Sir Walter, *Robert Louis Stevenson* (1895)

Rankin, Nicholas, *Dead Man's Chest* (1987)

Richardson, James D., *A Compilation of the Messages and Papers of the Presidents 1789–1897* (Washington 1899)

Ross, Angus, *New Zealand Aspirations in the Pacific in the Nineteenth Century* (Oxford 1964)

Ryden, George H., *The Foreign Policy of the United States in Relation to Samoa* (Yale 1933)

St. Gaudens, Augustine, *Reminiscences* (1913)

Sanchez, Nellie Vandegrift, *The Life of Mrs Robert Louis Stevenson* (1920)

Saposnik, Irving S., *Robert Louis Stevenson* (N.Y. 1974)

Schueller, Herbert M., & Peters, Robert L., eds. *The Letters of John Addington Symonds*, 3 vols (Detroit 1969)

Showalter, Elaine, *Sexual anarchy: gender and culture at the fin de siècle* (N.Y. 1990)

Simpson, Eve Blantyre, *Robert Louis Stevenson* (1906)

Simpson, Eve Blantyre, *The Robert Louis Stevenson Originals* (Edinburgh 1912)

Simpson, Eve Blantyre, *Robert Louis Stevenson's Edinburgh Days* (1914)

Sitwell, Sir Osbert, *Great Morning* (1948)

Slocum, Joshua, *Sailing Alone Around the World* (1900)

Smith, Janet Adam, *R. L. Stevenson* (1937)

Smith, Janet Adam, *Henry James and Robert Louis Stevenson* (1948)

Smith, Janet Adam, *John Buchan* (1965)

Smith, Janet Adam, *John Buchan and his World* (1979)

Starrett, *Bookman's Holiday* (1942)

Stephen, Leslie, *Studies of a Biographer* (1902)

Stern, G. B., *No Son of Mine* (1948)

Stern, G. B., *He Wrote Treasure Island* (1954)

Steuart, John A., *Robert Louis Stevenson*, 2 vols. (1924)

Steuart, John A., *The Cap of Youth* (1927)

Stevenson, Burton E., *Famous Poems and the Controversies which have Raged Around Them* (1923)

Stevenson, Fanny Vandegrift, *Cruise of the Janet Nichol among the South Sea Islands* (1915

Stevenson, Fanny Vandegrift & Robert Louis (ed. Charles Neider), *Our Samoan Adventure* (1956)

Stevenson, Margaret Isabella, *From Saranac to the Marquesas and Beyond* (1903)

Stevenson, Margaret Isabella, *Letters from Samoa, 1891–93* (1906)

Stoddard, Charles Warren, *Exits and Entrances* (n.d.)

Stoddard, Charles Warren, *The Lepers of Molokai* (1885)

Stott, Louis, *Robert Louis Stevenson and the Highlands and Islands of Scotland* (Stirling 1992)

Strouse, Jean, *Alice James* (Boston 1980)

Swearingen, Roger C., *The Prose Writings of Robert Louis Stevenson* (1980)

Swearingen, Roger C., *Edifying Letters of the Rutherford Family etc.* (Paisley 1982)

Swinnerton, Frank, *Robert Louis Stevenson* (1914)

Symonds, John Addington, *Recollections of a Happy Life* (1892)

Symonds, John Addington, *Some Further Recollections of a Happy Life* (1893)

Symonds, John Addington, *Our Life in the Swiss Highlands* (1907)

Taylor, Una, *Guests and Memories: Annals of a Seaside Villa* (1924)

Thwaite, Ann, *Edmund Gosse* (1984)

Trudeau, Edward Livingstone, *An Autobiography* (N.Y. 1916)

Turner, George, *Samoa a Hundred Years Ago and Long Before* (1884)

Veeder, William & Hirsch, Gordon, *Dr Jekyll and Mr Hyde after One Hundred Years* (Chicago 1985)

Wilbur, George B. & Muensterberger, W., *Psychoanalysis and Culture* (N.Y. 1951)

Wilde, Oscar, *Selected Letters*, ed. Rupert Hart-Davis (1979)

Wilson, A. N., *The Laird of Abbotsford* (1980)

Woolf, Leonard, *Essays on Literature, History, Politics* (1927)

Yeats, W. B., *The Trembling of the Veil* (1955)

INDEX